Disability Across the
Developmental Life Span

Julie Smart, PhD, CRC, LPC, ABDA, CCFC, ABPC, LRC, is professor and former director of the Rehabilitation Counselor Education Program, Department of Special Education and Rehabilitation, Utah State University. Her areas of specialization include multicultural rehabilitation, the rehabilitation of Hispanics, distance education, psychological aspects of disability, and disability studies. She is the author of *Disability, Society, and the Individual* (2008), chapter author of several books, and author of numerous professional articles in such journals as *Journal of Rehabilitation, Journal of Applied Rehabilitation Counseling, Journal of Counseling and Development, Rehabilitation Education, Directions in Rehabilitation Counseling,* and *Journal of Forensic Vocational Assessment.* She is on the editorial review board of *Continuing Education for Rehabilitation Nurses, Life Planning and Managed Care Nurses,* and the *American Disability Analyst* and on the editorial board of *Directions in Rehabilitation Counseling.* She was an NIDRR Switzer Scholar in 1989–1990. She is a site visitor and accreditor for the Commission on Standards and Accreditation.

Disability Across the Developmental Life Span

For the Rehabilitation Counselor

Julie Smart, PhD, CRC, LPC, ABDA,
CCFC, ABPC, LRC

SPRINGER PUBLISHING COMPANY
NEW YORK

Springer Publishing Company, LLC
11 West 42nd Street
New York, NY 10036
www.springerpub.com

Acquisitions Editor: Sheri W. Sussman
Production Editor: Lindsay Claire
Composition: Newgen Imaging

ISBN: 978-0-8261-0734-3
E-book ISBN: 978-0-8261-0735-0

14 / 5 4 3

The author and the publisher of this Work have made every effort to use sources believed to be reliable to provide information that is accurate and compatible with the standards generally accepted at the time of publication. The author and publisher shall not be liable for any special, consequential, or exemplary damages resulting, in whole or in part, from the readers' use of, or reliance on, the information contained in this book. The publisher has no responsibility for the persistence or accuracy of URLs for external or third-party Internet Web sites referred to in this publication and does not guarantee that any content on such Web sites is, or will remain, accurate or appropriate.

Library of Congress Cataloging-in-Publication Data
Smart, Julie.
  Disability across the developmental life span : for the rehabilitation
counselor / Julie Smart.
    p. ; cm.
Includes bibliographical references and index.
ISBN 978-0-8261-0734-3 (alk. paper) — ISBN 978-0-8261-0735-0 (e-book)
I. Title.
[DNLM: 1. Developmental Disabilities—rehabilitation.
2. Counseling—methods. 3. Human Development—physiology. 4. Mentally
Disabled Persons—rehabilitation. WS 350.6]
  616.85880651—dc23   2011040237

Printed in the United States of America by Gasch Printing.

For David

Contents

Preface

To my knowledge, there is no book that considers the experience of disability in relation to the grand theories of human growth and development. It is generally agreed that there are six grand theories, Freud, Erikson, cognitive learning, behavioral learning, Maslow, and Kohlberg. None of these theorists included people with disabilities (PWDs) in their theory development or in their research. On the other hand, the so-called "clinical" or "allied health" academic disciplines of medicine, nursing, physical therapy, occupational therapy, and rehabilitation counseling give little, if any, thought to stages of human development, concentrating solely on diagnoses and the resulting medical and rehabilitation treatment plans. In addition, the general counseling and psychology academic disciplines, and their textbooks, consider psychiatric disabilities and mental retardation, but not the developmental experiences and tasks of individuals with these disabilities. Unfortunately, the fields of psychology and counseling rarely include the experience of physical disabilities in their training.

The result is that the social developmental experiences of PWDs are not addressed in the university curricula. This may appear to be a broad, damning judgment. However, this lack of attention to the social developmental experiences of PWDs (and their families) has been longstanding, persisting for centuries. The disciplines of human growth and development, psychology, and counseling focus on the "normal," or, better stated, a narrow, illogical definition of normal and the clinical and allied health disciplines have focused on the medical model of disability in which attention was directed toward only the physical, biological, and medical needs of the individual. Certainly, there was no intentional malfeasance in ignoring PWDs in academic curricula or in physicians focusing solely on medical needs. Both were acting on the mandate given them by the larger society. Nonetheless, university graduates have little academic training in disability and physicians often do not conceptualize PWDs as individuals negotiating developmental stages and tasks.

In contrast, most PWDs, after medical stabilization, think of themselves as normal, ordinary people with the same types of needs, emotions, goals, and developmental tasks as everyone else. The difficulty lies in persuading PWODs (people without disabilities) to think of PWDs as typical, ordinary individuals. An ethical guideline found in all professions is the injunction to practice within the scope of one's training, education, and experience. Therefore, if PWDs are to be offered developmentally and socially appropriate services (in addition to the necessary medical care), it will be essential that university curricula include the experiences and needs of PWDs. Academicians, researchers, theorists, and scholars fall prey to the tendencies of the broader culture to sensationalize, exaggerate, and pathologize PWDs.

In some ways, the absence of PWDs in academic disciplines and the corresponding lack of professional services mirror that of other groups, such as women of all races and ethnicities, gay individuals, and those of racial and ethnic minority groups. Indeed, throughout this book, we shall learn that effective criticisms were leveled at the six grand theories for failing to incorporate the experiences of individuals who were not white, middle-class, straight men. This is not to suggest that white, middle-class, straight men were not worthy of study and research, only that there were other groups *also* worthy of study. Nonetheless, there are some differences between these other "disadvantaged" groups and PWDs. First, disability, until recently, was relatively rare. For millennia in medicine, the two-outcome paradigm of total cure or death dominated. Second, PWDs have been isolated, segregated, and institutionalized throughout history. In the United States, PWDs were not given their civil rights, protection under the law, and the right to a quality of life until 1990, long after other groups were enfranchised.

Obviously, the inclusion of PWDs into the social sciences and the addition of the social experiences of PWDs into the clinical disciplines will require an examination of the definitions of "normality" and "humanity." Defining and operationalizing these concepts are not a boring semantic exercise for a graduate seminar, instead, examining long-held assumptions often leads to an understanding that faulty definitions have resulted in the type of daily, lived life of PWDs and, in some extreme cases, whether they lived or died. Most academicians and textbook writers initiate the study of disability by defining disability. In contrast, a more fruitful discussion would result if the consideration of disability began with defining humanity and normality.

Almost one-fifth of the American population has some sort of government-recognized disability. However, this statistic is based on the broadest possible definition of disability. Each government agency defines disability somewhat differently and, therefore, the numbers of PWDs varies, depending on the source. The broadest government definition of disability is the Americans with Disabilities Act, which includes a large number of disabilities and, in addition, states that an individual who is *perceived* to have a disability is protected under the law. Furthermore, many would be surprised to learn that such conditions as arthritis, depression, and other chronic illnesses are defined as disabilities.

In this book, we shall first review some of the basic, general aspects of theories of human growth and development. Juxtaposed with this view of development theories, we shall consider great demographic shifts. These demographic changes were predicted; however, both the pace and the extent of these changes surprised demographers. One demographic change that is not typically discussed is the rapidly increasing numbers of PWDs and the appraisal of these increasing numbers as progress, both for the individual and society. Briefly stated, for many of these individuals, the alternative to living with a disability would be death. The two-outcome model of medicine has progressed to a three-outcome paradigm—death, total cure, or long-term care of PWDs or individuals with disabilities and chronic illnesses. The combination of medical, scientific, and technological advances and better public health have resulted in more PWDs (and fewer deaths).

The middle section of the book provides brief, general overviews of each of the grand theories, with a brief outline of the theorists' biographies, the main points of the theories, an evaluation of each theory and, finally, possible application to PWDs.

By necessity, each of these chapters is short, touching only on the main points and I hope I have not been simplistic, but rather concise and straightforward. Furthermore, most of these grand theorists had followers, often called "disciples," who continued and expanded the work of their mentors. However, with one or two exceptions, it is difficult to name these disciples or the way in which their theories differed from or expanded on the grand theorists. The fact that these grand theories continue to be used today attests to their usefulness and enduring quality. For example, it would be a daunting task to list all of the doctoral dissertations written in a single year that attempt to validate some aspect of these grand theories! With the passage of time, advances in testing instrumentation and sophisticated multifactorial statistical models provide the means to test and assess the validity of these grand theories, some which were developed almost a century ago. In spite of all these research methodological advances, these grand theories remain worthy of study.

Following the chapters on the grand theories, a short chapter outlining some basic concepts of disabilities provides some introductory information. In the next chapters, the basic stages of life are presented, typically two stages to a single chapter. Included in these chapters are the typical developmental tasks, a discussion of the ways in which demographic and historical changes have affected these life stages, a brief outline of two or three disabilities that are common to this stage of life, and a discussion of the ways in which the experience of disability affects passage through these particular life stages. The inclusion of two or three disabilities in the chapters on the life stages is not to suggest that these disabilities occur only in one or two life stages; but rather to show that the typical age of onset or diagnosis coincides with life stages presented in the chapter. Obviously, the exception is congenital disabilities, or disabilities which are present at birth; their time of onset occurs at a single life stage, birth. Nonetheless, individuals with congenital disabilities negotiate all the succeeding life stages. Note: the preferred term is "congenital disabilities" rather than the negative, pathologizing term of "birth defects."

There are four sections found at the end of each chapter, presented with the intention to provide further learning experiences and to allow students to engage more fully in the information presented. It is hoped that students will be able to integrate the material in the textbook, class discussion, additional readings, and topics of personal interest. Students are not expected to complete all of these exercises; but rather to choose one or two. These four sections are "Terms to Learn," "Videos to View," "Learning Activities," and "Writing Exercises." It is hoped that students will use these exercises to individualize their learning experiences. For example, students in the Allied Health fields may wish to learn more about developmental theories while students in counseling, psychology, and human growth and development will wish to apply their knowledge of the developmental stages and tasks to the experience of disability. These activities may be completed individually or as a group. Obviously, I think writing exercises are important, not only as a practice of a highly critical skill; but also as a way to clarify one's thinking to oneself.

I have attempted to write about these grand theories in a way that is congruent with the intent of the theorists and I have also attempted to write about disability from the perspective of PWDs and their families.

Acknowledgments

For a long time, I have wanted to write a textbook dealing with the developmental experiences of individuals with disabilities. This past year, writing this book has been both satisfying and challenging. However, I could not have succeeded and completed this book without the assistance, support, and encouragement of many individuals.

The books that I have written have often been termed "consumer oriented," and I consider this to be a positive judgment of my work. Without doubt, this book could not have been written without the many excerpts of first-person accounts that describe and explain the disability experience. I do not think that the work of these individuals with disabilities has received the recognition and consideration that it deserves; but rather is a vast reservoir of hidden scholarship. These excerpts form the basis of this book.

I wish to extend my gratitude to Utah State University and my department for granting me the time to focus on writing. I also thank two of my friends and assistants, Sharon Melton and Kris Wengreen, for their enthusiastic help, often going far beyond the call of duty.

I teach in a graduate program in Rehabilitation Counseling, and I am grateful to my students for the many stimulating classroom discussions, that have strengthened and broadened the scope of this book. Knowing that I am always interested in issues related to disability, students send me articles and books, and these, too, are incorporated in to this book. My students either currently work with people with disabilities or plan to do so upon graduation, and therefore, they assist me in viewing different aspects of the disability experience.

Sheri Sussman at Springer Publishing Company has been an enthusiastic advocate for this book throughout the entire process, and I am grateful to her. Finally, I thank my husband, David, a very patient and positive person, for his unflagging support and encouragement.

Major Developmental Theories

Introduction

Every time we buy a greeting card we see many different types of cards. Most greeting cards are written and illustrated examples of socially sanctioned developmental stages. These cards encourage or console those who are beginning new developmental stages and congratulate those who have completed an important developmental stage. Birthdays, graduations, wedding anniversaries, retirement, and widowhood are all considered socially sanctioned developmental stages. We would not find a card for significant changes in an individual's life that are not socially approved, such as a card wishing well an inbound prisoner.

In addition to greeting cards, significant changes are often marked by parties, gifts, special foods, and (occasionally) distinctive clothing such as wedding gowns, graduation robes, or military uniforms. Elaborate and expensive preparations are part of moving an individual from one developmental stage to the next. Gifts are given at some stages (think of baby showers) or family and friends travel great distances to attend ceremonies, all in order to help the developing individual assume new roles. At times the individual changes his or her name or gains a new title to reflect a major shift in identity; both self-identity and the ways in which others view the individual. Rites of passage are often part of one's religious or spiritual belief system and signal that the individual has achieved adult status in a church or synagogue. Birthday parties may also be considered rites of passage, communicating to children that more mature behavior is expected. All these rites of passage serve to connect individuals to the larger society. Especially in young children, these rites help people find their place in the world and assist in self-definition (Austrian, 2002).

Children begin to replace their deciduous teeth (baby teeth) with permanent teeth between the ages of 6 and 12. In the United States when small children lose a baby tooth, they place the tooth under their pillow. During the night the mythical Tooth Fairy takes the tooth and leaves money under the pillow. In Europe, however, it was common to bury the baby teeth up until the beginning of the 20th century. One author described the process of losing a baby tooth as "most unusual":

> It is initially difficult [for the child] to imagine part of the human body becoming so fragile that it ultimately disconnects itself. Children will very likely have parted with hair and certainly with nails by the time they lose their first tooth, but deliberately, as part of normal grooming and self-care. Teeth are the only part of the anatomy designed to fall out naturally and then grow back. Once the tooth is out, the lure is not over. (Austrian, 2002, p. 76)

This continued "lure" led to the creation of the Tooth Fairy. These traditions could be considered rites of passage because the Tooth Fairy, a uniquely American phenomenon, communicates to children that they are growing up and also assists children in relinquishing part of their "baby" identity. Of course, the parents could take the tooth and give the child a quarter; however, the loss (of babyhood) and the challenge (of growing up) are eased by the idea of a loving, kind, and mysterious fairy who is ever mindful of the number of teeth of every child. At no other time in life when we lose teeth—such as when we have our wisdom teeth extracted—do we expect a visit from the Tooth Fairy. Perhaps by then losing teeth is no longer considered a change of identity. Of course, most of us have given up the idea of the Tooth Fairy by the time we lose teeth as adults. Austrian considered this dichotomy between losing baby teeth in childhood and losing teeth later in life.

> Later in life, problems with teeth represent aging, the body's decline.... Throughout life, teeth remain something that connects adults to their early development—in this loss, in their symbolism, and in the memories provoked each time they see a child from this age period with missing teeth. (Austrian, 2002, p. 77)

Most socially approved rites of passage are considered to be signs of positive growth, development, and progress. However, there are some predictable, socially approved developmental stages and rites of passage that are not thought to be positive, such as the death of a loved one. Instead of parties, balloons, and cake, there are funerals, casseroles, and flowers. The death of a loved one is not hidden; others learn about the death by reading the obituary in the newspaper. The death of a loved one (especially a spouse) is a widely acknowledged (and somewhat predictable) stage of life.

Although the "hope you enjoy prison" card may appear funny, when an individual is incarcerated both the individual and his or her family experience "disenfranchised grief." There are no flowers, casseroles, ceremonies, or parties. Going to prison requires a major change in self-identity, the disengagement from many current relationships and tasks, and entry into new relationships and tasks. However, it is not considered a developmental task because very few individuals actually go to prison, and (more important) imprisonment is the results of antisocial behavior. Going to prison is not a predictable developmental stage. There are very few parents who look at their infant and consider that he or she might one day go to prison.

There is no greeting card for the acquisition of a disability or the birth of a baby with a congenital disability. Especially if it occurs at a young age, the onset of a disability is not a socially sanctioned developmental task. Still, acquiring a disability, being born with a disability, or having a disability diagnosed can be considered a developmental stage that requires a change in identity and completion of certain tasks. In addition, simply because most other developmental stages have widespread social approval and the acquisition of a disability does not, the individual (and his or her family) who experiences disability must encounter denial at best, or prejudice and discrimination at worst. To those who do not have a disability, disability may appear to be pathology, deviance, and inferiority although disability is in fact none of these. Indeed disability is very "normative" and "natural" in the sense that disabilities are very common and are frequently a part of the human experience. Nearly one in five Americans has a disability according to U.S. census data. Nearly 1 in 16 newborn infants has a congenital disability. Although it is true that parents never wish for their baby to be born with a disability and no adult ever wants to acquire a disability, most people with disabilities (PWDs) or parents of infants with disabilities state that a disability is not an unbearable tragedy; most report that they return to a "new normality," and some relate that there are positive aspects to the disability experience.

When an individual acquires traumatic disability, receives a diagnosis of a disability, or experiences the first symptoms of a psychiatric disability, he or she often retains a strong, detailed memory of when life changed, often termed a "flashbulb memory." The time of day or night, the exact circumstances (such as the color of the blanket when a patient awakes from a therapeutic surgical amputation), or the place in which the accident occurred divide the individual's life in two—before and after the disability. Many PWDs have a party every year to observe the day their disability occurred, such as a "day-I-broke-my-neck party." They invite friends and family members to gather together with balloons, party hats, cake, and ice cream.

We shall discuss disability as a developmental task at greater length and in much more detail. Following the six chapters on developmental theories, the remainder of this book will focus on an integration of disability concepts and developmental theories and stages of the life span.

WAYS IN WHICH DISABILITY AFFECTS DEVELOPMENTAL STAGES

Although there is some variation (both cultural and individual) in the definition and description of the developmental stages of life, these stages can be defined in a general way. Each stage will be discussed in greater detail in the third section of this book. For our purposes, the developmental stages are (1) pregnancy and infancy, (2) toddlerhood and early childhood, (3) school age, (4) adolescence, (5) adulthood and midlife, and (6) the young elderly and the old elderly.

None of the most well-known developmental theorists discussed in this book considered the development life span of PWDs. The absence of PWDs also mirrors the ignoring of women, racial and ethnic minorities, gays, and men and women with lower socioeconomic status. These grand theorists concentrated *mainly* on white, middle-class, straight males without disabilities, undoubtedly individuals worthy of study (Gilligan, 1977, 1982/1993, 1987). The criticism of these grand theories is a simple acknowledgment that other groups, often termed "minority groups" are *also* worthy of study. The absence of all these so-called "minority groups" is partially explained by the time these theories were evolving, when few societal opportunity structures were available for racial and ethnic minorities, women, gays, and PWDs. Without these opportunity structures, individual merit, hard work, and planfulness do not and cannot bring rewards. We shall learn that most of these grand theories are based on a range of choices available to the individual. Although no range of choice is ever unlimited, it is true that white, middle-class, straight males without disabilities experience a wider range of choices. It should be noted that all the longitudinal studies conducted in the 1920s, 1930s, and 1940s included both gays who chose not to disclose and men with invisible disabilities who also chose not to disclose.

Three Factors That Will Bring PWDs Into the American Culture

- The population explosion of PWDs
- PWDs as a group moving away from stigma management to a political identity group
- The media changing its portrayal of PWDs

Disability also presents another dimension: the concept of normality. Without doubt disabilities often involve functional losses; disability is expensive, requires management, and is difficult. However, disability is not as tragic as most people without disabilities (PWODs) think. Disabilities appear to be an assault on Americans' glorification of health, vigor, autonomy, freedom, and individualistic self-reliance. Disability makes PWODs uncomfortable because it is a visual reminder that anyone can acquire a disability at any time.

Nonetheless, three factors combine to bring PWDs into the American culture, including the study and research of "normal" development and growth. First, the sheer number of PWDs is increasing. Just as the population explosion of elderly people in the 1980s resulted in the creation of a new academic discipline and profession—gerontology—the population explosion of PWDs will result in more professional services for PWDs and greater awareness of the experience of disability in the university curriculum.

Second, PWDs resemble many other American minority groups by moving from a position of stigma management to one of identity politics. More than any other event, the passage of the Americans with Disabilities Act (ADA) (1990) and the Amendments to the ADA has produced an "identity cohort" of PWDs who were born after the ADA and thus have no memory of or experience with widespread prejudice and discrimination, institutionalization, or lack of opportunity. Frieden (2010) undertook a survey of leaders in the disability community in all 50 states and concluded:

> Overall, 90% of survey respondents believe that the quality of life for PWDs in communities across the United States has improved greatly since the passage of the ADA.... Two-thirds of survey respondents with disabilities believe that the ADA legislation has had more influence on their lives than any other social, cultural, or legislative change in the last 20 years. (p. 4)

The third and last factor is changes seen in media in the United States. The way in which books, films, and television portray a group of people has a powerful influence in either challenging or maintaining the social status quo of prejudice, discrimination, and limited opportunity. The media are forging an evolutionary path in portraying PWDs as people, rather than as a symbol for tragedy, pity, and deviance. For example, there is now less sad background music played when a PWD is shown onscreen.

In the not-so-distant future, PWDs may dominate the American social agenda as the Baby Boomers have for the last 60 years.

DISABILITY AND DEVELOPMENTAL STAGES

Some transitions in life are reversible, while others are irreversible. Birth and death are irreversible, while the transition to adulthood may not be. Adult children drop out of college, return to live in their parents' homes, and fail to enter the job market. Marriage is reversible. In contrast, disability and chronic illness are irreversible transitions. The very definition of disability and chronic illness means life-long, day-to-day management. The irreversibility of a disability is an aspect of acceptance of the disability, understanding that disability and chronic illness may have some opportunities for improvement through medical management, assistive technology, and social support. On the other hand, even the most stable-course disabilities have the probability of degenerating due to the acquisition of secondary conditions and the effects of aging. Therefore, birth, death, and disability are irreversible transitions.

For everyone, there are certain achievements and task completions expected at each stage. Many of the grand theories, especially Erikson's, include social expectations. However, there has historically been little social role guidance for PWDs, and the few social expectations were negative ones imposed upon PWDs by PWODs, such as (1) unquestioning compliance with all medical recommendations, (2) hiding or minimizing the disability, (3) showing the "public" that the individual is accepting of the disability to reduce the discomfort of others, and (4) keeping one's expectations at a modest level, thus accepting society's definition of oneself.

Most of the developmental theories view individuation as one of the end goals of development. Individuation is the process of becoming a unique individual, a result of one's experiences and pursuit of self-identified goals. Often PWODs view PWDs not as individuals but only as their disability. This categorization (instead of individuation) often leads to inaccurate stereotypes, such as "all deaf people are shy." PWDs recognize when they are seen only as a disability and not as individuals. Irving Zola illustrated the "all you PWDs look alike" experience:

> I use a cane, wear a long leg brace, and back support, walk stiff legged with a pronounced limp. All in all, I think of myself as fairly unusual in appearance and thus easily recognizable. And yet of years, I have had the experience of being "mistaken" for someone else. Usually I was a new place and a stranger would greet me as Tom, Dick, or Harry. After I explained that I was not he, they would usually apologize, saying, "You look just like him." Inevitably, I would meet this Tom, Dick, or Harry and he would be inches shorter or taller, 40 pounds heavier or lighter, a double amputee on crutches, or a paraplegic in a wheelchair. I was continually annoyed and even puzzled how anyone would mistake "him" for the "unique me." What eventually dawned on me was that to many I was handicapped, first and foremost. So much so that in the eyes of the "able-bodied," I and all the others "looked alike." (1991, p. 158)

Nevertheless, PWDs must negotiate all the developmental stages that PWODs experience and also manage the disability. In the last section of this book, we shall discuss each of these developmental stages in detail and how these stages interact with a disability. For now we shall discuss some general experiences of PWDs and developmental stages.

Ways in Which Developmental Stages Are Affected by Disability

- The developmental disorders, such as autism spectrum disorder, are diagnosed in relationship to normal developmental functioning.
- The developmental stage of the individual at the time of onset or diagnosis of a disability has an important effect on the individual's response to the disability.
- The acquisition or onset of a disability has a powerful impact on the individual's negotiation of developmental stages.
- The onset of a disability can define transitions of developmental stages.
- The onset of a disability or the treatment of the disability can cause the individual to miss out on important developmental learning and task completion.
- Society has traditionally not accorded adult PWDs adult status, infantilizing them and making them "eternal children."
- Observing friends and siblings achieve important developmental milestones is difficult for PWDs who understand that they will never be able to reach these milestones. As PWDs age they fall further and further behind, and the developmental gap continues to widen.
- There is little positive social role guidance for PWDs.

An obvious relationship between developmental stages and disability is seen in the developmental disorders. Developmental disabilities are diagnosed during childhood when deviations from typical or expected patterns of development are first noticed. Two general types of developmental symptoms now lead to a diagnosis. Mental retardation (now commonly referred to as "intellectual disabilities") is a developmental disability because there are two components of the diagnosis. The first is below-average intellectual functioning, and the second is below-average adaptive or developmental functioning. Sub-average adaptive functioning includes deficits in self-care and social skills.

The second general type of developmental disorders is characterized by behavioral and functional characteristics that are not typical of children of a particular age group, such as the pervasive developmental disorders of autism and Asperger's syndrome. Although there are far more individuals with intellectual disabilities, the autism spectrum disorder is the fastest-growing disability group in the nation.

Most developmental disabilities are diagnosed in childhood, which indicates that the signs or symptoms of these disabilities originate in childhood; however, this does not imply that developmental disorders disappear when the child grows older. Developmental disorders have lifelong consequences resulting from two sources. The first source is the continuation of characteristics or symptoms throughout life, and the second source is the disruption in learning childhood developmental and adaptive skills, such as social skills and communication abilities. Because childhood is an important time in which the brain changes and matures significantly, most children develop in a hierarchical, sequential pattern, learning one skill, then a more difficult one, and so on. Many development disabilities cause the individual to "lose out" on the typical learning and growth of childhood. When a young child is diagnosed with a developmental disability, some parents mistakenly think that their child will "grow out of it." However, the child never does outgrow the disability, and the effects of the disability in some ways become more pronounced in relation to the typical development of other children, including siblings. Thus when the child with a developmental disability is an infant, he or she may not seem very much different from other babies. However, the discrepancy gap becomes larger and more obvious as these infants become older. At each developmental stage of life, when other children ride bicycles, go to birthday parties, or attend school, both the child with a developmental disability and the child's parents may be confronted with more losses.

In order to determine developmental abnormality, it is important to understand normal development. Therefore, the study of disability must include some attention to the concept of normal development. There are universal, identifiable biological, psychological, and social milestones that are achieved at approximately the same age. Understandably, no definition or diagnosis of abnormality is without some flaw. However, there are basic guidelines that are followed, so an individual who displays only one aspect of abnormality would probably not receive a diagnosis of a developmental disorder. It is therefore important to understand what is "normal," "typical," or "expected" developmental growth. When making a diagnosis, a team of professionals will also take a detailed and thorough developmental history of the individual. Understanding the developmental history assists in both diagnosis and development of a treatment/service plan.

Most disabilities involve functional loss; generally, the older the individual, the greater the loss. Typically midlife is the time of peak professional and familial success when the individual has attained success as a result of hard work and sacrifice. Acquiring a disability in midlife often results in major losses. Of course, there are more losses in old age than at any other time of life, but these losses are offset by the social expectation of late-onset disability. Indeed, the acquisition or diagnosis of a disability at any developmental stage before old age is considered to be an "off-time" transition.

The type of disability has an impact upon the individual's negotiation of developmental stages. Degenerating and episodic (meaning having periods of symptoms alternating with periods of remission) disabilities make planning for the future difficult; indeed, planning for next week or tomorrow is difficult. A professor of English who was diagnosed with multiple sclerosis (MS), a chronic degenerating illness, described her MS as "global uncertainty" when she said:

> Our sense of who we are is intimately related to the roles we occupy, professional and personal…and to the goals we hold dear. Chronic, progressive disabling disease necessarily disrupted (or threatened to disrupt) my every role in ways that, at the outset, seemed to reduce my worth as a person. Moreover, the uncertainty of the prognosis transformed my goals and aspirations into foolishness. (Toombs, 1995, p. 16)

The public's reaction to the disability—which has nothing to do with the disability itself—also changes the individual's developmental growth. For example, most PWDs in the United States are unemployed. Perhaps it is thought that the disability makes the person unemployable; however, most PWDs express a desire to be employed. It is only society's misperceptions, the lack of accommodations, and the institutional financial disincentives that prevent PWDs from working. Eric Weihenmayer is blind and succeeded in climbing Mt. Everest. His "force of will, ingenuity, and tenacity" helped him to achieve the summit. However, he failed to obtain a job as a dishwasher while he was in college. In this excerpt, Weihenmayer (2001) described societal limitations as a locked door and concluded that this was the most difficult lesson he learned about blindness:

> Too big, too small, too fast, too hot, like a twisted version of the three bears—the story repeated itself again and again. I had thought somehow, that with my force of will, with my ingenuity, with my tenacity, I could eventually win people over and get what I wanted out of life. I hadn't realized there were doors that would remain locked in front of me. I wanted so badly to break through, to take a battering ram to them, to bash them into a million splinters, but the doors were locked too securely and their surfaces were impenetrable. I never got a dishwasher job in Cambridge, but I did choke down an important lesson, that people's perceptions of our limitations are more damaging than the limitations themselves, and it was the hardest lesson I ever had to swallow. (pp. 127–128)

The onset of a disability can define a transition. In her autobiography, the movie actor Mia Farrow stated, "My childhood ended at age 10. I contracted polio" (Farrow, 1997, p. 1). Farrow was transported to the adult world of hospitals, doctors, and physical therapy. Her disability provided a sharp boundary between two developmental stages, childhood and adulthood. While simply being elderly is not a disability, acute-onset (a sharp, sudden, clear-cut onset) disability often moves a middle-aged individual into old age.

On the other hand, many other PWDs feel that they are infantilized because of the disability. Society does not allow them to be adults. "PWDs have often been viewed as 'eternal children,' in need of control, management, and spiritual guidance" (Smart, 2009, p. 329). Infantilization of PWDs is practiced both on an individual level and an institutional level. In the film *My Body Is Not Who I Am*, a woman states, "It's as if I am a child and I have no boundaries." PWODs feel free to ask strangers with disabilities very personal questions and to touch PWDs and their assistive devices. Neither the questions nor the intrusive touching would be tolerated by someone without a disability. The medical model of disability in which PWDs are expected to be dependent recipients of services—in an inferior and subordinate position with little input into their treatment choices—also contributes to the infantilization of PWDs. Lack of physical accessibility infantilizes PWDs, including adults. An architect explained,

> [the built environment is designed for] adult, literate, numerate, physically fit specimens, with good hearing and 20:20 vision…As an architect, I am often struck how little people register about the spaces they are in and why they feel uncomfortable or otherwise. In a way, this lack of awareness places the individual in a child-like reliance on the spaces to contain them, as an infant does of its mother…. (Van Royan, 1997, p. 5; cf. Marks, 1999, p. 83)

The developmental stage of the individual at the time of acquisition of a disability is very important. The disability can be the same type of disability with the same level of severity. However, it is the time of life at the time of acquisition that is important.

For example, congenital deafness (deafness present at birth) is very different from old-age deafness. The level of hearing loss may be identical for two individuals of different ages. However, the individual who was born deaf and lived life as a deaf person would be very much different from an individual who developed deafness in old age. Another example of the importance of developmental stage is disfiguring disabilities. Because body image and attracting a romantic partner are important during the teenage years, adolescence would be a very difficult time to acquire a disfiguring disability.

Disappointment often accumulates when PWDs realize that they will never be able to achieve significant life tasks. Those with intellectual disabilities, seizure disorders, or legal blindness understand that they will not be able to obtain a driver's license. Thus the PWD falls further and further behind as his or her friends and family members continue to progress. The developmental gaps and performance discrepancies between the PWD and others continue to widen. Therefore the individual and his or her family must develop great coping skills and find different types of accommodations. For example, a mother described experiencing a sense of loss when her son reached "bicycle age."

> When my son Doug, whose disabilities were present from birth, reached bicycle age, I was dismayed that he could not ride a bike—something that had given *me* great pleasure as a child. And he couldn't climb trees. I spent many happy times as a little girl sitting and daydreaming in treetops. (Berry, 2009, p. xi)

A mother of two children—one with a disability and the other without a disability—described these developmental discrepancies between her "normal" child and her child with a disability:

> Without realizing it the process of parenting this normal child becomes a double-edged sword. We are thrilled and delighted with each accomplishment. It brings us great joy to see this child developing and progressing so well. However, at the same time, the experience can be one of pain—a spark that ignites the flames of chronic sorrow. This is especially true when the normal child surpasses the sibling with a disability. It is a very happy time that can produce, without warning, sadness. (Michalegko, 1993, p. 52)

A brother shared this story of his mother and his brother Marc, who has autism.

> My mother often told me how devastated she felt bringing Marc home after they had dropped me off at school. Watching other children his age getting dropped off with their siblings reinforced this pain. (Siegel & Silverstein, 1994, p. 8)

Many of the hardships of life can be anticipated; furthermore, role models are available from whom we can gain some insight into the management and negotiation of hardships, like death, divorce, and job loss. In the past few role models were available for PWDs because of the way society structured the lives of PWDs, keeping them hidden away, failing to provide physical accommodations for access into the community, or not allowing them to participate in education or the workplace (Imrie, 1996; Marks, 1999). Another difference between the hardships of death, divorce, and job loss is the relative lack of prejudice associated with these losses and the provision of a great deal of social support. Although the situation is improving, the acquisition or onset of a disability is often met with prejudice, discrimination, and blaming the individual for the disability (Martinelli & Dell Orto, 1991). Some PWDs are met with the remark "what did you do to yourself?"

The Three Major Theories

- Stage model
- Social moratorium or "time-out"
- Cognitive restructuring

ADAPTING TO A DISABILITY

There are three major theories on adaptation to disability. The first is a developmental stage model, similar to the stages of death and dying, first advanced by Kübler-Ross (1969). In the stage model, the individual—and often his or her family—experiences certain predictable stages in coming to terms with the disability (Livneh & Antonak, 1990, 1997). The stage theory is the most commonly used theory of adjustment to disability. In the second model the individual experiences a "social moratorium" or a "rupture." In this social moratorium the individual and his or her family engage in a period of introspection, most often during hospitalization and medical stabilization and perhaps during a long period at a physical rehabilitation center. During this time, the individual is released from his or her familial, occupational, educational, and social responsibilities. The third model of adjustment takes only physical disabilities into consideration. Wright (1960), a pioneer disability scholar who interviewed World War II veterans with physical disabilities, devised her theory of "cognitive restructuring," in which the individual redefines reality.

It is important to note that the correct term to use is *response* to disability rather than *adjustment* or *adaptation*. Choice of words is powerful. The use of adjustment and adaptation pathologizes disability, implying that a disability is automatically an undesirable experience. Also, the idea of adjustment and adaptation may imply that responding to a disability is a one-time event, rather than a lifelong process. Arnold Beisser clearly describes the constant, ongoing process of responding to a disability. Beisser (1989) was a physician traveling on a train to report for military duty during World War II. On the trip he became very sick with polio and was paralyzed from the neck down. He described his response to polio as a long-term marriage because it always changes. Nonetheless, adjustment and adaptation to disability are the most easily understood terms, so we shall use these terms in this book with the understanding that there are more accurate words to describe this experience.

It is also important to note that we are discussing only the individual's response to a disability without consideration of the environmental resources available. Good medical care, assistive technology, a caring and supportive family, and an accessible environment are resources that assist the individual in responding to a disability (Dunn, 1996;

Equal Access to Software, 1999). However, not every PWD had or has all of these resources. Nonetheless, we will consider these three models of adaptation to disability, understanding that an individual adjusts and society *accommodates*.

THE STAGE THEORY OF ADJUSTMENT TO DISABILITY

The stage model of adjustment to disability provides some helpful guidelines in the way an individual assimilates the disability into his or her identity and reorients his or her priorities and relationships. Similar to Kübler-Ross's (1969) stage theory of death and loss, the disability stage model differs in two important aspects. First, most people who die have some preparatory time, but for acute-onset disabilities, there is no time for preparation. Second, in losses such as death and job termination, the individual does not experience prejudice and discrimination as PWDs do. These stages are not irreversible, and not every stage is necessary. Some individuals skip stages or cycle back through the stages. This stage theory of adjusting to disability cannot be considered hierarchical (meaning that the preceding stage must be completely resolved before moving on to the next higher stage).

The Stages of Adjustment

- Shock
- Denial
- Depression
- Regression
- Anger, personal questioning
- Acceptance

Also, for some PWDs it is not the onset of the disability that requires adjustment, but some other meaningful event, such as being required to use a wheelchair or entering a residential care facility. The stage theory of adaptation to disability is more applicable to physical disabilities than to intellectual or psychiatric disabilities. Furthermore, the stage theory is more useful for physical disabilities that have a stable course.

The first stage is shock, in which the individual's thinking is often disorganized and the individual feels overwhelmed and confused. A woman whose husband acquired a disability after they had been married for 16 years described the state of shock as being "in the midst of a hurricane."

> When everything is over, I think I will be able to really sum up a lot of the feelings that I have inside that I find hard to express or I don't have the words for. When everything is over, I think I'll probably find a lot of things inside of me. Isn't that what happens? Like when you are in the midst of a hurricane it's real hard to kind of…figure out everything. But once you are out of it, you can kind of go, "Hey, yeah, I was in the middle of that hurricane, and this is what happened." (Buki, 2007, p. 339)

The second stage is denial, often called "defensive retreat." As the word *defensive* implies, this stage can be therapeutic because it may allow the individual to maintain his or her self-identity. However, denial is considered therapeutic only if the denial does not continue for too long (Naugle, 1991; Stewart, 1994). Denial of the disability is very rare, but denial of the permanence of the disability or the implications of the disability is more common. Remarks such as "I'll soon be my old self" are a denial of the permanence of the disability. President Franklin Roosevelt, who contracted polio, engaged in denial of the implications of his paralysis when he said, "I will walk again" (Gallagher, 1985). He never did walk again because the polio virus destroyed his hip and leg muscles. However, a few childhood disabilities, such as asthma, are not permanent, and the child eventually outgrows the disability. Still, most developmental disabilities are chronic, lifelong conditions.

A young man diagnosed with schizophrenia related the way in which the combination of the symptoms of the disability and society's prejudice and discrimination made shock and denial difficult to overcome.

> I cannot tell you how difficult it is for a person to accept the fact that he or she is schizophrenic. Since the time we were very young we have all been conditioned to accept that if something is crazy or insane, its worth to us is automatically dismissed.... The nature of this disorder is that it affects the chemistry that controls your cognitive processes. It affects your belief system.... It is exceedingly difficult for you to admit to yourself that the mind does not function properly. It fools you. (Frese, 1997, pp. 145–146)

A pediatrician (Batshaw, 1998) stated that physicians and other medical providers may engage in denial. Batshaw told of the tendency of many professionals to use the term *developmental delay* rather than *developmental disability* or *mental retardation*. Although Batshaw clearly states that it is not appropriate to use the diagnosis of a developmental delay for a child older than two to three years, it may be a type of denial on the part of physicians (which then perpetuates denial in the parents). Batshaw concluded: "It [the use of developmental delay] then becomes a way of avoiding the reality that may be painful both to the parent and to the professional" (p. 54).

The third stage is depression, in which the individual attempts to retain his or her former identity. The future is uncertain, and the individual may feel that he or she no longer has an identity. Often PWDs feel that "my family would be better off without me." In this stage, the individual does not have the motivation or energy to invest in a rehabilitation program. One man with a spinal cord injury stated,

> If someone is stuck in the grieving process... it's like an adjustment to a death. The only thing is, for an injury or disability, it's not as easy to adjust as with a death because with a death, the person's no longer there. With a disability, you have a constant reminder. So, sometimes, it takes even longer to grieve and adjust. A lot of people turn to alcohol and drugs, which is a way of going through denial. As long as you're smashed, you can forget about your disability. (Scherer, 1993, p. 115)

Another man, paralyzed from a diving accident as an adult, described his physical rehabilitation and the total lack of attention to his emotional needs. He, too, describes his depression as experiencing a death of a loved one (Hofsiss & Laffey, 1993):

> The one thing that surprised me through all of this was the real lack of either interest or concern about depression after an accident. There is much more concern about your physical therapy, making sure that your lungs are clear, all the things that might physically have happened to you. "Can you move this? Can you feel that?" But, for the emotional things, no psychiatric help was offered by the doctors who had been treating me and certainly knew my case very intimately.
>
> I began to see a therapist. I talked to her very much the way I think one would if one had gone through the death of someone close. Because there is that grieving process you must allow yourself—very essential to anybody whose life is altered as severely as mine was. (p. 86)

The fourth stage is regression, in which the person gives up and regresses to an earlier, less mature stage of life. Cohen (2004), who has multiple sclerosis, related that he received the diagnosis from his doctor by telephone and described his reaction to the diagnosis. "After the phone was returned to the cradle, immediately I wished I could be also [returned to the cradle]. This would be a great time to be an infant again, to be picked up and rocked" (p. 18).

The fifth stage is anger or personal questioning, in which the person may ask, "Why me?" or "Why did God allow this to happen to me?" Often PWDs will replay the accident or the prediagnosis period endlessly, trying to find someone to blame or looking for ways to have avoided the disability (Bordieri, 1993; Bordieri & Drehmer, 1993). Frequently PWDs believe in the erroneous assumption of a fair world in which everyone receives what he or she "deserves." Obviously, misguided belief in the "fair world" fallacy can lead to anger. A man with a spinal cord injury spoke of:

> anger that just sits there and grows. I wish I'd had counseling...on a fairly regular basis. I'm not sure what would've come out of it, but if you see someone enough, eventually you're going to say something. Try to bring things out, some of the anger, and things like that. That was something that was never done, and that anger just sits in there and grows. (Scherer, 1993, p. 160)

The stage model assists PWDs, their families, and their caregivers in understanding the process of accepting a disability. They can understand that these stages are "normal," or better stated, typical and to be expected. While some of these stages, such as anger and depression, are not pleasant to experience or to watch a loved one experience, understanding and tolerance can be given rather than abandoning the PWD. In addition, treatment plans can be developed. The man with the spinal cord injury stated that counseling could have helped him deal with his anger. However, the stage theory is not as useful with episodic disabilities, degenerating disabilities, or psychiatric disabilities such as mental illness.

Many practitioners and researchers are beginning to question the stage model of adaptation to disability asserting that the adaptation process is influenced by a broad array of factors, such as visibility of the disability, developmental stage and chronological age at onset, and functional limitations. Therefore, these individuals do not provide a "road-map" approach as does the stage theory of adaptation. Instead, an undefined, individualistic process is advocated. Harper and Peterson (2000) explained: "There are complex relationships among these variables between their rate of progression, pattern, and sequence, level, type, and context of adaptive functioning. Individual differences and variation is the rule between individuals with common phenotypic, chronic, physical disorders" (p. 127). It seems that the stage model accommodates and considers all of these factors.

Kübler-Ross's stage theory of death and dying is also being questioned for many of the same reasons as the stage theory of adapting to disability. However, even the sharpest critics of Kübler-Ross credit her theory and the interventions based on her theory with three positive outcomes. Kübler-Ross' theory (1) changed the way in which both professionals and the general public viewed death (as a process rather than a one-time event), (2) changed the way in which dying individuals were treated and cared for, (3) provided support to the family of the dying individual by allowing her to see her loved ones' responses to the dying process as "normal" or typical, and (4) created an entire profession and a system of caring for terminal patients: the hospice and death and dying counselors.

In the same way, even though criticism of the stage theory of adaptation to disability is growing, this theory can offer the same four benefits: (1) changing the way in which professionals and the general public view disability, (2) changing the ways in which PWDs are treated and cared for (by providing counseling and other emotional support), (3) providing support to the families of PWDs, and (4) creating a new set of professionals—disability counselors.

The Social Moratorium

The second model of adjustment to disability is called the "social moratorium," in which the individual is given time away from responsibilities. There is a clear separation between life "before the disability" and life "after the disability." This time is used to redefine oneself and (occasionally) to separate from past disadvantages, such as economic poverty, lack of education, difficulties with the legal system, or substance abuse. Marsh and Lefly (1996) explained: "A catastrophic event [such as a disability] generally results in disintegration of existing patterns, which in turn offers the opportunity for constructive reintegration" (p. 3).

Cognitive Restructuring

The third model deals only with physical disabilities and is considered to be the first model of acceptance of disability. Beatrice Wright developed her theory of cognitive restructuring immediately after World War II and published her seminal work in 1960 (McCarthy, 1993). Wright's theory is composed of four points. The first is enlargement of the scope of values that are not in conflict with the disability. First-person accounts of people with physical disabilities often have this statement: "I escaped into my mind," giving an example of an enlargement of scope of values. Individuals with more education, a longer work history, and a supportive family have been found to be accepting of disability simply because there are more options available to them and they are able to pursue a different type of life.

Wright's Four Points

- Enlargement of the scope of values
- Subordination of the physique
- Containment of disability effects
- Transformation from comparative to asset values

The second point is "subordination of the physique." Many people consider their body to be a symbol of worth, desirability, and competence, which is not surprising because we live in a culture that is obsessed with physical appearance. The acquisition of a physical disability prompts the individual to consider his or her self-identity. What makes you, you? What makes me, me? Intellect, personality, character, a spiritual soul, or past history often becomes the PWD's self-identity, rather than any physical characteristic or appearance. Incidentally, elderly individuals without disabilities also experience a subordination of the physique. Charles Mee, a writer who contracted polio as a teenager, resented his father's failure to see the way in which Charles's disability changed his identity. Mee stated that he "was filled with rage."

> For the rest of his life after I had polio, my father carried a picture of me in his wallet that he had taken at the halftime of a football game. I was sitting on the grass with my teammates while the coach talked to us. My father had come around to the side of the group, and as I turned to look at him, he took the picture: an adolescent boy in the vigor of youth, a strong jaw and neck, a crew cut, massive shoulders with the football pads....I always took the fact that he carried that picture with him as a sign of disappointment in me, and it filled me with rage....The photograph was still on a table not far from his bed when he died at the age of ninety-four. (1999, p. 170)

The third point of Wright's model is "containment of disability effects." The individual does not deny the disability but contains or limits the effects of the disability. This requires active management of the disability, the avoidance of secondary disabilities, and an active search for opportunities that are available. The PWD has a realistic view of the disability and neither exaggerates nor minimizes it. The individual wishes to return to normality—a new, redefined version of normality in which the absence of the disability or a cure for the disability is not considered necessary. Normality means the return of the individual's family life, work life, and social life, all with a disability. In a recent oral history of Canadian World War II veterans with spinal cord injuries, titled "Going Back to Civvy Street," the veterans describe the way in which they self-described normality.

> It didn't make much sense spending all that energy covering a short distance (on crutches)...when you could do it quickly and easily with a wheelchair.... It

didn't take long for people to get over the idea that walking was that essential. (Tremblay, 1996, p. 153)

The fourth and final point of Wright's model is "transformation from comparative to asset values." This is also termed "asset orientation," meaning that rather than considering one's losses, the PWD should focus on what he or she can do. Two aspects of shifting from comparative values include the necessity of not comparing oneself to PWODs and actively discovering one's strengths and talents. Randy Souders felt that his disability rescued him from a life in a "mediocre little ad agency."

> It's odd. If I had a crystal ball to see what would have happened had I not had the injury, I don't see myself having done what I've done at all. I would probably have a mediocre position in a mediocre little ad agency and be like the rest of society—up to my ears in debt, just trying to get by—and frustrated that I didn't go for something that would have truly inspired me all along. . . . I don't know that I would have dedicated myself to art. Art was a vital part of my recovery from my injury. I found myself in a situation of being the same person in a new body, one that didn't work, along with the loss of self-esteem and self-confidence and all the things that come along with a traumatic injury. Once I realized that I still had a chance at being creative and of value through my artwork, I just really focused in on that. It was a real part of my recovery. (Smith & Plimpton, 1993, p. 153)

DISABILITY AS GROWTH AND DEVELOPMENT

Most theories of human growth and development consider the process of development to be represented by an upward line and the goal to be greater competence, autonomy, and individuality. In contrast, disability is incorrectly thought to be deviance, weakness, and pathology, so life with a disability cannot be a life of competence, autonomy, and greater autonomy.

Erikson, a developmental theorist, viewed "ego disequilibrium" as a motivation to higher stages. Ego disequilibrium, or imbalance, is the result of wanting to progress to the next development stage, learning new skills, and conforming to societal expectations, while at the same, desiring to remain in the security and familiarity of the present stage. The "crises" of each of Erikson's stages are periods of great potential and heightened vulnerability. The onset or diagnosis of a disability can be considered a developmental task or crisis, or a turning point in an individual's life. There are PWDs who consider their disability to have been a catalyst for a transformation to becoming a better person and living a different type of life.

The idea that different people reach the same goals through different pathways seems appropriate to the disability experience. This is termed the *model of diverging pathways* (Kerckhoff, 1993). Longitudinal studies have the capability to show the effects of the model of diverging pathways. There have been no longitudinal studies conducted on individuals with a wide array of disabilities.

Finally, the concepts of growth, development, and maturation in old age have parallels with the disability experience. In the past, life-span theorists considered old age to be a period of decline and loss, which was and is true in a solely biological sense. However, some theorists assert that other types of growth and development occur in the presence of biological loss, such as the growth of wisdom and a wider and less judgmental understanding or view of the world and others. A mother of a man with a psychiatric disability described her son:

> Well, he is the most kind, wonderful human being—probably because all he has been through. He volunteers at our local crisis unit. Patients will go in because he is there. Other families request him to speak to their mentally ill loved one. Because of Clozapine (an anti-psychotic medication), he is in a master's of social work (MSW) [program] at our university, and he wants to work with severely mentally ill patients when he graduates. Our mental health center said they want him to work there. (Marsh & Lefly, 1996)

In another first-person account, a woman thinks of her missing arm as a Zen Buddhist koan, a paradox that is used to meditate upon in order to gain enlightenment.

> Being disabled is a deep wound, a source of pain. But like all wounds, it is also a gift. As Eastern wisdom has always known, it is hard to tell good luck from bad luck.... Having one arm is an endless koan. It is what it is, which is unknowable, and it attracts a lot of ideas, stories, and images. Caught up in the negative story, I felt ashamed, incomplete, and not okay. I drank to die. Later on, caught up in a more positive story, I felt pride and a sense of identity.... In such open being there is freedom and possibility for the new. (Tollifson, 1997, p. 111)

One article (Boerner & Jopp, 2007) discussed major life change and loss and how three major life-span theories describe adjustment to loss. Although disability is not specifically mentioned, one example provided considers two types of disabilities: blindness and arthritis. This may be because one of the authors (Boerner) is affiliated with Lighthouse International, a large research and service agency for individuals with all types of vision loss. This article is unique in human development literature because the authors refer to the acquisition of a disability and ways in which to respond:

> Life changes or losses (e.g., a physical impairment) often involve coping challenges that are both within and beyond one's control. For example, a person with a functional loss due to arthritis or vision impairment may be able to maintain prior levels of functioning in certain life domains by using technical aids, while having to reevaluate the importance of those life domains which are no longer manageable even with the help of such aids. Furthermore, it may be critical to achieve developmental gains during periods of loss. (p. 172)

Discussing the possibility for growth and development during old age, Baltes, Staudiner, and Lindenberger (1999) asserted:

> Deficits in biological status can also be the foundation for progress, that is, antecedents for positive changes in adaptive functioning.... In this line of thinking, the human organization is by nature (Gehlen, 1956) a "being of deficits" and social culture has developed or emerged in part to deal specifically with biological deficits.
>
> This "deficits-breeds-growth" mechanism may not only account for cultural–biological evolution, it may also affect ontogenesis. Thus it is possible that when people reach states of increased vulnerability in old age, social forces

and individuals invest more and more heavily in efforts that are explicitly oriented toward regulating and compensating for age-associated biological deficits, thereby generating a broad range of novel behaviors, new bodies of knowledge and values, new environmental features, and, as a result, a higher level of adaptive functioning. (p. 478)

Baltes et al. (1999) clearly stated that (1) biological deficits are natural ("by nature") and universal; (2) society should "invest" in people with biological deficits, assisting them to compensate and regulate these deficits; and (3) investing in people with biological deficits will benefit both these individuals and society as a whole due to "new bodies of knowledge and values." If the word *disability* is substituted for "biological deficits" and "old age," then PWDs will be viewed as valued members of the larger culture and society and the disability experience will become valued and less frightening. These authors clearly advocate for the "deficits-breeds-growth" approach.

In this short introduction we have touched on the topics of developmental theories and disability and chronic illness. Each of these two topics will be discussed in greater detail later in this book. The purpose of this book is to understand the relationship between developmental theories, developmental life stages, and disability.

This book consists of three major sections:

- Explanation and description of the major developmental theories and their importance and utility.
- Presentation of the major stages or periods of life, such as infancy, childhood, adolescence, adulthood, elderly, and how the acquisition or diagnosis of a disability influences each stage of life.
- Discussion how the major developmental theories can incorporate the experience of disability.

Terms to Learn

Cognitive restructuring	Infantilization	Transformation from
Containment of disability	Rites of passage	comparative to asset
effects	Social moratorium	values
Enlargement of the scope	Subordination of the	
of values	physique	

Videos to View

- View the 24-minute video *A Full Stride: Overcoming the Challenge of Amputation,* by Films for the Humanities and Sciences. The producers describe this video as follows: "Focusing on three people, this program shows the many sides of what is often a generic label: disabled or amputee. Old, young, partial loss, complete loss, each story is different. From the time of hospitalization to the triumph of accomplishing small and large tasks, we see the many challenges and the small victories: the psychological pain of losing a limb, the stigma of being 'disabled,' and the vivid 'phantom' pain of a lost limb, but also the process of adjustment to a prosthesis and the freedom and mobility it can bring."

- View the 30-minute video *Open to the Public: Complying with the Americans with Disabilities Act,* from Aquarius Productions. The producers describe this video as providing "an overview of the ADA as it applies to state and local governments. The ADA does not provide recommendations for solving common problems, but this film could provide enough information…to solve common problems."

Learning Activities

(Note: Some of these may be used for class presentations.)

- Read Beatrice Wright's book *Physical Disability: A Psychological Approach* (1960), published by Harper and Row. Write 10 paragraphs about her work with PWDs and her groundbreaking book. Why do you think Dr. Wright focused only on physical disabilities?
- Read and review the ADA, and learn the five titles of this law. Why were the 2008 Amendments necessary? ADA can be found at: www.usdoj.gov/crt/ada/adahom1.htm.
- Obtain the ADA technical manual, which will give precise measurements and specifications for accessibility. Visit various places in your community, such as entertainment facilities, sports facilities, schools, and churches or other places of worship, then give a class presentation on your findings. Explain the way in which your awareness of lack of accessibility has increased.
- Interview an individual who has acquired a disability. Explain the stage theory of adaptation and ask this individual if these stages apply to him or her. Explain Wright's theory of adjustment, and ask if this applies to him or her.
- Interview a parent or parents of a child with a congenital disability. Explain Wright's theory of adaptation to disability and the stage theory of adjustment to disability, and ask these parents if these apply to them.
- Read the article "An Integrated Model of Psychosocial Adjustment Following Acquired Disability," written by Kendall and Buys in 1998 and published in the *Journal of Rehabilitation.* Kendall and Buys raise serious questions about Wright's stage theory of adjustment to disability. Do you agree or disagree with these authors?
- Complete the *Acceptance of Disability Scale* (ADS). This instrument was developed using Wright's theory of adaptation to physical disability. Place each question on this scale into one of four categories based on Wright's four components.
- Read D. C. Linkowski (1987) *The Acceptance of Disability Scale.* Washington, DC: The George Washington University Medical Center, Department of Psychiatry and Behavioral Sciences, the Rehabilitation Research and Training Center.

Writing Exercises

- Write a six-paragraph paper defending this statement: "People with disabilities will soon dominate the national agenda." Consider services and public funding.
- Write a five-page paper describing a rite of passage of your religion or of some group you belong to. For example, how does your religion define, celebrate, and observe a wedding? What are the bases for this particular rite of passage? How does this rite of passage change the self-identity of the individual and change the identity of the individual in the view of others?
- Write a six-paragraph paper defending this statement: "Those hardships in life for which an individual can make preparations are typically easier to negotiate."
- Interview an individual who is 20 years old or older who has sustained a disability. Ask him or her about the adjustment period. Did this individual seem to follow the stage theory, the social moratorium theory, or the cognitive restructuring theory? Write a 10-paragraph paper explaining your findings.
- Do you think that using the phrase "response to a disability" rather than "acceptance/adjustment/adaptation to a disability" is important? Write three paragraphs that explain your reasons for agreeing or disagreeing with this statement.
- Write a three-page paper on the type of party you would have every year if you were involved in an accident and became quadriplegic. Name the party "the-day-I-broke-my-neck" party. Which people would you invite? What would be the activities? Do you think your party would be fun?

Basic Principles of Developmental Theories

2

It is important to examine the different theories of human development, because these theories often determine what is considered to be normal or abnormal human behavior. These theories describe the experiences of a large number of people, thus providing a framework that defines normal, or more correctly stated, what is considered to be typical. In this section, the basic principles and commonalities of several of these theories are presented. There is variability among all of the theories, and some of these theories continue to evolve. In the next chapters, overviews of the major theories and the differences among them will be presented. The distinctive features of each of the major theories will be emphasized. These major theories have affected the way in which testing and assessment is undertaken, the implementation of public policy, and many therapeutic and educational applications. Therefore, although these theories may appear abstract and merely theoretical, they have real-life consequences for individuals.

The study of life-course development began only recently in the 1920s. In the beginning, it tended to focus solely on childhood development because it was thought that most—if not all—development was completed by adulthood. The shorter life spans, the influence of Freud, and the lack of longitudinal studies all contributed to this focus on children.

The theories included in this book are often referred to as the "grand theories" of human development because they have continued to be used by scholars, researchers, and practitioners. These grand theories are typically referred to by the last names of their originators—such as Freud, Erikson, and Skinner—although it is probably more correct to label these theories by their guiding principles—such as psychosexual (Freud), psychosocial (Erikson), and behavioral (Skinner).

No single developmental theory provides a complete description and explanation of human development (Berk, 2001; Hunt, 2005). The problems and social issues with which counselors contend cannot be conceptualized by using a single theory. Life is complex; there have been no attempts to merge all of these theories into one "metatheory," or a single, all-inclusive theory. Magnusson and Torestad (1992) explained:

> These are considered grand theories because each provided powerful frameworks that guided all the questions used by practitioners in gathering information needed to understand issues involving human behavior (Renninger & Amstel, 1997). However, competing theories have existed side by side, and integration of theories has seldom or ever taken place. (p. 89)

Developmental theories are based on the assumption that predictable and common changes occur in individuals' lives. Most developmental theories look at the entire life span from womb to tomb, from conception to death. This is called "life-span perspective" and helps us understand both constancy and change (Berk, 1998). Life-span research has tended to generate knowledge on three components: (1) individual development, (2) interindividual commonalities, and (3) the degree of plasticity or adaptability of the individual. Developmental theories are interdisciplinary organizing frameworks for understanding the human life span (Mortimer & Shanahan, 2004). The professions and academic disciplines of sociology, psychology, education, anthropology, medicine, and rehabilitation counseling develop and refine these theories, conduct research to validate these theories, and incorporate them into practice applications. The terms *life span*, *life history*, *life course*, and *life cycle* are synonymous with each other.

Some practitioners and researchers study a single individual and his or her negotiation of these developmental stages: a case study. Others study a single developmental stage—such as old age or early childhood—and the way in which various groups of people pass through this stage. A few longitudinal studies have focused on designated individuals as they progress through many life stages, such as the Terman (1929) studies. Louis Terman, a professor at Stanford University, studied 1,500 very intelligent boys from 1921 into their maturity during the time of the Great Depression and World War II. Terman wanted to understand the relationship between intelligence and social adjustment, health, emotional stability, marital stability, professional success, and other variables. After decades of study, Terman concluded that intellectually gifted individuals reported better physical health, professional success, and higher levels of marital and emotional stability. The subjects in Terman's studies nicknamed themselves "termites."

A few of these theorists, such as Freud (1952, 1969), have not only created a theory of human growth and development but have also developed psychotherapies. However, most of these developmental theories do not emphasize any practice or therapeutic methods. Developmental theories describe, define, and explain the ways in which people mature and experience the stages of life.

Basic Principles of Developmental Theories
- Biological age as the basis of most developmental theories
- Cultural and social interpretations (or constructions) of biological age
- Formal and informal age-appropriate norms
- The meaning of "normative"
- The definition of "social clock"

CHRONOLOGICAL AND BIOLOGICAL AGE

Biology sets some limits. Therefore, chronological and biological age are often associated with each stage of development, such as infancy, early childhood, adolescence, adulthood, and old age, providing the basis for age norms. Behavioral changes occur during certain time periods, and these changes are based on biological growth and physical maturation, often referred to as the "biological clock." Every society and culture has age-normed role-functioning expectations. The expression "act your age" simply means that everyone is expected to act and think in a way considered appropriate for his or her age. This is referred to as the "social clock." Riegel (1975) explained, "The normal course of life is partially determined by inter-biological factors that find expression in the normative age-grading system of any society.... Physical maturation determines the boundaries of these normative events" (cf. Datan & Ginsberg, 1975, p. 101). Body image also changes with both biological age and developmental task. Age norms require that individuals engage in some behaviors and avoid other behaviors, thus requiring individuals to make choices. These decisions are often termed *critical decisions* because they are thought to be essential to a particular stage. Behaviors and attitudes are considered to be normative when they occur in a similar way for most people in any given group. More than 40 years ago Neugarten (1968) recognized that societal opportunity structures are built around large groups of people adhering to the social clock theory of human development and "being on time." These societal opportunity structures also penalize people who are "off-time," being too early or too late. In addition, most on-time changes and stages are considered to be less stressful to the individual simply because his or her age mates are experiencing these same changes; social support and understanding are available, and the individual feels understood and supported when "on time."

These age-normed stages provide direction and structure for developmental theories, and developmental theories based on chronological age just seem to "make sense" or are "intuitively appealing." Of course, many changes in chronological age are visible and measureable. We can see the teenager's growth spurt of three inches in a single year; however, the teenager's psychological and social maturation is not as visible or easy to measure and quantify.

Some of these age norms are codified in law and are universal and formalized. Examples of these include public school entry, compulsory school attendance, conscription into the military, the right to drive a car, the right to consume alcohol, the right to vote, the right to seek public office, or the right to retire with full social security benefits (Carr, 2009). Structured social roles and statuses tend to be related to biological age, probably because biological age is easily measured and documented. However, in the last century biological age changed dramatically. Longer life spans were not readily predictable when many of these theories emerged. All of the six major types of theories predated the longer life spans. Indeed, although demographers predicted these demographic changes, they were often surprised at the *extent* of these changes. For example, although the Baby Boomer generation was expected, the "boom" was larger (more babies) and longer (continued for more years until the birth rate fell to normal) than anticipated.

Both biological age and the formalized, written rules for the developmental stages based on age are easy to understand (Schu-Chen & Schmiedek, 2000). No one expects an infant (while in infancy) to enlist in the military or to go to college. However, when the infant becomes 18 years old, he or she may do either of those things. Mayer and Schoepflin (1989) wrote an article, titled "The State and the Life Course," in which they stated, "Age groups are a favorite way of dividing up social problems" (p. 200). There are services for children, for teenagers, for the elderly, and all other age groups. It is true that the continuing increase in life spans has led to more ambiguous interpretations of chronological age, and "organizational and governmental policies and practices have not kept pace with the realities of [a] changing and aging" population (Moen, 2004, pp. 275–276).

Unwritten, age-appropriate norms are more difficult to understand (Sheehy, 1976). At what age should an individual marry? When should an individual have children? Neither of these very important changes has been formalized in law but is instead more socially and culturally defined. In many societies and cultures, these unwritten proscriptions and prescriptions often have a greater influence on human behavior than written, formal law (Baltes, Reese, & Lipsitt, 1980). For example, religion is often associated with many developmental stages of life. Baptisms, confirmations, bar and bat mitzvahs, the Hispanic Quinceanera, and the Amish rumspringa are examples of rites of passage for children and adolescents at specific ages that require them to complete certain tasks, assume added responsibilities, and change their identities—both to themselves and to others (Clydesdale, 2009).

We can see that although biological age provides the basis for human growth and developmental theories, social and cultural *interpretations* of age often play a greater role in determining appropriate behavior. The importance of cultural interpretations is described in this way: chronological age is "meaningless unless there is knowledge of the particular culture and the social meaning(s) attached to chronological age" (Neugarten & Hagestad, 1976). For example, the "social clock" for people in the lower socioeconomic statuses tends to run faster. "Low socioeconomic status people in our society generally leave school, begin work, marry, and become parents at younger ages than those of higher socioeconomic statuses" (Rice, 1998, p. 450). This is often called "accelerated aging."

One developmental theorist (Elder, 1991, 1997) stated that conceptualization of the life course requires three different meanings of age: (1) chronological age, (2) social age, and (3) historical age. There are two other types of age: functional age (defined as the individual's functioning in a certain environment) and identity age (defined as the individual's perception of his or her age). However, chronological age is an objective measure that is easily obtainable and continues to be the marker used for administrative and government agencies.

In general, those theories of human development that are closely related to biological and chronological age tend to be more linear, are ordered more sequentially, and may incorporate the concept of irreversibility. Irreversibility means that the individual cannot return to an earlier stage of development. Biologically based theories of development tend to be unidimensional, unidirectional, and unifunctional (Baltes, Staudiner, & Lindenberger, 1999). For example, Freud's theory is based on the individual's biology, specifically sexual needs. Therefore, Freudian theory is considered to be unifunctional (meeting only sexual needs), unidirectional (growth and development is defined only as sexual maturity), and unidimensional (because the individual's biology explains all growth and development). Freud ignored such aspects as the person's work or family functions (multifunctional), as well as many dimensions of the person, such as his or her intellectual life or spirituality.

Freud's theory would also be considered a "noncontextual" theory because it is focused only on a biological machine—the individual's body—and not on the surrounding context or environment. More flexible theories tend to be contextual, multidimensional, multifunctional, and multidirectional; they tend to state that some reversibility is possible. These more flexible theories also assert that the same level of functioning can be achieved through different paths. Therefore, a developmental outcome can be a result of many different pathways.

Is human development defined by religion, by the medical professions, by governments, or by individuals themselves? The answer is all of the above. Religions (for religious people) give meaning to the various stages of human life. The medical professions assist in negotiating developmental changes simply because there are biological aspects to these various stages. Governments define the various life stages by enacting and enforcing laws and policies that provide opportunity structures—such as education—that enhance development. Individuals themselves, with the combination of religion, medicine, and government, define their own development within a historical context.

Developmental Stages

- Linear
- Sequential
- Epigenetic
- Hierarchical
- Stages involve ego disequilibrium

Chronological age is the starting point for each of these developmental stages as defined by various developmental theories (Bandura, 1982; Baltes & Schaie, 1973; Smith & Voneche, 2006). However, developmental stages are defined differently in each of the major theories, emphasizing different aspects such as Freud's psychosexual development, Erikson's psychosocial development, and Piaget's cognitive development. In all of the theories, there are similarities that characterize their underlying assumptions.

Developmental theories view the life span as a series of sequential, linear, epigenetic, hierarchal stages that involve ego disequilibrium. A developmental stage is a period of life with specific characteristics that distinguish it from the preceding and succeeding stages (Newman & Newman, 2009). Therefore, stages vary *qualitatively*, meaning that different cognitive, social, and emotional changes occur in the way the individual perceives himself or herself and the way in which others perceive the individual. Most individuals pass through each of these stages in a somewhat orderly fashion; in some of these theories, the sequence or order of the stages is considered to be fixed. Each stage allows us to look at a particular period of life and determine the interrelationships between physical growth and social and emotional development. Developmental stages show what is expected of the individual at different stages throughout the life span; therefore, developmental stages include societal and cultural expectations. The individual's behaviors at each stage are not isolated responses but rather general patterns of thought and behavior that are exhibited in a wide array of circumstances (Adams, 2006). These new behaviors and attitudes become part of the individual's personality and temperament.

At each stage, the individual encounters new developmental tasks that, if successfully completed, lead to greater mastery over the environment, along with more freedom and autonomy. Completing each stage may be compared to climbing a staircase in which every step mounted results in greater maturity, competency, and autonomy. Infants learn to walk and speak, children complete school, and adults marry and find meaningful work.

Developmental stages are considered to be epigenetic because the successful completion of one stage enables the individual to progress to the next higher stage with more complex developmental tasks (Bateson, 1998). The prefix *epi* means "upon," and *genesis* means "emergence." Epigenetic means that growth occurs as one component of a developmental stage arises out of another, and each has its own time. *Hierarchical* is a related term and describes the way in which the successful completion of one developmental stage results in competency and strength that can be utilized in the more complex and difficult tasks required in the following developmental stage. Epigenetic growth is both cumulative and continuous. For example, Piaget's theory of learning is epigenetic, because Piaget stated that higher levels of cognitive functioning can be found in elements of lower levels. Epigenetic and hierarchical development includes the individual's capacity to retain growth, strengths, knowledge, and insights obtained in an earlier stage. The individual incorporates these assets into an increasingly complex personality.

However, Kohlberg believed that this progression through the stages of cognitive moral reasoning is a result of the individual's thinking deeply about moral problems, rather than a result of biology. Like other epigenetic theorists, Kohlberg stated that the sequence of stages in his theory cannot be rearranged and that it is not possible to skip a stage. Therefore, Kohlberg's theory of cognitive moral reasoning is epigenetic, but not in a biological sense.

Another clear-cut example of epigenetic growth is biological maturation. As infants, we are born with all of our body parts (most of the time), and our physical growth is cumulative. For example, as we mature, our arms become larger, stronger, and more coordinated. Discontinuous growth might entail growing a third arm. Biological continuity also applies to negative experiences. Therefore, it is easy to see why, generally speaking, life-span theorists whose theories are closely related to biological stages have developed theories that tend to be epigenetic and describe continuous growth.

An additional type of epigenetic change might include the concept of "cumulating advantages" and "cumulating disadvantages" (Elder, 1997, p. 7). Choices made in an earlier stage, especially adolescence and young adulthood, set in motion long-lasting consequences and affect all subsequent transitions and changes. For example, substance abuse in adolescence may have long-term physical effects.

Most stage theories state that growth and development occur in all stages of life; however, the rate of change is greatest during infancy and old age (Bornestein & Lamb, 1984). Growth and development are thought to occur in old age because, although "biological sources of development deplete with increasing age," there is the possibility of "age-related growth in adaptive functioning" (Staudiner & Lindenberger, 2003, p. 8). Later in life, in addition to reaching new levels of capability, people deal with two additional demands: maintenance of levels of functioning and regulation of loss. Therefore, stages of development are considered *linear* because a line (not exactly a straight line) represents the successful completion of each stage. Because every stage has growth and development, the direction is upward. Freud's theory is an exception to the idea that there is growth in every stage, because he believed that development stopped at late adolescence, when the individual achieved sexual maturity.

Ego Disequilibrium

- Crises
- Turning points
- Increased vulnerability
- Heightened possibility

Ego disequilibrium, or tension, occurs in each stage of life because the individual is required to complete developmental tasks. Erikson refers to this disequilibrium as a "crisis," the resolution of which results in greater ego identity (or sense of self) and competence. The successful goal-directed completion of each stage results in a lifelong strength, competence, and mastery. Therefore, each stage has an outcome or goal, and when this goal is met, the individual moves to the next (higher) stage. These transitions can often be difficult and demanding. Perhaps, it is more helpful to consider disequilibrium or crisis as a turning point or critical decision point. The word *crisis* may imply a catastrophic event, but Erikson (1968) described a crisis as "a turning point, a crucial period of increased vulnerability and heightened potential" (p. 84). Another way in which to view these transition points is to consider the magnitude of the consequences of each decision (Datan & Ginsberg, 1975). For example, the decision each day of which clothes to wear probably requires less thought and emotional involvement than the decision of which university to attend. Daily clothing decisions, whether good or bad, do not typically have long-term consequences. Finally, everyone anticipates and plans for the next stage; however, the individual's present stage of life, and the tasks required, takes precedence.

In the section on changing demographics, we shall see that both social and biological clocks are changed by factors in the environment, such as demographic conditions found in pages 39–48, educational opportunities, and scientific advances.

Off-Time Transitions

- Early off-time transitions
- Late off-time transitions

The preceding section emphasized that developmental stages and tasks occur in a certain sequence and at an approximate time in an individual's life. Most of us have an expected order of life events. What happens when the timing and order of developmental stages are "off-time?" Off-time refers to development stages that occur either "early" or "late" in an individual's life or occur in a different sequence. Three Swiss developmental scholars, Freund, Nikitin, and Ritter (2001) stated that

> development is not only the result of a person's history, but also of the antici-
> pated future. More specifically, we argue that the extension of future time per-
> spective plays an important psychological role for developmental regulation.
> But what happens when the future is different from [what] the individual
> expected? (p. 1)

Off-time developmental stages or tasks are typically stressful. Whether considered to be positive, such as graduating from college early, or negative, such as not climbing a career ladder at the customary time, deviations from typical timetables cause stress. Angold and Costello (1991) described off-time transitions: "Normality requires us to take into account not only the symptom and the behavior, but also the developmental stage at which it occurs" (p. 84). Marcia (2002) stated that normal, expected life events are not as stigmatizing as off-time events. Marcia used the example of the midlife crisis to make his point, adding that on-time events are regarded more positively and receive more social support. For example, in the past, experiencing a midlife crisis was consid-ered stigmatizing, but as more and more people reported that they have had a midlife crisis, it was no longer considered to be shameful.

Generally, early transitions (or off-time developmental transitions that are earlier than typical) have enduring consequences. Early transitions affect later transitions and set in motion "cumulating advantages and disadvantages" (Elder, 1997, p. 7). For exam-ple, 9 out of 10 of the males in the Oakland Growth Study served in the military. It is no surprise that most of these men served in the military, because they came from economically deprived families of the Great Depression of the 1930s and World War II coincided with their young adult years. This example clearly shows the strong influence of historical events. Somewhat surprising was the difference found between those men who entered the military early in their life and those who entered the military at a later age. Men who entered the military "early" (defined as shortly after high school) expe-rienced a lifetime of advantages, including an early developmental change that pulled men from the past and created new beginnings for them. The early entrance into the military has been called a "knifing-off" period or a "social moratorium" (Shanahan, 2000, p. 673). Early mobilization into the military acted as a clear-cut break or "time-out," which gave these men time to contemplate their self-identity and their future plans. The military also provided a new set of opportunities and experiences for growth and development, including leadership skills, travel, and group processes. Young men in the military in this study were placed in highly demanding leadership positions.

Glueck and Glueck (1950, 1968) studied a large sample of young men who they labeled as "juvenile delinquents" and found that for them military service provided a clear-cut separation from past disadvantages, such as poverty, deviant peers, and the stigmatization of the legal system. Shanahan (2000) explained, "The positive effect of being sent overseas on wages and economic status…was significantly greater among delinquents than among a non-delinquent control group" (p. 674).

Social moratoriums are defined as those life events that provide a sharp bound-ary between developmental stages, especially the boundary between adolescence and adulthood. In adolescence, knifing-off experiences postpone the acquisition of adult roles and responsibilities (Elder, 1980, 1999). Finally, for White veterans, the G. I. Bill provided many advantages. For this generation, induction into the military shortly after high school provided a lifetime of opportunity. Early entrance into the military during World War II was very beneficial for men from disadvantaged backgrounds (Shanahan, 2000, p. 673).

In contrast, those veterans in the Oakland study who entered the military during World War II later in life, defined as after age 30, experienced a lifetime of disadvantage. The researchers termed this an "untimely point" in their lives, viewing their military service as "a life disruption" from which they never recovered. These men left established families and careers and, after their service, experienced more work instability, higher rates of divorce, and an often accelerated decline in physical health in their 50s (Shanahan, Miech, & Elder, 1998).

It is true that the strength of the idea of "timing" has waned (Schafer, 2009). The social expectations of the "correct" time to marry, to have children, or to graduate from college have been broadened. On the other hand, "some transitions remain quite normative on the chronological timeline, making them deviant if experienced at another juncture" (Schafer, 2009, p. 78). Disability in old age is considered to be an on-time, expected transition; however, the onset of disability (or its diagnosis) in adolescence or childhood is perceived to be off-time. Also, the death of a parent when the individual is a child is a very different experience than the death of a parent when the individual is middle aged. Parental death experienced as a child may hinder the individual's ability to form healthy adult relationships.

The Continuity of Development

- Gradual
- Stable
- Continuous
- Cumulative

Continuity of development states that individual growth and development is gradual, stable, and continuous. Theorists who advance the idea of continuity of development assume that any change in an individual is a process of gradually adding more of the same types of skills that were developed in infancy and childhood, or, stated differently, growth and development are cumulative (Schlossberg, 1991). The linear representation of this would be a straight line that rises. Gormly (1997) explained continuity of development by stating that the

> transformations that we see represent a long, gradual sequence of changes that begin in early childhood and culminate in adulthood in complex and mature behavior. After a person reaches maturity, change does not occur. Personality, for example, is viewed by many psychologists as developing in earlier parts of the life span and remaining stable throughout adulthood. (p. 9)

Freud, for example, believed that the individual's personality is formed by the age of five. Prior behaviors are incorporated into later periods. The concept of continuity of development assumes that individuals' behavior is somewhat predictable, simply by looking at their past behavior.

Does the student who was given the title of "Most Likely to Succeed" in the high school yearbook continue to succeed after graduation? Those theorists who assume epigenetic (or continuous) growth, would say, "Of course, success in high school predicts success in the later stages of life."

Discontinuous Growth

The theory of discontinuous growth, in contrast, postulates that growth occurs in spurts; some periods of very little growth are followed by periods of rapid and dramatic change. Individuals may vary in the rate at which they develop, but the order of the development from one stage to another is basically identical for everyone. Certainly, physical growth and maturation are considered to be continuous because the rate of change can be objectively measured, whether the change is growth or decline. Some theories of development stages view growth as discontinuous. Stated differently, stages are qualitatively different, meaning that the individual thinks, feels, and behaves differently at each developmental stage. Discontinuous growth implies that abrupt changes move the individual from one stage to another. The question of continuous or discontinuous growth applies to emotional, social, and mental changes in an individual.

Some psychologists and theorists advance the view that growth is both continuous and discontinuous. Marcia (2004) stated, "One remains who he/she was, but also becomes different in response to bodily changes and the accumulation of life changes" (p. 52). Marcia proposed that significant periods of an individual's life result in lifelong personality characteristics.

Continuity of change is related to the concept of remediation. If an individual did not successfully complete the tasks of one developmental stage before progressing to the next, is it possible to go back and resolve these issues? The consensus seems to say that the earlier the uncompleted tasks, the more difficult remediation becomes, because later developmental stages are also likely to be flawed.

CONTROL OR AGENCY

Almost everyone wants to be an active force in his or her own life. Theories of human growth and development are based upon the concept of agency, that even as an infant and small child the individual has choices and therefore agency. Of course, goals change throughout the course of life (Diessner & Tiegs, 2001). Strangely, the concept of control or agency is missing from the literature on human growth and development (Hitlin & Elder, 2007). Perhaps this is not so unexpected when considering the American theorists, who came from a very individualistic culture in which individual effort and talent were paramount. Viewed from this perspective, successful individuals can congratulate themselves, and unsuccessful individuals can blame themselves.

Two developmental sociologists Hitlin and Elder (2007) explained:

> From a social psychological point of view, these debates over the relative importance—and even existence—of agency are a bit peculiar. To maintain that social actors make decisions, no matter how socially circumscribed, is a fairly banal statement from a micro-analytic perspective. This is not, however, always the received wisdom in sociology, where there are those who render the actions (motivations, choices, and goals) of actors as irrelevant, epiphenomenal or error variation. (p. 170)

Agency involves choosing the right environment in which one's capacities are rewarded and in which one's preferences are filled. Gecas (2003) defined agency as "planful competence." Others define agency as "freedom," "free will," or "the ability to initiate self-change." Of the theorists presented in this book, Albert Bandura took agency into consideration and proposed that the individual is an active participant in his or her life rather than a passive spectator. Bandura identified four aspects of agency: (1) intentionality, (2) forethought, (3) self-regulation, and (4) self-efficacy or the idea that one can be successful.

It makes sense that "planful competence" is more important during adolescence, when the individual is making choices that will have both pervasive and lifelong consequences, such as life partner and career choice. Shanahan (2000) described planful competence as

> the self's ability to negotiate the life course as it represents a socially structured set of age-graded opportunities and limitations.... Drawing on extensive longitudinal archives from the Berkeley and Oakland samples at the Institute of Child Welfare, Clausen (1991a, 1991b, 1993) demonstrated that planful competence in senior high school (ages 15–18 years) had pervasive effects on functioning later in life, including marital stability, educational attainment for both males and females, occupational attainment and career stability for males, and life satisfaction in later adulthood. (p. 676)

Planful competence, or agency, has less importance in later adulthood because it is thought that there are fewer "choice points" and that older individuals have fewer resources. Also, in those societies that restrict individual freedom, planful competence is limited. With the reunification of Germany in 1989, studies have shown that West German youth considered their capacity to make choices much greater than did East German youth, who had been born and raised in a communist, soviet-bloc nation.

Agency and freedom of choice are defined by the type of government under which the individual lives (Keller, Edelstein, Krettenaur, Fang, & Fang, 2005). Leiserling (2004) wrote a chapter on "Government and the Life Course" in which it was noted that "North American and European approaches to the life course have different emphases that reflect distinct realities" (p. 207). Leiserling explained that "Continental Western Europe has a strong 'state tradition' (Dyson, 1980)—that is a stronger tradition of public law, public administration, and ideas about the essence of and the responsibility of the state—that permeates life course research" (p. 206). In Western Europe, the life course is much more institutionalized and structured by governments, and governments also define differing stages of life, such as youth, adulthood, and old age. In these types of government, it is the nation that manages the risk and exigencies. In the United States, with its culture of individuality and autonomy, most definitions of life stages are not considered the responsibility of the government; however, without governmental support, individual citizens are often vulnerable to historical, economic, and societal downturns.

Throughout the life span, individuals try to fulfill their potential, and empirical research has shown that self-efficacy, or the belief in oneself, helps the individual to achieve. "Structured agency" (Shanahan, Hofer, & Miech, 2002) reflects the idea that rules, one's gender, available resources, the available societal opportunity structures, the time in which the individual lives, define and determine the degree of freedom and agency.

These developmental theories are based on the illogical concept of *unlimited* choice (Cockerham, 2005). However, everyone is subject to historical, social, and economic constraints. Further, freedom of choice is not evenly distributed throughout society (Clausen, 1998). Those who are more advantaged and have been born into higher socio-economic statuses will have more choices in fulfilling their ambitions and preferences. Advanced technology may give the perception that there is more personal sense of control, but this idea can be questioned. In individualistic societies, agency and personal control are typically viewed as positive and constructive forces in the life course, but this premise leads to the conclusion that if our lives are not as we had intended, then we are responsible for regrets and failures.

Finally, no one can become or experience everything that he or she wants. Every choice and decision eliminates other opportunities. It is also interesting to consider how many of our choices have *personal* meaning, or whether choices and goals were based on societal expectations. Indeed, "making meaning" is an important part of the dying process in which the individual reflects on his or life, including important decision points. The Baby Boomers are different in many ways than previous generations, and the increased number and the wider range of choices available are also unprecedented in history (Moen, 2004).

A significant universal, lifelong function is the avoidance of loss and preparation to reduce the impact of those losses that cannot be avoided (Ebner, Freund, & Baltes, 2006; Valliant, 1990; Wasak, Schneider, Li, & Hommel, 2009). Over their entire life spans, most people experience far more gains than they do losses. Loss is inevitable for everyone, and there are challenges over which individuals have some control and challenges and losses for which the individual has very little control. One way in which to prevent loss is choosing an environment in which one can succeed. For instance, non-athletic people probably should not consider professional sports as a profession.

Individuals who possess a high degree of plasticity and adaptability are more likely to respond to loss with reorientation processes (Boerner & Jopp, 2007; Sherrod, 2001). "Reorientation" means disengagement from some goals, in some cases, highly valued goals. In reorientation or adjustment, the individual assumes an active role in changing aspects of his or her life. Maintaining a sense of control or agency when they encounter loss helps individuals to compensate or to re-evaluate the importance of certain goals, lifestyle, or individuals in their lives. Acquiring emotional resources throughout the entire life span with which to deal with loss and challenges can be viewed as a developmental task. Certainly there is empirical research that shows that a person's coping style and adaptive strategies developed in early adolescence are important in their later lives (Elder, Johnson, & Crosnoe, 2004; Moen, 1998).

Successful coping strategies are based on the ability to see oneself somewhat accurately. Erikson (1959) stated that a realistic self-appraisal is achieved both in retrospect (looking at one's past) and in prospect (planning the future). Coping with loss tends to become more effective as a person ages, because the individual has both experience in dealing with loss and a more realistic self-identity (Blanchflower & Oswald, 2008). On the other hand, coping with loss may become more difficult as the individual ages if he or she possesses fewer material resources.

Adaptive strategies to deal with loss include seeking out social support, channeling resources to new goals, increasing efforts, regulating emotions, and compensating for losses with other resources available. The search for new goals is often difficult and may require a great deal of time. Attributional style is important in responding to loss. Attributional style is the way in which the individual conceptualizes the loss: whom the individual regards as responsible for the loss and whom the individual considers responsible for responding to or "fixing" the loss.

There are different types of losses, and insurance companies are big businesses because they are able to offset some of the effects of losses. This planfulness is termed "anticipatory preparation." For example, a husband's foresight in obtaining life insurance would assist his wife in adjustment to widowhood. Anticipatory preparation is helpful in both instrumental and emotional ways. Very few people consider the possibility of acquiring a disability, except for the elderly or military personnel who experience combat. Many people without disabilities have never contemplated what they would do if they did acquire a disability because they deny the probability of acquiring a disability and lack any knowledge of or experience with disability. Of course, adolescents and young adults are more likely to experience acute onset disabilities, while older adults generally have chronic, insidious onset disabilities.

Generation Groups

- The historical time in which individuals live
- The Servicemen's Readjustment Act of 1944—the G. I. Bill
- Why the adolescent experiences of each generation are significant

The historical time in which individuals live influences their developmental process. Groups of individuals born in the same time period and who move through the life span at the same time, called generations, typically have similar values, attitudes, behaviors, and expectations (Dien, 2000; Schaie, 2007). As it crosses class, racial, and gender boundaries, the influence of one's generation lasts throughout one's life (Mellor & Rehr, 2005). Newman and Newman (2009) described generation groups and the effects of their shared experiences:

All the people who are roughly the same age during a historical period are referred to as a generation. The labels or names given to each generation are based on a major historical point or a social movement or simply a "noteworthy turn in the calendar." (Keeter & Taylor, 2009)

Differences in medical advances, occupational opportunities, educational resources, and the number of people in any one generation are four factors that may affect the pattern of life events for generation members (Newman & Newman, 2009, p. 409). Studying generation effects is also termed the "sociohistorical" approach to human development. Researcher Glen Elder (1998) described the relationship between personal choice (agency) and major historical events:

> Historical forces shape the social trajectories of family, education, and work, and they in turn influence behavior and particular lines of development. Some individuals are able to select the paths they follow, a phenomenon known as human agency, but these choices are not made in a social vacuum. All life choices are contingent on the opportunities and constraints of social structure and culture. (p. 2)

> Moreover, major crises, such as war, famine, and political unrest, may alter a trajectory by introducing unanticipated transitions—for example, closing off certain activities, as when young men interrupt their education to go to war, or opening up new opportunities as when women, and people with disabilities (PWDs), entered the labor market because many of the men were in the military. (p. 409)

The G. I. Bill (the Servicemen's Readjustment Act of 1944) extended social benefits to veterans of World War II, providing low interest mortgages for homes and farms, and paying tuition and stipends for veterans who wished to attend university or vocational programs. The G. I. Bill transformed the lives of millions of veterans (2.2 million used the benefits to attend college and 5.6 million completed vocational training). When educational attainments, quality of jobs, housing, and attainment of higher incomes are considered, the G. I. Bill transformed the United States (Mettler, 2005). However, the G. I. benefits were not extended to African American veterans and actually increased the gap between African Americans and White Americans (Katznelson, 2005). African American and Native American veterans understood that the combination of wartime service, talent, and hard work could not ensure life success if their institutional opportunities were unavailable.

Terman's longitudinal study of intellectually gifted individuals born between the 1900s and the 1920s showed that super intelligence had a buffering effect on the historical forces affecting the individual. Terman's "termites" entered adulthood during the Great Depression and World War II, but "[s]elected as the upper 1% of age peers at 19, these 'best and brightest' seemed to be invulnerable to the misfortunes of history" (Elder, 1999, p. 6).

Generation groups are history-graded events. For example, Baltes and Reese (1984) have speculated that the role of history-graded influences is particularly strong in adolescence and early adulthood:

> Adolescence and early adulthood are periods in which individuals show a high consciousness of about what society is and should be all about, and in the ways they can influence its future course. Moreover, much of one's foundation for

adulthood (career, lifestyle, family life) is centered in these periods mediated by the nature of the current and socioenvironmental climate. Therefore, we suspect that history-graded influences have their most prominent relative influence on development during the periods of adolescence and early adulthood. (Baltes & Reese, 1984, p. 518)

Ryder (1965) explained why the adolescent experiences of each generation are so significant:

The potential for change is concentrated in the generations of young adults who are old enough to participate directly in the movements impelled by change, but not old enough to have become committed to an occupation, a residence, or a family of procreation or a way of life. For whatever reason, youth seem maximally open to sociological influences of the time. (cf. Alwin & McCammon, 2004, p. 24)

It would seem reasonable that adolescents and youth in developed nations are given the gift of a lengthy youth with a great deal of flexibility and independence, combined with education, which makes them open to shaping their culture, making an impact on society, and shaping their individual identities.

There have been few, if any, longitudinal studies of PWDs. This, however, will change as there are more and more PWDs born after 1990, the date of the passage of the Americans with Disabilities Act (ADA). The discrimination and prejudice against PWDs born before 1990 will fade into history for those PWDs born after 1990—a sad and shameful history but still history. Currently, there are some cross-sectional studies and interviews conducted with activists in the Disability Rights movement, including Leonard Kriegel, Judith Huemman, Edward Roberts, and Harriet McBryde Johnson. Their accounts of this time period will document the changes and progress made that occurred during their particular generation.

The U.S. Baby Boom was sudden and large, lasted decades, and affected all racial, socioeconomic, and geographic groups. Although all of the developed nations (except Germany) experienced Baby Booms after World War II, the United States, Australia, and Canada experienced the largest generations. (Periods of low birth rates are called "Baby Busts.") Baby Boomers are the largest generation group in the history of the United States. Presently, the 76 million Baby Boomers compose more than 40% of the adult population, compared to their parents' generation of 26 million. The years from 1946 to 1964 saw phenomenal birth rates, and, after 1964, the birth rate fell to pre-1946 levels. The Baby Boomers' parents had matured rapidly due to World War II, and after the war, they married and gave birth to an unprecedented number of infants. Postwar Americans wanted to pursue the American dream of marriage and family. Thus, the Baby Boom was both large and sudden. One author explained:

One of the most popular songs among returning World War II veterans was, "I've Got to Make Up for Lost Time." The number of children per family in the 1940s jumped from 2.6 to 3.2. Birth rates doubled for third children, and tripled for fourth children, as the country's population increased by a record 19 million in this decade. At a time when birth control information was rapidly expanding, America's growth rivaled not England's but rather India's. (Oshinsky, 2005, p. 81)

Numerically large generations are at a significant disadvantage. Specifically, the Baby Boom generation has and will continue to confront a major socioeconomic disadvantage. Alwin and McCammon (2004) noted "the strain it places on the opportunity structure" and explained that "generation size affects not only the economic well-being of generation members, but many features of the family and individual functioning, including fertility rates, because there are many competing for the same resources at the same time." Larger generation groups generally experience lower quality and levels of education, lack of job mobility, and higher unemployment. This is called the "generation size hypothesis," which states that the average economic and social outcomes of a generation vary inversely with its size (Hughes, 2009, p. 362).

The large population bubble of the Baby Boomers has had a great impact on American cultural, social, economic, and political life. Accommodating the Baby Boomers throughout their life spans has been a recurrent issue. On January 1, 2011, the oldest Baby Boomers reached the age of 65, and for the next 19 years, on average 10,000 more Boomers will turn 65 each day. The upcoming retirement of the Baby Boomers will mean the potential loss of a large number of skilled and experienced workers who have maintained the economy for decades. Also, this large number of retirees may become a fiscal burden on the American economy (Hudson, 2009). In the 1950s, when these children began entering elementary school, classrooms were crowded. Societies often experience an increase in the crime rate when a large birth generation, such as the Baby Boomers, enters adolescence and early adulthood because these are ages in which individuals engage in crime (Macmillan, 2009). In the 1960s, when the first boomers entered university, competition was stiff for acceptance, and new types of post–high school education were initiated, such as the community college.

Both male and female Baby Boomers grew up in a time of unprecedented prosperity, and Baby Boomers were the most well-educated generation in American history. Due to these increased educational levels, Baby Boomers tend to be more tolerant and open-minded than their parents' generation.

Women in the Baby Boomer generation had more advantages in the prosperous postwar economy than women of the previous generations. In addition to a more favorable economy, women Baby Boomers took advantage of expanded opportunities for higher education and professional life, often due to the achievements of the women's movement.

Baby Boomers will redefine retirement and health care. It can be seen that belonging to a large birth generation has both advantages and disadvantages. One advantage is being part of a group that has a strong influence on public policy and economics. The disadvantage is the increased competition for scarce and valuable resources, such as entry into universities and entry-level jobs.

In addition to the sheer numbers of Baby Boomers, this group is unique in many other ways (Maples & Abney, 2006). They have grown up in a world without global wars; they are the most highly educated generation in history; they have had access to technology and therefore wider worldviews; they are more affluent than their parents (probably due to their higher rates of education), and they will live longer. The lives of American Baby Boomers parallel the postwar transformation of American life. In a Pew Research Center Study (2011), 61% of Baby Boomers feel younger than actual age (when compared with about 50% of American adults). Religious affiliation is stronger in Boomers than in the younger adult generations, but lower than in the generation of adults born between 1928 and 1945.

Without doubt, the Baby Boomer generation has had more dominance than any generation before and continues to monopolize public attention. Indeed, the name given to the generation that preceded the Baby Boomers is "the Silent Generation" (those born before 1946). Recently the name the "Greatest Generation" has been used to describe this age group of Americans who survived the Great Depression of the 1930s and who were young adults during World War II (Keeter & Taylor, 2009). Generations after the Baby Boomers are not as distinctly defined (Wuthnow, 2007). Generation Xers are the children of Boomers born between 1965 and 1980. The letter X applied to this generation because these young adults seemed to have little identity. The Millennial generation is the group of individuals who entered their 20s (or young adulthood) around the year 2000 (the "millennium"). It can be seen that each generation is stereotyped with certain characteristics and labels.

In the United States, Generation X is shaped by the end of the Cold War and the economic and oil crises of the 1970s. There are 51 million individuals in Generation X. This generation is also more heterogeneous than previous generations with great diversity in race, socioeconomic status, religion, ethnicity, and sexual orientation. However, as a total group, Generation X reports the highest educational attainment.

Generation Y (Gen Yers) was born between 1977 and 1998 and consists of 75 million people. As the name implies, individuals in this generation became adults around the turn of the 21st century. The "Generation of Trophy Kids" is also applied to the Gen Yers. The idea behind the word trophy reflects their childhood and adolescence in which they were given many advantages and experiences. On the other hand, these children and teenagers faced parental expectations that their large investments in time and resources would result in trophies, meaning high achievement. This generation is now beginning to enter the workforce. Sociologists predict that the American workforce will be composed of competitive, achievement-oriented workers.

However, the Gen Yers have also been labeled the "Peter Pan Generation" or the "Boomerang Generation" because economic circumstances have led many to delay becoming adults and they have not completed such developmental tasks as leaving their parents' home, entering their professions, and getting married. Three human developmental researchers offered another explanation for this delay in the passage from childhood to adulthood. Nelson et al. (2003) explained that Gen Yers delay these developemental tasks in order to avoid the mistakes their parents made by entering both marriage and professions early in life and then discovering that they were unhappy in both their jobs and marriages. Gen Yers want "to do it right, the first time."

Demography and Developmental Theories

- Longer life spans
- Growing economic inequality
- Changing labor markets
- Increasing racial/ethnic diversity
- Increasing rates of disability

Society has undergone vast technological, economic, and demographic changes—changes that have transformed social conditions. Today, demographic changes are occurring at a rate unknown to previous generations. Both the *extent* of these changes and their *pace* have rendered social, economic, and educational life very different than it was a century ago. These shifts have occurred in five general areas: (1) longer life spans, (2) growing economic inequality, (3) changing labor markets that require workers to acquire more education, (4) increasing racial/ethnic diversity, and (5) increasing rates of disability. We shall consider the increasing rates of disability in the next chapter and discuss these first four factors in this chapter.

Most of these developmental theories originated in the first half of the 20th century (1900–1960), a time in which demographic changes were neither rapid nor wide-ranging. The knowledge of these shifts was unavailable to the great theorists. For example, Sigmund Freud, who developed the theory of psychosexual development, lived from 1856 to 1939.

THE LONGEVITY REVOLUTION

In 1920 the average life expectancy for Americans was 55 years. In 2010, the average life expectancy in the United States is 76.1 years for White males, 70.9 years for Black males; 81.8 years for White females, and 77.8 years for Black females. Mellor and Rehr (2005) have labeled this the "Longevity Revolution." A White female born in 2015 will have an estimated life expectancy of 83.8 years, a White male 78 years, a Black female 78.9 years, and a Black male 71.9 years (see Figure 2.1). Americans may be unaware of the speed of this revolution. For example, a demographer stated, "Mortality declines since the 1950s have been more evenly distributed throughout the life cycle" (Edmundson, 1997). There has been a consistent increase of three months of life expectancy per year for the

FIGURE 2.1

Age distribution, 2000.

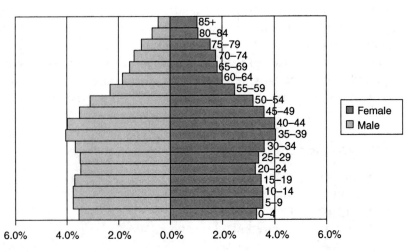

Source: www.censuscope.org.

past 16 years (Oeppen & Vaupel, 2002) (see Figure 2.2). Expressions such as "sixty is the new forty" and "you're only as old as you feel" illustrate the changing age structure of the United States and other developed, Western nations. Nonetheless, being old is typically viewed as a negative experience. Schafer (2009) explained, "Particularly in individualistic Western societies such as the United States, youthfulness is celebrated as a proxy for the cultural values of autonomy and self-sufficiency" (p. 75).

In developed, Western, industrialized nations, the population is aging due to the combination of low birth rates and longer life spans. For those nations which do not accept immigrants, their populations age at a faster rate. Medical advances, better public health, pollution control, safer workplaces, and increased access to medical care have resulted in population longevity. Population aging affects social, political, economic, and cultural conditions for entire societies (Putney & Bengtson, 2004). Age structures of large groups of people, such as the entire population of the United States, are often shown through a bar graph, with the younger people on the bottom and the older people on top. These bar graphs have been termed "population pyramids," because the percentage of the youngest people is the largest and appears on the bottom. As the pyramid builds, from youngest to oldest, the number of elderly people is very small; therefore, the top of the pyramid is very narrow. Demographers predict that by the year 2030, this pyramid bar graph will become square because the oldest and youngest generations will become equal. This "senior boom" has the potential to create intergenerational inequity in which the younger generations must work to provide retirement benefits and health care to the elderly. Typically, older individuals require more societal resources, including social, economic, and psychological resources, in order to maintain functioning. Berk (1998) has labeled the mounting responsibility of the younger generation to care for the elderly as a "public burden," in which the "elderly receive more than their fair share of public resources at the expense of the very young, who cannot vote and lobby

FIGURE 2.2

Growth rate of America's aging population.

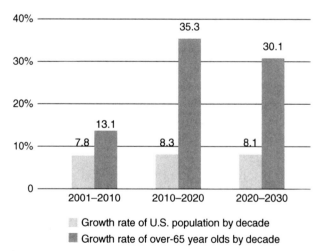

Growth rate of U.S. population by decade
Growth rate of over-65 year olds by decade

Source: U.S. Bureau of the Census, Projections of the Total Resident Population by Five-Year Age Groups and Sex, with Special Age Categories, Middle Series 1999 to 2100 (NP-T3), www.census.gov/population/www/projections/natsum.html.

for their needs" (p. 573). Jacoby (2011), somewhat tongue-in-cheek, termed the aging Baby Boomers as "greedy geezers." In a nation of limited resources, how are we to decide which life is more valuable—an infant's life or an elderly person's life? (Fishman, 2010). If we cannot provide unlimited health care to everyone, of every age, how do we make judgments between giving unlimited health care to one age group and not to another? Much like PWDs, older Americans are beginning to be perceived as a burden and drain on resources.

Throughout the entire life span, the social and cultural interpretations of biological age change as life expectancies increase. Longer life expectancies result in lengthening childhoods, more adolescent years, and longer adulthoods, and they create entirely new life stages at the end of life. Thus the increasing levels of education have been, in part, a result of these longer life spans. Longer lives also increase the probabilities that individuals will experience certain life events. There are two new developmental stages—"the young elderly," those 60 to 79, and "the old elderly," who are 80 years old and older. Certainly someone who is 60 is different from someone who is 95 years old. Speaking in terms of societal responsibility, medical care costs are a great deal higher for individuals past the age of 80 than for 65 to 70 year olds.

Everyone plans his or her life based on the number of years he or she expects to live (Newman & Newman, 2009). Moreover, these longer life plans also affect self-identities. When do individuals consider themselves to be "old?" (Elder, Johnson, & Crosnoe, 2004; Jacoby, 2011). At what age do individuals think of themselves as young adults? Certainly the expectation of a longer life span has the potential to lengthen all of the stages of life and add new stages (Arnett, 1997, 1998, 2000, 2004). In its time, Erikson's psychosocial developmental theory was considered a radical departure because it took into account the individual's entire life, including old age. Today, Erikson is considered to be somewhat outdated because his eight stages do not fully describe the entire life span, specifically the older elderly.

Human life expectancy is continuously increasing, allowing more time in which to accomplish goals (Freund, Nikitin, & Ritter, 2009). Nonetheless, scholars and practitioners are not clear: "What do people do with the additional time they have at their disposal? Or, more generally, what are the psychological consequences of having a longer life?" (Freund et al., 2009, p. 3). The definition of family is also affected by these longer life spans. For the first time in history, many families will consist of four or five generations, and many children will have close relationships with their great-grandparents. Thus, for the first time in history, there will be many years of intergenerational living and "co-survivorship among generations" (Putney & Bengtson, 2004, p. 152). Intergenerational families have the potential to increase family continuity and stability, but due to the combination of lifelong conflict and rising medical costs, they also have the potential to increase stress and strain.

Another impact of the longevity revolution is one that most people do not consider, the expanding numbers of disabilities, both the number of people who have disabilities and the number of types of disabilities. Succinctly stated, when death rates go down, disability rates go up. Statistically expressed, this relationship would be described as "the rate of disability is inversely related to the mortality rate." This makes the rising number of disabilities is progress for society. The Social Security Administration (SSA) is the largest insurance program in the world, and, therefore, SSA demographers develop projections of life spans, and these projections, are truly phenomenal when compared to the life spans of Americans 100 years ago.

The longevity revolution has created a large group of elderly people who might say, "Now what am I supposed to do?" Social expectations for the old elderly have not kept pace with the longevity revolution (Jacoby, 2002). Contrast this with the societal role expectations of infants and toddlers. Parents love to boast about their remarkable babies and their precocious completion of developmental tasks, such as walking, talking, and toilet training. These parents can boast because there are well-defined social expectations for babies and small children.

Inventing new stages of development is not new. For example, before the 1900s, there was no adolescence, and before the 1990s, the stage of emerging adulthood was not considered. Both of these newer stages are "transitional" stages since adolescence encompasses the years between childhood and adulthood, and emerging adulthood are the years (as many as 12) between adolescence and "real" adulthood. Perhaps a transition period of "emerging elderly" could be initiated in which individuals approaching the age of 60 could be given some time to reconsider another new transition period.

In the same way that it takes time for social norms to develop (in order to "catch up" to these longer life spans), institutions tend to lag behind in providing opportunity structures. Freund et al. (2009) explained:

> This *relative* lack of social expectations for older adults regarding which kinds of goals they are expected to set and pursue might stem from the fact that it takes some time for social norms to develop, just as institutions and societies tend to lag behind in changing their opportunity structures to conform to demographic changes.... Given that, historically, old age is a fairly young (new) phenomenon affecting a large number of people, it might simply take more time for such norms and expectations about age-appropriate tasks and norms to develop. (p. 7)

The longevity revolution, with other societal and cultural changes, has made the measurement of age and age groups more complicated (Settersten & Mayer, 1997). Furthermore, gerontological researchers assert that these longer life spans affect every developmental stage of the individual (Freund, Nikitin, & Ritter, 2009; Settersten & Mayer, 1997). Since development is the result of a combination of the individual's past, lived life, and the anticipation of the future, young people's lives are altered. Young people today have more time to plan. For example, some individuals might choose to work into their 70s, taking into consideration that they will most likely live many more years. Longevity increases time and also provides more choices for individuals. It is often stated that the longevity revolution is good for individuals, but bad for society.

The longevity revolution has had a powerful influence on professional practice. Gerontology, as a profession and as an academic discipline, did not exist until 1985 (Baltes, Staudinger, & Lindenberger, 1999). There was little gerontological research until the 1990s.

The experience of death has also changed. In the 19th and the early 20th centuries, the most prevalent cause of death was infectious diseases, which equally affected all socioeconomic groups, age groups, and both genders. After the initial manifestation of the symptoms, death often occurred quickly. In contrast, most deaths today are the result of chronic diseases and conditions, and these diseases and conditions are stratified according to socioeconomic group, gender, and age. These diseases and conditions are more common among older people, men (rather than women), and lower socioeconomic groups. Death is slow; the individual becomes more and more debilitated and is often in pain (Bryant, 2003). It is safe to state that modern medicine has changed the experience of death into a *process* (rather than an *event*) which, in turn, led to Kübler-Ross's (1969) theory of death and dying, a theory that is considered to be developmental, with a number of different stages.

THE INCREASING DIVERSITY OF THE UNITED STATES

The United States has always been a major destination for immigrants and is home to more than 500 Native American tribes and nations. Therefore, the United States has always been a diverse nation. Immigration has increased worldwide, and, as a result, there are more foreign-born individuals living in the United States than at any other time in history. The great migration waves of the late 19th and early 20th centuries were from European countries, while the current waves of migrations are from Mexico, Central American, and Asia.

However, the generation of children and adolescents is becoming increasingly racially diverse (Sarawathi, 2003). This is a radical shift from a nation whose children were once overwhelmingly White. In 2010, it was estimated that approximately 20% of school children were racially and ethnically diverse and that by 2020 one-third of all school children will be from culturally and racially diverse backgrounds (Rampal, 2003). Three factors have contributed to this diversity of children and adolescents: (1) high migration rates of individuals who are of child-bearing age, (2) declining birth rates of Whites, and (3) a large number of interracial marriages. It is estimated that by 2015 immigrant children will compose almost one-third of the public school population.

According to the Pew Research Center (Passel, Wang, & Taylor, 2010), "A record 14.6% of all new marriages in the United States in 2008 were between spouses of a different race or ethnicity from one another." Therefore, one in seven marriages in the United States is either interracial or interethnic, while in 1980, these rates were only one-half of those in 2008. In 1980 6.7% of new marriages were interracial or interethnic. The ongoing migration waves from the past four decades have enlarged the pool of available marriage partners.

Immigration to the United States has ameliorated the twin effects of the aging population and falling birthrates. Without immigration, the United States would soon approach the nonrenewal rate. In other words, there would be more Americans dying than babies born, and the population would begin to decrease (Table 2.1).

Very few, if any, studies have been done on the developmental experiences of individuals of American racial/ethnic/cultural/linguistic groups. If America wants to maximize the potential of all of its youth, it is important to initiate longitudinal and cross-sectional studies on nonwhite and immigrant individuals. Cross-national life span research has been conducted on Germans (Mayer, 1988), the British, and Canadians. One life span researcher explained:

> When compared with Whites, many racial and ethnic minorities—including some immigrant groups—are more likely to experience transition patterns that

TABLE 2.1

U.S. Immigration and Estimated Emigration, by Decade: 1931 to 2009

Period	Immigrants to the United States (thousands, rounded)	Emigrants from the United States (thousands, rounded)	Estimated net immigration (thousands, rounded)	Estimated ratio: emigration/ immigration
2001–2009	9,458	2,802	6,656	0.30
1991–2000	9,081	2,338	6,743	0.26
1981–1990	7,255	1,600	5,655	0.22
1971–1980	4,399	1,176	3,223	0.27
1961–1970	3,322	900	2,422	0.27
1951–1960	2,515	425	2,090	0.17
1941–1950	1,035	281	754	0.27
1931–1940	528	649	−121	1.23

Source: Information adapted from, for immigration, all years: U.S. Department of Homeland Security, Yearbook of Immigration Statistics, 2009 data tables available online at http://www.dhs.gov/files/statistics/publications/yearbook.shtm. For emigration, years 1931 to 1990: U.S. Immigration and Naturalization Service, Statistical Yearbook of the Immigration and Naturalization Service, 2000, GPO, Washington, DC, 2002. For 1991 to 2000: U.S. Census Bureau, Net International Migration and its Sub-Components for the Vintage 2000 Post-censal National Estimates: 1990 to 2000, Internet release date February 8, 2002. For 2001 to 2005: Population Reference Bureau, Estimates and Projections of Emigration from the United States, available at http://www.prb.org/Journalists/FAQ/USEmigration.aspx. For 2005 to 2009: Phillip Martin and Elizabeth Midgley, Population Bulletin Update: Immigration in American 2010, Population Reference Bureau, Washington, DC, June 2010, http://www.prb.org/pdf10/immigration-update2010.pdf.

cast a long shadow over their adult lives, including diminished prospects for socioeconomic achievement and for a fulfilling family life. Yet these groups will constitute an even larger segment of the population in the future. Will they continue to have diminished prospects, and, if so, what are the implications for social order, productivity, and national identity? (Shanahan, 2000, p. 686)

GROWING INEQUALITY

A researcher who commented on the widening gap between middle-class and lower-class Americans suggested that socioeconomic status may become more of an identifier. "Contrary to my prediction that the significance of gender, race, and ethnicity will diminish in decades to come, current evidence suggests that class differences that are now relatively invisible may become more prominent in structuring the life course in the 21st century, unless, of course, policies to counteract this trend are put in place" (Furstenberg, 2004, p. 665).

In 2006, approximately 17.4% of U.S. children were living in families below the poverty line (Federal Interagency Forum on Child and Family Statistics, 2007). This is an increase from 2001 (16.2%) but down from a peak of 22.7% in 1993. The figure of 17.4% of American children living in poverty is much higher than the figure for children from other developed nations (Associated Press, 2010). For example, Canada has a child poverty rate of 9%, and Sweden has a rate of 2% (Santrock, 2009, p. 13). The higher rates of childhood poverty are due to the lack of a large social safety net in the United States (Associated Press, 2009a, 2009b).

Using a revised formula, U.S. Census Bureau has determined that 15.8%, or almost 1 in 6 Americans, live in poverty. This revised formula included such factors as the rising costs of medical care, transportation, and children care. The formula that the U.S. Census previously used to calculate the rate of poverty was developed in 1955 and had not been revised to take into account rising costs (Associated Press, 2009a, 2009b).

These growing rates of poverty, particularly childhood poverty, play an important role in the rate of disability because childhood poverty is a predisposing factor for acquiring a disability (Himmelstein, Woolhandler, & Wolfe, 1992). Childhood poverty is also related to the diagnoses of disability. Generally speaking, children of poverty-level families tend to receive more stigmatizing diagnoses, such as mental retardation, while children of higher social classes are given diagnoses of learning disabilities.

Two social economists assert that the social distance between those in the higher socioeconomic levels and those in the lower socioeconomic may worsen as poverty increases:

> Economic inequality—particularly when overlaid with racial, ethnic, language, and other differences—increases social distance which, in turn, undermines the motivational basis for reaching out to those in need. Indeed, surveys consistently reveal that support for those in need is stronger in societies whose before-tax and—transfer are more equal. (Bowles & Gentile, 1999; cf. Pimpare, 2003, p. 113)

Social inequality affects the life course (Clark, Glick, & Bures, 2009). In the past, general wisdom stated that a combination of disadvantaged statuses, such as low socioeconomic status and membership in a racial/ethnic/cultural minority group, often led to a faster social clock, in which individuals marry and have children earlier, especially in the teenage years. Generally, a more accelerated social clock confers greater disadvantages throughout the life course. However, it is now thought that socioeconomic status plays a greater role than racial/ethnic minority group status in these social inequalities. Empirical research that controlled for parental education and income, family structure, and aptitude test scores found that differences between racial groups tend to disappear.

The institutionalized individuality of the United States is related to social inequality. Leisering (2004) explained:

> The United States has a comparatively small government—the state's share in Gross Domestic Product (i.e., the percentage of all generated wealth devoted to the public sector), social spending as percent of the GDP, and public employment as percent of total employment are worlds apart from most other developed countries.... The United States...with a last safety net (welfare) that is weaker and less rights-based than in most other countries, with a short duration of entitlement to unemployment benefit and without universal coverage of health insurance. For Americans, the very term "welfare" conjures up the idea of needs-based programs for the poor and weak. (Leisering, 2004, p. 206)

Solutions are difficult. It is safe to say that although most Americans desire to retain their individuality, freedom, and autonomy, they would also like to see a nation without poverty.

Changing Labor Market

- A labor market based on physical labor and well-defined gender and age norms
- The population becomes more well-educated
- Blurring of "normative" timetables

Socioeconomic conditions also influence human growth and development. Life changes are closely tied to the resources and opportunities available in the labor market (Heinz, 2004). We have seen the way in which the end of World War II brought prosperity and the "affluent society" to the United States. In an industrial society based on physical labor, work opportunities were governed by well-defined age and gender norms. Only relatively young, fit men could succeed in physical labor. In the developed nations, economic and political changes have transformed the labor market. Today's labor market is based on information and technology. Individuals of all ages, especially women, experience more opportunities in such a labor market. Even jobs such as farming, which previously required physical labor and were therefore male-dominated, are now mechanized and computerized, allowing women and older men to operate successful agribusinesses.

Work and professional life have changed, moving toward a society in which individuals hold more jobs of shorter duration and engage in multiple careers. In a changing labor market, the individual must take more initiative and control over his or her professional life. According to social scientists, during the 1990s the concept of a work-centered life was ending (Beck, 1992; Heinz, 2004; Rifkin, 1995). Also, if people live longer and continue to retire in their 60s, they will spend a smaller proportion of their lives in the workforce (see Figure 2.3).

Childhood as a stage of life is lasting longer as the job market changes and the labor of children becomes less valuable than in a job market based on physical labor. In a job market based on physical labor, children contributed to their families' finances. Indeed, this may have been a factor in higher birth rates. However, in a job market based on technology and information, children do not possess the education to make major financial contributions to their families. Furthermore, children now require education that can extend into their 20s, and sometimes, 30s. Therefore, they enter their work life at an older age (Furstenberg, 2004).

Before 1920, fewer than 16% of the population graduated from high school, and most people left school at 16 to start their work life (Roberts & Caspi, 2003). Life expectancy in the 1920s was approximately 55.

The combination of life-context factors and life-expectancy limitations during this earlier period in history meant that age 30 may have corresponded to middle

FIGURE 2.3

Analysis of Bureau of Labor Statistics data.

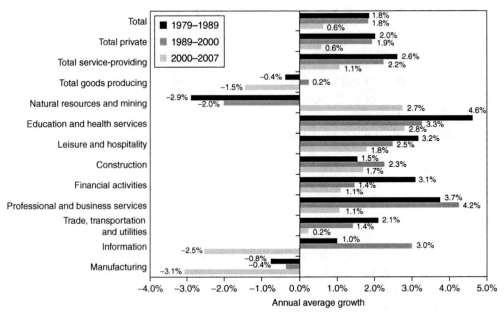

Source: Economic Policy Institute.

age. In contrast, the generations that followed increasingly acquired more schooling, delayed their careers, and delayed their development of a strong identity. Current generations now face a life course in which childhood and adolescence can stretch into their 20s, and identity-related decisions about work, marriage, and children can be delayed well into their 30s. Arnett (1998, 2000, 2004) refers to the period between ages 15 and 30 as "emerging adulthood" in a tacit acknowledgment that adulthood is now forestalled both demographically and psychologically until after age 30 (Roberts & Caspi, 2003, p. 205). Today 30 may not even be considered adulthood.

In developmental settings of high modernity, which are characterized as accelerated cultural change, growing interconnectedness (globalization) and pluralization of life forms, it becomes increasingly difficult to meet both demands of adaptive flexibility and personal continuity. Blurring of normative "timetables" that traditionally have served as guiding frameworks for organizing one's life and environment exerts a powerful influence to the developmental life course (Brandtstadter & Rothermund, 2003, p. 119). Some have termed this the "irrelevance of age."

More and more people of about the same age participate in the process of dying at the same approximate time. Due to better medical care, large-scale insurance coverage, and improved public sanitation, most people die in old age. This is termed the resurgent peak of age-graded influence in old age (Baltes & Reese, 1984, p. 518).

The Goal of Human Development and Growth

- Autonomy
- Self-determination
- Higher adaptive functioning
- Increased competence

Most of the theorists would agree that the object of life is to look back at its end and say, "I lived the life I wanted." Therefore, the goals of most theories of human development are autonomy and freedom, simply because these allow the individual to decide what type of life is desirable. Self-determination and self-expression are important, because they allow the individual to improve and optimize his or her self-defined goals and objectives (Riediger & Ebner, 2007). Most theories assume the importance of relatedness and being loved and supported by others, but self-determination is the primary goal. "Self-determination theory argues that people intrinsically strive toward integration and differentiation of the self…" (Kneezel & Emmons, 2006, p. 266). Ego strength, individuation, and autonomy are related words, meaning that as individuals grow and mature, they identify less with others and establish a strong self-identity. Infants and young children closely identify with their parents, children identify with their families, adolescents identify with their peer group but adults have developed a self-concept that is separate from these groups. Certainly, societies with great cultural diversity and increased access to education and technology tend to move toward individualistic worldviews and more egalitarian relationships (Newman & Newman, 2009).

Individuals are constantly moving toward more individual expression. Thus, adults tend to be a more heterogeneous age group than infants and children. Adults are very different from one another. Individual differentiation is also termed "ego strength" or "individuation." Thus, the individual becomes increasingly more complex as he or she ages, but at the same time, becomes more integrated. Individuation is a simultaneous process of differentiation (from others) and becoming whole, or integrated.

Many of the developmental theories include the concept of autonomy as a lifetime goal. Autonomy means that the individual is capable of controlling his or her environment in order to acquire self-identified desires, skills, and resources. Individuals become progressively better at making decisions in order to meet their needs (Mottern, 2008, p. 35). Decisions are defined as "good" if they increase the individual's autonomy, while not harming others. Of course, the individual's social/cultural/economic status does influence the individual's perception of autonomy and good decision making. Kneezel and Emmons (2005) commented, "Autonomous actions are fully self-endorsed and personally valued" (p. 267).

Another goal is greater competence, such as developing more effective coping strategies and successfully moving toward personal goals (Freund & Riediger, 2001). The wider the applicability of these developed adaptive skills is, the greater the potential for their use in other environments. Even better are those adaptive skills that can be generalized to other task demands while individuals simultaneously remain adaptive and open to developing new adaptive behaviors (Greve & Wentura, 2007). For example, Tarzan developed the highly adaptive skill of swinging on vines. However, vine swinging is not useful in large urban cities; therefore, his highly adaptive developmental growth and skills are not very generalizable. When Tarzan moved to the city, he lost his environment-based resources (the vines) and his jungle-based skills (vine swinging). The question then becomes, what are the upper limits of Tarzan's plasticity? Can he learn to live and thrive in a large urban environment? Of course, many developmental psychologists assert that for mature individuals one of their adaptive skills is increased competence in choosing their environment—one that allows them to use their skills. Hence, these psychologists would say that Tarzan would never move to a big city in the first place.

Other theorists, such as Maslow, proposed that transcendence is the motivator of all human behavior. Transcendence is defined as creativity, freedom of will, intuitive awareness, inventiveness, flexibility, and being exceptionally integrated. The virtues of faith, hope, and charity are achieved, and the individual becomes emotionally stable and well organized (Cloninger, 2003, p. 172). "The importance of personality coherence in adaptation across the life span has been recognized in social cognition research" (Cloninger, 2003, p. 161).

Most developmental theories assume that the goal of development is related to the concept of self that has been defined in industrialized Western nations, especially the United States (Cirillo & Wapner, 1986; Fowler & Wadsworth, 1991; Dien, 2000). As Thompson (1997) explained "the U.S. majority culture, considered by some to be the most individualistic in the world, lies at one extreme of a worldwide individualistic-collectivist continuum" (p. 16). Applying these developmental theories to cultures not based on individualism will be difficult:

> Many psychologists (Erikson, 1963, is a good example) use autonomy as the translation term for freedom. But it's not intuitively obvious that freedom to act in the service of one's desires is friendlier to human nature or more conducive to social harmony—if these are the criteria chosen. . . . Thus, it is appropriate to ask why autonomy is often chosen by Western theorists as an end point of preference. Chinese and Japanese societies regard a love of humanity as the primary goal of development, and I am persuaded that (love of humanity) is as reasonable a goal as autonomy. The ideals of compassion, nurture, and love place obligations on children and adults that restrict seriously each person's individual freedom. (Kagan, 1986, p. 88)

N. Smart (1969, 1978) has asserted that westernized religions are more individualistic, while Eastern religions tend to be focused on more mystical experiences with a unitary consciousness that is both nonspatial and nontemporal. Therefore, in Eastern religions, the emphasis is upon unity with God. In Christianity, the worshiper approaches God in prayer and meditation as an individual human speaking to an individual God.

All of the theories presented in this book were developed by Western theorists from developed nations, so all have the underlying assumption of ever-expanding growth and complexity of active, self-determining individuals (Heckhausen, 2003).

Also, their underlying assumptions of linear, upward progress and predefined ideal goals are considered to be Western in orientation (Keller, Edelstein, Krettenauer, Fang, & Fang, 2005; Steenbarger, 1991).

RELIGION AND DEVELOPMENTAL STAGES

Life transitions are often guided by religious traditions or spiritual orientations. Religion and spirituality serve two general purposes: (1) finding meaning and purpose in life and (2) maintaining a sense of hope and creativity. It was the Baby Boom generation that first made a distinction between religion and spirituality, viewing religious individuals as those who were affiliated with formal religious institutions and who accepted the doctrinal tenets of these institutions. In contrast, being spiritual means interacting with higher or nonphysical powers that assist individuals in finding meaning and purpose in life. Spirituality is further defined as a central philosophy of life that guides the individual in his or her daily life and composes a large part of the individual's self-identity. Baby Boomers were also the first generation in which many would identify themselves as spiritual rather than religious. Obviously, it is more straightforward for researchers to measure the religiosity of individuals or groups because they can use such measures as church attendance, self-reported belief in church doctrines, and participation in such rituals as baptism, confirmation, bar mitzvahs, weddings, and funerals.

In the United States, the proportion of adherents to Islam, Hinduism, and Buddhism has remained stable at a combined rate of 5%. Americans also identify with such faiths as Sikh, Bahaai, Shintoism, and Taoism. Native Americans tend to follow the spiritual heritage from their traditions. Approximately 2% of Americans identify as Jewish.

Walsh and Pryce (2003) described the relationship between religion and developmental stages:

> Rituals can celebrate family holidays, traditions, achievements, and reunions. They can ease difficult transitions or unfamiliar situations and summon courage through the darkest hours. In times of crisis and profound sorrow, they can script family actions and responses, as in funeral rites or memorial services. Rituals also connect a particular celebration or tragedy with all human experience, and a birth or a death and loss with others. (p. 349)

Developmental stages of life have always been guided by religion and by church and synagogue leaders. The birth of an infant is a religious event that is observed in baptism, in which the child often receives the name of an ancestor, thus providing generational continuity. Entrance into adulthood was and often still is a religious event during which the child demonstrates some sort of competence, such as learning catechism or reciting the Torah. In both cases, the priest or rabbi taught these children and judged when they had achieved these religious skills. Marriage, divorce, and death are also considered religious events; indeed, these events are often triggers either for religious participation or for dropping out. For example, divorce is often a catalyst for women to renew their religious participation, but for men divorce is generally a catalyst for ending church participation. Marriage ceremonies generally occur in a church or synagogue when the marriage occurs at a normative age and the couple desires to have children. Teenage marriages, late-life marriages, or second marriages typically do not take place in a religious or spiritual setting (Wuthnow, 2007).

Along with relationships and work, religious/spiritual identification is considered one of the three foundations of adult identity for Americans. National polls have shown that almost two-thirds of American adults believe in some sort of a god, and 61% claim membership in a religious organization. The most significant predictor of a person's religious orientation is the religion of his or her parents, although teenagers often stop attending church to express their need for individuation and autonomy.

Western Europe is becoming more secularized, with fewer adults claiming belief in a higher power and even fewer attending services at a church or synagogue. Even though the United States is becoming more secularized, church attendance still remains high. Some demographers posit that instead of becoming secularized, Americans tend to switch religions. The proportion of Americans who change religions has been estimated to be as high as one-third, especially conversion to conservative Protestant faiths.

Religious activity in the United States tends to be differentiated by gender, with women more likely to attend church or synagogue and to engage in weekday church activities (Neill & Kahn, 1999). Berk (2001) explained: "[women] turn to religion for social support and for a larger vision of community that places life's challenges in perspective" (p. 599).

In old age, individuals tend to view religion as very important in their lives. In a national survey, 76% of Americans age 65 and older stated that religion is very important in their lives, and 16% described religion as fairly important. More than half attend weekly religious services, and nearly two-thirds view religious television programs. Approximately 25% stated that they prayed at least three times a day (Princeton Religion Research Center, 1994). As individuals age, they tend to advance to higher levels of religiosity and spirituality, contemplating the deeper significance of doctrine, tenets, and rituals. Many individuals in late life state that they are more open to spiritual inspiration (Birren, 1990). It has long been known that religious participation has positive social and emotional results; however, one longitudinal study also found religious participation to be a strong predictor of better physical functioning over a 12-year period (Idler & Kasl, 1997).

Another developmental transition that often triggers a change in religious participation is the acquisition or diagnosis of a disability. For some, the disability acts as a catalyst to renew or begin church activity, but for others it can lead to questioning their beliefs and membership in religious organizations. For many disabilities, the cause (etiology or pathogenesis) is unknown; medicine and science simply cannot determine the cause. However, religion and spirituality can bring meaning and purpose to a disability, allowing the PWD to view the disability as something other than a random, unpredictable, undeserved occurrence. For others, dealing with a disability marks the end of their religious participation. Charles Mee was part of an active Catholic family. He contracted polio as a teenager and in the following excerpt he tells of a conversation with a Jesuit priest and his resulting resentment of the power differential and the failure of the priest to understand his feelings:

> "I've lost my faith. I no longer believe in God."
>
> "I see," the priest said. And then he made a mistake. Instead of honoring my thoughts and feelings—instead of gently exploring the anger that had taken me to this place I was in—he decided to bully me, to intimidate me back into the church with his superior reasoning. (Mee, 1999, p. 202)

Churches and synagogues have not, until recently, generally been accessible for PWDs. The ADA does not apply to private organizations, such as churches. Dr. Judith Heumann, former Assistant Secretary for the Office of Special Education and Rehabilitative Services, a polio survivor and wheelchair user, wrote about the inaccessibility of a Jewish synagogue:

> When the environment is made accessible, people have to start going out and becoming more independent, doing things they never did before. A simple example of this occurred in a synagogue that I attended when I lived in Berkeley. The bema, an area where people go to do readings and worship, was not accessible. One day, I told the rabbi, "The bema is not accessible." Two weeks later, it was accessible. The rabbi said, "OK, now it's accessible and you have to come up and do some of the things that other people do." I thought, "Oh my God, I've never been trained!" I didn't even know how to participate because I hadn't learned the things that a person needs to learn in order to participate. (Heumann, 1999, p. 53)

Religion and spirituality can guide a person's adjustment or adaptation to a disability through the principle of forgiveness. Many times, a disability is the result of human error or unwise risk taking. When the individual and his or her family, can forgive someone for causing the disability, the individual is more likely to forgive himself/herself. The psychology of forgiveness, both of others and oneself, has shown to lead to reduced negative feelings and to produce a positive change in well-being, both emotionally and physically. Failing to forgive one's self often leads to decreased acceptance of the disability, depression, and negative self-esteem.

THE VALUE OF THEORIES

Theories organize knowledge, provide hypothesized explanations, and generate research (Feist, 1990). As Lerner, Schwartz, and Phelps (2009) summarized, "It is important to appreciate that the issues raised . . . about the study of developmental processes are not simply theoretical abstractions" (p. 65). Practitioners apply their preferred theoretical orientations when conceptualizing cases and planning interventions. However, there is no universal theory that can be used with everyone in all circumstances. Certainly, none of these theories considered PWDs and their experiences or their developmental stages.

All theories, because they are created by humans, reflect the values of the theorists. Perhaps this explains why we find it interesting and helpful to read the biographies of these theorists. In addition, these developmental theories also reflect the time periods during which the theorists worked; it would be difficult to consider Freud's theory without thinking about Vienna in the late 19th century and early 20th century or Vygotsky without thinking about Soviet Russia immediately following the Bolshevik Revolution. Theories can change, or rather theorists have expanded and changed some aspects of their theories. In the face of contradictory research results, some theorists have modified their theories (Baltes & Reese, 1984).

The stage theory of dying proposed by Elisabeth Kübler-Ross in 1969 illustrates a once widely accepted theory that is now being questioned. Kübler-Ross was a psychiatrist at a Chicago hospital when she began interviewing dying patients. In her book *On Death and Dying* (1969), she describes five stages of the process of dying: regression, denial, anger, bargaining, and acceptance. At that time, there was no empirical research to either prove or disprove her theory, but her stage theory of dying seemed to make sense. Kübler-Ross's book became a national bestseller, initiated an entire new counseling specialty (grief counseling), and had a powerful influence in initiating the hospice movement in the United States. Her book also raised the standard of care for people who were dying as well as their survivors (Konigsberg, 2011).

Today, large-scale, tightly controlled research is beginning to challenge Kübler-Ross's stage theory of dying. Specifically, two basic premises are being questioned: (1) the progression through well-defined stages and (2) the encouragement for catharsis, or publicly expressing grief to others. Kübler-Ross's method of interviewing terminally ill patients, some of them only once, has been criticized. Furthermore, Kübler-Ross never directly asked these patients about the stages of dying.

In retrospect, it seems a logical step to construct a theory of death and dying in response to demographic, social, and medical changes. Demographically, the United States was becoming older; therefore, greater numbers of people were dying. Socially, the United States was becoming more secular, thus eliminating one of the main social institutions (the church or synagogue) that provided support for the dying and their families. Medically, the experience of death was changing from an event to a process, which often necessitated hospital care. Even if Kübler-Ross's theory was to be completely debunked, it would be credited with creating many innovations in dealing with death and, perhaps most important, changing the way in which society views dying, death, and grief.

Developmental theories are not systems of psychotherapies; however, a few developmental theorists developed complementary methods of psychotherapies, such as Freud. Nonetheless, therapists use these theories of human development in order to decide which information to gather for assessment and case conceptualization.

However, developmental theories do have practical applications, such as guiding government policies and programs. Federal social programs have incorporated the scientific principles of human growth and development. Government actions and programs, which serve millions of citizens, can be traced to the scientific research on human development. For example, Bronfenbrenner's research (1974, 1977) led to the establishment of Head Start. Head Start is a federally funded program: "One of the facets of (Head Start) was preschool intervention, which it was hoped, would provide young children with an inoculation against the ills resulting from poverty" (Zigler & Finn, 1984, p. 465). Bronfenbrenner recognized that early childhood is a very important period for academic development and enrichment, and his theory emerged during the "War on Poverty," a national effort to eliminate the inequities caused by poverty in the United States. In addition, developmental research and applied practice are circular endeavors. The Head Start program was a result of development research, and Head Start has provided a laboratory for developmental scientists to study childhood development. In short, developmental research is relevant to public policy.

The mental testing movement was a direct result of theories of development. Intelligence tests, such as the Stanford-Binet, were based on theoretical conceptions of normality. One of the most well-known and respected cognitive development theorists, Jean Piaget, worked with Alfred Binet in his Paris laboratory. Binet developed the first intelligence test, which was translated into English in 1916 at Stanford University in California and was from then on called the Stanford-Binet Intelligence Test. In fact, many paper-and-pencil psychological instruments, including intelligence tests, have used developmental theory as a normative base, which means that it was necessary to first determine what normality is before tests could be constructed to diagnose abnormality. Counselors and other professionals use developmental theories in their case conceptualizations, and many professional counselors and psychologists include the developmental theories they use in their disclosure statements. Disclosure statements are detailed written statements given to clients and patients before they enter into a counseling relationship. These disclosure statements provide information on the professional's education, experience, and their theoretical orientations (Remley & Herlihy, 2005).

In career counseling, Anne Roe's theories (1956) have been the basis of widely used classification systems, such as the *Occupational Preference Inventory,* the *Vocational Interest Inventory,* and the *Dictionary of Occupational Titles.* John Holland's theory of career choice has resulted in the most widely used career interest inventory, the *Self-Directed Search* (Zunker, 1998).

Most developmental research is cross sectional, studying individuals (or an individual) in one point in time. In contrast, longitudinal researchers follow an individual or groups of individual, over the course of many years. Obviously, with a life span developmental theoretical orientation, longitudinal research is more suitable. One example of a longitudinal study is the Stanford Studies of Gifted Children, which was begun in 1921 by Louis Terman and followed (indeed continues to follow) young boys who were identified as unusually intelligent, having IQs of at least 135 (Terman & Oden, 1959). Surveys were sent to these individuals at certain times throughout their lives to collect information on their adult years, including education, work, marriage, and children. This great body of information initiated new ways of thinking about human development by studying the life course of this group across several developmental stages. The participants nicknamed themselves "termites."

Surprisingly, the surveys asked the respondents only about their personal lives and did not consider the effects of social events on their lives. These intelligent young children of the 1920s are now elderly or deceased. After 60 years, the Stanford Studies concluded that a majority of these very intelligent men held advanced degrees, were superior achievers in their professions, and reported accomplishments far above the general population of men. However, in relationships such as marriage and children, these highly intelligent men looked like the general American male population (Rice, 1998).

As with any other longitudinal study, it is not always easy to generalize about other groups, because the termites lived in a specific historical time and were far more intelligent than the general population. Nonetheless, the studies produced important information about marital stability, longevity, and resilience in coping with stressful life events. Perhaps even more important, the Terman studies demonstrated that lengthy longitudinal studies could be undertaken, and would produce highly significant and valuable results.

Longitudinal research is expensive and difficult to implement, because many of the participants tend to drop out of the study. Therefore, there is a dearth of longitudinal studies. However, studies that cover the entire life span of individuals are much more useful than cross-sectional studies. (Cross-sectional studies result in a "snapshot" of a group of individuals at one specific time.) Terman's study focused on unusual people (highly intelligent young adults), while other studies have focused on people who have had unusual experiences or lived during extraordinary points of history. Of course, if the specific time period is very unusual or the group of individuals has experienced out-of-the-ordinary events, cross-sectional studies are extremely valuable. For example, Jewish survivors of the Nazi Holocaust were studied and interviewed. Four classic longitudinal studies that asked and answered important questions illustrate this type of study. First, Elder (1999) completed the first longitudinal study about the effects of the Great Depression. Second, Furstenberg, Brooks-Gunn, and Morgan (1987) followed 300 teenage mothers and their children over a 17-year period. Third, Laub and Sampson (2006) completed the longest longitudinal study of age, crime, and life course, following up on a study completed in 1950 (Glueck & Glueck). Fourth, Glueck and Gluck interviewed 500 men who had been incarcerated in "reform school" in the 1940s. Laub and Sampson collected data on the life course of these men when they were 70 years of age and Rossi and Rossi (1990) studied three generations of families in Boston. It would be interesting to design and implement a longitudinal study of PWDs in order to determine the effects of the ADA on their lives.

It is far easier to build a decontextualized theory than one that accounts for the myriad of ecological, social, cultural, and historical contexts. It is far easier to use the closed system of the medical model, which often focuses on only one variable. Due to the need to control the variables, research is simpler and more straightforward with decontextualized theories. In the Stanford Studies of Gifted Children, the surveys asked the respondents only about their personal lives and did not consider the effects of social events on their lives. "The men in Terman's study who had fought in World War II wrote about their war experiences in the margins of surveys that neglected to ask them about such experiences. They were puzzled by the study's indifference to the war" (Elder, Johnson, & Crosnoe, 2004, pp. 5–6).

One developmental theorist, Urie Bronfenbrenner, captured the difficulty of conducting research under controlled conditions. He stated that experimental laboratory research is the "science of the strange behavior of strange children in strange situations with strange adults for the briefest possible period of time" (1977, p. 513). Instead, Bronfenbrenner advocated reach in children's natural environments, such as their homes or schools. However, when natural settings are used, strict scientific control of all the important variables is decreased.

Today's sophisticated statistical tools and computers allow researchers to consider many different variables simultaneously. Advanced analyses, such as factor analysis and linear regression models, will lead researchers to undertake more contextual, multifunctional, multidimensional, and multicausality studies with a large sample of participants from many different groups. Most of the grand theories were developed before these statistical methods were available. Before the advent of computers, it was impossible (and perhaps unthinkable) to gather information on a large number of variables.

Developmental theories were biased toward middle-class individuals, and these theories have influenced the construction of career counseling and job placement. Almost all of the theories on human development have been justifiably criticized for their almost exclusive attention to White, middle-class males without disabilities. Hence, perhaps, a better description of these theories would be "theories of development for White, middle-class males in Western nations." Of course, everyone understands that these theories have never included all humans. Nonetheless, no published criticisms and evaluations of these theories have questioned the total absence of PWDs. In contrast, these theories have been criticized for their silence on women, gays, recent immigrants, and differing racial, ethnic, and linguistic groups. No one would suggest that White, middle-class males in Western nations are not worthy of study, but other groups should also be studied to help generate theories that will stimulate research, result in valid and reliable testing instruments, and assist professionals in their case conceptualizations.

Because most developmental theories have a goal of moving toward greater autonomy and independence, they may not be as relevant to women (Gilligan, 1982). The Harvard psychologist Carol Gilligan argued that women typically consider the values of attachment and relatedness more important than autonomy and independence. Indeed, Gilligan considered autonomy and independence to be *masculine* values.

Although the weaknesses and shortcomings of developmental theories have been pointed out, it must be noted that the strengths, practicality, and predictive value of these theories far outweigh their weaknesses, and they do demonstrate the capacity to accommodate many different life events. It is important to acknowledge the weaknesses, but we should also recognize that these theories continue to demonstrate strong explanatory value.

This chapter concludes with one last observation: these developmental stages, despite their flaws, have played a vital role in developing other types of developmental theories, including theories of career development (Super, 1972), theories describing the process of dying (Kübler-Ross, 1969), and theories describing adjustment to disability (Livneh & Antonak, 1997; Smart, 2001, 2009). These grand theories have provided direction to negotiating many life events, especially in viewing these life events not as events, but processes.

Terms to Learn

Agency
Contextual
Continuity of
    development
Differentiation
Epigenetic
Epiphenomenal

Equifinality
Generation or generational
    groups
Multicausality
Multifunctionality
Normative
Ontogenesis

Plasticity
Quinceanera
Rumspringa
Social and cultural con-
    struction of age
Social clock

Video to View

- View the 14-minute video *Freedom Chasers: The Importance of Independence for Teens with a Disability*. The producers describe the video in this manner: "Living with a disability means that you find yourself both struggling with the need to be independent as well as being dependent on others at the same time. The teens in this video share great insight on living a challenge like cerebral palsy, spina bifida, juvenile arthritis, and Down syndrome."

Learning Activities

(Note: These may also be used as class presentations.)
- Research the life of Albert Binet. Do you think that Binet's intelligence test is used in the way that Binet suggested? In 1895 Binet outlined the purposes of intelligence tests and considered them suitable only for use in academic settings.
- Research the Stanford-Binet Intelligence Test. Explain why the name Stanford appears in the title of this intelligence test.
- Research the life of Louis Terman. Why do you think that Terman decided to study boys who were highly intelligent?
- Read Valliant's (1997) classic book *Adaptation to Life*, published by Little, Brown. Consider the ways in which each of the concepts listed in "Terms to Learn" applies to Valliant's work.
- Research the California Study of Gifted Children. Do you recognize any of the names of the participants? Read L. Terman (1925). *Genetic Studies of Genius: Volume 1. Mental and Physical Traits of a Thousand Gifted Children*. Stanford, CA: Stanford University.

- Read L. M. Terman, and M. H. Oden (1959), *Genetic Studies of Genius: Vol. 5. The Gifted at Midlife: Thirty-five Years of Follow-up of the Superior Child,* Stanford, CA: Stanford University.
- As a class, develop a list of questions to ask individuals in the Baby Boom generation. These questions might include: "What do you remember as the most important historical event that occurred in your lifetime?" "Do you consider your generation to have had an unprecedented range of choices in lifestyle?" "How long do you expect to live?" "What would you do differently if you could go back in time?" After the questions have been developed, have each class member interview a Baby Boomer and ask the questions from the class-generated list.

Writing Exercises

1. Describe the way in which you think the longevity revolution will affect you. If you live to reach the age of 100 (or older), what do you think you will do and accomplish after the age of 80?
2. Defend this statement in four paragraphs: "America will become an age-irrelevant society." Then in additional four paragraphs provide an argument against this statement.
3. Write six paragraphs describing your own generational group. Give a name to your generation. Explain the tasks of your generation. Provide information on the way in which your generation is a logical extension of the generation that preceded yours.
4. In six paragraphs, explain why history-graded influences are especially strong during adolescence and early adulthood. Provide two examples of individuals who made great contributions to society while they were in late adolescence and early adulthood.
5. Write a three-page paper defending the use of contextualized theories of human growth and development.
6. Write a three-page paper describing the way in which autonomy and self-determination are part of the American culture and, therefore, how American developmental theorists have incorporated these values as the goals of human growth and development.

Acquisition and Diagnosis of Disabilities in Stages of the Life Span

Sigmund Freud 3

Freud was Freudian. If we were to state that, "Dr. X is Freudian," or "Woody Allen movies are Freudian," everyone would have some understanding of the concept of Freudian. Many of Freud's ideas are implanted in popular culture and, it is safe to state that the profession of psychiatry is a bastion of Freudianism. Of course, Sigmund Freud did not think of himself as Freudian; but, nonetheless, despite the controversy surrounding him and his theory, Freud developed the first theory of human development and the psychoanalytic method of therapy and remains the most famous theorist of human development (Strachey, 1964). In simple terms, Freud started a revolution in the way in which consciousness is viewed. For centuries, humans were thought to be entirely rational, controlled by reason and their conscious thoughts. Freud's core statement asserted that humans are also controlled by their emotions, their desires, and their ability to bond and attach to others. The unconscious mind controlled much of human life and the unconscious mind was emotional.

He wrote and compiled a great body of work (24 volumes), occasionally revising his theories while maintaining key elements. Freud thought of himself primarily as a scientist and writer, rather than as a practicing physician (Feist, 1990). Therefore, because Freud is the first and most famous of all the human development theorists, it seems appropriate to begin our discussion of the major human development theorists with Freud's work. However, Freud's stature and contributions often make it difficult to evaluate his work. One author explained:

> [Freud] looms as such a giant to both his advocates and his opponents that it is difficult to see him objectively even in our time.... Freud was deeply committed to his work, family, friends, colleagues, and principles. From youth he showed the brilliant intelligence, tenacity, and independence that marked him for greatness and the resulting social rejection. (Maddi, 1996, pp. 27–28)

THE LIFE OF SIGMUND FREUD

Freud lived for almost 80 years in Vienna, the capital of Austria. However, he was born in Moravia, a Germanic part of Czechoslovakia, in 1856 and died in London in 1939. Freud was the oldest child of his parents' eight children. As a child, he was close to his mother and distant from his father; and in his later life, Freud exhibited very hostile, angry feelings toward his father. He was barely 10 years old when he entered high school and he was only 17 when he entered medical school. He trained to be a physician, but he was always more interested in scientific research than in practicing medicine. While in medical school, his choice of student research projects included: (1) dissecting 400 male eels, demonstrating for the first time that male eels have testes; (2) discovering that cocaine was an effective anesthetic, using himself as a subject; (3) developing the first gold-chloride technique of staining nerve tissue; and (4) studying nerve cells in fish (Jones, 1957; Parisi, 1987). These topics chosen by Freud seem to foreshadow his later interests in sexuality and neurology. Freud also studied for a year with a French psychiatrist, Jean Charcot, who used hypnosis as a treatment method. If Freud had followed his first ambition to become a professor of medicine (Freud, 1952), he very well might have been forgotten by history.

After 8 years of medical school, he graduated at age 25 and entered private practice, treating many patients who did not appear to have physical illnesses, but rather experienced "nervous symptoms," such as hallucinations, fears, and paralyses, all which fell under the definition of hysteria. Freud's specialty was neurology. He began to theorize that some of his patients' physical complaints had mental causes and then reasoned that a therapy for the mind needed to be developed. In 1900, Freud published his first great work, *The Interpretation of Dreams*.

He was a family man, practiced medicine from an office in his home, was a devoted husband to Martha Bernays, and was the proud father of three sons and three daughters. In 1938, Freud's friends convinced him to leave his beloved Vienna due to Nazi persecution of Jewish people in Austria. Freud was Jewish but never practiced Judaism; in fact, he considered religion an infantile regression that people used in order to cope with feelings of helplessness.

Freud went to London and eventually died there. One author described Freud's death:

> Freud died from cancer of the jaw and mouth on September 23, 1939, only a year and a summer after he migrated to London. The malignancy undoubtedly stemmed from his lifelong addiction to cigars, which he chain-smoked from early morning to late evening. You may find this addiction quite interesting when you read about Freud's theory of orality.... On September 21, 1939, Freud asked his personal physician to continually administer morphine to him until he died (*Monitor of the American Psychological Association*, September 10, 1998, p. 10). Two days later the morphine ended his life. (Allen, 2000, p. 21)

Many biographers and Freudian scholars believe that it is important to understand the social and intellectual environment of late-nineteenth-century Vienna in the decades preceding World War I (Gay, 1988). At this time, Vienna was very sexually circumspect, and Freud's theory created a great deal of controversy because it is firmly based on sexual impulses and needs; indeed, Freud defined humans in terms of sexual instincts. Most people did not want to acknowledge that humans, including newborn infants, had sexual needs or that these needs formed the basis for personality development. In addition, Freud's deterministic views showed humans to be fallible, which contradicted some Western religious views of humans as perfectible.

He gathered a group of followers around him, consisting of young, ambitious, and intellectually gifted physicians who learned both his methods of psychoanalysis and his concepts of human development. Eventually, this informal group developed into the

Vienna Psychoanalytic Society. Membership in this group was very limited and highly valued, and the work of the group was extremely influential in European medical and scientific communities. With these younger professionals, Freud was almost paternalistic and somewhat possessive; with his strong personality and radical new ideas, these mentoring relationships were often very intense. A few of these followers made substantial changes to Freud's theories, and two or three members, such as Carl Jung, left the group and became estranged from Freud. A group of those who revised key elements of Freud's theories, called "neo-Freudians," include Carl Jung, Alfred Adler, Erich Fromm, and his daughter Anna Freud. Nonetheless, as one scholar summarized, "It is a tribute to Freud's intellectual impact on them that these outcasts typically went on to develop influential theories of their own that reflected their psychoanalytic parentage" (Maddi, 1996, p. 28).

Freud was both a gifted writer and translator. He was fluent in several languages and translated several major authors into German, such as John Stuart Mill (English) and Jean-Martin Charcot (French). In 1930, he was awarded the Goethe Prize for literature.

One scholar described Freud's personality:

Among other qualities, Freud possessed an intense intellectual curiosity; unusual moral courage demonstrated by his daily self-analysis; extremely ambivalent feelings toward his father and other father figures; the tendency to hold grudges disproportionate to the alleged offense; a burning ambition, especially during his earlier years, strong feelings of isolation even while surrounded by many followers; and an intense and somewhat irrational dislike of Americans, a feeling that became more intense after his trip to the United States in 1909. (Feist, 1990, p. 31)

Freud developed many ideas that are widely accepted today, such as the importance of early childhood and the family in the individual's development. Freud thought that early development influenced later development. The neo-Freudians accepted these components of Freud's theories, but they could not accept Freud's deterministic views. Indeed, Freud is considered to be "deterministic," because he believed that behavior was caused by intrapsychic dynamics that were outside the control of the individual. Another concept discarded by the neo-Freudians was the idea that humans are driven by instincts that they somehow manage to camouflage. Freud thought that humans are controlled by forces inside (instincts) and pressures outside (society), and (even more critical) humans did not understand their situation (unconscious motivation).

Unlike the other theorists discussed in this book, Freud developed a method of psychotherapy in addition to producing a theory of human development. We will not discuss Freud's methods of psychoanalytic therapy or those aspects of his theory that do not directly relate to human development.

Freudian Theory

- Instincts are motivators of behavior
- Early childhood development is important
- Emotion is more powerful than reason

Freud's theory involved instincts, the sources of punishment and guilt, and the ways in which humans protect (or defend) themselves from guilt, tension, and punishment. An instinct is an inner drive or impulse that acts as a motivator. Because an instinct is internal, individuals cannot escape or avoid their instincts. Instincts can be powerful or weak and originate from a region or zone of the body, typically a sexually stimulated region. Tension results when the organism lacks something it needs; therefore, sexual tension is a sign of sexual deprivation. Each instinct has its own form of energy. Instincts cannot be changed, but the way in which pleasure is obtained or tension reduced can be modified and, indeed, is modified throughout the individual's life in order to conform to the conventions of society. Freud considered instincts to be the core components of personality. He defined sexuality in very broad terms, considering many parts of the body as erogenous.

Second, Freud recognized the importance of early childhood experiences on adulthood. His theories, however, are not considered to cover the entire life span, because in his theories psychosexual development ends at adolescence. According to Freud, new developmental skills are not achieved or learned in adulthood or old age because he believed that psychosexual development has been completed by then.

Freud was an innovator when he postulated that emotion is a stronger motivator of behavior than reason. This was not only new but also unpopular, because all people liked to think (and still do like to think) that they are rational, thoughtful individuals who act after logically considering all the alternatives. One scholar explained:

> Even among highly educated people, emotion is always more powerful than reason. Intelligent people can use their talents and their abilities to justify what they *want* to believe. As history shows, intellectuals have consistently committed themselves to false ideologies. We need look no further than the history of ideas in the 20th century, in the course of which many philosophers, scientists, and artists have unapologetically supported all kinds of ideas, ranging from totalitarian politics to religious orthodoxies. (Paris, 2000, p. 73)

Three Components of the Personality

- Pleasure principle
- Reality principle
- Idealistic principle

The three components of personality, according to Freud, are the id, the ego, and the superego. The id is present at birth, the ego emerges during infancy and childhood, and the superego appears during early childhood. All three of these components must be successfully integrated into an effective pattern in order for the individual to function in an adaptive way.

The id is the primary source of psychic energy and demands satisfaction through the *pleasure principle*. At its simplest, the id is biologically rooted, seeking pleasure and attempting to avoid pain, and because it is in a person's unconscious, the individual is not aware of the id. The id cannot recognize the difference between reality and fantasy. For example, an infant sucks his or her thumb, not understanding that the thumb provides no nutrition. Also, the id is illogical because incompatible ideas can coexist; Freud would say that someone may want to have a sexual union with another person while also wishing to kill him or her. The id is not immoral—merely amoral. Although chaotic, illogical, unorganized, and unable to distinguish between good and evil, the id also possesses great stores of energy. The id, therefore, is completely egocentric and does not regard the conventions of society or the feelings of others. The id does not recognize the existence of others and thinks that all of its desires can be satisfied. The id does not grow and develop; it remains the same throughout a person's life. For example, no adult would cut in line at Disneyland, but many of us on a sinking ship might be tempted to cut in line in order to get the last place in a lifeboat. We would probably hate ourselves for allowing others to die, but we really want to survive.

The ego is developed during the first 6 to 8 months of infancy and early childhood and is psychic energy directed toward self. The ego is the mental structure that experiences and interprets reality. Therefore, the ego is composed of cognitive capacities, such as perception, memory, and problem solving. Freud thought that infants and children exhibit self-love and an interest in their bodies, their experiences, and their sense of choice and agency. The ego operates on the *reality principle,* meaning that the ego tries to satisfy its impulses in a socially accepted form. The ego grows and develops throughout an individual's life. Often, the ego is considered to perform executive functions for the individual, mediating between the impulses of the individual and the conventions of society. Therefore, the ego is realistic when it performs cognitive and intellectual functions, but it is unrealistic when trying to satisfy the needs of the id. This conflict between the realistic and unrealistic parts and functions of the ego results in anxiety. The ego tries to reduce anxiety by preventing undesirable elements from reaching consciousness. Therefore, in a lifeboat story, it might be true that we shoved people aside in order to get the last seat on the last lifeboat, thus allowing people to die. However, we probably would remember this experience in a different way in order to avoid self-condemnation and to defend ourselves. In our remembered story, we acted heroically and saved many lives. We helped others to get into the lifeboats and surrendered our seat to others.

The superego is often thought of as the individual's conscience and begins to develop at about age 5 or 6. The superego operates on the *idealistic principle.* Most people try to avoid self-condemnation and, therefore, engage in only those behaviors that are acceptable and proper. The superego represents the ideal self, with firmly established concepts of the behaviors and thoughts considered to be admirable, praiseworthy, and ethical. The superego guides humans to seek rewards, praise, and self-respect and, at the same time, avoiding punishment and self-condemnation. For most people, if they had survived a sinking ship by pushing to the head of the lifeboat line, they would live the remainder of the lives filled with guilt and self-recrimination. Indeed, according to Freud, the more the individual is capable of repressing the id, the more self-confident he or she becomes.

Freud thought that not all individuals experience growth of the superego after childhood and that, for most individuals, the ego and the superego alternate in controlling personality, resulting in extreme fluctuations of mood.

Domains of Consciousness

- The conscious
- The unconscious

Freud proposed that there is an area of the mind, called the unconscious, that is a storehouse of powerful, primitive motives of which the person is unaware. Both unconscious and conscious motives govern behavior, sometimes simultaneously. The unconscious mind is further divided into two levels, the unconscious and the preconscious, making a total of three domains. The individual can become aware of the unconscious, but only with great effort and difficulty. The idea that most people do not know themselves or understand the reasons for their attitudes and behaviors was considered very radical. Freud described the mind as an iceberg. The conscious mind is the tenth of the iceberg that protrudes out of the water. However, although the conscious mind is available to our awareness and the tip of the iceberg is visible, they both compose a small part of the mind or a small part of the iceberg. The preconscious mind is compared to the part of the iceberg near the water line. Preconscious thought can be accessed through focused attention, most often by retrieving memories. The part of the iceberg with the greatest mass is not seen above the waterline, and this is what makes icebergs dangerous. An iceberg may appear to be small chunks of floating ice when, in reality, there are often unseen mountains of ice below the water.

Freud considered the unconscious domain of thoughts, feelings, wishes, fears, and repressed memories to be analogous to the part of the iceberg that is hidden from view. Freud believed that the unconscious is outside of awareness; furthermore, most individuals actively work to keep the unconscious from intruding upon their conscious. Through the techniques of psychotherapy, it is possible to find the link between the unconscious and the individual's behavior. To cite a simple example, Freud had a patient who either forgot his wife's name or did not call her by her name, even though the man said he loved his wife very much. Freud hypothesized that it was not acceptable to the man to have negative, hostile, unloving feelings toward his wife, so he simply forgot her name, which was more acceptable to his conscience.

Old Aunt Pamela Loves Gorillas: Freud's Five Psychosexual Stages

- Oral
- Anal
- Phallic
- Latency
- Genital

According to Freud, there are five psychosexual stages of human development, each of which has a form of sexual instinct. Freud defined sexuality very broadly to include the full range of physical pleasure. The mnemonic phrase, Old Aunt Pamela Loves Gorillas, serves as a memory aid to remember the five stages of psychosexual development: oral (old), anal (aunt), phallic (Pamela), latency (loves), and genital (gorillas). The gratification of sexual instincts often conflicts with societal expectations; therefore, for each of the psychosexual stages, there is a corresponding defense mechanism. Each of these stages has a type of personality associated with it.

Each developmental stage is qualitatively different from the other stages and is associated with the sexual instinct; thus, Freud's theory is based on the sexuality (and biology) of human nature. These psychosexual stages are sequential and hierarchical, and each is associated with a specific age range. If the individual does not resolve conflicts successfully at each stage, there will be lingering effects on later behavior. This lack of resolution is called "fixation," which simply means that the individual is stuck at the stage or that the individual remains fixed at one stage of development. Fixation is defined as seeking gratification or anxiety reduction appropriate to earlier stages of development. For example, Freud thought that people who smoked, constantly chewed gum, or overate were fixated in the oral stage.

According to Freud, the most important development takes places in the stages before the age of five. Describing these stages may make them appear to be simplistic, but each stage is very complex and involves a great deal of conflict and competing impulses, all which must be resolved in a way that is acceptable to both the individual and the society.

The oral stage involves sexual gratification experienced through the mouth. Freud reasoned that since the nervous system proceeds from the brain downward, the mouth would be the first body part to experience pleasure and pain. Moreover, because the mouth is used for eating and drinking, it is important for physical survival. The mouth, according to Freud, can express both pleasure and tension through eating and exploring the environment. The infant craves and enjoys stimulation of the mouth through touch, taste, and the use of muscles. To satisfy the needs of the id, the infant may be very demanding, such as requiring feeding every 2 hours; parents and other caregivers, in spite of these demands, love and care for the baby. Individuals who are fixated at this stage may either be optimistic, gullible, and full of admiration for others, or they may be pessimistic, envious of others, and full of suspicion and sarcasm.

The anal stage begins during the second year of life; the anus is the most sexualized part of the body. During this time, the child begins to control his or her body and becomes toilet trained. In this way, the child is beginning to be aware of and to satisfy the demands of his or her culture. Because children in the anal stage wish to maintain the affection of their parents, they submit to the demands of toilet training. Someone who is fixated at this stage is either anal expulsive or anal retentive. Someone who is anal expulsive is messy, disorganized, reckless, careless, and defiant. Someone who is anal retentive is precise, orderly, careful, stingy, obstinate, and passive aggressive.

Freud described children in the phallic stage as bisexual. This stage, which begins at age three, is a period of heightened genital sensitivity and self-stimulation. During the phallic stage, the child has competing impulses, wanting to satisfying sexual feelings but at the same time understanding that it is not socially acceptable to do so. During the phallic stage of the child's life, he or she also begins to identify with his or her parents, adopting and internalizing the parents' values and ethical guidelines. In the anal stage, the child has become aware of his or her parents' value system; however, in the phallic stage the child internalizes the value system, and the ego begins to control more and more of the child's behavior. The child gains more autonomy and freedom and yet manages to please his or her parents, thus earning a place within the family. Repression of the id increases as parents strive to teach and guide their children toward obedience and self-control. According to Freud, children have a strong sexualized attraction to the parent of the opposite sex and a strong identification with the same sex parent. The Oedipal complex, which is found in boys, is characterized by strong sexualized feelings for the mother, and the Electra complex is the strong sexualized attraction of young girls for the father. Fixation at this stage results in individuals who are reckless, self-assured, narcissistic, proud, and vain.

The latency period begins after the conflicts of the phallic stage are resolved, and it lasts from about age 7 to the onset of puberty. During this period, there are no conflicts or impulses, and the ego matures. The word latent means either present and potential but not evident or active, or dormant and hidden. Freud's use of this term indicates something that is present in the unconscious mind but not consciously expressed. In the years of elementary school, children's sexual and aggressive urges are redirected toward more appropriate outlets due to their developing cognitive and social skills. These newly developed skills help them to strengthen their superegos. According to Freud, the psychosexual urges of the oral, anal, and phallic stages of infancy and the preschool years have been resolved, so the elementary school years are relatively calm.

The genital stage begins with the onset of puberty and ends with the sexual maturity of the individual. Teenagers begin to develop sexual relationships with individuals outside of the family and, in this way, obtain some measure of autonomy from the family. Adolescents may withdraw emotionally from their parents and families at this time, culminating in a more egalitarian relationship with their parents. The conflicts and tensions that arise during this period result from a failure to satisfy or express one's sexuality in a socially appropriate way. No one can completely satisfy all of his or her impulses or needs. Therefore, it is necessary for the id and superego to channel the energy of these needs in socially accepted ways. The ego (the value system of one's culture) and the regulation of the superego (the individual's conscience) work together to assist the adolescent in fulfilling his or her needs. Eventually, young adults develop and maintain long-term sexual partners.

EVALUATION

Freud's theory is considered to be pessimistic. Stefan Zweig (1962) spoke at Freud's funeral and stated

> So long and so abundantly has Sigmund Freud been a physician that he has gradually come to look upon mankind at large as ailing. His first impression, therefore, when he looks outward from his consulting-room into the outer world, is a pessimistic one.... (p. 208)

Due to the fact that Freud considered the individual's anatomy chiefly sexual, many experts have characterized his theories as foreordained, instinctual, and mechanistic. In this context, mechanistic means that individual does not possess a great deal of freedom of choice; he or she is governed by sexual drives.

Allen (2000) concisely lists the criticisms leveled at Freud:

> Freud capriciously changed his position, was inconsistent, self-contradictory, and tautological, borrowed ideas from others, and supported his theory by inventing evidence.... Reexamination of Freud's case histories shows that he did not actually have certain case subjects in therapy, he made up childhood traumas for certain case subjects, and he misrepresented the efficacy of his therapy. (p. 50)

Allen then concluded that, in spite of these criticisms, Freud's theory continues to be supported and used in professional practice.

> The intensity, number, and perhaps convincingness of the assaults on Freud's theoretical fortress may seem to have increased so much over time that its walls appear sure to soon come tumbling down. However, there is another perspective. Detractors, though increasing in number, may be a mere platoon compared to the vast army of psychological professionals who either explicitly support Freud or imply support by making his ideas central to their own. Even as detractors seek to obliterate each of Freud's ideas great and small, others are finding support for his concepts. (Allen, 1997, p. 47)

Another author emphasized the respect accorded to Freud. Although this author recognizes that today's psychoanalysts have updated Freud's theories and methods, he refers to Freud's writing as "scripture" and to Freud and other psychoanalysts as "gods."

> Like liberal theologians, analysts can reinterpret scripture to support a contemporary point of view....
>
> This, if one peruses recent issues of the *International Journal of Psychoanalysis* and the *Journal of the American Psychoanalytic Association,* it quickly becomes clear that that only a minority of articles represent a new eclecticism. The movement remains highly conservative, and most papers pay homage to the founder....
>
> In science, theories come and go as new evidence is collected, As Wilson (1998, pp. 182–183) wittily stated, "Progress in a scientific discipline can be measured by how quickly its founders are forgotten. Yet psychoanalysis retains all previous gods in its pantheon, rather like the multitude of deities worshiped during the Roman Empire." (Paris, 2000, p. 75)

In its most simplified form, Freud's theory of human development may be viewed as the tension or conflict between one's needs and the demands of society and the way in which this conflict shapes the development of the individual. The ego is tasked with maintaining relationships with others and giving personal meaning to the expectations of society. Specifically, a person's sexual impulses and needs continue throughout the life span, so because of this, everyone must resolve the conflict between his or her needs and societal conventions. Therefore, human behavior is as much the result of emotion and impulses as of rational decision making. It is easy, therefore, to understand why Freud also developed psychotherapeutic techniques. If individuals experience strong emotions, impulses, and sexual needs but are not able to channel these unconscious motives, they will often engage in behavior that does not make sense to the individuals themselves. Therefore, they need psychoanalysis in order to uncover their motives and explore new, socially acceptable ways to satisfy their impulses. Freudian theory holds that individuals act in illogical, often self-defeating ways without understanding why, or even worse, at times they do not recognize that they are engaging in self-defeating behaviors.

Perhaps the most difficult aspect to accept in Freud's theory is the insistence that infants and small children have sexual impulses. Furthermore, Freud postulates that if these sexual impulses are not successfully resolved at the right stage of life, adults may not be able to form loving, successful sexual relationships with others. Everyone agrees that babies and children require love, cuddling, and snuggling, but some find it more difficult to accept that babies and children need sexual stimulation. In spite of this, it is apparent that sexual dysfunction continues to plague society, with the continuing presence of rape, infidelity, sexual harassment, sexually transmitted diseases, and homophobia. True Freudians believe that these types of societal psychopathology are the result of unsuccessful resolution of psychosexual stages of development. The psychopathology of individuals can be resolved by psychoanalysis.

Freud never undertook empirical research; instead his method of research was the case study, using clinical records. Most critics consider these case notes to be indirect methods. Freud treated only one child, but he was able to develop an entire system of child development based on his adult patients' memories of their childhood, his observations of his children, and his memories of his own childhood, all of which are somewhat questionable practices. Freud considered humans to be closed systems who only had a "finite set of cause and effect sequences" (Horowitz, 1987, p. 54).

His theory and concepts of human development closely align with the biomedical model of disability. Today, most disability scholars subscribe to the sociopolitical model of disability, in which disability is viewed as a social and political concern rather than a private, individual concern. In this newer model, not only the individual must change but also society is required to change attitudes, laws, and institutions and provide full accessibility to people with disabilities (PWDs). Freud's theory fits the biomedical model because the pathology exists solely in the individual (a closed system) rather than in any environmental causes. Therefore, all treatment is aimed at "fixing" the individual, without regard to the individual's social or physical environment.

Freud defined human development in terms of males, and many critics, especially feminists, think that Freud deliberately consigned women to the lesser status of "nonmen." Freud ascribed negative characteristics to women and thought that women, in comparison with men, had greater tendencies to neurosis and also did not possess fully developed superegos. He also clearly stated that women functioned at a lower ethical level than men and tended to use defense mechanisms more frequently than men. Macmillan (1997) wrote a book that evaluates Freud and his theories, concluding that Freud considered civilization to be an entirely male creation. Gloria Steinem, a journalist and women's rights advocate, asked, "What if Freud had been a woman?" and wrote an article titled "Phyllis Freud" (1994), in which she reversed the genders in many of Sigmund Freud's theories and case studies. In a later chapter, we will learn about

Lawrence Kohlberg (1981) and his theory of cognitive moral reasoning. Kohlberg also thought that (in comparison to men) women functioned at relatively low levels of moral reasoning.

Nonetheless, Freud developed the first theoretical framework for human development and was among the first to state that the family environment, parenting practices, and early childhood experiences influenced a person's thoughts and behaviors throughout the entire course of his or her life. All the theorists discussed in this book owe some debt to Freud for providing a foundation for their theories.

Freud's Theory Applied to PWDs

- The use of defense mechanisms in adapting to a disability
- The significance of the individual's body image
- The importance of the early stages of development

Ego defenses can contribute significantly to helping an individual understand his or her response to a disability. According to Freud, ego defenses are unconscious processes whose primary task is to prevent anxiety by distorting or denying stressful realities, such as a disability (Livneh & Cook, 2005). Also, ego defenses help the individual deny unpleasant emotions. When an individual is adjusting to a disability, perhaps the most important ego defense is denial.

Denial is also termed defensive retreat; it prevents the individual from being flooded and overwhelmed with the reality of the disability, the functional limitations, and the necessary change in identity and life style. Denial occurs when there is a discrepancy between the "real self" and the "ideal self." Coping behaviors (which are goal-directed positive steps to rehabilitation) are encouraged, but ego defenses are typically discouraged. If the individual does not persist too long in this stage denial may facilitate the first phases of rehabilitation. Denial of a disability may take three forms: (1) denial of its presence, (2) denial of its implications, or (3) denial of its permanence. Denial of the disability is rare, but denial of its permanence ("I'm going to walk out of this hospital") and of its implications ("My life will be unchanged") is far more common.

In her book *Recovery: The Lived Experience of Rehabilitation*, Patricia Deegan (1991) described the denial of her psychiatric disability—schizophrenia. Note that she describes denial as normal and that the denial is not permanent; it lasts "those few awful months."

> Needless to say, we didn't believe our doctors and social workers. In fact, we adamantly denied and raged against these bleak prophesies for our lives. We felt it was all just a mistake, a bad dream, a temporary set-back in our lives. We just knew that in a week or two, things would get back to normal again. We felt our teenage world was still there, just waiting for us to return to it. Our denial was an important stage in our recovery. It was a normal reaction to an overwhelming situation. It was our way of surviving those first awful months. (p. 48)

In Deegan's example, we can see that several individuals ("doctors and social workers") tried to tell her that she had schizophrenia. Freud's idea that individuals unconsciously distort reality in order to relieve conflict, stress, and tension explains Deegan's behavior and provides a rationale for the behavior.

Another of Freud's ego defense mechanisms is regression, in which the individual returns to an earlier developmental stage, becoming childlike and dependent. Becoming childlike relieves the individual of the anxiety and stress of responding to the disability, the responsibility of changing one's identity, and the requirement to plan for a future with a disability.

These ego defenses are common and are not counterproductive if they are used for short periods of time. It was Freud who first asserted that the individual's unconscious will protect him or her from conflict and stress.

BODY IMAGE

Livneh and Cook (2005) described body image and its importance:

> The unconscious representation of one's own body is believed to be at the root of the individual's self-concept and personal identity. The body image is formed early in life but is continuously changing. It is invested with symbolic, emotional, and cognitive significance, and includes personal, social, environmental, and temporal components. (p. 190)

The term "unconscious" implies that none of us is fully aware of how we think and feel about our bodies. An individual's body image may be very different from a photograph of him or her. It is the way in which the individual "appears" to himself or herself that is important. Body image is important in another aspect: the individual's perception of how others view his or her body has an important influence on body image. Much of a person's self-esteem is based on his or her body image.

Infants begin to develop body images during adolescence, the developmental stage in which body is most important. Many visible disabilities are considered to be unattractive or the adaptive technology (such as hearing aids or insulin pumps), rather than the disability itself, make the disability visible to others.

THE IMPORTANCE OF EARLY DEVELOPMENTAL STAGES

One of the greatest strengths of Freud's theory is his concept of "sensitive periods in adjustment and development." Freud pioneered the concept that events that happen early in an individual's life can affect the individual for the remainder of his or her life. An example of the importance of sensitive periods is the attachment theory: the concept that the infant and small child who has been nurtured, loved, and cared for by a loving caregiver (typically the mother) will grow into an adult who can establish and maintain healthy relationships (Bowlby, 1958, 1969, 1973, 1980). Neuropsychiatry has expanded Freud's concept of attachment, stating that an infant's brain is physically changed (or "wired") by his or her relationship with a caregiver, most often the mother.

The infant and mother read each other's emotions by using touch, gaze, smell, rhythm, and imitation, becoming very intimate even though the infant does not speak a word. Researchers have been able to look at the attachment patterns of children at 42 months and predict with 77% accuracy who will graduate from high school (Brooks, 2011), and men who had experienced unhappy childhoods were three times more likely to be solitary at age 70. Freud and today's neuropsychiatrists are not deterministic but rather state that early experiences set pathways, which can be changed or reinforced by later experiences.

Attachment Theory and Infants with Disabilities

Although newborn infants with severe and multiple disabilities or infants who are technology dependent are no longer automatically institutionalized, these infants must often be hospitalized for long periods of time. Developing an attachment to an adult caregiver is difficult when the caregivers change with each 8-hour shift. Even when the infant is cared for at home, the parents may be sleep deprived, depressed, and withdrawn. Parents of a child born with a disability may be struggling with their own adjustment and feelings of loss. They have lost the dream of a healthy baby. Grandparents may be fearful of providing baby care because they believe they lack the technological skills needed to care for the baby.

The widely accepted but patently false theory of causation of autism may have been fostered by the influence of attachment theory. Bettelheim (1967) hypothesized that autism was caused by "refrigerator mothers." Fathers were not blamed quite so directly; instead, Bettelheim termed them "absent fathers." Therefore, in the absence of any objective evidence, a theory was advanced. Refrigerator mothers were aloof and unloving. In the brains of individuals with autism spectrum disorders, neuroimaging has shown structural differences. Therefore, mothers encountered two challenges: first, finding services and treatment for their children with autism and, second, enduring the implied blame of professionals.

Attachment Theory and Attitude Toward PWDs

Attachment theory postulates that adults who have enjoyed a close, warm, loving relationship with their primary caregiver, typically the mother, experience ego-strength, self-esteem, a sense of security, and self-awareness (Takahashi, 2005). Thus, infancy and early childhood can be considered a critical period, because the quality of attachment produces a lifelong orientation toward oneself and toward others. Further, attachment orientation is composed of one's own memories, expectations, and attitudes toward relating to others in a warm and intimate way. "Attachment orientation is conceived as a global and stable orientation..." (Vilchinsky, Findler, & Werner, 2010). Those with an attachment orientation have been given a strong secure base (the care and love of the mother) that, in turn, allows these individuals to explore the world and engage actively with others of all types of groups. Those with strong attachment orientations also have a positive self-image and project these positive views onto others. They sense that the world is a safe place; they feel that they can rely on others. Finally, emotional regulation is a characteristic of those with a strong attachment orientation. This is especially important in managing fear and stress.

Those without an attachment orientation tend to avoid relationships and have high levels of self-reliance. Indeed, the expectation of relationships may initiate anxiety (Bowlby, 1969). Vilchinsky et al. (2010) described:

> the negative self-models of anxiously attached persons should lead to appraisals of helplessness, uncontrollability, and an inability to cope during stress may, in fact, lead to suppression of attachment needs.... This passive coping with stressors should lead to heightened distress and negative thoughts about the person.... Negative models of others (as reflected in an avoidance of closeness) may lead to discomfort and a desire to distance oneself from the situation so as to minimize the distress associated with the encounter (Mukulincer & Florian, 1998). Both processes may result in overall negative attitudes.... (p. 299)

Therefore, attachment theory can assist us in understanding the reaction of people without disabilities (PWODs) to PWDs. Could attachment theory provide insights into the irrational reactions of fear, hostility, and anxiety toward PWDs? Do PWDs provoke stress and avoidance in PWODs? Information on the attitudes that lead to either acceptance or rejection of PWDs could be gained through empirically validating attachment theory. In addition, interventions and training protocols could be developed to help others accept PWDs.

Terms to Learn

Anal stage	Idealistic principle	Phallic stage
Defense mechanisms	Instincts	Pleasure principle
Denial	Latency stage	Psychosexual theory
Domains of consciousness	Old Aunt Pamela	Reality principle
Fixation	Loves Gorillas	
Genital stage	Oral stage	

Videos to View

- View the 52-minute video *The Interpretation of Dreams* by Discovery University Production. The producers describe this video: "Few figures have had so decisive an influence on model cultural history as Sigmund Freud, psychology's grand theorist—yet few figures have also inspired such sustained controversy and intense debate. In this program, Freud historian Peter Swales; Freudian psychoanalyst Barbara Jones; Peter Kramer, author of *Listening to Prozac*; and others analyze *The Interpretation of Dreams,* the concepts it contains, and the growing movement to reject them. Biographic details, dramatizations of Freud at work, and archival footage and photos add a personal dimension."
- View the 53-minute video *Refrigerator Mothers* produced by Fanlight Productions. The producers describe this video: "From the 1950s through the 1970s, mental health and medical professionals claimed that autism was caused by mothers who were cold, rejecting, unable to 'bond properly.' They were labeled 'refrigerator

mothers.' This film profiles seven courageous women who refused to be crushed by the burden of blame. Today, they have strong, supportive relationships with their now adult sons and daughters and, in a variety of ways, have helped them to find their place in the world." Do you think that vestiges of Freudian theories contributed to blaming mothers for their children's autism?

Learning Activities

(Note: These may also be used as class presentations.)
- Read the following articles and then consider the ways in which Freud's pessimistic, pathological theoretical orientations relate to the biomedical model of disability. Freud thought that "biology is destiny," and the biomedical model considers only the medical needs of PWDs. Do you see a relationship?
  - Smart, J. F., & Smart, D. W. (2006). Models of disability: Implications for the counseling profession. *Journal of Counseling and Development, 84,* 29–40.
  - Smart, J. F. (2009e). The power of models of disability. *Journal of Rehabilitation, 75,* 3–11.
  - Smart, J. F. (2006). Challenging the biomedical model of disability. *Advances in Medical Psychotherapy and Psychodiagnosis, American Board of Medical Psychotherapists, 12,* 41–44.
  - Smart, J. F. (2004). Models of disability: The juxtaposition of biology and social construction. In T. F. Riggar & D. R. Maki (Eds.), *Handbook of rehabilitation counseling* (pp. 25–49). Springer Series on Rehabilitation. New York: Springer.
- Read P. Gay (1988), *Freud: A Life for Our Time,* New York: Norton. Describe the effects of the following upon Freud's theory:
  - The city of Vienna in the late 1890s
  - Freud's birth family
  - Freud's Jewish identification or lack of Jewish identification
- Read J. Bowlby (1958), The nature of the child's tie to his mother, *International Journal of Psycho-Analysis,* 350–373. Then read D. M. Buss (1999), *Evolutionary Psychology: The New Science of the Mind,* Allyn & Bacon. Bowlby posited that the infant's attachment to his or her mother had lifelong effects, while Buss stated that infants with disabilities were more often abandoned (institutionalized or put up for adoption). Consider both of these viewpoints and their effects of infants with disabilities.
- Discuss various television programs and films in which Freud's theory is used. Include your reactions.

Writing Exercises

- Write a five-page paper on the way in which Freud changed how consciousness is viewed. During Freud's time period, why was this viewpoint a radical departure from the long-held view of the mind?

- Write a five-page paper titled "Biology Is Destiny," using Freud's principles to make your argument.
- Consider ways in which you (or others) reconcile the pleasure principle with the reality principle. Write six paragraphs describing this struggle.
- Write a humorous stand-up comedy routine of five pages on the topic "Why Is It Always the Mother's Fault?" Incorporate Freud's theory into your comedy.
- Write a 10-page paper listing and describing various instances in your life that seem to support the idea that much of human experience is supported by unconscious motivation.
- Assume that you have acquired a disability. Which of Freud's defense mechanisms do you think you would use? Write a two-page paper describing the choices and detailing the reasons for choosing these particular defense mechanisms.

Web Sites

http://www.freudfile.org/
http://psychology.about.com/od/sigmundfreud/p/sigmund_freud.htm
http://www.pbs.org/wgbh/aso/databank/entries/bhfreu.html
http://learningdisabilities.about.com/od/pr/g/psychoanalysis.htm
http://www.notablebiographies.com/Fi-Gi/Freud-Sigmund.html
http://webspace.ship.edu/cgboer/freud.html

Erikson's Psychosocial Theory of Human Development

4

Erik Erikson considered himself to be a Freudian psychoanalyst or a neo-Freudian, although many scholars believe that Erikson's theory deviates so radically from Freud that Erikson cannot be considered in "the Freudian tradition" (Hall, Lindzey, & Campbell, 1998, p. 191). Like Freud, Erikson conceptualized human development as progressing in stages that closely parallel biological maturation. However, Erikson differed from Freud in two important respects: (1) Erikson deemphasized biological sexual conflicts in favor of psychosocial conflicts, and (2) Erikson provided a life span perspective from birth to death, while Freud was clear in his belief that development was complete when sexual maturation (or late adolescence) was achieved. Both Freudian and Eriksonian concepts have become widely known and part of the popular culture; however, Freud and his theory are very controversial, but Erikson is widely accepted. For example, concepts such as "identity crisis" and "identity confusion" were first proposed by Erikson. Hall, Lindzey, and Campbell (1998) summarized, "If Erikson had to be pinned down by a name, he would probably prefer to be called a post-Freudian" (p. 191). Another author stated, "Many have seen Erikson's work as a continuation of what Freud might have done had he lived another 50 years" (Feist, 1990, p. 109).

THE LIFE OF ERIKSON

Erik Erikson was born in Frankfurt, Germany to a Danish mother in 1902. His mother's family was Jewish; Erikson never knew his biological father, although in his late 40s Erikson tried to discover his father's identity but failed. Erikson's mother married his German pediatrician, Dr. Homburger, and Erikson was raised and adopted by Homburger. Erik was 3 years old when his mother married Homburger, and the two of them moved into Homburger's home. Erikson took his stepfather's surname of Homburger, but when he became an American citizen in 1939, Erik changed his name from Erik Homburger to Erik H. Erikson, which literally means "Erik, son of Erik."

Erikson's mother told two stories that explained Erik's paternity (Friedman, 1999). On the birth certificate his mother listed her estranged husband as Erik's biological father, but this was not possible since she had not seen her husband for several years (Capps, 2008). Then she told young Erik that Dr. Homburger was his biological father, and in Erikson's words, he "more or less forgot the period before the age of three, when [his] mother and [he] had lived alone." Perhaps because young Erik wanted to believe his mother, he did. However, neither story was true. Most unsettling to the young boy was his Scandinavian appearance even though his mother, his mother's former husband, and his stepfather were Jewish. According to Erikson's autobiographical essay, he was "blond, and blue-eyed and grew flagrantly tall" (Erikson, 1970).

Allen (2000) summarized both the origin of Erikson's surname and the conflicts surrounding his adult choice of a surname.

> A look at Erikson's childhood makes it easy to see where his interest in "identity crises" originated. He was a child with an identity dilemma. As most boys are, he was pressured to pin his identity to his biological father, but it is almost impossible to tack anything onto a virtual void. Thus, he turned to his adopted father, who loved him and treated him well (Hall, 1983). As a reflection for his esteem for his adopted father, Erikson initially chose "Homburger" as his surname. Even early in his career…he went by Erik Homburger. Yet his ambivalence showed when later he relegated Homburger to a middle initial. This display of confusion about his stepfather was only a rare outward sign of the identity crisis that occurred to him repeatedly. An ideal Aryan in appearance—he was tall and blonde—Erikson faced taunts served up by the children at his father's synagogue. At the same time he was shunned by his German schoolmates because of his stepfather's religion…. Later in his life, Erikson aptly expressed how uncertainty about his identity affected him during his youth, "I was," he recalled, "morbidly sensitive." (Erickson, 1970, p. 87)

Erikson was a professor at the University of California and Harvard, although he never earned a college degree. Immediately after high school graduation in Germany, Erikson spent a year touring Europe in an attempt to determine his life's direction. He moved to Vienna, took up painting, and was asked to teach art at a private children's school. Most serendipitously, the parents of his students were undergoing psychoanalysis with Freud, and through this connection Erikson became a member of the Vienna Psychoanalytic Society. Originally a portrait painter of children, Erikson was persuaded to become a child psychoanalyst. Erikson's lack of a medical degree was very unusual for a member of the Psychoanalytic Society, but Erikson's membership in the society and mentoring from the great Sigmund Freud allowed him to practice child psychoanalysis without degrees. When the Nazis came to power, Erikson and his American wife, Joan Serson, moved to Denmark and attempted to establish citizenship there. When this failed, they immigrated to the United States.

Rare among the great theorists of human development, Erikson worked with varying cultural groups (R. Coles, 1970). In his early career Erickson worked at the Sioux Indian Reservation and with the Yurok, a Northern California Native tribe, comparing the childhood training practices of Native Americans of the Plains (Sioux) with those of Native American coastal fishing societies (Yurok). Erikson also wrote biographies of famous individuals such as Gandhi and the Protestant reformer Martin Luther, individuals whom Erikson thought to be highly developed. Throughout his career, Erikson was a prolific writer, producing seminal works such as *Childhood and Society* (1950), *Insight and Responsibility* (1964), *Identity: Youth and Crisis* (1968), all of which made him famous. Erikson died on May 12, 1994 in California.

> **Components of Erikson's Theory**
> - Epigenetic stages
> - Psychosocial
> - Polar opposites

ERIKSON'S EIGHT PSYCHOLOGICAL STAGES

Erikson believed that humans progress through eight, sequential, epigenetic stages. At each stage, there are various tasks of life to be completed; therefore, humans possess the potential to progress and become more robust and resilient until their death. In spite of the biological declines of old age, personalities continue to develop. Indeed, Erikson did not think that individuals "achieved maturity" but rather approximated maturity to varying degrees. Although Freud believed that development stopped (or was greatly reduced) after adolescence, Erikson thought that development was dynamic and that it continued throughout the life span. These tasks are conceptualized as "crises" that provide the motivational power for the individual to progress to the next stage. Although sequential and epigenetic, these stages are not tied to a strictly chronological timetable, nor do they have a rigidly prescribed duration. Erikson recognized that each of the eight stages has its roots in previous stages and its consequences in subsequent stages. Epigenetic growth implies that the individual becomes an improved version of himself or herself; however, Erikson also thought that new accomplishments and the completion of tasks have the capacity to make individuals of more benefit to themselves and to others.

Rather than concentrating on the resolution of psychosexual conflicts, Erikson proposed that individuals worked to resolve conflicts with the society around them. Hence, Erikson's theory of development is labeled psychosocial. Erikson conceived humans as socialized into a culture at a particular historical time. Although Freud stated that biology (and sexuality) is destiny, Erikson stated that destiny was a combination of biology, society, culture, and a historical time period. Inner readiness reacts to outer opportunity. When the individual is blocked from meeting goals, he or she simply renews efforts and does not give up. The conflict of the individual with society is termed a "crisis," meaning a turning point or a decision, which is a time of heightened vulnerability but also of great potential. Rather than viewing a crisis as something to be avoided or minimized, Erikson believed that humans thrived and grew by resolving crises. Indeed, he thought that individuals actively and joyfully seek out crises.

Through the successful resolution of each stage, the individual's world becomes larger. This broadening world has been described as "a radiating network of significant relationships" (Newman & Newman, 2009, p. 21). The infant interacts with a few caregivers and family members; the school child's social circle expands to include friends, classmates, and teachers; the adolescent's horizons expand; and networks of significant relationships continue to grow throughout adulthood. Erikson's theory of psychosocial stages takes into consideration cognitive and physical maturation but emphasizes social and cultural expectations placed upon individuals.

In each of Erikson's stages, individuals are posed between qualities that are polar opposites, or they are caught in dilemmas. One quality is very idealistic and optimistic and communicates positive growth, while the other quality is pessimistic, which communicates losses. Some authors have labeled the positive quality "syntonic" and the negative quality "dystonic" (Feist, 1990). Understandably, it is important to move (or migrate) in the direction of positive qualities, but a small degree of the negative quality is also necessary for survival. For example, in infancy the conflicting qualities of trust and mistrust need to be learned and developed. Obviously, it is more important to develop trust and to feel that the world is a safe and trustworthy place. Nonetheless, a little realistic mistrust is necessary throughout the life span in order to avoid being gullible. Erikson, in his later writings, acknowledged that the ratio between the positive and negative poles was not 100% to 0%. Erikson recognized that a small part of the negative characteristic is essential. Generally, empirical research and the statistical tools of factor analysis have supported Erikson's ideas of conflicting qualities.

Erikson's Eight Psychosocial Stages

- Infancy—Trust versus mistrust
- Toddlerhood—Autonomy versus shame and doubt
- Early school age—Initiative versus guilt
- Middle childhood—Industry versus inferiority
- Adolescence—Identity versus identity confusion
- Early adulthood—Intimacy versus isolation
- Late adulthood—Generativity versus stagnation
- Late adulthood—Integrity versus despair

Infancy — Trust Versus Mistrust

Infancy is the first psychosocial stages and lasts from birth to 2 years of age. Infants begin to develop sensory, perceptual, and motor functions. However, the most significant task involves emotional development. A baby's main and most important relationship is with the caregiver, typically the mother. In this relationship, the infant learns trust or mistrust. If the infant can rely on the mother to be available, sensitive, and willing to satisfy all of his or her needs, then the infant develops trust, and the entire world seems to be safe and nurturing. In addition to providing nutrition, warmth, and comfort, a trustworthy mother also smiles at her baby, speaks in a sweet voice, and uses rhythmic motions. However, the infant develops mistrust and a helpless rage against the world if he or she is neglected or abandoned, because the world seems an uncertain and frightening place. Erikson believed that infants who have not developed basic trust in their first 2 years of life develop into adults who are insecure and mistrustful. Basic trust leads to other positive emotions and (eventually) personality strengths, such as faith, hope, and feelings of safety and security. Trust allows a person to form and maintain social relationships, and our willingness to take social risks and reach out to other people is certainly related to our levels of trust. Long-term relationships are also related to levels of trust, because maintenance of relationships requires the expectation of future mutual trust despite difficulties. Adults who have developed trust during infancy typically are able to consider the needs of others. Some mistrust is needed, because individuals without a small measure of mistrust become gullible and easily taken advantage of, and all babies experience times when their mothers (or other caregivers) do not respond to them. Older adults who have developed a strong sense of trust and security are able to reduce the impact of life's difficulties and problems. Erikson also believed that those who develop a strong sense of trust often have strong religious beliefs and view the universe as a great source of love and goodness.

Toddlerhood — Autonomy Versus Shame and Doubt

The next stage occurs during the ages of 2 to 3 years, when children develop the basic motor abilities that give them some degree of independence. Toddlers must learn to control their muscles in order to crawl, walk, and become toilet trained. Like Freud, Erikson considered toilet training an important part of the toddler's development. Learning to control one's body is a major task of this stage. Erikson conceptualized the two poles of crisis and motivation of this stage as autonomy versus shame and doubt. The toddler wants to become independent, yet at the same time he or she wants the love and security of others. This dilemma becomes one of separateness competing with the need for protection, love, and security. After infants have developed a sense of trust, hope, and security, they are then required to become self-willed to become worthy to receive the trust of others. Erikson termed this the "dilemma of freedom." Self-esteem for toddlers is directly related to their ability to do things for themselves and to the degree of self-control and will power they develop. Both initiative and restraint are necessary, so to some extent toddlers are expected to determine when each is appropriate. Naturally, toddlers do not want to be controlled by others, they develop shame, doubt, and anger when parents and others restrain them. Although autonomy is considered to be a positive quality toddlers should learn and develop, autonomy must also be contained; therefore, societies have principles of justice and law.

Self-regulation is the ability to control impulses, direct actions toward a goal, and inhibit undesirable emotions. Considered a marker of maturity by Erikson, self-control begins to develop in toddlerhood. Infants have very rudimentary methods of self-regulation such as rocking and sucking, but toddlers learn that their behavior is unacceptable at times, and they become willing to change their behavior. Obviously, self-regulation is part of social competence, and those who lack it are often isolated and lonely.

Erikson considered toddlerhood as a time of fantasy play and thought that fantasy play facilitates the toddler's social, intellectual, and emotional development. Because fantasy play is not required to represent reality—or even the viewpoints of others—toddlers can work out angry feelings by punching a baby doll (punching their baby sibling would not be allowed) and thus reduce their anger, tension, and frustration. Fantasy play allows the toddler to think about problems, act out these problems, and devise suitable solutions. The child capitalizes on the flexibility of fantasy play in order to structure his or her play in ways that are personally meaningful. Sometimes it is important for the toddler to assume new roles while engaging in play, such as mother, father, cowboy, or cowgirl. Fantasy play helps the child to understand his or her emotions, to learn new ways to express these feelings, and to develop empathy and understanding of the feelings of others.

Early School Age — Initiative Versus Guilt

The third stage encompasses the third and fourth years of life, in which the conflicts to be resolved are initiative versus guilt. In addition to maturing physically and increasing coordination and control over their bodies, toddlers are also increasing their cognitive skills. In addition, the world of toddlers is larger and broader than that of infants. There are more friends (perhaps preschool teachers), and the toddler interacts with a larger number of people and individuals of more varied groups.

Adults who have successfully resolved this stage demonstrate a joyful spontaneity while also exhibiting a sense of responsibility. Initiative involves carrying out self-defined goals. Initiative, therefore, is composed of two components: defining one's goals and completing these goals. Guilt results when the child is not able to meet his or her goals. Erikson believed that toddlers begin to develop moral reasoning because they identify with their parents and the parents' ethical viewpoints. Children in this stage define and strive toward goals that are within their moral structures; children begin to develop a conscience. In a book titled *Insight and Responsibility* (1964), Erickson defined the crisis as the "virtue of purpose," which is "the courage to envisage and pursue valued goals, uninhibited by the defeat of infantile fantasies, by guilt, and by the foiling fear of punishment" (p. 122). Toddlers who grow up to become guilty adults become repressed, inhibited, and hesitant to take on new challenges. An adult who has not resolved this crisis may become self-righteously intolerant of others or—in extreme cases—experience psychosomatic illnesses. On the other hand, adults who have an overdeveloped sense of initiative may feel that they must constantly achieve in order to maintain self-esteem.

Play is an important part of this stage, as is the awareness of the differences between the sexes. In this stage children develop their own gender identification. Children in this stage typically engage in sex-role playing. Generally speaking, girls role play nurturing women, and boys fantasize about being competitive, athletic males.

Middle Childhood — Industry Versus Inferiority

In the fourth stage, the child begins school, and the crisis to be resolved is industry versus inferiority. The virtue to be acquired is competence. The age range for this stage is 6 to 12 years of age. School requires serious effort; children must learn and master many tasks and have many peers with whom to compare themselves and their efforts. Many school tasks and athletic endeavors also require the cooperation of others, so children need to learn to work with others. Therefore, this stage requires both competitive and cooperative competence.

When children develop industry, they feel competent, adequate, and skilled. Inferiority results if children feel inadequate, are unable to succeed at school, and view themselves as failures. School is work for children. They must learn a wide range of tasks, such as reading, the physical requirements of writing, arithmetic, the ability to complete homework assignments, and often athletic skills. These are all practical tasks. Children in this stage must also learn the way in which to work; that is, how to use self-control, planning, self-monitoring, and appraisal of results. Completion of schoolwork helps children to understand the value of successful work performance. In short, children in middle childhood are learning adults' rules of work. Their task is to develop industry rather than inferiority; however, if children become overly concerned with work and see it as their only basis for identity, they can become workaholics.

School introduces children to society, and, certainly, schools teach children the skills of their culture. The school day requires that children spend time away from their family homes and their parents. Nonetheless, most children report that their most significant relationships are with their parents, especially their mothers, and after parents, the most important relationships are with their grandparents. Successful completion of this stage results in children who are capable of cooperative participation in society.

Adolescence — Identity Versus Identity Confusion

Adolescence (the fifth stage) is the time when individuals begin to develop their lifelong identities. Teenagers deal with the question, "Who am I?" Erikson believed that identity is the integration of all previous identifications and self-images, including negative ones. Thus, identity development is epigenetic (or continuous) because it synthesizes the identities of previous stages, but identity development is also a result of adding new aspects, that especially determine or predict one's future identity. Of course, identity formation is lifelong; however, it is in adolescence that individuals question and then either accept or reject their parents' values.

An individual's identity formation is also influenced by the historical times in which he or she experiences adolescence. Teenagers are often given a time-out, or psychological moratorium, from making long-term commitments. Erikson believed that adolescents vacillate between regression to childhood behaviors and attitudes in which they either are confused or enthusiastically embrace fads and cults, or, as Erikson stated, adolescents often respond to siren songs that are simplistic and promise to answer all questions and solve all problems. The other side of this vacillation is premature decision making, which commits the adolescent to ill-considered choices and courses of action. For example, Erikson believed that adolescent intimacy differs from adult intimacy because teenagers have not yet developed strong self-identities and are thus incapable of entering into adult relationships.

Adolescence is the time for developing romantic and sexual relationships. Adolescence is also the time to begin considering career choices. The virtue to be acquired in this stage is fidelity, which involves sustained loyalty, faith, and a sense of belonging to a social movement, such as ethnic group, an ideology, and or a religion. Fidelity also includes a sense of belonging with friends and loved ones. Friends and peers provide the individual with opportunities for comparison and identification, helping the adolescent in identity formation through self-evaluation. Social approval, affiliation and friendship, leadership, and power are also available in friendships. Often, sociologists and psychologists refer to these friendship groups as "reference groups." Peer groups typically do not replace the attachment to the parents and extended families. In fact, family ties help adolescents to develop their identity because it is through family that racial, ethnic, cultural, and sexual identities are developed.

Combining the virtue of fidelity with the need to determine a possible vocational identity and the beginning of romantic and intimate commitment contributes to the individual's self-identity. Successful completion of these tasks and conflicts leads to a strong sense of identity.

Erikson believed that identity confusion, along with the need to reduce or eliminate this confusion, prompts teenagers to form cliques and be intolerant of differences. Basing one's entire identity on one group and refusing to question and challenge the values of the group's ideology can lead to weak self-identity. Remembering that Erikson's life was marked by the Nazi movement helps to understand the importance he placed upon the individual's choice of the people, organizations, and ideologies with which he or she identified. Erickson considered unquestioned fidelity a "narcotic."

Physical maturation leads to concern about one's physical appearance, attractiveness, and desirability. Love is another path to identity formation because individuals see themselves reflected in their loved one. When we share our thoughts and feelings with our mate, we gain in return some clarification of our identity. Another source of identity clarification is our choice of a romantic partner, because we tend to choose individuals whom we consider to be like ourselves.

Early Adulthood—Intimacy Versus Isolation

The sixth stage of life provides the opportunity to develop the virtue of love. The other pole in this crisis is isolation and self-absorption, the failure to make close, long-term commitments to others. According to Erikson, intimacy was the ability to develop close loving relationships with others while maintaining one's own identity. In the previous stages, the formation of one's self-identity and the resulting differentiation from others were important developmental tasks.

The age of 24 is often considered the beginning of the psychosocial stage of young adulthood (Newman & Newman, 2009). However, entry into any developmental psychosocial stage is based more upon the individual's successful resolution of the tasks and crises of the previous stage than upon chronological age.

Late Adulthood—Generativity Versus Stagnation

Generativity means the ability and desire to facilitate the development of the younger generation, most often one's own children. The virtue of this period is care, meaning that the individual "has an ever-widening commitment to take care of the persons, the products, and the ideas one has learned to care for" (Erikson, 1975, p. 67). Stagnation means inactivity and a lack of commitment to improving life for future generations, which frequently leads to narcissism, self-preoccupation, or periods of depression. Individuals in late adulthood have succeeded in their careers and established friendships and intimate relationships, so they are now able to focus on trying to make a difference in the lives of others. Often, individuals describe this need for generativity as "wanting to make a difference in the world."

In Erikson's theory, late adulthood spans a long period of time, from ages 34 to 60. Individuals in this psychosocial stage experience raising teenage children, relating to adult children as friends, becoming grandparents, enjoying career success, and taking care of aging parents. As individuals move from the role of parent to that of grandparent, they often experience generativity needs because the next generation of a family represents continuity.

Empirical research has provided support for Erikson's concept of generativity, suggesting that individuals who scored high on measures of generativity reported great happiness and life satisfaction (McAdams, de St. Aubin, & Logan, 1993). Erikson's belief that generativity was associated with late adulthood was also supported in the same study, for those in the middle adult group scored highest on generativity. Erikson expanded this concept to include "grand generativity," meaning that individuals engage in leadership and creative roles that create and promote growth for more than those in their immediate family or circle of friends and associates. Grand generativity focuses on humankind.

Late Adulthood — Integrity Versus Despair

At this stage individuals are required to confront both the realities of the lives they have lived and the certainty of death. According to Erikson, late adulthood begins at age 60; if the individual lives into his or her 90s or even 100s, late adulthood may continue for two or three additional decades. Individuals in this stage contemplate the lives they have lived; if they are satisfied with their accomplishments, they develop a sense of integrity. However, if for any reason older individuals feel that their lives have been disappointing and deficient, they often feel despair. Thus the conflict to be resolved is integrity versus despair. Integrity means feeling the satisfaction that the goals, aspirations, and dreams that they have had in their earlier life have been fulfilled. In Erikson's theory, the use of the word integrity refers to the ability to integrate past history with one's hopes and dreams. Integrity also means that the individual has lived the life that he or she wanted; therefore, both the individual's goals and satisfactions have been self-defined. At this stage of life, it is not possible to relive life, so it is important to view one's past life as coherent and whole. Erikson (1950) described integrity:

> Only he who in some way has taken care of things and people and has adapted himself to the triumphs and disappointments adherent to being, by necessity, the originator of others and the generator of things and ideas—only he may gradually grow the fruit of these seven stages. I know of no better word for it than ego integrity. (p. 231)

Because they have lived many years and are now disengaged from many of the demands of the life, older individuals try to "make meaning" of the lives they have lived. Old age is the culmination of all the previous life stages. Until this stage most adults have been preoccupied with work duties and family obligations. During this stage they engage in self-evaluation and review their past life. When they have passed through all of the developmental stages of life and successfully completed the tasks and developed core strengths, older individuals feel a sense of satisfaction and meaning, which Erikson described as "the dignity of one's life" (1950, p. 232). Of course, everyone develops some core pathologies and has regrets over missed opportunities or the failure to achieve some goals. Nonetheless, to achieve integrity individuals must balance these failures, regrets, and personality weaknesses with their successes and present circumstances. A sense of integrity in Erikson's theory may be compared to a sense of serenity and fulfillment in which individuals realize that although life has not been perfect, it has been positive and satisfying. The individual resolves the feelings of failure and regrets. Bitterness and disappointment over the past result in despair, which is often a feeling that one did not have the life he or she wanted or expected. At this age "do-overs" are no longer possible, meaning that the individual cannot go back and do things differently.

Older individuals often begin to define themselves more broadly, seeing themselves as more than their work and family roles. The core virtue to be attained is wisdom. Successful resolution of the previous seven stages allows older individuals to integrate their lives (or their memories of their lives) into the broader society.

Older individuals often desire to leave a legacy through their children, grandchildren, or their body of work, thus creating a sense of continuity with future generations. Feeling that their lives have been meaningful and rich, they wish to pass on what they have learned and discovered. Older adults see themselves as having mature judgment and as being repositories of knowledge and experience. They view themselves as a link between the generations. Although it may appear that older adults are engaged in self-reflection and self-evaluation, they also want to connect to the larger society through a legacy of some type.

Somewhat in contrast to this is the idea of mutual disengagement, in which the older individuals reduce their activities and involvements with others and "society" begins to lower its expectations of and demands on older adults. This has been termed "mutual withdrawal" (Papalia & Olds, 1992).

Because one's goals and aspiration are self-defined and self-evaluated, life satisfaction is subjective and difficult to measure.

Evaluating Erikson's Theory

- Erikson's eight stages have not kept pace with longer life spans
- Questions about polar opposites

There is an intuitive logic to Erikson's theory of development, and Erikson's theory has undoubtedly stimulated a large number of research studies. Unlike Freud or B. F. Skinner, Erikson was never considered controversial, and his view of humankind is essentially optimistic because his theory proposes that humans have a life-long potential to grow and develop. Although there are few criticisms of Erikson's theory, it is considered to be relatively free from widespread criticism when compared to the other theories. All theories of development suggest that changes are universal and inevitable, but the trajectory of Erikson's theory is upward. Erikson also believed that positive growth is possible in any stage of life, including old age and that, regardless of the nature of past resolutions, individuals can resolve the crises of their present stage.

However, there are no therapeutic techniques associated with Erikson's theory, although Erikson did develop standardized play situations in which children could reveal their concerns (conflicts). Erikson did not engage in empirical research, but rather replied on observation. However, other researchers have applied empirical methodology to Erikson's theory and have found support for many of Erikson's principles, and his theory is still considered to be a rich source of hypotheses. Erikson himself acknowledged that observational methods are subjective and impressionistic.

The greatest criticism of Erikson's theory by far concerns the time frame of each developmental stage and the fact that there are only eight stages. For Erikson, development follows a definite age-linked sequence, but the longevity revolution and social redefinition of age roles have made Erikson's demarcation of stages somewhat obsolete. Although the sequence and the epigenetic nature of Erikson's stages are still valid, the age ranges are becoming increasingly outmoded. Some scholars (Newman & Newman, 2009) have added two additional stages, later adolescence (spanning the ages of 18 to 24) and very old age (ranging from the age of 75 until death). More stages may be necessary, and the age ranges may require realignment as demographic, societal, and medical advances continue. Because of societal and cultural changes, Arnett (1992, 1998, 2000, 2004) added a new stage to the life span that he termed "emerging adulthood."

Some have also questioned the way in which Erikson chose the bipolar labels that describe the conflicts of each stage (Hoover, 2004). For example, the psychosocial crises in infancy are identified by the bipolar labels trust versus mistrust. The questions asked include "would not some other terms be more appropriate?" and "does not the development of these strengths occur throughout the individual's life, rather than being permanently resolved at a single stage? Don't individuals deal with these bipolar crises throughout life?" However, Erikson believed that the epigenetic base of his theory rests on the successful resolution of each of these crises as the individual progresses throughout the stages and that these conflicts persisted only to a small degree throughout the remainder of the individual's life. Finally, some criticized the very bipolar, either-or orientation of Erikson's developmental tasks, stating it is important to develop some degree of the negative pole. For example, some small degree of mistrust is necessary in order to protect oneself from being taken advantage of.

The final criticism of Erikson's theory has also been directed at many of the other developmental theories. Many have found a gender bias in Erikson's theory, meaning that the theory is more useful for men than for women. The positive labels of "autonomy," "initiative," and "industry" describe men better than women, especially White men of European origin (Ochse & Plug, 1986). Erikson was not as gender biased as Freud, who said that "anatomy is destiny." Instead, Erikson stated that "anatomy, history, and personality are our combined destiny." He also made a comparison between the liberating aspects of science and technology on socially constructed gender roles when he stated that "as birth control goes to the core of womanhood, the implications of arms control go to the core of the male identity, as it has emerged from evolution and history" (Erikson, 1975, p. 245). Women can choose roles other than motherhood, and men would not be required to engage in war.

This lack of applicability to other cultures is understandable because Erikson conceived of development as a response to social demands, and social demands of one culture may not apply to another culture. Even the criticism of obsolete age ranges and the insufficient number of stages due to greater longevity is understandable, because Erikson considered his theory to be historical. Erikson stated that his theory was a historical theory, related to one particular time. Hall et al. (1998) explained: "It is the placing of the ego in a cultural and historical context—a space–time frame—that is one of Erikson's most creative contributions..." (p. 206).

APPLICATION TO INDIVIDUALS WITH DISABILITIES

Paradoxically, Erikson's psychosocial stages are very difficult to apply to people with disabilities (PWDs) on the one hand, and on the other they do have a great deal of applicability for PWDs. None of the grand theorists discussed in this book considered PWDs and their development. Yet most PWDs negotiate and complete Erikson's eight stages; in fact, many more PWDs are surviving longer, especially those with congenital disabilities, so that more PWDs survive to middle age and old age.

Further, PWDs must complete these developmental stages while simultaneously managing a disability, avoiding secondary complications, treating symptoms, and maintaining the highest quality of life possible. Therefore, in many ways Erikson's psychosocial stages can be appropriately used with PWDs. This does not mean that *all* PWDs reach *all* of the stages; some PWDs may be required to alter these stages, to delay them, or relinquish some of the tasks of the developmental stages.

However, there is a difficulty. Erikson's theory is described as "psychosocial," meaning that the individual (the psyche) responds to the demands of his or her society and culture. For centuries, it was thought that PWDs could not participate in society; therefore, there were no socially sanctioned roles or identities for PWDs. The concept of normality was confused with the concept of humanity. Normality was defined as the absence of deviance, pathology, illness, or disability. Of course, the definition of normality changes with time, but assumptions, including wrong ones, can persist for centuries. It is becoming more common to challenge and question the existence or the value of enshrined norms. A bumper sticker on a car reads, "Normal at our house is a setting on the clothes dryer."

Developmental theorists were primarily concerned with the regularities and universals of life. Those theorists who regarded biology as destiny perhaps thought that PWDs could not be considered biologically normal, and theorists who looked at social demands perhaps thought that PWDs either could not or would not want to participate in society. In addition, the experience of disability and the people who experience disabilities were the responsibility of the medical professions. Medical practitioners tended to focus solely on the diagnosis and functional limitations of the disability and to ignore all other attributes of the individual, such as roles, relationships, goals, and needs. The developmental stage of the individual was also ignored. This attitude also is changing.

There is a revolution in the way in which society view PWDs today because of the greater number of PWDs, their integration into all social settings, and the Americans with Disabilities Act. PWDs are beginning to be viewed as ordinary people or, more accurately, normal people who have the same needs, aspirations, and goals as people without disabilities (PWODs).

Erikson and the other developmental theorists considered increased competence, autonomy, and freedom to be the end goals of development. In contrast to other theorists, Erikson asserted that increased adaptive functioning was possible in old age, because he defined adaptive functioning to include moral and social awareness rather than just biological functioning. However, many PWDs do not appear to experience a great deal of adaptive functioning, autonomy, and freedom. Some PWODs look at

PWDs and think, "I'd rather die than not be able to...." However, PWDs redefine freedom and autonomy and consider themselves to be both autonomous and free. Here are two examples. The first is an Academy Award winner for Best Documentary, Mark O'Brien. Mark is a poet and journalist who is a polio survivor.

> It is tempting to pity a man in an iron lung. But pity has become a lethal weapon. On January 8, 1997, the Supreme Court heard arguments in favor of killing people like me—out of pity—to end our suffering. An iron lung has been my second skin since the 1955 polio epidemic. For 40 years, people have said, "That poor thing—how he must suffer!"..."Don't waste your pity on me. I want to live." (O'Brien, 1997, p. 3)

An iron lung is a breathing machine in which the person lies. Polio often paralyzed individuals, especially if they were adults when they contracted the disease. Some individuals, like O'Brien, were paralyzed from the neck down and therefore could not breath on their own.

Some PWDs require a personal care attendant to bathe them, feed them, and attend to all their physical needs. Therefore these individuals might appear to have little freedom or autonomy. Here is how one woman described her autonomy.

> My attendant is an extension of my body. It takes a very emotionally strong as well as spiritually strong person to understand that and not resent it. If I don't direct that person, then I'm dependent on that person. Then I'm not autonomous and ultimately it's harder on the attendant. (Panzarino, cf. Rousso, 1993, p. 111)

Another explanation for the absence of PWDs in developmental theories concerns the unpredictability of most disabilities. All these theories are based on the concept of predictable phases of life that are experienced by most people. This predictability allows individuals to make plans and establish goals. When life tasks are universal (that is, almost everyone encounters these tasks), it is possible to have multiple role models and mentors. Disability seems unpredictable and random in most of the developmental stages, with the exception of old age.

Erikson also considered "ego identity" as the culminating stage of life. Erikson's definition of ego identity is "the acceptance of one's own life cycle as something that had to be and that, by necessity, permitted no substitutions" (Erikson, 1950, p. 268). Erikson might include disability as a life experience that permits no substitutions, from which the individual can develop great ego strength. Instead of the "problem" of PWDs, society will think of the "promise of PWDs."

Terms to Learn

Autonomy versus shame
  and doubt
Developmental task
Dilemma of freedom
Generativity versus
  stagnation

Identity crisis
Identity versus identity
  confusion
Industry versus inferiority
Initiative versus guilt
Integrity versus despair

Intimacy versus isolation
Normative crises
Psychosocial crises
Psychosocial theory
Trust versus mistrust

Learning Activities

(Note: These may also be used as class presentations.)

- In class, discuss the ways in which the negative characteristics of the bipolar labels of the developmental stages may have some positive aspects. For example, in trust versus mistrust being somewhat mistrustful is a positive adaptive characteristic because an individual could otherwise be the victim of scam artists. In other words, most people lock their homes and cars (which is somewhat mistrustful of others).
- Discuss the differences between "psychosexual" stages and "psychosocial" stages.
- In class, discuss the ways in which Erikson's theory can be viewed as a product of a historical and cultural period (20th-century America) and the ways in which his theories can be applied universally across various time periods and cultures.
- Which of Erikson's concepts would help you most in understanding the process of adjusting to a disability?

Writing Exercises

- Write a 10-page autobiography that describes your life in terms of Erikson's eight psychosocial crises.
- Write a five-page paper explaining this statement: "Many have seen Erikson's work as a continuation of what Freud might have done had he lived another 50 years" (Feist, 1990, p. 191). Include your ideas on why Erikson's psychosocial theory is considered optimistic, while Freud's psychosexual theory is considered pessimistic.
- Research the life and biography of Erikson, with emphasis upon the way in which his own life influenced the development of his theory of human development. Write a 10-page paper titled: "The Relationship Between Erikson's Life and His Theory of Human Growth and Development."

Web Sites

http://www.learningplaceonline.com/stages/organize/Erikson.htm
http://psychology.about.com/od/profilesofmajorthinkers/p/bio_erikson.htm
http://www.simplypsychology.org/Erik-Erikson.html
http://www.learning-theories.com/eriksons-stages-of-development.html
http://allpsych.com/psychology101/social_development.html

Cognitive Theories of Development: Piaget, Vygotsky, and Bronfenbrenner

5

This chapter will focus on three cognitive theorists: Jean Piaget (1952, 1954, 1962, 1965), Lev Vygotsky (1962, 1978, 1987), and Urie Bronfenbrenner (1974, 1977, 1986, 2005). Piaget's theory is based on biological maturation, Vygotsky's on environmental factors, and Bronfenbrenner's on a systems theory. Cognitive theories explain the way in which infants, children, and adolescents change and progress in all their cognitive functioning, including reasoning, thinking, memorizing, and problem-solving. Cognition also includes organizing, synthesizing, systematizing, and interpreting information and transforming information into logical systems. Piaget has had more influence on cognitive theories and their application than any other theorist.

JEAN PIAGET

Jean Piaget, a Swiss developmental psychologist, was born in 1896 and died in 1980. His theory came to the attention of American educators and psychologists late in his life (in 1960), after he had produced an enormous body of writings. As a young man he began working in the Paris laboratory of Alfred Binet, where modern intelligence testing is thought to have originated. Piaget observed infants and small children (including his own three children) and afterwards asked questions about how these children had devised problem-solving strategies.

Components of Piaget's Theory

- Adaptation
- Assimilation
- Accommodation

Piaget hypothesized that cognition has its base in the biological capacities of the infant. Cognitive development results from the maturation of the brain and the nervous system. IQ measurements (or intelligence quotients) are derived by comparing the person's chronological age with his or her mental capacities; therefore, biological age may be considered a logical starting point for constructing a theory of cognition. Children begin learning by manipulating the environment, in particular by touching and sucking. Adults, on the other hand, learn by comprehending abstract, elaborate ideas. Piaget was the first to emphasize that an active individual, of any age, possesses a mind filled by rich structures of knowledge. The different stages of cognitive development determine the way in which these structures of knowledge are acquired.

Piaget stressed both discontinuous and continuous growth and theorized that all humans seek equilibrium in motor, sensory, and cognitive functions. Change and transition are termed disequilibrium, and equilibrium is re-established by adaptation.

Adaptation is a two-step process: first, assimilation and second accommodation. Assimilation is the tendency to interpret novel experiences in terms of what is already known and in terms of an existing scheme. Accommodation is the tendency to modify existing knowledge and familiar schemes to account for new information revealed through experience. For example, a small child may think that all four-legged animals are dogs because the only animals he or she has seen are dogs, thus demonstrating the process of assimilation. However, when the child sees and learns about cats, he or she is then accommodating new knowledge. When the child reaches a balance (or equilibrium) between assimilation and accommodation, he or she has achieved adaptation. Thus the concepts of adaptation in Piaget's theory can be considered ones of continuous growth, because in them a person forms newer, more complex schemes.

Piaget's Four Stages

- Sensorimotor stage
- Preoperational stage
- Concrete operational stage
- Formal operational thought

Piaget proposed that cognitive development occurs in four distinct stages, each of which is characterized by a unique capacity for organizing and interpreting information, or adaptation. Because each of these stages is qualitatively different, this part of Piaget's theory describes discontinuous growth. Certainly, small babies and adults think in different ways. Babies cannot understand abstract concepts, such as the differences between democractic and totalitarian governments. Nor would the same system of logic apply to individuals in each of Piaget's different stages. The thinking of adults is more flexible and comprehensive.

The first stage, sensorimotor intelligence, begins at birth and continues to approximately 18 months of age. In this stage the infant exercises some control over the environment. Thus, the infant "knows" a toy through his or her senses of touch, taste, sight, smell, and hearing, or what is termed sensorimotor learning. By using very simple cause-and-effect reasoning, infants are capable of problem-solving. The thinking and perceptions of infants are egocentric, meaning that they are not able to separate their perspective from someone else's nor do they have the capability to feel empathy for others (Santrock, 2009). Therefore, in this stage egocentrism is typical and should be expected. Piaget's theory clearly showed that infants are active learners and thinkers "whose minds contain rich structures of knowledge" (Berk, 2001, p. 20).

The sensorimotor stage has a substage, which is the symbolic functioning stage and occurs between the ages of 2 and 4. Children vastly expand their knowledge, skills, and experiences while retaining their egocentric view of the world. Primarily through pretend play, children become able to use symbols as a representation of objects, albeit at a very simple level.

The second stage, preoperational stage, begins when the child learns a language (approximately age 2) and ends about age 5 or 6. In this stage children learn causal relationships and can manipulate categories, classification systems, and hierarchies in groups. Their knowledge is tied to their own perceptions. In this stage, the toddler "knows" a toy by its functions, mainly through his or her own actions while playing with the toy, but also sees symbols, words, and pictures as representing physical objects. Therefore, a 2-year-old recognizes a picture of a doll in a book as a doll.

> Children in this stage assume that others recognize their inner thoughts and feelings, but they lack the role-taking abilities necessary to distinguish their own thoughts and feelings from those of others. Consequently, the preschooler's emerging sense of self does not include a stable set of self-feelings or self-attitudes, but is limited to one's name, aspects of gender identity, age, body image, possessions, personal characteristics, and favorite activities. (Demo, 1992, p. 304)

However, in this stage the child does not engage in mental operations; hence the name of the stage is preoperational thought.

The third stage, the concrete operational stage, comprises the ages of 6 or 7 years old until approximately 11 or 12. While in this stage, children are not able to think in terms of abstract or metaphorical concepts. However, children in this stage focus on physical reality and arrange objects into hierarchical classifications, they understand class inclusion, they know the meaning of reciprocity and symmetry, and they understand the principle of conservation. The principle of conservation is the awareness that altering an object's or substance's appearance does not change its basic property. For example, the amount of liquid in a container is equal, whether the liquid is in a tall thin glass or a short wide glass. Through direct experience, children teach themselves relations, classes, and quantities. Children in this stage are capable of judging the reactions of others or making social comparisons. Attending school with other children and with adult teachers, which expands their social world, enables children to consider the feelings of others.

The fourth and final stage, formal operational thought, begins in adolescence and persists through adulthood. Adolescents are able to think in abstract, symbolic terms, refining and developing more sophisticated cognitive skills. They are able to project themselves into the future. In this stage, individuals simultaneously conceptualize many different variables—a skill that allows them to problem-solve and create new systems and categories. Moreover, in this stage the individual is capable of *metacognition,* or thinking about thinking. At this stage individuals are capable of understanding and evaluating the way in which they perceive, remember, and learn.

Discovery Learning

Piaget's theory supported the concept of "discovery learning" as the best way to promote cognitive development, because he considered individuals capable of developing their own learning systems. Many early intervention programs described in later chapters are based on Piaget's stages of development.

According to Piaget, children engaged in play in order to learn by handling the objects and learning about the limits of their own bodies within their environment. For example, it is not a good idea for a child to jump off the roof even while wearing a Superman (or Superwoman) cape. Later in childhood, children engage in pretend play and make-believe in order to practice their symbolic understanding of the world. In contrast, Freud believed that children engaged in play in order to relieve their emotions and tensions in an acceptable manner. Piaget considered children's play as a very important part of practicing their sensorimotor understanding.

Evaluation of Piaget's Theory

Perhaps the most criticized area of Piaget's theory is his conclusion that no major cognitive development takes place after adolescence (Bruce & Muhammad, 2009). In addition, there is a lack of evidence demonstrating that Piaget's stages are universal. For example, not all adults reach the higher stages of formal operational thinking; furthermore, not all adults require the ability to think in formal operations. Kohlberg and Gilligan (1971) estimated that one-third of American adults never attain the stage of formal operations. On the other hand, Piaget has been criticized for not recognizing the ability to handle "real-life" problems. Another shortcoming of Piaget's theory is that it underestimates the effect of such environmental factors as school and home in developing cognitive abilities. This underestimation of environmental factors is probably a result of his focus on biological maturation (Klein & Safford, 2001).

Until fairly recently, Piagetian theory has been applied only to the cognition and development of infants and children, not to that of adults. Like Freud's, Piaget's work was clinical and did not employ empirical research methodology, but relied on flexible interviews and meticulous observation. Finally, Piaget's theory ignores the role of emotion in learning; some critics have stated in response that emotional processing is important to memory function, because the memories associated with strong emotions are the ones we remember most easily (Plutchik, 1980).

Application of Piaget's Theory to People With Disabilities

Development during the sensorimotor stage is based on active interaction with the environment through physical actions and sensory input. Active interaction with the environment is essential, and learning to orient oneself with the environment is important as a base for the higher stages (Klein & Safford, 2001). For an infant or a child with a congenital disability, either a sensory loss or a motor impairment, motorsensory learning will be impaired. Children born blind or deaf (or both) will miss much of the learning of this stage (Wachs, 2001). Because the disability of autism includes tactile defensiveness, children with autism tend to avoid sensory stimulation from touch as much as possible. Indeed, these children generally tend to avoid all sensory stimulation. Children with cerebral palsy, muscular dystrophy, spina bifida, and osteogenesis (brittle bones) are not able to manipulate their environment physically. Interestingly, occupational therapists use sensorimotor methods with young children having these disabilities, so these infants and children learn to integrate sensory input with motor development.

An interesting study conducted in 2010 sought to determine the role of sequence learning in deaf children who received cochlear implants (CIs) after many years of deafness (Conway et al., 2011). The authors stated that

> Deaf children with cochlear implants (CIs) provide the fundamental premise [that] was: Exposure to sound may provide a kind of "auditory scaffolding" in which a child gains vital experience and practice with learning and representing sequential in the environment. If true, then a lack of experience with sound may delay the development of domain-general processing skills that rely on the encoding and learning of temporal or sequential patterns, even for non-auditory input. (p. 69)

Research with children who had CIs studied hearing input—such as auditory perception, speech perception, and spoken language perception. This study was the first to study more global learning and cognitive capabilities. The authors stated that "Deaf children with CIs provide a unique opportunity to study brain plasticity and neural reorganization" (p. 69).

The nonauditory input consisted of visual patterns (p. 69). Two groups of children were participants: 27 hearing children and 25 prelingually (deaf before they learned to speak) profoundly deaf children who had received CIs. All of the children were shown squares of different colors on a computer screen and asked to remember the pattern of the squares, a visual memory task that did not require hearing. The CI children did not remember the colored squares as well as the hearing children did; the authors summarized:

> Consistent with the hypothesis that a period of deafness (and or language delay) may cause secondary difficulties with domain-general sequencing skills, the present results reveal that deaf children with CI (cochlear implants) display atypical visual implicit sequence learning abilities. Moreover, the partial correlations suggest that both the length of auditory deprivation and the amount of exposure to sound via a cochlear implant has secondary consequences not directly associate with hearing or consistent with the hypothesis that a period of deafness (and or language delay) may cause secondary difficulties with domain-general sequencing skills, the present results reveal that deaf children with CI (cochlear implants) display atypical visual implicit sequence learning abilities. Moreover, the partial correlations suggest that both the length of auditory deprivation and the amount of exposure to sound via a cochlear implant has secondary consequences not directly associate with hearing or language development *per se*. The amount of experience with sound, or lack thereof, appears to affect the ability to implicitly learn complex visual sequential patterns. (p. 75)

Although this is only one study, it does lend support to Piaget's cognitive theory which states that sensory input (from all of the senses) is critical for learning.

LEV SEMYONOVICH VYGOTSKY

Lev Vygotsky was a Russian developmental psychologist whose work and writings gained attention in the Soviet Union during the 1920s after the Bolshevik Revolution. In an article titled "The Rise of Soviet Sociolinguistics from the Ashes of *Volkerpsychologie,*" Brandist (2006) described Vygotsky's work as having been influenced by the German fusion of linguistic and social sciences. Certainly, the Bolshevik Revolution required the formulation of a soviet identity.

He was born in same year as Piaget, 1896, but died at the early age of 37 of tuberculosis. Horowitz (1987) explained why Vygotsky's work was not known in the United States until the 1980s and the end of the Cold War, 50 years following his death.

> His death at the age of 37 in 1934 and prevailing world conditions contrib-
> uted to a general ignorance of his highly original ideas concerning language,
> thought, and culture in relation to developmental processes. The work was
> largely unknown until relatively recently. Translations into English of his papers
> and monographs (Vygotsky, 1962, 1978) and the work of his student and col-
> laborator, Alexander Luria (1976, 1981) introduced important ideas that are
> now entering the mainstream of developmental theory. (p. 4)

Vygotsky was born in Belarus (which was then a part of Russia) into a nonreli-
gious Jewish family in 1896. He was a prolific writer, producing six books in a 10-year period. Interestingly, Vygotsky had no formal training in psychology, and his life's work included many diverse topics, such as the psychology of art, the philosophy of science, the methodology of research, the study of learning disabilities, and the study of abnormal human development. During his life and after his death, the government of the Soviet Union severely criticized Vygotsky, his theory, and his methods of learning, but a group of students circulated his ideas and kept them alive. As a result of this criticism and harsh repression by the Stalinist regime, his students (including Luria) were forced to leave Moscow and went to Ukraine.

Lev Vygotsky's Sociocultural Cognitive Development Theory

Both Piaget and Vygotsky developed theories about how children think and how thinking changes throughout life. Similarities between Piaget and Vygotsky include their emphasis on the ways in which children construct their own knowledge and understanding. Although Piaget considered the cognitive development of children universal, Vygotsky thought that it is necessary to focus on the child within his or her culture (Daniels, 2007). Some have held that Piaget emphasized the natural line of development, while Vygotsky followed the cultural line of development (Berk, 1998). However, both theorists proposed that parents and educators should be sensitive to the child's readiness to learn and capitalize on ways to challenge the child. On the other hand, parents and teachers should not push children if they are not cognitively prepared. Both Piaget and Vygotsky believed in the importance of accepting individual differences.

Components of Vygotsky's Theory

- Individuals in differing cultures have different cognitive structures
- Language shapes thought
- Culture as a mediator of self-regulation
- Movement from intermental to intramental
- Inner speech
- Zone of proximal development (ZPD)

Unlike Piaget, Vygotsky stressed the sociocultural context for learning and did not propose general stages of development. Developmental cognitive theories that are based on biological maturation tend to be more universal (because biology is very universal), but sociocultural theories such as Vygotsky's often propose that individuals reared and educated in different cultures will display different thinking structures and problem-solving skills (Cole & Gajdamaskchko, 2007). "Vygotsky directs attention to the guiding role of social interaction and culture in shaping and orienting cognition, thus bringing the study of cognitive development into much greater harmony with the concepts of psychosocial theory than are seen in Piaget's theory" (Newman & Newman, 2009, p. 59). Vygotsky also stressed the importance of language in shaping thought. Naturally, Vygotsky viewed humans across cultures as similar to the extent that they shared basic biology; however, he considered the sociocultural environment to be the most significant factor determining the individual's cognitive development. Individuals from differing cultures use different symbolic systems, organize information differently, have different ways of recording and remembering information, and they have different relationships to the natural environment. Furthermore, Vygotsky believed that people fully understand their native language only when they can contrast it with another language. Bilingual children learn that there is no fixed relationship between the world around them and the words they use to describe the world. Therefore, language is somewhat arbitrary, because objects can be renamed or relabeled. Individuals who speak more than one language are more flexible because they see the world from two different perspectives.

Vygotsky believed that speech and language play an important role in self-regulation, self-directed goal attainment, and problem-solving. His theories are based on four components: (1) culture as a mediator of cognitive structure and self-regulation, (2) movement from the intermental to the intramental, (3) inner speech, and (4) the zone of proximal development.

Vygotsky argued that all higher planning and organizational functions appear twice in the individual's life: first when a child interacts with adults and second after the child has internalized what others have taught him or her. The caregiver engages the infant and encourages intramental (egocentric) functioning. When interacting with the caregiver, the infant is not a passive recipient but is beginning intermental (social) learning. Play with other children is a very important component in Vygotsky's theory, because it is a social/cultural teaching method. So-called "expert" members of a society or culture teach child culturally relevant knowledge and skills, often using "guided participation."

Small children engage in "private talk," which Vygotsky considered to be social speech turned inward. Further, it is adults who have taught the child speech. Although the child learned private speech in a social setting, private speech may not have a social intention; it simply helps the child to problem-solve. Eventually audible private talk disappears, and the child substitutes inner speech.

The concept of the zone of proximal development has led to the creation of guided learning methods. Vygotsky (1978) described the zone of proximal development as "the distance between the *actual* developmental level as determined by independent problem-solving and the level of *potential* developmental as determined by problem-solving under adult guidance or in collaboration with more capable peers" (p. 86). Parents help their children to complete all sorts of tasks by guiding them with appropriate questions or providing hints or clues. As the child becomes able to do more, the parent helps less and less. In this way children learn a new competency, such as dressing themselves, and this new information and ability is internalized into existing developmental skills and finally becomes synthesized at a newer, higher intermental (social) level. The zone of proximal development has been described as the juxtaposition of cognition with culture.

The word *scaffolding* is used to describe the temporary support and assistance the parent or teacher provides to help the child accomplish a task or learn a new concept (Gindis, 1995). As one author noted about scaffolding, "there is an inverse relationship between the child's current ability and the amount of support needed" (Papaila & Olds, 1992, p. 198). Scaffolding helps children (actually, everybody) to incorporate new information into existing cognitive structures. Naturally, the success of scaffolding is related to the sensitivity of the parent or teacher in providing individualistic, finely tuned support. The practice of scaffolding has been extensively researched.

Evaluating Vygotsky's Theory

Criticisms of Vygotsky's theory have focused on what many consider to be an oversimplified reliance on the sociocultural environment, in which the child becomes a product of teaching, toys, and television. Critics argue that the focus is removed from the child, and the environment instead becomes the major explanation of development and growth. Vygotsky's theories have led to research on the effects of television and different parenting styles. Certainly Vygotsky proposed that a child's cognitive and social development is only as good as the environment, both the formal institutions such as school and daycare and the informal institutions such as play and access to toys and books (Tudge & Rogoff, 1999; Zigler & Finn, 1984).

In the history of developmental psychology, Vygotsky has been described as an exception in the 20th century because he developed a contextualized theory: "With the exception of Vygotsky, the contextual developmental psychology appears to have lain dormant for much of this century. Recently, however, numerous psychologists have rediscovered contextualized thinking" (Dixon & Lerner, 1984, p. 24). Vygotsky's theory is more flexible in responding to historical shifts and rapidly changing demographics.

URIE BRONFENBRENNER

Urie Bronfenbrenner was an American psychologist born in Moscow, Russia in 1917, the son of Jewish Russians. At the age of 6, he and his parents immigrated to the United States, where he attended Cornell University and received his PhD in developmental psychology from the University of Michigan. Anne Levine (Scarr, Weinberg, & Levine, 1986) interviewed Bronfenbrenner. Some excerpts from that interview are included below:

> I grew up on the grounds of what was called an institution for the "feeble-minded" in the 1920s: 3,600 morons, imbeciles, idiots—and me. These were my friends and companions. My father was a physician, a neuropathologist. In those days, it was hard for a Russian immigrant to establish a private practice. You got a job at a state institution. We lived at Letchworth Village in upstate New York—a marvelous place, really.... Two things that happened at Letchworth stand out in my mind. Some of the kids who were sent there didn't belong in a home for the mentally retarded.... My father would examine them when they arrived and see that they were not mentally retarded. His problem was to get them tested before the institution had its effect, for then they would be stuck there for life. The Binet was the hand of God. It was the only way he could get them out. [The Binet was the first intelligence test.]
>
> The second thing that happened was that the inmates worked in the physicians' homes as maids and helpers. I was brought up by Hilda and Anna and Marilyn. These were my caregivers. They were supposed to be mentally retarded. But, when they worked in our homes, their IQs would go up. So you can see the beginnings of an interest in development right there. (p. 45)

Bronfenbrenner described his mother in this way:

> My mother was a lover of literature, art, and music, and there was none of that at Letchworth. Psychologically, she never came to the United States. She lived in her own world of Russian literature. I learned to read and write Russian before English, and read all the great Russian poetry and novels with my mother. You know what Russian novels are about? Human development. Do you remember how *Anna Karenina* begins? "All happy families are alike: every unhappy family is unhappy in its own way." (p. 45)

Levine asked Bronfenbrenner: "Your comparative study of the United States and the Soviet Union, *Two Worlds of Childhood,* is a classic. Could you summarize the differences between these two worlds, for children?" (p. 47).

> The Russians have a word, *vospitanie,* which doesn't translate very well into English. It means upbringing, building character, becoming cultured. *Vospitanie* is a national hobby. Everyone is preoccupied with children. They are given the best clothes, the best food available. Adults speak to children wherever they are, and see themselves in the role of aunt or uncle, to all children.... Russian children grow up surrounded by affectionate adults, but also under constant surveillance. Adults feel they have a right to love—and to correct—any child. (p. 47)

Bronfenbrenner is considered to be the cofounder of Head Start, a federally funded preschool to assist children from families of lower socioeconomic status as a part of President Lyndon Johnson's War on Poverty. He was a highly productive writer and lecturer whose theory has had widespread acceptance.

Bronfenbrenner's Ecological Systems Theory

In his theory Bronfenbrenner combined both biological maturation and the environment (or ecology) in which the child develops. Therefore, in contrast to psychosexual theories, Bronfenbrenner characterized humans as open systems that interact with the environment. (Freud's psychosexual theory is a closed system because the individual's sexual urges are internal.) However, Bronfenbrenner's greatest contribution was his theory that children developed in a complex system of relationships that are affected by multiple levels of the environment. These levels are also termed "nested systems" or "layered systems." Before Bronfenbrenner's theory, most developmental researchers viewed the child's environment as limited to only those events and conditions immediately surrounding the individual. In contrast, Urie Bronfenbrenner conceptualized the environment as consisting of complex inter-nested structures that all play a role in the individual's development. Conflicts and changes in one system will ripple throughout the other systems, so Bronfenbrenner advocated looking at both the immediate environment of the child and the larger environment. These complex and interrelated relationships compose the systems theory.

Components of Bronfenbrenner's Theory

- Microsystem
- Mesosystem
- Exosystem
- Macrosystem

Each level may be considered to be another level of analysis in which each becomes increasingly distanced from the individual's direct experience. With the exception of the exosystem, the relationships in these levels are bidirectional or reciprocal, meaning that the individual is affected by but also affects the system. It is important to remember that Bronfenbrenner's systems approach did not consider stages of the individual's development within these varying systems. Finally, these systems and the individual interact to form sets of "correlated constraints." The individual is not free to do anything or everything that he or she desires (Shanahan, Hofer, & Shanahan, 2004).

The innermost level of children's environment, their home and family, is termed the *microsystem*. This is the environment closest to children. Parents and caregivers affect the children's growth and development, but infants and children also affect and influence the behavior of parents and caregivers. Therefore, Bronfenbrenner stated that relationships between the infant and family are bidirectional. Berk (2001) described the infant's effect on parents: "a friendly, attentive child is likely to evoke positive and patient reactions from parents, whereas an active distractible youngster is more like to be responded with restriction and punishment" (p. 26). Children with congenital disabilities may not be physically attractive or responsive to their parents; furthermore, they may make many demands on their parents and caregivers. In short, parents may view the child with a disability as a source of stress.

In the microsystem (typically the family and the home), every member of the family is affected if the mother receives a pay increase or the father goes to prison. The microsystem adjusts by redefining roles and relationships, adjusting boundaries, and modifying patterns of communication.

The second level of the individual's environment, the mesosystem, comprises the interrelationships between two or more settings in which the individual develops. For children, the mesosystem is often composed of their school, neighborhood, and peer relationships. For adults, the mesosystem is primarily the workplace outside the home. The mesosystem is nested within the microsystem, because these two systems are reciprocal. For example, the child's academic progress (mesosystem) depends on family and parent involvement (microsystem), and the child's relationships at home are influenced by his or her school performance.

The third level of the individual's environment, the exosystem, does not involve the individual as an active participant; however, the exosystem environment does affect the experiences of the individual. The exosystem includes both informal and formal organizations. Informal organizations are social relationships, extended family support, and other community-based support. Formal organizations include the written regulations and policies of health care, school, and the workplace. For example, a child may not be aware of the policies of his mother's employers, but his daily life is affected by the way in which his mother's workplace provides daycare. The exosystem is the only system that is not bidirectional. Although the exosystem affects the individual, the individual does not influence the exosystem.

The fourth and outermost level in Bronfenbrenner's theory is called the macrosystem, which consists of the values, laws, and customs of a particular culture. Also included in this level are the resources of the culture, such as education, work opportunities, gender equity, and access to opportunities for self-development.

For Bronfenbrenner, an individual's life is a series of reciprocal exchanges between the individual and these four levels of development. Events in the adjoining systems affect each other. It has been noted that the child's academic progress affects both the mesosystem and the microsystem, but we can also see that the exosystem affects the child's academic progress simply by providing an appropriate education. These relationships are considered to be reciprocal because individuals have the capability to select, modify, and create many of their own environments. Therefore, Bronfenbrenner believed that freedom and autonomy were based on the degree to which individuals can select and determine the appropriate environment.

Bronfenbrenner's theory also considers the historical time period, which is labeled the *chronosystem*. Obviously, changes in life events can be imposed by external events, and the relationships between various systems change over time. In the macrosystem, worldwide economic depressions or global wars affect the lives of individuals. The individual's changes in development, such as biological maturation or university graduation, change with the passage of time. For example, a longitudinal study

(Glueck & Glueck, 1950, 1968) of children of the Great Depression of the 1930s found that many children were required to assume adult roles earlier in life; some of these children expressed pride and satisfaction in helping their families, but others felt resentment at being robbed of a full-length, carefree childhood.

Rather than independence and autonomy, systems theory considers interdependence as the ultimate goal. Equilibrium is defined as the maintenance of balance between an individual's systems. Much of family therapy case conceptualization has been based on Bronfenbrenner's systems theory, which focuses on the quality of the child's environment (Zigler, Piotrkowski, & Collins, 1994). However, Bronfenbrenner was also concerned that a

> deficit model is used to determine the level of support granted by the public to struggling families. Parents must declare themselves deficient in some way in order to qualify for help in solving problems that may come about because of our cultural value of independence. A larger degree of failure means a larger amount of support. By working from this deficit model, we expect families to hold their hands up from deep inside a black hole of helplessness. Then, we expect them to have the psychological strength to climb up the thin rope we throw down. (Paquette & Ryan, 2001)

Bronfenbrenner's emphasis upon dyadic interaction (that between two people) and its influence on teaching has also been used to support the concept of mentorship (Languis & Wilcox, 2001). A great deal of research has been designed to study the parent–child or the teacher–child relationship, but little attention has been focused mentoring relationships between adults. Longitudinal studies have shown that many successful adults have established meaningful mentor relationships, but little is known about the process of choosing a mentor, the relationship between adult mentoring dyads, and the developmental stage at which these relationships are most effective.

Application of Bronfenbrenner's Theory to PWDs

Bronfenbrenner's systems theory is able to describe, define, and explain the experience of disability. In the past, disability was considered a private concern of the individual; therefore, the onus of responding to the disability rested on the person with the disability (PWD) and his or her family. More and more, disability is thought to be a public concern that affects everyone, so that disability is a societal issue.

Before the formulation of Bronfenbrenner's theory, most developmental psychologists and theorists viewed the environment in a fairly normal way and saw is as only the individual's immediate environment, such as the home and family. Bronfenbrenner clearly stated that there are many layers of environment that directly affect the individual. For example, without opportunity structures for certain groups of individuals such as PWDs, even the most well-adjusted, hard-working, well-educated PWD could not succeed. Bronfenbrenner defined the macrosystem as the culture surrounding the individual. It is clear that a macrosystem can cause, define, or exaggerate disability (and in fact has). As Hurst (1998, p. 322) explained, "disability is viewed as...a product of disabling, unresponsive, insensitive environment."

Environments limit physical access and opportunities for work, education, and social participation.

American Polio Epidemics: Macrosystem Involvement in a Disability Experience

The American polio epidemics from 1893 to 1955 provide a clear example of the way in which the disease of polio was a part of the macrosystem, but the individuals (and their families) who survived polio were not considered part of the macrosystem. The polio epidemics could be considered part of a chronosystem, because the times of both the first and last epidemics is well established. The polio epidemics also coincided with the widespread introduction of electronic media and the American post–World War culture of prosperity and optimism. There were all sorts of public responses to *avoid* and *prevent* polio, which culminated in the discovery of the polio vaccine in 1955; however, there was little public response to the polio survivors. After 1955, in the United States, polio and polio survivors were abruptly forgotten. Shell (2005) wrote a book of first-person accounts of polio survivors with the subtitle *The Paralysis of Culture.* The author strongly made the point that the American government and general public had failed Americans who had contracted polio.

It was thought that everyone was susceptible to the polio virus, making polio a universal macrosystem. During the polio epidemics, movie stars made television and film appeals for charity. Indeed, beginning in 1946, more than one-third of all funds donated came from monies collected in movie theaters (Shell, 2005). The print media and radio described ways to avoid polio and also solicited funds for treatment and research. Iron lungs were displayed in department store windows. The American president Franklin Roosevelt was a polio survivor. Charity telethons and poster children were invented during the polio epidemics. Roosevelt's image on the dime is an allusion to his charitable fund-raising foundation, the March of Dimes.

The first Americans with Disabilities Act could have been enacted during the polio epidemics rather than in the 1990s. There was a slogan: "You have given us your dimes. Now give us our rights." Polio survivors had no accommodations, no psychological counseling, and no work opportunities. Many children were required to drop out of school because their schools had stairs. Like all other disabilities, polio was considered a shame and embarrassment to the survivor and his or her family. Contracting polio was considered a moral failing, and polio survivors were advised to hide and minimize their disability. Today the survivors of the last polio epidemics are dying, but unlike World War II veterans, there has been no effort to collect and archive their first-person accounts.

Bronfenbrenner's system theory makes disabilities a public concern, not only a medical, clinical concern. The macrosystem can facilitate and improve the experience of disability for everyone. Although the family of a PWD can have tremendous restorative powers, that family cannot provide physically accessible environments, entrance into educational institutions, opportunities for meaning work, and equal social status relationships. The nation could understand the concept of *vospitanie;* that all American children were the responsibility of society.

Terms to Learn

Accommodation	Exosystem	Private talk
Adaptation	Formal operational	Scaffolding
Assimilation	thought	Sociocultural cognitive
Concrete operational	Inner speech	development theory
stage	Macrosystem	Symbolic function
Discovery learning	Mesosystem	stage
Ecological systems	Microsystem	Zone of proximal
theory	Preoperational stage	development

Videos to View

- View the 57-minute video *Cognitive Development* by Films for the Humanities and Sciences. The producers describe this video: "The aim of this program is to examine Piaget's theory and to critically examine it in light of modern research. The study of child development in the 20th century revolved around Jean Piaget's theories, and the program clearly describes their central themes, covering the cognitive stages of development from birth to 12 years old, giving illustrations of children's behavior at each level."

- View the 31-minute video *Learning in Context: Probing the Theories of Piaget and Vygotsky* produced by the Open University and available from Films for the Humanities and Sciences. The producers describe this video: "This program presents recent work by developmental psychologists that emphasizes the influence of contextual factors in learning and performance. Three sets of experiments involving children are examined: tasks in which deliberately gender-biased instructions are provided; tasks requiring cooperation between asymmetrical pairs of peers; and tasks involving training of students by adults and peers. The intriguing results of these tests shed light on the impact of stereotyping on performance; the effects of self-perception on competence; and the influence of different teaching approaches on learning. Implications for adults are considered as well."

- View the 26-minute video, *Cognitive Development: Piaget's Influence* available from Insight Media. The producers describe this video: "Presenting a brief discussion about Jean Piaget's life and theories, this program describes the four stages of cognitive development and illustrates the major achievements of the concrete operational stage. It emphasizes the importance of conservation, seriation, and categorization in a child's cognitive development."

Learning Activities

(Note: These may also be used for class presentations.)
- Discuss the ways in which Bronfenbrenner's concept of *vospitanie* contributed to his theory of child development and the founding of the Head Start program.

Do you think that the Head Start program has helped to reduce the effects of poverty and disadvantage?

- Bronfenbrenner moved away from the deficit model to the systems model. Explain why this change in emphasis was important.
- Interview one or two parents whose children have attended Head Start programs and ask them about the positive results for their children and for their families.
- In class consider if Vygotsky's sociocultural theory of learning is the most appropriate theory for today's globalization.

Writing Exercises

- Write a four-page paper on the life and work of Alfred Binet. Include a discussion of how Binet's ideas influenced Piaget and the development of his cognitive theory.
- Write a four-page paper on the life and work of Alexander Luria. Include a discussion of how Vygotsky influenced Luria and the development of his cognitive theory.
- According to both Bronfenbrenner and Vygotsky, children's environments affect their learning. Write a 10-page paper that explains and expands upon this idea.
- Write a 10-page paper that compares and contrasts Piaget's theory with Vygotsky's. Note that Vygotsky's theory does not include stages.
- Both Piaget and Vygotsky thought that teachers should serve as facilitators and guides rather than as active directors. Does this make sense to you? Would you like teachers who would guide you in discovery learning? Should children be allowed to develop their own interests? Write a 10-page paper answering these questions.
- Write a five-page paper in which you describe the ways in which Piaget's, Vygotsky's, or Bronfenbrenner's cognitive theories explain your educational experiences.

Web Sites

http://psychology.about.com/od/developmentecourse/a/dev_cognitive.htm
http://www.learningandteaching.info/learning/piaget.htm
http://psychology.about.com/od/piagetstheory/a/keyconcepts.htm
http://www.learning-theories.com/vygotskys-social-learning-theory.html
http://www.simplypsychology.org/vygotsky.html
http://www.gulfbend.org/poc/view_doc.php?type=doc&id=7930&cn=28
http://www.newworldencyclopedia.org/entry/Urie_Bronfenbrenner

Behavioral Theories of Development: Ivan Pavlov, B. F. Skinner, and Albert Bandura

6

In earlier chapters we looked at Maslow's humanist theory, which generally has an optimistic view of people and their ability to change and develop. If humanists are too optimistic, behaviorists are too pessimistic, mechanistic, and deterministic. They are mechanistic when they emphasize mindless reactions to stimuli, and deterministic in their beliefs that the individual does not have freedom to make choices. The humanist theorist Maslow said that behaviorism is like exploring a continent with a microscope. According to the behavioral theorists, "human behavior is subject to the laws of science and can be studied without reference to internal motivations" (Feist, 1990, p. 349). The leading behavioral theorist, B. F. Skinner, considered it possible to study human behavior, to predict it, and finally to control it.

> Science is more than the mere description of events as they occur. It is an attempt, to discover order, to show that certain events stand in lawful relations to other events.... Science not only describes, it predicts.... Nor is prediction the last word: to the extent that relevant conditions can be altered, or otherwise controlled, the future can be controlled. (Skinner, 1953, p. 6)

Behaviorists believe that the individual's development is closely related to the opportunities for learning that are available to that individual. Therefore, the behaviorists thought that controlling or manipulating the environment made it possible to control human behavior. If there is any concept of choice in the behaviorist theories, it is in choosing the environment.

The "radical behaviorists" (Maddi, 1996, p. 520), such as Pavlov and Skinner, began the development of their theories by experimenting on animals because there are fewer ethical constraints on strictly controlling the environments of nonhumans. The behaviorists experimented on animals; the other developmental theorists studied people in their natural environments. Simply understanding this distinction helps to understand behaviorism and its underlying assumptions. In the past, it was also accurate to state that it is possible to observe behavior but not to observe the mind working. This is perhaps still true, but today it is possible to observe the structure of the brain through several neural imaging techniques, including computed tomography scans, and magnetic resonance imaging. It is possible to view the functioning of the brain by using electroencephalography and positron emission tomography.

Strictly speaking, behaviorism is not a theory of human development, and, indeed, it is often paired with learning theory. All other theories in this book describe certain unlearned, inherent, universal aspects of human nature. For example, Freud considered humans to be sexual beings, Erikson considered humans to be social beings, and Maslow thought humans to be self-actualizing beings. The theories of the behaviorists made no assumptions about the core aspects of humans, considering newborn infants to be blank screens. Behaviorism is more explicit on motivation because it states that any behavior that is reinforced will continue. In contrast, Freud stated that sexual conflicts motivated behavior, Erikson stated that desires to resolve socially defined "crises" were motivators, and Maslow stated that the fulfillment of needs motivated behavior. Because behavioral theory clearly states that there are no inherent human traits, it focuses solely on the process of learning. For this reason, behavioral theories are often not considered theories of human development.

However, some consider both respondent and operant conditioning to be theories of development because new coping strategies are adopted. Both types of conditioning are processes through which a culture's norms and rules are adopted. Learning both coping strategies and society's rules can also be generalized to similar situations. However, Pavlov and Skinner stated that there are only sequences of learning rather than stages of development. It should be noted that Skinner never considered respondent conditioning to be a complete theory.

Components of Respondent Conditioning

- Involuntary responses
- Unconditioned stimuli or neutral stimuli

IVAN PAVLOV

The work of Ivan Pavlov, a Russian psychologist, formed the basis for the behavioral theories. The theory of Pavlovian learning, respondent conditioning, or classical conditioning is based on involuntary responses and intrinsically reinforcing stimulus. Involuntary responses are not automatic and include rapid heartbeat, sweating, or salivating.

Respondent conditioning is a form of learning through association; this means that when a previously neutral stimulus is paired with an unconditioned stimulus, the neutral stimulus elicits a response. Therefore, emotional responses can be acquired through respondent conditioning. Everyone knows about Pavlov's dogs that salivated when a bell was rung. All dogs salivate at the sight of food; however, Ivan Pavlov discovered that dogs began to salivate when they heard the sound of the approaching attendant, before they saw the food. Simply hearing the approaching footsteps of the attendants produced salivation. Pavlov then devised experiments that sounded a metronome and a bell before the dogs were fed. The dogs became conditioned to associate the sound of the bell or the metronome with food, even when the food was not present. Events that occur close together in time often acquire similar meaning. Pavlov was not interested in salivation rather but in discovering the conditions under which other stimuli in the environment could elicit salivation. Pavlov was interested in studying these other stimuli.

Learning occurs when two unrelated stimuli are presented at approximately the same time (repetitively), and, as a result, the two unrelated stimuli acquire similar meaning. Therefore, food was a necessary stimulus but the neutral stimulus in Pavlov's experiment could have been almost anything, as long as it was paired with food. Neutral stimuli common to humans include money, promotions, and good grades. People are not born to desire money or promotions; however, because they are born to want to eat, they learn to value money, promotions, and good grades, which eventually provide food (and other physical necessities).

The associations made in respondent conditioning do not require language skills. Babies and toddlers develop both positive and negative emotions in response to certain environments or individuals.

Newman and Newman (2009) describe respondent conditioning:

> Your emotional reactions to the taste of a certain type of food or the feel of a particular material may be the result of conditioned learning that has persisted until adulthood. For example, the idea of "comfort food" suggests the conditioned link between certain foods and feelings of security and warmth that were established in childhood when family members gathered together to enjoy a meal. (p. 62)

Therefore, meat loaf and mashed potatoes make us feel secure and warm.

Respondent conditioning can also produce fears that are associated with a specific cue, such as a noise, smell, or light. These fears can result in systematic, lifelong avoidance of these cues and the environments in which they occur. Almost everyone has a fear resulting from a painful, unpleasant, and frightening experience from childhood. Fears of swimming, dogs, or certain foods may be the results of nearly drowning, being bitten by a dog, or choking on a peanut.

Senator John McCain, who was a prisoner of war in North Vietnam, said that long after he had returned home the jingling of car keys made him very anxious and frightened. The neutral stimuli of the sound of car keys elicited fear. During the years of his imprisonment, his captors would come to his cell, jingle their keys, unlock the door to his cell, and take him for brutal interrogation sessions. After he came home, everyone around Senator McCain learned not to jingle their keys, because the sound of keys evoked strong memories of the brutality he had experienced as a prisoner of war.

Respondent conditioning is an important concept because it provides the foundation for the behaviorism of B. F. Skinner (and others) and because behaviorism in turn provides the foundation for Bandura's social learning theories. Pavlov also demonstrated the importance of consequences in shaping and determining behavior. According to Pavlov, learning was a response to events, rather than a result of unconscious forces.

Components of Operant Conditioning

- Behaviorists state that humans are *reactive*
- Humanists state that humans are *proactive*

Pavlov experimented on animals, while Skinner began his research with animals and subsequently studied people. The use of animals freed them from ethical restraints and allowed them to control the experimental environment. They could deprive the animals of food and water, which is not allowed on humans. Theorists *experiment* on animals, but *study* or *observe* humans.

Operant conditioning differs from respondent conditioning in that the individual performs a conscious, deliberate behavior. Simply by understanding the individual's past behaviors and the corresponding rewards and manipulating his or her environment, one can often predict accurately the individual's future behavior. The difference between operant conditioning and respondent conditioning is that operant conditioning involves the individual *learning* a response while respondent conditioning involves a *reflexive, involuntary* response, such as emotions. However, in both responsive and operant conditioning individuals react to the environment, or better stated, to stimuli in the environment. Although the humanist theories state that humans are proactive, the behaviorists state the humans are reactive.

B. F. SKINNER

When B. F. Skinner was a child and young man, it would have been difficult to predict that he would eventually become a world famous psychologist and scientist and a widely published author. Indeed, as a child he was attracted toward the arts, and because of the sudden, unexpected death of his younger brother, Skinner's parents kept him closely attached to them. During his college years B. F. Skinner did not show much promise, and many of his later major projects ended in failure. Moreover, many of his projects, such as the Skinner Box, were both widely praised and widely criticized.

Burrhus Frederick Skinner, the son of a successful lawyer, was born in 1904 in a small Pennsylvania town. He was called "Fred" as a child, never Burrhus or B. F. During his first year of college, when he had returned home on Easter vacation, his younger brother Ed died. Ed's death had a devastating impact on Skinner, and some of his biographers have claimed that it was at this point that Skinner began to minimize the importance of human emotions. After he graduated from a small, all-male liberal arts college with a major in English, Skinner returned home and spent a year working on creative writing in an attempt to start a career. In his later autobiography, Skinner refers to this year as his "Dark Year." Skinner's yearlong attempt at writing ended in failure, in spite of encouragement from the poet Robert Frost.

The next year, 1928, he was accepted into a graduate program in psychology at Harvard, even though he had never taken a single course in psychology. Skinner received his PhD (1931) and spent five additional years in a prestigious laboratory research, but he felt he was ill-suited to teaching psychology because he had "never even read a text in psychology as a whole" (Skinner, 1979, p. 179). In spite of this attitude, Skinner accepted a teaching and research position at the University of Minnesota.

In Minnesota Skinner married and became the father of two daughters. Skinner is well-known for his experimental methods in caring for and raising his younger daughter, Deborah. He constructed a crib for Deborah that had a large window and a continuous supply of warm, fresh air, sometimes called the Air-Crib, Heir Conditioner, or the Skinner Box. The infant Deborah wore only a diaper; the crib was filled with lots of toys and Deborah was removed from the crib frequently in order to play, interact with her parents, and receive cuddling and affection. However, the Air-Crib was abandoned after Deborah physically outgrew it, and several attempts to market the crib ended in failure.

During World War II Skinner trained pigeons to pilot missiles, bombs, and torpedoes into enemy targets. Skinner presented his project in Washington, DC in 1944, and the pigeon performed without a mistake. Indeed, in all the simulations, the pigeons performed unerringly. Nonetheless, the federal government did not use Skinner's pigeons. Afterwards, Skinner returned to academia and used behavioral techniques to train pigeons to play ping pong.

In 1945 he left the University of Minnesota in order to take a position as the chairperson of the psychology department at the University of Indiana. One biographer has termed the years 1945 to 1948 Skinner's "midlife crisis" (Elms, 1981). In 1948 Skinner published *Walden Two,* a widely read and popular book, and his crisis ended. *Walden Two* is a novel that describes an experimental society based on behavioral principles. The main character of *Walden Two* is Professor Burris, apparently an alter-ego of Skinner. Thus, Skinner had merged his interests in creative writing and scientific inquiry into a single book. Skinner returned to Harvard, became a much-honored psychologist and scientist, and died in 1990.

Above all, Skinner desired to make the world a better place by advocating that people should be placed in utopian environments in order to allow them to fulfill their full potential. Therefore, although Skinner's methods may appear deterministic, his goals were the advancement of human race. Skinner's theories dominated much of the academic field and professional practice of clinical psychology during the 1940s and the 1950s, but his influenced has gradually decreased (Perven & John, 2001).

Components of Skinner's Theory
- The importance of the environment
- All behavior is learned

Most of Skinner's work was experimental and conducted in laboratories, focusing on observable behavior and describing the conditions under which behavior occurs. Empirical, observable, quantifiable study of both behaviors and stimuli is necessary, and Skinner's work has its roots in experimental psychology; indeed, his initial research efforts used animals, such as rats and pigeons, and shaped their behaviors in eating and avoiding danger. For example, rats and pigeons were trained to press a lever that automatically dispensed food pellets. He continued his research by focusing on humans, specifically on individuals rather than large groups. He did a great deal of research on small children because they were easier to control than adults. Skinner concentrated on the present or used the "here and now" approach, thinking that an individual's past or future was of little importance in determining his or her behavior.

Skinner understood that everyone has feelings. However, he did not believe that feelings provided any explanation of an individual's behavior, nor do behaviorists take much interest in unconscious motivation. The theory of operant conditioning states that humans are not influenced by any internal motivator (whether cognitive or affective). Skinner said that human freedom and dignity are myths; furthermore, the environment shapes behavior. Behaviorists claim that operant conditioning excludes the role of thinking, attitudes, beliefs, preferences, and values.

Human behavior is the sum total of learned responses to stimuli in the environment, and all behavior continues (or is maintained) by stimuli or consequences. Therefore, all behavior, both healthy and unhealthy, is learned. For behaviorists this explains why habits are so difficult to break. Behaviorism proposes that development, or learning, does not occur in stages but rather in sequences. Behaviorists are only interested in quantitative changes.

Types of Reinforcement

- Positive reinforcement
- Negative reinforcement
- Punishment
- Extinction
- Shaping behavior

Skinner believed that *operant conditioning* occurs when a behavior produces consequences, either good or bad. Stimuli *operate* on the individual to produce a specific effect or consequence. The nature of the consequence, therefore, determines the probability of the behavior happening. The individual produces a behavior and then is either rewarded or punished by the situation. Skinner is careful to state that the reinforcement does not cause the behavior but simply increases the probability that the behavior will be repeated. Understanding the concept of operant conditioning helps to understand the importance of controlled conditions in laboratory settings that were used to test the validity of behaviorism. For Skinner, behavior was simple; it was not a complex, internally driven response or a product of the individual's personality. Skinner believed that if behavior were based on the individual's personality, then the individual would respond similarly across a variety of environments. Instead, behavior is simply the product of the individual's history of reinforcement.

Extinction is continuous nonreinforcement that results in lowering the rate of the behavior or, stated differently, the response weakens. It also means the eventual total absence of the behavior. Often, the term "unlearning" is used instead of extinction.

Reinforcement is anything that strengthens the behavior, rewards the individual, and increases the likelihood that the behavior will be repeated. Reinforcement can be divided into positive reinforcement and negative reinforcement. Positive and negative refer to the presence or absence of a consequence. A positive reinforcer, therefore, is a stimulus that is both *present* and pleasant to the individual, and a negative reinforcer is the *removal* of an unpleasant, or aversive, consequence. Money is often termed a general positive reinforcer because most people like to receive money. The removal of pain is a negative reinforcer because most people do not like to be in physical pain. There is a wide array of positive reinforcers, some of which are not tangible but are still very powerful motivators. These include social approval, fame, comfort, and security. There is also a wide array of negative reinforcers, all of which include the removal of something, including both tangible and intangible consequences. Removing electric shock would be a tangible negative reinforcement, while eliminating anxiety would be an intangible negative reinforcer. Individuals refrain from some behaviors that are often contingent on negative reinforcers. Skinner would say that most people do not lie or steal because anxiety and guilt are negative reinforcers. When we do not engage in immoral, unethical, or illegal behavior, the fear of being discovered and feelings of guilt or shame are removed.

Unlike negative reinforcement, punishment does not remove or eliminate a stimulus, but presents an aversive or unpleasant stimulus, such as an electric shock, a loud noise, hunger, bad grades, or time in jail. Unlike negative reinforcement, which increases the likelihood that a behavior will increase, punishment decreases the likelihood that a behavior will reoccur. For example, most individuals will stop behavior that leads to electric shocks, bad grades, or prison. Of course, although punishment stops a behavior, it does not indicate which behavior should be substituted. Therefore, punishment does not actually improve behavior but only suppresses bad behavior.

Behavior is then controlled by the environment or the individual who is controlling the environment by having access to rewards and punishments. Learning is simply the result of remembering the consequences, good or bad, of certain behaviors. If (and when) the individual understands and evaluates the reinforcers (and the reinforcement schedule), he or she can choose to resist operant conditioning. Obviously, operant conditioning works best with small children because parents, caregivers, and teachers possess the capability to control the environment. Operant conditioning also works well with well-defined treatment processes, such as smoking cessation or pain management.

Certainly, the use of small children or other vulnerable populations, such as individuals with intellectual and developmental disabilities, raises questions of exploitation and denial of basic human rights. For example, the ethical principle of informed consent may not be possible with these types of populations, because informed consent means that the participants in a research study are capable of evaluating and understanding what participation in research studies means.

Shaping of behavior is the process of breaking down a complicated or multistep behavior into small components. According to the principles of successive approximations, the first step of a final behavior is reinforced and then other behaviors are gradually reinforced until the complicated final behavior is achieved. Whether the final behavior is a complicated athletic move, dressing oneself, or memorizing the alphabet, individuals begin learning by doing gross approximations. It may take years for the individual to reach the desired behavior.

Schedules of Reinforcement

Schedules of reinforcement refer to the interval of time between the desired behavior and the delivery of the reinforcement. Fixed intervals are unchanging, such as payday every two weeks. The individual knows that invariably he or she will be paid every two weeks. With variable interval schedules of reinforcement, reinforcement is provided at random time intervals. Behaviors reinforced on an intermittent schedule are much more difficult to extinguish. Frankel (1971) illustrated both types of schedules—continuous and intermittent—by using bubble gum as a reinforcer. Two children have asked their fathers for money to buy bubble gum.

> It is not uncommon in our experience to find ourselves trying harder after frustration. However, as the nonreinforcement of the operant response continues over trials, the weakening of the response manifests itself in lower and lower rates of responding, until finally it returns to its initial level (prior to the first reinforcement), or disappears altogether. In our example, both children will stop asking their parents for bubble gum. However, the child who has been reinforced on a continuous schedule will extinguish faster than the child who has been reinforced on an intermittent schedule. If we observe an individual seemingly struggling in vain, and we wonder how someone can work so hard when achieving so little reinforcement, we may speculate that a history of intermittent reinforcement [was provided] for that individual. (pp. 452–453)

Skinner also claimed to have found an explanation for superstitious behavior, which he defined as those behaviors in humans for which there is no causal link between the response and the reinforcer. Superstitious behavior is continued only because there is an occasional totally random reinforce. This is termed "accidental conditioning" (Hall, Lindzey, & Campbell, 1998, p. 514). The example most often given in textbooks is of the rain dance.

> The members of a primitive tribe may practice rain making by the performance of some ritualized dance. On some occasions rain does happen to follow the performance. Thus the rain-making dance is reinforced and tends to be repeated. The natives believe that a causal connection exists between the dance and the production of rain. Actually the dance is accidentally conditioned; the rain occasionally happens to follow the dance. The same type of behavior can be seen with superstitious people who carry lucky charms, rabbits' feet, and other talismans. It may even be the case that the generally superstitious person is distinguished from the less superstitious person by the fact that many instance of accidental conditioning, by chance, figured to a relatively large extent in that person's life. (Hall, Lindzey, & Campbell, 1998, p. 514)

Many of our reinforcers are termed "secondary reinforcers," such as money. Money itself (the paper bills) has no intrinsic value. However, money has been paired with many other reinforcers, which include everything that money can buy (such as bubble gum). There are also idiosyncratic reinforcers, which are reinforcers specific to one individual. Individuals who will work for caramel popcorn, for example, are individuals with idiosyncratic reinforcers.

Skinner did not avoid controversy and seemed to enjoy healthy debate among theorists. Indeed, Skinner stated that behaviorism was not a theory but simply an explanation for the way in which behavior is learned. According to Allen (2000),

> Skinner often played the iconoclast (Dinsmoor, 1992). He seized every opportunity to tweak the nose of the psychological establishment. For example, he was often accused by humanitarian and libertarian critics of devising fascist methods for the coercive regulation of human behavior. Noticing that his critics

blanched at the mention of the word *control,* he used it often. This tactic also served to bait his adversaries. (p. 325)

ALBERT BANDURA

Albert Bandura was born in 1925, in a small town in northern Alberta, Canada. In this town, there was only one school that consisted of both elementary and secondary grades, with 20 students and two teachers. From this remote small town, seemingly with few academic resources, Bandua went on to a distinguished career in teaching, research, and writing.

After graduation from high school, the young Bandura worked one summer building the Alaskan Highway, meeting and associating with a wide array of individuals, many of whom manifested various degrees of psychopathology. His work on the Alaskan Highway was a turning point that led Bandura to an interest in clinical psychology. He earned a PhD at the University of Iowa and eventually taught, wrote, and conducted research at Stanford University.

Bandura's Social Learning Theories

Albert Bandura considered respondent conditioning and operant conditioning to be theories of performance, not theories of learning. In Bandura's concept of reflective self-consciousness, which is the capacity to think (or reflect) on behavior and learn from others, humans have the ability to monitor their own behavior. Unlike Skinner, Bandura did not consider the environment to be the primary determinant of human learning. Rather, social learning theory proposes that behavior is learned (Bandura, 1997a, 1997b). Therefore, the research on social learning theories did not use animals as subjects. Bandura believed that humans are the product of learning and that biology plays only a small role.

Components of Bandura's Theory

- Consideration of internally driven motivations
- Observational learning
- Vicarious reinforcement
- Modeling and imitation

Bandura perhaps qualifies as a humanist theorist (or a "moderate behavioralist") because he believed that humans were both flexible and resilient and that they "must develop their basic capabilities over an extended period, and they continue to master new competencies to fulfill changing demands throughout their life span" (Bandura, 1986, p. 20). Social learning theory is optimistic (meaning that all humans seek to develop their full potential) and has a life span perspective. People are able to control and change their behavior, so that people continue to learn and to grow throughout the various stages of life. Bandura's social learning theory combines operant conditioning and observational learning. Finally, Bandura never used animals in his research, so his theory is less empirically oriented. Empirical research requires very precise, accurate definitions of variables, such as a behavior, and complete control of the experimental environment. Therefore, empirical research, which is the hallmark of both respondent and operant conditioning, tends to oversimplify behavior into simple, specific responses, which greatly limit the generalizability of the experimental results. In contrast, social learning theory considers more internally driven motivations and is more generalizable to other individuals and other types of environment.

Bandura (1977b) stated his attempt to "provide a unified theoretical framework for analyzing thought and behavior" (p. vi). Social learning theory introduced several concepts, such as observational learning, vicarious reinforcement, and self-efficacy. Bandura believed that an individual watches others, learns about the consequences of their behavior, and then learns new behavior without actually engaging in trial-and-error behavior. Social learning theory holds that learning occurs through social interaction. Termed observational learning, it also includes hearing or reading about other individuals' behaviors and the resulting consequences. Observational learning means that the individual does not have to engage in specific behaviors in order to learn. Reading, listening to others, and watching others can result in learning. In contrast, both respondent and operant conditioning theories state that individuals are required to act in order to learn.

Vicarious reinforcement refers to the component of observational learning in which an individual observes the results (or reinforcers) of others' actions. Seeing someone receive rewards or punishment for his or her behavior can be vicariously rewarding or vicariously punishing. When an individual observes that someone who engages in illegal behavior is caught and sent to prison, there is vicarious punishment that might deter the individual from criminal acts (Bandura, Ross, & Ross, 1963).

Observational learning requires a model (a person who performs the behavior) demonstrating the way in which the behavior is performed and showing the rewards gained as the result of the behavior. As individuals become older, they become skilled at seeking out models who can display the behaviors in which they are interested. For most people, their environments are expanded as they mature, and they have more models from whom to choose. The environment of small children is often limited to their home, where only a few role models are available.

Bandura elaborated on the characteristics of models most likely to be imitated. Individuals who demonstrate authority, prestige, and, of course, the ability to perform the desired behavior are chosen. Successful individuals are often models. Almost everyone is drawn to attractive people, as we can see when fads copy the wardrobe of an attractive and influential person. For example, the style of hat worn by Jacqueline Kennedy when she was First Lady of the United States became wildly popular with American women. Models are not required to be actual people, and Bandura recognized the importance of "symbolic models," such as fictional characters in books, television, and films. Bandura also recognized that the expansion of electronic media would increase the importance and availability of models. The Internet is also a source of symbolic models.

Modeling and imitation are very effective ways in which to learn; however, without some capability or familiarity with the behavior being modeled, the individual could not benefit from the modeling. Watching the performance of a surgery would not make most people capable of performing that same surgery. Even if the model, the person who performs the surgery, is an excellent surgeon, the observer must have some previous knowledge of anatomy and experience with surgical techniques to benefit from this type of observational learning. Individuals take the information received from models and relate it to information they already have.

Components of Self-Efficacy
- Self-regulating
- Coping behavior

Self-efficacy, according to Bandura, is a powerful self-regulatory process. Self-efficacy is the belief concerning one's ability to perform behaviors and that the reward for this behavior will be worthwhile. The important word in the last sentence is belief, because self-efficacy is not the individual's actual capabilities but rather the individual's perception of his or her abilities. Self-efficacy is much like self-confidence. Self-efficacy influences an individual to attempt a behavior and also determines the quality of the performance. Coping behavior is influenced by a history of previously successful responses to problems and other adversities.

Individuals with high levels of self-efficacy tend to attempt novel behaviors, and these individuals demonstrate a great deal of tenacity in the face of failure. Many great scientists and novelists persisted in pursuing their goals even after experiencing obstacles, failures, and rejections. Obviously these individuals were able to maintain their self-efficacy by viewing failure as a learning opportunity and by seeing their work as a reward in and of itself. In contrast, we sometimes see individuals who quit after a few feeble, half-hearted attempts. It is not difficult to see why self-efficacy is the most researched aspect of social learning theory. Why do some people persist and others do not? Under what conditions do these differences occur? Two developmental theorists commented on the differences in self-efficacy between two individuals and the way in which their perception of obstacles was an important factor.

> Bodily alterations, transitions, and turning points have the potential to open up new opportunities, alter life goals, and create stress. Their influence on the life depends on how individuals interpret them and respond to them, as well as the constraints that limit those responses (Elder, 1997; Rutter, 1998). Although constraints are often conceptualized as structurally based, people differ in their perceptions of the limitations imposed by similar structural contingencies and in their perceptions of their abilities to surmount them (Bandura, 1986). As a result, different persons faced with the same situation will assert different types and levels of effort to change it, creating diverse life pathways. (McLeod & Almazan, 2004, p. 395)

Self-efficacy has been researched extensively, especially in the 1980s and 1990s. Self-evaluation is part of self-efficacy, because it is necessary to assess our performance continuously. With each assessment, we can make adjustments, stop the behavior, and find some other way to attain the same goal; if our efforts are judged to be successful, we redouble them.

Related to self-efficacy is diffusion of innovation, which occurs when a large number of individuals try something new. Fads, such as hula hoops, are examples of diffusion of innovations. By definition, fads are short-lived because the incentives to maintain the innovation are not permanent. In the beginning cars were compared to horses, and some thought that cars would never replace horses. However, the incentives for maintaining cars as an innovation were very powerful, so that no one would now consider cars to be a passing fad. For an innovation to become permanent, it is important that a large number of people think that they have the skills (self-efficacy) to perform those behaviors associated with the novelty.

Bandura recognized the importance of "social comparison," in which the value of rewards is relative. Individuals evaluate how well they are doing in life by comparing themselves to others in their same situation. Perhaps this is why many children reported during the Great Depression that "We didn't know we were poor. Everybody we knew was poor." Finding suitable groups with whom to compare oneself (or a reference group) has a powerful influence on happiness and well-being.

Bandura's theories have been applied to the management of physical disabilities, such as pain control, depression, addictions, heart disease, diabetes, and arthritis. Symptoms are reduced and wellness promoted when individuals make deliberate efforts to develop their sense of self-efficacy and sense of accomplishment. There is an increase in self-management behaviors for a disability when the individual makes deliberate sustained efforts to develop a sense of self-efficacy and a sense of accomplishment. Bandura's theories have been found to be relevant to chronic disabilities, because for lifelong disabilities the focus is on care, rather than a cure. In most cases, the pathology of the disability will not change. Bandura might say that the disability is the environment, and self-efficacy is under the control of the individual who has the disability.

In conclusion, Bandura's theory of social learning has had wide-ranging positive results with many types of individuals in many types of settings (Rosenthal & Bandura, 1978). Is Bandura a humanist or a behavioralist? He is both. Bandura conceptualized humans in very positive ways, considering them possible of great growth and achievement. In this sense Bandura is a humanist. He also defined (and empirically demonstrated) the necessary behaviors and how to use these behaviors in order to become a fully functioning individual. In this sense he is a behaviorist. Bandura's book *Self-Efficacy* (1997) has had a wide readership.

EVALUATION OF BEHAVIORAL THEORIES

Behavioral theories have been criticized as simplistic, segmented, and fragmented, unable to explain or predict human behavior very well. Rather than viewing the individual in a holistic manner, behavioral theorists break down behavior into small fragments (or chunks). Behavioral theories are also thought to be somewhat artificial, because little research has been undertaken to study people in their natural environments. Of all the theories discussed in this book, behavioral theories are the most laboratory oriented. Although laboratory research has the advantage of rigid control, it also has the disadvantage of not allowing the individual to be understood in a real-world environment. True behaviorists such as Skinner did not believe it was necessary to go beyond the principles of behaviorism, because these principles described, explained, and predicted human behavior and development (Ferster, 1961). On the other hand, Bandura and some others who used Skinner's behavioral theory as a foundation for more social and therefore more real-life theories did not have Skinner's sophisticated, precise methodology. However, Bandura's theory seems more useful and understandable than Skinner's. Also, Bandura's social learning theory has not received the same degree of criticism as Skinner's theory.

> In summary, (behavioral) theory is a theoretical position that in many respects is singularly American. It is objective, functional, places much emphasis on empirical research, and is only minimally concerned with the subjective and intuitive side of human behavior. As such, it provides a striking contrast to many of the theories...that are deeply indebted to European psychology. (Hall, Lindzey, & Campbell, 1998, p. 599)

In spite of these limitations, it is undeniable that positive reinforcement occurs every day in the life of every person.

Application to People With Disabilities

Behavioral principles and techniques are used to treat anxiety disorders, depression, substance abuse, eating disorders, domestic violence, and pain management. The entire system of applied behavior analysis (ABA) is based on Skinner's theory (Cataldo et al., 2007). The behavioral technologies derived from Skinner's research and single-subject research design are used in medicine, education, and a growing variety of behavioral therapies. All the behaviors listed above are considered to be maladaptive, so behavioral techniques are used to reduce or extinguish them (Murphy & Barnes-Holmes, 2009).

Since the 1960s, Skinner's theory has gained wider acceptance by professionals who work with people with disabilities (PWDs). The terminology "applied behavior analysis" (ABA) or "positive behavioral support" seems more acceptable than Skinner's term of behavior modification (Cataldo et al., 2007). More important, Skinner's theories and methods are being used to further social skills, independence, and greater autonomy (Jahoda, Dagnan, Kroese, Pert, & Towler, 2009). The high success rates and the goals of Skinner's techniques and theory are reviving the use of behavioralism. Successful behavior change has been demonstrated for language acquisition, self-care, activities of daily living, and vocational functioning. Empirical studies have demonstrated the success of behavioral techniques in extinguishing behaviors such as self-injury, inappropriate sexual contact, stereotypes (repeated behaviors that serve no purpose such as rocking and head-banging), and aggression toward others. As Cataldo et al. noted, "these approaches have been shown to be successful with almost every diagnosis in the spectrum of developmental disabilities" (p. 541).

ABA is used with individuals who have severe disabilities, especially with young children. A very specific set of behavioral objectives is identified and then broken down into very specific components. These behavioral objectives are shaped by providing reinforcements and (in a few cases) punishment. Two researchers (Sautter & LeBlanc, 2006) reviewed empirical studies from 1989 until 2005, looking for the use of ABA with humans, specifically in the acquisition of verbal behaviors. They found that "autism professionals comprise one of the larger potential clinical consumer groups of Skinner's approach to language" (p. 44). Sautter and LeBlanc concluded:

> It is also critical to continue investigating the conditions under which functional interdependence is demonstrated... and how clinicians might best use this knowledge in applied settings to facilitate rapid acquisition of functional language in individuals with disabilities. (p. 44)

Bandura's Theory and PWDs

Bandura's concept of self-efficacy has been employed in many skill acquisition programs for PWDs. In particular, a self-identity of self-efficacy assists PWDs in responding to social and physical environments that are not always accessible. A high degree of self-efficacy is also related to higher levels of tenacity and persistence. If people view their success as dependent upon their own behavior and characteristics, they are less likely to develop a self-identity as victims. So-called victims are less likely to see the relationship between their behaviors and consequences (Ng, Sorenson, & Eby, 2006). PWDs do not like others to use the word "victim" to describe them, such as, "He was a polio victim." They prefer the word "survivor," which implies strength and resilience rather than weakness.

Advocacy training is a type of training that has the goal of helping PWDs learn self-efficacy. Advocacy training assists PWDs to view themselves as capable of creating optimal environments for growth and development. For PWDs as a group, the focus is on changing public policy and enforcing the Americans with Disabilities Act. For PWD, as individuals, the focus is on skill development in empowerment, stigma resistance, and insistence on full integration into society.

Terms to Learn

Coping behavior
Extinction
Fixed interval schedules
Modeling and imitation
Negative reinforcement
Observational learning
Operant conditioning

Positive reinforcement
Punishment
Respondent conditioning
Schedules of reinforcement
Self-advocacy
Self-efficacy
Shaping behavior

Social learning theories
Unconditioned stimuli or
    neutral stimuli
Variable interval schedules
Vicarious reinforcement

Videos to View

- View the 57-minute video *Further Approaches to Learning*, available from Films for the Humanities and Sciences. Although this video includes several approaches to learning, the producers note that "the program includes archival film featuring B. F. Skinner and Dr. Robert Epstein, who demonstrated apparent 'insight' learning in pigeons using behaviorist techniques. Skinner, speaking just before his death, claims that reinforcement rather than higher mental processes is at work in learning. The behaviorists think differently!"
- View the 55-minute video *Classical and Operant Conditioning*, available from Insight Media. The producers describe this video: "This program examines the nature of behaviorism and considers it applications in clinical therapy, education, and childrearing. Featuring footage of laboratory experiments, the program discusses the classical and operant conditioning theories of Ivan Pavlov and B. F. Skinner."

Learning Activities

(Note: These may also be used for class presentations.)
- As an in-class activity, role-play a debate between Freud and Skinner.
- Play the group game "Pigeons and Experimenters." This game demonstrates successive approximations (or shaping) of target behaviors. Divide the class members into two groups. Have one group, called the Pigeons, leave the room. With the remaining group (the "Experimenters") in the room, decide upon a desired behavior, such as standing on a chair. Bring the Pigeons back into the classroom, but do not tell the Pigeons the target behavior. Pair a Pigeon with an Experimenter. Whenever a Pigeon comes close to the chair, reinforce him or her with cheers and applause. When the individual walks away from the chair, provide no reinforcement. See which Experimenter can shape his or her Pigeon's behavior most quickly.
- Read B. F. Skinner's novel *Walden Two* and discuss the book in class. One discussion point may be the way in which Skinner's behavioral theories are used in the book.
- In a class discussion, share some of your self-efficacy strategies. Which ones work and which ones do not? How can these strategies be related to behavioral theories?

Writing Exercises

- The learning that occurred during the game of Pigeons and Experimenters may also be considered observational learning, which is a concept of Bandura's theory. Write a five-page paper in which you consider whether (1) the learning was strictly operant conditioning or if (2) the learning was also observational.

- Write a five-page paper that explains this statement: "Behaviorists state that humans are reactive."
- Bandura stated that he wanted to "provide a unified theoretical framework for analyzing thought and behavior." Write a 10-page paper in which you provide evidence either (1) that Bandura succeeded or (b) that Bandura did not quite succeed.
- Write a five-page papter considers the value of behavioral techniques in learning. Emphasize the lack of importance ascribed to internal motivation in behavioral techniques.

Web Sites

http://webspace.ship.edu/cgboer/skinner.html
http://www.sntp.net/behaviorism/skinner.htm
http://psychology.about.com/od/profilesofmajorthinkers/p/bio_skinner.htm
http://webspace.ship.edu/cgboer/bandura.html
http://psychology.about.com/od/profilesofmajorthinkers/p/bio_bandura.htm
http://www.learning-theories.com/social-learning-theory-bandura.html

Abraham Maslow the Humanist

7

The next theorist we shall discuss is considered a humanist because he believed in the inherent goodness of humans and in their capacity (indeed, their innate need) to grow, develop, and eventually self-actualize (Maslow, 1971). (Self-actualization means reaching one's full potential.) Maslow believed in the vast potential of humans. Rather than emphasizing biological or social stages of development, humanists have organized their theories around a hierarchy of needs. Psychosexual theories propose that development is a result of biological and sexual changes. Psychosocial theories consider development closely linked to societal expectations, and cognitive theories view development primarily through the development of thought and language. Erikson's psychosocial theory proposes that transitions are the main motivators of human behavior. Erikson believed that because transitions between the various stages of development are periods of heightened vulnerability and increased potential, successful negotiations of these transitions are motivators. Humanists, on the other hand, base their theories on human needs or motivators. Maslow believed that human nature is inborn, not made, and that given a supportive environment, humans naturally mature into trouble-free, effective adults.

Humanists substitute the word "striving" for "development," which indicates that self-actualization is the end goal. Other theorists have suggested that hedonistic pleasure-seeking, pain avoidance, or reduction in internal tension is the motivator of behavior. Humanists believe that after the tension level has been reduced, individuals strive to fulfill their potential. Pleasure-seeking, pain avoidance, and tension reduction are sometimes called drives, but self-actualization has been called a motivation. Motivation and goals transcend personal life situations; because it is self-defined, all humans can seek self-actualization, regardless of their culture, environment, generation, or historical time period.

ABRAHAM MASLOW

Maslow was born in Brooklyn, New York in 1908, the oldest of seven children. His parents were Jewish immigrants from Russia who were also first cousins. He taught at Columbia, Brooklyn College, and Brandeis University and died in 1970. As one reviewer noted, "Maslow considered himself an abused and neglected child and a victim of prejudice.... He seethed with suppressed anger" (Allen, 2000, p. 219).

Maslow's father was rarely present at home, and his mother was a very religious, punishing woman. He always did well in school, attending a select all boys' high school.

Speaking of his childhood, Maslow stated that he grew up in libraries among books. At his parents' request, Maslow entered law school at Columbia University but dropped out after three semesters and transferred to Cornell University. Not liking Cornell, he once again transferred, this time to the University of Wisconsin, after he married his first cousin, Bertha, in spite of his parents' objections. Maslow received all of his degrees at Wisconsin, earning his PhD in 1934.

At Wisconsin he worked with Harry Harlow, a famous researcher who studied attachment theory by using baby rhesus monkeys as subjects. Maslow watched the monkeys under various experimental conditions and observed that they fulfilled some needs first. For example, he concluded that thirst is a stronger need than hunger but need for oxygen was even more important than thirst.

A biographer described Maslow's next step. "During the interval between getting his PhD and finding a permanent position, Maslow searched desperately for a stable means of livelihood. Because the depression was ongoing, he opted for future security and entered medical school. However, as always, when he did something for reasons other than intrinsic interest, he became bored and dropped out" (Allen, 2000, p. 223). Luckily, the famous learning psychologist Edward L. Thorndike became interested in his work and hired Maslow.

During this period, New York City was a heaven for psychologists. Most of the important American psychologists were working there, and many psychologists who were European refugees came to New York. Maslow associated with great innovators, but his most influential mentor was Kurt Goldstein, whose book *The Organism* originated the idea of self-actualization.

After a short stint teaching at Brooklyn College, Maslow gained a faculty position at Brandeis. He retired to California and died in 1970. Maslow was a leader of humanistic psychology, which became a "third force" in psychology. In the study of human development, Freudian theory is considered the "first force," and behaviorism is considered the "second force."

MASLOW'S THEORY

Stating that Freud had emphasized the "sick half" of human nature, Maslow emphasized that he would focus on "the healthy half of human nature." Freud would say that the "child had to be kicked upstairs," meaning forced against his or her will toward maturity and very resistant to change. Maslow, on the other hand, believed that children did not have to be forced to master developmental tasks and that children have an innate need for creative growth. Everyone has universal, positive needs, and everyone is self-directing. Maslow stated, that "what a man *can* be, he *must* be" (1970, p. 46).

Maslow criticized human development scientists who he thought had "desacralized" science. (Desacralized is a word whose root means sacred.) Scientists, in his opinion,

> had removed the emotion, joy, wonder, awe, and rapture from their study in order to purify and objectify it.... They [the scientists] must be willing to "resacralize" science or to instill it with human values, emotion, and ritual. Astronomers must not only study the stars, they must be awestruck by them;

psychologists must not only study human personality, they must do so with enjoyment, excitement, wonder, and affection. (Feist, 1990, p. 598)

Maslow also felt that because most human development research studied samples of individuals who were not well-adjusted, these studies and their results had a pathological/deficit orientation. The few uses of samples of well-adjusted individuals were often statistically averaged with samples of maladjusted people, "resulting in a concoction that is neither vintage champagne nor cheap wine" (Allen, 2000, p. 233).

Maslow wrote extensively and produced a complex and complete theory of development. However, he did not develop a system of psychotherapy. Carl Rogers did base his client-centered therapy on Maslow's humanist principles.

Hierarchy of Needs

- Lowest—Physiological needs
- Second—Safety needs
- Third—Belongingness and love needs
- Fourth—Esteem needs
- Fifth—Self-actualization

Maslow proposed a hierarchy of needs, in which lower-level needs must be satisfied before higher-level needs become motivators. Each ascending need, therefore, requires that the needs below it are satisfied. Maslow's hierarchy ranges from the lowest level needs of the biological person to the higher level of abstract, uniquely human needs. When one need is met, the individual will then become motivated to fulfill higher-level needs. Once a need has been met, it loses its motivational power. For example, after obtaining enough food and water, the individual will then begin to seek safety. The needs are universal, but they are culturally and socially shaped.

Maslow's hierarchy of needs as motivators can be applied to other cultures because even biological needs (and certainly the higher needs) are met in different ways in different cultures. Although needs are the same basic motivators, the manner in which they are met is culturally and individually determined.

The lowest or first level of needs is the *physiological* needs of water, food, oxygen, sleep, and sex, which are termed "deficit needs." If these basic needs are not met, the individual's life becomes dominated by fulfilling these needs. For most people living in the developed countries these needs are met; however, during wars or natural disasters these physiological needs often take precedence. As Maslow explained, "a want that is satisfied is no longer a want. The organism is dominated and its behavior organized only by unsatisfied needs. If the hunger is satisfied, it becomes unimportant in the current dynamics of the individual" (Maslow, 1970, p. 3).

The next level consists of *safety* needs that include security, protection, stability, law and order, and freedom from fear and chaos. For example, children often do not like disruptions in their routine and prefer structure, and when adults are subjected to stress, anxiety, chaos, and violence, they feel threatened and frightened. Adult individuals construct their environments to be safe, predictable, and stable. Obviously, in a choice between growth and safety, the individual will choose safety. It is children and babies for whom safety needs are most clear cut; for example, some children are afraid of strangers or dogs. Especially in time of natural disasters or in war, the need for safety dominates.

The third level of needs consists of *belongingness and love needs,* which motivate the individual toward affectionate relationships with other people and a sense of place in a family and other groups. Also termed *affiliation and acceptance,* this need is brought to the forefront by divorce, homelessness, and other types of alienation. Everyone needs friends and "affectionate relationships" with others; if this need is not met, Maslow believed that individuals cannot develop unconditional giving and nonpossessive love.

The fourth level, the *esteem needs,* consists of self-esteem and esteem from others. Therefore, this need is to a degree based on obtaining success. For children, success can be academic, athletic, or interpersonal; adults may find success in their professional lives, communities, or long-term intimate relationships. Maslow recognized the circular nature of self-esteem; that is, individuals gain much of their self-esteem from internalizing the perceptions and opinions of others. Therefore, he warned against basing one's self-esteem on fame, status, and dominance, but rather ensuring that self-esteem is based on true competencies. It is important for an individual to develop self-acceptance and achieve a sense of trust in himself or herself.

The highest level of needs, which represents the pinnacle of the hierarchy, can be achieved only when all four of these lower levels of needs have been met. Maslow termed this highest level the need for *self-actualization.* Many books have been written on the concept of self-actualization; self-actualization is a very broad concept that is individually defined. Basically self-actualization is the discovery and fulfillment of one's own potentials and capacities. Self-actualization is also based on the proper fit between the individual and the environment; the individual has constructed and/or discovered the environment in which he or she can thrive. Obviously this environmental fit is individually defined. Maslow stated that ordinary individuals can be self-actualized, not only extraordinary heroes such as Martin Luther King, Jr., Mother Teresa, or Albert Einstein.

The first two levels of needs, physiological needs and safety needs, are deficiency needs that are necessary for physical survival and self-preservation. All human possess these two levels of needs that must be filled through external means, either tangible things or other people.

The third, fourth, and fifth levels of needs are termed growth and being needs. Healthy individuals are open to these needs because they bring satisfaction and growth. Therefore, it is much more satisfying to meet a higher need rather than a survival need. Unlike the deficiency needs, growth and being needs are unique to each individual. Maslow stated that it takes courage to be responsible for one's own development. If individuals have freedom from deficiency needs and other mundane worries, they then have the independence to develop their innate potential.

Later in his career Maslow qualified his previous statement that a higher need can be a motivator only when the lower needs have been completely satisfied. Instead Maslow stated that the typical individual is satisfied when approximately 85% of physiological needs, 70% of safety needs, 50% of love needs, 40% of esteem needs, and 10% of self-actualization needs are met. Therefore, as an individual ascends the hierarchy of needs, the percentage required for satisfaction is reduced (Hall, Lindzey, & Campbell, 1998).

SELF-ACTUALIZATION

Maslow believed that self-actualization is a matter of degree and that most of the time the self-actualized person demonstrates maturity, constructive behavior, happiness, creativity, and wisdom. In addition, a self-actualized individual views the horizon as limitless and is always striving for greater insights and new experiences. Self-actualized individuals are not free of weaknesses or shortcomings but simply accept these without feeling ashamed, guilty, or defensive. Self-actualizers have greater self-acceptance; they are also more tolerant and less judgmental of others. Because they have a more complete picture of themselves, self-actualizers understand their own motives, emotions, abilities, and potentials. With this increased self-knowledge, self-actualized individuals have a more accurate view of reality because they are less inclined to impose their own perceptions on experiences and people.

Self-actualized individuals typically have some consuming passion in life that involves much of their energy and time, such as art, human rights, or science. Self-actualizers tend to require some solitude and privacy (which Maslow called "detachment"), and they tend to be autonomous, independent, and less concerned about the social role expectations of others or external rewards. However, self-actualized individuals also have the capacity to develop and maintain deep, intimate, and loving relationships with a few close friends, while at the same time they tend to have high levels of social interest, a genuine interest in others, and a desire to help them. Self-actualizers are more democratic, meaning that they can associate with all types of people.

Self-actualized individuals have a more highly developed sense of justice and strongly oppose injustice, inequality, and exploitation of others. They have high moral and ethical standards and accept responsibility for their actions, whether good or bad. They exhibit a greater discrimination between good and evil and can also distinguish between the means and the end, meaning they understand the immorality of doing bad things for the right reasons. Self-actualizers also tend to enjoy doing something for its own sake, rather than as a means to an end. Also, self-actualizers tend to engage in social action and philanthropic endeavors.

A self-actualized individual tends to have a sense of humor that is nonhostile and does not hurt others, often serving a purpose such as to teach or to point out ironies. They live daily life with creativity and freshness, whether they are homemakers, teachers, hairdressers, or carpenters; indeed, Maslow emphasized that creativity can be expressed in all human endeavors when he stated that a first-rate soup was better than second-rate poetry. Nor do self-actualizers believe that they have all the answers, but they are still open to novel ideas and experiences and seek them out. Perhaps because of their high levels of autonomy and individuation, self-actualizers are not threatened by the achievements of others.

PEAK EXPERIENCES

Maslow was the first to write about peak experiences, those transcendent experiences that are extremely important and valuable to the individual. After a peak experience, the individual feels that he or she has been transformed, strengthened, and renewed. Maslow described the peak experience as that is only "beautiful, good, desirable, worthwhile, etc. and is never experienced as evil or undesirable" (1970, p. 63). Therefore, peak experiences are periods of intense joy and heightened insight. Others have described peak experiences by using the word "perfect," while others have characterized peak experiences as "creative possibility." Feist (1990) provided this description of peak experiences:

> First, though peak experiences have a religious core, they are not supernatural events. They are quite natural and are part of our human makeup. Second, during the experience, the whole universe is seen as unified or all in one piece and people clearly see their place in that universe. Also, during this mystical time, peakers feel both more humble and more powerful at the same time. They feel passive, receptive, more desirous of listening, and more capable of hearing. Simultaneously, they feel more responsible for their activities and perceptions, more active, and more self-determined. Peakers experience a loss of fear, anxiety, and conflict. They become more loving, more accepting, more spontaneous, less an object, and more likely to get something practical from the experience. Peakers often report such emotions as awe, wonder, rapture, ecstasy, reverence, humility, and surrender. There is often a disorientation in time and space, with persons less conscious of self or ego, more unselfish, and more able to transcend everyday polarities. (1990, p. 591)

EVALUATION OF MASLOW

Maslow's theory has been criticized for being too optimistic and overestimating the human potential for growth. Also, some have questioned Maslow's use of historical figures whom he had never met, such as Abraham Lincoln, Gandhi, and Albert Einstein, as a basis for his principles of self-actualization. His research to validate his theory did include major empirical studies, in addition to clinical observation.

In spite of these criticisms, Maslow's theory has had a major influence on the growth on positive psychology and wellness psychology. Carl Rogers developed his client-centered system of psychotherapy by implementing Maslow's humanist principles. Maslow's theory makes intuitive sense; everybody knows that a starving man would rather eat than compose a sonata.

APPLICATION TO PEOPLE WITH DISABILITIES

The important question of self-actualization theory is, "What is so essential to humans that without it they would no longer be defined as humans?" For centuries society has not viewed people with disabilities (PWDs) as fully human. In contrast, Maslow stated that humans were resilient and capable of responding to a wide array of demands and circumstances (Chang & Page, 1991). Maslow also thought that individuals often seek tension in order to grow and realize their full potential. Therefore, Maslow stated that one of the costs of self-actualization is increased tension, which forces the individual to encounter and deal with challenges.

The disability scholar Carolyn Vash (1981) described transcendence as the final stage of adapting to a disability. Until Vash, most disability specialists considered acceptance to be the final stage, but according to Vash, many PWDs reach the acceptance stage though only a few reach transcendence. Because self-actualization is personally defined, people with disabilities can view the lower stages of the needs pyramid as management of the disability and the highest stage as transcendence. During medical stabilization and physical rehabilitation, the individual's focus is obviously on meeting physical needs. However, after these physical needs are met, higher needs can be fulfilled. Often transcendence of a disability is considered to be some sort of denial or detachment, or inability to accept the realities of the disability. For many people without disabilities (PWODs), it seem unrealistic that some PWDs (though perhaps only a few) view their disability as a gift and to consider themselves to be better people *because* of the disability rather than *in spite* of the disability.

With Maslow's hierarchy of needs, for PWDs to experience transcendence, they first must be released from the mundane physical aspects of life. PWDs must have good medical treatment and management, an accessible environment, appropriate access to assistive technology, and social support and acceptance.

Components of Transcending a Disability

- Finding meaning and purpose in the disability
- Reevaluating goals and identities
- Discovering personal strengths
- Finding positive aspects of the disability
- Taking pride in the mastery of the disability
- Seeking out new experiences
- Assisting other PWDs (Smart, 2009, p. 411)

A disability is difficult, time-consuming, and expensive, but most PWDs would not describe either their disability or their lives as tragic. In a discussion of transcendence Reed (1991) noted:

> There is a universal human desire for transcendence and connectedness. Transcendence is defined as a level of awareness that exceeds ordinary, physical boundaries and limitations, yet allows the individual to achieve new perspectives and experiences. Awareness of self-transcendence refers to the developmental maturity whereby there is an expansion of self-boundaries and an orientation toward broadened life perspectives and purposes. (p. 64)

Patricia Deegan, who has the psychiatric disability of schizophrenia, describes transcendence:

> In fact, our recovery is marked by an ever-deepening acceptance of our limitations. But, rather than being an occasion for despair, we find that our personal limitations are the ground from which spring our own unique possibilities. This is the paradox of recovery, that is, in accepting what we cannot do or be, we begin to discover who we can be and what we can do. (p. 50)

Robert Owen, a polio survivor who became a physician, estimated that before he was 12 years old he had read a grand total of three books. He recalls that before polio struck when he was 12, he was constantly in trouble and fought while going to and from school. In addition to fighting, he also "loved to play football and things like that." When he returned to school after a year of rehabilitation, he focused on his studies. Owen is convinced that if he had not had polio, he probably would not have become a physician (Wilson, 1990, p. 202).

A movie prop man who was diagnosed with multiple sclerosis found that through helping other PWDs, he felt attractive, creative, and powerful in self-defined ways.

> Before my disability, I was a superficial person, caught up with competitiveness and machismo. The disability gave me the opportunity to find out who I really am. I had to start from square one to become a member of a community that from time immemorial has been discriminated against and viewed as defective by mainstream society. Transferred to a world of disability culture, I developed deep and meaning relationships with people in the disability rights movement.... They encouraged me to feel attractive and creative and powerful in my way. (Fleischer & Zames, 2001, p. 202)

Another woman described her pride in her disability, despite its negative aspects. She compares her disability to her ethnic identity.

> I'm proud of being Italian. There are things I am ashamed of, like the existence of the Mafia—but these things do not stop me from embracing my Italian-ness. I love being a woman, but I hate going through menopause. But I wouldn't want a sex-change operation just because of menopause. Certainly the pain and physical limitations of disability are not wonderful, yet that identity is who I am. And I am proud of it. (Fleischer & Zames, 2001, p. 202)

Many PWODs would not consider that PWDs can experience transcendence *because* of their disability rather than *in spite* of it. Some PWODs think that PWDs are continuously bitter, angry, and have not accepted their disability. Yet some PWDs and their families have found transcendence.

Jack Hofsiss is a theater director in New York who directed *The Elephant Man*, the story of an Englishman, Joseph Merrick, who was born in 1862 and was the first to develop neurofibromatosis, a disfiguring disability in which large bony lumps appear on the head and limbs. Because there was then no medical diagnosis to explain neurofibromatosis, his family ascribed the disease to a superstitious cause, although neurofibromatosis is the result of a chromosomal abnormality (Morris, Morris, & White, 2005). Merrick survived the cruelty of his family and the Victorian workhouse. Hofsiss won both a Tony and an Obie for his direction of the play *The Elephant Man*. In the following paragraphs, Hofsiss describes his transcendence as a sweetness and peacefulness. First he tells of the way in which he became paralyzed:

> Then on January 20, 1985, on Fire Island, I was taking an early-morning dip—you know, "Oh, I think I'll take a nice bracing dip, rather than taking a shower." There were stories that it happened in the dead of night at a wild party, with me doing backflips off a garage roof. All untrue. It was one of those pools with a very severe incline from the shallow end to the deep part, very deceptive. Essentially, I dove into a wall. (Hofsiss & Laffey, 1993, pp. 79–80)
>
> It's odd, but I'm beginning to see a greater unity in my life. I came to terms with the worst experience of my life, which was this accident, and the best experience of my life, which was the pure, really sweet sense of satisfaction that the *Elephant Man* gave me—the sweetness of working on that piece of material and being responsible for a large number of people knowing about that man and what he was like and how much we have to learn from him. I think it all relates. I don't know if I'm fooling myself. I found a way which has given, thankfully, a certain peacefulness. The good and bad have interrelated in my mind in my mind. I can't crystallize that into a precise moment, but evolving over the year or two after my accident happened, I began to see those things relating to each other: somehow, the unities were met. (Hofsiss & Laffey, 1993, p. 87)

Stephen Hawking, the British theoretical physicist and cosmologist, was diagnosed with amyotrophic lateral sclerosis at age 21 when he was a graduate student at Cambridge University. He told of his response to the diagnosis of an incurable degenerative terminal illness:

> The realization that I had an incurable disease, that was likely to kill me in a few years was a bit of a shock. How could something like that happen to me? Why should I be cut off like this? . . . Now knowing what was going to happen to me, or how rapidly the disease would progress, I was at a loose end.
>
> My dreams at that time were rather disturbed. Before my condition had been diagnosed, I had been very bored with life. There had not seemed to be anything worth doing. But shortly after I came out of the hospital, I dreamt that I was going to be executed. I suddenly realized that there were a lot of worthwhile things I could do if I were reprieved. Another dream, that I had several times, was that I would sacrifice my life to save others. After all, if I were going to die anyway, it might as well do some good. But I didn't die. In fact, although there was a cloud hanging over my future, I found to my surprise, that I was enjoying life in the present more than before. I began to make progress with my research. (Hawking, 2011)

Terms to Learn

Belongingness and love
   needs
Esteem needs
Hierarchy of needs

Humanist theories
Needs as motivators
Peak experiences
Physiological needs

Safety needs
Self-actualization
Transcendence

Learning Activities

(Note: These may also be used as class presentations.)

- In class role-play a debate between Freud and Maslow. Remember that Maslow thought that Freud emphasized the "sick half" of human nature.
- Research the psychotherapeutic methods of Carl Rogers, and discuss the way in which Maslow's humanist theory provided the basis for Rogers's methods.
- Discuss Maslow's idea that a first-rate soup is better than second-rate poetry. Was Maslow trying to say that it is the *quality* of the work that is most important, rather than the *prestige* of the work?
- As a class share examples of "peak experiences." Interview friends and family members and ask them about their peak experiences and report these to class.
- As a class discuss this question: "What is so essential to humans that without it they would no longer be defined as humans?"

Writing Exercises

- Write a 10-page paper describing someone you know who you think has achieved self-actualization. Be sure to include both the ways in which this individual demonstrates self-actualization and how this person reached this point.
- Write a 10-page paper describing a historical figure who you think achieved self-actualization. Be sure to include both the ways in which (in your opinion) this individual demonstrated self-actualization and how this person reached self-actualization.
- Read the book *Flow: The Psychology of Optimal Experience* by Mihaly Csikszentmihaly (1991). Write a 10-page paper comparing and contrasting Maslow's concept of "peak experiences" with Csikszentmihaly's concept of "flow."
- Write a 10-page paper describing examples from your life that illustrate Maslow's hierarchy of needs.

Web Sites

http://webspace.ship.edu/cgboer/maslow.html
http://psychology.about.com/od/theoriesofpersonality/a/hierarchyneeds.htm
http://www.pbs.org/wgbh/aso/databank/entries/bhmasl.html
http://www.edpsycinteractive.org/topics/regsys/maslow.html
http://allpsych.com/personalitysynopsis/maslow.html

The Stage Model of Cognitive Moral Development: Jean Piaget and Lawrence Kohlberg

8

According to some authorities, "moral development is one of the important aspects of childhood and one of the most important responsibilities of families and societies" (Tichy, Johnson, Johnson, & Roseth, 2010, p. 765). The stage model of cognitive moral development is based on two assumptions: (1) in order to think and act morally, it is necessary to first judge or cognitively reason about the appropriateness of behaviors, and (2) the ability to reason cognitively develops in sequential stages. The most respected theorist of cognitive development of children, Jean Piaget, focused on cognitive functioning in general and learning in particular; he introduced the concept that learning takes place in stages in the child's life. As you will remember, Piaget's cognitive theories apply only to children younger than 14 years old.

Nonetheless, in addition to his theories about general cognitive development, Piaget also developed theories about two broad stages in cognitive moral reasoning. Lawrence Kohlberg, who is most widely known for his theory of moral development, was influenced by Piaget's broad stages of cognitive moral development, and subsequently expanded greatly on Piaget's stages. Kohlberg is certainly the most well-known theorist of cognitive moral development.

Cognitive Moral Reasoning

- A result of cognitive and biological functioning
- The ability to think, reason, and problem-solve

Piaget's stages of general cognitive development were related to the child's biological age; in fact, he postulated that an infant's roots of cognition were based in his or her biological abilities (1952, 1954, 1962, 1965). Cognitive moral reasoning, therefore, is a result of biological and cognitive maturation. The systematic development of moral reasoning begins in early childhood. Cognitive moral reasoning is the ability to think, judge, and reason about the appropriateness of a certain behavior. As a child matures, he or she organizes these moral principles into a more sophisticated, complex, and comprehensive structure. Logical ability is necessary in order to reason at a certain moral level or stage. Therefore, it is not possible to act morally if one does not possess the necessary cognitive ability. Strictly speaking, cognitive moral reasoning does not include emotional aspects. Cognitive moral reasoning includes only the way in which the person thinks about morality.

The Stage Theory of Cognitive Moral Development

- Qualitative changes in moral reasoning
- Kohlberg's theory covers the entire life span
- Thinking becomes more abstract, relativistic, and complex

The stage theory of cognitive moral reasoning is much like the concept of stages in other types of theories. Because a small child is not very developed cognitively, he or she has a very naïve and simplistic way of thinking, reasoning, and judging morality. As the child progresses, qualitative changes in his or her cognitive abilities allow the child to become increasingly morally sophisticated and more developed. In addition, the child's life becomes more and more morally complex, which requires more cognitive flexibility and ability. Like other stage theorists, Kohlberg thought that interrelationships between various stages are characterized by increasing differentiation and that each stage includes everything that took place at previous stages (Kohlberg, 1973, 1981). Kohlberg also thought that as individuals develop morally, they consciously choose to discard certain moral principles that they learned in the past (Kohlberg, 1984). Each succeeding stage allows more developed cognitive reasoning. Kohlberg's stage theory shows the way in which individuals develop and grow morally throughout life (Kohlberg, 1987). Although Piaget's theory of cognitive moral reasoning only included children until they were 14 years old, Kohlberg's stages covered the entire life span. Indeed, Kohlberg stated that only in adulthood do individuals have the freedom to make their own judgments and choices, while at the same time adults assume long-term responsibility for others, further expanding their moral reasoning.

Higher stages of cognitive moral reasoning require abstract thinking, the ability to coordinate more than a single idea at one time, and the capability to take the perspective of others. All of these capabilities are the result of higher levels of cognition and a broader array of both knowledge and experience. Thinking becomes more relativistic and complex, with the result that the individual is able to integrate complex and occasionally divergent pieces of information. Kohlberg postulated six stages of moral reasoning, although few individuals achieve stage six. However, in his later writing Kohlberg amended his view on stage six and stated that only a very few individuals have achieved or achieve stage six. Kohlberg named three such individuals (all historical figures): Mahatma Gandhi, Mother Teresa of Calcutta, and Dr. Martin Luther King, Jr. Instead, Kohlberg considered stage six to be a "theoretical stage." Certainly the individuals mentioned had developed their moral standards based on universal human rights.

Kohlberg's idea of hierarchical integration has been supported in empirical research. Hierarchical integration means that individuals do not lose the insights gained in earlier stages, but instead integrate these insights into broader perspectives. Therefore, each stage of cognitive moral development transcends the lower levels. Frequently individuals understand their reasoning at earlier stages, but when looking back, they think of their earlier moral reasoning as inferior and occasionally morally reprehensible.

OTHER THEORISTS' CONCEPTUALIZATION OF MORAL DEVELOPMENT

Freud thought that moral standards are the result of the unconscious, irrational motives to keep antisocial impulses from entering the individual's consciousness. Therefore, Freud generally thought moral behavior is the result of avoiding guilt. The superego keeps individuals from immoral and unethical behavior.

Learning theorists, such as Skinner, would state that morality is based on the simple use of rewards and punishment. If the individual's environment is very closely controlled, it would be possible to elicit any type of behavior through punishment and rewards.

Components of Piaget's Theory

- Moral realism (ages 5–10)
- Autonomous realism (ages 10–14)

The Swiss theorist Jean Piaget, considered children ages 2 to 5 to be *premoral.* Children in this age group do not perceive the need for rules and do not possess the cognitive ability to make moral judgments; indeed, most toddlers are unaware of rules. Piaget believed that society tolerated the misbehavior of young children because people understood that little children were not aware of rules or capable of understanding them.

Piaget used two methods to develop his ideas of cognitive moral development. First, he interviewed children and told them a series of two stories of child-like misbehaviors. After each pair of stories, Piaget asked the children, "Which outcome is the naughtiest? Why is it the naughtiest?" His second method was observing children playing a game, usually marbles. After some time watching, Piaget would ask the children if he could play with them. When he was playing, Piaget would casually ask, "What are the rules of the game? Who invented these rules? Can these rules be changed?" Piaget wrote a classic book, *The Moral Judgment of the Child* (1965), that used the results and conclusions gained from interviewing and observing children. According to Piaget, younger children think about moral dilemmas in a more simplistic way than older children do. Piaget's second stage of moral reasoning was more cognitively complex than the first stage. Thus, Piaget postulated only two stages of cognitive moral reasoning. Children younger than 10 or 12 think about the rules of morality differently than older children do.

Younger children told Piaget that the rules for marbles "just came into peoples' hands" and that "Daddies show little boys how to play." When Piaget asked a little boy why he played marbles in a certain way, the boy replied, "Because God didn't teach them any other way" (Ambron & Brodzinsky, 1979). Young children believe that rules are absolute and fixed, and no questioning is either necessary or allowed. For them, rules are handed down from God or from their parents.

THE BROKEN TEACUPS

One pair of stories involved a little boy breaking china teacups. In the first story, the boy is helping his mother clear the table and puts 15 teacups on a tray in order to carry them to the kitchen. The little boy accidentally drops the tray and breaks all 15 cups. In the second story, a boy is told not to climb on the kitchen counter to get cookies. The boy does climb up on the counter and gets a forbidden cookie, but he accidentally drags a teacup off the counter and breaks it. Piaget asked children 5 to 10 years old which story was naughtier.

The children said the little boy in the first story was naughtier. Why? According to these young children, the degree of naughtiness, was based on the *amount* of damage and not on the *intention* of the little boy. Although the first story involved an accidental breakage of the china cups by a little boy who had the good intention of helping his mother, the second story involved a little boy who broke a single cup through willful disobedience. Nonetheless, very young children considered that 15 cups had been broken in the first story and only a single cup in the second story. Therefore the first little boy was the naughtier one. In addition, Piaget concluded that children in this age group determined the severity of the punishment also based on the amount of damage done. Therefore, they believed that the boy who broke 15 cups should be punished much more severely than the boy who broke only one cup.

Children ages 5 to 10 thought of rules and morality as firmly fixed, absolute, and unchangeable. Rules are absolute authority, given by God or by parents. Therefore, rules should not be questioned or modified. Because they judge solely on consequences, children do not differentiate between accidents and intentional behavior. They see misbehavior and wrongdoing as external, something that is outside of themselves because wrong is whatever adults forbid and punish. At this stage, children often thought that wrongdoing had not occurred if the offender was not caught. Hence, if the cookie-stealing boy was able to sweep up the pieces of the broken cup and avoid getting caught, he had not done anything wrong. Children often suggest very severe and harsh punishments, viewing punishment as a way to deter rule-breaking. Piaget termed this stage *moral realism*.

When Piaget interviewed children ages 10 to 14, he found that there was a marked shift from blind obedience to rules and authority and a corresponding awareness that rules are meant to help people and that rules can be changed. In the teacup story, they judged the degree of naughtiness by the person's intentions and not by the consequences or amount of damage done. Therefore the boy who broke a single cup was naughtier, because his intentions were disobedient. These older children also proposed less severe punishments and viewed the purpose of punishment as a way to teach the offender that his or her behaviors were inappropriate. Included in punishment was the concept of restitution, with the purpose of helping the offender to understand the perspective of the individual he or she had harmed. Piaget termed this second stage *autonomous realism*.

In the stage of autonomous realism, the children often thought that the punishment should be equal (or proportional) to the harm or pain the offender had inflicted on others. Children begin to understand moral principles and the concepts of mutual respect and mutual consent. In this stage, there are cooperative, social, and logical aspects to the child's moral reasoning.

LAWRENCE KOHLBERG

Lawrence Kohlberg, who was influenced by Piaget, eventually, expanded on Piaget's theories, oftentimes using the same research method of proposing a pair of moral dilemmas and then presenting two solutions. Kohlberg also used a stage theory, and Kohlberg's stages for younger children are very similar to Piaget's. However, Kohlberg's advanced stages describe adults; therefore, Kohlberg's theory goes beyond Piaget's and is considered more complete.

Like Piaget, Kohlberg was not interested in the emotional or behavioral aspects of cognitive moral reasoning. Kohlberg never asked the children how they *felt* about these moral dilemmas, nor was he interested in their behavior. Both Piaget and Kohlberg focused on cognitive aspects, such as interpreting, reasoning, judging, and making logical comparisons.

Lawrence Kohlberg was born in 1927 in Bronxville, New York and attended Andover Academy, an exclusive boarding school that was a high school for wealthy and high-achieving students. When he graduated from Andover immediately after the end of World War II, Kohlberg became a seaman in the U.S. Merchant Marine. During this time, Kohlberg volunteered to help smuggle Jewish refugees and Holocaust survivors out of Europe to British-controlled Palestine. Because Jewish immigration to Palestine was then against British law, when Kohlberg was captured he was put into a detention camp on the island of Cyprus, from which he was rescued by the Haganah, a Jewish fighting force.

Kohlberg returned to America and began college in 1948 at the University of Chicago; however, because his scores on the admission examination were so high, he was required to take only a few courses to earn his bachelor's degree. In 1958 Kohlberg received a PhD in psychology from the University of Chicago. He taught at both Harvard and the University of Chicago. His seminal work, *Stages in the Development of Moral Thought and Action* was published in 1969.

According to Crain (1985, pp. 118–119), "Kolberg is an informal, unassuming man who is also a true scholar; he has thought long and deeply about a wide range of issues in both psychology and philosophy and has done much to help others appreciate the wisdom of many of the 'old psychologists,' such as Rousseau, John Dewey, and James Mark Baldwin." Kohlberg contracted a tropical parasite in 1971 while doing cross-cultural work in Belize. As a result, he struggled with depression and physical pain for the rest of his life. On January 19, 1987, he requested a day of leave from the Massachusetts hospital where he was being treated and reportedly committed suicide by drowning himself in Boston Harbor.

KOHLBERG'S THEORY OF COGNITIVE MORAL DEVELOPMENT

Piaget had studied poor Swiss children, but Kohlberg studied 72 boys with the same IQ, aged 10, 13, and 16, who were from upper-middle-class families. (Because Kohlberg was studying the cognitive aspects of morality, the boys had to have the same measured intelligence score to hold the important variable of intelligence constant.) Kohlberg presented the boys moral dilemmas and told them that there was no "right" or "wrong" answer. Kohlberg and his colleagues presented many different invented moral dilemmas in order to obtain a large sample of each child's reasoning; however, each dilemma had only two solutions: one solution involved obeying authority figures even when the action violated legal or social rules, and the other solution involved doing what was best for the welfare of others. After the boys had stated their choices, Kohlberg and his colleagues conducted a clinical interview in which the boys were questioned about *why* and *how* they had chosen each solution. Kohlberg was interested only in reasoning (or cognitive aspects) and not in the emotional or behavioral aspects. Kohlberg was not interested in the boys' behavior or the way they felt about these dilemmas; he was studying their reasoning. Kohlberg and his associates studied this group of boys for more than 20 years. As he expected, Kohlberg found consistent evidence that cognitive reasoning changed as the boys became older. After some professional criticism, Kohlberg eventually expanded his research to include girls, progressed to comparing popular and unpopular children, and finally interviewed children of different religions. He published two well-known books, *The Psychology of Moral Development: The Nature and Validity of Moral Stages* (1984) and *Childhood Psychology and Childhood Education: Cognitive Developmental View* (1987).

Kohlberg's Six Stages of Cognitive Moral Reasoning

- Stage One—Preconventional
- Stage Two—Instrumental purpose
- Stage Three—The "Good Boy, Good Girl" orientation
- Stage Four—The law-and-order orientation
- Stage Five—The social contract orientation
- Stage Six—Universal ethical principle orientation

Kohlberg proposed three major levels, each with two different motivations, for a total of six different stages. In each stage a person has a different approach to determining right or wrong and a different motivation for being moral (Kohlberg, 1976). Kohlberg proposed that higher stages showed more advanced and well developed cognitive reasoning and thus indicated higher levels of morality. Kohlberg found that moral development is both slow and gradual, but individuals do progress through the stages in the order that Kohlberg expected (Berk, 1998). At each level, the moral reasoning of the previous stage begins to decrease and decline. Kohlberg believed that at age 16 the individual begins to self-define morality.

Level One—Preconventional (Early School Age)

This stage is also termed the punishment and obedience orientation. Behaviors are considered good if they result in reward, but if behaviors lead to punishment, they are considered bad. Parents or other caregivers establish the rules, and fear of authority and avoidance of punishment are the motivators for acting morally.

Stage One: Preconventional Orientation

Children in this stage view morality as external, or outside themselves. Rewards and punishments are external because parents and other authority figures determine when and how much to reward or punish the child. At this stage, children are not influenced by internal feelings of conscience, guilt, or shame. The importance of behavior (or the interpretation of behavior) is simply the result of being punished or rewarded, so children are very obedience-versus-punishment oriented. Rules are fixed and cannot be changed; furthermore, rules are not to be challenged or questioned, and a small child would obviously not have the cognitive capabilities to question or challenge. At this stage children are very egocentric, meaning that they think that everyone views the world as they do. It would not be possible for a small child to consider that others have differing perspectives or interpretations of the same event. Egocentrism leads to maximizing one's own interests and validating one's choices and decisions.

Stage Two: Instrumental Purpose Orientation

Children begin to become aware that people can have different viewpoints about a moral dilemma. In this stage, the child satisfies personal needs when making moral choices and assumes that everyone else acts out of self-interest. Furthermore, children believe that everyone focuses on the pleasure motive. Reciprocity is beginning to develop in the child; however, children in this stage understand reciprocity as an equal or fair exchange of favors, such as "I'll do this for you, if you do this for me." This stage in Kohlberg's theory corresponds to Piaget's concrete operational stage.

Level Two—Conventional (Late Middle Childhood Until Age 13)

At this level, behavior is moral when it is acceptable to others. Generally, children in this level seek to avoid guilt and try to maintain the affection and approval of friends and family. The child also identifies with emotionally important individuals. Moral dilemmas in this level focused on the choice between doing something helpful for someone else or meeting one's own needs. This level is sometimes referred to as "The Letter of the Law" orientation.

Stage Three: The "Good Boy, Good Girl" Orientation

As the name implies, children in this stage follow conventions, the widely accepted standards and rules of society. Conventional people, especially children in this Kohlberg stage, think it is important to justify, maintain, and support the social structure. Because of their concern with the larger society, children in this stage are thus more sociocentric and become less egocentric. However, children continue to view morality from a two person perspective—oneself and a loved one. Children begin to understand that good behavior also involves good intentions. Kohlberg acknowledged that children must reach Piaget's formal operational level of cognition before they can engage in either the conventional stage or the one above it, postconventional reasoning.

Stage Four—The Law-and-Order Orientation

Children obey rules for their own sake. This law-and-order thinking and reasoning continues to develop until about age 13. The child reasons that everyone has a duty to follow rules and uphold the law, demonstrating that he or she has a larger perspective (rather than simply thinking of oneself). Moral choices are no longer based on close ties to others. Laws cannot be violated under any circumstance because society would break down if a large number of people broke the law. This stage in Kohlberg corresponds to Piaget's formal operational stage. Kohlberg found that most adolescent boys were at Stage Four.

Level III — Postconventional Morality (Late Adolescence Until Early Adulthood)

As the name implies, teenagers and young adults move beyond unquestioning obedience of the laws and rules of society. They begin to define morality in more abstract terms and support values that apply to all humans. Moral dilemmas in this stage were based on asking the individual to violate a law or break a promise in order to achieve some other goal, thus placing justice in conflict with rules, laws, and authority figures. People do not obey the law because they are required to but because they want to. This level is often referred to as the "Conscience and Principle Orientation." Those at this stage act morally because they want to avoid self-condemnation.

Stage Five — The Social Contract Orientation

Individuals in this stage can see that rules and law exist to serve human purposes and are therefore flexible and subject to change. The social contract orientation means that each individual is a free and willing participant in devising rules and laws and in agreeing to uphold them. Rules are based on the need to protect the rights of individuals and the needs of the majority. Individuals in late adolescence begin to self-define morality and question their parents' systems of morality instead of blindly accepting them. The individual also seeks to avoid lapses in self-defined morality.

Stage Six — Universal Ethical Principle Orientation

Principles that serve all of humanity are the guiding force for this stage. However, later in his career Kohlberg questioned whether most individuals moved beyond stage five.

MORAL DILEMMA: HEINZ STEALS A DRUG

The most well-known moral dilemma Kohlberg created and used in his research is called "Heinz Steals a Drug." Most developmental textbooks use Heinz's story to illustrate each of the six stages of Kohlberg's theory.

> In Europe, a woman was near death from a special kind of cancer. There was one drug that the doctors think might save her. It was a form of radium that a druggist in the same town had recently discovered. The drug was expensive to make, but the druggist was charging ten times what the drug cost him to make. He paid $200 for the radium and charged $2,000 for a small dose of the drug. The sick woman's husband, Heinz, went to everybody he knew to borrow the money, but he could only get together about $1,000 which is half of what it cost. He told the druggist that his wife was dying and asked him to sell it cheaper or let him pay later. But the druggist said, "No, I discovered the drug and I'm going to make money from it." So Heinz got desperate and broke into

the man's store to steal the drug for his wife. Should the husband have done that? (Kohlberg, 1973, p. 19)

Because this is a story invented for research and interviewing purposes, we will naturally not question the rather remarkable coincidence that the one druggist who invented the cure for Mrs. Heinz's cancer just happens to live in the same town as Mr. and Mrs. Heinz. The story is also arranged to show that Heinz has exhausted every possible honest way to obtain the drug, such as asking to borrow the money and asking the druggist to delay payment. The drug is important because someone's life is at stake. The druggist is shown to be a somewhat morally dubious character because he openly states that his motive is to make money. Kohlberg knew that it was important to include these details in order to make the story truly a moral problem. "The hypothetical case of Heinz shows pits two legal norms, the right to life, and the right to property are in conflict" (Keller, 2006, p. 171). The respondent is given a forced choice, steal the drug or allow Mrs. Heinz to die. Respondents are not permitted to offer other solutions in spite of the fact that a wide range of solutions could be determined.

A child in *Stage One* who says that Heinz *should steal* the drug typically reasons that the drug only costs $200. However, the overwhelming majority of children in Stage One reason that Heinz should not steal the drug. A child in Stage One who says that Heinz *should not steal* the drug would reason that stealing is a crime. It can be seen that whether they answer yes or no, children are concerned with authority figures and what they will or will not allow. Punishment is thought to be tied to an absolute concept of wrong.

A child in *Stage Two* who says that Heinz *should steal* the drug would reason that Heinz really doesn't want to steal anything, but he is forced to steal in order to save his wife's life. A child in Stage Two who says that Heinz *should not steal* the drug would reason that, regardless of the druggist's motivation, the drug is his invention and he has the right to make money. One boy stated that Heinz should not steal the drug because after his wife died, Heinz would be free to marry someone younger and better-looking. Several boys stated that Heinz should not take the drug because he would end up in prison for many years. Regardless of whether they think Heinz should steal, children in Stage Two are concerned with self-interest and consider punishment a risk to be avoided.

A child in *Stage Three* who says that Heinz *should steal* the drug would reason that Heinz is stealing because he loves his wife; indeed, it would be wrong not to steal the drug because that would show that Heinz did not really love his wife. A child in Stage Three who says that Heinz *should not* steal the drug would reason that no one would blame Heinz if his wife died. Instead, everyone would blame the heartless druggist. Children in Stage Three dichotomize the motives of Heinz and the druggist. Heinz's motives are good; the druggist's motives are selfish, greedy, and self-interested. Some children volunteered that the druggist should be put in jail.

A teenager in *Stage Four* who says that Heinz *should steal* the drug would reason that simply doing nothing would be allowing his wife to die. Heinz is obligated to steal the drug; however, he could always repay the druggist later. The teenager in Stage Four who says that Heinz *should not steal* the drug would say that it is absolutely wrong to steal. Although it is understandable that Heinz would like to save his wife's life, it is still wrong to steal. Teenagers in Stage Four have shifted their perspective from the egocentric views of their childhood to a concern with society as a whole. Because laws function for the good of society, stealing the drug harms not only the druggist but the entire society. In contrast, young children in Stage One reason that it wrong to break the law; their only rationale is that someone in authority says it is wrong.

The individual in *Stage Five* who says that Heinz *should steal* the drug would reason that the law against stealing does not take into account Heinz's circumstances. Taking the drug is not legal, but is justified. The individual in Stage Five who says Heinz *should not steal* the drug would reason that the ends do not justify the means. Saving a life (the end) does not justify stealing (the means). If everyone stole (or broke other laws) whenever he or she thought it was justified, then society would break down. Kohlberg considered the reasoning of Stage Five to be "prior-to-society" reasoning (Colby et al., 1983, p. 22). Individuals in this stage evaluate the laws of their society, theoretically considering the rights and values a society should endorse. Would a good society punish a man who stole in order to save a life? Society is formed by a social contract; individuals enter into it freely and it protects the welfare of all individuals, including poverty-stricken dying individuals. One young man answered: "It is the husband's duty to save his wife. The fact that her life is in danger transcends every other standard you might use to judge his action. Life is more important than property." This young man continued to say that Heinz should steal to save a life of a stranger because the value of a life means any life (Kohlberg, 1976, p. 78). As can be seen, individuals in stage five tend to be more independent thinkers. Although children in the first stages of moral reasoning tend to think in terms of what society is, teenagers and adults in the higher stages tend to think in terms of what society should be.

The individual in *Stage Six* who says that Heinz *should steal* the drug would reason that Heinz's circumstances have forced him to choose between stealing and allowing his wife to die. Although this is a very rare occurrence, certainly the value of a life is more important than violating a law. The individual in *Stage Six* who says that Heinz *should not steal* the drug would reason that others might need the drug just as much as Heinz's wife does. Heinz must consider the value of these other lives. The mode of moral reasoning in this stage is to acknowledge the importance of individual rights but simultaneously use democratic processes to settle differences.

According to Kohlberg, the highest level of moral reasoning requires individuals to see the viewpoints or perspectives of others. In the Heinz story, the druggist would see that he should give the drug to Heinz because the druggist can understand Heinz's predicament. One day the druggist might also find himself in a situation in which his life was endangered because another person valued money and personal gain.

Stages five and six sound much like the principles of civil disobedience, and Kohlberg would agree. Justice is regarded as a higher principle than obedience to a law. Perhaps Kohlberg's experience as an 18-year-old in assisting Jewish refugees to immigrate to Israel shaped his theory.

FACILITATING HIGHER LEVELS OF COGNITIVE MORAL REASONING

Kohlberg proposed that certain child-rearing practices and school environments can promote higher levels of cognitive moral reasoning in children. If parents and teachers are aware of the developmental stages of morality, they can help young people move to higher levels. Both Piaget and Kohlberg thought that the higher the cognitive level of the individual, the more advanced his or her moral reasoning becomes. Therefore, Kohlberg thought higher levels intelligence, a great deal of education, the ability to think abstractly and consider the motives and feelings of others, and diversified social experiences are all positively correlated with higher levels of cognitive reasoning. Remember that Kohlberg was interested only in cognitive moral reasoning and not moral behavior.

Parents can teach higher moral reasoning by providing a home that is democratic, warm, and loving. Instead of just being punished for breaking rules, children are allowed some input into the rules of the home or are at least told the rationale behind the rules. Schools that provide students with rule-making opportunities help students to understand that autonomous rules are the products of cooperative agreements.

Children can be helped to learn moral reasoning when the parents or teachers help children to understand the feelings and viewpoints of others, to question their motives of their own behaviors, and to reflect on the consequences of their actions. Simply helping children to understand and interpret their problems and conflicts (or the problems of characters on television or the movies) will assist children in moving to the next stage of moral reasoning. Listening without lecturing and asking clarifying questions provide a template for higher levels of moral reasoning. When answers are not readily available, children can be taught to question assumptions and rules. For small children the world is relatively small and not very complex morally; however, as children become teenagers they are exposed to a broader social context and more ambiguous situations. Thought-provoking discussions and volunteer work in the community provide a larger social world while also demonstrating that the motivations and moral reasoning at Kohlberg's lower stages are no longer appropriate. These experiences help the individual's thinking to become more complex and relativist. For example, teenagers begin to view Heinz as not all good and the druggist as not all bad.

Enlarging the social and educational world of teenagers often includes the loosening of family ties, the acquisition of a college education, and social relationships with a widening group of diverse individuals. All these experiences stimulate moral reasoning because they present moral questions that the teenagers have not previously confronted. Obviously it is not necessary to totally abandon one's childhood moral code; it is necessary to examine and evaluate childhood moral codes and methods of reasoning. Kohlberg also suggested that moral exemplars often demonstrate the cognitive moral reasoning of higher stages, so that others can use these individuals as role models to advance to higher levels.

According to Kohlberg, awareness and appreciation of social diversity are associated with higher levels of cognitive moral reasoning (Snarey & Kello, 1991). Most individuals feel empathy or understand the viewpoint of those with whom they identify and closely associate. In contrast, it is more difficult to feel empathy for or appreciate the perspective of those they consider very different from themselves. By simply expanding our world, we therefore learn other perspectives and higher levels of cognitive moral reasoning. Kohlberg stated that higher levels of moral reasoning in adulthood are closely linked to a wide range of experience. Kohlberg stated that individuals with higher levels of moral cognitive reason were able to deal more constructively with significant losses in their lives, such as divorce or the death of a loved one.

EVALUATION OF KOHLBERG

Without doubt, Kohlberg and his theories have had a major impact on theories of development, have contributed to the thinking about moral development, and have stimulated a great deal of research. Nevertheless, Kohlberg and his theory have been criticized. Kohlberg responded to some of these criticisms, amending or adding to his theories. These criticisms are:

- Moral cognitive reasoning does not always result in moral behavior.
- Kohlberg's theory is often considered to be elitist because it emphasizes higher intelligence, college education, and a wealth of social experience as precursors to more advanced moral reasoning.
- Kohlberg's research methods are considered simplistic and unrealistic because of his reliance on simple either-or dilemmas. Both Piaget and Kohlberg were criticized for characterizing small children as "little moral philosophers."
- Kohlberg's theory is thought to be male oriented.
- Although Kohlberg insisted that his theory applied to other cultures, others believe that Kohlberg's theory applies only to urban, middle-class, Western societies.

The critics have a basis to question the association between reasoning and action. For example, all schoolchildren know that it is unethical to cheat in school, but some children do cheat. All teenagers and adults understand that it is both illegal and dangerous to speed on the highways, but many do speed. Also, Kohlberg's theory does not take into account the individual's emotions (such as guilt or empathy) nor does it include the individual's history and past experiences. Both emotion and past experience are thought to be powerful determinants of cognitive reasoning, but Kohlberg did not consider these factors. Toward the end of his life, Kohlberg developed a participatory democracy program for use in the classroom, attempting to bridge the gap between moral reasoning and moral action.

Kohlberg's theory is considered individualistic, because only individuals are questioned about these moral dilemmas. As individuals become older, they frequently solve moral dilemmas through group discussions. Some cognitive development researchers state:

> Kohlberg's (and Piaget's) theories are considered individualistic because each individual is presented with a moral dilemma and asked to respond without discussion with anyone. Recent research suggests that "constructive controversy" in which moral dilemmas are resolved by listening to the discussion and conclusions of others, thus gaining more information and the insights of others, resulting in better quality decisions. (Tichy et al., 2010, p. 767)

Kohlberg asserted that his theory was culturally universal, and studies were conducted in India, Turkey, and Israel. However, moral reasoning was more advanced in Turkish metropolitan areas than in remote, non-technological Turkish villages. For example, Kohlberg concluded that in Turkey, "individuals in technological societies and urban settings moved through Kohlberg's stages more quickly and advanced to higher levels than people from isolated villages or non-technological societies"

(Gormly, p. 271). Kohlberg argued that although cultural beliefs varied, the process of cognitive moral reasoning was basically identical in all cultures and that the overall moral development of people in other cultures parallels the maturation of American children. His critics stated that Kohlberg's methods did not capture or show evidence of higher moral reasoning in non-Western cultures (Keller, Edelstein, Krettenauer, Fang, & Fang, 2005). It was not because individuals did not reason at higher levels but because Kohlberg's measuring instruments were not sensitive enough to show this. Because systems of logic are so different between cultures, it is not possible to generalize Kohlberg's theory to non-Western cultures. The following examples demonstrate the ways in which important research variables (in this case definitions of moral reasoning) often are not equivalent in different cultures:

> [Asian] Indians perceived interpersonal responsibilities as duties, while US Americans saw them as more voluntary. Similarly in reasoning about moral dilemmas, Chinese people frequently mentioned issues of interpersonal welfare and mutual benevolence which, in more elaborate forms, could not be captured in Kohlberg's theory (Keller, 2006, p. 176).
>
> [In Keller et al., 2005], we interpreted this finding that close friendship is a more dominant value with the Icelandic youth than it is for the Chinese.... This again indicates that the Chinese experience interpersonal obligations stronger than Icelanders. They never were "happy victimizers," but always "unhappy moralists (Oser & Reichenbach, 2005), living up to the expectations of others." (Keller, 2006, p. 186)

The most forceful and widespread criticism of Kohlberg's theory was based on its perceived gender bias (Ryan, David, & Reynolds, 2004). Specifically, Carol Gilligan of Harvard University stated that Kohlberg's theory was based on the masculine values of individualization, impersonality, and justice. Gilligan described Kohlberg's theory as "utopian, outdated, impractical . . . the outworn philosophies of hippies" (Gillian, 1987, p. 75). The fact that Kohlberg had initially studied only boys and men does lend some credibility to this criticism.

Gilligan argued that girls and women use different perspectives in defining morality (Gilligan, 1977; 1982). Although not all moral dilemmas pit justice against caring, men typically choose justice and women choose caring in a choice between justice and caring. When dilemmas focus on justice alone, women reason on the principle of justice.

Gilligan stated that girls and boys are socialized differently. Girls are taught to show concern for the feelings, rights, and welfare of others, but boys are taught to be fair and obedient to abstract principles. According to these critics, Kohlberg's theory would obviously not be useful in cultures and societies with well-defined gender roles. Because of the emphasis upon caring for others, the social distance between the self and the other is an important determinant of moral reasoning for women, but the type of relationship is not as important for men who base their morality on principles of justice and fairness. According to Gilligan, women tend to care more about others who are close to them, and men tend to use the same justice orientation toward everybody. Some research has supported Gilligan's male–female orientations toward moral reasoning (Galotti, Kozberg, & Farmer, 1991; Garmon et al., 1996).

Gilligan proposed three main stages of cognitive moral reasoning for girls: (1) concern for self and survival, (2) concern for being responsible and caring for others, and (3) concern for the consequences for all individuals. Gilligan and Kohlberg engaged in debate, and they had begun to address these criticisms (Kohlberg & Gilligan, 1971).

APPLICATION TO PEOPLE WITH DISABILITIES

Some real-life conflicts often require moral reasoning below the individual's actual capacity, but other conflicts require moral reasoning above the individual's capacity. Each individual draws on a range of moral reasoning responses that vary with the context. Kohlberg stated that child-rearing practices and the degree of diversity to which children are exposed influence individual cognitive reasoning.

Individuals with intellectual disabilities present challenges to moral reasoning, simply because of their lowered cognitive abilities. A greater challenge to cognitive moral reasoning, however, is the lack of experience of most people without disabilities (PWODs). As we shall read throughout this book, the social distance between people with disabilities (PWDs) and PWODs is often great, so that many PWODs believe that PWDs are not fully human or like normal people. Does this lack of first-hand experience and these false beliefs affect the way in which PWODs resolve moral dilemmas that involve PWDs?

Because Kohlberg's moral dilemmas were developed in the 1960s, they are somewhat dated and obsolete. For example, the case of Heinz and the drug involves a life and death situation. Throughout this book, we shall learn that disabilities are chronic, lifelong conditions. Therefore, the dichotomy of life and total cure or death without a cure does not apply to PWDs. Hypothetical moral dilemmas could be constructed that feature PWDs. The next section presents a brief list.

Moral Dilemmas of Disability

- Should a fetus with severe and multiple disabilities be allowed to be born? What about the lifelong financial costs of raising this child?
- Should individuals with an invisible disability (for example, a psychiatric disability) disclose their disability? What are the costs of disclosure and what are the benefits? What if they knew they would not get a job or a promotion if the psychiatric disability was disclosed?
- Should society pay the costs to educate a child with a disability when public funds are very scarce?

While reading about Heinz's dilemma throughout the years, I have never seen a solution that asked Mrs. Heinz what *she* wanted. I have wondered why no one ever thinks to ask Mrs. Heinz. Perhaps she would not want Mr. Heinz to go to prison or does not want him to steal for some other reason. PWDs would consider Heinz's failure to ask his wife paternalism and a violation of her rights to self-determination.

Direct experience with PWDs would clearly change one's attitude toward these dilemmas. For example, many parents of children with disabilities become active, effective advocates on moral dilemmas such as ones listed above.

Terms to Learn

Autonomous realism
Cognitive moral reasoning
Hierarchical integration
Moral realism
Stage One—preconventional

Stage Two—the instrumental purpose orientation
Stage Three—the "Good Boy, Good Girl" orientation

Stage Four—the law-and-order orientation
Stage Five—the social contract orientation
Stage Six—the universal ethical principle orientation

Video to View

- View the video *Kohlberg's Moral Developmental Stages,* available from Symptom Media: Visual Learning for Behavioral Health. The video presents Lawrence Kohlberg's stage theory about morality. Vignettes play out various conflicts within stages of human development.

Learning Activities

(Note: These may also be used as class presentations.)
- Devise hypothetical moral dilemmas that involve PWDs. As a class, discuss the criteria you would use to create a scoring protocol for determing the level of moral reasoning.
- Discuss the ways in which higher levels of cognitive moral reasoning can be facilitated both at home and in school.

Writing Exercises

- Kohlberg thought that very few individuals reach the level of stage six, naming a few historical individuals such as Mahatma Gandhi, Mother Teresa of Calcutta, and Dr. Martin Luther King, Jr. Write a five-page paper that disputes this view.
- Write a 10-page autobiography that describes the development of your moral reasoning. In what ways does your life support Piaget's and Kohlberg's stages of moral reasoning? How does your life differ from these theories?
- Write a five-page paper in which you argue that Kohlberg was an elitist. Write another five-page paper in which you argue that Kohlberg's theories are culturally relevant.

Web Sites

http://webspace.ship.edu/cgboer/maslow.html
http://psychology.about.com/od/theoriesofpersonality/a/hierarchyneeds.htm
http://www.pbs.org/wgbh/aso/databank/entries/bhmasl.html
http://www.edpsycinteractive.org/topics/regsys/maslow.html
http://allpsych.com/personalitysynopsis/maslow.html

The Experience of Disability

Understanding Disability

9

The purpose of this chapter is to promote a basic understanding of the broad scope of disability. The definitions, listing, and categorization of disabilities provided here give only a minimal broad overview of disabilities.

Defining disability is complex, because it is not limited to the medical and biological aspects of the condition (Barnes, Mercer, & Shakespeare, 1999; Brown, 1991; Smart, 2004, 2005a, 2005b, 2006, 2007; Smart & Smart, 2007, 2008; Walkup, 2000; Zola, 1993). Most individuals with little or no experience with disability generally think of disability only in terms of physical disabilities (such as orthopedic impairments, amputations, or limb deficiencies) or sensory losses (such as blindness, deafness, or both). The popular media often perpetuate and reinforce these misconceptions in movies, books, and television (Mirzoeff, 1997; Norden, 1994; Safran, 1998; Zola, 1983, 1985). These media tend to focus on presenting only those individuals with disabilities who have accomplished remarkable tasks, such as Eric Weihenmayer, a blind man who climbed Mt. Everest (2001); Helen Keller, who became a worldwide celebrity while deaf and blind (Herman, 1998); or Christopher Reeve, a movie actor who became a public advocate for those with quadriplegia (Reeve, 1998). Although all of these individuals obviously had severe disabilities, they also had a great many resources to manage their disability—far more than most people with disabilities (PWDs). Furthermore, most of the disabled heroes developed their skills or celebrity before they acquired a disability. Weihenmayer climbed mountains as a child and teenager, and Christopher Reeve was a famous movie actor. Even Helen Keller had the remarkable resource of a full-time companion, Annie Sullivan, for 47 years (Brueggemann & Burch, 2007). When we consider Helen Keller's case, we realize that most people without disabilities (PWODs) could not name another deaf/blind individual.

Disability also includes cognitive disabilities and psychiatric disabilities. Cognitive disabilities include intellectual disability, learning disabilities (LD), and developmental disabilities, such as autism. Psychiatric disabilities include all types of mental illness, alcoholism, and other forms of chemical and substance abuse. Many disabilities are not visible; therefore, it is not possible simply to look at a person and to tell if the person has a disability or whether the disability is severe. The degree of visibility is not correlated with the degree of severity (Smart, 2009). A very severe and limiting disability can be invisible, and a very visible disability may not limit the individual to any great extent.

THE UNWARRANTED FEAR THAT PWDs PROVOKE IN PWODs

There are medical and biological realities to all disabilities; all disabilities include functional losses and limitations, they require management and control, and many are expensive. However, most PWDs and their families state that their greatest difficulty is responding to the prejudice, discrimination, unnecessary limitations, and lowered expectations of the general society (Davis, 1997, 2010; Scotch, 1984). For most PWDs the greatest barriers are those imposed by society. No one seeks to acquire a disability or have a child with a disability, but many PWDs nevertheless state that there are positive aspects to the disability, that they are proud of their mastery of the disability, and that their experience of disability is not an unending tragedy. For example, in a Gallup poll 42% of the respondents agreed that "blindness is the worst thing that can happen" (The Lighthouse, 1995). Dr. Geerat Vermeiji, an evolutionary biologist and a professor at the University of California at Davis, has been blind since early childhood. In his book *Privileged Hands* (1997), Vermeiji explains how uninformed and naïve but widely held perceptions of blindness contribute to society's fear of it:

> Yet opinion polls almost unanimously portray blindness as the most feared of human conditions. Sight is *perceived* as the means by which we gain the bulk of our information about one another and about our surroundings. Accordingly, educators have built curricula almost entirely on a foundation of visual learning. For this reason, blind people are widely regarded as being incapable of learning or interacting fully with others. Skeptics despair that blind people cannot see facial expression, cannot witness a baby's first tentative steps, cannot respond to a smile, cannot see how others behave. Without such quintessentially visual experience, the argument goes, the blind are denied a basic dimension of what it means to be human. Naively, [they] fear or loathe blindness. (p. 16)

Those PWDs who have reached transcendence, the highest stage of acceptance of disability (Vash 1981), often feel that they are better people because of their disability, wish to assist others with the same type of disability, and feel that they have had opportunities and experiences that would not have been open to them if they did not have the disability.

Perhaps the combination of lack of knowledge about the experience of disability and the uncomfortable feelings that disability arouses in most PWODs leads them to see PWDs as one of two stereotyped opposites: a heroic or a pathetic PWD. Neither stereotype allows the PWD to be seen as an individual, and both are extreme roles, prompted by the intense discomfort of PWODs (Elliot, Frank, Corcoran, Beardon, & Byrd, 1990).

PWDs often provoke anxiety in PWODs because PWDs remind them that it is possibile (perhaps even probable) that they will acquire a disability. Paul Longmore (2003) described this fear:

> Disability happens around us more often than we generally recognize or care to notice, and we harbor unspoken anxieties about the possibility of disablement to us, or someone close to us. What we fear, we often stigmatize and shun. (p. 32)

Heinemann and Rawal (2005) stated,

Spinal cord injury resulting in permanent paralysis and loss of sensation would seem to be one of the most devastating experiences imaginable. Emptying one's bladder with a catheter, using a wheelchair, having difficulty entering one's home and public buildings, being unable to participate in enjoyed activities, and disrupted sexual expression may seem to the outsider like a life not worth living....People who sustain SCI [spinal cord injury] do live independent lives and fulfilling lives. (p. 610)

Despite the general feelings about blindness, Kleege, a university professor who is blind, worries about "Normals," and feels that "they need a lot of help."

I worried about a lot of them so much, the Normals I know. If some of them never became disabled...it will be a bad business. If they could just let go of the fear, I think, I have fear, too. I am afraid of losing my hearing. But I know that if or when it happens, I'll make do somehow. Making do is not such a foreign concept to me. For the Normals, making do is dreadful even to contemplate. What would life be without a leg, without eyesight, without hearing, they worry. Life would be life...I say. Flawed and limited in some ways, rich and various in others.

I don't enjoy feeling like we [PWDs] exist to offer illuminating insights to the Normals. But in my more generous moments (few and far between as they are), I feel like it's something worth doing. They [Normals] need a lot of help. (Kleege, 2006, p. 182)

Most PWDs report that the most limiting aspects of their disability have nothing to do with the disability itself; it is instead social conditions, such as lack of accommodations and other civil rights, and the inaccurate perceptions of PWODs that unnecessarily limit the lives of PWDs. Moreover, if "society" has constructed these limitations, then it seems logical that society can also deconstruct, or at minimum, greatly reduce these limitations (Higgins, 1992a, p. 6). Madeline Will (as cited in Weisgerber, 1991), former assistant secretary for education and head of the Office of Special Education and Rehabilitation (OSER), stated:

Most disabled people...will tell you that despite what everyone thinks, the disability itself is not what makes everything different. What causes the disabilities is the attitudes society has about being disabled, attitudes that make a disabled person embarrassed, insecure, uncomfortable, dependent. Of course, disabled people rarely talk about the quality of life. But it is has precious little to do with deformity and a great deal to do with society's own defects. (p. 6)

PEOPLE MEET MY DISABILITY BEFORE THEY MEET ME

PWDs do not define themselves primarily as persons with a disability, nor do PWDs view the disability as the most important part of their self-identity. Although the disability is an important part of the individual's identity, like everyone else PWDs define themselves by multiple roles and functions (Fine & Asch, 1988a, 1988b, 1988c). PWODs, in contrast, often view a PWD as only the disability, as shown by the words they use—a quad, a schizophrenic, "the blind guy," or "the woman in the wheelchair." Nothing else about the PWD is recognized or acknowledged; the disability is the PWD's "master status." Thus the PWD is always viewed as the "other," "someone who is not like us." As one woman with a disability explained, "people meet the disability before they meet you" (National Public Radio, 1998a. "Inventing the Poster Child"), and another PWD stated that "you want to be yourself and the world wants you to be the disability" (National Public Radio, 1998a, "Inventing the Poster Child"). PWODs often think that every thought and behavior of the PWD is a direct result of the disability, thus ascribing much more importance to the disability than the PWDs do.

PWDs do not view themselves as heroes or pathetic cripples, and they often resent when PWODs describe them in these two ways. Especially insulting to PWDs is the label of "hero" or judgments such as "I don't know how you do it" or "I know I couldn't handle your disability." Occasionally, professionals who work with PWDs are told, "God bless you for doing this work." Even though all of these judgments are well-intentioned, they are often insulting and demeaning to the PWD to whom they are addressed. Such perceptions do not allow the PWD to be an ordinary person with a full range of characteristics and instead communicate to the PWD that he or she is viewed only as the disability. These perceptions are not accurate because most PWODs do not understand the experience of the disability or the demands in responding to the disability. When PWODs view the PWD as a pathetic cripple who is an object of pity, sympathy, and charity, they are most often well-intentioned, but PWDs resent these attitudes. The only role for the pathetic cripple is to be a recipient; the PWD is not viewed as a contributor. These false perceptions are seen in the accounts of many individuals with a visible physical disability who report that when they were shopping at a mall, strangers try to give them cash.

Categorizing Disabilities

- Categorization according to symptoms, not causes
- Three broad categories:
  - Physical
  - Cognitive
  - Psychiatric

Most PWODs would be surprised to learn that the most common disability in the United States is arthritis (U.S. Census, 2006). Perhaps because arthritis is a chronic illness, the general public does not recognize it as a disability, but individuals with such chronic illnesses compose a large segment of the disability population. Traumatic injuries may often result in disabilities, but not always. Following medical stabilization some individuals are restored to complete functioning, while others survive with a lifelong disability.

TABLE 9.1

Prevalence of Disability Among Non-Institutionalized People of All Ages in the United States in 2008*

Disability type	Percent	MOE	Number	MOE	Base population	Sample size
Any disability	12.1	0.05	36,169,200	157,070	299,852,800	2,949,415
Visual	2.3	0.02	6,826,400	71,880	299,852,800	2,949,415
Hearing	3.5	0.03	10,393,100	88,160	299,852,800	2,949,415
Ambulatory	6.9	0.04	19,203,700	118,020	278,976,400	2,770,321
Cognitive	4.8	0.04	13,462,900	99,810	278,976,400	2,770,321
Self-Care	2.6	0.03	7,195,600	73,750	278,976,400	2,770,321
Independent living	5.5	0.04	13,179,300	98,800	238,826,000	2,384,789

* Children under the age of five were only asked about vision and hearing disabilities. The independent living disability question was only asked of persons aged 16 years old and older. MOE, margin of error.
Source: http://www.ilr.cornell.edu/edi/DisabilityStatistics/reports/report.cfm?fips=2000000&subButton=Get+ HTML#prev-all.

CATEGORIZATION OF DISABILITES

Categorization of disabilities is usually based on the symptoms and rarely on the causes. The etiology is the cause of the disability, and for many disabilities the cause is unknown or there are multiple causes. There are thus three general categories of disability: physical disabilities, cognitive disabilities, and psychiatric disabilities. Those with physical disabilities exhibit physical symptoms, those with cognitive disabilities experience cognitive symptoms, and those with psychiatric disabilities experience psychiatric symptoms. If disabilities were categorized by cause, however, everyone with a disability would have a physical disability because all types of disabilities, including psychiatric disabilities, have physical causes. Nor does this categorization system correlate with some major diagnostic manuals. For example the *Diagnostic and Statistical Manual of Mental Disorders,* published by the American Psychiatric Association (2000), includes both psychiatric disabilities and cognitive disabilities. This makes sense because psychologists and psychiatrists serve individuals who have cognitive or psychiatric disabilities (see Table 9.1).

Physical Disabilities

- Blindness and vision loss
- Hearing loss and deafness
- Dual sensory loss: deafness/blindness
- Mobility impairments
  - Autoimmune diseases
  - Cerebral palsy
  - Spina bifida
  - Muscular dystrophies
- Chronic illness and health disorders
- Disfigurements

Physical disabilities include mobility impairments; sensory loss, such as blindness and/or deafness; neurologic impairments, such as cerebral palsy (CP) and seizure disorders; traumatic brain injury (TBI); and musculoskeletal conditions, such as muscular dystrophy and arthritis. Physical disabilities are frequently diagnosed with the use of standardized, objective, quantifiable laboratory procedures, such as blood tests, magnetic imaging, and X-rays. For many disabilities, there are standardized levels of severity: for example mild hearing loss, moderate hearing loss, and severe hearing loss. Each of these levels of severity is based on the loss of a specific number of decibels of hearing (standardized), and different audiologists would arrive at the same diagnosis (objective).

Blindness and Vision Loss

Visual impairments include total blindness from birth; the gradual loss of vision, such as retinitis pigmentosa (RP); muscular disorders, such as strabismus or "crossed eyes"; and loss of acuity across the visual field, such as tunnel vision (Rosenthal & Cole, 2005). People who wear eyeglasses or contacts are not considered to have a visual impairment and are not protected under the Americans with Disabilities Act (ADA) because the provision of widely used and easily obtainable adaptive technology (eyeglasses and contacts) restores the individual to full functioning. Indeed, testing for vision loss takes into account the individual's best corrected vision.

The age distribution of vision loss is different from that of other types of disabilities (Table 9.2). Blindness and severe vision loss typically occur either at the beginning of life (before age one) or at the end of life. It is estimated that 60% of all visual impairments occur before the age of one. More than 100,000 Americans have RP, a degenerative disease that destroys the center of the retina and for which there is no cure. Most individuals with RP are blind by the age of 40. Relatively speaking, few individuals become blind in middle age. By the year 2030, an estimated 6.3 million Americans will have some form of macular degeneration, which results in blindness or vision loss (Brain Awareness Week, 2001). Macular degeneration is most common among elderly people.

Another interesting aspect of blindness is that it is considered the disability with the least stigma. The PWODs in the general public typically do not blame individuals for their blindness and, mistakenly think that they understand blindness. Finally, blindness is a disability for which there are objective and standardized diagnostic procedures that include measuring visual acuity. The best estimate of the number of Americans

TABLE 9.2

Percentage of Americans With Vision Loss by Age

Age	Percentage of Americans with vision loss (%)
18–44 years	5.40
45–64 years	12.20
65–74 years	13.60
75 years and over	21.70

Source: CDC.

(of all ages) with visual impairments is 1.5 million, although disability demographers caution that vision impairments are underreported.

A large percentage of visual impairments have no known cause. Degenerative conditions affecting the retina or optic nerve include RP, retinal detachment, and glaucoma. Vision loss may be caused by genetic factors such as malformation of the eye, or it may be acquired from infections, accidents, or tumors.

Presently, there is a larger percentage of individuals with vision impairments than ever before in the United States. However, advances in medicine, especially neonatal medicine, have greatly reduced the number of infants born with blindness. The answer to the puzzle is that there is a larger percentage of elderly people in the American population, among whom vision loss is quite common. Vision loss is a secondary condition of diabetes, a condition that affects millions of Americans. Macular degeneration, another common disability among older individuals, causes blindness.

Two factors have been eliminated that formerly contributed to the high number of infants who were born blind. These two factors are maternal rubella (a pregnant woman contracting German measles) and excess oxygen administered to premature infants, which resulted in retrolental fibroplasias. There is now a rubella vaccine, and incubators developed in the 1960s control the amount of oxygen given to infants. However, many adults born before 1960 are blind because these medical innovations were not available.

Individuals with severe vision loss cannot learn by observation or demonstration, and those with congenital blindness have no memory or visual experiences of such concepts as color, distance, depth, or proportion. Falvo (1991) explained:

> [Individuals who have congenital blindness] because of their lack of visual experience in the environment, such as the observation of tasks or behaviors of others…must learn by other means concepts that sighted individuals often take for granted. This adaptive learning of tasks then becomes a natural part of their developmental process so that the adjustment to visual limitations is incorporated into their self-perception and daily activities as a normal part of growing up. Individuals who lose their vision later in life have the advantage of being able to draw on visual experiences in the environment as a frame of reference for physical concepts, but they may find it more difficult to accept their blindness than those who have never had vision. (p. 255)

Erik Weihenmayer, the blind man who climbed Mt. Everest, became totally blind as a teenager as a result of a degenerative condition. He was a skilled, experienced climber before he became blind. Because his blindness resulted from gradual degeneration, he also had time to adapt to and accept his eventual blindness. Interestingly, his blindness proved to be an asset on Everest because he was highly skilled at night climbing (unlike his sighted companions), and his keen sense of touch and hearing alerted him to the presence of crevasses. Weihenmayer could "feel" snow that sounded hollow. The one adaptation to his blindness that was not available when he was climbing was his well-developed sense of touch, because he had to wear gloves. This description of Weihenmayer's assets and compensations does not mean that it is easier to climb mountains when one is blind. It does mean that his team of climbing companions assisted him, especially when vision was required, but Weihenmayer also contributed to the climb, using abilities that his sighted companions did not have. Incidentally, one of the greatest contributions Weihenmayer provided his sighted climbing companions was funding and sponsorship. The National Federation of the Blind and the Glaucoma Society have funded many of Weihenmayer's climbing expeditions.

Interestingly, the head of the biomechanics group at the Massachusetts Institute of Technology, Hugh Herr, lost both of his legs at age 17 in a mountain climbing accident. In a book named *Design Meets Disability* (Pullin, 2009), Herr's disability is considered to be such an advantage that other climbers want to have him disqualified from competitions:

> As he came to terms with his disability, his prostheses became an important part of his self-image. But he still thought of himself as a climber, not an amputee. He fashioned himself climbing prostheses that gave him a foothold where others couldn't even gain a fingerhold, and telescopic legs that could be extended during a climb to any length, shorter or longer than his original legs—even each leg a different length. Then he witnessed the reaction of his fellow climbers turn from pity to calls for him to be disqualified from competitive free-climbing for having an unfair advantage. (p. 33)

Hearing Loss and Deafness

Hearing loss and deafness can be congenital (present at birth) or acquired at a later time. Most deaf infants are born to hearing parents. Individuals with hearing impairments have achieved some degree of recognition in and integration into the broader American culture. (Moore, 1987; Smart, 2009). College students are familiar with sign language interpreters in the classroom, we all are able to watch television with closed captioning, and many of us have a grandparent or great grandparent with some degree of hearing impairment (see Figure 9.1).

However, deafness and hearing impairments differ from other types of disability because they bring additional barriers and unique complications: (1) Speech may be impaired, especially in the case of congenital deafness; (2) Many individuals with hearing impairments are isolated and excluded from employment; (3) Parents with deaf children must make important decisions about their children's education very early in the child's life, including whether the child will be educated in a community school or a residential school for the deaf and whether the child will learn American Sign Language (ASL) or try to become a speaking person. Many individuals with severe hearing loss attend residential schools, being required to leave their families and homes at a very age and deafness is the only type of disability that some consider not a pathology, deviance, or impairment but instead the mark of a society. The Deaf Culture has a long and rich history of providing an environment for deaf people, producing art and literature, and advocating for the deaf.

The cause of 25% of all hearing loss is unknown. Hearing loss is measured in decibels; therefore, the levels of hearing loss are diagnosed by standardized, objective procedures. However, the most important distinction of severe hearing loss/deafness is whether the loss is congenital or acquired later in life. Those with congenital deafness typically experience great difficulty in learning speech, and many never learn speech. Those who experience late-onset deafness cannot hear themselves (or anyone else) speak, but they can speak. Congenital hearing loss is often caused by hereditary genetic factors,

FIGURE 9.1

Age at which hearing loss begins.

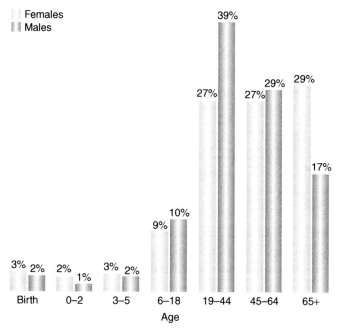

Source: National Health Interview Survey, 2002. Chart created by the NIDCD Epidemiology and Biostatistics Program.

such as those that cause otosclerosis, and by prenatal disease, such as rubella. One expert estimates that 35% to 50% of all cases of deafness are the result of genetic conditions.

Acquired deafness is often caused by postnatal infections, such as scarlet fever, measles, mumps, influenza, typhoid fever, meningitis, or otitis media (ear infections). Helen Keller and her brother had a fever that was never diagnosed at the time. It was thought that both children would die; her brother died, however, Helen survived though she was consequently both deaf and blind. Obviously, the development of antibiotics has greatly reduced the incidence of deafness from infection. Hearing loss, including deafness, can also be caused by environmental factors, such as physical abuse and prolonged exposure to loud noise.

Hearing impairments may become very rare due to a combination of medical and technological advances. Antibiotics cure infections, and surgical procedures can repair structural anomalies in the ear. Cochlear implants are surgically implanted into the ear (called the cochlea) and provide small electrical currents that stimulate the auditory nerves and provide the sensation of hearing. Other types of technology are also available, including programmable digital hearing aids and disposable hearing aids. Hearing aids can be programmed to amplify the frequency at which the individual cannot hear. Therefore, hearing aids are custom designed.

Dual Sensory Loss: Deafness/Blindness

Helen Keller is perhaps the most famous individual who was both deaf and blind. The fact that the general public can name only one deaf/blind individual (Helen Keller) illustrates the low incidence of the disability and the severe communication deficits of deaf/blindness. Before Helen Keller, individuals (including children) who were blind and deaf lived with their families, never attended school, and communicated with gestures. Unlike Helen Keller, they did not attend college, and no plays or movies were made about them. These other deaf and blind individuals lived in obscurity. As with any low-incidence disability, services and education are very difficult to obtain, and few professionals are trained to work with individuals with low-incidence disabilities. In addition, children with low-incidence disabilities are typically educated in residential schools.

A biographer of Helen Keller explained the disability of deafness/blindness:

> Today, relatively few D/deaf-blind people suffer from Helen Keller's condition—that is, being completely D/deaf and blind from an early age. The life-threatening childhood infections such as meningitis and scarlet fever have been for the most part eradicated, and the simultaneous onset of blindness and D/deafness seldom occurs. (Herman, 1998, p. 340)

Almost 50% of all deaf/blind individuals now have Usher syndrome, a genetic condition characterized by hearing loss and gradual loss of vision due to a condition called retinitis pigmentosa, in which the individual begins to experience vision loss in adolescence and gradually losses more and more until the onset of total blindness, usually in middle age.

Mobility Impairments

The category of mobility impairments covers many different types of disabilities, including spina bifida, cerebral palsy (CP), spinal cord injuries (SCIs), paraplegia, quadriplegia, muscular dystrophy, amputations, congenital limb deficiencies, and motor neuron diseases, such as amyotrophic lateral sclerosis (Lou Gehrig's disease) or muscular dystrophy. Mobility impairments interfere with the individual's movement and coordination, and most people with these impairments require some type of assistive technology, such as a cane or a wheelchair.

Most mobility impairments are visible to others, and many individuals with mobility impairments experience other disabilities, such as hearing loss or an intellectual disability. Causes include hereditary causes (muscular dystrophy), lack of oxygen at birth (CP), or abnormal fetal development (congenital limb deficiency). Trauma causes a significant number of orthopedic impairments, such as SCIs. Eighty percent of all individuals with SCIs are men (see Figure 9.2). This is an interesting statistic; however, the fact that most of SCIs are men means that many treatments and services are often not designed with women in mind. How many female wheelchair athletes are there?

Autoimmune diseases, such as rheumatoid arthritis, also cause mobility impairments. With these diseases, the immune system attacks the joints and slowly destroys them. Women are almost three times as likely to develop rheumatoid arthritis, with ages 20 to 45 as the peak onset years.

Motor neuron diseases include ALS, polio, and muscular dystrophy. ALS is a progressive terminal disease in which the motor neurons degenerate and are replaced with scar tissue. ALS is more common in men. Although it does not affect cognitive or

FIGURE 9.2

Causes of spinal cord injury since 2005.

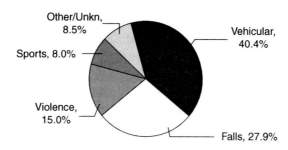

Source: https://www.nscisc.uab.edu, February 2011.

sensory functioning, it results in muscle weakness, including the muscles used for swallowing, speech, and breathing. Age of onset is typically during middle age; 47 is the average age of onset. Most patients die 2 to 4 years after the onset of symptoms, but 20% live 5 or more years after the onset (Bronfin, 2005).

Like many congenital disabilities, there is a wide range of severity in CP, which occurs when the brain is injured in the fetal period, during the birth process, or in early childhood. The most common cause of CP is perhaps lack of oxygen (*anoxia*) during the birth process. CP is a lifelong disability because the brain injury is permanent. In mild cases, there are symptoms that are not very visible, but in severe cases there are muscle disorders, such as lack of accuracy of muscle movement and involuntary movements that are visible. Falvo (1999) described these symptoms:

> Some individuals with CP have *ataxia* (disorder in the accuracy of muscle movement), which affects their balance and coordination of gait. Still others have *dyskinesia*, involving unwanted, involuntary muscle movements. Specific types of dyskinesia include slow writhing; purposeless movements (*choreoathetosis*). Some individuals have a combination of spasticity, ataxia, and dyskinesia. (p. 10)

If other parts of the brain are injured, additional problems may result, such as vision and hearing impairments, seizures, or intellectual disability. Experts expect an increase in the incidence of CP as an increasing number of extremely low-weight infants survive. This is not to say that all low-weight babies will have CP (or any other disability). Rather, the probability of CP is greatly increased in these infants, and physicians provide respiratory support to the infant immediately following birth. Also, in utero treatment (treatment given to the fetus in the uterus) can be provided. Twins, triplets, and other multiple births have an increased probability of CP because infants in multiple births tend to be of low weight.

Spina bifida is a congenital disorder in which the spinal column has excessive spaces between one or more vertebrae; the Latin word *bifida* means divided, and spina bifida is divided spine. In mild cases, there are few, if any symptoms, but in severe cases, muscle paralysis, loss of sensation, and loss of bowel and bladder control are much more likely. In one type of spina bifida, the membrane surrounding the spinal cord pushes out through an opening in the spinal cord, and in another type of this disability, both the membranes and the nerves of the spinal cord push out through the opening. Physicians describe the condition as the "extrusion of abnormally formed neural elements" (Gold, 2005, p. 461). Surgery (sometimes multiple surgeries) is required to repair these defects and to prevent further or permanent damage to the spinal cord. Infants born with spina bifida may also have hydrocephalus (fluid on the brain), which can result in intellectual disability if the fluid is not surgically drained and a shunt placed to continue draining the fluid as it accumulates. Children and adults with spina bifida are susceptible to infections in their spine, and, because of this, they typically experience several hospitalizations each year. Spina bifida is a lifelong disability, with severe impairments in many areas of functioning.

In the last decade, there has been a 27% decrease in the number of infants born with spina bifida; this decrease is attributed to the folic acid supplements added to grain products, such as cereal. It is important that pregnant women take folic acid because it aids in neural tube development. However, Gold (2005) noted that there are many other causes of spina bifida: "Although folic acid supplementation plays a role in prevention, the etiology for neural tube defects is likely multifactorial and has a genetic basis" (p. 463).

Muscular dystrophies (there are several types) are hereditary conditions that are characterized by progressive muscle degeneration. Congenital muscle dystrophy is apparent at birth; in severe cases, obstetricians and pediatricians must guard against respiratory failure in the newborn. The infant shows weakness and restriction of joint movement (Bronfin, 2005).

There is a large number of causes of mobility impairments, including birth trauma, later-in-life injuries, and degenerative conditions. John Hockenberry, a reporter for National Public Radio and Middle East correspondent, describes the variability in paraplegia and quadriplegia:

> "Paralyzed from the waist down" describes so little of the experiences of a spinal-cord injury that most crips use it as kind of shorthand joke. In my case, I am paralyzed from the nipples down. When people learn this they are shocked to realize that there is no international checkpoint at the waist. It is an arbitrary demarcation. In actual fact, relatively few people are paralyzed from the waist down. Everyone has their particular separating sensation from numbness. Each line of separation is invisible to the eye. In some people the aspects of temperature and pressure and muscle control are separate. Some spinal-cord injured people can feel pressure but not temperature in some parts of their body and vice versa. There are people with almost total sensation but with no motor control...a partially damaged fiber-optic cable...picture, but no sound...bad reception. All these metaphors aid understanding, but none is precise. The trace of each paraplegic and quadriplegic's sensory border zone is unique as a fingerprint. Each person has a different answer to the question: What does paralysis feel like? (Hockenberry, 1996, p. 97)

Chronic Illness and Health Disorders

We have discussed some chronic illnesses in the section on mobility impairments. In addition, diabetes, cardiovascular disease, brittle bone disease (osteogenesis imperfect), rheumatoid arthritis, Parkinson's disease, ankylosing spondylitis, and Huntington's chorea are recognized to be disabilities. All of these chronic, lifelong conditions limit functioning.

- Diabetes is a condition of carbohydrate metabolism which results in an imbalance of the availability of the hormone insulin. Diabetes must be managed on a daily basis and is almost a gateway disability because its complications lead to limb amputations, blindness, and other disabilities.
- Cardiovascular disease, because of its limiting chronic nature and the need for treatment and management, is a disability. The arteries that supply the heart are the most important blood vessels in the body.
- Huntington's chorea (or disease) is a slow, progressive hereditary disease of the central nervous system that is typically diagnosed in young adulthood. Individuals with Huntington's have jerky, involuntary movements and intellectual deterioration. Death occurs approximately 15 years after the first onset of symptoms.
- Rheumatoid arthritis is a chronic, progressive systemic disorder in which the joints become inflamed and swell. It is thought to be an autoimmune disease. Autoimmune diseases occur when the body's immune system attacks itself, leading to inflammation and cell death.
- Parkinson's disease is also a slow, progressive disorder of the central nervous system. Characteristics of Parkinson's include involuntary tremors, extreme slowness of movement, and lack of spontaneous movement. The actor Michael J. Fox has Parkinson's and has become an advocate for research and greater awareness of this disease.
- Ankylosing spondylitis is a type of rheumatic disorder that occurs mainly in young men and affects the joints and ligaments of the spine. It can also affect the hips, ankles, or elbows. Kyphosis (hump back) may result. As with other rheumatic disorders, the joints become inflamed, which causes pain and often results in fusion of the joints and restriction of motion.

Disfigurements

Advances in surgical techniques have given individuals more options to reduce or remove their disfigurements. Interestingly, disfigurements typically do not include functional limitations, but they are still legally considered to be a disability (Patterson et al., 1993). It is the stigma of the disfigurement and other negative responses of society that limit individuals with disfigurements. For example, lower limb amputations (one or both of the legs) are considered to be more functionally impairing, while upper limb amputations (one or both of the arms) result in fewer functional limitations. However, upper limb amputations are thought to be a greater disability because of the disfiguring aspects of lacking one or both arms. Most disfiguring disabilities have an acute onset, many of them traumatic. For example, individuals who experience severe burns often have lifelong facial disfigurements after medical stabilization, although there are no functional limitations.

Cognitive Disabilities

Examples of Cognitive Disabilities

- Intellectual disabilities (formerly termed mental retardation)—such as Down syndrome
- Learning disabilities
- Pervasive developmental disorders—such as autism

Cognitive disabilities include intellectual disabilities, Down syndrome, learning disabilities (LD), and developmental disorders such as autism spectrum disorders. Traumatic brain injuries are often grouped in the cognitive category. Cognitive symptoms are impairments in perception, memory, and information processing. These disabilities are grouped together because of their similar symptoms, yet the range of their symptoms is broad. One aspect of cognitive disabilities that is different from physical disabilities concerns the education and services provided to people with intellectual disabilities. Government-funded public special education provided in community schools began in the 1960s, and employment opportunities before this time were limited to sheltered workshops. Before the 1960s most adults with intellectual disabilities simply stayed at home (and many still stay home today). Doctors advised parents whose infants had these types of disabilities to put their babies into institutions. Many older individuals with intellectual disabilities were born before the 1960s and have lived their entire lives in institutions. Adult services (the state-federal Vocational Rehabilitation system) for these individuals were not provided until 1943, while individuals with physical disabilities began receiving VR services in 1920.

Therefore, the limitations experienced by individuals with intellectual disabilities were not a part of the disability but a creation of society at the time. It can be said that American society, including government entities, further disabled these individuals by segregating them from society and not educating them (according to their potential). Society made intellectual disabilities more limiting than necessary.

Mental Retardation or Intellectual Disabilities

The preferred term now is intellectual disabilities instead of mental retardation, a stigmatizing label. However, many diagnostic manuals use the diagnosis of mental retardation in very precise, standardized ways, so the term mental retardation will be used here when necessary. An estimated 3% of the American population has an intellectual disability, of whom 90% have mild intellectual disability (Joseph P. Kennedy, Jr. Foundation, 1991). Severe intellectual disability, therefore, is relatively rare. Intellectual disabilities are more than seven times as prevalent as blindness or deafness and 10 times more prevalent than physical disabilities. Although there are standardized and quantifiable levels of severity (mild, moderate, and severe), the diagnostic procedures include both standardized paper-and-pencil intelligence testing and clinical impressions. As expected, it is more difficult to diagnose a mild intellectual disability than it is to diagnose severe or profound intellectual disabilities. Frequently a lack of educational and cultural opportunities or a lack of English-language skills is difficult to distinguish from a mild intellectual disability. Moderate intellectual disabilities are typically discovered when children enter school, though severe and profound intellectual disabilities are frequently apparent at birth because other disabilities are often present, such as sensory loss, mobility impairments, seizure disorders, or a combination of these disabilities.

Intellectual disability is defined by the American Association on Intellectual and Development Disabilities (AAID). The AAID defines intellectual disability as "significantly subaverage general intellectual functioning resulting in or associated with concurrent impairments in adaptive behavior, and manifesting during the development period" (Grossman, 1983, p. 1). Social functioning is included in the definition of adaptive functioning (American Association on Mental Retardation, 1992).

In order to distinguish intellectual disability from cognitive disabilities that occur later in life (e.g., senile dementia), this diagnosis is determined during the individual's developmental period, which is birth to 22 years (Drew, Logan, & Hardman, 1992). Individuals with IQs in the range of 55 to 70 would be considered to have mild intellectual disability; individuals with IQs in the range of 40 to 54 are considered to have moderate intellectual disability; and individuals with IQs below 40 are considered to have severe intellectual disability.

Most intellectual disability is associated with neurologic damage. Damage to the central nervous system (which typically occurs at birth) from causes such as lack of oxygen, abnormal fetal position, or infections that lead to intellectual disability. However, some cases of intellectual disabilities have known organic causes. These include maternal infections, maternal use of alcohol, or incompatible blood types between the mother and the fetus. Changes in metabolic functioning, especially in the fragile X syndrome, result from genetic-chromosomal factors and often lead to an intellectual disability. Down syndrome is caused by a chromosomal defect in the developing fetus. (Dr. Landon Down was the physician who first described Down syndrome. Many conditions are named for the individual who first described them, such as Alzheimer's, Turner's syndrome, Asperger's syndrome, or Tourette's.)

A pediatrician (Batshaw, 2001) made clear distinctions between the terms developmental delay, developmental disability, and mental retardation:

> Physicians used the term *developmental delay* to describe a young child who is slow in developing but has the potential to catch up. This contrasts with the term *mental retardation*, which implies a permanent and significant slowness in development. The term *developmental delay* is often used in describing a premature infant; it is rarely appropriate to be used for a child older than 2–3 years of age. Unfortunately, professionals often use the term *developmental delay* long after it has become clear that the child has mental retardation. It then becomes a way of avoiding the reality that may be painful to the parent and to the professional. (p. 54)

Learning Disabilities

Learning disabilities (LD) are becoming one of the most prevalently diagnosed disabilities. The actual rate of LD may not be increasing as much as it appears, but because more and more individuals are being screened, there are more frequent diagnoses. Once considered a disability that the individual outgrew, it is now known to be a lifelong disability.

Diagnosis of an LD first begins by eliminating other possible causes, such as a sensory loss, an intellectual disability, or autism. Children who are suspected of having an LD are initially identified because of a discrepancy between their measured academic potential (IQ) and their actual academic performance. The causes of LD can only be speculated, although functional magnetic imaging has shown that children with LD have reduced physiological functioning in the cerebellum. Other suspected causes include lack of communication between the hemispheres of the brain or one hemisphere that is larger than the other (termed "asymmetrical development").

Pervasive Developmental Disorders

In 1943 Leo Kanner described a group of 11 children who displayed a similar pattern of symptoms that were very different from those of other childhood behavior disorders. Kanner used the term "early infantile autism" to describe the disorder (Morris, Morris, & White, 2005). Pervasive developmental disorders is the term created by the American Psychiatric Association, which is used to describe a pattern of neurologically based impairments in social interactions and communications. Pervasive development disorders, including autism and Asperger's syndrome, are discussed in Chapter 11.

Psychiatric Disabilities

Psychiatric Disabilities

- Mental illness
- Mood disorders

Psychiatric disabilities include mental illness, depression, alcoholism, and chemical and substance abuse. Both the diagnostic criteria and the diagnostic process are based on clinical judgment and the use of paper-and-pencil tests, such as the Minnesota Multiphasic Personality Inventory. Of all disability groups, psychiatric disabilities are most often thought of as self-inflicted or (at best) disabilities that could have been avoided if the individual simply "tried harder." Psychiatric disabilities are also the ones that produce the greatest degree of societal prejudice and discrimination. This prejudice and discrimination is experienced in daily life in social interactions. However, prejudice and discrimination are also seen in reduced funding for services, unequal insurance coverage, and a very short history of government funding (Mannion, 1996; Marsh, 1992). After all, legislators are subjected to the same societal misperceptions as everyone else.

Recent federal legislation is mandating insurance coverage for those with psychiatric disabilities. Also, while the treatment of individuals with any type of disability has been of low quality or nonexistent, the treatment and rehabilitation of individuals with psychiatric disabilities have lagged behind (Orrin, 1997).

Mental Illness

Psychiatric disabilities are diagnosed using the *Diagnostic and Statistical Manual of Mental Disorders, IV-Text Revision* or *DSM* (American Psychiatric Association, 2000). This manual provides information such as diagnostic criteria (those symptoms that are necessary for the diagnosis to be made), prevalence rates, the course of the disorder, and gender features, but the *DSM* does not give treatment plans. Because the diagnostic criteria are objective, there is an inconsistency in diagnosis among various practitioners. The *DSM* is a serial endeavor, meaning that there have been many editions since 1952. The use of the manual requires specialized training, and it is typically used by psychiatrists, psychologists, and social workers. Although most disorders listed in the *DSM* are defined as disabilities, several disorders, such as kleptomania or sexual addition, are not considered to be disabilities; therefore, individuals with these disorders would not be protected under the ADA nor would they be eligible for government-funded disability programs, such as vocational rehabilitation.

According to the American Psychiatric Association, mental illness includes schizophrenia, delusional disorders, bipolar affective disorders, major depression, and anxiety/panic disorders. Many psychiatric disabilities have courses that are episodic or relapsing, in which symptoms may disappear for a time and then reappear. Relapses or the onset of symptoms is called the active phase, and the disappearance of symptoms is termed remission.

There is a wide range of subtypes of schizophrenia; however, all of these include distortion of reality and disturbances of thought, speech, and behavior. Schizophrenia affects many areas of functioning and is a lifelong disability. Most cases of schizophrenia begin in late adolescence and early adulthood, although there are a few cases of onset in middle age. Men tend to experience an earlier onset (around ages 20–24) than women and also tend to have a more severe form of schizophrenia than women. Schizophrenia is also more prevalent in men, with a ratio of three men with schizophrenia to every two women who develop this disability.

The characteristic symptoms of schizophrenia are delusions, hallucinations, disorganized speech, and bizarre behavior. Hallucinations are sensory experiences that seem real to the individual for which there is no external stimulus. Hearing voices is an auditory hallucination. Delusions are erroneous beliefs that are firmly held despite clear evidence to the contrary.

Mood disorders or affective disorders occur at least 15 to 20 times more frequently than schizophrenia (Butcher, Mineka, & Hooley, 2010). Mood disorders are divided into two broad categories, depressive disorders and bipolar disorders. Affective disorders are not always considered to be disabilities; some government agencies recognize the various types of depression (including bipolar depression) as disabilities and others do not. Those agencies acknowledge depression to be a psychiatric disability because of the pervasive impairment depression causes in all areas of the individual's life. Falvo (1999) noted that with severe depression, "the incapacitation can be so great that individuals are unable to attend to their own daily needs, such as basic hygiene and nutritional needs" (p. 133). Depression can be fatal, since about 10% of those with depression successfully commit suicide. Not all depression is considered to be pathological; for example, grief following the death of a loved one is not considered a disorder or disability unless it is unresolved after a lengthy period of time. This is an illustration of the adage, "unpleasant does not mean pathology." In other words, everyone has down or blue days; if this were the only manifestation, the individual would not receive a diagnosis of depression. The depressive symptoms must be long term, typically unremitting, and impair the individual's functioning.

The depressive disorders are characterized by some combination of the following symptoms: feelings of sadness, hopelessness, decreased energy, feelings of worthlessness and guilt, an inability to concentrate, and disturbances in sleep, eating, and activity level. There is considerable overlap in the symptoms of depression and bipolar disorder. However, individuals with bipolar disorder also experience manic episodes in which they have an inflated self-esteem and a decreased need for sleep; they also become excessively involved in activities, either work or pleasure. It is estimated that that between 10% and 50% of individuals with depression will, at some point, have at least one manic episode. Manic episodes tend to begin suddenly. Strictly speaking, depression without manic episodes are termed unipolar depression, and correct differentiation between unipolar and bipolar depression is important (but often difficult) because different treatments are used.

The most frequent age of onset for depression is the early 20s, but depression can be diagnosed in infants, children, and adolescents. Individuals are often hospitalized in order to stabilize the symptoms. Typically, the more severe depressions have an acute onset (sudden), while the less severe depressions have a gradual (insidious) onset.

Psychiatric disabilities, including mental illness and affective disorders, require lifelong management and there are few total cures. Thus we can see that psychiatric disabilities parallel physical and cognitive disabilities in that they are chronic, not curable, and require careful management and monitoring. The one difference between psychiatric disabilities and other types of disabilities may be the frequency and intensity of relapses.

WHY CATEGORIZE DISABILITIES?

Categorization of disabilities is necessary in some circumstances and often is totally irrelevant in many others. Government agencies are required to develop some system of counting and data collection about disability in order to ensure government services and funding. Advocacy groups need information on disabilities in order to pursue their legislative and public interests. For example, the nonprofit Muscular Dystrophy Association probably does not have funds to collect national data on the incidence of muscular dystrophy. Therefore, in order to provide funding and services, it is both ethical and logical to categorize disabilities. When accessing various large-scale systems, such as the U.S. Census, it is important to understand first the way in which a disability is defined before looking at the numbers. For example, some systems include only "activity limitations," or "work limitations," but other systems have a much broader definition, and the number of PWDs will thus be higher.

Categorization of disabilities often is not relevant and may even be harmful. The following section provides a list of the ways in which categorization is not useful.

Ways in Which Categorization if Disabilities Is Not Useful

- Many individuals have more than one disability, such a physical disability and a psychiatric disability. One category would not describe their experience accurately.
- Categorization of disability exerts a powerful influence on the degree of stigma directed toward PWDs. Broadly speaking, there is a great deal more prejudice and discrimination toward psychiatric disabilities than there is toward physical disabilities.
- Any categorization system that lumps greatly diverse individuals, experiences, and needs in a single group can erroneously lead to stereotypes, such as "all individuals who have an amputation also have a cognitive disability."
- Disability rights advocates support the "cross-disability" perspective. Instead of organizations for different disabilities competing with each other for resources and civil rights, it makes more sense to include individuals with all types of disability or to use the "cross-disability" perspective (Fleischer & Zames, 2001). PWDs are developing a collective identity. In fact, if PWDs were considered a minority group, they would outnumber any of the racial/ethnic minority groups.

There are biological and physical components of all disabilities, and it is important to understand the number of individuals affected by each type of disability. Therefore this book will occasionally use this categorization of physical, cognitive, and psychiatric disabilities. However, most of this book will view the disability experience and PWDs as including all types of disabilities.

Reasons for the Increasing Rates of Disability

- Advances in neonatal medicine
- Advances in emergency medicine
- The aging population
- Longer life spans for PWDs
- The liberalization and expansion of the definition of disability
- Greater accuracy in counting

INCREASING RATES OF DISABILITY

There are more individuals with disabilities than ever before in history. Indeed, the U.S. Census found that 18% of the American population has a disability of some sort. Furthermore, this percentage probably underestimates the rate. It is safe to state that everyone will either have a disability, marry someone with a disability, attend school with students with disabilities, have a baby with a congenital disability, or work with colleagues with disabilities. The combination of the civil rights bill for PWDs, the Americans with Disabilities Act (ADA), and the increasing rates of disabilities ensure that PWDs will no longer be hidden and segregated from the broader society (Rehabilitation Act of 1973). Moreover, the integration of PWDs into society will enrich and broaden American life.

A review of the causes of these increased rates of disability reveals that a higher standard of living results in more disabilities. Included in the higher standard of living are better nutrition, more insurance coverage, more workplace safety, better public sanitation, and wider access to medical care (Smart, 2009a, 2009b, 2009c, 2009d, 2009e). This may appear to be incongruous at first. There are six reasons why there are more disabilities; four are due to medical and scientific advances, and two are termed "statistical" causes, meaning that refined diagnostic techniques and more accurate counting methods have simply found more PWDs.

In many ways, the increasing numbers of PWDs parallel the increasing numbers of elderly people. Such parallels include some of the same causes, such as scientific and medical advances and the higher standard of living. The lack of societal opportunity structures available to these greater numbers of PWDs also mirrors the experience of the elderly. This is termed a "structural lag" (Freund et al., 2009), meaning that governments and societies often do not keep up with demographic changes. However, the general public is more aware of the increasing number of elderly people than of the increasing number of PWDs. This greater awareness is shown by the well-known phrase, "the graying of the population."

Advances in Neonatal Medicine

There are more congenital disabilities (disabilities present at birth) than ever before because of scientific advances in neonatal medicine. Indeed, neonatal medicine is a relatively new specialty of medicine. Neonatal medicine is concerned with the treatment of newborns (neonates), including fetuses before birth. More infants survive, and the infant mortality (death) rate has decreased markedly, but many of these infants survive with a disability. This relationship may be stated in this way: Infant mortality rates are inversely correlated with the rate of congenital disabilities.

It is now commonplace for infants as small as 1.5 pounds to survive, and premature and other low-weight newborns have a much higher risk of congenital disabilities. Most premature infants develop well and have no complications or disabilities. However, premature babies have a much high probability of developing cognitive, physical, and behavioral disabilities. A premature birth is any birth that occurs before the 37th week of pregnancy (Glass, 2001). These "kilogram babies" often have problems related to their underdeveloped organs. Premature infants are susceptible to brain hemorrhages. Societal conditions contribute to low-weight newborns, including births to teenage mothers; and worldwide, one baby in 10 is born premature (Neergaard, 2009). Neergaard reported that the two areas with the highest percentages of premature births are Africa and North America. She explained why more than 13 million babies are born prematurely each year.

How? "That's the 13-million-baby question," said March of Dimes epidemiologist Christopher Howson, who headed the project being debated at a child health meeting in India (Neergaard, 2009, p. A6).

> Different factors fuel prematurity in rich countries and poor ones. Wealthy nations such as the United States have sophisticated neonatal intensive care units for the tiniest, youngest preemies. That produces headlines about miracle babies and leads to a false sense that modern medicine conquers prematurity—without acknowledging lifelong problems including cerebral palsy, blindness, and learning disabilities that often plague survivors. (Neergaard, 2009, p. A6)

Teenage mothers have higher rates of babies who are premature or low weight. Fertility treatments are becoming more common, and these treatments have a higher rate of multiple births. There is a much higher rate of congenital disability in multiple births, such as twins or triplets. For example, infants who are part of a multiple birth are four times more likely to have CP. Before 1957 there were no children who survived with spina bifida, although some infants were *born* with this condition. However, all spina bifida babies then died a few days after their birth. In 1957 a shunt was developed that drained fluid from the brains of infants with spina bifida, helping babies with severe cases of spina bifida survive (Stefan, 2001). Today there are relatively high rates of the congenital disabilities CP, Down syndrome, intellectual disability, and spina bifida.

A cause of congenital disabilities that is completely avoidable and therefore would not be considered progress is a lack of insurance coverage. When a nation experiences an economic depression or recession, insurance coverage decreases because of job loss and the loss of employer-based insurance ("Census Numbers Show 51 Million in U.S. Uninsured," 2011). Lack of insurance is associated with more congenital disabilities and more late-onset disabilities. When pregnant women cannot afford prenatal care, there are more congenital disabilities. When middle-aged people cannot afford routine preventive check-ups, diabetes and other asymptomatic disabilities develop.

Advances in Emergency Medicine

The death rate from accidents and other types of trauma has been greatly reduced by developments in emergency medicine and trauma care. The Vietnam War provided the impetus for many advances in emergency care at the scene of the trauma. It is interesting to note that many medical advances were a direct result of military innovations in time of war. The American military in Vietnam used helicopters to transport injured soldiers and evacuate them quickly, treating and stabilizing them while they were being transported to the hospital. These methods were quickly adopted by the civilian population. Before the Vietnam War, most ambulances carried no medical equipment and only provided transportation. Now fewer individuals die before they reach the hospital, not only in combat, but in civilian life as well. The death rate from accidents has now declined dramatically, but the disability rates resulting from injuries, accidents, and trauma have increased. For example, "in 1980, less than 10%

of individuals with trauma brain injury (TBI) or spinal cord injuries (SCI) survived; today the survival rate for these individuals with these disabilities is higher than 90%" (Smart, 2009, p. 39).

Therefore there are now many individuals with SCI, including quadriplegia (paralysis of all four limbs). However, individuals with any kind of paralysis experience many secondary health conditions, such as decubitus ulcers or pressure sores, respiratory infections, and bladder infections. The use of antibiotics has allowed those with paralysis to live a much longer life (Crewe, 1993). After World War I, there were only 400 American men with battle injuries that paralyzed them from the waist down. Ninety percent of the men with these injuries died before reaching home from secondary infections, such as pneumonia. After World War II and the discovery of antibiotics, there were 2,000 veterans with paraplegia (paralysis of the legs), and 85% were alive 20 years later (Shapiro, 1993). Most individuals with paralysis consider themselves to be healthy, controlling their secondary conditions with antibiotics. Of course, individuals with paraplegia or quadriplegia do not live as long as those without disabilities. Therefore, if they are young when injured, these individuals can plan for education, employment, and family life. Wheelchair sports illustrate the good health of many of those with orthopedic impairments.

TBI is an acquired damage to the brain that alters functional capacities such as motor control, sensation, perception, cognition, memory, personality, and emotion. TBI is a lifelong disability with pervasive limitations of motor and cognitive abilities, as well as changes in personality. The condition has mild, moderate, and severe levels of severity. Because mild TBIs frequently do not result in impairments, it is thought that the incidence of TBI is underreported. The Centers for Disease Control (CDC) estimates that approximately 1.5 million people acquire a TBI. Dixon, Layton, and Shaw (2005) explain the relationship between medical advances and the increase in TBIs: "The rate of survival from TBI has increased over the last 20 years due to advances in emergency medicine, neurosurgery, and intensive care. As a result, the cumulative number of people with TBI is increasing. Many people who formerly would have died as a result of accidents or assaults now are saved in the acute period following injury" (p. 120). Typically, individuals (mostly males) between the ages of 15 and 24 have the highest rates of TBI; the risk of sustaining a TBI decreases dramatically after age 24, but it increases again after the age of 75 because elderly people tend to fall. Alcohol is frequently associated with accidents that result in TBI. Corrigan (1995) found a 36% to 51% occurrence of intoxication at the time of injury.

Because of the combination of (1) the growing survival rates of individuals with TBI, (2) the typical severity of this disability that limits many areas of functioning, and (3) its frequent occurrence in the late adolescent years and the early twenties, there is a fairly large group of individuals with TBIs who will progress through most of the life span developmental stages.

Aging of the Population

The rate of disability is positively correlated with age. As individuals age, they have a greater probability of acquiring a disability; in other words, old age and disability are highly correlated. This correlation holds true both for individuals and for large groups of people. Therefore, nations that have "graying" populations will have higher rates of disabilities, and those nations with younger populations will have lower rates. Medicine and medical technology have lengthened the life span. Arthritis, diabetes, mobility impairments, and sensory impairments (vision and hearing) are disabilities often associated with the elderly. The following examples show the way in which the longevity revolution has increased the rate of disability.

- In the United States today, 75% of all therapeutic amputations are performed on people older than the age of 65, mostly as a secondary condition of diabetes.
- Since the 1970s stroke mortality rates have decreased, but the incidence of a stroke has not decreased. Thus more individuals are surviving strokes and many survive with disabilities; most of those who experience strokes are elderly (although younger people can have strokes).
- The percentage of vision impairments is increasing dramatically due to the aging population. For example, 17% of Americans in the age group 65 to 74 years have vision impairment, and 26% of Americans who are 75 or older have vision impairments. Vision impairment is diagnosed when the person's best vision with eyeglasses or contacts falls below a certain threshold (The Lighthouse, National Survey on Vision Loss, 1995).
- Individuals with diabetes have a 25 times greater risk for blindness than the general population (Rosenthal & Cole, 2005).

People With Disabilities Are Living Longer

The longevity revolution has allowed individuals with disabilities to live longer, although not as long as those who do not have disabilities. Hence, as the rates of congenital and acquired disabilities continue to rise, the life spans of these individuals are lengthened. Nearly 90% of children with disabilities survive into adulthood (Jones, Stanford, & Bell, 1997; Lublin, 1998; White & Lublin, 1998). In the past, parents of children with congenital disabilities, such as CP, Down syndrome, or intellectual disability, were told "take your baby home and enjoy him or her. You won't have this baby for long."

Children with Down syndrome (a genetic condition that causes intellectual disability) are living twice as long as they did 20 years earlier. In 1983 the average life span of an individual with Down syndrome was 25 years, but in 2007 the average life span was 56 years; moreover, the life span for these individuals is expected to increase further. This increase is the results of advances in surgery and the use of antibiotics (Smart, 2001, 2009).

The increased life spans will create the need for more and more varied programs for PWDs, especially gerontological programs, and will require medical practitioners to enlarge their scope of practice to include skills in treating various types of disabilities in individuals at a wide range of developmental stages. For example, sex and marriage education will become important services to provide to individuals with Down syndrome. More important, the experience of disability will be different for the individual and his or her family. Harriet McBryde Johnson (2003, 2005) was a disability rights lawyer who died in 2009 at age 51. When she was born with a degenerative muscle disease, her parents were told that she would die in early childhood. In an article titled "Too Late to Die Young," she explained her response to living past the time when doctors predicted that she would die.

> The death sentence hangs over my childhood like a cloud (2005, p. 44)....As my body continues to deteriorate, my life looks more and more like normal. At 25 I leave the cozy comfort of home to go to law school. I figure I'll be 27 when I finish; if I go now I can probably practice law for a couple of years. By this time, the thought is almost subconscious: when I die I might as well die a lawyer. "My plan to die young hasn't worked out.... It's too late to die young." (2005, p. 46)

The causes of increasing rates of disability described in the next two sections are considered statistical causes, which indicates that the actual number of PWDs did not increase but the way in which disability is defined and counted changed.

Liberalization and Expansion of the Definition of Disability

Not very long ago, all disabilities were physical disabilities. Disabilities such as LD, mental illness, and alcoholism were not thought to be disabilities, so the individuals who experienced these diseases were not eligible for government services or funding. After 1990 and the passage of the ADA, individuals who did not have a documented disability defined by ADA were not protected by the act. The old adage "If you don't have a label, you don't get services" is true. More recently defined disabilities include AIDS, post-polio syndrome, and chronic fatigue syndrome.

Major medical and psychiatric diagnostic manuals continue to expand and list more and more disorders. It should be noted that not all of these disorders are considered disabilities. The fourth edition of the *Diagnostic and Statistic Manual IV (DSM-IV)* (2000) lists 120 more diagnoses than the third edition did. For example, LDs were formerly lumped under a single category of dyslexia. In the *DSM-IV-TR*, LD are divided into three categories, dyslexia (impairment in reading), dyscalculia (impairment in math), and dysgraphia (impairment in writing.) Asperger's syndrome was not added to the *DSM-IV* until 1994 (American Psychiatric Association, 1994).

LDs provide an illustration of how the definition of disability has been liberalized and how such liberalization decreases the stigma from the general public and allows for accommodations and services (Cruickshank, 1990). Children (usually boys) with LD were thought to be stupid, lazy, and oppositional. Often their family experienced stigma because schoolteachers felt that the family did not value education. Instead, these children had central nervous system impairments, which are now beginning to be seen in resonance magnetic imaging. Butcher, Mineka, and Hooley (2010) explained:

> It is unfortunately the case that LD, despite its having been recognized as a distinct and rather common type of disorder for more than 40 years, and despite its having generated a voluminous research literature, still fails to be

accorded the status it deserves in many school jurisdictions. Instead, many classroom teachers and school administrators resort to blaming the victims and attributing the affected child to various character deficiencies... a youngster who learns academic skills slowly or in a different way is treated as a troublemaker.... Thus even when LD difficulties are no longer a significant impediment, an individual may bear, into maturity and beyond, the scars of many painful school-related episodes of failure. (p. 551)

These painful episodes result in poor self-concepts. If powerful and authoritative individuals, such as teachers, tell a child something, the child often believes it. John R. Horner described his self-image:

Back in the days when I was growing up, nobody knew what dyslexia [a type of LD] was.... So everybody thought you were lazy or stupid or both. And I didn't think I was, but I wasn't sure. (Gerber & Brown, 1994)

Horner flunked out of the University of Montana six times, but later "his brilliant synthesis of evidence...forced paleontologists to revise their ideas about dinosaur behavior, physiology, and evolution" (West, 1994, p. 334; cf. Gerber & Brown, 1994).

When large-scale screenings are used, more disabilities are discovered. For example, there are screening tests in elementary schools for both hearing and vision. In many hospitals, there are simple hearing tests given to all newborn babies. There are frequent announcements of screenings for depression at universities. Screening tests discover individuals who might (or might not) have the particular disability and send these individuals for further diagnostic testing.

Different government agencies define disability differently. For example, some agencies include affective disorders, such as depression, in their definition of mental illness, and other agencies do not consider affective disorders to be a mental disorder. Agencies that define mental illness more broadly will report higher rates of the disability of mental illness. Some government agencies include only "work limitations," thus eliminating children and elderly PWDs.

Overdiagnosis, however, is a negative aspect to broadening the definition of disability. For example, there is some disagreement over the incidence of autism, the fastest growing disability in the United States. Some have indeed termed the large number of newly diagnosed autism cases an epidemic. Autism is a childhood developmental disorder that involves a wide range (or "spectrum") of deficits, such as language, motor, and social skills. Some experts assert that autism is overly diagnosed because a child must have a diagnosis (or a "documented disability") in order to be eligible for services and accommodations. Therefore, children with fairly mild impairments may be diagnosed as autistic, because physicians and psychologists understand that the child must have a disability to receive services and autism seems the best fit for the child's problems.

More Accurate Counting

There is a difference between the number of disabilities and the number of *reported* disabilities. Smart (2009) explained:

As both the general public and government policymakers become clearer on the definitions of disability, the numbers of all individuals *reported* to have disabilities continues to climb. Essentially, more accurate counting is another "statistical" cause for the higher disability rates, because the number of people with disabilities did not increase, only the number of people who are counted or reported as having a disability. Furthermore, disability and health demographers consider the reported number of disabilities to be an underestimation, simply because there are many individuals who do not wish to identify themselves as having a disability. (p. 44)

In the same way that the profession and academic discipline of gerontology was a result of the growing number of elderly people, perhaps a new profession and academic discipline will emerge as a result of the growing number of PWDs.

The combination of longer life spans PWDs and the liberalization of the definition of disability will serve as an impetus for developmental psychologists to consider the developmental stages and transitions of PWDs. For example, the first generation of adults who were formally diagnosed with LD as children and (hopefully) received services and accommodations can reflect on their experiences; in so doing, they may help parents, teachers, and other professionals to provide sensitive, supportive, and effective services (McNulty, 2003).

As the number of PWDs increases, societal perceptions of disability will change (Linton, 1998). For example, in the future, the use of hearing aids will not be viewed any differently than the use of eyeglasses. There is little, if any, stigma in wearing eyeglasses; however, those who need hearing aids often refuse to use them because they know that this type of sensory adaptive technology can be stigmatizing.

DO WE WANT MORE DISABILITIES?

Do we want to have more individuals with disabilities? The answer is both "yes" and "no." Yes, we want more PWDs when the alternative would be death or lack of services. No, we do not want more PWDs when these disabilities are a result of or are related to societal conditions. Society does not want more disabilities if they can be avoided.

Let us turn to the "no" part of the answer. There are many widely disseminated disability prevention and reduction programs, including the use of seat belts, helmets, and other safety equipment for recreation or the workplace (Nagi, 1991). These programs are geared at avoiding a disability altogether. However, when accidents and injuries do occur, disability is preferable to death. Other disability-prevention programs include government-funded access to prenatal care for pregnant women, free or low-cost screening programs to catch the early onset of diabetes, high blood pressure, and other silent (asymptomatic) conditions that can lead to further disability. Early diagnosis and programs to prevent disabilities or reduce their severity save money—for insurance companies, the government, and the individual. More important are the unquantifiable emotional costs for the PWD and his or her family.

However, if the disability cannot be or was not preventable, the survival of the individual with a disability is considered to be a positive for both the individual and for society. Cook (as cited in Stalcup, 1997, p. 175) stated that "we want more disabled people, not fewer." With the increases in medicine, science, and technology, it seems reasonable to expect greater numbers of PWDs. Further, because President's Obama health plan will result in more Americans having access to health care, it seems reasonable to expect that more disabilities will be detected.

Another way to understand that society and government have the capability to reduce the number of disabilities is to look at the higher disability rates for racial/ethnic minority groups in the United States (U.S. Department of Health & Human Services, 2000; Vernellia, 1994). African Americans, Native Americans, and Hispanics have higher rates of disability than do Asian Americans, Pacific Islanders, or non-Hispanic White Americans (Smart & Smart, 1992, 1993, 1997d). Disability demographers hypothesize that the lack of insurance coverage, lower educational levels, employment in physically dangerous and demanding jobs, and high levels of poverty are related to these higher rates of disability. Better education typically leads to safer jobs and more insurance coverage. More insurance coverage means more prenatal care, more routine physical examinations, and more gerontological care, all which results in fewer disabilities. Smart (2009) concluded, "If these societal conditions could be changed, reduced, or improved, it stands to reason that the higher rate of disabilities for minorities could be reduced" (p. 73).

One other point should be considered in this discussion. Science and medicine have increased the number of PWDs; however, science and medicine also have the capability to decrease the number of PWDs through abortion or assisted suicide. This question will be considered later. However, it is important to remember that the use of either of these two methods requires reflection and resolution of the definitions of humanity, normalcy, and quality of life (Douard, 1995). These three concepts have confounded humankind for millennia.

DISABILITY IS BOTH COMMON AND NATURAL

It is true that one important source of an individual's identity is his or her body; however, is it true that normalcy (or the lack of a disability) is a criterion of humanity? When stated in this way, it seems silly to think that a PWD is not a human. Nonetheless, there may be deep-seated, almost subconscious feelings that an individual with severe and multiple disabilities is "not quite human," while those with less severe (or invisible) disabilities are thought to be "more human." The increasing numbers of PWDs and their longer life spans add more meaning to the question: "What is humanity?" (Douard, 1995). In Western cultures, the value of each individual contributing to the larger society is deeply ingrained. Of course neither children nor elderly people contribute, but children have the potential to contribute, and most elderly people have devoted a lifetime to working and contributing. If humanity is defined in terms of the capability to provide for one's self and others, then many individuals with severe and multiple disabilities would not meet this standard. It must also be remembered that many, if not the majority of PWDs, are not allowed to contribute because of societal barriers (Gill, 2001).

According to the U.S. Census, disability is a very *common* experience; moreover, the potential to acquire a disability is *universal.* Clay Haughton, director of the Civilian Equal Opportunity for the Department of Defense, explained:

> No one is immune to developing a disability, and almost no one, regardless of race, gender, religion, or economic status, will go through life without suffering from some form of physical impairment. It's truly the equal opportunity situation, and those of us who are disabled are a constant visual reminder of the frailty of each member of the human [race]. And so, accepting this possibility and adjusting to disability, those are matters that concern us all. (Fleischer & Zames, 2001, p. 109)

Often we confuse normalcy (or the lack of a disability) with the ideal, a standard against which everything is measured. When carried to the extreme, this misperception equates normalcy with perfection. These false assumptions can, and remain, strongly maintained throughout centuries. These false assumptions have also been projected into the future. In all of the futuristic books of the 1950s that envisioned great scientific and technological advances of the 21st century, not one mentioned PWDs. In the past, PWDs have been absent or at least marginal, but society is now changing to one that provides a social identity to PWDs. Most people probably do not consider the possibility that they could acquire a disability before old age. They rationalize this by saying that "disability is something that happens to other people, not to me." However, Smart (2009) summarized: "So rather than thinking of disability as something abnormal, exotic, or marginal to our interests, we see that disability concerns all of us" (p. 12).

Others Factors in the Disability

- Type or time of onset
- Type of course
  - Stable course
  - Degenerating course
  - Episodic stable course
  - Episodic degenerating course
- Degree of visibility
- Prevalence of the disability—low incidence or high incidence
- Degree of prejudice and stigma

Both the type and severity of the disability exert powerful influences on the individual's development. There are other factors that also influence the individual's development such as type of onset, course of the disability, and the degree of stigma directed toward the disability.

Type of Onset

Type of onset includes *time* of onset. Broadly speaking, there are two types (and times) of onset: congenital or acquired. Congenital disabilities are present at birth or shortly thereafter. "Congenital disability" is the preferred term, rather than "birth defect." Acquired disabilities are those whose onset occurs any time after the first year of life. Typically, the earlier the age of onset, the better the individuals respond and adjust (Alfano, Nielsen, & Fink, 1993; Krause 1988a, 1988b, 1992, 1997; Krause & Crewe, 1991). This may be due to several factors: children have cognitive and affective resiliency children with congenital disabilities do not have a premorbid (pre-disability) identity, children have not internalized society's prejudices and discriminations about disability, and children have not fully developed their body image. For example, children with a congenital limb deficiency adjust better than children or adults who undergo therapeutic amputations (such as for cancer or diabetes). Certainly congenital blindness is a different experience from blindness acquired in old age.

With both types of onset, differentiating time of onset from time of diagnosis is important. In most disabilities, diagnosis and onset occur at the same time. For example, before the widespread use of neonatal (newborn) hearing tests immediately following birth, the average age of diagnosis for congenital deafness was 15 months. During these first 15 months of life, the parents and other caretakers were aware that something was "not quite right," but there was no definitive diagnosis. Therefore, the infant lost 15 months when he or she could have been learning to communicate through the use of sign language. For adults with many types of disabilities, such as autoimmune diseases, it is typical to experience symptoms for months and years before the diagnosis is made. In these cases, the time of onset is never accurately known.

Acquired disabilities require a change of identity. Some acquired disabilities are the result of traumatic injuries, which occur unpredictably. The person thus has no time to prepare emotionally for this major life transition. In his book *Talking to Angels: A Life Spent in High Latitudes* (1996), Robert Perkins described the shock of the diagnosis/onset of his mental illness:

> In the spring of 1968, I was nineteen and a freshman at Harvard College. I was soon to leave school, without even passing "GO" or finishing the year, to start a journey. A journey I have yet to complete. . . . To have the wind knocked out of you, hard, at nineteen. To give you the feeling of it [how it felt], I'd [have to] hit you on the side of the head, when you were not expecting it, with a flat board or a piece of rubber tubing. The shock of the thing! (pp. 5, 15)

A young man named Roy went on a trip to the American West with friends to celebrate their college graduation. The driver fell asleep at the wheel and rolled the van. Roy was the only one seriously hurt. Roy expresses in a single sentence the sudden, unexpected onset of his disability: "I was 22, a recent college graduate, and all of a sudden, I'm a T8 bilateral paraplegic, whatever the hell that is!" (Crewe, 1992, p. 32).

Richard Cohen, the husband of television personality Miera Vera, wrote a book about his diagnosis of multiple sclerosis. Describing his reaction to the diagnosis, he called the diagnostic process "a journey into a strange land. That place would be exotic and rude" (2004, p. 17). Cohen related that he had no experience with or expectation of a disability; nothing in his earlier life had prepared him for a disability. He felt that the label "winner" had been replaced with the label "damaged goods" (p. 27).

Both Perkins and Cohen compare the onset of their disability and the subsequent adaptation and acceptance to a journey. The concept of a journey may be a way in which to describe two aspects: the ongoing process of adaptation and the necessity of leaving one's home to start the journey, or the need to change one's identity. Older individuals have stronger, more developed self-identities and may have earned prestige and status in the community. Middle-aged individuals tend also to have more responsibilities for spouses, children, and elderly parents. Therefore, the onset of a disability in middle age requires a great deal of adjustment.

Type of Course

The course of a disability refers to the time after medical stabilization, especially the day-to-day experience of living with a lifelong disability. There are basically three types of courses: (1) stable, (2) episodic (sometimes referred to as recurring or relapsing), and (3) degenerating.

Stable course disabilities are those whose symptoms do not vary after medical stabilization. Some examples of stable course disabilities are intellectual disabilities, deafness, and SCIs. The stability of the course is based upon good management and treatment so that the individual does not acquire secondary disabilities. A plateau of functioning has been attained, and the individual (presumably) knows what he or she is dealing with. Life has changed for these individuals, but stable course disabilities tend to present fewer adjustment demands for both the individual and the family.

Examples of episodic disabilities include several types of mental illness, asthma, and seizure disorder. (Note: seizure disorder and not elilepsy is the preferred term.) Disabilities with episodic courses are the most difficult to adjust to. In episodic disabilities, symptoms become worse at times but then disappear or become much reduced. Typically, the course of episodic disabilities is very unpredictable; therefore, the individual is subjected to ambiguity and lack of control (Falvo, 1999). Episodic disabilities are also ambiguous for the family, work colleagues, and society in general. Indeed, when only the three types of courses are considered, there is more prejudice and discrimination against those with an episodic course disability. After all, at times, the individual "seems herself/himself," but at other times the individual is severely limited in functioning. This unpredictability is sometimes confusing to the individual with the disability. When symptoms remit, he or she may overexert or may discontinue medication and treatment. Ambiguous situations are stressful, and we generally tend to ascribe negative and hostile characteristics and motives to people and situations that appear ill-defined. Ambiguity creates discomfort, tension, and stress in others, and those with episodic course disabilities appear ambiguous. Almost everyone tries to avoid ambiguity. Stefan (2001) explained:

Society is most comfortable with disabilities that are permanent and chronic; either one is disabled or not. Even with people who sometimes have to use a wheelchair find themselves regarded with skepticism and suspicion bordering on hostility. (p. 10)

Stefan asserted that the prejudice and discrimination against those with episodic disabilities (especially mental illness) are part of the larger legal and economic structure of the United States.

The economic, mental health, and legal structures, however, cannot accommodate the central truth of alternating or concurrent crisis and functioning at all. The U.S. legal system, mental health system, and labor market are marked by a static and dichotomous vision: One is either disabled or not, and once identified as disabled, residence in the category is presumed permanent. There is no place for the complexities and contradictions of people's real lives....Defeats...are also not seen as temporary, but as permanent. One bad episode can mean the termination of parental rights, an involuntary commitment or involuntary medication. It is all or nothing in American society. (p. 59)

Episodic course disabilities present the greatest adjustment demands. Toombs (1995), a university professor with multiple sclerosis, described her disability as "global uncertainty."

Our sense of who we are is intimately related to the roles we occupy, professional and personal...and to the goals we hold dear. Chronic, progressive disabling disease necessarily disrupted (or threatened to disrupt) my every role in ways that, at the outset, seemed to reduce my worth as a person. Moreover, the uncertainty of the prognosis transformed my goals and aspirations into foolishness. This sense of diminishment was accompanied by a sense of guilt. But still, in my heart of hearts, I felt in a myriad of ways that I was failing to do as I ought. (p. 16)

Individuals with episodic disabilities cannot afford to forget the disability, even in times of normal functioning. They must take their medication, adhere to all treatment regimens, wear a medical bracelet, ensure that they do not engage in any activities that might trigger a relapse, and control their environment at all times, understanding that symptom exacerbation could occur at any time. Often families with a member with an episodic disability practice "relapse drills," in which all member, including the youngest children, are trained to perform certain activities when a relapse occurs.

In the brief section that described disabilities, we saw that some disabilities were terminal, such as amyotrophic lateral sclerosis (ALS or Lou Gehrig's disease). On average those with ALS die 3 years after diagnosis. Many other disabilities are degenerating but do not necessarily result in death. Degenerating disabilities have a steady rate of worsening of symptoms, and degenerating episodic disabilities have cyclic periods of degeneration coupled with periods of remission. In both types of degenerating courses, the disability becomes worse.

Accepting the reality of the degeneration of abilities and functioning and facing greater limitations and losses place great demands on the individual and his or her family. As the disability degenerates, the environment tends to become more and more inaccessible. Robert Neumann (1988) described the damage to his joints caused by rheumatoid arthritis as "Joint of the Month Club." (Note also his relief in being diagnosed "at last.")

> Early in 1960, I went to the Mayo Clinic, where my arthritis was diagnosed at last, and where more appropriate treatment was prescribed. Nonetheless, even this was not able to halt the progression of the disease to my other joints. First, it my other knee, then my ankles, then my fingers, then my elbows, then my neck, then my hips. . . . With a sort of gallows humor, I'd say that I had joined the Joint-of-the Month Club. But, behind this façade, I was terrified at how my body was progressively deteriorating right before my eyes. (p. 157)

Degree of Visibility

It is not possible to discern if an individual has a disability, including a very severe disability, simply from his or her appearance. Many health conditions, psychiatric disabilities, and many other disabilities are invisible. Often the disability is not apparent but the accommodations are, such as hearing aids or insulin pumps. Occasionally PWODs mistakenly think that an invisible disability cannot be very serious or impair the individual's functioning very much. Nonetheless, some visible disabilities are very mild (such as some orthopedic impairments), while many invisible disabilities can be both severe and limit functioning in many different areas. For example, many psychiatric disabilities are considered invisible but are often very serious. Some individuals with episodic disabilities often appear to be normal. We may become angry when a seemingly able-bodied person parks his or her car in a handicapped parking space, but the individual may have multiple sclerosis and need to conserve his or her energy for shopping. One woman wrote to Ann Landers, the newspaper advice columnist, stating:

> I am handicapped, but one would never know it by looking at me. I have had two back operations and four knee surgeries. If I do any walking or standing, even for a few minutes, I get very tired and must sit and rest. Recently, I parked in the handicapped spot at the supermarket. I have a handicapped tag hanging on my rear view mirror. Before I could get out of the car, a "gentleman" walked up and said, "You certainly don't look handicapped to me. You should not be parking in that space." I looked at him and said, "And you, sir look intelligent, but I guess looks can be deceiving." (*Salt Lake Tribune* 2010, October 31)

Individuals with invisible disabilities confront the challenge of disclosure. When, where, and to whom should the individual disclose his or his disability? It is difficult to hide something that is so central to one's identity, such as a disability. Furthermore, the disclosure decisions are not based on anything about the individual or the disability. Disclosure decisions are necessary because of the prejudice and stigma toward PWDs.

Richard Cohen, a journalist who was diagnosed with multiple sclerosis, described his quandary.

> I learned a valuable lesson then and there. Honesty is not the best policy. Candor about health problems works in the confines of academia and maybe in the movies. Full disclosure does not work so well in the real world. Hard times in a competitive industry at a tough moment in history leave little room for dealing fairly with a serious illness. People with serious problems can be perceived as weak candidates for employment in the dollars-and-cents world. The right to do has currency when nothing is at stake.... Don't tell nobody nuthin.... My stealth approach bothered me enough to write my private rulebook outlining when dishonesty went too far and when it was permissible. (Cohen, 2004, pp. 54–55)

A reporter for *Time* magazine tells of his decision not to hide his disability. In an article entitled "How I Lost My Hand but Found Myself," Weisskopf (2006, p. 37) related that he acquired his disability when covering the war in Iraq. Weisskopf's hand was amputated when he caught a grenade and threw it out of the Humvee. This action probably saved the lives of the soldiers with whom he was riding.

> Before Iraq, the technology of arm prostheses hadn't changed much since World War II. The tiny population of amputees created little market incentive. Miguelez (the prosthetist) used the burst in demand from Walter Reed [Hospital] to lean on manufacturers for progress. Before long, he was outfitting Iraq war amputees with an electronic hand that opened and closed 2½ times faster and could be programmed to function at different speeds and grip strength.
>
> The cosmetic arts had also improved. I received a silicone hand that was so lifelike it passed for real in social settings. But Pretty Boy, as I called it, kept tearing and afforded the precision of a boxing glove. It was too spongy to grasp anything small and too slippery to hold most objects for long.
>
> Function was only part of the problem. The idea of trying to pass had begun to trouble me. It made me as if I had something to hide or to be ashamed of. When I started to go bald, I shaved my head. No comb-overs, no transplants or toupees for me. So why try to conceal a handicap? I was proud of how I had lost my hand. The stump had a story to tell. (p. 37)

As we read in Weisskopf's story, those who try to "pass" as not having a disability often sacrifice functioning. The silicone prosthetic hand was very lifelike, yet it was almost useless. The only function "Pretty Boy" served was to decrease the discomfort of PWODs. There are many examples of people who do not wear their hearing aids in public (others may think the person is rude and aloof when in reality he or she cannot hear) or of individuals who try to walk when the use of the wheelchair is available. President Franklin Roosevelt was a polio survivor who had no hip muscles, yet, in public his sons and other aides would take his arms and make it appear as if he were walking. In private he was carried in the arms of the Secret Service men or used a wheelchair. Of course, in this case the public *knew* Roosevelt was a polio survivor, but Roosevelt did not want to *remind* the public.

Sometimes it is better to disclose the disability instead of allowing others "to think the worst." We have seen that ambiguity is stressful and uncomfortable; in the absence of knowledge, we tend to ascribe negative aspects to the individual or the situation. For example, a gap of time of months or years in a resume as a result of a hospitalization may raise more questions than simply telling the job interviewer the truth. In cases of motor-neuron disabilities, it is best to disclose an invisible disability. When symptoms reoccur, especially when the individual is fatigued or stressed, the individual loses coordination and stamina and may stumble, stagger, trip, or fall. In many cases these individuals were thought to be intoxicated. An individual who requires time off from work to attend Alcoholics Anonymous meetings (or other types of treatment and support meetings) may appear to coworkers as a goof-off. An individual with a psychiatric disability who chooses not to disclose it must remain silent and listen to friends' jokes about "wackos," "fruitcakes," and "loonies" (Weingarten, 1997).

Prevalence or Incidence of the Disability

Prevalence or incidence of disability means the number of people who experience the disability. Old age deafness is very common, termed high incidence, while spina bifida is very uncommon, called low incidence. Typically, high-incidence disabilities place fewer adjustment demands on the individuals. There are three reasons for this: (1) the public has more awareness and experience with the disability; (2) services and accommodations are more readily available; (3) individuals with high-incidence disabilities and their families can find more social support with others who have the disability; and (4) the lack of role models.

We have learned that the perceived ambiguity of the disability often leads to prejudice and discrimination (Pfeiffer, 2005; Phillips, 1990). Those who are blind and those who use a wheelchair experience less prejudice and discrimination because the public has had more experience with these disabilities; therefore people think that they understand blindness and orthopedic impairments (Mirzoeff, 1997). Blindness and orthopedic impairments do not elicit the fear and hostility that psychiatric disabilities often do. Ambiguity can also be experienced by those who have the disability. Due to all the medical and scientific advances, physicians are treating patients with conditions that they have never seen; in some cases, very few physicians are familiar with the conditions. In these cases, the diagnosis is delayed or changed while the physicians try to describe the condition accurately.

In telling the story about his amputation, Weisskopf stated that prostheses were becoming more functional and available because of the increasing number of soldiers with amputations in the Iraq and Afghanistan wars. Thus the *demand* or need for better prostheses accelerated their development. For individuals with low-incidence disabilities, there is no market demand for supplying their accommodations or services. People living in rural areas who have a family member with a low-incidence disability often must move (or travel long distances) to receive services, treatment, and monitoring from a large university hospital.

Individuals with low-incidence disabilities experience less social support; although with the internet, this is somewhat ameliorated. Social support helps to "normalize" the disability ("Oh, other people are experiencing what I am!"), provides role models and validity to their experience, and in general improves the quality of life for PWDs. Anne Finger had polio (which was then not a low-incidence disability). She described her first experience of associating with other polio survivors at a conference on post-polio:

> I sat for the first time in my life in a room filled with other disabled people. I remember how nervous I felt. I'd always gone to "regular" schools; I had been mainstreamed before there was a word for it. I had moved through the world as a normal person with a limp. (Finger, 1991, pp. 16–17)

One 9-year-old boy was born without any functioning muscles, due to a type of muscular dystrophy. He is on a ventilator (because he cannot breathe on his own), is fed through tubes in his stomach (because he cannot swallow), and uses a motorized wheelchair. Every year, this boy attends an Easter Seals camp for children with MD. Although he loves going to this camp with other children with his disability, he reports that "no one is as bad(ly disabled) as me."

There are no role models for those with low-incidence disabilities. The following are three examples of the value and life-changing aspects of role models. In the first example, the mentor assists by assuring the newly disabled person that her feelings are normal, or typical, and that the future will be good.

> I didn't want to admit that I was also handicapped. . . . She [the mentor] tells me that she felt like that, too, and that you get over this feeling. And you know that life goes on and that there's a lot out there that you can do, anything you want to. . . . You can still be just as much a person without [your legs]. (Veith, Sherman, Pellino, & Yasui, 2006, p. 293)

In this next personal experience, Joan Tollifson (a woman born without one of her arms) feels a greater sense of self-worth and self-empowerment after learning that others have experienced what she has. Rather remarkably, she sees that the prejudice and discrimination she has experienced all of her life is not the result of her own failings, but society's.

> They shared so many of what I had always thought was my own isolated, personal experiences that I began to realize that my supposedly private hell was a social phenomenon. We had eye-opening, healing conversations. We discovered, for example, that we had all had the experience of being patronized and treated like children even though we were adults. It wasn't simply some horrible flaw in my own character that provoked such reaction, as I had always believed, but rather, this was a part of a collective pattern that was much larger than any one of us. It was a stereotype that existed in the culture at large. Suddenly, disability became not just my personal problem, but a social and political issue as well. (1997, p. 107)

Role models provide practical information and can share their own experiences. They help answer such questions as, "How long will it take to go through my morning routine?" or "Who is your doctor? Does he or she understand your disability?" A woman with a spinal cord injury related the information she received from her mentor about specific questions:

[H]ow [the mentor] got around and what had happened to her and how she dealt with cooking and how she dealt with her kids, how she had sex, and what kind of bed she had. Lots of different questions [about] life and living.... Spasticity and, oh God, just everything.... And the more I learned, the less scared I got. (Veith et al., 2006, p. 291)

The Degree of Stigma and Prejudice

Nothing inherent in either the disability or the individual who has it warrants the prejudice and discrimination of PWODs. The expression of this prejudice and discrimination (often termed "handicappism") ranges from minor inconveniences for PWDs to differences in the type of housing, government services, education, and employment they receive (Frank & Elliot, 2000). The ADA (1990) and the Amendments (2009) to it have done a great deal to reduce handicappism.

The general society holds more prejudice for some types of disabilities than others. Generally society holds the least prejudice toward physical disabilities, more prejudice toward cognitive disabilities, and the greatest prejudice toward psychiatric disabilities. This is called the "hierarchy of stigma" (Antonak, 1988; Livneh & Antonak, 1991; Horne & Ricciardo, 2004; Smart, 2009; Tringo 1970); although it is a theoretical concept, this hierarchy of stigma is seen in the daily lived experience of PWDs. For example, the history of federal funding for disability services follows this hierarchy. Those with physical disabilities were granted services first, those with cognitive disabilities were then given services, and those with psychiatric disabilities were the last to be given services and legal protection. It is thought that the general public perceives physical disabilities more readily considers them understandable. Cognitive and psychiatric disabilities appear strange, ambiguous, and fearful, so individuals with these disabilities are often blamed for having the disability. Blaming the individual for his or her disability in attitudes such as "he brought this upon himself," or in beliefs that the individual should have done something or not done something to avoid the disability. Especially with psychiatric disabilities, the general public often feels that "these people should just try harder" (Leete, 1991). One author (Lewis, 2006) illustrated the hierarchy of stigma by referring to all nonpsychiatric disabilities as "the whole flock" and psychiatric disabilities as "the most vulnerable lamb." He also warned that after the wolf takes the lamb, he might also return to take the entire flock. "When a wolf wants to target a whole flock, it looks for the most vulnerable lamb. The Bush administration is targeting psychiatric survivors today, but the whole disability movement is the target tomorrow" (p. 348).

Perceptions about the way in which the disability was acquired also play a role in determining the degree of prejudice and stigma. Individuals who are thought (or known) to have caused their disability experience the most prejudice. Those with congenital disabilities experience less prejudice because the public feels that the individual could not have avoided the disability, and those who receive the least stigma are individuals whose disability is the result of "noble" endeavors, such as a workplace accident or a combat injury. Obviously, it is impossible to know by simply looking at a person the type of onset of the disability. Empirical research has shown that those individuals whose disability is a result of dangerous behavior, such as drunk driving or riding a motorcycle without a helmet, experience a great deal of prejudice.

Other aspects of the disability determine the degree of prejudice and discrimination encountered. Invisible disabilities and even mild disabilities elicit more prejudice. Under the ADA, PWDs cannot request accommodations if they do not disclose their disability. However, because individuals with invisible disabilities and mild disabilities often do not appear to have a disability, unreasonable expectations may be placed upon them; when these PWDs fail to live up to these expectations, PWODs think the worst. It is somewhat surprising, but individuals with mild disabilities often wish that their disability was more apparent so they could receive more services and accommodations. Invisible disabilities are also more ambiguous than visible disabilities; as the case of the woman in the Ann Landers column illustrates, others (even strangers) feel they can voice their negative and irrational criticisms.

Stigma and prejudice are complex but entirely unwarranted (Goffman, 1963; Leytens et al., 2000). Those who hold these prejudices literally pay for them in dollars and cents (May 2005). Not allowing a group of individuals (in this case PWDs) to develop their potential and talents, to be educated, and to contribute to the national economy is expensive (Lynch & Thomas, 1994).

FROM STIGMA MANAGEMENT TO IDENTITY POLITICS

Stigma directed toward PWDs, with all its false beliefs, can become self-fulfilling. When societies and governments (incorrectly) assume that all PWDs are totally economically dependent, laws and economic policies are enacted that simply provide financial resources to PWDs (National Organization on Disability, 2004). Accepting this false premise (of economic dependence), governments and societies can feel that such laws and polices discharge their responsibility to PWDs. Economic dependence and exclusion from the work force lead to segregation (O'Keeffe, 1994).

Stigma management means recognizing that regardless of one's accomplishments and resources, the PWD must understand that he or she is a member of a devalued, politically disenfranchised group (Lefley, 1991). PWDs with visible disabilities (or those who disclosed an invisible disability) understood that society did not value them and did not view the provision of accommodations for them as desirable or necessary (Frank, 1995; Pelka, 1997; Pfeiffer, 2005). The author of the book *The Anatomy of Prejudice* (Young-Bruehl, 1996) summarized:

> Unkind words against homosexuals, African Americans, Hispanics, and other minorities at least prompt rebuke from people who, though not members of these stigmatized groups, still recognize the prejudice. But prejudice against individuals with disabilities commonly goes undetected by a general public too unaware of its own feelings to recognize what has been said or written is prejudicial. (Fleischer & Zames, 2001, p. xv)

Individuals with disabilities could manage this stigma by refusing to internalize society's stigma by feeling self-doubt and humiliated. One PWD explained that he considered this prejudice to be justified: "The worst part about it is that I felt it my fault" (Holzbauer & Berven, 1996, p. 481). For those PWDs who have been teased and harassed since childhood, managing stigma as an adult may be overwhelming (Coleman, 1997; Huemann, 1997).

The passage of the ADA (1990) resulted in a group social identity for PWDs that crosses all diagnostic lines (Batavia & Schriner, 2001; DeJong & Batavia, 1990). No longer were PWDs divided into competing groups, such as "the blind," "the deaf," or the "mentally ill" (Berkowitz, 1987). Large national cross-disability groups, such as the American Coalition of Citizens with Disabilities and the Disabled Peoples International, began to organize. Americans with disabilities began to view themselves as a large citizen body with interests and needs, with the goal of creating disability policies and services (Humphrey, 1999). They modeled a great deal of their political movement on the Civil Rights Movement of the 1960s; indeed, much of the language for the ADA was borrowed from the Civil Rights Act of 1964.

Naturally not all, or even a majority of PWDs, are politically active. However,

> Once a shared identity is established, those defined as having a disability can become a distinct interest group which may become capable of mobilization.... By the 1990s, many appointed government officials responsible for making and enforcing government disability policies were recruited to their posts from...organizations of people with disabilities. (Asch & Scotch, 2001, p. 224)

This new political and social identity of PWDs has encouraged a new view of PWDs. Some social scientists term this "a narrative of emancipation." Life course developmental theory that positions individuals in various historical periods of time, such as World War II or the Baby Boom, allows us to view their lives through a historic lens. This has been termed, "cohort specificity" (Elder, 1998). Erikson (1950, 1964) believed that self-identities were formed by social expectations and social definitions. Presently a cohort of young adults with disabilities was born after the passage of the ADA. It will be interesting to observe and study their lives (Hahn, 2005).

What Do PWDs Want?

- American public education is a free entitlement program
- Disability is still considered to be a private, family concern

PWDs and their families want full civil rights and legal protection under the law when these rights are violated. They want a quality of life comparable to that of most Americans, including housing, transportation, education, and work (Burgdorf, 2002).

Most of all, they would like to see disability conceptualized in the same way as education. By law American children are entitled to a free, appropriate public education. Education is not viewed as a private family affair (except for the small minority who home-school their children). All citizens pay taxes that support public education, regardless of whether they have children enrolled in school. The rationale behind free public education for all children is based upon the benefits to the nation of an informed, educated citizenry.

American public education is a free entitlement program; proof of age and American citizenship are the only requirements to enter school. In contrast, disability is still considered to be a private, family affair (Friesen, 1996). Families are often over-burdened; parents are sometimes forced to leave the workforce in order to care for the family member with a disability, and PWDs are not given the services and financial work incentives that would let them use their potential to benefit the American people. Of course, there are some government-funded services for PWDs, but these are eligibility programs with long, difficult application processes. In addition, many PWDs are not able to access these services. There are private charities that serve and provide funds to PWDs and finance research to eliminate various types of disabilities. Although well intentioned, charity is not always reliable, and many PWDs resent the costs to their dignity and self-respect these charities extract. American public education is not based on charitable contributions, nor are application and eligibility processes required to enter school.

Continuing to conceive of disability as a private family affair is costing the American nation in many ways: one is a literal financial way, because any time individuals are prevented from fulfilling their full potential, the nation loses tax dollars and assumes responsibility for public assistance programs. When America's response to the disabilities of its citizens is not seen as a public entitlement, it also perpetuates the fear of disability. When PWDs are not integrated into American public life, PWODs continue to fear disability. Furthermore, PWDs have a term for PWODs—TABs (temporarily able-bodied).

The disability itself has many aspects, among them

- Type of disability
- Time of onset
- Type of onset
- Type of course
- Degree of visibility

However, most PWDs state that neither the disability itself nor its aspects make their lives difficult. Rather, it is the unearned prejudice and discrimination in the general public that limits them. Causes of prejudice and discrimination against PWDs include:

- Perceived type of disability
- Perceived type of onset
- Perceived type of course
- Perceived degree of visibility

All these causes have the word "perceived" because PWODs do not truly understand the individual's experience of disability; they simply *think* they know.

Terms to Learn

Anoxia	Dyskinesia	Syndrome
Ataxia	Normalization	TABs, normals
Choreoathetosis		

Videos to View

- View the 30-minute video *Abandoned to Their Fate: A History of Social Policy Toward People with Disabilities,* available from Insight Media. The producers describe this video: "This program traces the origins of social stereotypes of exclusionary practices toward individuals with disabilities from the Middle Ages through modern times. It explores the moral, aesthetic, and economic policies that have shaped the lives of individuals with disabilities."

- View the 42-minute video *Recollections of the Institution 1: Personal Reflections* available from Insight Media. The producers describe this video: "Featuring rare archival footage and excerpts from individuals who once lived in institutions for individuals with mental retardation, this program explores daily life in institutions."

- View the 20-minute video *What Is Mental Retardation?* available from Insight Media. The producers describe this video: "Explaining that mental retardation is a development disorder with many known and unknown causes, this program describes mental retardation, using the criteria of the *DSM-IV-TR.* It covers known causes of mental retardation, outlines normal growth and development from birth to age five, and explores associated comorbidities."

- View the Walter Brock film *If I Can't Do It,* which is "an unflinching portrait of one cantankerous and courageous disabled man, who, with many others, is pushing for independence and an equal slice of the American pie. Born with cerebral palsy in an isolated cabin in the Kentucky mountains in 1944, Campbell spent the first 38 years of his life at home, sheltered by his overprotective parents." This film was seen on PBS on the series P.O.V and was partially funded by the Corporation for Public Broadcasting.

- View the 56-minute video *Without Pity: A Film About Abilities* available from Insight Media. The producers describe this video: "This DVD celebrates the efforts of people with disabilities to live full, productive lives. Profiling diverse individuals with such disabilities as cerebral palsy, blindness, polio, quadriplegia, and missing limbs, this program emphasizes the resilience and potential of individuals who are determined to be self-sufficient." Emmy Award. Gold Apple, National Educational Media Network.

- View the HBO-produced video *Baghdad ER,* available from Films for the Humanities. This 65-minute program includes some nudity. The producers describe this video: "Combat-zone medicine has inspired innovations in civilian trauma care for decades. A particularly compelling model can be found in Iraq, where injured troops have a 90 percent chance of survival. This program follows U.S. Army medevac teams to crash and combat sites, depicts surgeries and amputations, and records the feelings of those who treat the effects of war every day. Viewer discretion is advised."

Learning Activities

(Note: These may also be used for class presentations.)
- Using the following variables in your analysis, discuss two physical disabilities, two cognitive disabilities, and two psychiatric disabilities:
  - Type of onset
  - Time of onset
  - Type of course
  - Degree of visibility
  - Prevalence of disability
  - Degree of prejudice and discrimination
- Visit these websites: The U.S. Census Bureau, Disability Selected Characteristics of Persons 16–74, http://census.gov./hhes/www/disability/cps105.html and The Disability Statistics from the American Community Survey (ACS) at Cornell University in Ithaca, NY, www.disabilitystatistics.org. Note the two levels of disability: severe and not severe. Which age group reports the greatest number of disabilities? Are there conditions that you had not considered to be disabilities?

Writing Exercises

- Go to the library and access the second edition of the Radius CD-ROMs. These data sets on these 19 CD-ROMs are the largest single source on disability. Their website is www.socio.com, and their e-mail address is socio@socio.com. Write a paper on the prevalence of one disability. In this 10-page paper, address the following demographic variables: sex, age, geographic area, income, level of education, and racial/ethnic groups.
- Write a 10-page paper with the title "Disability Is a Natural and Common Part of Life."
- Write a 10-page paper in which you describe and conceptualize two PWDs that you know. In case study style, compare their disabilities and their impact, using the terms described in this chapter.
- Write a 10-page paper in which you agree with this statement, "Biological deficits and disabilities can be triggers for growth and development."

Web Sites

http://www.teachingld.org/understanding/default.htm
http://www.easterseals.com/site/PageServer?pagename=ntl_understanding
http://dsc.ucsf.edu/main.php?name=understanding

Pregnancy and Infancy: Conception to 2 Years

10

Pregnancy is a well-defined, biologically based period that is critical because events occurring in pregnancy will have lifelong effects on the individual. Critical periods are those stages in life in which events have their greatest effect; in some cases, such as pregnancy, the individual cannot attain this type of growth in any other period. Perhaps more than any other developmental stage, pregnancy is the least socially defined. However, this does not imply that pregnancy is not somewhat socially defined. Unlike other stages, pregnancy also has well-defined starting and ending points—conception and birth.

The developmental period of infancy, typically defined from birth to 2 years of age, is a time of great development, including physical, neurological, and psychosocial development. Babies triple their weight during their first year of life, and the synapses in their brains become more elaborated. In the first 2 years of life, the brain grows to more than half its adult size; overall, the infant grows to half his or her adult size (Ashford, LeCroy, & Lortie, 2001). Infants learn to engage their environment in a social context; they begin to learn to regulate their emotions and are exposed to a large number of environment stimuli.

NEUROGENESIS

Demographic changes in the life periods of pregnancy and infancy include the larger numbers of congenital disabilities—ones that are present at birth. The term birth defects is now not used because of its negative, deviance-oriented bias; the preferred term is congenital disabilities. The U.S. Census estimates that nearly 1 in 16 infants is born with a congenital disability. Pregnancy and infancy are becoming more of a public and governmental concern rather than a private family affair. Generally speaking, congenital disabilities have a low rate of incidence and are considered severe disabilities. Each of these factors complicates the response and adaptation to the disability. Nonetheless, "the prevailing norms of the modern American family presume the absence of a disability" (Couser, 1997, p. 252).

Ethical issues have proliferated with advances in medicine, science, and technology. The combination of medicine, science, technology, and the irreversible outcomes of pregnancy has resulted in ethical dilemmas never before encountered. Prenatal screening in pregnancy makes it possible to accurately predict many types of disabilities. After the presence of a disability in the fetus is determined, the woman or the couple must choose whether they will continue the pregnancy and deliver an infant with a disability or terminate the pregnancy. Science and technology have thus provided more choices for a larger number of individuals. Prenatal screening is another example of medicine serving society and individuals in the society. However, it is not the place of science, medicine, or technology to render moral or value statements.

Developmental guidance can be considered a treatment service (Cicchetti & Toth, 1991). The developmental needs of children with disabilities (CWDs) and the ways in which to meet those needs can be discussed with the parents. Certainly parents of infants without disabilities who do not sleep through the night or of toddlers who resist toilet training ask their physicians and other medical service providers for advice. In the case of infants with disabilities, it might be more difficult for medical professionals to provide such developmental guidance because parents might interpret this as blame or criticism. The timing of the guidance is important. We have learned that many parents of infants with disabilities grieve the loss of the expected child, so it is more productive to wait until some of these emotions have subsided. Another source of developmental guidance is support groups of parents whose children have the same type of disability (Chesler & Chesney, 1988).

This chapter will discuss the following topics:

- the developmental stage of pregnancy
- the developmental stage of infancy
- gene-linked abnormalities
- chromosomal abnormalities
- hearing loss
- vision loss
- cerebral palsy
- spina bifida
- responses to a congenital disability
- the parents' needs
- positive aspects of having a child with a congenital disability
- congenital disabilities and the developmental theories
- ethical concerns
- screening tests
- abortion

PREGNANCY

Until the beginning of the 19th century, it was thought that the fetus began as a pre-formed, miniature human being who simply grew larger throughout the pregnancy (Scarr, Weinberg, & Levine, 1986). In the 1950s and 1960s, newly developed photo-graphic techniques literally allowed a picture of fetal development. We now know, for example, that at about 7 weeks of gestation, sexual development begins and the fetus becomes either a male or female. At about 8 weeks, bones begin to develop. In the first third of the pregnancy (the first trimester), the fetus develops basic structures, including internal organs, limbs, and sense organs. In the second trimester, the fetus continues to grow from 3 inches to 1 foot in length and from 1 ounce to 1.5 pounds in weight. In the third trimester, the fetus grows about 8 inches in length and gains 6 pounds.

Only recently has the need to provide the fetus with a safe prenatal environment been recognized. Until about the 1960s, it was assumed that every infant was safe in the mother's uterus. It was also thought that only beneficial substances ingested by the mother crossed through the placenta to the fetus. Gormly (1997) stated:

> It was assumed that the fetus was cut off from the outside world and safe from harm within the mother's body. But in the early 1960s, this belief was shattered by medical research that linked the birth of grossly deformed babies to the drug thalidomide, prescribed to their pregnant mothers to alleviate morning sickness. These babies were born either without limbs or with embryonic-like flippers. When thalidomide was taken during the critical period of limb formation (27 to 40 days after conception), the drug drastically altered the normal course of limb development. (p. 65)

Thus, two major (albeit recent) insights in the developmental aspects of pregnancy have greatly changed the experience of pregnancy for both the parents and the unborn child. When it was learned that the first trimester was the time of greatest development during which nearly all congenital disabilities occurred, more attention was focused on early prenatal care for the mother. The importance of the prenatal environment (the mother's uterus) focused attention on maternal nutrition and maternal drug intake.

Fetal Development During Pregnancy

- Cephalocaudal development
- Proximodistal development

The central nervous system and body parts begin to develop early in the pregnancy. By the end of the fourth week, the head and the body are visible, and the forerunners of the forebrain, midbrain, hindbrain, eyes, and ears are being formed. Although the brain grows greatly in size and complexity throughout the second and third trimesters, most of the brain structure is completely formed by the fourth month of pregnancy. Cephalocaudal development is related to many congenital disabilities. (Cephalo refers to the brain, and caudal means tail, and cephalocaudal development means head-to-toe development.) The brain forms first, then the trunk, then the arms and legs, and finally the fingers and toes. A primitive tail develops in this stage but disappears as the spinal cord develops.

Cephalocaudal development means that the brain is formed very early in gestation, often before the woman realizes that she is pregnant. In addition, during fetal development the brain grows at a faster rate than any other part of the body. Part of the brain tissue remains brain, and other parts of the brain tissue develop into the eyes and the face. A physician described:

> At one month gestation, the top end of your body is a brain, and at the very front end of that early brain, there is tissue that has been brain tissue. It stops being brain and gets ready to be your face...Your eyeball is also brain tissue.

It's an extension of the second part of the brain. It started out as brain and "popped out." So, if you are looking at parts of the brain damaged from alcohol during pregnancy, eye malformations and midline facial malformations are going to be very actively related to the brain across syndromes. (O'Rahilly & Muller, 1987, pp. 246–247)

Fetal proximodistal development parallels motor skill growth and development after birth. Proximodistal development means that physical and motor skill growth takes place from the center of the body outward. During the fetal stage, the head and upper trunk develop before the stomach, and the arms develop before the legs. Therefore, after birth (and into adolescence) upper body motor skills develop before lower body motor skills. Infants can raise their heads and sit up before they can walk. In the fetus, arms and legs develop next and fingers and toes after the arms and legs. After birth, infants are capable of controlling their arms or shoulders before they can use their hands and fingers.

CONGENITAL DISABILITIES

Most babies born in developed nations are healthy and considered to be normal. Furthermore, for many congenital disabilities it is impossible to determine the cause, and for others there are multiple causes. Premature births (or infants who are small for gestational age) are one of the leading causes of congenital disabilities. Nonetheless, only one in eight births is premature, and many premature infants do not have a disability. Santrock (2009) explained:

The number and severity of these problems (lower I.Q. scores, less effective information-processing skills, and at risk for behavior problems) increase when infants are born very early and as their birth weight decreases (Marlow et al. 2007). Survival rates for infants who are born very early and very small have risen, but with this improved survival rate have come increases in the rates of brain damage. (Allen, 2008; Casey, 2008)

At school age, children who were born with a low birth weight are more likely than their normal birth weight counterparts to have a learning disability, attention deficit hyperactivity disorder, or breathing problems such as asthma (Greenough, 2007; Joshi & Kotecha, 2007). One study revealed that 17-year-olds who were born with low birth weight were 50 percent more likely than normal birth weight individuals to have reading and mathematics deficits (Breaslau, Paneth, & Lucia, 2004). Approximately 50 percent of all low birth weight children are enrolled in special education programs (p. 101).

One study found that of the children who received intervention services before the age of 12 months, 33% were born at low birth weight, 17% were born at very low birth weight, 37% had been in neonatal intensive care (NICU), and 44% were required to stay in the hospital after birth (Howard, Williams, & Lepper, 2010).

Low birth weight infants are more common in multiple births (twins and triplets) and in teen-aged mothers, older mothers, and mothers who live in poverty. Maternal poverty is considered to be a constellation of pre-disposing factors for low-weight and premature infants, including poor nutrition, lack of prenatal care, and lack of insurance

FIGURE 10.1

U.S. children born with or develope long-term medical conditions each year.

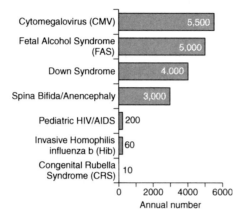

Source: CDC, 2008.

coverage. Many nations report lower rates of premature and low weight newborns than the United States, rates that are probably related to their health care systems, which provide free or very low-cost prenatal care (see Figure 10.1). Incidentally, the provision of prenatal care to low-income women has also been found to be related to higher rates of preventive care for their newborns and other children. It appears that the prenatal care links mothers to other social and medical services. The lack of prenatal care for a large segment of the American population is another illustration of the way in which society or the government can create disability. Developmental surveillance and early intervention programs and treatments should be provided for premature and low-weight infants (Collins-Moore, 1984).

Overview of Causes of Congenital Disabilities

- Maternal teratogens
- Maternal diseases
- Gene-linked abnormalities
- Chromosomal abnormalities

Maternal Teratogens

A maternal teratogen is any substance that crosses the placenta and harms the developing fetus. The word teratogen is derived from the Greek word *teras*, which means malformation. The prenatal environment is important to the fetus's development, and the mother is responsible for providing an optimal environment. Examples of teratogens are tranquilizers, narcotics, alcohol, marijuana, heroin, and cocaine. The effect of these teratogens on the developing fetus is based on the dosage, duration, and (perhaps most important) the timing of the exposure. Certainly exposure during the first trimester is especially harmful. Infants exposed to heroin and cocaine in the uterus have increased risks of congenital disabilities, low birthrates, and high rates of infant mortality.

Although maternal teratogens have a much greater effect on the fetus, the effect of paternal drug use on the fetus has also been recognized. Drug use among men can produce abnormalities in the sperm that can cause congenital disabilities (Pollard, 2000).

Tranquilizers, barbiturates, and analgesics depress the central nervous system and can result in pre-birth and post-birth bleeding. Nicotine intake (typically cigarette smoking) often results in low birth weight. Most studies indicate that infants born to smoking mothers, on average, weigh six ounces less than infants born to nonsmoking mothers. Marijuana use has also been associated with premature birth, low birth weight, and developmental delays.

Those drugs that act as vasoconstrictors (reducing blood and oxygen flow to the fetus) often stimulate early labor-induced separation of the placenta from the uterine wall and hemorrhaging. Cocaine is a vasoconstrictor. Drinking one or two alcoholic drinks every day substantially raises the risk of growth malformation as well as mental retardation. Fetal alcohol spectrum disorders (FASDs) are disabilities that are completely avoidable (Centers for Disease Control and Prevention, 2007) and are the leading cause of mental retardation in the Western world. There is no cure for FASD, although there are treatments and services available. Maternal alcohol use disrupts fetal brain development and the maturation of the central nervous system. A fetus metabolizes alcohol much more slowly than the mother does; therefore, the level of alcohol in the fetus's blood is much higher than the mother's. Alcohol interferes with the delivery of nutrition to the fetus' developing tissues, organs, and brain. FASD results in abnormal facial features, growth deficiencies, problems with learning, memory, attention span, communication, visual and verbal learning, or some combination of these. Maternal alcohol ingestion during pregnancy is a common cause of eye malformations and midline malformations because of alcohol's effects on cephalocaudal development.

Berk (2001) summarized the effects of fetal alcohol damage:

> Distinct physical symptoms also accompany it [fetal alcohol damage]. These include slow physical growth and a particular pattern of facial abnormalities: widely spaced eyes, short eyelid openings, a small upturned nose, a thin upper lip, and a small head, indicating that the brain has not developed fully. (p. 91)

Although the damage is not considered a congenital disability, it is now known that teratogens can also increase the infant's probability of developing a disability later in life. For example, children of mothers who smoke 10 or more cigarettes per day are at 50% greater risk of developing cancer during childhood (Stjernfeldt, Berglund, Lindsten, & Ludvigsson, 1986).

Maternal Diseases

Maternal diseases often result in congenital disabilities. These include rubella (German measles), diabetes, and sexually transmitted diseases such as syphilis, genital herpes, gonorrhea, acquired immunodeficiency syndrome (AIDS), and chlamydial infections. Because bacteria and viruses can cross the placenta, the fetus may be infected if a pregnant woman becomes infected.

Rubella is becoming increasingly rare because most women of child-bearing age were vaccinated againt rubella when they were children. On their first prenatal visit many women are given a rubella immunity test to ensure that the effects of the vaccination have not worn off. Like most teratogens, the earlier in the pregnancy the mother is infected with rubella, the greater the risks of damage to or death of the fetus. Rice (1998) summarized the effects of maternal rubella:

> If the mother is infected with the virus before the 11th week of pregnancy, the baby is almost certain to be deaf and to have heart defects and visual and intellectual deficiencies. The chance of defects is 1 in 3 for cases occurring between 13 and 16 weeks, and almost none after 16 weeks. (p. 71)

Many sexually transmitted diseases (STDs) result in the death of the baby shortly after birth. For example, between 50% and 60% of newborns who contract herpes die, and half of the survivors suffer brain damage or blindness.

Gene-Linked Abnormalities

Most congenital disabilities are part of a large number of similar disabilities or a family of disabilities. Therefore, the following discussion considers only the most common disability in any particular group or family, with the awareness that there are many more related disabilities. Genetic defects are inherited via a single defective dominant gene or a single defective recessive gene. Approximately 20% of all congenital disabilities are inherited. There are approximately 1,200 gene disorders and 124 sex-linked disorders. Many of these 1,200 disorders involve the interaction of several genes.

- Huntington disease—Although it is considered a congenital disability, symptoms of Huntington's do not appear until the individual is about 30 years of age. Symptoms include gradual deterioration of the nervous system, mental retardation, and eventually death.
- Cystic fibrosis—Babies born with cystic fibrosis do not have an essential enzyme. The absence of this enzyme results in mucous obstructions in the lungs and digestive system. Death eventually results.
- Phenylketonuria (PKU) is caused by an excess of phenylalanine, an amino acid that causes mental retardation.
- Tay-Sachs disease is caused by an enzyme deficiency and is most common in families of Eastern European Jewish origin. "One in every 27 Jews in the United States carries this gene" (Newman and Newman, 2009, p. 89). Symptoms include progressive retardation of development, paralysis, blindness, dementia, and death by age 3 or 4.
- Thalassemia is an inherited disease in which the blood does not carry enough oxygen. This disease occurs most often in individuals of Mediterranean, Middle Eastern, or Southeast Asian origin.

Obviously listing only five congenital disabilities caused by genetic defects disregards more than a thousand others. The five listed above are those that are most commonly known. Genetic counseling is available for couples who have a family history of these inherited disabilities. If a couple has genetic counseling before initiating a pregnancy, it can assist them in determining the probability of having a baby with this type of disability. Also, many of these genetic defect disabilities can be discovered by prenatal testing.

Muscular dystrophies are caused by X-linked recessive inheritance for which women are carriers. The many types of muscular dystrophy are all inherited diseases characterized by muscle degeneration. Diagnosis is usually made with boys when they are between the ages of 3 and 5. The most common type is called Duchenne muscular dystrophy (DMD) and was discovered in the mid-1800s. At about 2 years old, the child with DMD cannot walk, falls often, and has difficultly going up and down stairs. Between the ages of 8 and 12, there are significant declines in motor functioning, and these children must use braces, walkers, or wheelchairs. The young person dies in late adolescence or in his or her early 20s. Later in this chapter, we shall discuss the experience of a mother, Pat Furlong, who had two sons with DMD. Reading her experiences allows us to see that physicians subtly blamed her for the DMD because she was the carrier of the gene that caused DMD.

Chromosomal Abnormalities

There are two types of chromosomal abnormalities; sex chromosomal abnormalities and autosomal chromosomal abnormalities. Infants can be born without a specific chromosome or born with an extra chromosome or, more rarely, with the loss of a large portion of a chromosome. A syndrome is a pattern of traits which has a single cause, such as a genetic syndrome (Meyer, 2001). Examples of disabilities caused by chromosomal abnormalities are:

- Fragile X syndrome affects both males and females, although it is twice as common in males. It typically includes mental retardation.
- Turner's syndrome affects only females and typically includes incompletely developed internal and external sex organs, short stature, deafness, and mental retardation. Turner's syndrome is caused by the deficiency of a chromosome and "is the only disorder in which a fetus can survive despite the loss of an entire chromosome. Even so, more than 99% of... [Turner's syndrome] conceptions appear to miscarry" (Batshaw, 2007, p. 7).
- Kleinfelter's syndrome affects only males and results in feminine appearance, infertility, and occasionally mental retardation.

DOWN SYNDROME

The most commonly known autosome chromosomal abnormality is Down syndrome. (Dr. Landon Down was the physician who first described the syndrome.) Down syndrome is the result of having an extra chromosome and is also related to maternal age, with women over 40 more likely to have an infant with Down syndrome. Congenital heart disease is very common. Both physical and mental development is delayed. The average IQ for someone with Down syndrome is approximately 50. Down syndrome is the best known example of a genetic syndrome and is the second most common genetic cause of mental retardation. Fragile X syndrome is the common genetic cause of mental retardation.

Until the 1960s, the most common term used to describe Down syndrome was mongolism, which referred to the facial anomalies. According to Fishler and Koch (1991) more than 50 traits are associated with Down syndrome, although most individuals with this disability may have only a few of these traits. Physically children with Down syndrome may be of short stature, have clubbed short fingers, and have skin at the inner corner of each eye that forms a fold, making the eyes appear slanted. Other physical characteristics of Down syndrome are rosy cheeks, malformed ears, flat nose bridge, and often a tongue protrusion. One of the most dominant physical characteristics of Down syndrome is low muscle tone (hypotonia); therefore, children often have delayed motor and speech development.

Down syndrome is an example of the longer life spans of PWDs. At the first of the 20th century, the average life expectancy of an individual with Down syndrome was 9 to 12 years, but today the life expectancy for infants who survive their first year of life is 60 years. Before the discovery of antibiotics, upper respiratory infections often resulted in death for individuals with Down syndrome.

SCHIZOPHRENIA

Schizophrenia is a disability that has both hereditary and environmental causes. It cannot be said that children inherit schizophrenia from their parents. However, it has been shown that children inherit a predisposition toward it. Although the general incidence of schizophrenia is about 1% of the population, about 12% of their children will be affected if one parent has it. If both parents have schizophrenia, 39% of their children will also have this psychiatric disability (Rice, 1998). Twin studies have also demonstrated a genetic component.

HEARING LOSS

Nongenetic congenital hearing loss results from both pre-birth and post-birth factors, such as infections, lack of oxygen during the birth, prematurity, physical trauma, or exposure to antibiotics. There are also genetic causes of hearing loss, one of which is Usher syndrome. In Usher syndrome, the infant is born with a profound hearing loss, then (typically in adolescence), develops retinitis pigmentosa, a degenerating loss of vision. Most individuals in the United States who are deaf and blind have Usher syndrome. Before the advent of antibiotics, most individuals who were deaf and blind had survived a severe case of a bacterial infection. These individuals then recovered but were deaf and blind.

It is widely believed that it would be worse to be born blind than deaf. Although both are disabilities with many limitations, deafness has the potential for greater and more generalized interference with development because the deaf child finds it very difficult to learn oral language. Without spoken language skills, cognitive skills are negatively affected. Language skills and cognitive development are closely associated. Allen and Cowdery (2009) explained:

> Children who are blind learn language with considerably less difficulty than children who are deaf. They benefit from the many incidental learning opportunities every day. They hear casual conversations containing bits of information that add up to valuable learning. They hear teachers' and parents' instructions and suggestions. All of this contributes to cognitive development.
>
> Because of the influence of language in forming and maintaining relationships, children who are blind also have more options for social learning than children who are deaf. (p. 147)

Many researchers believe that deaf children miss the "critical period" in which language is learned. Deaf children who cannot hear sounds and verbal stimulation during infancy and early childhood may never fully master language.

VISION LOSS

Most infants with congenital blindness experience other disabilities, such as cerebral palsy or intellectual disabilities. Indeed, it has been noted:

> The incidence of blindness in children with multiple developmental disabilities is more than 200 times that found in general population. One third of children with partial sight and two thirds of children with blindness have other developmental disabilities, the most common being intellectual disability, hearing impairments, seizure disorders, and cerebral palsy. (Miller & Menacker, 2007, p. 152)

Common causes of blindness in children include traumatic brain injury, severe eye infections, and tumors.

Children who are born blind or become blind in the early years of life have no concept of what they supposed to be seeing, because they have no visual experience with such concepts as colors, shapes, distance, depth, or proportion. Falvo (1991) summarized:

> [Individuals who have congenital blindness] because of their lack of visual experience in their environment, such as the observation of tasks or behaviors of others... must learn by other means concepts that sighted individuals take for granted. This adaptive learning of tasks then becomes a natural part of their developmental process so that the adjustment to visual limitations is incorporated into their self-perception and activities as a normal part of growing up. (p. 225)

Therefore, although those who with congenital blindness have the advantage of early development of compensating abilities, the blindness also affects their motor development, cognitive development, and social development. The child's ability to interact with others is decreased. Often children who are born blind experience learning problems, even if they have average or above-average intelligence. Total blindness, the inability to distinguish between light and dark, is relatively rare.

The use of Braille is declining in the United States. Braille is a writing system with raised writing that is very difficult to learn. Indeed, most individuals with late-onset blindness never attempt to learn Braille. The decline in learning Braille is thought to be caused by two factors: (1) use of speaking technology and (2) the lower attendance rates at residential schools for deaf and blind children. Although advanced speaking technology has many uses, relying solely on such technology means that without Braille blind people would not be able to read or write. It would be difficult for most people, blind or sighted, to learn and remember everything simply by hearing. Children who attend residential schools learn Braille early in life and become proficient. Of course, children, parents, and families want all of their children to live at home and to be educated in the neighborhood school. Nonetheless, when the shift from residential schools to community schools occurred, the use of Braille began to decline.

CEREBRAL PALSY

According to Livneh and Antonak (1997) approximately 9,000 children in the United States are diagnosed with cerebral palsy (CP) each year and about 1 million individuals have this disability. Approximately one out of every 200 children has some form of cerebral palsy.

Cerebral palsy means "brain weakness." Like most other developmental disabilities, cerebral palsy is diagnosed on the basis of functional characteristics rather than on the cause of the disability. CP is diagnosed when there is severe functional mobility that is thought to be associated with signs of neurological dysfunction. It is non-progressive (has a stable course) and is thought to a result of a non-mature brain, hence the word cerebral in the name. Cerebral palsy is one of the disabilities for which the hypothesis of causation has changed. Traditionally CP was thought to have been the result of a lack of oxygen during birth. Now it is thought that most cases of CP are a result of brain injury or genetically based abnormalities in development of the brain. CP is much more common in premature infants, infants who are a part of a multiple birth (such as twins or triplets), or those who are full term but small for their gestational age (Pellegrino, 2007).

Cerebral palsy often involves secondary disabilities, such as speech and language impairments and cognitive deficits. According to Kopriva and Taylor (1993), one-third to one-half of children with CP have some level of intellectual disability. It is difficult for children with CP to speak because of dysarthria (lack of speech fluency); therefore, they are often isolated because others do not take the time to understand these children.

CP causes multiple disorders of movement and posture, along with abnormal muscle tone. Children with CP often walk with abrupt, involuntary movements. Therefore medications to reduce spasticity are necessary. Orthotic straightening devices, such as braces, improve posture and movement. Children may need orthopedic surgeries throughout their childhood (Pelletier, 1988).

SPINA BIFIDA

Spina bifida means "split spine" and is the most common neural tube defect (NTD). The correct term is meningomyelocele. It "also has been called the congenital malformation most compatible with life" (Liptak, 2007, p. 419). More than a spinal lesion, spina bifida is incomplete development of the brain and the meninges (the protective covering around the brain and spinal cord). It is the most common neural tube defect in the United States, affecting 1,500 to 2,000 of the 4 million babies born in the United States each year (see Figure 10.2).

The exact time of the malformation is known; most NTDs occur 26 days after conception during the period of neurulation, which is the first step in forming the central nervous system. The most serious form of spina bifida includes paralysis, sensory loss below the lesion in the spine, and learning problems. There is no cure because the damaged nerve tissue cannot be repaired or replaced, nor can function be restored to the damaged nerves.

Some infants with spinal bifida also experience hydrocephalus (water on the brain), which requires immediate shunting after birth in order to drain the fluid. Therefore, some (but not all) children with spina bifida demonstrate unusual language and learning problems.

Catheterization in order to assure that the bladder is completely empty is often necessary. It is important to keep catheters clean in order to avoid infection. Most parents learn these skills. By the ages of 8 to 10 years, children will begin to learn self-catheterization skills, but during the elementary school years, someone must assist the child when he or she is in school. Complicated daily treatments, such as catheterization, demonstrate the difficulty of obtaining babysitters or allowing the child to participate in sleep-overs.

FIGURE 10.2

Prevalence* of U.S. children with spina bifida, ages 0 to 11.

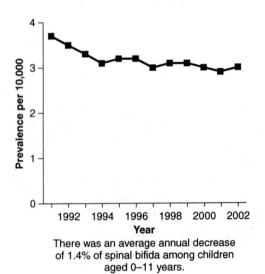

There was an average annual decrease
of 1.4% of spinal bifida among children
aged 0–11 years.

*Proportion of spina bifida cases in the population to the total live births.
Source: CDC, 2010.

FIGURE 10.3

Spina bifida estimates.

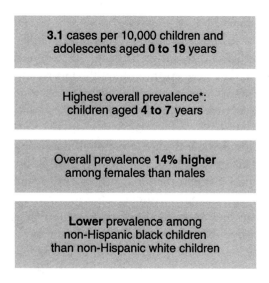

*Proportion of spina bifida cases in the population to the total live births
Source: CDC.

Spina bifida can be treated before the birth of the baby. The mother's abdomen and uterus are opened, and physicians close the opening over the developing baby's spinal cord. This is a risky procedure for both mother and child that cannot restore lost neurological functioning; however, it can prevent further loss from occurring (see Figure 10.3).

One mother told of the birth of her daughter with spina bifida:

> My husband will never forget that trip to Boston, being asked whether to treat the baby—a decision, really, whether to let her live. He was told that she was paralyzed from the waist down, would never walk, and would be retarded if she lived at all—and then he had to return to me to go through it all again. With essentially no guidance from anyone, we were asked to make a decision regarding a child for whom we had waited for 6 years and about a condition we had never heard of until just hours earlier. (Winske & Lingerman, 2007, p. 410)

INFANCY

Infancy is generally considered to be the first 2 years of life, and the 2-year-old child is very different from a newborn infant. From birth to age one, very rapid physical growth takes place. In the second year growth slows, following a linear annual increase. A National Academy of Sciences task force determined that the first 3 years of life exert a powerful influence on future development. Although learning takes place throughout life, plasticity (the ability of the brain to change in function and anatomy) decreases after the third year. Neuroplasticity means the brain's capability for growth and is a relatively new idea because historically science and medicine thought that the brain did not change, other than to decline in old age.

It is now known that while the greatest neuroplasticity takes place during infancy, the brain can rewire itself, resulting in a reconfiguration of the neural networks. We often say, "I've changed my mind." We now understand that it is also accurate to say, "I'm changing my brain."

Developmental tasks include developing gross motor skills and fine motor skills, along with acquiring verbal and receptive language. However, the sensory/perceptual system of the newborn infant develops more rapidly and functions at more advanced level than motor skills. Infants learn to attend actively and respond to their environment through all their senses. In order to learn and to interact socially, the five senses must be developed.

Following birth, vision is the least developed of all the senses; however, at approximately 6 months visual acuity is normal. Infants have the ability to hear and can discriminate their mother's voice from other voices by as early as three days old.

The mother typically has the most intimate relationship with the baby. Infants who have secure attachment to their mothers develop into children, adolescents, and adults who (paradoxically) feel free to explore the world, attempt new things, desire to meet different types of people, and accept others with nonjudgmental tolerance. The sense of freedom is the result of the secure base that the mother provides. Attachment to the mother (or the caregiver) also results in more enthusiastic, persistent, cooperative, and effective individuals.

Responding to a Congenital Disability

- Today, medically fragile and technology-dependent newborns are not automatically placed in an institution
- The parents must adapt to the disability

The practice of neonatal medicine has changed and improved. For example, not very long ago, tracheostomy and gastrostomy tube placement were considered "extraordinary" measures (especially if the infant had very severe cognitive impairment) but are now considered to be ordinary measures (Silber, 2007). Tracheostomies allow newborns to breathe and gastrostomies provide nourishment.

In the past medically fragile and technology-dependent newborns were automatically institutionalized. There were no community services, such as in-home health care, respite care for parents, or special education. Many of these newborns did not live long after placement in an institution, although others spent decades in these settings. As a result of past practices, many parents of older children with severe disabilities feel that they have been unjustly maligned for putting their children in these institutions. However, others do not understand the combination of the total lack of services at the time of the child's birth. When other living arrangements were made available, adults who had lived their entire lives in an institution often preferred to stay instead of attempting some type of supported living setting in the community. These adults who had arrived at these institutions as infants had no other home or family.

Most of the research on congenital disabilities has focused on the infant, and very little attention has been given to the parents or the family (Scarr & McCartney, 1983). When an infant is born with a disability, it is obviously the parents (and the extended family) who must respond and adapt (Berube, 1996, 1998). With the introduction of prenatal testing, it is now possible for some parents to know in advance that disabilities are present. Other parents do not know that the baby has a disability until he or she is born. If the parents decide to have the baby with a known disability, they have a few months' time for preparation, such as seeking out other parents who have a child with the same disability and allowing the extended family (especially grandparents) time to adjust. Most of these parents simply state, "We got our worrying done before the baby was born and we were able to greet the baby with love and concrete plans for treatment and care." These parents must deal with caring for the infant even as they simultaneously grieve the loss of the baby they had imagined, a baby without a disability, a normal, healthy baby (Heller, Rafman, Zvagulis, & Pless, 1985). Parents find that "everyone was shocked, confused, and uncomfortable."

One grandmother told of her family's reaction when her grandson was born with multiple disabilities:

> [The baby's diagnosis] was a multisyllabic disease, very rare and genetic. Grandparents and great-grandparents gasped! That diagnosis set both sides of the family busy rattling skeletons trying to prove that each was pure and not responsible for the present suffering. (McPhee, 1982, p. 13)

One mother of a child with an intellectual disability (or mental retardation) told of her experience of giving birth to this child in the 1970s.

> When the baby was born, they said, "Oh God, put her out." This is the first thing they said, "Oh my God, put her out". . . and the next thing I remember was waking up in the recovery room. . . . I had my priest on my left hand and my pediatrician on my right hand . . . and they were trying to get me to sign a paper. . . . I just couldn't believe that this was happening to me and I said to my priest, "Father, what's the matter?" and he said, "You have to sign this release. Your daughter is very sick." And I said to the pediatrician, "What's the matter with her?" and he said, "Don't worry honey, she'll be dead before morning. . . . " He said that she had something that was too much to talk about, that I shouldn't worry myself. . . . Nobody was telling me what this was . . . I was very depressed. (Darling, 1979, p. 130)

Babies with congenital disabilities often have medical crises that occur later and cause the parents more grief and adjustment to the disability. Ambiguity or fear of the future is a major concern. What will my baby be able to do? How long will my baby live? Will my baby go to school? (King, Scollon, Ramsey, & Williams, 2000). Pat Furlong, the mother of two sons with Duchenne muscular dystrophy (DMD), is a nurse and her husband is a physician. When she was in graduate school at Ohio State University, she ran the intensive care unit at the campus medical center. She explained how unprepared she was in trying to determine what was wrong with her sons:

If an adult was sick, I could go through it systematically and say, "What are we looking at?".... But with the children I didn't have those tools. (Colapinto, 2010, p. 64)

Her husband later admitted that he had considered the possibility of DMD, "But, it's not a diagnosis you want to make." This physician-father's denial could be considered a Freudian defense and is an example of the way in which emotion can overwhelm rational, logical thought processes.

Low-Incidence Disabilities

- Difficult to diagnose
- Difficult to find services and treatment
- Difficult to find role models
- Often considered "orphan diseases"

Although many more infants are born with congenital disabilities than ever before in history, many of these disabilities are termed "low-incidence" disabilities, which means that very few individuals have these disabilities. Low-incidence disabilities are more difficult to respond to than high-incidence disabilities. Reviewing the chart of congenital disabilities, one can seen that for *each type* of disability only a small number of babies each disability. As neonatal medicine continues to allow more babies to survive, physicians and pediatricians will be treating disabilities that they may never have heard of before.

Most congenital disabilities are relatively rare, meaning that there are few infants with each type of disability. This statement may not appear congruous with the statement that the *number* of congenital disabilities is increasing and is expected to continue to increase. These statements make sense when we understand that there are many more types of disability. One author explained:

Unlike adults, where the type[s] of chronic illnesses [disabilities] are few in number but are prevalent, each of the hundreds of different conditions in child is relatively rare.... Except for a few common disorders such as mild asthma, the prevalence of any single condition is less than 1 per 100 children. (Patterson, 1988)

Debbie Jorde is the mother of two adult children with Miller's syndrome. In her book *Eight Fingers, Eight Toes: Accepting Life's Challenges* (2010), Jorde described the experience of the birth of her children. Miller's syndrome is an example of a low-incidence disability: only thirty people worldwide have this disability. Indeed, Jorde's family was the first family to have their entire genome sequenced. Miller's syndrome is characterized by facial and limb malformations.

Congenital low-incidence disabilities are difficult to diagnose, and often the diagnosis changes as the infant manifests more or different symptoms, or as more information becomes available. Some disabilities may be so rare that there is medical debate on naming the diagnosis, prescribing treatment, or planning for the future. Ambiguity and lack of clarity are common with low-incidence disabilities, regardless of the age of onset.

Low-incidence disabilities, acquired at any age (but far more common in congenital disabilities) are often termed "orphan diseases." Orphan diseases are disabilities and illnesses for which the National Institute of Health (NIH) and other similar government organizations do not fund research because not enough people are diagnosed. The National Organization for Rare Diseases (NORD) publishes a newsletter and lists 140 nonprofit health organizations serving people with rare disabilities.

It is difficult to find services and treatments for low-incidence disabilities, especially if families live in remote rural areas. Living in a large urban area with a university teaching hospital, especially a children's hospital, makes it easier to obtain diagnosis, treatment, and services. There are few role models or parent support groups for low incidence disabilities, although the internet is a great advantage. One mother of an 8-year-old boy was born without muscle control. He uses a respirator, a feeding tube, and a computerized wheelchair. John has never breathed on his own, eaten anything by mouth, or spoken. He communicates with a computerized communication board. The physicians told the parents that John's condition does not have "an official diagnosis" and that it is a result of "a random genetic mutation." His mother says that John loves to go the Easter Seals camp for children with muscular dystrophy and described his experience, "He was in heaven knowing that there were kids a little like him." However, she also says, "We get stared at all the time, even at the Easter Seals camp."

Most congenital disabilities are also severe disabilities that require expensive treatment and technology, many visits to doctors, and decisions by the parents about medical treatments, living arrangements, and type of education for their child very early in their child's life. Smart (2009) summarized:

> Faced with an array of needs—a complicated structure of services and payment requirements—parents make decisions. Occasionally, as would be expected, these children grow up and later question or resent the decisions by the parent(s). (p. 432)

Remember the man in the video, *My Body Is Not Who I Am* who said, "I resented my parents jumping at the requests of the doctors." This man had undergone many corrective surgeries during his childhood.

THE FAMILY

Each family unit is a small culture that transmits traditions, values, religious beliefs, and ethnic identity. Families are also the major disability-defining institution, transmitting perceptions, values, and definitions of disability. Families are also the major source of disability services. Because society rarely thinks about disability (even professionals who work with families), often the importance of family in the provision of disability services is rarely considered.

Families who have an infant with a congenital disability must deal with all the typical family needs but at the same time respond to all the demands of caring for their baby. These parents are faced with a staggering amount of medical and technological information, some of which may be contradictory. John's parents lived in a small trailer at the married students' housing complex at a large university. A nurse came every night to watch John and listen for the alarm that sounded if the respirator failed. As a newly married couple who had their first child while the husband was attending the university, they felt that their life was stressful before John was born. Now their privacy was compromised. One set of grandparents was willing to learn the technology and the complicated care routines, but the other grandparents were intimated by the risks involved.

Typically the mother provides the majority of care given to an infant with a disability, although men are participating more than in the past. Obviously good parenting skills, a strong marital relationship, financial stability, and excellent problem-solving competencies contribute to feelings of achievement and competence in caring for an infant with a disability (Cook & Ferritor, 1985). One mother described her experience:

> I am the mother of this child. While it is she who must bear the trauma, the pain, and the limitations, it is I who suffers with her and sometimes, truthfully, because of her.
>
> After writing the brief medical history, I thought I would try to compute the hours spent in and traveling to and from hospitals. I found it impossible—the hours are uncountable. Which is worse, I think, life-or-death surgery with comparatively little follow-up or routine orthopedic surgery, which requires trips to Boston (20 miles away) three times a week for physical therapy. It has been almost a year since the last surgery and we are still making the trip twice a month. The exercises are never ending, the casts must be continually replaced, and trying to motivate acceptance of these responsibilities by Karen was, until recently, next to impossible. (Dell Orto & Power, 2007).

An adult born with cerebral palsy described the way in which her mother's response to the daughter's disability "greatly complicated" her life. Note also that in spite of birth trauma, she was not diagnosed with cerebral palsy in the first year of her life. Note also the way in which she describes two contrasting responses to having an infant with a disability: to not bond with child at all, anticipating that the child will die at an early age or to become "desperately afraid" of having the child die at an early age.

> After I was born, they were unaware that anything was wrong with me for almost a year. It was only when I could not perform the expected developmental activities—such as rolling over by myself, reaching for objects, and beginning to crawl—that they began to realize that there was problem. I was not quite a year old when my pediatrician informed them of his diagnosis of cerebral palsy.... Research indicates that mothers of congenitally disabled children exhibit a tendency of being afraid to become close to their children due to the fear that they will die.... One of the complications of... birth trauma was that I was more susceptible to respiratory infection. From reading about the reactions of mother parents, I can now see that my mother was desperately afraid

of losing me. Her acute anxiety in this regard greatly complicated my life in childhood and adolescence. (Pellitier, 1988, p. 55)

These are heavy demands even for a highly functional two-parent family that is financially stable and has helpful, willing members of the extended family nearby to offer support and care. Demographically, this type of ideal family is becoming more uncommon. There are many single-parent (most often mothers) families, and there are families who do not live close to extended families. The Family Caregiver Support Act of 2001 recognizes the heavy responsibilities placed upon families and offers some assistance and services for families. This law also recognizes the contribution of family caregivers. For example, it is estimated that family care giving saves the federal government more than $196 million a year. It is also important to support the marriage of parents with a child with a disability. They must meet many demands and frequently do not have enough resources, all of which places stress on the marriage. One parent stated, "It's easy for both of us to have a bad day."

In an article entitled, "Uncommon Children," the mother and aunt of a child with severe disabilities succinctly described this dilemma:

We expect parents of children with disabilities to "rise to the occasion," but some don't or can't. As a nation we were recently horrified by the Kelsos, who left their profoundly disabled ten-year-old at a Delaware hospital with a note saying they could no longer care for him. Certainly, they did the wrong thing. But their desperate act should not be dismissed lightly as simply aberrant. (O'Connell & Foster, 2000, p. 18; cf. Ginsburg & Rapp, 2010, p. 242)

Such legislation as the Family Caregiver Support Act also acknowledges that disability is no longer only a family concern but a public issue. The following news story is an example of the way in which the macrosystem (state government) failed the microsystem (the family). The economic recession of the late 2000s required workers at Indiana's Bureau of Developmental Disabilities Services to tell parents to leave their children with severe disabilities at homeless shelters during the day while the parents worked. "There have been no confirmed cases of families dumping severely disabled people at homeless shelters because Indiana wouldn't provide the care needed. But some families have been on waiting lists for waivers [to receive Medicaid funding] for 10 years. The lists contained more than 20,000 names last month" (Kusmer, 2010). One mother described the lacks of services for her daughter:

Becky Holladay of Battle Ground, Indiana, said that [was] exactly what happened to her, [the Bureau of Developmental Disabilities Services telling her to leave her son at a homeless shelter] when she called to ask about the waiver she's seeking for her 22-year-old son, Cameron Dunn, who has epilepsy, autism and attention deficit hyperactivity disorder.

Holladay, a school nurse, said that she and her husband would go bankrupt trying to pay for services themselves, so Cameron spends most days sitting in his stepfather's truck while he works as a municipal employee.

"It's heart-wrenching as a parent to watch it. We are the people and they are the people," Holladay said, referring to her son and others with disabilities. "They have lives that are worth something." (Kusmer, 2010)

Cameron Dunn, who is 22 years old, has graduated from special education because federal law states that an individual must leave special education at age 22. This lack of services for PWDs will probably result in more abortions of fetuses with disabilities. Without lifetime support, mothers and their partners will feel compelled to terminate the pregnancy. Therefore, although abortions are a highly personal and private choice, society shares some of the responsibility for providing these types of services.

PARENTS' ADAPTATION

First-time parents idealize their babies and their infancies. Many parents of babies without disabilities feel powerless. The baby requires around-the-clock care and creates a need for almost every aspect of the household to change. The fantasies of imagined parenthood and are quickly discarded. For parents of children with disabilities, there are more demands for adjustment, and these demands are more pervasive and life-long.

Parental guilt is very common when an infant is born with a disability. If one reviews the short overview of maternal teratogens, chromosomal and genetic disorders, it can be seen how easy it would be for the parents to look for both a cause and a source. The so-called "cause" is often falsely interpreted as something the parents did or did not do, and the so-called "source" may be the attempt to determine "which side of the family did this come from?" Often the family or neighbors may ask the mother what she did or did not do during the pregnancy. This is an example of implied blame. Occasionally professionals have implied that one of the parents (especially the mother) may be responsible for the disability. Remember the "refrigerator mother" theory of causation for autism?

These are futile questions for two reasons: first, the cause and the source are often not known. Physicians call the disability "idiopathic," which means unknown, or the physicians state that cause of the disability is "multifactorial" or from many different sources. Second, whether it is self-blame or implied blame from others, blame has been shown to be detrimental to adjustment and adaptation. Parental self-blame is common in some cases because an unknown etiology (cause) of a disability is stressful (Nixon, 1993). Everyone wants to know (with any type of disability) the cause, but often the cause is unknown. This is difficult to accept; therefore some parents prefer self-blame to the stress of ambiguity. When parents blame each other for their baby's disability, it places stress on their marriage. Occasionally older siblings think that they are to blame for the disability of their baby brother or sister. The following excerpt shows a mother's stages of adaptation, her feelings of self-blame, and her feeling that she had failed her husband, the baby, her family, and society.

> I had read many times about the grief surrounding the birth of a child with defects, but the literature had not seemed to apply to me. My life certainly included denial, anger, bargaining, depression, and acceptance. But, these were not milestones on a timeline, but were aspects of every day, sometimes every hour. Furthermore, there was little grief attached to the "expected baby." The grief was tied up with the whole mental picture I had for myself, my family, and our future. Feeling that I had failed myself, Kurt [her husband], Beth [the baby], the family, and even society itself, what I really had lost was my whole sense of self-esteem. (Miller, 1988, p. 145)

Another mother related her growing awareness of her son's cerebral palsy as a door closing slowly and a ghost drifting away. Notice also her awareness that there would be neither a cure (a miracle) or death,

> Later, the words which have already reverberated in my head are pronounced by the neurologist: cerebral palsy. As he reviews the findings, a door slowly shuts. There will be no miracle, neither will Robbie die soon. As we leave the clinic carrying our reprieved son, the ghost of Robbie-might-have-been begins to drift away. (Currey, 1995, p. 26)

A French woman who was born deaf described her parents' denial (Laborit, 2010):

> Uncle Fifou, my father's older brother, was the first to say, "Emmanuelle makes shrieking sounds because she can't hear herself." My father claims it was my uncle who "was the first to arouse our suspicions." "The scene is frozen in my mind," says my mother.
>
> My parents didn't want to believe it. To such an extent, in fact, that it was only much later that I found out my paternal grandparents had been married in the chapel of the National Institute for the Deaf in Bordeaux. What's more, the institute's director was my grandmother's stepfather. In an attempt to hide their concern, perhaps, or to avoid facing the truth, my parents had forgotten all about that! (pp. 599–600)

In the National Public Radio Disability History Project *Tomorrow's Children* (May 1998c), parents of children with congenital disabilities report that physicians have told them, "This should have been caught" (Wilson, 2006). Parents who have undergone prenatal testing, discovered the presence of a disability, and chose not to have an abortion may be viewed as selfish and irresponsible. Pat Furlong is a mother with two sons with Duchenne muscular dystrophy, both of whom eventually died when they were teenagers. Furlong related this experience:

> The doctor upbraided her, she says, for having had a second boy. "You should have known about this," she recalls him telling her. "This is a familial disease, it's genetic, you have it in your family." I said, "I don't." (She learned later that she was among the one-third cases of cases in which the mutation appears spontaneously.) The doctor insisted, "You could have prevented the second pregnancy, or you could have aborted the second pregnancy." Patrick, then four, was sitting on Furlong's lap. "Before that day, I was relatively mild-mannered," Furlong says. She remembers grabbing the doctor's tie and pulling him up to her nose. I said, "If somebody should have been aborted today, you're the one." (Colapinto, 2010, p. 65)

In a textbook on life span developmental psychology (Callahan & McCluskey, 1983), a chapter heading asks: "The Birth of a Defective Child: Permanent Crisis?" However, for most parents and families, the sadness decreases. The family develops a routine of care, accesses early intervention programs, and obtains support and services. Eventually they begin to see development in their infant, development that is specific to the disability. One family expressed it this way, "Little steps and small progress are really important to us." Families and parents adjust their expectations and aspirations and gain both meaning and control over the situation (Darling, 1983; Darling & Baxter, 1996). Occasionally, families and parents seek counseling services that help them to balance the emotional needs with the physical demands of caring for an infant with a disability.

One of the tasks of families who have a child with a disability is to prove to the world that their child and their family are normal (Green, 2007). One mother wrote to the newspaper advice columnist Ann Landers. The mother described her daughter's disability:

> I gave birth to my first child last April. "Crystal" was 12 weeks premature and weighed less than 2 pounds. We were afraid that she would die or have severe handicaps, but we were blessed with good fortune as her only remaining requirement is the extra oxygen she receives through a nasal tube worn 24 hours a day.
>
> Because the nasal tube makes her look different, I have received a lot of unsolicited and rude comments. People ask, "What's wrong with her? Was she born that way? What's her problem?" I do not wish to discuss my daughter's medical condition with strangers, and considering the handicaps she might have had, my husband and I feel there's nothing wrong with Crystal at all.
>
> Ann, please alert the boneheads out there that if they see a child who is "different," to coo over the baby the way they would a "normal" child.

From Crystal's mother, we can see that the family considers themselves "normal." In another example, John's mother expressed the same need to be considered normal but related many pleasant experiences. "It is so fun when people do normal things with John." The Ann Landers letter is another illustration of the number of babies who survive premature birth but with a disability. Crystal's parents feel fortunate that she survived and believe that a nasal breathing tube is small price to pay for Crystal's life. Also, this short letter shows that the attitudes of others are often more difficult than managing the disability.

It is necessary to separate the disability and its functional limitations from the "disabled role" of being inferior and facing a life of limited choices. An elderly lawyer who was born blind was interviewed upon his retirement. The interviewer could not mask his amazement that the man had graduated from law school and had had a successful law practice. "How did you do it?" the interviewer asked. The lawyer responded in one short sentence: "My parents never taught me that I was disabled." Of course, his parents knew he was blind. The lawyer communicated, however, that his parents did not view blindness as an obstacle to a life of achievement and contribution.

For children with congenital disabilities, as with any other children, it is the parents who interpret the child to himself/herself. For children with disabilities, parents also define the disability and its implications. What one family would consider a mild disability may be a severe to another (Scorgie & Sobsey, 2000). One author described these differing perceptions:

> Families with strong beliefs in high achievement and perfectionism tend to equate normality with the optimal, to define normality or successful family functioning in terms of ideal or problem-free circumstances. Families that

define normality in this way are prone to apply (disability) standards that are inappropriate because the kind of control they are accustomed to is impossible in this situation.... The fact that life cycle goals may take longer or need revision may require some modification in beliefs about what is normal and healthy. Sustaining hope, particularly in situations of long-term adversity, demands an ability to embrace a flexible and broad definition of normality. (Rolland, 1994, p. 135).

Components of Disability Identity

- The disability itself
- The "disabled" role imposed by society
- The PWD's self-identity

The disability, the "disabled" role imposed by society, and the individual's self-identity are often considered to synonymous, especially by those who do not have disabilities. However, very important distinctions should be made between these concepts. Indeed, most PWDs refuse to be defined by others, in the same way that everyone likes to define himself or herself.

Joan Tollifson (1997) described her life long experience dealing with societal responses to her congenital disability. An important distinction is that Ms. Tollifson was speaking not about her disability but about others' reactions to it.

I'm missing my right hand and half of my right arm. They were amputated in the uterus, before I was born, by a floating fiber. The question "what happened to your arm?" has followed me through life.... Total strangers come up to me on the street and inquire. Children gasp in horror and ask. People tell me with tears in their eyes how amazingly well I do things, such as tie my shoes. Or they tell me they don't think of me as disabled. (I guess they mean a "real cripple" would be totally incompetent, and I always wonder if they would regard the amputation of their own right arm as no loss at all, no disability.) Or people try desperately to pretend that they don't even notice. Nobody says a word. People swallow their curiosity and conceal their discomfort, hoping that the Great Dream of Normalcy is still intact. One of the central memories of my childhood is of children asking me what happened to my arm. (pp. 105–106)

The definition of disability includes the losses, the functional limitations, the financial demands, and day-to-day management of the disability. Disability is not a minor inconvenience. In contrast, the "disabled role" is the rules and expectations that society places upon PWDs (and often their families). It is not a self-identity. These rules include: (1) always be cheerful; (2) answer all questions asked by strangers; (3) actively manage the disability, or better stated, *the PWD must appear as if he or she is managing the disability*; (4) ignore prejudice and discrimination; (5) appear and behave as "normal" as possible; and (6) do not seem demanding when requesting accommodations. Of course, since the ADA and the greater number of PWDs, some of these role expectations are changing. Nonetheless, when a PWD refuses to accept society's "disabled role," he or she is often considered to be denying the disability or to be an angry, bitter, tormented individual. When we clearly outline the "disabled role," we can see that the disability and the disabled role are two different concepts. The disability is not curable; but society is curable.

Finally, many PWDs consider their disability to be an integral or inextricable part of themselves. Is it possible to love a PWD and not his or her disability? PWDs want to be loved for who they are (as everyone does) and part of who they are is the disability. These last two sentences may seem either counterintuitive or a semantic exercise. For those without a disability and who have had little or no experience with PWDs, it is difficult to understand how it would be possible to love someone's blindness or schizophrenia, or paralysis. If offered a "magic pill" that would completely eradicate the disability, would not every PWD automatically seize the chance? Surprisingly, some PWDs say no and many hesitate, stating that they would need to consider the possibilities. Dr. Temple Grandin, a woman with autism explained:

> If I could snap my fingers and be nonautistic, I would not—because then I wouldn't be me. Autism is part of who I am...As I have said, it has been only recently that I realized the magnitude of the difference between me and most other people. During the past three years I have become fully aware that my visualization skills exceed those of most other people. I would never want to become so normal that I would lose these skills. (1995, p. 180)

Of course, there is no "magic pill." However, later in this chapter, we shall discuss abortion, an issue of actually possessing a "magic pill." The debate over abortion of fetuses with disabilities requires the clear definition of (1) the disability itself; (2) the disabled role imposed by society; and (3) the capability of PWODs to love the individual and his or her disability.

Nick Vujicic is an Australian motivational speaker who raises more than $1 million a year to build hospitals and orphanages. He is the oldest child of a nurse and a church minister (Basheda, 2006). Nick was born without arms and legs and asks people who try to tell him that his life is a tragedy, "How do you know what it feels like to be me?" His disability was not known until he was born despite the fact that his mother had ultrasound tests during the pregnancy. He considers this prenatal lack of knowledge to have been a gift, stating: "I'm so thankful that they knew nothing and were not confronted with the choice of abortion." The cause of his congenital limb deficiencies is not known. He is a university graduate, is a very successful stock market trader, and has written a book titled, *No Limbs, No Limits*.

Nick credits much of his success to his parents' small church congregation who provided his parents (and him) with ongoing, unquestioning support. He summarizes his disability: "I have something to give the world that no one else can." He has a sense of humor, telling audience members, "If you walk out, I'll have someone throw me at you." He drives a car with hand controls and likes to freak out other drivers by turning completely around in the driver's seat.

What Do Parents Need?

- Access to information and services
- Financial support
- School and community inclusion
- Family support
- Respite from the stress of being on "high alert" for safety concerns

The concern expressed most by parents of a newborn with a congenital disability is the need for information and services. One parent described her experiences, "I mean it's been a fight for anything, it's unbelievable," and another parent explained, "You have to understand where we are coming from first. We get so many no, no, no, no, no" to requests for information and assistance (Resch et al., 2010, p. 142). Parents' first reaction to having a baby with a congenital disability is often the feeling of being over-whelmed and not knowing how to access information and services, and at the same, understanding the importance of starting treatment as soon as possible. One parent described the importance of information:

> I mean, I was like "information!" I couldn't get enough...just anything, every-thing...You find something, your first help....whatever it was that [makes you go] "oh thank God, somebody can talk to me." (p. 143)

Simply informing parents about the disability and referring them to parent support groups can be considered a type of "service" or "treatment" (Pearson & Sternberg, 1986; Santelli, Turnball, Lerner, & Marquis, 1993). Many parents (and PWDs of all ages) relate that they learned about available services from other parents of children with dis-abilities. Physicians recognize the importance of parent support groups and view them as an adjunct to their services. Parents of an infant born with dwarfism (achondroplasia) related the importance of support groups in helping them to overcome their denial. The last line is: "He's really going to stay small." (This statement is an illustration of denial of the permanence of the disability.) These experiences were helpful; but they also made them physically ill. Also, note the generosity of Paul and his wife in inviting the new parents into their home.

> Paul said, "Why don't you come over to our house after the meeting. We're going to have dessert in the evening." I remember sitting on the couch. These people had all their furniture cut down. Well, we had the best time. We got up ready to go and when we stood, that's when it hit me. Because when we were sitting, everyone was the same. But when we stood up, these people were down below my waist. Our heads were spinning and our stomachs were churning and we went home. We ended up being involved, and going to other meetings that they had because we felt that it was important for Joey to have that exposure at that time, if he was indeed a dwarf, which is a permanent condition. These people were real people in different professions and a lot of members were a big

help during that time. But we used to have to take Pepto-Bismol when we got home, because even though we'd had a good time; it was the reality of it all. And I think that's what's good. I think that's good for parents, to be hit with the reality. You find you're enjoying it, but when you go home, you suffer the effects of that reality—that my child is not going to grow. He's really going to stay small. (Albon, 1989, p. 357)

The most common cause for dwarfism is achondroplasia and individuals with this disability use the self-identifier of "little people" (Albon, 1984). Achondroplasia manifests as defective bone growth, resulting in short stature (adult height averages 4 feet). There is also a disproportionate shortening of their arms and legs relative to their body and, therefore, as these parents discovered, their sitting height is closer to average than their standing height. Babies born with achondroplasia have an arched skull to accommodate an enlarged brain and they have a low bridge across their nose. Their hands are typically short and broad, with the index and middle finger close together as are the ring finger and the pinkie (Mackelprang & Salsgiver, 1999).

A secondary condition can be deafness because poor growth of the facial bones increases the frequency of ear infections which, in turn, lead to permanent hearing loss (Kelly, 1996). In some types of dwarfism, retinal detachment results in blindness and compression of the spinal cord can result in neuromuscular changes.

In today's world of neonatal medicine, there are disabilities for which there is no definitive diagnosis or no known cause. Often, the diagnosis changes. Many, if not most, congenital disabilities are low incidence disabilities and therefore, there are few treatment protocols. Both eligibility and funding for services is closely associated with the diagnosis. When an infant is born with more than one disability, it is often difficult to determine which agency or medical specialty should take primary responsibility (and the funding) for the care of the infant.

Pat Furlong, the mother of two sons with DMD, explained her methods of gaining information from the doctors:

Furlong began travelling to medical centers around the United States and Europe. "I wanted to understand the landscape—who the players were, what they thought, how they thought about Duchenne, what priorities, what plans," she says. She found that very little was being done, and that few doctors were willing to talk to her. "Most researchers and physicians will do anything to avoid meeting with distraught mothers," she said. To get past secretaries, she would impersonate a doctor on the phone, then arrive at meetings dressed for the part. "I would wear something very professional and the highest heels possible," she said. She added, "Of course, I'd start crying the minute I sat down with them—so they knew." (Colapinto, 2010, p. 66)

Some parents become "crusaders," becoming increasingly immersed in support groups as mentors and becoming involved in groups advocating for increased funding, better services, and more research. Typically, crusader families have many resources at their disposal. Reading Furlong's story, we can see that she has a strong will, the ability to challenge professionals, organizational skills, and has financial resources which give her the time and money to travel to research hospitals and centers. In 1984, Furlong relates that she withdrew $100,000 from a bank account to pay for her sons' treatment, giving some indication of her financial resources.

Another concern is the financial barriers to obtaining services. A stay in the Neonatal Intensive Care Unit (NICU) can cost hundreds of thousands of dollars. Even with excellent insurance, the deductible costs are large. For parents who must travel to a university teaching hospital, travel and child care costs for other children quickly accumulate. For those parents who can access services, the financial burden can be overwhelming (Andrews et al., 2009). However, many parents cannot access services because they do not qualify for financial assistance. These parents make too much to qualify for government-funded services and, yet, do not make enough to be able to pay for these services. One parent explained:

> You can't get anything if you're . . . I mean we are working paycheck to paycheck and we don't qualify for anything, but then we can't get anything because we can't pay for it . . . if you are at the poverty level, you might get some kind of help, but if you're not, you can't get any assistance if you can't pay for it. (Resch et al., 2010, p. 143)

Some families become experts in obtaining multiple sources of funding and quickly learn all the entitlements available (Agosta & Melda, 1995). Other families struggle with these demands. A mother of a child with spina bifida described the weekly paperwork required.

> My husband's role and mine did not change a great deal, but they expanded instead to include more tasks, some of which were traded or shared. He spent many hours each week on the paper work and financial mix-ups of insurance, handicapped license plates, taxes and the like. (Lingerman, 2007, p. 414)

In addition, most parents must reduce the time spent at work in order to care for their child. Typically, it is the mother who becomes the care-giver. The mother in the following excerpt has two daughters, the oldest Lindsey without a disability and the younger, Beth, with spina bifida.

> It was my husband who helped me see that I was over involved with Beth, not that Lindsey was lacking my attention. Both girls were thriving.
>
> Once I gained some time and the distance that Beth's schooling provided at age 3½, I was able to see our enmeshment more clearly. I had not been prepared for the sense of responsibility I would feel toward a child, perhaps even an able-bodied one. The enmeshment had been understandably born out of our desires for a child and the related needs of this particular one. Enmeshment was also fostered by the system that taught me all the care and treatments. I once realized that I was expected to carry out 9 hours of assorted treatments per day, while meals, baths, groceries, a social life, laundry, errands, and recreation were to come out of the little remaining time. (Lingerman, 2007, p. 414)

Round-the-clock nursing care for infants and children who are technology-dependent (such as using a breathing tube) is expensive. "John," who was born without muscle control requires surgery every six months to replace the rod in his back in order to facilitate his growth. John has had his saliva glands removed so that he doesn't drool. Assistive technology must be purchased frequently because infants grow rapidly. Adaptive technology, such as wheelchairs, are expensive because they must be customized to fit the needs of each child, another aspect of a low-incidence disability: the technology cannot be purchased "off-the-rack."

Parents are worried about school and community inclusion. Often, when parents take their CWD in public, they are the subject of disapproval because onlookers mistakenly believe that the parents are not disciplining the child or that the parent is overprotective (Bendell, 1984). Many parents, in order to avoid these encounters, keep the child at home. These mistaken perceptions are especially common in children who have invisible disabilities. Smith (2010) described these incidents.

> Social isolation may be an adaptive mechanism for families with a child who has an unobservable disability. In my family's situation, my son looks and usually acts like a child who is developing typically, yet this mirage can easily be blown away by loud noises, small spaces containing several people or a busy street with too much traffic. I protect my son from these possible threats with great care. As a result, I am often the recipient of disapproving glances. The label of "helicopter mom" might apply to me—*if* my son didn't actually require that level of care. (p. 55)

A different view of parental care is described by a woman as "destructive."

> My mother's overprotection was also a destructive element in my development. She assumed complete care of all my physical needs. This meant that I was lifted in and out of bed, onto the toilet, and in and out of our car. I was bathed, dressed, groomed and fed without my lifting a finger to help myself. I realize now that it would have been extremely difficult for her to sit by passively and watch me to struggle to perform these basic activities of daily living. Although my mother meant well by catering to me in this way, it retarded my physical development because I was never given the opportunity to work on doing these essential tasks. Such a relationship caused me to be completely dependent upon my parents. (Pelletier, 1988, p. 58)

Another parent described her experiences with professional service providers:

> Many times, as parents, we'll go to an agency and the social worker sees the disability and she automatically labels our children. For them, your child is not going to accomplish anything in this life. Some people think that way and parents are confronted with those people. Unfortunately, it happens a lot of times. (Resch et al., 2010, p. 144)

Frequently, parents feel that they must become political activists in order to encourage others to view their children as individual children with needs and potential.

The need for support and assistance from family members is often expressed. It is said that it takes a village to raise a child; but for children with disabilities, often there is no village. A mother said her infant "cried" for months, day and night. Caring night and day for a child with multiple and severe disabilities puts the caregiver in the high stress position of being on "high alert" for safety concerns. Infections in shunts and catheters could require immediate hospitalization for intravenous antibiotics. Devices may become clogged at each end. Planning and organization are difficult because when the child with a disability becomes sick or has to be hospitalized, all plans are cancelled. One parent expressed,

> I know in our situation we rely on my mom who lives 2 hours away, in the summertime she takes our kids one on one..... We are relying on this distant grandmother to just spoil these kids rotten and give us a break. And we don't have a real severe situation in the home, we, you know, it's not intense. But, it's a wonderful break just to get to be individual with this other kid. (p. 145)

Susan Smith (2010, July) is a counselor who provides counseling services to parents of children with disabilities. She has a son with Asperger's. Smith described her services as a combination of psychoeducation, referral services, and grief counseling.

> As a counselor, I envision myself gathering information and collaborating with specialists to uncover the facts so I can assist families in restructuring their perspectives to start from a realistic framework.
>
> This does mean glossing over the truly difficult and overwhelming feelings that accompany these families' situations. When I work through my own circumstances, I find that I need to marry grief work and psychoeducation—honoring my feelings of loss while also gathering information about expectations and alternatives, some of which are positive in nature. (p. 56)

POSITIVE ASPECTS OF HAVING A CHILD WITH A DISABILITY

Surprisingly, many parents relate the positive aspects of having a child with a disability. Indeed, one of the conclusions of the Resch et al., study was, "Being the parent of a child with a disability is not a devastating experience as one might assume." In other studies, families experience an increase in hardiness, cohesion, and state they have met individuals and had experiences that they would have never had, if their infant did not have a disability (Summers, Behr, & Turnball, 1989). The supportive environments of support and advocacy groups provide social acceptance and understanding of their experience. The family develops self-esteem as they gain mastery over the disability and the care of their new baby. Many feel that their life has been enhanced and enriched.

Siblings of infants with congenital disabilities often demonstrate an increased maturity, a sense of responsibility, and tolerance and compassion for others who might be considered different. Many siblings of individuals with disabilities enter the helping professions (Trachtenberg, Batshaw, & Batshaw, 2007).

It is predicted that, eventually, there will be education classes for parents of infants with congenital disabilities (Andrews et al., 2009). Since parents are vulnerable to psychological distress, counseling, both individual and group counseling, should be provided to them to help them negotiate the adjustment process.

Smith, the counselor with a son with Asperger's summarized the positive aspects of their disability experience. Note that many of these abilities and skills were present before the birth of their son; but the family "strengthened" or "fine-tuned" these abilities.

I considered the positive ways that my son has affected our lives. Our family experienced an initial readjustment of our values and a reconsideration of life's priorities. We fine-tuned our teamwork skills, strengthened our family bonds and discovered that husbands/fathers are capable of cleaning toilets. Most important, we all learned the true meaning of love—an engaged, full-throttle, unconditionally accepting love that I wonder if we would have learned otherwise. (2010, p. 56)

The Individual's Adjustment to Congenital Disability

- Generally, congenital disabilities are easier to adjust to than disabilities acquired late in life.
- Adults with congenital disabilities have no pre-disability identity.
- Infants and small children are flexible and adaptive.
- Infants do not have a well-developed body image.
- Children and adults with congenital have developed compensation strategies.
- Typically, infants and small children do not encounter prejudice and discrimination until they attend school.
- Those with congenital disabilities have not internalized society's prejudices and discrimination about disability.
- There is less societal prejudice and discrimination against individuals with congenital disabilities.

Adults and older children with congenital often state, "For me, abnormal is normal." Generally, the earlier the age of onset, the adjustment is less difficult and more complete. For example, research has shown that children with congenital limb deficiencies tend to adjust better than children with acquired amputations (for example, due to therapeutic surgeries for cancer).

Gerri Jewell is a stand-up comedian who appeared on a Public Broadcasting System (PBS) comedy special, "Look Who's Laughing." She was born with cerebral palsy. In her comedy routine, she jokes: "It's not like I wake up every morning and say, 'Oh my goodness, I have cerebral palsy!' I was born like this." In contrast, Christopher Reeve, the actor who played Superman and who acquired a spinal cord injury in a horse-riding accident, told a television interviewer that upon awaking in the morning, he is momentarily surprised to find that he is paralyzed. Christopher Reeve was required to change his identity and Gerri Jewell had no identity except as a PWD. Remember, we are not discussing the type or severity of the disability; we are discussing the time of onset, or the developmental stage of onset.

Society's false beliefs about the tragic, limited life of those with disabilities are not accepted (or even recognized) by infants and small children with disabilities. Infants and small children have not acquired the prejudices and discriminations about PWDs and therefore, their disability is not an emotionally fraught experience. Typically, the older the individual, the more he or she has accepted the ideas of the wider society, such as disability is an unbearable tragedy. Of course, the small child with a congenital disability understands that he or she has a disability which must be managed; he or she simply does not view the disability as unbearable sadness.

There is less societal prejudice and discrimination directed toward individuals with congenital disabilities because others do not blame the individual for the disability. We have learned that one of the causes of prejudice is the idea that the individual brought the disability upon himself or herself. Stated in such a forthright manner, it seems absurd that anyone actually accepts this notion. However, these widely held beliefs are not often clearly expressed. Furthermore, false assumptions against many different types of individuals have persisted for centuries.

Infants and children with congenital disabilities develop idiosyncratic compensation strategies and coping abilities. The management of the disability is a daily experience and, often, the child is taught to execute these techniques independently. The acquisition of these skills may be due to the innate flexibility and adaptability of infants and small children. Brenda Premo explained her compensating skills:

> The fact that I was born with my visual disability has had advantages. I have what my eye doctor calls "compensating skills." My brain has compensated and fills in the pictures of what I cannot see with my eyes. For example, I remember where steps are if I have been on them before. I see the steps because the brain is filling in what the eyes can't see. Sometimes I make mistakes, so I have to be careful, but my brain gives me the picture. It's easier for me than someone who has been blinded later in life. (Mackelprang & Salsgiver, 1999, p. 140)

Magee, a philosopher from the U.K., is blind. He wrote about his blindness when he was a small child.

> I had a vivid nonvisual awareness of the nearness of material objects. I would walk confidently along a pitch black corridor in a strange house and stop dead a few inches short of a closed door, and then put out my hand to grope for the knob. If I woke up in the dark in a strange bedroom and wanted to get to a light-switch on the opposite side of the room I could usually circumnavigate the furniture in between, because I could "feel" where the larger objects in the room were. I might knock small things over, but would almost invariably "feel" the big ones. I say "feel" because the sensation, which I can clearly recall, was as of a feeling-in-the-air with my whole bodily self. Your phrase "atmosphere-thickening occupants of space" describes the apprehension exactly. I suddenly "felt" a certain thickness in the air at a certain point relative to myself in the blackness surrounding me.... This illustrates your point that the blind develop potentialities that the sighted have also been endowed with but do not develop because they have less need of them. (Magee & Milligan, 1995, pp. 97–98)

DEVELOPMENTAL THEORIES AND INFANTS WITH DISABILITIES

The theorist who placed the greatest significance on the developmental period of infancy is Freud. Socializing experiences between the mother (or other caregiver) and the infant are reciprocal, or bi-directional. The mother responds to the baby and the baby responds to the mother and thus an attachment is formed. In spite of the age differential between mother and infant and the power differential between the mother and baby, both members of this dyad contribute to these attachments. On a very basic level, the mother remains close to the baby in order to ensure his or her safety and survival. The mother responds to the baby's physical needs and provides love, comfort, and security, remaining attentive to her baby's changing needs.

Freud's theory of attachment (or the oral stage of development) has been confirmed in empirical research conducted with both animal babies and human babies, starting in the 1960s. This research has shown that the emergence of these attachment bonds is both normative and universal (Bowlby, 1969, 1973, 1980). Infant animals who were not allowed to form attachment bonds were found to have experienced *physical* changes, in addition to emotional changes.

> In animal studies, it was found that even minor deprivation of contact results in abnormal neuoranatomical structures and impaired endocrinological sensitivity related to stress and coping (e.g., Ginsberg, Hof, McKinney, & Morrison, 1993). Studies of human children adopted from orphanages, some having impoverished opportunities for human interaction, also reveal neuro-hormonal sequelae of restricted social contact. (Chisholm, 1998; Collins, 2002, p. 12; Gunnar, 2001; Rutter et al., 1998)

Infants with neuromuscular disabilities may be difficult to hold and comfort and often, an occupational therapist teaches the parents these techniques (Harper & Peterson, 2000).

Babies with osteogenesis imperfect (OI), or brittle bone disease, are subject to bone fractures and deformities, and some infants die (Zarestsky, Richter, & Eisenberrg, 2005). There are two basic types of OI, congenital in which fractures are present at birth and latent in which the condition first appears in childhood. In congenital OI, the infant may be born with broken bones and many of these children die within the first few years of life. In both types of OI, the bones are fragile, the limbs are thin and may be misshapen. Due to the fact that the bones fail to form correctly, a slight bump or jolt or even carrying the infant down a staircase could break the baby's bones. Occupational therapists work with parents, especially when braces and crutches are used. In some cases, surgery is required and the bones are cut and threaded over a rod. It is easy to understand why some parents might be anxious when caring for their infant with OI.

Researchers also study "relationship histories" of older children and adults. Anna Freud, Freud's daughter, spent 60 years developing techniques of psychoanalysis for children and adolescents. She became interested in the impact of the environment upon the development of the child. One author described Anna Freud's work:

> During World War II, she observed many children who were orphaned, had survived concentration camps, or in other ways were affected by the war, and she became very aware of their resilience.
>
> Although trained and analyzed by her father, who arrived at his theories through reconstruction of childhood events as he analyzed adults, Dr. [Anna] Freud was more interested in directly exploring a child's life history through observation as the child lived it. Child analysis, she believed, is needed when

development is impaired due to the possibility of threatened fixation at some phase; the goal must be healthy future functioning. The child's ego and super-ego are immature and subject to physical, psychological, and environmental threats. Full-blown "neurotic symptoms" are not usually observed in children. (Austrian, 2002, p. 21)

Erikson understood the importance of the infant-mother relationship, terming the developmental task of infancy to be the development of trust rather than mistrust. Erikson thought that as an infant gradually increases the number of waking hours, "he finds that more and more of his senses arouse a feeling of familiarity" (1959, p. 219).

Capps (2008) explained:

This feeling—especially recognition of the mother and sense of her presence—enables the infant, in time, to let the mother out of sight without undue anxiety and rage, because she has become an inner certainty as well as an outer predict-ability. In effect, the infant trusts her as much when she is absent as when she is present. Erikson called this the infant's "first social achievement."

Erikson's theory clearly stated the importance of the quality of attachment to later social competencies and outcomes of the infant. Individuals who have strong infancy attachment bonds are able to form relationships with others, successfully resolve con-flicts with others, and are able to commit responsibly to others. Naturally, adults do not replicate the relationship they had with their mother when they were infants; but the attachment bonds formed in infancy provide a foundation for all later relation-ships. Strong attachment bonds formed in infancy provide *expectancies* about the world and the people in it. When considering Erikson's dichotomy of trust vs. mistrust, it is easy to understand that those individuals who established strong attachments in their infancy view the world as safe, friendly, welcoming, and interesting and are more open to the positive influences of other people. Strong attachment bonds allow the infant and young child to build the ego strength to deal with future challenges and to survive and, at times, thrive when difficulties arise.

According to Erikson, mistrust develops, when the mother is rejecting, avoiding, or depressed. The absence of a once-loving mother is devastating to the infant. Infants with disorganized relationships with their mothers tend to experience less ego strength later in life. If the needs of the infant are not met, the infant may feel worthless and insecure. In order to develop trust, infants need continual, routine, loving care or maximum comfort with minimal uncertainty.

Congenital disabilities are considered to be a challenge to the attachment pro-cess. For infants born with severe and multiple disabilities, long stays in the Neonatal Intensive Care Unit (NICU) or prolonged treatments at a specialized hospital distant from the parents' home may disrupt the attachment process. In hospitals, caregivers change with each eight hour shift. On the other hand, if the infant is cared for at home, the parents might be depressed, exhausted, overwhelmed, or withdrawn, attempting to respond to a future of caring for a child with serious, significant disabilities. Of course, parents can be depressed, whether or not their infant has a disability; it is simply more common in parents who are required to face a different reality than they imagined. However, most parents with infants with disabilities do form strong attachment bonds with their babies. Medical providers understand the importance of the attachment process and, therefore, provide opportunities for the parents to form these bonds.

The polio epidemics provide a clear example of parental separation. Marc Shell (2005) compiled a collection of first-person accounts of polio patients, survivors, and their families, constructing what he termed a "metapathography" (p. 6). Shell defined metapathography as comparing and contrasting hundreds of accounts, some book-length of the polio experience. Shell discovered some idiosyncratic experiences and perceptions; however, he found many more commonalities among the survivors from Canada, the United States, the U.K., South Africa, Australia, New Zealand, France, the Scandinavian countries, Mexico, and Singapore. He also defined the metapathography of polio as "the sociology of a childhood disease" (p. 7). Childhood separation from parents and family was one of the most common experiences:

> Polio narratives almost always involve children being separated physically from their parents because of the legal need for quarantine or the medical need for treatment. . . . The military aspects of the enforced sequestration in New York City—of the sick population (concentrated in guard camps) from the healthy. . . . This separation from family and home could last weeks, months, or years. Tom Atkins's first-person account *One Door Closes, Another Opens: Personal Experiences of Polio,* describes how he was entirely isolated from his family from the age of three to the age of seven. In many cases, the end of the quarantine period meant legal orphanhood or permanent institutionalization by the states. . . . This separation usually affects a person quite as much as the lasting physical disabilities that polio imposes. (pp. 33–35)

The supreme irony of separating polio patients from the families was the fact that when the polio symptoms appeared in the individual, the entire family and anyone who lived in the house had already been infected. It was the physicians and the nurses (and their families) who were risking their lives. Since medicine and science did not understand the polio virus, it was falsely thought necessary to quarantine polio patients.

THE BEHAVIORISTS AND INFANCY

The underlying premise of behavioral theorists is that all behaviors are learned. Regardless of the complexity of the behavior, it has been acquired through simple behavioral learning techniques. One extreme form of behaviorism is described:

> Give me a dozen healthy infants, well-formed, and my own specified world to bring them up in and I'll guarantee to take any one at random and train him to become any type of specialist I select—doctor, lawyer, artist, merchant, chief, and yes, even beggar-man and thief, regardless of his talents, penchants, tendencies, abilities, vocations, and race of his ancestors. (Watson, 1926, p. 104)

The behaviorialists were confident and often made these types of claims. Further, we can see by the words, "healthy" and "well-formed" infants born with congenital disabilities were never included in these theories. Behavioral therapy techniques are more often used, especially behavioral-cognitive therapy, which combines the cognitive theories with behavioral theories.

For Piaget, the infant begins life by developing intelligence, although he or she cannot differentiate between self and non-self. Piaget termed this lack of differentiation as global causality. This does not mean that the infant is passive or completely helpless or that he or she does not interact with others and the environment. Since the infant does not use language, activity is the dominant form of learning. Moreover, one of Piaget's most important contributions is his idea of sensory-motor learning which, in the absence of language, the infant learns by using the senses and movement. For infants born with a sensory loss or a nueromuscular disease, pediatric occupational therapists have devised treatment protocols to ameliorate some of these losses.

The ecological framework of Bronfenbrenner's theory can be very useful in understanding the experience of a parent of an infant with a congenital disability (Sontag, 1996). Bronfenbrenner's Systems Theory allows us to view disability as a public concern which affects everyone, rather than a private, family experience. Considering the section of this chapter about the needs of families, we can see that parental and infant well-being is influenced by many systematic factors, such as family support, access to medical care and assistive technology. The financial concerns coupled with the loss or decreases in employment are other types of stressors found in the macrosystem. In the past, when disability was thought to be a private, family concern, the responsibility for the treatment of the disability was located in the microsystem. Families felt unsupported and isolated from others and they were. There are still gaps between needs and services; however, as these gaps are discovered and needs are articulated, resources, funding, and environmental and government resources are allocated to families. Families with children who have disabilities want the same quality of life that other American families enjoy.

Ethical Dilemmas

- Screening tests
- Abortion of fetuses with disabilities

Screening tests for fetuses and infants are based on the assumption that their use will have a benefit (Bailey, Skinner, & Warren, 2005). The Apgar scale is routinely administered to newborns within five minutes of birth. This short screening device gives numerical scores on heart rate, respiration, reflexes, muscle tone, and color. The Apgar scale was named for Virginia Apgar, who developed it in 1952. Not only health benefits have resulted from the use of screening tests, but other educational and social programs have been developed to provide early treatment or intervention. However, in the past, most of these screening tests were for relatively common conditions and medical treatments and services were available. For example, most infants born today in the developed nations have a screening for phenylketonuria, which is a lack of an enzyme which can result in mental retardation. This test is relatively inexpensive, non-invasive, and there is a treatment available if the condition is found. Furthermore, parents report a high degree of satisfaction with this type of screening.

Another type of neonatal screening is hearing tests. Hearing tests at birth are important because they "catch" or "find" hearing loss early, while the child is in a very sensitive period of development, thus preventing years of lost opportunity to acquire (spoken) language. These screening tests alter the experience of congenital deafness. In the past, many first-person accounts of both children and the parents of children with congenital hearing losses related the difficulty of diagnosis and the lost months and years of language development.

Another way in which fetal and infant screening tests can benefit the child is the prevention of the "diagnostic odyssey" and its financial and emotional costs (Bailey et al., 2005, p. 1890). A diagnostic odyssey is the frustrating process of seeking out doctors and tests in an effort to determine a diagnosis and may take months or even years. The value of screening tests will increase as more treatments, services, and supports become available. Parents desire the earliest possible information on their child's health in order to make informed, considered opinions. Screening tests are proliferating and becoming more advanced as medicine and the scientific study of genes push new borders.

Advances will bring numerous challenges to medical ethics and social and moral ethics? Are there disadvantages and risks to screening tests? With greatly expanded screening programs, can it be possible to screen for and find conditions for which there are no treatments? How much health risk is justified for a screening test? Will screening tests lead to more selective abortion? (Fenigsen, 1997) Will there be insurance discrimination in screening procedures? Do screening tests violate the parents' privacy? Will parents who decide to have a baby with a disability be considered irresponsible and selfish? Will PWDs be considered a financial "luxury"?

Most of these questions are appropriate for discussion in public arenas, such as task forces, disability groups, public focus groups, and educators (Silber & Batshaw, 2004). Whatever the conclusion, the first step is to educate the public about the complex issues surrounding fetal and newborn screening, including the availability of treatments, funding, and services. To date, there has been no research on the meaning of the experience of prenatal testing for the woman. Medical technologies have been developed in societies "which are entrenched in disability discrimination" (Saxton, 2006). A physician explained medicine's ethical obligation to first, be aware of their own beliefs and second to recognize the inherent power differential in the relationship:

> People come to their professions with certain core beliefs and biases, and they must be careful to "disarm" or at least acknowledge these in all clinical, educational, and ethical considerations. This awareness is particularly important in the traditional hospital environment, where there is the potential for a power differential between professionals and the families they serve. This disparity, fortunately, is changing. (Silber, 2007, p. 591)

Even if parents can receive and process information, some clinicians maintain that parents still are not in a position to give informed consent. They argue that parents faced with a child with severe disabilities and so overwhelmed by fear, guilt, and horror, that they are not capable of making an informed decisions.

Physicians, therefore, provide information and referrals to other parents with children with similar disabilities, and other service providers. They allow the prospective parents time to consider their choices and, perhaps most important, physicians communicate to the couple that they will be supported in the decision for abortion or in the decision to have the baby (Fenigsen, 1997).

SELECTIVE ABORTION OF FETUSES WITH DISABILITIES

The disability rights movements are clear in stating that they support the right of women to have an abortion. However, they are against women being pressured to have an abortion solely of the basis of a disability.

> There is a key difference between the goals of the reproductive rights movement and the disability rights movement regarding reproductive freedom: the reproductive rights movement emphasizes the right to have an abortion; the disability rights movement, the right *not to have an abortion.* Disability rights advocates believe that…all women have the right to resist pressure to abort when the fetus is identified as potentially having a disability. (Saxton, 2006, pp. 105–106)

Another scholar (Hubbard, 2006) expressed the same viewpoint, that all women should have the right to abortion. However, Hubbard believes that pressuring women to have an abortion solely on the basis of a disability is wrong.

> To say again, I am not arguing against a woman's right to abortion. Women must have that right because it involves a decision about our bodies and about the way we will spend the rest of our lives. But for scientists to argue that they are developing these tests out of concern for the "quality of life" of future children is like the arguments about "lives not worth living." No one these days openly suggests that certain kinds of people be killed; they just should not be born. Yet that involves a process of selection and a decision about what kinds of people should and should not inhabit the world. (p. 101)

Today's genetic science and reproductive technology have the capability to eliminate entire categories of disabilities and the people who experience these disabilities. Fetuses found to have spina bifida and Down syndrome can be aborted and eventually there would be no one with these disabilities (Bayles, 1987).

Considering the financial demands (which are only one aspect of disability), disability is expensive and much of the costs are covered by the "public purse," meaning government funds or insurance policies, so there is some basis for government and public intervention in policy-making. This does not consider the emotional costs and lifelong obligations of a child with a disability. Some believe that arguments for selective abortion are based only on the premise that disability only results in suffering. This is a vague, unsubstantiated statement and does not consider that society imposes much of the suffering of PWDs and their families. Most physicians understand the experience of disability and have opportunities to see ordinary PWDs living their lives successfully in their communities and among families and friends. In contrast, those without disabilities tend to exaggerate and sensationalize disability and its effects (Hubbard, 2006). This explains why many parents of children with disabilities are irritated when they are told, "I don't know how you do it," or "I couldn't do it." The answer is "you could do it, if you had to and it's not as tragic as you think it is."

The disability rights advocates often wish that some of the funds used for genetic research to eliminate specific disabilities would be spent on raising the quality of life for individuals who have the same type of disability. Mothers of children with disabilities are told, "This could have been prevented," or asked, "Didn't you get tested?" How will adults with these disabilities be treated? Will adults with disabilities be forced to justify and defend their lives? These are unnecessary burdens imposed upon PWDs. One mother told of her son being asked to be in the March of Dimes charity drive:

> "I'm sorry," I explain, "but I don't feel comfortable telling my son that he is doing this to prevent other children like him. We're trying to help him understand where he fits into a world that is often more confused than he is about his problem. I can't put him out there as something to 'prevent.' This poster thing also seems to use these kids to collect money, yet you tell me none of it goes toward their problems now. That feels sort of dishonest.
>
> I realize that I have given away potential "celebrity" status for Robbie by declining their invitation. I have also risked being labeled an ungrateful parent. But I think I have been true to what I really want for him. Free lunches and pictures in the newspaper are not going to help push his wheelchair into a community that sees him as something that should not have happened. (Toombs, Barnard, & Carson, 1995, pp. 32–33)

On the other hand, a woman's decision to abort a fetus with a disability should be honored and supported. Parents should not be made to feel guilty or anxious or that they have taken the "easy way out." Oppression can also work in both directions. Women who choose not to have an abortion should not be pressured by arguments of public expense, the difficulty of caring for a child with a disability, or the severity of the disability.

Most of the American public believes in the benefits of prenatal screening tests. If the parents choose not to abort, the test results allow them time to prepare for their baby, to consider treatment choices, and to meet with parents of children with similar disabilities.

INFANTICIDE OF NEWBORNS WITH DISABILITIES

Peter Singer is a professor of philosophy at Princeton University who has written several books (Singer, 1981, 1995). Singer's first books dealt with animal rights and the prevention of cruelty to animals. His publisher's blurb states: "Singer has written the book that sparked the modern animal rights movement" (*Animal Liberation*, 1975). In his next book, *Writings on an Ethical Life* (2000), he advocates that newborn infants with disabilities should be killed at birth:

> Regarding newborn infants as replaceable, as we now regard fetuses, would have considerable advantages over prenatal diagnosis followed by abortion. Prenatal

abortion still cannot detect all major disabilities. Some disabilities, in fact, are not present before birth; they may be the result of extremely premature birth or of something going wrong in the birth process itself. At present parents can choose to keep or destroy their disabled offspring only if the disability happens to be detected during pregnancy. There is no logical basis for restricting parents' choices to these particular disabilities.

Obviously, to go through the whole of pregnancy and labor, only to give birth to a child who one decides should not live, would be a difficult, perhaps heartbreaking, experience. For this reason many women would prefer prenatal diagnosis and abortion rather than live birth with the possibility of infanticide; but if the latter is not morally worse than the former, this would seem to be a choice that the woman herself should be allowed to make.

Nevertheless, the main point is clear: killing a disabled infant is not morally equivalent to killing a person. Very often it is not wrong at all. (Singer, 2000, p. 193)

Thus, Singer's arguments are based upon three premises: (1) the "replaceability" of newborn children (a newborn with a disability could be replaced with a "normal" baby); (2) the belief that if abortion is allowed, infanticide is not morally different; and (3) the utilitarian argument that resources are limited and should be allocated to "normal" babies. Singer's definitions of person, fetus, infant, disability, abortion, and killing are important to his argument. He also believes that withdrawal of life support (which society appears to sanction), also justifies outright killing (Scholar under fire for views on infanticide, 1999).

In a *New York Times* article (Johnson, 2003) titled, "Should I Have Been Killed at Birth?" a disability rights lawyer and activist with a severe congenital disability, Harriet McBryde Johnson, describes going to Princeton to participate in a debate that was attended by university students. Even though Dr. Singer was very pleasant, cordial, and welcoming to Ms. Johnson and Ms. Johnson had a long and distinguished career with many accomplishments, Dr. Singer very clearly stated that she should have been killed at birth.

MARKERS ON THE SLIPPERY SLOPE

We may disagree with Singer's conclusions, but there is some logic to his arguments. By understanding his arguments, we can gain a better understanding of the difficulties and complexities of these decisions. Although Singer does not use the phrase "slippery slope," part of his argument does include a slippery slope (Wolbring, 2001). If abortion is allowed, then infanticide may be legal in the future. If one accepts the utilitarian argument that PWDs are not as happy as PWODs, then some might consider it kindness "to put PWDs out of their misery."

The solution to slippery slopes is to define the boundaries (or the length of the slope) very clearly. Societies and governments have the right to state: "The slope ends here and this is why it ends here." To state that abortion and infanticide have the same moral standing is repugnant to most.

Terms to Learn

Alpha-fetoprotein blood
  screening
Anoxia
Apgar neonatal
  screening
Apgar scale
Cephalocaudal
  development

Chromosomal
  abnormalities
Developmental guidance
Down syndrome
Fetal alcohol syndrome
Gene-linked disorders
Low-incidence
  disabilities

Neural tube defects
Neurogenesis
Neuroplasticity
Proximodistal
  development
Screening tests
Selective abortion
Teratogens

Videos to View

- View the 20-minute video *Baby's First Year,* available from Insight Media. The producers describe this video: "Examining the physical, emotional, social, and intellectual changes that occur during the first year of life, this program discusses important issues associated with infant development. It highlights strategies for promoting development."
- View the 29-minute video *Fetal Development and Birth,* available from Insight Media. The producers describe this video: "This DVD describes the development of fetal systems during pregnancy and details the hormones involves in regulating fetal development, birth, and lactation."
- View the 28-minute video *Abilities to the Extremes: Pursuing the Dreams,* available from Aquarius Health Care Media. The producers describe this video: "When Justin was just a baby, he suffered amputations on both arms due to a rare blood disease known as meningococcemia. Being enrolled in the Shriner's system, Justin learned how to adapt to his new condition and to make him grow to be the person he is today, an avid skateboarder."
- View the 27-minute video *Raising a Child with Down Syndrome,* available from Aquarius Health Care Media. The producers describe this video: "When a child is born with Down syndrome, a family may feel that their lives will be forever changed. Experienced parents and doctors know that a child with Down syndrome will grow into a loving, contributing member of the family."

Learning Activities

(Note: These may also be used for class presentations.)
- Listen to the National Public Radio program "Tomorrow's Children." This audio program was one of four programs produced for *The Disability History Project* (May 1998c). In this program, parents speak about the abortion of fetuses with disabilities.
- Watch the video *The Terror of Tiny Town: Little Guys with Big Guns.* This is a Hollywood film produced by the legendary director Sam Newfield, who

produced more than 270 films. *The Terror of Tiny Town* is considered to be his most popular movie. This movie is described as "the cult western tale of an Innocent Girl (Yvonne Moray) saved from the Villain in Black (Little Billy) by the Hero in White (Billy Curtis). Comic relief is provided by the Foreign Cook (Charles Becky), whose kitchen cooks up continual culinary calamity while Tiny Town's saloon singer (Nita Krebs) is a miniature Judy Garland who delivers indelible interpretation[s] of Lew Porter's soul searching songs." This film is available from Alpha Video, Box 101, Narberth, PA 19072 or www.oldies.com.

- Discuss or write a paper on one of the following two opinions: (1) *Tiny Town* is an exploitative film that presents little people in a demeaning ways, or (2) *Tiny Town* is not exploitative.
- Watch the Discovery Channel series *Little World.*
- Research the disability of achondroplasia (dwarfism). What are the causes? What is the incidence of achondroplasia? What are some assistive/adaptive technology devices? (Hint: Go to ABLE database and type in achondroplasia.)
- Read Harriet McBryde Johnson's article about the debate with Peter Singer at Princeton University. Singer, a philosophy professor at Princeton, has lectured and written books about killing infants with severe disabilities at birth. Johnson is a disability rights lawyer who was born with a progressive neuromuscular disease. Johnson and Singer debate this issue at Princeton. Singer clearly states that he believes Johnson should have been killed at birth. The article is entitled "Unspeakable Conversations" and was published in the *New York Times,* February 16, 2003. It is also available online.
- Read about Pat Furlong in an article published in *The New Yorker* magazine (J. Colapinto, (2010) December 20 and 27, "Medical dispatch: Mother courage. The Duchenne Campaigner," pp. 64–75. Write a five-page paper on Furlong's crusading techniques.
- Visit Nick Vujicic's website and view his 15-minute video, www.lifewithoutlimbs.org.
- Go to Debbie Jorde's blog and view the 15-minute video showing her presentation on her two children with Miller's syndrome to medical students. What is Ms. Jorde's message to these physicians-to-be? This may be found at the website "Eight Fingers and Eight Toes: Accepting Life's Challenges," www.createspace.com/.
- As a class read and discuss "The Impact of Childhood Disability: The Parent's Struggle" by Ken Moses. This may be found at www.pediatricservices.com.

Writing Exercises

- Interview an adult with a congenital disability. Interview another adult with the same disability that had a late onset. Write two pages on the ways in which their experiences are alike, then write another two pages on the ways in which their experiences are dissimilar.
- Research one of the following disabilities: spina bifida, cerebral palsy, or prelingual deafness. Write a 10-page paper covering such topics as prevalence,

onset, functional limitations, adjustment demands, and the course of the disability.

- Write a five-page paper in which you defend the use of prenatal screening tests.
- Write a five-page paper in which you discuss the commonalities between abortion of fetuses with disabilities, infanticide of newborns with severe disabilities, and assisted suicide of PWDs.

Web Sites

http://www.ncbi.nlm.nih.gov/pmc/articles/PMC2517190/
http://www.familyvillage.wisc.edu/
http://www.thearc.org/page.aspx?pid=2530
http://www.marchofdimes.com/Baby/birthdefects.html

Toddlerhood and Early Childhood: Ages 18 Months to 5 Years

11

Toddlers and preschoolers are beginning to control their bodies and master their environments. During this time children begin to understand sex roles, learn to communicate, and gain some independence from their parents. They also learn to regulate their emotions, and their motor abilities improve greatly. Physical development increases rapidly during these years. For example, in the third year of life, the individual grows 4 inches on average.

The toddler and preschool years are thought to encompass the ages of 18 months to 5 years. More specifically, toddlerhood is considered to be 18 months to 2 or 3 years. In the past, there was little research on children in the toddler and preschool years. Attention was instead focused on the developmental periods of infancy and school age. However, this is changing because awareness is increasing that the toddler and preschool years are a critical period of life. Research has proven that enriching experiences during the toddler and preschool years have long-term benefits and provide the building blocks for the rest of the child's life. Physically, socially, and (especially) mentally, preschoolers are open to new experiences. At this stage the brain has a great deal of neuroplasticity, or stated differently, the brain changes greatly in the first few years after birth. The way in which these early years of life unfold

> results in a basic "package" of a person in terms of appearance, personality, and skills that they will carry forward into the rest of life, that can be modified and altered in various ways, but is rarely fundamentally reconstituted. (Carr, 2009, volume 1, p. xxi)

Socially, children begin to develop speech (or sign language), which provides cognition and communication. Emotionally, during preschool years the home and the family are the primary sources of love and acceptance. After the preschool years are completed, children spend most of their waking hours away from home. The combination of these factors makes these years between infancy and school age a window of opportunity. Research on preschool and other early intervention programs for both children with disabilities (CWDs) and children without disabilities (CWODs) has shown that graduates of these programs benefit from the foundation provided.

Children in these developmental stages who do not have disabilities begin to develop some awareness of children with disabilities. It is the responsibility of parents of CWODs to interpret the meaning of the disability and provide access to children with disabilities. Of course, integration of children with disabilities into preschools and other early developmental programs provides some awareness of children with disabilities (Leininger et al., 2010). Questions arise, however. Will these CWDs be invited for play dates, birthday parties, and other out of school activities? Will parents of CWODs encourage their children to play with CWDs during recess? The parents of CWODs will make these decisions. Inclusion of CWDs into typical early childhood experiences may well benefit CWODs more than CWDs. In ideal circumstances, CWODs will learn about disabilities (and the people who have them) in a natural, happy environment.

Children in this age range who have congenital disabilities or who acquire disabilities during these years encounter additional developmental tasks; those with severe physical or intellectual disabilities perhaps will never be able to complete these tasks. Early intervention programs and developmental surveillance are important. In most written accounts of preschool children with disabilities, the tenacity, crusadership, and advocacy efforts of their mothers are apparent.

The parents of children with congenital blindness (or severe vision loss) and children with prelingual deafness are required to make decisions concerning the type of education, the type of school, and the type of communication in which their children will be trained. Deafness has two types of onset: either before the acquisition of spoken language or after the acquisition of spoken language. Deafness is the only disability for which the time of onset is not divided into congenital or acquired. Of course, most prelingual deafness is present at birth (congenital), but onset of deafness before the ages of 2 or 3 years is considered prelingual deafness. Therefore, a prelingual time of onset is generally considered to be from birth to about 5 years of age, and postlingual from 5 years onward.

In the past, the relative low incidence of prelingual deafness and congenital blindness and the need for teaching communication skills made it necessary to educate children with these disabilities in boarding schools or residential schools. Presently, most children with these disabilities are educated in community schools and live with their families. The history of residential schools has not always been positive, but such schools had some advantages, mainly the ability to teach small children to read and write Braille or to become native signers of American Sign Language.

Another responsibility of parents with toddlers and preschoolers with disabilities is to arrange for continuous access to professional services. In the past parents were more willing to unquestioningly accept physicians' treatment plans. The following physician's statement shows how the relation between parents and physicians is changing:

> In the old prototype, parents came as supplicants to receive care for their child; professionals were the ones with all the knowledge. In the new prototype of family-centered care, recognition is given to the role of the parents who, through time spend caring for their child, have become "experts" in the disease and intricate care issues, including the availability or lack of availability of appropriate services. (Silber, 2007, p. 591)

Thus parents are becoming more empowered to question or challenge the advice of physicians, seek second opinions from other physicians, and ally with parent support groups. Medical caregivers encourage such actions, understanding that the parents live 24/7 with the child and the disability. It is true that it takes a village to raise a child, with or without a disability. However, as Rooehlkepartian and others (2001) stated, the family is the "first village" (p. 298). Before the child enters elementary school, the "first village" is the most significant influence.

In this stage body image begins to develop, although this image will change throughout the individual's life span. Body image is the mental and emotional picture an individual has about his or her body. Therefore, the physical body is a reflection of one's self (Berkman, Weissman, & Frielich, 1978). As the word "image" implies, body image is not a realistic, objective picture of one's physical self, but an emotional judgment closely tied to the macro trends of what society considers to be health, beauty, and athleticism. A great deal of body image is based on social comparisons, and preschoolers begin to compare themselves with others; therefore, body image becomes somewhat circular. The way in which young children think that others perceive them influences the way in which they view their bodies. Not only do preschoolers begin engaging in activities outside the home, they also watch television and movies and internalize these media's beliefs about a "good" or "beautiful" body. Therefore, preschoolers begin to evaluate their own physical attractiveness. For young children, body image changes as cognitive and social skills develop.

Developmental Tasks of Toddlerhood and Early Childhood

- Language development
- Locomotion
- Play
- Self-control
- Development of empathy

This chapter will first discuss the developmental tasks of toddlers and preschools and the way in which these tasks are conceptualized by the major developmental theorists. It will then discuss the disability experiences of CWDs and their unique developmental tasks and experience. Finally, the chapter presents the disabilities of the autism spectrum disorder and hyperactivity.

Interestingly, the word infant is derived from a Latin root that means "without speech." Almost all children learn their native language, whether spoken or signed, without formal teaching, and it is clear that an infant can distinguish his or her mother's voice from other voices. Deaf infants and preschoolers make up their own sign language when their parents do not know American Sign Language. Therefore, evidence points to children's innate (inborn) capacity for acquiring speech and language. In addition, most child development specialists believe that learning enhances language development. Skinner and the other behaviorists stated that infants and toddlers learn to speak because they are reinforced and the infant's random sounds are shaped into meaningful words by the adults in the environment. "Communicative competence" (Newman & Newman, 2009) begins in the newborn and continues throughout life. Deaf infants learn to sign in the same gradual, incremental manner. Adults reinforce signing and shape childish or incorrect signs into more sophisticated language.

Children learn their culture through language; therefore, the more language children learn, the more they become integrated into their culture. Language development creates a group identity and transmits the values, myths, and wisdom of the culture. The idea of language as culture is important to understand when we discuss the Deaf Culture. Another important concept that helps us understand the Deaf Culture is the language environment. Infants and children need an interactive environment so they can learn to understand and speak. An optimal interactive environment gradually raises the expectations of the infant or toddler and helps him or her to develop more language skills. The stepwise, progressive process of language acquisition is clear when one observes that adults speak to infants and toddlers differently than they speak to other adults. Simplifying speech, restricting the vocabulary (a horse becomes the "horsie"; a train becomes the "choo-choo"), paraphrasing and repeating, speaking slowly with many pauses, and using simple sentences are all examples of the nonformal teaching of language to infants and toddlers. Many books are devoted solely to language acquisition of infants and toddlers, including the acquisition signed languages. Language is a form of social communication and a powerful socializing tool. With language children can share and interact with their family and their friends. The ability to ask questions or to request assistance helps the child to become more independent.

The word toddler refers to the way in which a 1-year child walks, typically precariously and ungracefully. Locomotion is the act of moving oneself through walking, running, and jumping. According to Adolph and Berger (2006), the infant/toddler develops lifelong movement patterns during the first 2 years of life. Five factors influence the development of locomotion: (1) the physical characteristics of muscles, joints, and limbs; (2) changes in body weight and mass; (3) new capacities in the central nervous system that improve coordination of feedback from the arms and legs; (4) motivation to move; and (5) opportunities for practice. Walking, running, and jumping expand the child's world and make him or her more self-confident. Many toddlers consider jumping the precursor to flying. Therefore, although the possibilities of locomotion are not limitless (humans cannot fly), the small toddler continues to enlarge and elaborate his or her powers of locomotion. The child views locomotion as fun, an activity to be enjoyed just for the sake of moving; toddlers and preschoolers run just for the fun of it. Toddlers continue to develop their large muscles and can run and jump progressively faster and higher and can throw a ball with more accuracy. According to Bashford, LeCroy, and Lortie (2001), "Three year olds exhibit the highest activity level of any age group" (p. 254).

As we learned in the chapter on infancy, infants and children develop their large muscle movements before movements of their small muscles. Children learn to use their arms and legs before they use their fingers. Therefore, infants and toddlers learn locomotion before writing (or picking up Cheerios). Toddlers can find this lack of dexterity and precision in fine motor tasks frustrating because they may be incapable of buttoning their clothes, printing letters, or putting together small puzzles.

Play is an important developmental task of toddlerhood and the preschool ages, because it helps the child develop independence within his or her social group (which at this time of life is quite limited). Play helps the child individuate so he or she can make independent choices and accomplish tasks such as dressing and feeding independently. Piaget considered play to be a sensorimotor activity because children are required to coordinate sensory input with their movements. According to Piaget, play allows children to understand (or assimilate) their experiences and events in their environment. Piaget would have loved computer games because such games require the simultaneous use of touch, vision, and eye–hand coordination.

In fantasy play or pretend play, children create characters and situations that have private meanings. For children, fantasy play is a retreat in which the rules and social sanctions of the physical world no longer apply. According to Erikson (1972), fantasy play allows children to soothe their feelings and reduce stress, because children construct (make up) a story in which the problem is represented and children conquer the it and become heroes. Children as young as 2 years old can distinguish between reality and pretend play. Some children may become fascinated with a certain heroic figure, and such a fascination gives them a feeling of self-mastery of their environment. Fantasy play has also been found to increase children's language competence.

Children also engage in imitative play, in which they learn the social roles of their culture. It is easy to understand how imitation helps the small child (and everyone else) learn skills. In addition, imitation assists in learning social cognition. Social cognition consists of understanding which gestures, actions, and expressions are appropriate. Toddlers observe and learn voice tones, vocabulary, body language, and acceptable behavior by watching others. Eventually toddlers learn that these rules change in different circumstances. Social cognition is a form of autonomy and independence. Parents who take an active role in modeling correct behavior and telling the child why a certain behavior is acceptable or not acceptable become active models. Active models take imitation a step further, allowing the child to both *see* the behavior and then *discuss* the behavior.

Self-control is defined as the ability to control impulses, direct action toward a goal, express and inhibit the expression of emotions, regulate or restrain behavior, and resist temptation (Newman & Newman, 2009). To achieve it, the toddler must gain control both over the environment and over himself or herself. Children as young as 2 or 3 years are able to modify and control their impulses and tolerate delays in gratification. Toddlers typically sleep through the night and are able to find ways to manage their frustration, such as distracting themselves by finding another toy or activity. Some toddlers self-regulate by the use of comfort items, such as pacifiers, stuffed animals, or a beloved blanket. By simply observing a toddler seeking comfort, we can see that he or she has learned to self-regulate emotions.

Toddlers begin to see distress and discomfort in others. Parents, family members, and school teachers may point out to the toddler that he or she caused distress in others. In this way, the child is beginning to develop more advanced social competence. By age four most children are able to share, a skill learned through parental encouragement and observing their peers. Preschool children begin to understand emotions, both their own and the emotions of others. Parents provide "word-labels" that name, identify, and describe emotions. At first the child understands only basic emotions, such as happiness and sadness, but the child subsequently progresses to understanding more complex emotions such as embarrassment and frustration.

Preschool children also conceptualize gender as part of their self-concept, including the sex-role requirements. Preschool girls understand that "I am a girl. I will grow up to be a woman. I am a lot like Mommy and I want to be like her when I grow up."

Children also establish a sex-role preference, such as "I like being a boy." By age 2 ½, children can accurately identify other children as boys or girls and can sort photographs of boys and girls. Indeed, preschool children are very interested in the differences between boys and girls, but these differences are based on outward indications, such as clothing, toys, and activities.

Childhood Disabilities

- Traumatic brain injuries
- Seizure disorders
- Childhood infections
- Asthma
- Pervasive developmental disorders
- Autism spectrum disorders

Parents of toddlers and preschoolers with congenital disabilities have experienced the diagnostic period and the subsequent adjustment process. For these children, early treatments and services will be continued, with adjustments made to accommodate the "typical" developmental stages (Bernstein & Batshaw, 1998). Additionally, some types of disabilities are diagnosed only in the preschool years, especially those disabilities that have communication deficits. Because toddlers and preschoolers are vulnerable to those who care for them, disabilities can be exacerbated or acquired through neglect or physical abuse.

TRAUMATIC BRAIN INJURIES

Traumatic brain injuries (TBIs) can occur at any age, but often have more disabling effects on a young, developing brain (Mangeot, Armstrong, Colvin, Yeates, & Taylor, 2002). In 1937 Symonds made this observation: "It is not only the kind of head injury that matters but the kind of head." TBIs are classified as either closed head or open head, depending on whether the skull is penetrated. Bullets and other objects cause open-head TBIs. Closed head TBIs occur when the brain undergoes a sudden change in momentum through either acceleration or deceleration (Dixon, Layton, & Shaw, 2005). Falls, for example, cause the brain to move rapidly within the skull and to strike the hard interior surface of the skull with considerable force and speed, resulting in stretching, and swelling of the brain. In addition, the fall may produce small lesions throughout the brain. Often the brain stem is injured, and unconsciousness may or may not follow.

Traumatic acute-onset disabilities can occur during toddlerhood and the preschool years, especially TBIs. The number of early childhood onset TBIs is increasing. According to Chapman et al. (2004):

> Traumatic brain injury (TBI) is the leading cause of acquired disability in children in the United States. As many as 435,000 children between the ages of 0 and 14 years are treated in the emergency department each year with TBI. An additional 37,000 are hospitalized for TBI and 2,685 die annually. (p. 37)

Early childhood onset TBI is defined as one that occurs between the ages of birth to 7 years; it is typically the result of injuries sustained by physical abuse, falls, car accidents, and play accidents. Falls from grocery carts, walkers, and windows are common causes. A new term, shaken baby syndrome, describes the form of TBI that results from repeated severe shaking of an infant, in which the movement of the brain within the hard shell of the skull causes serious injury. The definition of TBIs in the Individuals with Disabilities Act (IDEA, 1992) shows the pervasiveness of the effects:

> An acquired injury to the brain caused by an external force, resulting in total or partial functional disability or psychosocial impairment, or both, that adversely affects a child's educational performance. This term applies to open and closed head injuries resulting in impairments in one or more areas, such as cognition; language; memory; attention; reasoning; abstract thinking; judgment; problem-solving; sensory, perceptual, and motor abilities; psychosocial behavior; physical functions; information processing, and speech. The term does not apply to brain injuries that are congenital or degenerative, or brain injuries induced by birth trauma. (34 C.F.R., Section 300.7[6] [12])

TBIs, at any age of childhood typically result in post-injury behavior problems; therefore a TBI requires early, intensive interventions if the child is very young (Lamphear, 2005). Chapman et al. hypothesized that infants and preschoolers who acquire TBIs show "similar acute and longer term behavioral consequences of their injuries as children who experience a TBI at an older age" (p. 56). Obviously, young children with TBI have a longer future of behavioral problems, so developmental surveillance and individualized intervention programs are required. As the demands of the environment increase when the child enters school adolescence, or the workforce, the deficits and problems often become more evident (see Figure 11.1).

Closed-head TBIs are difficult to diagnose accurately at any age, but for a small child or infant who is unable to speak and report accidents, diagnosis becomes a more

FIGURE 11.1

TBI annual estimates.

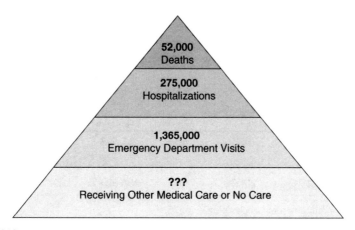

Source: CDC, 2010.

complex process. TBIs are often diagnosed many months after the injury, only after behavior changes occur. Another difficulty in diagnosis with young children is the lack of a preinjury baseline measurement (Pellegrino, 2007). Physicians must rely on the reports of the parents, who often cannot be sure of the exact time of injury. Sadly, TBIs associated with shaken baby syndrome are relatively easy to diagnose because they are typically accompanied by other signs of abuse, such as broken bones, bruises, and contusions. The use of bicycle helmets and child-restraint car seats has reduced the numbers of early-onset TBIs; however, physical abuse and play accidents have increased.

SEIZURE DISORDERS

Seizures are the result of abnormal electrical discharges in the brain; as many as 10% of people will have at least one seizure in their lifetime. Everyone has a "seizure threshold," beyond which one will experience a seizure. However, for most individuals the threshold is so high that they never have a seizure. Those with seizure disorders (SDs) have very low thresholds, caused by a combination of genetic and environmental events. More than 150 causes of seizures have been identified, but in 70% of individual cases, it is not possible to determine the cause (Howard, Williams, & Lepper, 2010).

SDs in which there are no other disabilities or cognitive delays are termed "epilepsy only," and SDs in which there are additional disabilities, such as cerebral palsy or mild mental retardation, are termed "epilepsy plus." Epilepsy plus is further exacerbated by its resistance to drug therapies. In infantile SDs, the prognosis tends to be poor, and there is mental and neurological damage in 80% of the cases. As a general rule, the earlier the onset of the seizures, the poorer the prognosis (see Table 11.1).

At any age, the response to a SD includes careful medication compliance and ensuring the individual's safety. Adjustment to SDs may be complicated by the episodic nature of the disability; most of the time, the individual is free of seizures. However, when a seizure does occur, it could be life-threatening. Society's lack of understanding about SDs may be more impairing than the actual disorder. Seizures tend to be frightening to

TABLE 11.1

Prevalence of Recurrent Unprovoked Seizures in a Population-Based Door-to-Door Survey Study of All Ages

Region	Reference (First author)	Publication date	Gender	Population	Number of cases	Prevalence (per 1,000) Crude	Age adjusted to 2,000 U.S. standard population
Mississippi	Haerer (Haerer et al., 1986)	1986	M>F	23,597	160	6.8	7.1
New York	Kelvin (Kelvin et al., 2007)	2007	M<F	208,301	42	5.2	5

Source: www.ncbi.nlm.nih.gov/pmc/articles/pmc2696575.

others, and for many of individuals with SDs their greatest fear is the embarrassment of having a seizure in public. In addition, safety and independence are often incompatible. The individual with a SD must never swim alone, for example, and when the individual becomes a teenager, he or she may not be able to obtain a driver's license.

CHILDHOOD INFECTIONS

Meningitis and encephalitis are infections that involve the central nervous system, especially the brain. Both diseases generally affect infants and small children or older people who are chronically ill. Meningitis occurs when bacteria enter the meninges, the coverings of the brain and spinal cord. Encephalitis is an inflammation of the brain and spinal cord resulting from a viral or bacterial infection spread by the circulatory system. Meningitis and encephalitis appear to be similar; indeed, ruling out a diagnosis of meningitis is part of the process of diagnosing encephalitis.

The presenting symptoms of both diseases are the same: fever, vomiting, severe headache, and drowsiness. For meningitis, 90% of those infected survive, but 25% of survivors have residual effects, including such disabilities as a SD or deafness. Deafness may be the result of either the swelling brain places pressure on the auditory nerve or the antibiotic therapy. It is also thought that some children experience hyperactivity after meningitis due to brain damage.

Helen Keller's "brain fever" was never diagnosed. Both she and her brother were infected. Although he died, Helen survived but was both deaf and blind. Before the introduction of antibiotics, meningitis was the leading cause of deaf/blindness. A modern story of meningitis is told by a mother, Kim Shafer (2010):

> When Maddy was only 2 months old, she woke one day, listless and not herself. Just to be safe, I took her into the doctor's office and he didn't seem that concerned until he touched the top of her head. Within 30 seconds, he was back in the room telling me that we were going to the hospital by ambulance and that she possibly had meningitis.
>
> It was then that I learned what that soft spot was on the top of her head and how important that was. It's where the two pieces of the brain haven't merged yet. And that soft spot actually tells you if there is any swelling in the brain. Usually, it should be soft and dipped, but this time it was swollen, which meant the fluid and swelling from Maddy's spine had already built up around her brain. (Howard, Williams, & Lepper, 2010, p. 364)

Baby Maddy lost all of her muscle control, was not able to lift her head or roll over, and became deaf. Maddy's mother had never known a deaf person. At 4 ½ months, Maddy began sign language classes and by 7 months, she was signing.

Encephalitis typically occurs in the United States during the summer months because children then swim and play outdoors, where mosquitoes transmit the infection. In addition to the early symptoms of meningitis, a child with encephalitis may have an unsteady gait, seizures, and decreased consciousness. Although most people contracting encephalitis recover without long-term effects, herpes encephalitis can result in severe language disorders, muscle weakness and paralysis on one side, deficits in hearing and vision, and SDs. Mental retardation may also result from herpes encephalitis.

Polio epidemics occurred mostly in the summer, primarily from contact with the virus while swimming. However, the polio virus was not transmitted by mosquitoes.

ASTHMA

Asthma is considered "the most disabling childhood disease" (Lanphear, 2005). Almost 5 million children under the age of 18 have asthma, the leading chronic illness among children. Prevalence rates have been as high as one in 10 children. Asthma is considered the one of the most undertreated and underdiagnosed disabilities. It is a respiratory disease that narrows the bronchial tubes, making breathing difficult. When the bronchial tubes constrict, the child's breathing sounds like wheezing. The most common risk factors for asthma are maternal smoking during pregnancy, exposure to second-hand smoke, and low birth weight. An asthma attack can last for days and may also be life-threatening.

There are two types of asthma. The first type is extrinsic or allergic asthma, in which the attacks is precipitated by allergens, such as pollen, dust, animal dander, molds, foods, or medication. The second type is known as intrinsic, and attacks are precipitated by infections. Most individuals with asthma have symptoms of both types, although intrinsic asthma is more common in childhood and extrinsic is more common in adulthood. Another name for extrinsic asthma is adult-onset asthma. Childhood asthma presents two developmental challenges: first, the child must be taught to prevent attacks, and second, the child needs to understand how to respond to attacks. Until the child is able to self-monitor, he or she will require continuous adult supervision. Even small children can be taught which environments to avoid and how to use their bronchodilators when necessary. Asthma accounts for more hospital admissions and absences from school than any other childhood disability.

With severe asthma, children often require frequent hospitalizations in spite of consistent monitoring and management. Hospitalization of a child, for whatever reason, necessitates the child's reintegration into preschool or school upon release. Often teachers and social workers explain to schoolmates why the child has been away. Asthma medications often affect children's attention spans due to fatigue and loss of sleep. However, the most difficult aspect of childhood asthma is convincing others of its severity and the need for monitoring and avoidance of some activities. For example, exercise, certain foods, or common medications such as aspirin can precipitate attacks, and serious attacks can result in death. The difference in power and status between a small child and a teacher or athletic coach often makes it difficult for a child with asthma to explain why he or she cannot participate in certain activities. This problem is especially difficult when there is a substitute teacher or coach who may (or may not) be aware of the child's asthma. Asthma is an invisible and intermittent disability, both of which make the individual appear "normal" (even to himself or herself) most of the time. In contrast, a child in a wheelchair is more likely to be monitored carefully and consistently by teachers and other adults.

The number of children with asthma continues to increase, and health demographers have tried to determine possible causes. One expert stated:

> A rapid and largely unexplained growth in rate of childhood asthma threatens the health of society.... Indoor air degraded by tobacco smoke exposure,

[and] organic allergens (such as carbon monoxide, volatile organic compounds, pesticides) presents a high risk for allergies, asthma, and other respiratory disabilities. Because people in modern societies spend approximately 90% of their time indoors and 66% of that time, in their home, indoor air quality plays an ever important role on human health.... It has been estimated that improving indoor air quality in homes and public buildings could reduce asthma symptoms by as much as 10–30% and save $2–4 billion annually in associated health care costs in the United States. (Howard, Williams, & Lepper, 2010, p. 375)

JUVENILE RHEUMATOID ARTHRITIS

The most common form of childhood arthritis is juvenile rheumatoid arthritis (JRA), which is characterized by pain, swelling of one or more of the joints, and redness. The average age of onset is typically before age 17, and it is a low-incidence disability, with about 1 child in 1,000 children experiencing JRA. The treatment goal of JRA is the preservation of physical functioning. A small number of children may have joint deformities, in spite of good medical management and physical and occupational therapy. These joint deformities make JRA a disfiguring disability, which adds another dimension to social acceptance, especially among small school children who may not understand why the child with JRA looks "crooked and bent." A secondary disability or complication of JRA is blindness. Since these children also have inflammation of the eyes, regular examinations by an ophthalmologist must be scheduled in order to prevent blindness. Pain is a part of JRA, and at any age pain may be difficult to manage; for children, it is often difficult to gauge the correct dosage of medication. Indeed, it is the child's complaint of pain that usually prompts the parents to see a physician.

Pervasive Developmental Disorders

- Relatively low incidence
- First described in the German language
- Only recently defined as a diagnosis
- Some debate whether there are five distinct PDDs
- Difficult to determine prevalence rates
- Parents often encounter blame, either for the cause of the disability or the management

The term pervasive developmental disorders (PDDs) was created by the *Diagnostic and Statistical Manual* (*DSM*) of the American Psychiatric Association in 1980. These diagnoses are therefore relatively recent, but this does not mean that these disorders did not exist before 1980. Instead, these PDDs were mistakenly thought to be a part of another diagnosis, or (more commonly) these children were considered to have an intellectual disability or were thought to be odd, weird, or eccentric. There has been confusion about the diagnosis of PDDs in the profession of psychiatry. The later, updated edition of the *DSM* has also changed the diagnostic criteria for autism. For example,

Asperger's syndrome was added to the *DSM* in 1994 (Morris, Morris, & White, 2005). Some of the first terms physicians used to describe PDDs were autistic psychopathy, dementia infantilis, and infantile schizophrenia.

There are five PDDs, which the *DSM IV-Text Revision* (APA, 2000) lists as (1) Autistic Disorder, (2) Asperger's Disorder, (3) Rhett's Disorder, (4) Childhood Disintegrative Disorder (CDD), and (5) Pervasive Developmental Disorder Not Otherwise Specified (PDDNOS). However, these disorders are more commonly referred to as autism spectrum disorders (ASDs), so this chapter will use the popular term ASDs.

AUTISM

ASDs are a class of pervasive neurodevelopmental disorders that affect almost every aspect of the child's life, hence the use of the term "pervasive." ASDs are first diagnosed in childhood, although autism is present at birth (Hyman & Towbin, 2007). The word spectrum is used because there are different levels of severity, or (to state it differently) these disorders occur along a continuum, with mild impairments on one end, the most severe impairments on the other end, and a great many variations in the middle. These disabilities are termed developmental because they appear in childhood; nevertheless, these are lifelong disabilities. Indeed, the discrepancy between individuals with ASDs and those without ASDs continues to widen as these individuals grow up and mature.

In all the ASDs, three areas of functioning are involved. There are deficits in social reciprocity, communication, and repetitive behaviors. To render a specific diagnosis of one of the five ASDs (and distinguish it from the other four diagnoses), medical professionals consider the following diagnostic criteria: the pattern of early childhood language development, cognitive ability, timing of regression, and the pattern and number of symptoms.

Dr. Leo Kanner (1943, 1949), a child psychiatrist working at Johns Hopkins University in 1943, first described a group of 11 children who displayed a similar pattern of symptoms that were different from those of other childhood disorders. Kanner used the term "early infantile autism" to describe the disorder (Morris, Morris, & White, 2005). Eventually, the term "autism" evolved, which comes from a Greek root that means self-involvement. During the 1950s, autism was thought to be caused by poor parenting or "refrigerator mothers." At first, it was thought that autism was a type of childhood schizophrenia, but it was eventually found to be an organic condition.

Diagnosis is typically made before the age of 3 years. Autism is defined by a pattern of six symptoms found in three areas: lack of social reciprocity, delay or total lack of language, and repetitive or stereotyped motor movements. Lack of social reciprocity includes failure to use nonverbal behaviors such as eye contact or changes in facial expressions, failure to develop peer relationships appropriate to developmental level, and lack of interest in others (Films for the Humanities, 1999). Individuals with autism have often been described as being in their own world. However, because they lack social awareness, individuals with ASDs may move inappropriately into the personal space of others, and some teenage girls have reported incidents of stalking by boys with ASDs who did not understand appropriate boundaries or that their behavior was frightening to the girls.

Delay or impairment of language may include a total lack of spoken language, marked impairment in the ability to carry on a conversation with others, and stereotyped or repetitive use of language. Stereotyped and repetitive movements include hand or finger flapping, rocking the body, spinning around in circles, or biting the hands. Stereotyped movements or speech includes the persistent and inappropriate repetition of words and phrases or of gestures and behavior. In addition, stereotypical behaviors and speech are also characterized by a lack of purpose of function, sometimes being called rituals or ritualization. Echolalia is defined as stereotyped speech in which the individual repeats (echoes) what others have said, including the intonation. Although repeating and mimicking the speech of others is a common and adaptive development task that assists infants and toddlers to learn language, echolalia is neither typical nor adaptive. Approximately 70% to 80% of children diagnosed with autism also have intellectual disabilities.

Individuals with autism are often hypersensitive to sensory stimuli. This hypersensitivity may present as a dislike of being held, touched, or hugged and an aversion to the feeling of their clothes. Many children with autism tend to insist on routine and do not tolerate changes in their schedule or environment very well (Dotson, 2010).

Although they were once considered fairly rare, ASDs are the fastest growing disability group in the United States. Indeed, when all five ASDs are considered, some prevalence estimates are as high as one in every 110 births (Centers for Disease Control and Prevention, 2007b; Wallis, 2007; Zimmerman, 2010). Other estimates place the prevalence rate even higher, at one in every 91 births. In addition, these prevalence rates continue to rise. Forty-one percent of children with ASDs have an intellectual disability, which is defined as an IQ of less than 70 (see Figure 11.2).

ASDs have multiple causes, but the general consensus is that ASDs are caused by abnormalities in both the structure and functioning of the brain. Also, the physiology of neurochemicals is impaired. Chromosomal mutations can also raise an infant's risk of

FIGURE 11.2

Changes in the prevalence of ASDs among children 8 years old, 2002 to 2006.

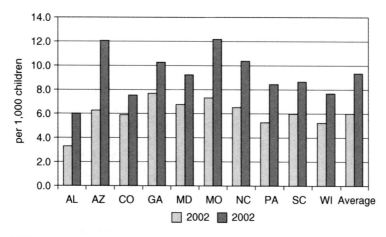

Source: CDC, 2007.

developing ASDs. Therefore, all of the causes are of biological origin. A genetic component is suggested by the fact that if families that have one child with autism, they have a 5% to 10% risk of having another child with this disability. Environmental pathogens combined with an increased genetic sensitivity have been hypothesized as factors in the higher rates of ASDs (Interagency Autism Coordinating Council, 2010). This theory would be difficult, if not impossible, to test (or prove) due to the large number of uncontrolled variables. Males are more likely to develop ASDs, with the male to female ratio at 4:1.

The increase in the *reported* rate of ASDs can be attributed to several sources: (1) different agencies use varying definitions of ASDs (which probably result in underestimates); (2) older children with ASDs are underestimated because the *DSM* diagnoses were not in place when they were young, and (3) many younger children are not counted as having ASDs because assessment interests do not identify the symptoms as well as they do for older children. Varying diagnostic criteria and the resulting disagreement about the types of care and education that would aid these children combine to make ASDs difficult (Lavaas, 1987). However, parents and physicians clearly recognize that the child needs a diagnosis in order to receive services and funding.

Although ASDs are lifelong disabilities, it is also true that appropriate treatments and interventions allow individuals to experience progress and success (McEachin, Smith, & Lovaas, 1993; Moreno, Neiner, & O'Neal, 2010). For example, some people with autism develop some self-awareness. However, approximately one-third of all individuals with autism never develop speech and other may refuse to speak even though they can. These individuals are also very routine bound and do not tolerate change very well. Children with autism do not like novelty or change and demonstrate an inflexible adherence to specific routines and rituals. They also have very restricted but intense interests.

Starting in the late 1940s and up until the 1980s, there was a large body of professional literature (Bettelheim, 1969; Ferster, 1961; Kanner, 1943, 1949; Cox, Rutter, Newman, & Bartak, 1975) that thought autism was caused by cold, rejecting perfectionistic parents with high IQs. Therefore, the parents of the first generation of children to be diagnosed with autism were given little support, but rather misplaced blame.

ASPERGER'S SYNDROME

In 1944 Dr. Hans Asperger published his observations of children who had difficulties with socialization and displayed repetitive behaviors. Asperger's syndrome (AS), which he was the first to describe, is "a relatively mild autism spectrum disorder in which the child has relatively good verbal language, milder nonverbal language problems and a restricted range of interests and relationships" (Santrock, 2009, p. 290). The average age of diagnosis of AS is 8 years. According to the *DSM-IV*, the clinical presentation of Asperger's includes (1) severe and sustained impairment in social interaction; (2) restricted, repetitive patterns of interests, behaviors, and activities; (3) significant impairments in social, occupational, and other role functioning; and (4) no significant delays in cognitive or language acquisition. Often individuals with AS speak in monotonic, robotic language and are unable to read the body language of others. Like the other ASDs, Asperger's is thought to be a neurological disability. Individuals with AS have been described in this manner:

> Although individuals who have Asperger's tend to have a marginally late onset of speech, once it is acquired the person tends to have one-sided conversation and frequently uses questioning as a social tool (Attwood, 1998). Attwood explains that individuals with Asperger's disorders are generally disinterested in game, sports, and play activities, are indifferent to peer pressure, and lack precision in expressing emotion. Issues regarding the differential diagnosis of Asperger's Disorder, high functional Autism, and nonverbal learning disabilities remain unresolved. (Morris, Morris, & White, 2005, pp. 324–325)

Infants often show signs of AS when they do not shift their attention easily. Typically developing children play with a toy for a short time and then pick up another one. Parents of children with AS have reported that as infants their children played with only one toy for prolonged periods of time and that it was difficult to shift their attention. When older, those with AS often find it difficult to leave a task uncompleted. Instead they feel compelled to complete the task before moving on to another activity.

The specific difficulties in communications for those with AS include failure to understand idioms, such as "The grass is always greener on the other side." They do not understand sarcasm or cute nicknames. Those with AS tend to think in very literal terms, without a great deal of abstraction.

Children with AS often have difficulty in regulating their emotions because they do not understand emotions and are not able to label emotions, either in themselves or others. Because they lack these labeling and recognition skills and have high impulsivity, those with AS cannot control their emotions. Rather than being a sign of rudeness or insensitivity, emotional outbursts are symptoms of AS; while they are annoying to parents and teachers, it is important to remember that these outbursts are not deliberate. The child is not misbehaving "on purpose."

As with most other disabilities, some children are diagnosed with AS extremely early because their symptoms are very recognizable. Children who sit in the corner while rocking back and forth and flapping their hands are easier to diagnose than older children who have long histories of social awkwardness, inattention, and poor organizational skills. Individuals with AS sometimes have learning disabilities, motor clumsiness, and hypersensitivity to sensory stimuli. Temple Grandin, an animal science professor with AS, described noise as literally painful: "When I was little, loud noises were a problem...they actually caused pain. When I was in college my roommate's hair dryer sounded like a jet airplane taking off" (p. 67).

Children with AS may therefore be prescribed a daily "sensory diet" that limits the number of stimuli. The sensory stimuli to be limited can include bright lights, verbal input, environments with lots of visual stimuli, situations that involve touch, and computer games. After the individual has experienced a certain predetermined amount of stimuli, he or she is allowed to be alone in a quiet place. Individuals with AS can find haircuts a terrible experience because the scissors are shiny, bright, and loud; the mirrors reflect blinding light; and there is a great deal of light. Often barbershops are filled with people who seem to be yelling at each other. AS individuals tend to be aversive to touch, which includes hugs, kisses, and other signs of affection. They may find wearing clothes unbearable because the cloth feels like sandpaper against the skin. They may not eat certain foods because the textures are unpleasant.

Some AS symptoms may be thought of as strengths and skills. Some individuals with AS have excellent mathematical skills, may be musically talented, have exceptionally early and advanced reading skills (which is termed hyperlexia), have advanced skills in chemistry and physics, or may excel in creative writing, such as poetry (Moreno, Neiner, & O'Neal, 2011). Individuals with AS tend to think in original ways, prefer detail more than broad generalities, remember details that are often forgotten by others, demonstrate remarkable perseverance in problem solving, and have remarkable memories. Their interests tend to be very narrow and esoteric; in the extreme form, they may include such interests as memorizing telephone directories or railroad schedules.

One educator (Herbert, 2011) described the social functioning of those with AS in positive terms:

> Peer relationships [are] characterized by absolute loyalty and impeccable dependability, free of sexist, "age-ist," or culturalist biases, speaking one's mind irrespective of social context or adherence to personal beliefs, listening without continual judgment or assumptions. (p. 5)

RETT'S SYNDROME

Rett's disorder (or Rett's syndrome) is a neurogenetic syndrome that involves the loss of previously obtained language and social milestones. In 1966 the Austrian physician Andreas Rett described children with mental retardation who engaged in stereotypical hand wringing. Rett's syndrome (RD) is a progressive neurodevelopmental disorder caused by a genetic mutation on the X chromosome. Infants with this syndrome develop normally until 6 to 18 months old, when Rett's symptoms appear. These symptoms include microcephaly (decreased head circumference and growth), loss of muscle tone, cognitive and functional regression, and the beginning of stereotyped hand movements. These symptoms become progressively worse.

This syndrome occurs far more frequently in females than in males; however, the precise number of infants with RD is not known. It is thought to affect one in every 10,000 to 15,000 live female births (Morris, Morris, & White, 2005).

CHILDHOOD DISINTEGRATIVE DISORDER

In 1908 Theodore Heller wrote about "dementia infantilis" (Hendry, 2000) which the *DSM* termed childhood disintegrative disorder (CID) in 1994. The prevalence of CID is very low, estimated to be 1.7 child in every 100,000 individuals. The symptoms of CID are similar to those of autism, and the presentation of symptoms is similar to Rett's disorder. In other words, the infant develops normally until a significant loss of communication, social relationship, and adaptive skills (such as bladder and bowel control) emerges in a period of 2 years up until the age of 10. With both Rett's and CID, the child develops normally for a period of time, after which regression occurs. Like those with autism, children with CID have impairments in communication and engage in restricted, repetitive, stereotyped patterns of behavior.

PERVASIVE DEVELOPMENTAL DISORDER NOT OTHERWISE SPECIFIED

Pervasive Developmental Disorder Not Otherwise Specified (PDDNOS) does not have specific diagnostic criteria listed in the *DSM*. PDDNOS is rarely diagnosed and is only identified in those cases in which the individual's symptoms developed after 30 months of age. Often the diagnosis of PDDNOS is later changed as the child becomes older and more definitive symptoms emerge.

ASPIES

There are more than 178,000 web sites (according to Google) for those with AS and their families. Those with AS often refer to themselves as "Aspies" and to those without AS as "neurotypicals." These web sites speak of the need for more understanding and compassion for Aspies, rather than seeking a cure. One joke is: "In school the Aspie is called a nerd. At work, the Aspie is called the boss." These types of jokes reveal the pride Aspies have about themselves and about AS.

PARENTAL AND FAMILY RESPONSIBILITIES

Disability is a family affair, and the demands of caring for a small child with a disability are great (Drotar, Crawford, & Bush, 1984). Nonetheless, many families state that there are positive, strengthening aspects of having a CWD and that after the initial period of shock and adjustment, family life returns to "normal" or a redefinition of "normal." After medical needs have been met, families report three important needs and resources: money, time, and friends. Caring for a disability is expensive, and having a CWD often requires one of the parents to leave work in order to care for the child or at least to reduce the amount of time spent at work. Not all jobs offer the flexibility to accommodate care for a CWD; consequently, there is no choice other than termination of employment. The unpredictability of exacerbations or infections makes employment difficult. Even small expenses can be burdensome when the family is living from paycheck to paycheck. Exactly when disability expenses increase, the parents' earning capacities are decreased. One family resorted to extreme measures:

> For a number of years, our family has made sacrifices that no family should ever have to make. Some of the things that Jennifer requires are common needs for a child with disabilities, and we had to be flexible enough to ensure she received what she needed. The cost of her equipment is incredible. For example, the braces that she has on her feet have to be replaced at least once a year, sometimes twice a year, and they cost $700 each time. We just got a brand new seat and back for her wheelchair, and they were $1,000. Jennifer's [wheel]chair alone cost $3,500.
>
> Our family got to a point of desperation, and my husband and I separated so that our income could be low enough to receive state funding for Jennifer's needs. At the time, Jennifer had been denied state funding although we were only $147 over the monthly eligibility limit on our income. We were stuck; we were struggling just to make enough for food, shelter, and clothing even with two blue-collar people working. It wasn't like we had a lot of money and we

were trying to cheat the system out of something. We felt like we were being punished because we had this child with special needs, and we didn't have jobs that paid $20 an hour. (Howard, Williams, &Lepper, 2010, p. 27)

As more types of community support are developed, such as qualified respite care, parents may be afforded more opportunities for working. Caring for any child is continuous and time-consuming; however, parents of CWODs anticipate a time when child care duties will decrease and will eventually become unnecessary. Caring for a CWD consumes more time, and there may not be any end in sight. Indeed, one of the greatest concerns of parents of CWDs is the future of their children. Who will care for CWDs when their parents no longer can?

Role flexibility is a requirement in most families; at times mothers are the primary wage earners while fathers are stay-at-home caregivers. For families with a CWD, role flexibility is not an occasional, short-term solution, but a continuous, long-term requirement. The primary caregiver of the CWD, typically the mother, frequently experiences role strain because the demands of caregiving are greater than her capabilities and resources. A child with a disability often requires constant attention in order to avoid infections, secondary complications, and hospitalizations. One infected catheter can mean immediate emergency hospitalization. When no one else can manage these complicated medical procedures, the caregiver feels isolated and overburdened. The caregiver's relationships with other family members (including marital relations) are often negatively affected. One mother looks at her wedding photograph and often thinks that the woman (herself) "in that picture is gone." Becoming the mother of an infant with a disability caused the young bride to disappear. Note how also she states that nothing in her life has been planned since the age of 23.

> In my house there is an eight-by-ten picture of me taken on my wedding day. It is just my face, looking somewhat seriously into the camera. When I am in a particularly melancholy frame of mind, it is sad for me to see it, for the woman in that picture is gone.... I was 23, my husband Jim had just turned 22 and we knew little about anything then. Eleven months later,... Maggie was born. She was not a planned child, and I do not think much else in my life has been since that day. As my husband peered into the nursery he saw Maggie turn, in his words, "navy blue." He came running into my room yelling, "There's something wrong with the baby!" and my life changed forever... I wish that the woman in that picture could have left me less suddenly, less painfully. But the person she left behind is smarter, wiser, more confident.... She has tested the love of her family and friends and has found it to be strong and enduring. She knows there is little life can put in her path that she will not be able to face and conquer head on. (Klemm & Schimanski, 1999, pp. 109–110)

This excerpt illustrates the shock of learning that an infant has a disability. Most parents state that they can remember in exquisite detail the time they were first aware that their child may have a disability. This is illustrated in this story when her husband screamed the words "navy blue." This excerpt also illustrates the ongoing support these parents and their baby received from friends and family. Finally, in spite of all the difficulties and heartache, this excerpt illustrates the positive growth of the mother.

The combination of stress, anxiety, and constant vigilance required to care for a small child with a disability can be exhausting and often overwhelming (Case-Smith, 2007). Families also experience role strain when all family activities are centered on the CWD, such as the child's daily care and medical or therapy appointments. There is familial role strain when typical family recreational activities are curtailed, such as movies, dinners in restaurants, or vacations. Even if there is time and money for recreational activities, does the family have the energy? Michael has a trach tube for breathing and a TPN (a transcutaneous peritoneal nutrition) device for feeding. Michael's mother describes "a typical Michael day."

> He gets tube fed for 4 hours a day.... Then he comes home (from school) and he gets more medicine, more breathing treatments, another diaper change, goes to bed for a nap. Then we have to wake him up for therapy...so we get him up, change him again, and it's either speech, OT (occupational therapy) or PT (physical therapy) depending on which day of the week it is. Some days it's doctor appointments.... We do that and then usually between 4 and 7 we're driving everyone else to their stuff, taking them to piano lesson or choir or scouts, or whatever it is, ice-skating lessons.... A couple of times a week we give him a bath in the evening, and when we do that, we have to go through changing all of the dressing, which takes about an hour. About 8:30 he goes to bed. I'm usually up two or three times in the night suctioning him or something like that.... So that is a typical Michael day. (Case-Smith, 2007, p. 316)

Families and parents of CWDs often feel socially isolated because friends and extended family members often are uncomfortable and may stay away. Sometimes the only respite care available comes from professional nurses, due to the medical technology and complicated care procedures. As the CWD grows older, the gap between development of CWODs and that of the CWD often grows wider, so, long-term family and social support is important. The family is required to adjust continuously to these discrepancy gaps. A 13-year-old boy, Matthew, told about his relationship with his brother, Alex.

> My brother Alex and I used to roll around on the ground for hours while I tickled him. We had so much fun. As we got older, I realized that Alex was different from other kids. It never changed my love for him, but we could not share in things as much as we used to. (Fennel, 1999, p. 132)

Whether significant milestones in a CWD's life are met or not met, they often result in "transition stresses" for parents and families (Howard, Williams, & Lepper, 2010). If the milestone is met, the CWD may be required to attend a different school or receive other types of medical services. If the milestone is not met, the CWD and his or her parents must adjust to another level of loss.

The parents and the family are responsible for the care and development of children with disabilities, including children with severe and multiple disabilities. As we have learned, only recently have families been entrusted with these responsibilities. In the past babies with severe disabilities died before, during, or shortly after birth, and infants who did survive were automatically institutionalized. Therefore, a combination of health advances and the societal expectation that all children should live with their parents has radically changed the care of CWDs. These advances have also changed the experiences of parents and families. In the 21st century, there will be very few adults who have spent decades in institutions, which represents a departure from literally centuries of institutionalization of PWDs.

Although these advances are considered progress for CWDs, for their parents and families, and for society, simply because this family-centered approach is new, it must be monitored for gaps between family needs and what medical and educational systems provide. Demographics and medicine often produce changes and progress for which society is not completely prepared. Parents want to feel included in all treatment and educational decisions and fully accepted as active partners with medical providers and educators (Austin, 1990). One parent expressed her perception: "The doctors thought I was a thorn in their side" (Guralnick, 2001, p. 135); another parent stated, "I wish that I would not have to be such a policewoman. I just wish that it could happen without me" (Guralnick, 2001, p. 135). Helping parents to understand the differences between "typical" development and the development of CWDs helps parents in developing realistic expectations. Services are required that provide support for parents, such as information and referrals to appropriate professionals and respite care.

In the United States, the Individuals with Disabilities Education Act (IDEA, Amendments, 1997; IDEA 2004) requires states to identify infants with disabilities and to provide referrals for services to the family.

OVERPROTECTION, NECESSARY CARE, AND REALISTIC EXPECTATIONS

Every parent of a toddler or preschooler has heard the phrase "Me do it!" It is a universal and typical developmental task of this stage of life to desire and achieve some independence, competence, and mastery. Doing too much for any child (with or without a disability) or protecting him or her from new experiences and possible failure may often result in helplessness, passivity, and a lack of self-esteem. Of course, parents must protect their children by not allowing them to play in the street, to drink cleaning fluids, or to engage in a host of other potentially dangerous actions. Nonetheless, there is a difference between realistic protection (the street and poison) and overprotection. Some parents have left their children on the first day of preschool with both the child and parent crying. Directing a reluctant child toward necessary independence is considered the duty of parents. Therefore, it is necessary to seek some sort of balance between independence and protection. Not all children with disabilities have behavior problems. However, some do and others have deficits in social skills, all of which requires parental intervention. Deficits in attention and control of impulsivity; aggressive, disruptive behaviors; and self-injurious behaviors are generally considered to be behavior problems, especially if the problems occur frequently or are inappropriate to the child's developmental level. In spite of the fact that parents need to adjust their expectations of a CWD, it is important to teach the child appropriate behavior. For CWDs, behavior problems that are allowed to persist can create significant barriers later.

For parents with a CWD, support groups composed of parents of CWDs who have the same disabilities can provide direction and guidance on supporting and developing the child's autonomy and independence. These support groups are the best source of information, because these parents have had both successful and unsuccessful experiences. Service providers, such as physicians, physical therapists, counselors, and others, have often not had the experience of living with a child with a disability. As we have learned in previous chapters, caregivers without CWDs or extended family members, in spite of their kind intentions, simply do not understand the disability and the limitations. Finally, if the child lacks the ability to do something, it is not a matter of motivation. For example, telling a blind child to see something has nothing to do with how much the child wants to please the parents or how much effort is expended. Neither rewards nor punishment will work. Phillips (1992) termed this the "try harder syndrome." Motivation is the need to succeed, avoid failure, and a sustained interest in a topic or activity. Many teachers and parents do not understand the relationship between effort, motivation, achievement, and capability so they tend to attribute the child's failure to do or achieve something to negative traits. The child is thought to be lazy, disobedient, or unmotivated. Americans tend to place a high value on motivation, often stating that "I can do anything I set my mind to."

Developmental Tasks of Toddlers With Disabilities

- Learn to monitor and manage their disabilities at a very early age
- Learn to bridge the power differential between themselves and adults, such as teachers, coaches, and other leaders
- Manage the disability while away from home
- Learn stigma management techniques

A congenital disability or one acquired during toddlerhood often results in appointments with medical caregivers, physical therapists, and speech and language therapists. Daily medications and frequent hospitalizations and surgeries are also part of many childhood disabilities. These surgeries may be required because the children grow at a rapid rate. For example, children with spina bifida must have spinal rods reinserted frequently to accommodate growth. Diminished strength, decreased activities, and compliance with treatment combine to communicate to the child that he or she is different from other children.

Children should be told about their disability in developmentally appropriate terms, and the child should understand that he or she is far more than the disability. Although it is important to manage the disadvantage and medical service providers are required to focus on the disability, the child should be told that the disability is only a single aspect of his or her identity. Harper and Peterson (2000) provided some guidelines in telling a child about his or her disability:

> The issue of what to tell others should be discussed with all children who have a chronic illness [and disability], explanations and understandings should be reviewed periodically, and each individual should be given a specific set of explanatory strategies to offer to peers and friends. These explanations obviously require some individualized tailoring for the child...related to his or her conceptual level, current and ongoing medical condition, prior experiences and

understanding of the disorder, and social and emotional status. They should be rehearsed to ensure that the dialogue is used and easy to deliver. The "tone" of these dialogues has a major impact on these social interactions with peers; how one says something may be more crucial than what one says. (p. 129)

In these types of situations, the family's religious affiliation or spiritual orientation is often used to discuss the disability (Kaye & Raghavan, 2002). The preschooler with a disability will begin to ask, "Why is did this happen to me?" "What did I do wrong?" Helping the child (or his or her siblings) ask these questions in an open and supportive environment and then providing developmentally appropriate explanations helps the CWD develop a strong, positive sense of self. If the questions are hidden, ignored, or minimized or if euphemistic words are used, the CWD understands that his or her parents think of the disability as too unbearable and tragic to discuss openly. Also, with increasing integration of CWDs in social settings, such as preschool, neighborhood activities, and church services, most CWDs are not the only child with a disability in a social setting. Of course, the CWD may be the only child with severe and multiple disabilities.

Peer relationships become important when a child enters preschool, and the relationship between the preschooler and his or her teacher tends to be more personal than at any other level of school. Preschoolers are beginning to be influenced by sources outside of the home and the extended family, and they begin to question the assumptions and beliefs of their parents. Erikson stated that very young children identify with their parents, and the values and standards of parents are internalized. For instance, a boy may think "I want to be just like my Dad." Although young children are not identical to their parents, they do incorporate their worldviews.

For many young children, preschool is the first time they develop relationships with adults outside their family. Indeed, for many children preschool is the only period of schooling in which a personal relationship with a teacher is very meaningful. Later in this chapter, we shall read about the mother of Mary, a preschooler with Rett's syndrome. The mother stated, "The most important thing any educator can do for me is to love my Mary."

Preschool expands the social world of children and brings external evaluation and new opportunities for success and failure. It is not an exaggeration to state that preschool changes a child's self-concept. Preschool also brings opportunities for self-evaluation when preschoolers compare themselves to their schoolmates. Piaget's theory holds that preschoolers are capable of thinking in categories, and preschoolers understand that people come in categories, such as gender, size, and disability. Children are capable of understanding which differences are important; for example, the fact that "I am a Catholic" may be important, but the fact that "I am an American" may not be important when everyone in the group is an American.

At any developmental stage, self-evaluation is partially based on the individual's judgment of his or her own specific competencies and attributes. Through comparison with others, the individual gains a self-concept. Even preschoolers are able to recognize the discrepancies between themselves and others. Some preschoolers may be the "class klutz," the "class clown," or the only child with a disability.

Preschool brings higher expectations because children are expected to complete certain tasks on a designated schedule and become aware of more social norms, such as sharing toys, not shoving people, not talking when others are speaking, and using a Kleenex to wipe to their noses. At home, the child may have received messages that communicated only love, support, and approval from others. On the other hand, the preschool may have a designated corner in which the offending child must sit, and the first corner experience can be shocking to the child. Preschoolers are learning not only preschool behavior but their culture's moral code. For the first time, preschoolers become aware of social norms; as Kohlberg asserted, these young children become aware of judgments of "good" and "bad." They may not completely understand the rationale behind these rules and standards, but they do know that it is "better" to use a Kleenex rather than their sleeve to wipe their nose.

Children between the ages of four and seven hold concepts of illness and disability that "are laden with irrational themes such as punishment or blame, magic, or even witchcraft" (Buchbinder & Clark, 2009, p. 254). As children mature, develop cognitively, accumulate more experiences, and acquire greater language skills, they are capable of more accurate and realistic conceptions of disability and illness and their causes.

Preschool children with disabilities must learn to take responsibility for the management of their disabilities. For example, a mother might say to her child, "Remember to take off your prosthesis before you go into the swimming pool." Preschoolers may have service animals, so these young children and their parents will be required to teach the etiquette of service animals to their schoolmates and teachers. Medications, suctioning of breathing tubes, and the use or maintenance of other specialized assistive technology are a part of the day for many preschoolers with disabilities. A study in New Zealand found that children as young as three or four were aware of the first onset of symptoms before an asthma attack, in spite of the fact that their teachers and other adult caregivers did not see these prodromal symptoms (Mavoa, 1999). For some of the more involved procedures with technology-dependent children, an aide might be assigned to attend preschool with the child. All of these services and treatments allow a CWD to attend preschool, but they also serve as very clear reminders that a CWD is different from other preschoolers.

Preschoolers are capable of observing physical differences in others. For example, they know their own gender, and they know the gender of other children. Toddlers (and infants) are capable of social referencing, seeking emotional information from caregivers and other children. During toddlerhood, self-awareness begins and adult instruction increases (Berk, 2001). Most CWDs do not recognize stigma until they begin activities out of the house without their parents. Hence, precisely when the toddler gains some self-awareness and the development of emotions such as shame, embarrassment, or pride, he or she must deal with unearned stigma and prejudice. A little girl, Amy Hagadorn, was born with cerebral palsy that limited the use of her fingers on her right hand and resulted in a limp and speech impairment. In the following story, she asked Santa Claus for a gift:

> [Amy] wrote a letter to Santa Claus sponsored by a local radio station: "Kids laugh at me because of the way I walk and run and talk. I want just one day where no one laughs at me or makes fun of me." (Holzbauer & Bervin, 1996, p. 479)

None of the grand theories of human development discuss the prejudice and discrimination that young children may encounter when they enter preschool. Small children with disabilities are asked about their disabilities by other children, and parents can tell their CWDs how to respond to these questions (Lindenberg, 1980). "My legs don't work right but I am very smart" is one example. Such an answer teaches the child (and his or her friends) that even though one part of his or her body does not function, other parts of the body work just fine. When the parents provide such learning experiences, they also help the siblings of the CWD respond to the questions of others. Although it is often considered rude and inappropriate for strangers to ask PWDs about their disability, it is appropriate for those who will have an ongoing relationship with a PWD to ask such questions. Certainly other preschoolers will be interested.

Like everyone else with a visible disability, CWDs will encounter some misconceptions about their disability, its causes, and its results. Therefore, when CWDs tell their parents what others have said, parents need to be able to explain and interpret these false beliefs. Stigma management skills are necessary at a very young age. An explanation such as "My legs don't work but I am very smart" provides stigma management, both for others and for the child himself or herself.

Stigma is not inherent in any disability nor deserved; society creates stigma (Wright, 1983, 1991). The PWD certainly does not think of himself or herself in stigmatizing terms. Small children can understand that a disability does not automatically include social inferiority.

THE PREJUDICE OF PRESCHOOLERS WITHOUT DISABILITIES

Parents teach children about disabilities. Very young children tend to internalize their parents' attitudes about disabilities, whether the attitudes are expressed openly or communicated emotionally. Preschool children possess the necessary cognitive skills to recognize differences, but their parents communicate which differences are important. Parents teach their children the characteristics of CWDs, the causes of disability, and the meaning of the behaviors of CWDs. Unfortunately, mothers and fathers can communicate to their young children that disabilities are tragic and that CWDs are very sad people all the time. Finally, parents teach their children how they should behave with CWDs. Some parents might teach their children to avoid CWDs.

Parents also control their children's access to and experience with extended family members and friends. At this stage of life, parents also tend to have more control over their children's peers and friends. Therefore, although it becomes increasingly more difficult, parents may choose to disallow their preschoolers any awareness of or experience with CWDs. Access to toys, books, and media is also highly influenced by parent preferences. Parents also choose their children's preschools, and some parents do not want CWDs in their children's preschools, claiming that seeing CWDs is too distressing to the CWODs, that learning experiences are compromised, or that standards are lowered when CWDs are in the classroom. However, research and anecdotal evidence has shown that inclusive preschools are enriching to all the students and that CWODs become more altruistic and empathic in integrated classrooms.

THE EFFECT OF PHYSICAL ATTRACTIVENESS

Parents of CWDs understand that others do not consider their children "trophy children." Trophy children are physically attractive, socially adept, and intelligent. In Chapter Two we learned that children of an entire generation (Generation Y) are nicknamed "trophy kids." Families who value high achievement and set perfectionistic standards may have difficulty in accepting a CWD. There will be no beauty pageants, no sports tournaments, or awards ceremonies for CWDs. Fortunately, this attitude is changing as public awareness increases that CWDs deserve recognition and honors. Parents of CWDs also know that teachers and other adults tend to respond more to children who are attractive.

Parents of CWDs groom these children, dress them according to their age and gender, and find ways to attract others to their children. For example, some parents colorfully decorate their children's wheelchairs in order to encourage CWODs to play with their CWDs. This what most parents do for their children, with or without disabilities.

Another more subtle response to a child's disability is the tendency of some parents to conceal the disability. This encouragement is well-intentioned, because parents understand the stigma directed toward disabilities and may also want to avoid "stigma by association" for their other children. If the disability is mild or invisible, the parents may have the possibility of hiding or minimizing the disability. For child with severe disabilities or visible disabilities (or who uses visible adaptive technology, such as wheelchairs or hearing aids), this is not possible. Although attempts at concealment are usually well-intentioned, a CWD may be burdened with trying to be someone that she or she is not. Two authors explained:

> In stressing the importance of "passing" as able-bodied, parents may also be communicating that being able-bodied is good and being disabled is bad. . . . Children with disabilities are thus being told, "As you are, you are inferior, and to the extent that you emulate able-bodied, this is the extent to which you can overcome your inferiority." Yet achieving full able-bodied status is inherently impossible, so children with disabilities may be condemned to always feel inferior, always to work to cover up their deficiencies, and always be on guard lest their disabilities show. They can rarely be at ease with who they are. (Weinberg & Sterritt, 1991, p. 69)

The desire to normalize the appearance of CWDs is decreasing. Facial plastic surgery is now available, but many parents refuse it. One author explained:

> Children with Down syndrome present an ethical question in regard to disfigurements. In contrast to disfigurements caused by burns and other traumas, children with Down syndrome are born with "facial anomalies," including an enlarged tongue, flattened nose, and large folds of skin on their eyelids. Facial cosmetic surgery is now available which has the capacity to minimize or remove many of these irregularities. Proponents of cosmetic surgery for these children cite the advantages of social integration and greater opportunities for marriage. Nonetheless, in a study (Goeke, 2003) of 250 parents with children who have Down syndrome, 88% stated that they would refuse the surgery. Most opposed

the surgery on the grounds that "society does not have the right to decide what is 'normal' or 'beautiful,' and by extension, to determine who is a candidate for physical alteration" (p. 327). Many of these parents stated that they thought their children with Down syndrome were beautiful. Others said that to reconstruct a child's differences through painful surgery sends a strong message to both the child and the larger community that they find their child physically unattractive (p. 328). Some parents "equated the decision to expose one's child to unnecessary surgery with child abuse." Several parents described it as "revolting" and "barbaric" (p. 329). (J. Smart, 2009, p. 533)

POSTER CHILDREN

In describing her daughter, one mother referred to poster children.

> My child will never be considered a poster child. She does not give professionals the satisfaction of making great progress, nor is she terribly social. But I need the same type of investment by professionals as any other parents of children with disabilities. The most important thing any educator can do for me is to love my Mary. [Carol Maloney, mother of a daughter with Rett syndrome.] (Howard, Williams, & Lepper, 2010)

Ms. Maloney recognizes that beautiful infants and children, with or without disabilities, receive more attention and better care, all of which agrees with both Freudian and Eriksonian theories of early attachment and the developmental tasks of establishing trust. When babies are beautiful, mothers tend to give them more attention and care and are less likely to abuse, neglect, or abandon them. At any age, beautiful people tend to attract other people.

Poster children were created during the polio epidemics, specifically in the 1950s. The correct medical term for polio is infantile poliomyelitis, and as the word "infantile" implies, it was primarily infants and small children who became infected in the beginning of the epidemics. However, as the decades passed, the age distribution of those who caught polio became older. As with most childhood diseases, the symptoms and effects are generally more profound if the the individual is older when he or she contracts the disease.

Poster children and infantile paralysis seemed to be a natural combination. Innocent children who had been struck down with polio pulled at both heartstrings and purse strings (Alder, Wright, & Ulicny, 1991). There were never poster adults because adults would not elicit the same sympathy. It was stated, "The larger the lump in the throat, the larger the check" (Smart, 2009, p. 323). To discover a vaccine that would end these epidemics and to provide care for Americans who had survived polio with some paralysis, the United States was unique in using a combination of public and private charity instead of government funding. Poster children were recruited to raise charity funds. Franklin Roosevelt, President of the United States, was a polio survivor, and he and his associates established the polio charity the March of Dimes. Roosevelt's image on the American dime is an allusion to this polio fundraising organization. Only after Roosevelt's death was it decided to use posters of children who were polio survivors. Canada also had polio epidemics, but the Canadian government financed services and research. The Canadian prime minister Jean Chretien was a polio survivor whose face was paralyzed asymmetrically (on one side). However, Chretien did not engage in fundraising activities (Shell, 2005).

Today the National Infantile Paralysis Foundation acknowledges the the use of these poster children was both manipulative and exploitative. The posters used only attractive young white children who were minimally disabled. African American and Hispanic children also contracted polio, but these children never appeared on a single poster (Shell, 2005).

EARLY INTERVENTION PROGRAMS

Federal legislation mandates early intervention for infants and small children who have disabilities or for infants who are considered at-risk for developing disabilities. Early intervention programs provide systematic and continuous treatments that are individualized for each child. These programs often begin soon after birth, providing services such as infancy stimulation for babies with hearing and vision loss. Research has proven the effectiveness of early intervention, and these programs continue to be refined in the types of treatments and services offered and to be broadened to include more young children.

The purpose of early intervention programs is to reduce the effects of the disability, prevent further disabilities or secondary complications, and capitalize on the child's strengths and capabilities. For children both with and without disabilities enriched experiences have been found to result in maintaining capabilities and accelerating development. Such simple interventions as nutrition planning have a profound effect on an infant's brain development.

Specialized therapies, preventive health care, and the right amount of stimulation that begins as early in life as possible are the goals of early intervention. Parents now have many choices available. Those intervention programs that have proven to be most successful include the components discussed in the next section.

Components of Successful Early Intervention Programs
- Direct engagement of the child such as sensory stimulation and early education
- Appropriate timing (beginning early in infancy and continuing through school age)
- Careful monitoring of progress and subsequent modifications
- Sufficient intensity (often daily treatments and activities)
- Follow-through to maintain early benefits

There is some debate as to whether the benefits of early intervention programs and services are lifelong or whether these benefits begin to diminish when the child begins elementary school. Young children, with or without disabilities, certainly develop and grow rapidly. Research has shown that all children perform better within and outside of school when they receive early intervention.

Aside from the human benefits of early intervention, these programs also result in cost savings for the government. These programs pay for themselves, or (better stated) "their costs are recovered." The earlier in life CWDs receive services, the more likely they are to stay in school and require fewer services throughout their school years. Families whose CWDs receive early intervention services and education are less likely to use other public funds, such as welfare and unemployment benefits. CWDs who have received these services are more likely to obtain gainful employment after leaving school, to pay taxes, and to avoid legal problems.

Early intervention programs provide a well-defined contrast to the automatic institutionalization of children with severe disabilities. Early and lifelong institutionalization resulted in further disablement of these children; the intellectual and social deprivation of these institutions produced children whose intelligence continued to decrease. Early intervention proved that society, government, and professions can work with families to provide the highest quality of life for CWDs.

Emmanuelle LaBroit is a French woman who was born deaf. As an adult, she wrote a book titled *The Cry of the Gull* (1998). The title of the book is derived from two sources: first, as a small child neither she nor anyone else in her family knew sign language and she made noises that sounded like the cries of sea gulls; second, the French word for "seagull" and "mute" were practically the same (*mouette/muette*). When she was 7 years old, her father heard a radio program about French Deaf Culture. The man "speaking" was both deaf and mute. He used sign language, and an interpreter was speaking the words.

Emmanuelle's father took her to another town to a Deaf Social and Cultural Center where she met a man, Alfredo. This one day in her life is frozen in her memory; she remembers the physical aspects of the Social and Cultural Center and also remembers seeing two men signing to each other. At 7 years old, Emmanuelle had never seen sign language being signed. Upon meeting Alfredo, she was surprised by three things: (1) Alfredo was an adult deaf person; (2) Alfredo did not wear hearing aids; and (3) Alfredo used sign language. It totally amazed her.

> Alfredo comes up to me and says, "I'm deaf, like you, and I sign, that's my language."
>
> So Alfredo is deaf, but doesn't wear a hearing aid. What's more he's an adult. I think it took me a while to grasp the threefold oddity.
>
> What I did realize right away, however, was that I was not alone in the world. It was a startling revelation. And a bewildering one because, up till then, I had thought, as do so many deaf children, that I was unique and predestined to die as a child. I discovered that I could have a future because Alfredo was a deaf adult!
>
> The cruel logic about early death persists as long as deaf children haven't encountered a deaf adult. They need to be able to identify with an adult. It's crucial. Parents of deaf children should be made aware of the importance of having their children come in contact with deaf adults as soon as possible, right after birth. The two worlds need to blend—the world of sound and the world of silence. A deaf child's psychological development will be quicker and much better, and the child will grow up free of the pain of being alone in the world with no constructed thought patterns and no future.

Imagine that you had a kitten and never showed it a full-grown cat. It might spend its entire life thinking it was a kitten. Or imagine that the little cat lived only with dogs. It would think that it was the only cat in the world and wear itself out trying to communicate in dog language. (Laborit, 2010, pp. 615–616)

THE "WHY BOTHER?" SYNDROME

The "why bother?" syndrome contrasts with the attitude that "every individual is worthy of investment." The "why bother" syndrome was shown in the reluctance to provide services to children with very severe and multiple disabilities, services that would automatically be provided to children without disabilities (Ferguson, Ferguson, & Taylor, 1991). For example, if a child has both severe intellectual abilities and poor eyesight, it may not be thought necessary to provide the child eyeglasses because "he won't know what he's seeing, anyway."

INCLUSIVE PRESCHOOLS

Because CWDs are increasingly being included in regular preschools instead of specialized preschools, the university training of preschool teachers now includes both didactic and practical components on CWDs. The first longitudinal study of parental perspectives on the early inclusion of their CWDs in nonspecialized preschools (called "inclusive" preschools) showed that parents liked the "real world" exposure their CWDs received and the opportunity for increased community acceptance for their children. However, a consistent criticism has focused on the preschool teachers' lack of competency in dealing with CWDs and the lack of specialized materials. True inclusion of CWDs in preschool does not mean putting the CWD alone in a corner to color pictures all day. Inclusion of PWDs in all levels of the American educational system will require modifications and additions to university teacher training programs. The definition of inclusion varies widely, and the actual day-to-day implementation of integration of all the children also varies from preschool to preschool. For children with severe disabilities, inclusion is not easy, even in preschools that have a long history of including CWDs. At the time of the following story, Jessica was 3 years old and was enrolled in a university-affiliated inclusive preschool:

Jessica started attending the child care center. The care providers, who had taken other disabling conditions in stride, found this child frightening. Jessica didn't help matters when she pulled part the ventilator tubing, setting off the alarm. This met with their immediate and undivided attention. Jessica couldn't make any sounds for days and would only sign "naughty nurse." She seemed fragile and thin and not nearly strong enough to play with toys or participate in activities. There was worry that they might inadvertently harm her, so the care providers subtly drew a circle around themselves and the other children, leaving Jessica on the outside. If Jessica was ready for a tube feeding, the other children's lunches were delayed, and they were kept outside until Jessica was finished. Jessica's cot was set up in an alcove, away from the other children, so that "she could rest undisturbed." She was rarely touched by the other children or interacted with playfully (McWilliam& Bailey, 1993, p. 172).

Jessica's parents were not satisfied with these arrangements and argued that they not only failed to include Jessica but (even worse) made her feel different from the other children. Jessica's mother was especially concerned that Jessica was not allowed to eat with the other children, recognizing that there are many social aspects of sharing a meal. The care center providers decided to change their approach. First, they began to recognize how frightened they were of Jessica's technology, especially the alarms. They consulted with medical professionals and decided to make some changes. She began to eat lunch with the other children and was placed in a sitting position and wheeled into the playroom. Teachers began to look for more ways to include Jessica. The results began to show.

The impact on Jessica was revealed at home first. Sharon (her mother) would bring her to the center each morning bubbling with news.

> "She signed to us last night to sing your songs, 'Twinkle, Twinkle, Little Star' and 'The Itsy, Bitsy Spider.' We sang them over and over. It was great!" One day she reported, "Jessica pulled herself up to stand last night! I couldn't believe it!" Another morning, she [Sharon] announced that they were going to Gramma's and Jess signed, 'No, I want school!'" (McWilliam & Bailey, 1993, p. 173)

In preschool, adults and teachers often consider the age of the child to be reflected by his or her height; as a result children with achondroplasia are thought to be younger than they are. In elementary school, the other children also think that the child with achondroplasia is younger than he or she is, simply because the child is short. However, most children with achondroplasia are healthy and intelligent, and their concerns (and those of their parents) are psychosocial in nature. These children often have trouble reaching the water foundation, getting on the bus, and using the bathroom. More significantly, "Such children may assume or be assigned the mascot role, which over the long term may impede their social development" (Kelly, 1996, p. 137). At times, a mascot role is, the only one available to someone with a visible and unusual characteristic. Mascots are "cute" representatives of the entire group, serve as the cheerleader for the group, and are not given credit for their achievements and accomplishments. Because a mascot is certainly viewed only as his or his disability, most PWDs consider the mascot role demeaning. Furthermore, if the mascot wishes to shed this role, he or she often meets resistance and resentment.

Achondroplasia can be detected in utero (before birth), so it is a type of disability that may be eliminated if women decide to abort their fetuses with achondroplasia. The community of "little people" has a strong tradition in Hollywood as actors and has powerful national organization designed to provide support and fellowship.

Parents of CWDs want schools and other programs that share their vision of what they want for their CWD. Preschools that offer specialized services (in addition to "regular" preschool), such as speech-language therapy, physical therapy, and occupational therapy, provide both the inclusion experience of learning with CWODs and specialized care for the disability. Such enriched preschools are usually located in large cities, especially those urban areas that have a university teaching hospital. Parents often feel that they have to advocate and fight for their CWDs in order to receive the necessary services and preschool education. This need is expressed when parents say, "I wish it all didn't depend on me."

Research has shown that some mothers of CWDs did not want their children placed in inclusive preschools that included other CWDs who had what they considered to be more stigmatizing disabilities, such as mental retardation (Turnball & Winton, 1983; Winton, 1990). These mothers voiced concern that the needs of their CWDs would not be met. In contrast, other research showed that mothers of CWDs reported that inclusive preschools resulted in more benefits, with a higher percentage of their child's needs met (Bailey & Winton, 1987; Reichart et al., 1989). Research has also shown that families of CWDs feel that families of CWODs do not have knowledge or understanding of CWDs, nor are they particularly inclined to learn. In these studies (Bailey & Winton, 1987; Turnball & Winton, 1983), the parents of CWDs did not feel included with the other preschoolers' parents.

Other mothers have expressed the advantages of an inclusive preschool for their CWDs:

> They're all just wonderful teachers. And I think that all the kids are benefiting from Charles being in the classroom. They have this aide now that not only helps Charles but helps everyone. They have this wonderful occupational therapist coming in and doing activities for all the kids. (Guralnick, 2001, p. 135)

THE DEVELOPMENTAL THEORIES

Freud termed the years of toddlerhood and preschool the anal stage because this is the time when children are toilet trained. Toilet training increases the child's sense of competence and mastery and provides greater independence. If children require catheterization several times a day to empty their bladders and do not start to learn self-catheterization skills until about age 12, they find it difficult to feel mastery over their own bodies. For children with neuromotor disabilities, such as cerebral palsy, the struggle to achieve control over their bodies will be a great deal more difficult than it is for CWODs.

Empirical studies with toddlers and preschoolers have provided some support for Freud's theory of attachment. Toddlers and preschoolers who are hospitalized (or placed in another type of institution) were found to demonstrate a decrease in responsiveness to hospital caregivers. When these small children returned home, their responsiveness to their mothers typically returned to prehospital levels. Researchers hypothesized that the decrease was due to the children's lack of motivation to perform for strangers (Clarke-Stewart, 1977; Skeels, 1966). Bowlby (1969) coined the term "separation anxiety" while observing hospitalized 15-month to 30-month-old infants. A very practical result of these theories and studies has been changes in hospital policies. "Total replacement of a child's primary caretakers and familiar environment in an institutional setting" is now uncommon (Papalia & Olds, 1981, p. 175). Parents are allowed to stay with their children; hospitals often provide prehospitalization visits to acquaint and prepare young children for leaving their home, and many hospitals have "foster grandmother" programs to ensure that the child receives a great deal of attention during the hospitalization.

Implementing Erikson's theories requires a very careful definition of exactly what he meant by positive and negative tendencies. For Erikson, the developmental crisis of toddlerhood is developing autonomy (rather than shame and doubt), and the developmental crisis of preschool years is developing initiative (rather than guilt). Initiative is sometimes defined as purpose. The feminist psychologist Gilligan disagreed with Erikson, considering his emphasis upon autonomy and initiative to be male oriented, because little boys are raised to be independent and little girls are raised to value relationships. A careful reading of Erikson, according to Capps (2008), may resolve this disagreement. Erikson intended autonomy to mean self-governance, and the child, whether boy or girl, becomes more relationship oriented, not less. Further, the negative tendencies of shame, doubt, and guilt are associated with the child's relationships. The toddler and preschooler feel that he or she has lost the respect of others.

The task required in the second stage of Erikson's theory is the development of will, initiative, or self-determination. As the toddler gains greater control over his or her physical body, he or she is also attempting to gain the love and respect of others. Both changes require self-control. According to Erikson, will is the ability to control one's own actions, rather than the capability to do anything one wants. The development of language provides another way to regulate emotion. The development of self-awareness also leads to the individual's first efforts to take the perspective of others and to compare himself or herself with others.

Kohlberg believed that children of these ages comply with rules out of a sense of shame, and a great deal of discipline is based on inflicting guilt and shame as a type of punishment. Often children will hide their faces in shame and doubt. Erikson was concerned about parents' use of shame, for he thought it exploited the power differential (between the preschooler and the parent) and might actually result in shamelessness. Shamelessness, according to Erikson, results because the child resolves to break the rules without being caught. Erikson saw a relationship between empathy, self-control, and compliance, considering that the ability to understand others and to control oneself assists the preschooler in obeying rules.

Freud, Erikson, Piaget, and Bronfenbrenner are all considered to have contributed to the early intervention programs because these theorists focused attention on the importance of early development. In different ways, all these theorists focused on the necessity of providing infants and young children with a stable, strong foundation.

Urie Bronfenbrenner thought that early development of preschool children was important, and that early deprivation of preschool children conversely produced lifelong negative consequences. As part of the government's War on Poverty initiated by President Lyndon B. Johnson, the Head Start program began as a highly individualized, intensive preschool program for children of lower socioeconomic groups. The empirical research generated by the Head Start program has shown that providing preschoolers with enriched learning opportunities gives children an advantage in later schooling. Television programming such as *Sesame Street* was also based on theories of the importance of the early development. Bronfenbrenner's contribution was a combination of his awareness of the importance of the toddler and preschool years with his advocacy that the macro system (in this case the federal government) should supplement the efforts of the microsystem (the family). As a boy living at Letchworth Village, Bronfenbrenner saw that environments of deprivation produced individuals with reduced capacities while enriched environments produced individuals with expanded capacities. Bronfenbrenner and his theories captured national attention at the right time, at the beginning of President Lyndon Johnson's War on Poverty, a wide-ranging governmental program to provide services for at-risk Americans. One author described the poverty and deprivation of American preschoolers:

> The risk factors for the 12 million American children under the age of three are enormous. Twenty-five percent live in poverty, 25% are in single-parent homes, 33% of those under age one are victims of physical abuse, and over 50% of mothers of children under three work outside of the home. (Carnegie, 1994, p. xiii)

It is well-known that adverse prenatal and postnatal environmental conditions, including poor nutrition, environmental toxins, premature birth, chronic illness, and central nervous system injuries, can affect child development in ways that may compromise brain functioning and lead to cognitive, physical, and behavioral problems, some of which may be irreversible. Impoverished minority children have less frequent contact with medical professionals than middle-class white children and often are sent to school with respiratory, ear, or gastrointestinal problems if their mothers lack medical information or have to go to work when no child care is available. In addition, children living in poverty may suffer from malnutrition (Austrian, 2002, p. 61).

In addition to providing preschool education, Head Start programs also provide comprehensive services related to health and nutrition. These young children are provided regular physical check-ups, including routine screening for vision and hearing and preventive dental care. Head Start programs provide meals for the children and thus ensure that their nutritional intake is supplemented.

Although Piaget never applied his theories to education, many educational programs and techniques are based on his theories. Piaget posited that recognizing the child's readiness and motivation to learn allows parents, family members, and teachers to provide the toys, books, and adult time at the right time to assist the child in learning and developing at his or her own pace and also pursuing individual interests. Piaget believed that learning was a result of using all five senses, but for CWDs the use of all the senses may obviously not be possible (Warren, 1984). For example, children with autism tend to be very touch aversive, avoiding being touched and refusing to explore their environment through touch. Indeed, one treatment for ASDs is a "sensory diet." Children with autism are often overwhelmed by sensory stimuli; therefore, parents, teachers, and occupational therapists develop a daily sensory diet to regulate the amount of sensory stimuli the child receives. As children with autism mature, they learn to self-regulate and devise methods to avoid excessive sensory stimuli.

Not all children of the same age have the same physical or cognitive abilities, and CWDs have a wider range of these abilities. If the child does not have the capability to do an activity, it is not a matter of motivation. For example, telling a blind child to see something has nothing to do with how much the child wants to please the parent. Neither giving rewards and punishments nor spending more time teaching the child will result in gains. For example, if children have not gained sufficient eye muscle control to move their eyes across the page, they have not acquired sufficient physical coordination to learn to read. Therefore this delay in reading is not result of the child's lack of motivation or the teacher's poor teaching skills.

Terms to Learn

Asthma
Autism spectrum disorders
Diagnostic and Statistical Manual IV-TR
Fantasy play

Pervasive developmental disorders
Poster children
Prelingual deafness
Role flexibility
Role strain

Seizure disorders
Sex-role requirements
Stigma management
Traumatic brain injury

Videos to View

- View the 29-minute video *Study of the Child: Theories of Development* by Films for the Humanities and Science. The producers describe this video: "This video presents child development theories in action: cognitive, psychosexual, psychosocial, behaviorist, social learning, and sociocultural. The video focuses on the fact that theories often force caregivers to dwell on 'parts' rather than 'the whole child.' A realistic interpretation of theories from Piaget, Freud, Erikson, Gesell, Skinner, and Vygotsky will clearly show the contradictions and lead to powerful discussion about how these theories have impacted child development in education."

- View the 13-part series *Child of Our Time: A Year-by-Year Study of Childhood Development.* These 1-hour videos were produced in the U.K. The producers describe this series: "In the year 2000, producers for the British Broadcasting Company (BBC) began documenting the growth and development of 25 newborn children from a wide range of social, ethnic, and geographical backgrounds. This series shows viewers the results so far, capturing pivotal stages in each child's learning process, manner of socialization, and physical development. Students of child psychology, early childhood education, and multicultural education will encounter detailed information and numerous case studies in these programs, while course instructors will find a wealth of material with which to launch lectures and discussion."

Learning Activities

(Note: These may also be used as classroom presentations.)
- As a group, view the film *Temple Grandin* by HBO Films. This film tells the story of a woman (Temple Grandin) with autism, and received seven Emmy awards. It stars Claire Danes and Julia Ormand. Temple Grandin, who earned

a PhD, was one of the first children to be diagnosed with autism who was not institutionalized. Note the following in the film:

1. The physician blames Temple's mother for not being affectionate during Temple's infancy.
2. The length of time required to arrive at a diagnosis.
3. Temple's lack of social skills and the way in which her aunt helps Temple to identify and correctly label her emotions.
4. The way in which the film shows lack of abstract thinking, such as "Get up with the roosters."
5. Temple's hypersensitivity to visual and auditory stimuli and the way in which she "self-treated."
6. The difficulties Temple experiences in school settings.
7. The significant impact of a high school science teacher who was able to look past Temple's deficits and see her strengths.
8. The one age mate who understood and accepted Temple was a PWD; her roommate who was blind.

- Google "aspie" (to find a website about individuals with Asperger's by individuals with Asperger's.) The name "aspie" is a self-identifier.

Writing Exercises

- Research one of the following disabilities: traumatic brain injuries, seizure disorders, asthma, or autism spectrum disorders. Write a 10-page paper about this disability that includes information on prevalence, onset, course, and adjustment requirements.
- Write a five-page autobiographical paper that traces your preschool development (or your memories of your preschool development). Focus on your physical development, the importance and function of play, the way in which you began to regulate your emotions, and your language development.

Web Sites

http://learningdisabilities.about.com/od/infancyandearlychildhood/p/
  24to36monthsdev.htm
http://nichcy.org/
http://www.kidsource.com/kidsource/pages/toddlers.disabilities.html

Most American children spend 13 to 17 years in school, beginning as very young children and leaving school as young adults. The developmental stage of the school years includes the ages 5 to 12 years, and certainly a 12-year-old differs greatly from a 5-year-old. During these years the child becomes more of an individual, using newfound freedoms, improved cognitive skills, and school experiences to become more of a unique individual. Erikson considered "industry versus inferiority" the developmental task of these years, thinking that young school children must learn to complete schoolwork (industry) rather than failing to conform to the demands of school and experiencing inferiority. Society allocates resources to ensure that children learn the skills valued and required in the community, believing that (most) children are worthy of public governmental investment. Obviously, the completion of the developmental tasks of school age is based on the resources of the society, which Bronfenbrenner (1977, 1986, 2005) termed the macrosystem. Until they enter kindergarten or first grade, most children have little or no direct interaction with the macrosystem. In children's early school years, there is a close link between the number and quality of resources available to them and their development. In most developed nations public education is an entitlement program, meaning that by demonstrating proof of age, such as a birth certificate, most children are allowed (indeed mandated) to attend public schools. There are no waiting lists or eligibility applications for public schools, and state governments fund most of the costs, regardless of the cost each student incurs.

According to the U.S. Department of Education (2006), approximately 12% of students between the ages of 6 and 17 are educated under the Individuals with Disabilities Education Act (IDEA) of 2004. Hundreds of thousands of schoolchildren are considered to have some sort of a disability, including children who are not receiving services under IDEA. Some experts (Judson, 2004, Perrin, 2004) estimate that approximately 15% to 18% of children in the United States have a disability. However, education for children with disabilities (termed special education) is a relatively recent addition to the public schools. In the past, for most children with disabilities (CWDs) the emphasis was upon custodial care rather than education (see Figure 12.1).

Even though nearly one-fifth of all children experience a disability, child development specialists have not shown much interest in the experiences of CWDs, nor have sociologists. McLeod and Almazan (2004) reviewed the literature on "childhood adversity" and found that the term was defined as traumas and childhood separations:

> Researchers from diverse disciplines have contributed to our understanding of how early experiences in a child's life influence adult attainments and

FIGURE 12.1

Percentage of youth ages 3–21 served under the individuals with Disabilities Education Act (IDEA), by Disability: Selected Years, 1976–77 through 2005–06.

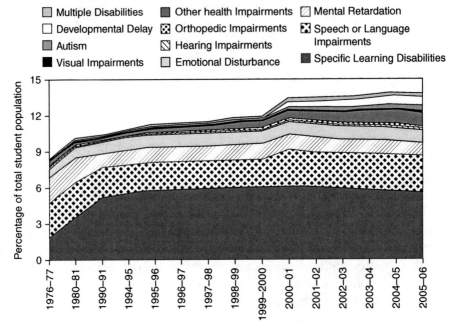

Source: National Center for Education Statistics. Table 7-2.

well-being. Psychologists and psychiatrists tend to focus on the psychopathological outcomes of childhood separation and traumas, whereas, demographers, economists, and sociologists have been more concerned with the economic or marital sequelae of parental divorce, living in female-headed households, or early economic disruptions. (p. 400)

The Demographics of School-Age Children

- A very large generation
- A very racially and ethnically diverse generation
- Most school children do not live with two parents who have been continuously married

The number of school-age children in the United States is at all-time high (Carr, Vol. 1, 2009, p. xx). These large numbers are attributed to two sources: the number of Baby Boomers who had children and the large influx of immigrants. As we learned in previous chapters, it is primarily the larger number of immigrants combined with their high birth rates that enables the United States to maintain its population replacement rate. Many nations that do not welcome immigrants, such as Japan, will soon report declining population numbers (Carr, 2009). For those countries who do not admit immigrants, it may be difficult to find enough workers to support old-age pensions. American school-age children are racially and ethnically diverse, with little over half the children of non-Hispanic white origin. In contrast to other nations, American has a very heterogeneous youth population. As generation, current American children differ from other generations of school-age children in another aspect. Most of today's school-age children do not live in two-parent households that have continuously married parents and one parent who stays home to care for the children. For example, in the 1980s and 1990s the widely used term "latch key children" described school children who came home to a house without a parent because both parents worked. This term is no longer used because the majority of children have working parents.

The next generation of American young adults will experience an increasingly diverse marriage market, with opportunities to meet and date many individuals from a much larger pool.

THE SOCIAL DEFINITION OF CHILDHOOD

Although most American institutions provide services based on the individual's age, we have learned that the social definitions are more important than biological age. There are two differing views on the time period when a basic shift occurred in the social definition of childhood.

The fundamental nature of childhood has changed in a single generation. In the past childhood was a carefree, unstructured, and unsupervised period when (other than school and perhaps church) most children were allowed to play all day. With most of the day devoted to active play, there was little childhood obesity (Vasta, 1998). With this type of childhood, there were also few demands for achievements in music, sports, dancing, or karate. Carpools, after-school piano lessons, and swim meets would have been viewed by both children and parents as unnecessary and burdensome. Breggin (2001) described the typical childhood of previous generations in which children did not spend a great deal of time indoors involved in sedentary activities, such as video games, in computer chat rooms, and watching television. No longer are children told to "be home for dinner," having taken off on their bicycles for an entire day or an afternoon. According to Breggin, today, most outdoor activities for children are both adult-monitored and scheduled.

Although Breggin focused on the lack of experiences of nature and physical movement in the childhoods of today, it may also be true that the earlier type of childhood did not provide children with much adult interaction, especially in the summer, nor did adults interact with children who were not within walking distance when school was not in session. Parents were not as concerned for the physical safety of their children, nor did there seem to be as much reason to be worried. On the positive side, children were not exposed to demands and high expectations for achievement nor held accountable for their use of time. This type of childhood was probably more common among boys, who were often given more freedom than girls.

Swartz stated that "children's skills at sustaining paradoxical truths" are an important part of childhood. In the book *Where Did You Go? Out. What Did You Do? Nothing* (Smith, 1957, 2011), the author illustrated the importance of childhood paradoxical thinking: Children believe wholeheartedly, for instance, that they've built a boat, while simultaneously knowing that in fact they've just hauled "an orange crate ten blocks and stuck it in a muddy brook and gotten wet up to [their] armpits" (p. 101). According to Smith, children, want magic, which requires both time and a space away from adults in which to daydream. Another book *Children at Play: An American History* (Chudacoff, 2011) asserts that modern societies have reverted back to the 18th-century view that child's play is a waste of time. In the 18th century, children were expected to work and produce; today, children are required to take lessons from professionals or learn foreign languages. Chudacoff, like Breggin, feels that these changes occurred only in the second half of the 20th century, but recently these changes have both accelerated and intensified.

The social definitions of childhood have changed: children are no longer viewed as miniature adults who assumed adult roles early and whose labor was valuable to both the family and society. When the labor market changed and governments enacted laws to protect children, children were allowed to have unstructured childhoods without adult supervision.

One professor (Austrian, 2002) described the change in children's clothing as related to the changing functions of childhood:

> Children once dressed exclusively in play clothes that accommodated that their higher levels of physical activity, propensity toward outdoor play, and use of expressive art materials. Today, they often wear expensive designer clothes and footwear, miniature adult apparel, including items which may be sexually provocative. (p. 71)

Thus, Austrian believes that societal views of childhood changed the way in which children dressed, but another author (Cook, 2009) believes that the way in which children dressed changed societal views of childhood. In the book *The Commodification of Childhood* (Cook, 2009), it is noted:

> Throughout the 1920s and the 1930s, children's goods in department stores steadily acquired their own spaces (departments) with specialized personnel and specialized selling techniques. For the first time, these departments (the height of the fixtures and the mirrors) were intentionally designed to appeal to children, rather than the mother.

> The children's clothing industry helped to reshape childhood, especially girlhood. In 1920, only three size ranges in girls' clothing existed—newborn to 1.5 years, 1.5 years to 6 years, and 6 to 14 years. By 1950, there were seven size ranges: Infant, toddler, children's girls, subteens, junior miss, and miss, which covered girls from birth through about age 16. The increasing differentiation of the life course for young females over this time stemmed, in part, from the age grading in the educational system. The finer distinctions in clothing sizes and styles both reinforced and help produce differentiations in age and social lives of girls.

Consumership of children and youth had the cumulative effect of identifying and defining youth and childhood as distinct and internally differentiated phases of life. The designation of "toddler"—which is now a general, named stage of the course—arose initially almost entirely as a merchandising and manufacturing category of children's clothes. (p. 49)

Because "society" defines all the developmental stages of life, it is accurate to state that both authors are correct. The functions and demands of any developmental stage change the definition, and societal expectations change the functions. It is a circular relationship.

PHYSICAL GROWTH FROM AGES 5 TO 12

Compared to infancy, toddlerhood, and preschool years, the early school years are a time of slower physical growth and development. At age six, the typical child weight about 45 pounds and is 3 feet, 6½ inches tall. In the years between 6 and 12, children typically add about 2 to 3 inches in height and 5 pounds in weight each year (Berk, 2001). At 12, the average child weighs about 86 pounds, although children in this age range gradually lose fatty tissue. Many girls are taller than boys because they experience a growth spurt at approximately age 10, 2 years earlier than the growth spurt for boys.

During this developmental stage children often appear awkward, gangly, and uncoordinated, with teeth too large for their mouths. During these years children's bodies begin to appear more proportionate. For example, head circumference and waist circumference decrease in relation to body height. At the age of 8, the brain is nearly at its mature size and brain growth is almost complete. Santrock (2009) described changes in the brain during the age period of 5 to 12 years, which he referred to as "middle and late childhood."

Total brain volume stabilizes by the end of middle and late childhood, but significant changes in various structures and regions of the brain continue to occur. In particular, the brain pathways and circuitry involving the prefrontal cortex, the highest level in the brain, continue to increase in middle and late childhood (Durston & Casey, 2006). These advances are in the prefrontal cortex are linked to children's improved attention, reasoning, and cognitive control (Anderson, Jacobs, & Harvey, 2005).

As children develop, activation of some brain areas increase while others decrease (Dowker, 2006). One shift in activation that occurs as children develop is from diffuse, larger areas to more focal, smaller areas (Trukeltaub & others, 2003)....The activation change was accompanied by increased efficiency in cognitive performance, especially in *cognitive control*, which involves flexible and effective control in a number of areas. These areas include controlling attention, reducing interfering thoughts, inhibiting motor actions, and becoming flexible in switching between competing choices (Munkata, 2006, p. 283). (Santrock, 2009, p. 283)

Muscle mass increases, and bones lengthen and broaden, causing children to have great flexibility of movement. Their leg bones grow faster than their arms and trunks, and children between 5 and 12 often appear "long legged." The first permanent teeth seem too large for the child's face, but facial bones, especially the jaw and the chin, grow and lengthen to accommodate the permanent teeth.

Another gender difference in physical attributes is the greater accumulation of body fat for girls and more muscle development for boys. Girls' bodies become more rounded and contoured, due to their greater amount of fatty tissues, while boys become more muscular appearing. The genetic advantage of greater muscle development makes boys more skilled in large motor skills such as throwing and kicking. Girls, however, tend to have better fine motor coordination than boys, making them more skilled at handwriting and artwork. Girls are also more adept than boys at skills that require balance and agility. Nonetheless, child development specialists warn that these gender-typed discrepancies are not defined as much by physical aspects as once thought. These specialists also point out the influence of the environment, the opportunities provided to boys and girls, and (perhaps most important) the expectations of the parents.

With greater physical capacities, children are able to master more complicated physical tasks that involve strength, endurance, and dexterity. Most children learn to ride bicycles, increasing their independence and allowing their world to expand. Indeed, most adults can remember getting their first bicycle because the bicycle represented a physical achievement and greater autonomy. Many people with disabilities (PWDs) remember receiving their first wheelchairs or other pieces of assistive technology (AT) because these pieces of technology also represented an achievement and greater autonomy. Leonard Kriegel received his first wheelchair in the New York State Reconstruction Home in 1945 (Wilson, 1990). During World War II wheelchairs were rationed for use by wounded soldiers and sailors, so Kriegel had to wait for his wheelchair. In his 1964 memoir Kriegel wrote, "The wheelchair was the way home. [I] loved that wheelchair with passion that embarrasses me now." The wheelchair provided a "newly won mobility and a gift of overwhelming mobility" (Kriegel, 1964, pp. 52, 55).

Fine motor coordination improves steadily during the first years of school due to increased myelination of the central nervous system. This increased fine motor coordination gives children the ability to print the alphabet and write the numbers from one to 10. Six-year-olds can also tie their shoes, cut with scissors, and button their clothes. Because they use their entire arm to write, their writing is quite large. By the third grade, most children have mastered more control and write with their wrist and fingers. During the age of 6 to 12 years, many children begin to learn to play a musical instrument, a skill made possible by their increasing cognitive abilities and improving fine motor skills.

DEVELOPMENTAL TASKS OF AGES 5 TO 12

Transition to First Grade

Children begin to move through the macrosystem, the institutional structures designed to serve and educate them. Entry into first grade is timed to coincide with a cognitive spurt experienced by most 6 year olds. Nonetheless, some authors believe that entry into first grade is defined socially, not cognitively.

The first-grade transition is profoundly social in nature. It signals the move from being a "home child" to being a "school child." This move is a big change, for one reason, because preschools and kindergartens are discretionary with caregivers directly answerable to parents. At the end of the preschool day parents often get a tally of the child's meals, naps, and problems. By contrast, first grade is not under parents' control in that way. Grade school is legally compulsory, the atmosphere is formal, and parents are not expected to make surprise visits. Teachers have authority over the child during the school day and jealously guard their prerogatives. Direct communications between teachers and parents are relatively infrequent and mostly in written form. (Entwisle, Alexander, & Olson, 2004, p. 230)

School, therefore, requires children to develop both cognitive and social skills. In turn, these improved cognitive and physical skills result in greater requirements placed on school-age children. A "school self-concept" is developed in these early grades and continues until high school graduation and beyond. Children see themselves as having unique capacities, the commitment and responsibility to complete schoolwork, and the ability to establish friendships. Children are expected to remain on task and complete their work in a timely manner. Therefore young children are expected to develop good work habits. As one child explained, "in kindergarten all we did was played. In kindergarten we get playtime more often than work.... In first grade we have to get finished. We can't monkey around" (Schnorr, 1993, p. 427).

Moreover, perhaps for the first time, children develop personal relationships with adults who are not their parents. Therefore, according to Harker (1990, 1998), elementary-age children develop three types of self-esteem: academic, social, and physical. However, these three types of self-esteem do not contribute equally to the child's overall self-esteem. Harter found that during childhood (and adolescence), perceived physical appearance was correlated most strongly with overall self-worth.

Another aspect of first grade is formalized evaluations in which children are compared to their classmates, in contrast to kindergarten and preschool where the child's work was compared to his or her prior achievements. The following excerpt shows the way in which elementary school children accept standardized external evaluation:

The director of our program had accepted the teachers' recommendation that we substitute descriptive evaluations for grades. The students participated in assessing their learning. Students met with the teachers to determine if their work in each subject showed improvement. Peter and I had a conference at my desk about his progress. "Do you think your reading has improved?" I asked him. "What do you mean?" He replied. "You know, are you getting better at reading?" I asked. "How should I know?" Peter said, "you're the teacher. It's your job to give me a grade so I'll know if I've learned anything." (Henley, Ramsey, & Algozzine, 1996, p. 231)

Children are expected to work on task and complete work in a timely manner. Little children are expected to develop good work habits and an awareness of the rights of others. School children know the schedule and the importance of adhering to it.

Social comparison becomes very important in first grade. Children judge their school achievement, appearance, behavior, and abilities in relationship to their peers. Feedback from others becomes the measuring instrument, or more correctly, the measuring instrument is what the child thinks (or infers) others think of him or her. As children become older, they naturally gain greater ability to understand the messages they receive from others. As children become older, they also enter ever-widening social groups in both the school and community. Therefore, in some ways the limited cognitive skills of elementary students, combined with the rather narrow social group of first grade, makes first grade very influential on children's self-concept.

Young school children who view themselves as cooperative, well-liked, and competent have gained this self-concept through interactions with their teachers, parents, and other children. For the first time in their lives, they receive formal written evaluations (report cards.) Their parents attend parent–teacher conferences. All these external sources (adults, children, report cards, and conferences) contribute to children's expectations about their abilities. Until first grade or perhaps second grade, children lack the cognitive skills to make systematic use of feedback and evaluation. Entwisle and others (1987) found by the end of the first grade, children are more aware of others' expectations of them, so children try to meet these expectations. Before this time there are few expectations in preschool and at home. For example, just about any scribble is considered a work of art. Of course, there are only a few expectations in preschool and at home, but a child younger than six or seven does not have the cognitive skills to understand fully those expectations or to evaluate his or her performance relative to them.

Self-esteem becomes increasingly more refined as children progress through elementary school. Increased cognitive abilities, a larger circle of social contacts, and the ability to begin to choose those environments in which they can succeed all help to provide more a realistic self-esteem. For example, when children are allowed some choice over the specific courses they take, the team sports they play, or any other of a host of activities, they naturally gravitate to environments in which their strengths can be used and further developed. Therefore, children from ages 8 to 11 develop their understanding of themselves through increasing interpersonal relationships. Their self-descriptions reflect this when they describe themselves as "smart," "dumb," "nice," or "mean." Although children in first and second grade tend to have either a positive or a negative self-concept, children in the later years of elementary school are able to integrate judgments that are both positive and negative, or evaluations of both strengths and weaknesses, into a more balanced or global self-concept. A sixth grader may understand that although she is not good at writing, she is an excellent athlete, a good friend, and a math whiz.

The achievements of first grade can be considered "high stakes" in that both educational achievement and job status in young adulthood have been found to be correlated with first-grade performance. It is somewhat daunting to consider that the transition of beginning school sets the stage for all that follows. Children's achievement trajectories are remarkably stable. Academic self-concept is somewhat circular, because the self-concept is based on academic achievements, which in turn are based on the child's concept of his or her ability to perform the task or on his or her academic self-esteem. Children with high academic self-concepts attribute school successes to their abilities, their work habits, and the perception that, they can complete school tasks if they work hard and are tenacious. On the other hand, children with low academic self-esteem tend to attribute their school failures to external factors such as luck.

The circular relationship between academic self-concept and academic achievement becomes apparent when children with high academic self-esteem believe in their own skills and therefore see failure as something that they can change, while students with low academic self-esteem attribute their failures to factors outside their control. After experiencing failures, children with high academic self-concept will continue to try harder because they believe that they can surmount difficult challenges, but children with low academic self-esteem will feel a loss of control and stop trying, thinking that their efforts will not make a difference. These children may also think that their failures are due to their lack of ability.

School success thus becomes cumulative because children with high academic self-esteem can develop refined self-regulatory processes that include persistence, a sense of self-mastery, control of their emotions, and other idiosyncratic (specific to the individual) traits for completing academic work. Those with high academic self-esteem tend to set high standards for themselves; they monitor their progress and are capable of self-correcting actions. Individuals with high academic self-esteem are able to seek support, such as asking the teacher for further explanation or organizing a study group. Both parents and teachers can assist children, including first and second graders, to develop a strong academic self-esteem by guiding them through some of these strategies.

School failure also becomes cumulative. Beginning in first grade, teachers and classrooms that are supportive and provide warm, accepting, positive learning environments can reduce low academic self-esteem among students. We shall discuss learning disabilities later in this chapter and learn how academic success or failure can be cumulative. Indeed, in the past it was thought that children with learning disabilities *dropped out* of school, but today it is thought that these children were *pushed out* of school.

Parents also communicate their expectations about school achievement to children. Young school children understand their parents' attitudes about school, and school success, as well as their judgment of their children's abilities and potential. At this age children tend to internalize their parents' belief systems, including beliefs about the value of academic achievement and the way in which academic achievement should be developed. On the other hand, teachers become powerful adult influences, and children are eager to please their teachers both socially and academically. For the first time, children may come home from school with beliefs that contradict those of their parents. For example, a teacher may tell the children that breakfast is the most important meal of the day, even though the parents may disagree. At an early age, children are capable of "apple polishing" or "kissing up" to their teachers. Newman and Newman (2009) described this behavior:

> In this age period, with the skills of metacognition and perspective taking, children come to understand that people may alter their behavior in order to project an image that will receive a favorable evaluation from others. They can recognize that under certain circumstances they may wish to alter their own self-presentation in order to receive positive social evaluation from parents, teachers, or peers. (p. 301)

Individuals, including children, cannot complete tasks if they do not have the basic ability. No amount of encouragement to try harder will result in success. Therefore, teachers and other school professionals are faced with the difficult task of helping children reach their full potential within the limits of their capabilities as they simultaneously assist each child in acquiring high academic self-esteem.

Public schools tend to be geographically defined, so children in schools tend to be of one socioeconomic status simply because they live in the same neighborhood. Schools located in areas with lower socioeconomic status tend to have lower standardized test scores. In contrast, children from more affluent neighborhoods tend to have higher test scores upon entering first grade. Most of these discrepancies are related to the lower quality of resources (including teachers) provided to schools in poorer neighborhoods. Community disadvantages, which include more than inferior schools, can have lifelong reverberations, adding a "social embeddedness of the life course" (Crosnoe, 2000, p. 385). A poor elementary education can result in "cumulating disadvantages."

Developing Friendships

Children depend upon adults for protection, security, and teaching. Adults (typically parents and teachers) are not equals or peers to children; moreover, adults have rules, expectations, and a substantial investment in each child, with strong and clear ideas of how the children should behave and mature. Friendships early in life tend to be play-oriented dyads, and friendship needs peak in adolescence, perhaps due to social anxiety (Crosnoe, 2000). One developmental psychologist coined the term "homophilous" (Crosnoe, 2000, p. 381) to indicate that children and adolescents are attracted to those who share their same characteristics, such as gender and race. The concept of homophilous friendships plays an important part in friendships between CWDs and children without disabilities (CWODs). If CWDs are considered to be "not like the other kids" or are educated in segregated settings, they will find it difficult to make friends with CWODs. Often the adults (parents and teachers) interpret the concept of "who is one of us."

In the school-age years, children tend to play in same sex groups, although there are some boy–girl friendships. These boy–girl friendships are often kept hidden from the other children in order to avoid embarrassment. Boys tend to play in larger groups and in more structured games. In the early school years, 40% of a child's time is spent with peers (Hartup, 1983). Girls' friendship groups tend to be smaller and based upon closeness and sharing secrets, and boys' friendship groups are based on activities and status. These gender-based differences in friendship groups tend to persist throughout life.

Friendships are peer relationships that are usually reciprocal and determined by choice. Children begin to learn that friendships do not disintegrate at the first sign of a disagreement. In order to establish friendships, school-age children must outgrow their egocentrism and develop the ability to see the perspectives of others. Preschoolers cannot imagine that their perceptions may not be true. Before age six, most children cannot recognize or understand the feelings of others, so they are not then faced with the need to develop empathy for others. For some children, it is quite surprising to learn that others have feelings, needs, and attitudes that differ from theirs. Assuming the viewpoint of other person is both a cognitive and social skill, and some developmental psychologists term the ability to make friends "social cognition." Parents often teach perspective taking and empathy when they ask children such questions as: "How does Johnnie feel when you take his toy away?" Nonetheless, when first developing empathy and awareness of others, the 6- or 7-year-old does recognize that others may have different perceptions but does not understand why. In fact 6- and 7-year-old children believe that others would feel the same way if they had the same information (Rice, 1998).

Social cognition is the capacity to understand others, both as individual and as groups. This includes understanding the motivations, emotions, and attitudes of others. The knowledge of what others think and feel is basic to all human interactions. Obviously these skills develop gradually.

As egocentrism decreases, skills in cooperation begin to develop. Some individuals become more socially skilled (they are "team players" or "people persons") and are "very socially intelligent." All these skills have their beginning in the first years of school. We have discussed how self-esteem is based on what we *think* others think of us, making social cognition and self-esteem related concepts. Social competence or social cognitive skills become more refined as children become able to read social interactions and then change their behavior to accommodate these interactions.

During the first few years of elementary school, children tend to seek friends who they *think* are most like them, generally making friends with same-sex children of about the same age. School provides an environment in which children of approximately the same cognitive level are grouped together. These young children also choose friends based simply on proximity and familiarity (for example, children in the same neighborhood or school). As children become older, they tend to choose friends based on common experiences and values, and schools that serve children from a wide geographic area can offer their students friendship opportunities they may not have in their neighborhoods. Friendships offer companionship, a safe environment in which to try out new behaviors, and (perhaps most important) approval, loyalty, and social affirmation.

Forging Relationships With Siblings

More than 80% of American children live with siblings (Gormly, 1997). Indeed, when a survey asked married couples why they wanted more than one child, the most frequent reason given was sibling companionship (Berk, 1998). As families become smaller and have fewer children, relationships among siblings become more intense and more significant. At age five most children are still deeply attached to their families, especially their parents. However, at age 12 children have begun to assert their independence, forging relationships with peers and significant adults in their lives. This independence from the parents does not include diminished sibling relationships. Most children and adolescents continue to have close relationships with their brothers and sisters throughout their childhood and teenage years.

Sibling relationships are generally the longest social relationships, beginning in childhood and ending only at death. Older siblings serve as powerful role models and teachers, and whether younger or older, siblings can be a powerful source of comfort and support throughout the life span. Older siblings often act as protectors, even at a young age. For example, an older child may watch over his or her new baby sibling, alerting the mother when the baby begins to cry and demanding that she respond immediately.

Sibling relationships are not determined by choice (as are friends) nor are sibling considered to be a source of authority (as are parents.) However, sibling relationships can provide a safe environment in which to practice social skills that can then be transferred (or not be transferred) to social interactions.

Siblings (unless adopted) share both the home environment, the same parents, and some genetic inheritance. Of course, siblings differ from one another, especially in terms of gender, birth order, and the particular time in the family history when they were born. For example, older children may be born when the family does not have a great deal of financial security, but the "baby" of the same family may be born when the family is financially secure. In terms of gender, it is typically the adult females who maintain family ties, planning reunions, newsletters, and other family activities.

Developing Concrete Operational Thinking

Piaget stated that at age seven children begin to develop concrete operational thoughts in which they continue to rely on concrete, tangible, observable objects or events. Children find it difficult to understand abstract concepts that cannot be directly perceived with one of the five senses, such as the concept of freedom, until they enter the formal operations stage, which typically begins at ages 11 or 12. Nonetheless, young school-age children become much more flexible in their thinking. Children learn decentration, reversibility, conservation, and classification or categorization. When children use these skills, both singly and in combination, they become more cognitively sophisticated. Therefore, a combination of brain maturation with experience facilitates learning more abstract concepts.

Decentration is the ability to shift one's attention from one object to another. Reversibility is the ability to retrace or reverse actions mentally. Piaget considered conservation to be the single most important learning task of this stage. You will remember that conservation is the awareness that altering an object's or substance's appearance does not change its basic properties. The most famous example of decentration, conservation, and reversibility involves pouring the same amount of liquid into a tall thin glass and then into a short wide glass. Decentration is required because the child is required to change the focus of his or her attention from one container to the other. A preschooler thinks that there is more liquid in the tall thin glass while a school-age child understands that the shape of the glass does not change the amount of liquid (using his conservation skills), and he or she also can retrace the steps of pouring the same amount of liquid into the tall and into the short glass (using his or her reversibility skills.) Conservation is typically learned in a certain order. Children first learn number, then length, then mass, and finally liquid.

Children are taught categorization or classification skills on children's television programs such as *Sesame Street*. On *Sesame Street,* a box with four objects is shown and Big Bird then asks the audience "Which one does not belong?" The box may contain pictures of three different types of birds, an owl, an eagle, and a robin, while the fourth object is an apple. At first young children must focus and think carefully before concluding that the apple does not belong. This example illustrates the simplest type of classification. Because children in this stage have developed the skill of classification, they love to have collections, such as dolls, stamps, butterflies, or coins. As they mature, children are able to arrange objects in many different ways.

Seriation is the ability to arrange objects along a quantitative dimension, such as a hierarchy, or according to some other arrangement, such as objects from short to tall, coins according to their value, or sticks according to size.

Developing Other Types of Cognitive Skills

Memory, attention, and problem-solving are other important cognitive skills young school-age children develop. Younger children have problems paying attention, and are easily distracted by irrelevant stimuli. The first grade helps children to focus attention on the necessary information and to filter out (or ignore) the unimportant details. For example, when the teacher is teaching the letters of the alphabet, children can focus away from the caged hamster in the corner of the classroom and direct their attention to the teacher. One of the developmental tasks of school is to increase children's control of attention. As children mature cognitively, they can both determine what is important and selectively direct their attention. Older children also become proficient in focusing attention for longer periods of time and on more complicated, multistep processes.

By ages six or seven, children's capacity for memorization improves, and school (especially elementary school) requires a great deal of memorizing. Memorization requires the use of attention, then the use of encoding, and finally the ability to retrieve the information. Encoding means finding a set of cues or prompts to help recall the information; therefore, organizational skills are important. By organizing new information into categories, the individual is able to encode or retain more information. As children progress through elementary school, they begin to organize their knowledge into meaningful chunks or categories and also to use seriation techniques.

Children now begin to become aware of their personal memories and are able to think about them. Most theorists consider this metacognition to be the result of an interaction between two factors: increased cognitive skills and advanced language skills. For example, until the age of 12 children learn either their first language or a second language very quickly, because of the plasticity of their brains. These language skills enable the child to encode (or store) memories. Increased cognitive skills in other areas also help children to develop and retain memories. For example, completing the simple task of learning to tell time and read a calendar helps children to gain a more sophisticated sense of time. Childhood memories become an important source of self-identity, although children are not always able to discern if they actually remember an event or if they simply remember someone speaking about the memory.

Learning Team Play

In Breggin's definition of childhood, there were probably fewer team sports, so children played in more unorganized ways, or at least their team sports were spontaneous, not very well organized, and not supervised by adults. Today, team sports are viewed as an important advance in the quality of play (Berk, 1998). Understanding rules, organization, and the roles of the other members of the team requires children to take the perspective of others. Of course, physical athletic skills are also required, but the need for these skills is perhaps not as great as it would be in individual sports. Team sports may also permit children to have athletic experiences, including losing, without a great personal risk. School-age children also develop a sense of community though sports team. Relationships with adults who are neither parents nor school teachers also develop as a result of team sports. Sports coaches often become significant mentors and role models.

Not all children participate in team sports or in individual sports. In addition to the physical skills and strengths developed, team sports are thought to provide leadership training, assist children in dealing with competition, and encourage them to learn how to work with others.

Early Career Exploration

Children and teachers differ in their perceptions of the goals of education. Elementary school teachers consider the goal of education to be long-range preparation for career and work, while children have very short-range goals, often waiting only for the school day to end. Most preschoolers and children in the early grades of elementary school think of careers in emotional terms, planning on jobs that are rather unrealistic and that they consider very active and very glamorous. They children often want to be firefighters, astronauts, cowboys, or astronauts. Of course, some adults do these types of jobs, but most young children have little or no conception of the realities of these careers. If asked about the job duties of an astronaut or the training to become one, most young children could not provide an answer. Nonetheless, they are becoming aware that adults do not attend school forever and most work at jobs.

Young school children begin to develop an awareness of different work occupations and professions, and simultaneously begin to have realistic images of their potential contribution to the larger community (Grotevant & Cooper, 1988; Kerchoff, 1995). Often elementary schools will have the children's parents come to the classroom and speak about their jobs and careers.

THE GRAND THEORISTS' VIEW OF EARLY SCHOOL AGE

Freud used the term "latency" to describe the psychosexual stage of the early school years, by which he meant that the child's sexual and aggressive urges during these years become latent or are rechanneled into other more appropriate outlets (Cincotta, 2002). The sexual urges of the oral, anal, and phallic stages have been resolved, so the early school years are a time of relative sexual calm. Early school-age children have also developed greater cognitive abilities and social skills that help them to strengthen their superego, or conscience. This seems intuitively correct because early school-age children progress from egocentrism to companionship, learn to complete schoolwork rather than playing all day, and learn responsibility rather than irresponsibility. Children gain greater capacity to control or inhibit impulses.

Freud also thought that as children are given the opportunity to compare their parents with other adults, such as teachers and children's leaders, they gradually become aware that their parents are not as perfect and ideal as they had thought.

ERIKSON'S VIEW ON THE EARLY SCHOOL YEARS

I Am What I Learn

Erikson recognized play as the major task of childhood; both play and artwork are the major means of expression for small children. Erikson considered the school the child's workplace. When children enter school, they leave the safety and security of their homes and families and become responsible for learning and achievement. Therefore Erikson (1959) stated that the child's self-identity through these years was closely tied to what he or she learned. The crisis to be resolved was industry versus inferiority.

In school, children are subject to formal, written evaluations while at the same time, these school children are comparing themselves and their achievements to other children. According to Erikson, a sense of inferiority or inadequacy can result if the child believes he or she cannot perform tasks up to standard. Of course, all children feel inferior at times and that their physical, emotional, social, and cultural efforts are not adequate. However, Erikson was speaking of continuous, longstanding efforts. Continuous, cumulative failure leads to a lifelong sense of inferiority. Certainly children who have approval, support, and encouragement from adults are more likely to develop a sense of mastery and industry. Erikson would also state that the more the child succeeds, the more he or she enjoys work; in other words, work become intrinsically motivating. Almost everyone wants to be good at something and takes pride in accomplishments; therefore Erikson believed that the early school years formed the basis for learning to work and cooperate with others throughout the later stages of life.

PIAGET

Piaget stated that early school-age children progress from concrete thinking to operational thinking, are able to consider many different objects or ideas at one time (decentration), understand the principle of conservation, and also categorize and rank objects in order. Piaget also sought to determine how children develop moral judgment. In the early school years, children gain a measure of freedom and autonomy from their families and homes simply because they spend a great portion of the day away from home. At home, even though the child may not quite understand the rationale behind family rules, he or she is required to obey these rules. Entering school means exposure to more authority figures (who may not love each and every child as most parents do) and peers. However, teachers are the major source of approval and support for young students. Therefore, school-age children are required to learn and obey new rules and to cooperate and compete with peers, and they also begin to form their own moral codes. For the first time, children become aware that others have different rules than their parents do. The realization that not everyone has the same rules and opinions as their parents may be disconcerting for children. The concept that there is more than one set of rules appears radical to early school-age children. In addition, when they understand that children have reached this stage of moral maturity, teachers often allow the children to formulate classroom rules in a democratic fashion. These teachers know that children are more likely to obey self-imposed rules.

Kohlberg was very influenced by the moral development work of Piaget. However, Kohlberg's research methods were different; he presented dilemmas to different groups of children and focused not on their decisions but the reasoning behind their decisions. According to Kohlberg, early school-age children function in the instrumental morality stage because they are aware of exchange and reciprocity. Because early school-age children are in the company of the same 20 or 25 children each weekday, they develop an awareness of the needs and opinions of others. By the end of the early school years (approximately age 11 or 12), children have morally matured to the stage in which they want to please others and gain approval, thus becoming less self-involved.

Bandura (1977a, 1977b) recognized the importance of early school experiences in building and enhancing a child's sense of self-efficacy. School provides experiences in which children feel a sense of accomplishment because their beliefs in their academic abilities contribute to their efforts, which subsequently result in positive outcomes. School children are often able to use their cognitive-behavioral learning techniques to sustain motivation and to reach their goals, whether the goal is a simple matter of learning the multiplication tables or learning their weekly spelling list. Children quickly learn to anticipate the consequences of their behaviors; failing to study for the weekly spelling tests results in failure. In this way children learn the ability to anticipate the consequences of their future behaviors based upon their past behaviors. Preschool children tend to react to the immediate, present environment, but elementary school children begin to develop the capability to self-reflect and then self-regulate. Bandura stated this principle as: "Future events cannot serve as determinants of behavior, but their cognitive representations can have a strong causal impact on present actions" (Bandura, 1986, p. 19).

Maslow identified feelings of safety and belonging as major individual needs that are, in part, based upon the environment. Piaget and Vygotsky considered the environment to be essential to both cognitive and social growth, and Bronfenbrenner, who growing up on the grounds of the New York state mental hospital as a young boy, learned that when individuals are placed in high-expectation environments and provided a wide circle of social relationships, the effects of their disability are diminished. Therefore, Maslow, Piaget, Vygotsky, and Bronfenbrenner placed great importance on both the social and educational aspects of school (Berk, 1986). As we have seen in the Chapter 2, the school environment and education provided to children is dependent upon the resources of the government.

SENSORY LOSS AND SCHOOL

Before universal screening exams for vision and hearing, many children discovered their disabilities in school. Typically, in school children first begin to understand that other students do not have their same experiences. For example, in the areas of hearing impairment and vision loss, most young children assume that everyone sees or hears in the way in which they do. In the first years of school differences become apparent to children. Brenda Premo was born with a degenerating type of vision loss. In the following story, note that she did not discover until the second or third grade that not everyone saw as she did.

> The first time I remember understanding that my vision was different from other people was in the second or third grade when I realized that other students

could read the blackboard. Before then, I couldn't understand why the teacher would bother to write on the board. When it dawned on me that other kids could read the board and I couldn't, it was one of those "aha" moments in my life. It was a new discovery. (Mackelprang & Salsgiver, 1999, p. 140)

Eric Weihenmayer was a teenager when his vision began to deteriorate, and he realized it during a math class (although he chose to deny it). Weihenmayer wrote: "While I couldn't see well enough to see an equation on the blackboard, I also couldn't accept myself as being blind" (2001, p. 47).

David Wright is a poet and professor in England. When he was 7 years old, he contracted an illness that destroyed his auditory nerve. Neither his parents nor doctors told him that he was deaf, for these adults did not know that David had lost his hearing. Wright can recall the first time he became aware that he was deaf:

> "How was I to know? Nobody told me." He had to "deduce the fact of deafness through a process of reasoning." He heard guns, motorbikes, lorries [trucks], crowds and drills by touch: "There can't be much I miss of the normal orchestration of urban existence." He could appreciate music too, resting his finger on a piano or a loud speaker. And in a room with a wooden floor he would listen to drum and string instruments through his feet. (Wright, 1994, p. 22)

Mild sensory losses or other mild disabilities are not as easy to discover through universal screening. In contrast, severe or clear-cut symptoms are easily discerned, and these children can be sent for diagnostic testing. Episodic disabilities are also difficult to discern in screening tests.

Children in the early school years are dependent upon adults for the diagnosis of their disability, typically their parents. Tosca Appel (1988) has multiple sclerosis (MS). She described the "diagnostic odyssey" that began when she was 11 years old. Perhaps because she was so young when she was affected by a disease whose most common age of onset 20, not only was she not believed, but she was also given negative, demeaning labels.

> I was 11 years, 9 months old when my first symptom appeared. My first attack of MS took the form of a lack of motor coordination of my right hand. I was unable to hold utensils and my hand was turned inward; my parents in their concern rushed me to the emergency room of the hospital. The intern who saw me at the emergency room told my parents, without any exam, that I had a brain tumor.... I was admitted to the hospital, where I stayed for 12 days. Ten days later after the initial attack the symptoms abated.... The doctors put the blame of the attack on a bad case of nerves.... My second attack occurred when I was 16 years old and in the 11th grade.... One day...my history teacher asked me a question. I stood up to answer and my speech came out all garbled. I was unable to string the words into a sentence. I was even unable to utter words. All that came out were sounds. I clutched my throat to help the words come out easier.... I remembered the teacher's look. He looked at me in utter surprise and a little helplessly.... Again, my parents rushed me to the emergency room where another intern did his initial workup on me.... The intern, in his

wisdom, thought this behavior was an attention-getter. He thought I was faking the whole thing. (pp. 253–254)

LEARNING DISABILITIES

The study of learning disabilities (LDs) is so recent that it is possible to trace its specific beginnings. It began on April 6, 1963 in Chicago, when Sam Kirk coined the term "learning disabilities" at a meeting of an organization that evolved into the Learning Disability Association of America or LDAA. (Smith & Tyler, 2010). In the beginning, this organization was composed of concerned parents of children with learning problems. These parents understood that their children had academic and intellectual talents and potential, but they were perplexed at their underachievement in school. Since the 1960s LDs have been recognized worldwide, and children with LDs are the largest single disability group served by special education. Does this short history indicate that no one had LDs before 1963? No, it does mean that the same academic underachievement in intelligent children was observed, but teachers and parents typically ascribed the cause to laziness, lack of motivation, retardation, or oppositional behavior. Often children with LDs were the "class clowns," using humor to deflect the stress and embarrassment of underachievement.

The U.S. Department of Education (2006) defined LD as:

Specific learning disability means a disorder in one or more of the basic psychological processes involved in understanding or in using language, spoken or written, that may manifest itself in an imperfect ability to listen think, speak, read, write, spell, or to do mathematical calculation, including such conditions as perceptual disabilities, brain injury, minimal brain dysfunction, dyslexia, and developmental aphasia. The term does not include learning problems that are primarily the result of visual, hearing, or motor disabilities, mental retardation, emotional disturbance, or environmental, cultural, economic disadvantages. (p. 1264)

Reading this definition, we can see that before they can diagnose an LD medical professionals must screen for and eliminate certain other disabilities and conditions, such as mental retardation, sensory loss, intellectual disability, or impoverished environments (Dean, Burns, Grialou, & Varro, 2006).

Central to the definition of LD is the possession of normal intelligence levels or innate capabilities, talents, and potential that are higher than the individual's actual achievement. These students with LDs have difficulties in processing and remembering information. Perception, memory, and attention are processes central to learning that each build upon the other (Cook, 1979). If children cannot differentiate distinctive features (perception), organize and make sense of information (attention), or receive and encode information (remember), learning is impaired (Pickar & Tori, 1986). Children with LDs have difficulty in transferring and generalizing knowledge and skills. For example, these students are not able to use knowledge or study skills learned in an English class in their history class.

Distinguishing a learning disability from simple underachievement is difficult. Therefore, a great many plausible explanations for academic achievement must be considered before arriving at a diagnosis of LD. As the knowledge of LD has increased, LDs are now divided by type, such as *dyslexia,* an impairment in reading in which the individual does not understand what he or she reads; *dysgraphia,* an impairment in handwriting; *dysacusis,* impairment in understanding speech; *dyscalculia*, impairment in mathematical ability; *dyskinesia,* an impairment in physical coordination; *dysnomia,* difficult in finding the right word; and *dysrhythmia,* a poor sense of rhythm. All of these specific learning disabilities (SLDs) begin with the prefix *dys*, which means impaired or abnormal. By far the most common SLD is dyslexia, which is typically discovered when the child's reading skills are below grade level. If the LD is not diagnosed in the early grades, its deficits are compounded because these children fall further behind (Reid, 1988).

Students with LDs tend to have behavioral and social deficits, in addition to their academic underachievement (Baird, Scott, Dearing, & Hamill, 2009). Seventy-five percent of children with LD may seem immature, inattentive, impulsive, disorganized, shy, and withdrawn. They have difficulties making friends; their interactions with others appear odd and eccentric (Weiner, 2004). They often have difficulty reading body language, and their poor information processing skills impair verbal communication.

It is now known that individuals with below average intelligence, such as those with Down syndrome, can also have LDs. The same definition of a *discrepancy* between innate ability and achievement is used to diagnose a LD in someone with mental retardation. However, individuals with mental retardation are rarely diagnosed as having a LD because it is usually assumed that all their academic underachievement is due to the mental retardation, even when the retardation may be mild and the underachievement very apparent.

Estimates of the number of children with LDs served by special education differ from 40% to 50% (U.S. Department of Education, National Center for Education Statistics, 2003; U.S. Department of Education, 1993). Another way to conceptualize the growing numbers of children with LDs is to consider that between 1977 and 1985, there was a 16% increase in special education students while during the same time period, the number of children with LD rose 119% (Gartner & Lipsky, 1987).

LDs are a neurological disability resulting from a central nervous system dysfunction (Turnball, Turnball, & Wehmeyer, 2010). New neuroimaging technologies have shown that there is a strong genetic contribution to LDs, and often many members of the same family exhibit the symptoms of LDs. Shapiro, Church, and Lewis (2007) explained: "Genetic studies using linkage and association techniques have shown a relationship between specific reading disability and loci on chromosomes 1, 2, 3, 6, 15, 18" (p. 370). There is also a strong environmental influence to LDs, but this relationship is difficult to understand because parents with LDs often have children with LDs.

HYPERACTIVITY AND ATTENTION DEFICIT DISORDER

Attention deficit hyperactivity disorder (ADDHD), like LDs, is a neurodevelopmental disability first diagnosed in childhood. It was originally thought that ADDHD did not persist into adulthood, but it is now known that ADDHD is a lifelong disability. Much like that of LDs, the diagnosis of ADDHD first requires ruling out (or excluding) other disabilities; however, unlike LDs, there are no neuroimaging tests. (One exception to this is deficits in the frontal/prefrontal cortex that impair executive functioning.) Rather, a list of symptoms clustered into three groups is used.

These three groups are (1) inattention/distractability, (2) hyperactivity, and (3) poor impulse control.

According to Glanzman and Blum (2007), these symptoms differ according to developmental stages. In preschool ADDHD is difficult to diagnose because most preschoolers have a high activity level and a short attention span. Glanzman and Blum described the way in which the presence of ADDHD is suspected with early school-age children: "Upon entering elementary school, problems with listening and compliance, task completion, work accuracy, and socializing are common concerns of parents and teachers" (p. 347).

The environmental demands of elementary school, such as sitting in one's seat throughout most of the day, completing worksheets correctly, and dealing with the increased demands of reading and writing thus make the symptoms of ADDHD more apparent (Baird, Scott, Dearing, & Hamill, 2009). In adolescence, observable hyperactivity tends to decrease, because of better management of the disability due to self-insight, medication compliance, and the capability of teenagers to choose environments in which the symptoms of the ADDHD are not as apparent or act as strengths. For example, teenage boys with ADDHD often participate in sports in which their hyperactivity may be an asset.

Often ADDHD is divided into three subtypes: the predominantly inattentive type, the predominantly hyperactive–impulsive type, and the combination type. The *Diagnostic and Statistical Manual IV-TR* (*DSM-IV-TR,* 2000) requires a minimum of six or more symptoms, such as difficulty in sustaining attention in schoolwork, avoiding or disliking to engage in tasks that require sustained mental effort, or being easily distracted by external stimuli.

Children who are diagnosed with the second subtype (hyperactive–impulsive) display these types of behaviors: often fidgeting with their hands or feet, talking incessantly, having subjective feelings of restlessness, or leaving their seats at inappropriate times. Impulsivity is shown through blurting out answers before the question has been completed, interrupting others, or having difficulty taking turns. The third subtype is a combination of the first two subtypes.

Heredity places a role in the development of ADDHD, with siblings of children with ADDHD five to seven times more likely to be diagnosed with ADDHD than children with unaffected families. Each child of a parent with ADDHD has a 40% to 57% chance of being ADDHD. Siblings are five to seven times more likely to have ADDHD than children whose siblings do not have ADDHD. Prenatal exposures to smoking, lead, and alcohol are known to affect brain development and may result in ADDHD. Complications during the birth process and the neonatal period also increase the risk of ADDHD. For example, premature infants who experienced low cerebral blood flow during labor and delivery were found to have an increased risk of ADDHD.

ADDHD is difficult to diagnose because there are many associated impairments such as LDs, intellectual disabilities, Tourette's syndrome, personality disorders (including oppositional/defiant disorders), conduct disorders, and depression (Conrad, 2004; Living with Tourette Syndrome, n.d.). Turnball, Turnball, and Wehmeyer (2010) described the high incidence of other disabilities in children with ADDHD.

A high overlap exists between the categories of AD/HD and emotional or behavioral disorders. For example, approximately 40 percent to 90 percent of students identified as having AD/HD have been identified as having oppositional defiant disorder and/or conduct disorder; additionally, approximately one-third have been identified as having an anxiety disorder.... Sleep problems are also more frequent within this group of students, which can have ripple effects in terms of behavioral manifestation throughout the day due to fatigue. Frequently occurring behavioral, social, and emotional challenges consist of the following: conflicts with teachers, low self-esteem, higher rates of using alcohol and tobacco, increased risk-taking behaviors, and significantly higher likelihood of receiving behavior management programs, mental health services, social work services and family counseling. (pp. 216, 218)

Diagnosis begins with evaluating the symptoms to rule out different conditions that may cause the same symptoms and taking a developmental history, typically using parents and teachers as informants. At this point, checklists of symptoms are completed. Paper-and-pencil tests of intellectual ability and academic achievement are also used, and several rating scales have also been developed specifically for assessing ADDHD.

Children with ADDHD are *quantifiably* different from their peers. Most children experience fidgeting and fail to pay attention to the teacher *some of the time*; however, for children with ADDHA, these symptoms are present *all of the time* (Lambie and Milson, 2010). Most children with ADDHD are boys and there has been discussion of the concept of the "normal" and ADDHD. Some question if ADDHD is actually a disability or impairment for which treatment and interventions should be provided and point out that the symptoms of ADDHD were considered valuable male traits when the labor market was based on physical labor and compulsory education was not enforced. Those who state that ADDHD is a disability state that the genetic basis of ADDHD and the nascent brain imaging techniques provide evidence that ADDHD is a neurological, lifelong disability.

Both LDs and ADDHD have been very stigmatizing disabilities (Reid, 1988), partially because PWODs have assumed that individuals with these disabilities had caused their disability through some moral or character weakness or flaw. Families of individuals with LDs or ADDHD were often "stigmatized by association," often blamed for not disciplining their children or not being invested in their children's education. With the information from genetic testing and neuroimaging, it is now understood that these disabilities are caused by physical, neurological factors.

Another similarity between LDs and ADDHD is the number of professionals involved in diagnosis, treatment, and care. Often a physician makes the initial diagnosis. Ramsey and Algozzine (1996), speaking of only LDs, described the number of professionals involved and the ensuing confusion:

The study of LDs can be traced to several diverse disciplines including psychology, medicine (i.e., ophthalmology, otology, neurology, pharmacology), linguistics, and education.... Researchers and practitioners in all of these specialized fields have made important contributions to the study of LDs. Paradoxically, these diverse contributions have played a significant role in confusing the understanding of LDs. Because each profession tends to view phenomena from a distinctive perspective, it is difficult to get professional agreement about what a learning disability is and how it should be treated. To a pediatrician, a learning disability is a mild neurological disorder. To an otologist, a learning disability is an auditory discrimination problem. To a teacher, a learning disability is a reading or math deficiency. To an ophthalmologist, a learning disability is a visual tracking problem. To a pharmacologist, a learning disability is a metabolic disorder. Each of these professionals will evaluate, describe, and treat LDs in terms of his or her own professional point of view. (p. 117)

An article in the *Journal of Learning Disabilities* titled "Dyslexia and the Life Course" (McNulty, 2003) reported interviews of adults whose dyslexia had been diagnosed when they were children. McNulty explained that his interviewees were "the first generation of individuals formally diagnosed as children with neurologically based, developmental reading disorders that meet the criteria for dyslexia [who] are now adults who are able to reflect on their experiences over the course of life" (p. 363). Eight men and four women were participants. Three of the participants attended high schools especially designed for students with dyslexia, a resource available to them because 10 of the participants were from the Chicago area. Most of the first-person accounts use the word "trauma" to describe their childhood school experiences. Bob, a commodities trader, described the humiliation and degradation of Sunday School:

> That was another place where everybody had to read, you know, passages out of the Bible. This teacher I had. I had the same teacher from first grade all the way through eighth grade. This guy knew I couldn't read and every fricking week he'd make me try to read. I don't know if you've experienced this, but you don't know how humiliating this is, to try to read something you... you can't read. It's a paragraph this big and it takes you 10 minutes, with him "helping out" to read the thing. It would take 10 minutes to read this paragraph. And the kids were all chuckling and laughing. I would get hot. I remember my cheeks would be burning on fire. And I'd get to a point where I couldn't even concentrate. I couldn't read anymore. It was so humiliating, so degrading to me. (pp. 371–372)

McNulty found common themes in the lives of these adults with LDs. During elementary school their coping techniques included finding alternative ways to achieve, finding other areas for achievement where their LD was not a factor (such as sports), or becoming passive or often absent from school. For experiences in adolescence, "finding a niche in adolescence and young adult" resulted in either success (with improved adaptation and self-esteem) or the failure to find a niche that produced a continuing experience of failure, loneliness, and self-doubt. For the adulthood experiences, McNulty discovered three common themes. The adults engaged in "gifted overcompensation," "alternative compensation," or "compensation."

One of the values of longitudinal studies is the opportunity to ask informants what they would have done differently or what would have helped them. All of McNulty's respondents were advocates of early intervention programs (which would also require the early identification of children with LDs), and many of them could recall by name an understanding teacher or tutor who made a tremendous difference in their school experience. Many of the participants had children with LDs, and they felt that they were able to promote their children's self-esteem and to find services, accommodations, and interventions for their children. However, the need most often expressed by all the participants was protection from humiliation, criticism, harassment, and teasing. McNulty explained:

> Such misunderstandings publicly call into question fundamental qualities of the self, such as work ethic, emotional state, or intelligence, and lead to intense feelings of shame and humiliation on the part of the individual in question. Repeated episodes along these lines appear to result in heightened emotional insecurity and self-doubt. (p. 377)

Interestingly, as these individuals approach midlife, all of them said that developmental transitions were difficult and caused them self-doubt about their capability to succeed in the next stage.

Developmental Tasks of Children With Disabilities in the Early School Years

- Find role models
- Stigma management
  - Resist internalizing the limited view of disability from others
  - Manage the disability while at school
  - Manage assistive technology
- Respond to atypical childhood experiences

School-age children are adaptive and flexible, characteristics which help them in responding to a disability and fully engage in medical and physical rehabilitation. Leonard Kriegel contracted polio in one of the epidemics of the summer of 1944. Like many school-age children with polio, Kriegel spent 2 years at the New York State Reconstruction Home, dreaming of playing baseball in Bronx Park. At age 11 he gained a role model:

> When I think back to those two years in the ward, the boy who made his rehabilitation most memorable was Joey Tomashevski. Joey was the son of an upstate dairy farmer, a Polish immigrant who had come to America before the Depression and whose English was even poorer than the English of my own *shetl*-bred father. The virus had left both of Joey's arms so lifeless and atrophied that with pinky and thumb I could circle where his biceps should have been and still stick the forefinger of my other hand through. And yet Joey assumed that he would make do with whatever had been left him. He accepted without question the task of making his toes and feet into fingers and hands. With lifeless arms encased in a canvas slide that looked like the breadbasket a European peasant might carry to market, Joey would sit up in bed and demonstrate how he could maneuver fork and spoon with his toes.

I would never have dreamed of placing such confidence in my fingers, let alone my toes. . . . We boys with dead legs would gather round his bed in our wheelchairs and silently watch Joey display his dexterity with a vanity so open and naked that it seemed an invitation to being struck down again. (Kriegel, 1997, p. 40)

Eleven-year-old Leonard's role model did not have the same impairments, but it was Joey's attitude toward rehabilitation that changed Leonard's attitude toward both his disability and the long, painful rehabilitation process. Joey seemed to have enjoyed the attention. Living with other boys with polio for 2 years provided a long-term, up-close view of the way in which others of the same age responded to the disabilities caused by polio. (On the other hand, Leonard missed 2 years of family life and "regular" school.) Note, also that Leonard ascribes a quasi-religious cause to polio when he states that Joey's vanity and self-confidence could lead to "being struck down again."

Joey illustrated many of the concepts of Bandura's theory of self-efficacy, especially the idea of behavior change and maintenance of this behavior change. Feeling a sense of accomplishment is a strong motivator (or reinforcement) to perform the tasks required. Obviously, without the use of his arms Joey was required to make changes. Rather than trying to change the reality of his disability, Joey chose goals of which he was capable. Joey's sense of self-efficacy led to accomplishment, and his accomplishments led to a greater sense of self-efficacy. Bandura would probably state that Joey invested in a plan of action and persevered until this own personal standards of success had been met. Obviously he did not want to be spoon-fed by an attendant.

Leonard Kriegel identified with Joey, not only because both were paralyzed at approximately the same age but because both were the sons of immigrant parents. Joey served as a role model in making the transition from the acute phase of the disability to the chronic phase. Why did Leonard and the other boys watch Joey eat? Perhaps they watched because they had failed in their rehabilitation programs and because watching someone who was succeeding increased their own sense of self-efficacy. The principle of "If he can do it, so can I" often motivates individuals to put forth greater effort and tenacity in their own goals. These boys, whose arms were not "dead," watched Joey and decided that they, too, were capable of rehabilitation. Bandura termed this "vicarious reinforcement." Joey provided a role model of both physical rehabilitation (eating with his feet) and emotional rehabilitation, eating with "confidence" and "vanity."

Perhaps Kriegel or some of the other children had "maxed out"; they had attained some level of physical improvement, but then their rate of improvement slowed and they did not make efforts to reach higher levels of rehabilitation. Joey's vicarious modeling was a stronger motivator than all the verbal persuasion of parents, physicians, and physical therapists.

STIGMA MANAGEMENT

As an adult Henry Viscardi described his first day of school. Viscardi's legs were congenitally deformed.

My sister Terry took me to school the first day. Clutching her hand, I hoisted myself up the steps to the schoolyard. It was crowded with children.... I heard laughter, "Hey Louis, look at the ape man." Three big boys came toward me.... The crowd of jeering boys had grown. One of them.... came over and shoved me. I shoved back against his knee. "Oh, you wanta fight, kid?"... "I want to go home." I hung on to Terry's arm, tears rolling down my cheeks. "Sissy. Sissy." (Holzbauer & Berven, 1996, p. 479)

We have read that all of the adult participants with LDs in McNulty's study stated that their schools lacked teacher protection from humiliation, teasing, and harassment was lacking and each advocated for such protection. Harassment and bullying are perhaps not as commonplace as they once were. In Vicardi's story there was an imbalance of power when three older boys taunted him and his sister; however, 5- or 6-year-old Henry tried to resist the bullying. If there were other children present, they did not try to help or stop the harassment. When harassment and bullying occur, often the targeted students "skip[ped] classes and avoided school to avoid the oppressive culture created by these boys" (Crosnoe, 2000, p. 380).

This is a disheartening story, but it is also noteworthy that after the passage of the Americans with Disabilities Act (ADA), all public schools are now required to have elevators so that children do not have "to hoist themselves up steps."

The cognitive growth of children, occurring at approximately the time of entrance into first grade, also allows CWDs to manage their disability, respond to social situations concerning their disability, and reflect upon and analyze their disability experience. For children with cognitive disabilities, such as intellectual disabilities, there may not be a cognitive growth spurt at the time of first grade. However, for other types of disabilities, this cognitive growth spurt allows children to regulate their emotions, alter their emotional and behavioral strategies, and employ other methods of self-regulation. Bandura believed in the power of self-defined goals and personal agency and for CWDs, and individuals who believe that they can obtain goals perform better and have higher self-esteem.

In much the same way that CWODs view their bicycles as independence, CWDs see their wheelchairs as freedom. Many wheelchairs today are electrically powered chairs that often have many technological applications in addition to mobility. These power chairs are expensive and heavy, and they can be hazardous to the student and to others. Training is required for the student using the chair, the teachers, and the other students. Although these power chairs provide freedom, their heavy weight also presents transportation problems, and necessitates the use of customized vans and buses. Power wheelchairs may cost as much as a car, and if the chair is disabled (a little disability joke), repairs can required a lengthy period of time during which the child must remain at home in bed (Pullin, 2009; Scherer, 1993).

Because many PWDs of all ages consider their assistive technology (AT) to be an extension of their body, they may not like others touching their wheelchairs or attempting to manipulate them. Because much of PWDs' functioning is dependent upon their technology, it is important to remember that these devices are personal tools and a medical necessity. Moreover, PWDs value their AT in a way that PWODs cannot understand. Remember how Leonard Kriegel stated that he loved his first wheelchair with a love that embarrasses him now, or Weisskopf named his prosthetic arm "Pretty Boy," or Mark O'Brien referred to his iron lung as his "second skin."

Early age school children are therefore required to explain these issues to others, ensure that others are not harmed by their technology, and monitor for battery outages or other simple repair and maintenance problems. School teachers may be required to position the child in the chair throughout the day without harming the child. Nonetheless, it is the CWD who understands what he or she needs. The following story is told by Brenda Premo, who eventually became director of the California Department of Rehabilitation. As a child she had progressive vision loss that resulted in legal blindness. She tells of an early school experience.

> One time my mother got called into the principal's office because I wouldn't use big print books. Instead of just bringing me in and chatting with me, the principal brought my mother in. In the meeting, my mother turned to me and said, "Sweetheart, why don't you want to use big-print books?" I said, "Mom, it's like this: I've got four academic classes and all the teachers assign several chapters to read. In large print books, chapters are in volumes. So if I have four academic classes and I have to have three volumes each, I need a wagon to take my books home." I told her I needed a magnifier, a $1.50 magnifier, but nobody asked me. (Mackelprang & Salsgiver, 1999, p. 41)

Brenda was an intelligent student, and (to the its credit) the school did not lower its standards because she was legally blind. Nonetheless, both Brenda and her mother were surprised at the principal's need to ask Brenda's mother about AT. This story also illustrates that AT is often both simple and inexpensive.

Young school-age children with disabilities often are not aware, nor do they understand, the emotionally fraught and distressing response of others to their disability or to their AT. One young child said, "Putting on my prosthesis is no more upsetting to me than you putting on your shoes and socks is to you" (Eisenberg, Sutkin, & Jansen, 1984). Until they reach school, they have known they have a disability but are unaware that their disability often elicits painful feelings in others (Wolfensberger, 1972). Children who have acquired their disability at birth or at a very early age have not acquired all the prejudices and limited views of society. Therefore, it may be difficult for CWDs to understand these types of reactions. In contrast, an adult with a disability understands why strangers tell them, "God bless you," "I don't know how you do it," or "I could never handle a disability."

ATYPICAL CHILDHOOD EXPERIENCES

Children with disabilities are socialized into the macrosystem of medicine in contrast to most children who see a doctor occasionally and rarely are hospitalized (Weinberg, 1982). CWDs experience repeated hospitalizations, frequent surgeries, fitting of prostheses and other AT, and occasionally travel to a large teaching hospital for treatments. Thus the young child is socialized into the role of the patient. Although all of these are atypical childhood experiences, they do not seem unusual to the CWD. However, when adults with disabilities consider their childhoods, they realize that their lives were very different from those of other children. One PWD related a childhood filled "of having things constantly *done to them*, often by a series of strangers but with the agreement of a trusted figure such as a parent, can be disruptive to their 'continuity of being,' and therefore traumatic" (emphasis original).

> Other children play, but you do therapy. Other children develop, but you are "trained." Almost every activity of daily living can take on the dimension of trying to make you *less like yourself* [emphasis mine] and more like the able-bodied. The world is often quite happy to reinforce this. (Mason, 1992; cf Marks 1999, p. 69)

Most CWDs do not form long-term relationships with their hospital caregivers, mostly because they have a large number of caregivers who change with each work shift. The risks for children who are exposed to a great many adults include the lack of peer relationships. Zach's mother described her experience of meeting with many medical professionals and the difficulties this presented:

> It took me a while to catch on to the game at the teaching hospital. Different doctors at different times would come in and start asking me questions about my family history, the pregnancy, was Zach ever dropped on his head, etc. I kept thinking that each was *the* doctor, but no, then he or she would gather up the notes, and minutes later a new person would appear. "Look," I said impatiently after the third one. "Why do I have to keep repeating this same story: why don't you get together with this?" What I didn't understand that all these people were medical students, interns, residents; Zach was part of their curriculum. So, of course, they didn't answer any of my questions. They were interested in asking their own. (Berry & Hardman, 1998, p. 110)

A woman with cerebral palsy remembered her childhood:

> My early childhood was unique, different from that of other children. From my earliest memories, I can recall being aware that there was something different about me that caused me to be the focal point of much attention and solicitude. I was an only child and had no brothers or sisters to relate to, or to use as standards by which I could measure my normality or lack of it. Every waking moment of my parents' lives was devoted to me and to my care. I naturally came to regard myself as the center of the universe because everything revolved around me. (Pelletier, 1988, p. 54)

CWDs who live at home and attend community schools have daily reminders that they are different from other children. Many elementary schools have simulation exercises in which CWODs "try on" a disability for a short time, such as blindfolding their eyes or using a wheelchair (Gaier, Linkowski, & Jacques, 1968). How do these simulation exercises affect the self-esteem of the few students who have real disabilities? These exercises can create social distance between CWODs and a CWD by creating pity for the CWD. One mother wrote about simulation exercises. Although her daughter, Tara, does not have a disability, the mother is a polio survivor and the father is blind.

> My daughter Tara had come home from school in tears. It was Disability Simulation Day at Greenwood…School. Blindfolded students were being led around by sighted students, others were bumping into walls. The students were terrified of their newly created disabilities. Some had told Tara they thought persons with disabilities had horrible lives; a few thought they would be better off dead.
>
> I contacted the school's psychology teacher once and tried to get Disability Simulation Day stopped. It was a lost cause. She (the teacher) liked having Disability Simulation Day featured in the local newspaper, and saw no need for me or my husband—or anyone from our local independent living center—to come to her classroom to talk with students.
>
> I am baffled as to why nondisabled people see a need to simulate a disability. Across our nation in February, we celebrate Black History Month. Is it necessary for people with white skin to paint their faces black to better understand this minority? (Brew-Parrish, 2004, p. 1)

Simulation exercises are unpleasant for most PWDs of any age and also give a false impression of the experience of disability (Kiger, 1992). For example, one classmate told Tara that she thought blind people would "be better off dead." We do not know if this classmate knew that Tara's father was blind. Children of early school age who do have disabilities are made to feel different and inferior on the annual school Disability Simulation Day. An alternative is suggested by Tara's mother: ask adult PWDs to come speak to students about their disabilities.

For children with disabilities that have an episodic course or life-threatening relapses, it is understood that unexpected emergencies result in aggressive emergency treatment (Featherstone, 1980). When these emergency treatments or other types of acute care become necessary, the CWD understands that hospitalization and treatment are more important than school, even if it means missing the spelling bee, the Halloween carnival, or an important test.

Reintegration into the classroom after a long hospitalization may be difficult for both the CWD and the other students (Hardman, Drew, Egan, & Wolf, 1993). Friends and peers may avoid the CWD, not knowing exactly what to say or do. Teachers and other adults can model acceptance and communicate a sense of normality to both the CWD and the other students (Taylor & Achenbach, 1975). Prolonged absences from school affect peer relationships and interrupt education, both which may result in school failure and/or peer rejection. Two teachers, Ellen and Rhonda, related the way they learned to feel comfortable around a "medically fragile" student. Ellen is a teacher in a residential facility for CWDs, and Rhonda is a teacher in community school.

Ellen talked about a student with severe spasticity who was automatically placed in her class because he had a gastrostomy and tracheostomy and required frequent suctioning. She advocated for this student to be moved from her class to a classroom in the school facility because he did not have frequent illnesses and had no problem tolerating a 6-hour day. Rhonda explained,

> "Ten years ago, I would have described medically fragile or complicated students differently." "Experience had altered her view about what constitutes medically fragile." [She said] "Many students who seem very fragile keep bouncing back even after surgery and repeated illness, and many have less problems that you would expect."... She believes that "the kids have taught me to be comfortable with them,... I don't like to see people back off from these kids because they are 'medically fragile.' They need to be handled and played with." (Brown & Lehr, 1989)

Children with chronic illnesses may experience limited strength, vitality, or alertness from their conditions or the medications used to treat it. The power differential between the adult teacher and the early school-age child may make it difficult for the CWD to ask for help.

On the other hand, CWDs should be held to the same standards (within their capabilities) as the other children. In the long run such practices as relaxing discipline or lowering academic standards for CWDs who are capable of meeting these standards are harmful to CWDs. Lowering standards communicates to the CWD that he or she is not considered capable and does not allow the CWD to receive honest, constructive feedback because any attempt at a task is accepted as satisfactory. One university counselor (Harris, 1992) found that high school transcripts for PWDs were "splattered with the milk of human kindness." Harris found that PWDs who were experiencing academic difficulties in college had excellent high school transcripts, thus making their early college failures perplexing. He finally decided that these PWDs had been given "mercy graduations" and "pity grades," motivated by misguided acts of kindness on the part of teachers. However, in the long run the transcripts and the PWDs' lack of academic preparation disadvantaged them. Honest feedback, in the long run, is more helpful to the individual.

Eric Weihenmayer, the blind man who climbed Mt. Everest, wrote about lowered expectations. When he appeared on a popular daytime talk show, he did not feel proud but "embarrassed and a little sick."

> Throughout the rest of the segment, I squirmed in my seat. I should have been proud to be picked out as being "amazing and inspirational," but strangely, I felt more embarrassed and even a little sick. I was no more accomplished [than the other blind guests]. I was simply a blind person who planned to climb a mountain and nothing more. But people sensationalize the lives of blind people when, often, all they did was to exhibit a semblance of normalcy. I have been receiving these accolades my whole life: give someone directions to my house—incredible. Make eye contact in a conversation—amazing. Each of us on the panel was being honored for our heroic tales, but the recognition spoke more loudly of low expectations than of accomplishment. (Weihenmayer, 2001, p. 167)

SIBLINGS OF CWDs

The sibling bond is one of the most important relationships in life (Santrock, 2009). Brothers and sisters of CWDs understand that their families are different from most others, and we have learned that any change in self-identity, whether individual self-identity or family self-identity, is stressful (Lefley, 1991; Singer & Irwin, 1989; Singer, Powers, & Olson, 1996). However, most research has shown that these relationships are positive and induce growth.

When an infant is born with a disability or when a child in the family acquires a disability, it is the parents who will interpret the disability to their children (Graliker, Fishler, & Koch, 1962; Green, 2003; Huberty, 1980). Siblings may blame themselves if their brother or sister has a disability, thinking that they are responsible for everything that happens to their family. Using language that is appropriate to the siblings' age and developmental stage to discuss, explain, and communicate fully is the first step (Chilman, Nunnally, & Cox, 1988). At first it may be appropriate to tell small children that "Johnnie has a problem we can't fix, but we still love him." It is also necessary to tell small children that the disability is not "catching." Second, the siblings should be allowed to ask questions and should also feel safe enough to express negative emotions about the disability and their sibling with the disability, such as anger, sadness, and anxiety (L'Abate, 1994). Parents can acknowledge to their children that they have negative feelings at times. Children can also be guided so they know what to say to those who ask about their sibling's disability and understand that they are not obligated to answer every question.

Developing intentional strategies is much more effective than simply responding to events as they occur, so family meetings or family councils in which the disability is openly discussed can be useful. There are three types of intentionality: (1) behavioral, (2) cognitive, and (3) affective. Behavioral intentionality might be framed as, "This is what we're going to do," meaning that the family has concrete and realistic plans for the CWD. Some families have "relapse drills" that are much like fire drills, in which the response to a relapse is planned and each family member's role assignment is reviewed and rehearsed. Cognitive intentionality is "This is what we're going to think," viewing the disability as a challenge and opportunity instead of a crisis, loss, or threat. Affective intentionality is "This is what we're going to feel," helping family members respond to the disability with hope and optimism. These three types of intentionality follow Bandura's self-efficacy principle.

At times there are failures in intentionality strategies because it is not possible to continuously maintain these behaviors and feelings. These lapses are acknowledged and dealt with then family revises strategies or devises more appropriate attitudes and behaviors (Ryan, et al., 2010). The way in which these lapses are resolved teaches children that it is possible to reorganize and reestablish family emotional equilibrium (D. L. Johnson, 1993). The following is advice for parents:

> Even more important, however, is your ability to convey to your other children that their feelings are *normal*—whether these feelings consist of irrational self-blame or resentment because of the extra attention you may need to give to your child with a disability. "It's okay to feel angry. Mommy and Daddy sometimes feel like that ourselves," is often the best response, even as you remind

your other children that it is *not* okay to act out these feelings of resentment in ways that can hurt other people. Saying this may be difficult for you, but it is preferable to responses such as "How can you say that about your brother? Don't you know he has a problem?" The ability to listen sympathetically to your other children in this fashion is directly linked to how well you have been able to deal with such feelings yourself. (Coplan & Trachtenberg, 2001, p. 7)

Siblings should be facilitated in their transition through the developmental stages, and individuation should be encouraged to allow each child in the family to develop strengths, skills, and talents (Cate & Loots, 2000). Encouraging peer relationships for all of the children is another step to encouraging self-identity. This means that all the family resources are not devoted to the needs of the CWD. The emotional and psychological needs of all the children in the family are met.

At times behavioral intentionality includes providing support, information, and resources to other families who have a child with the same type of disability (Kosciulek, 1998). A book entitled "The Sibling Slam Book" (Meyer, 2005) asked siblings of brothers and sisters with disabilities a set of questions. These questions included "What do you want people to know about your sib?" "Got any good stories about your sib?" "Is your outlook on life any different from your friends' outlook on life? How?," "When you were younger, did you ever wish you had a disability so your parents would pay more attention to you?" "Do you think being a sib has affected your life?" "Do your friends get along with your sib? Do you tend to pick friends who are likely to get along with your sib?" "Does you sib ever frustrate you? How?" and "What are some advantages—good parts—of having a sibling with a disability?" Overwhelmingly, most of these responses were positive, even to the question about being frustrated. Most siblings reported that they considered themselves better people who were more accepting of others and differences, and they felt very protective toward their sibling with a disability. To the question "What are the advantages of having a sibling with a disability? Cassandra from Iowa responded:

I get to meet so many great people, not only people with disabilities, but also people who work with them. My sib's teachers and aides are some of the nicest people I've ever met. They have given us ideas that have helped Keaton and our whole family. They are more than just teacher, though—I can honestly say that they are great friends. (Meyer, 2005)

On the first page of a book on the history of the disability rights movement, Doris Zames Fleischer wrote:

The most important thing that ever happened to me occurred two years before I was born. My sister (and now my coauthor) contracted polio....I imagined myself the hero for rather absurdly holding up my five-year-old fingers to traffic in the middle of the rather empty streets near our house as she slowly crossed using her crutches and braces. (Fleischer & Zames, 2001, personal notes)

An example of a close and supportive siblings relationship is seen with the Zames sisters. Freida's paralysis from polio created a lifelong bond between the two sisters. Frieda Zames spent 5 years in a polio hospital, and her younger sister Doris did not actually meet her sister until she was 5 years old, although her parents spoke about Frieda and she saw Frieda wave from the hospital window. Doris became a member of the Humanities and Social Sciences Department at New Jersey Institute of Technology, and Freida was Associate Professor of mathematics at the same institute. Both of the sisters lived in New York City. They co-authored a book, *The Disability Rights Movement: From Charity to Confrontation* (2001). Freida Zames passed away in 2005.

SPECIAL EDUCATION

In previous chapters we have learned that the resources available in the macrosystem directly affect the lives of individuals. These resources are not always distributed equitably; certain groups receive resources easily as a basic right while other groups must fight for these same services. This is not a part of our society of which we are proud, but it is necessary to understand history in order to move forward. Special education for all American children who need it is based on the premise that justice demands not that we give everyone the same thing but give everyone what he or she needs (IDEA of 1990). In the video *How Difficult Can This Be?* the narrator (who is an expert in LDs) describes consultations with teachers on simple accommodations they can make for their students with LDs. He states that the teacher invariably replies, "I can't do that if I don't do it for all of the students." He responds, "If I were giving a lecture to a large group of people and one person has a heart attack and stops breathing, would the emergency medical technicians (EMTs) have to give CPR to all the people in audience, simply because the EMTs gave CPR to the one man who had collapsed? The answer is of course not, because the other audience members would not need or want CPR. The ADA is based on this definition of justice: giving Americans what they need in order to succeed."

When PWDs ask for accommodations, it is often perceived as a request for preferential treatment. The following example shows the negative results of refusing a rather simple testing accommodation. Brenda Premo is legally blind and has albinism.

> I remember this bullheaded psychologist who gave me a small-print IQ test and told my mother that I was retarded. What he had really tested was my ability to read small print. Even my mother knew that his diagnosis was not correct. After all, why would someone give me a small-print test when they knew I couldn't read small print very well? Because I was very determined to go regular school, my mother told the resistant school officials, "You'll have to fight with her. She wants to go here." So this bullheaded psychologist then said to my mother, "Well, we'll let her go there so she can learn about failure." So my mother says, "Yeah, OK." She only had an eighth grade education, but she understood intuitively that that I was brighter than they gave me credit for. (Mackelprang & Salsgiver, 1999, p. 141)

Ms. Premo was an academically gifted young girl and did very well in "regular school."

There were thousands of school-age polio survivors during the 1893 to 1955 polio epidemics (Oshinsky, 2005). Many of these children were not allowed to return to school, often simply because there were no elevators. Marc Wilson undertook an analysis of hundreds of first-person accounts of polio survivors in Scandinavia, Canada, the U.K., Western Europe, and the United States (Public Broadcasting System, 1999). Wilson summarized:

> There were many teachers who did not know how to work with students with disabilities, had no desire to learn, and openly displayed their displeasure. For example, Jennifer Williams's second-grade teacher "just couldn't relate to a child with a handicap." This teacher was always hard on the young girl and refused to believe she was any different. As Williams remembers, "[S]he would always say things like, 'They're doing it, so you have to do it too. You know we can't play favorites.'" And Wanda Peterson's sixth grade teacher would talk about her in front of the class. The teacher would declare, without naming Peterson, "Some people in this room think they are so great because they aren't supposed to run in P.E." The teacher also made her move her desk away from everyone's else's.... The attitudes and actions of teacher could make all the differences in the class. Those who were supportive helped polio survivors to fit in as best they could and to excel where they were able. The worst helped make school a living hell. (Wilson, 1990, pp. 187–188)

Recently 4.5 million students in the United States received special education services. Special education costs almost twice as much as general education, and more children are being diagnosed with disabilities. Two special education professors, speaking only of LDs, explained:

> The more students receiving services, the higher the overall costs. Although variation exists across the nation and even district by district, every student with a disability costs more to educate than their classmates without disabilities (Chambers, Shkolknik, & Perez, 2003). On average, school districts spend 1.6 times more to educate a student with learning disabilities than they spend on the education of a general education student. Because the federal government does not fully cover these costs, the public and the media make the case that students with disabilities are being educated at the expense of their classmates without disabilities. (Smith & Tyler, 2010, p. 167)

The Advocacy Institute (2002) stated that in a single year (2000), more than $77 billion was spent on students with disabilities, an average of more than $12,000 for each CWD. In comparison, the average cost for a year of education for a CWOD is $6,556. Disability activists state that these increased educational expenses will be recovered when PWDs can go to work, pay taxes, and reduce the numbers of Americans on public assistance and disability insurance. In addition, these activists believe that standards of education are enhanced for all students when CWDs are in the classroom.

Federally mandated public special education in the United States has a very short history, beginning in 1975 with the passage of two federal laws, the Education for all Handicapped Children Act and the Developmental Disabilities Act. Before 1975 some court cases had attempted to require states to provide education for CWDs by invoking the Fourteenth Amendment, which guarantees every individual to full protection under the law (Stone, 1984; Stubbins,1988). In the 1960s federal law and intervention forced the states to allow African American children to attend school with other

American children. Disability advocacy groups began to lobby for the same rights for their children, with the goal of creating federal legislation that would force the states to allow CWDs to attend community schools. Racial minority advocacy groups knew that separate was not equal and would not tolerate the education of minority children in different schools from white children. Disability rights advocacy groups, such as the Association for Retarded Citizens and United Cerebral Palsy, learned a great deal from the civil rights struggles of the 1960s and also advocated that CWDs be educated in their neighborhood schools. Indeed, the landmark 1954 Supreme Court decision in the case of *Brown vs. Board of Education,* which upheld minority children's rights to educational equality, was often invoked in court cases seeking educational equality for CWDs. Thirty years ago, two disability rights scholars summarized this history:

> While the nation was seeking to improve the quality of the minority child's schooling, the handicapped child's educational needs remained forgotten, even though these needs were easily as great as those of the most cruelly disadvantaged able-bodied children. At that time perhaps one handicapped child in eight— over one million handicapped—received no education whatsoever, while more than half of all handicapped children did not receive the special instructional services they needed. (Gliedman & Roth, 1980, p. 173)

Passing federal laws and winning court cases was only the beginning. The next struggle was the implementation and enforcement of these laws. Federal monitoring helped ensure that CWDs gained access to American public education. Nonetheless, throughout the nation groups of parents continued to provide schooling for their CWDs in church and synagogue basements, with volunteer parents as teachers (National Public Radio, 1988b). Elizabeth Boggs, a mother of a child with an intellectual disability, has a PhD in theoretical chemistry and mathematics and was established in a scientific career. She "changed careers when she and her group organized classes for her son and other developmentally delayed children, in order to enable them to register at public schools" (Fleischer & Zames, 2001, p. 89). Dr. Boggs was described as "perhaps the nation's greatest authority on programs that affect the mentally retarded,... a woman of encyclopedic knowledge and enormous energy" (Berkowitz, 1987, p. 13).

In 2004 the Individuals with Disabilities Education Improvement Act was passed, recognizing a large number and types of disability and mandating that every CWD should be accommodated within the public school system, in the "least restrictive environment" (LRE). The principle of LRE requires that students with disabilities are educated, as much as possible, with their peers who do not have disabilities (Clair, Church, & Batshaw, 2007). Many accommodations can be provided that allow CWDs to attend school in the same classroom as their age mates without disabilities. Aides for children with medical needs, such as tracheosomies or gastrointestinal tubes, sometimes attend school with these children. Sign language interpreters, books in Braille, computers, communication boards, and other accommodations can assist in providing high quality education for both CWDs and CWODs (see Table 12.1).

The following example, told by a special education teacher in the 1970s (before the passage of the ADA), provides an example of school segregation. As you read this story, note that the students did not have intellectual disabilities but motor impairments.

TABLE 12.1
Number of Children and Students Served Under IDEA, Part B, by Age Group and State, Fall 2009

State	3–5	6–11	12–17	6–17	14–21	18–21	3–21
Alabama	7,258	33,714	36,693	70,407	30,090	5,332	82,997
Alaska	1,987	8,181	6,725	14,906	5,244	1,000	17,893
Arizona	14,340	54,157	51,817	105,974	38,640	5,552	125,866
Arkansas	12,865	24,643	24,695	49,338	19,413	2,836	65,039
California	71,783	271,527	291,060	562,587	231,376	39,058	673,428
Colorado	11,327	34,624	33,145	67,769	25,835	4,669	83,765
Connecticut	8,019	26,502	30,577	57,079	23,750	3,640	68,738
Delaware	2,572	7,604	8,041	15,645	6,371	1,131	19,348
District of Columbia	683	3,773	5,754	9,527	5,089	1,161	11,371
Florida	34,944	153,973	164,296	318,269	132,701	23,363	376,576
Georgia	16,491	74,727	77,239	151,966	59,017	8,613	177,070
Hawaii	2,455	7,767	9,092	16,859	6,754	643	19,957
Idaho	3,932	12,162	10,449	22,611	7,942	1,244	27,787
Illinois	36,962	125,530	133,605	259,135	106,768	17,486	313,583
Indiana	18,602	72,158	71,110	143,268	57,494	10,225	172,095
Iowa	6,267	26,180	30,664	56,844	23,977	3,525	66,636
Kansas	10,354	27,454	25,434	52,888	19,725	2,977	66,219
Kentucky	18,865	47,953	35,144	83,097	26,733	4,083	106,045
Louisiana	9,952	37,809	32,890	70,699	25,964	4,468	85,119
Maine	3,843	13,262	14,114	27,376	10,894	1,547	32,766
Maryland	12,532	40,965	43,851	84,816	34,587	5,670	103,018
Massachusetts	16,271	66,684	75,970	142,654	58,160	8,372	167,297
Michigan	24,245	92,851	97,647	190,498	77,868	13,230	227,973
Minnesota	14,706	48,881	49,980	98,861	40,824	7,792	121,359
Mississippi	9,649	27,583	23,232	50,815	19,672	3,524	63,988
Missouri	15,720	53,776	52,934	106,710	42,278	7,456	129,886
Montana	1,722	7,375	7,436	14,811	5,592	680	17,213
Nebraska	3,712	20,371	17,463	37,834	13,198	1,924	43,470
Nevada	6,872	19,188	20,180	39,368	15,087	1,875	48,115
New Hampshire	3,090	10,852	14,662	25,514	11,405	1,606	30,210
New Jersey	16,451	98,316	104,386	202,702	78,961	9,913	229,066
New Mexico	6,585	18,950	17,707	36,657	14,105	2,540	45,782
New York	64,903	177,055	196,342	373,397	152,801	23,170	461,470
North Carolina	18,144	80,657	76,166	156,823	58,901	9,926	184,893
North Dakota	1,660	5,477	5,426	10,903	4,238	699	13,262
Ohio	23,336	99,555	121,490	221,045	100,776	19,015	263,396
Oklahoma	7,808	41,595	41,421	83,016	31,448	4,362	95,186
Oregon	8,946	34,377	32,578	66,955	24,718	4,161	80,062
Pennsylvania	30,186	111,295	135,287	246,582	109,678	17,827	294,595
Puerto Rico	14,681	51,877	48,843	100,720	35,245	5,758	121,159
Rhode Island	2,903	9,794	12,035	21,829	9,756	1,600	26,332
South Carolina	10,878	43,369	40,496	83,865	33,316	6,296	101,039
South Dakota	2,688	8,406	5,968	14,374	4,628	845	17,907
Tennessee	12,858	51,323	48,292	99,615	38,635	6,543	119,016
Texas	40,706	168,716	208,976	377,692	165,801	25,800	444,198
Utah	8,679	31,308	24,988	56,296	18,338	2,806	67,781
Vermont	1,750	5,276	6,313	11,589	4,986	824	14,163
Virginia	17,057	66,117	71,458	137,575	58,677	10,139	164,771
Washington	13,858	56,006	49,754	105,760	38,213	6,406	126,024
West Virginia	5,754	20,765	17,215	37,980	14,118	2,435	46,169
Wisconsin	15,729	50,355	53,141	103,496	42,530	6,278	125,503
Wyoming	3,276	6,125	5,044	11,169	3,801	653	15,098
BIE schools	394	3,188	2,829	6,017	2,094	336	6,747
50 States, D.C., and P.R. (including BIE schools)	731,250	2,692,128	2,822,054	5,514,182	2,228,212	363,014	6,608,446
American Samoa	177	333	566	899	417	30	1,106

(continued)

TABLE 12.1 *(continued)*

State	3–5	6–11	12–17	6–17	14–21	18–21	3–21
Guam	182	743	1,033	1,776	865	130	2,088
Northern Marianas	78	322	405	727	325	65	870
Virgin Islands	145	443	747	1,190	685	144	1,479
United States and outlying areas	731,832	2,693,969	2,824,805	5,518,774	2,230,504	363,383	6,613,989

Note: Please see the Part B Child Count Data Notes on www.IDEAdata.org for information that the state submitted to clarify its data submission.
Source: U.S. Department of Education, Office of Special Education Programs, Data Analysis System (DANS), OMB #1820–0043: "Children With Disabilities Receiving Special Education Under Part B of the Individuals With Disabilities Education Act," 2009. Data updated as of July 15, 2010.

Also, consider the importance of the school years in the formation of a social identity and the type of message communicated to these CWDs when children with a wide range of disabilities were placed in a classroom separate from "normal" children. Some messages are "You are different and you should stay away from the others who are normal," and "The school is going to 'lump' you kids with disabilities together; therefore, your primary self-identity should be as a PWD."

> The approximately twenty children in my class, ranging in age from nine to sixteen, had a wide variety of motor impairments. Even though they were very different mentally, emotionally, physically, and socially, they were inappropriately segregated from the nondisabled kids and lumped together in one class. As a result, it was almost impossible to teach them. But they were very intelligent and high-spirited. So when the principal prohibited them from using the playground at the same time as their nondisabled peers, my class was outraged. While I was out of the room, they prepared signs expressing their indignation. Some wore them on their bodies; others attached them to the back of their wheelchairs. They planned to stage a demonstration, and I decided to encourage them. Exhibiting their signs, they marched around the inside foyer that served as the entrance to the school. They didn't change the principal's mind, but they made a statement, and they felt terrific about it. There were no curb cuts or accessible buses at the time. But there was something in the air, and they sensed it. (Fleischer & Zames, 2001, p. 2001)

A disability scholar in the U.K. (Oliver, 1996) wrote eloquently and somewhat radically of the inferiority of many "special" schools.

> If able-bodied children were taken from their local school, sent to a foreign country, forced to undertake physical exercise for all their waking hours to the neglect of their academic education and social development, we would regard it as unacceptable and the children concerned would rapidly come to the attention of the child protection... [services]. But in the lives of disabled children (adults too), anything goes as long as you call it therapeutic... conductive education is not regarded as child abuse but as something meriting social applause. (p. 107)

THE CONTINUUM OF SCHOOL PLACEMENT

The number and range of educational choices for CWDs has expanded due to three factors, (1) increasingly refined educational methods, especially in special education, including professional training of special education teachers; (2) advances in AT; and (3) the growing numbers of CWDs. Many authors have conceptualized these different environments as a pyramid (see Figure 12.2). The broad base of the pyramid represents the greatest number of CWDs—those who (with accommodations) can be educated in general education classrooms (Sailor, Kleinhammer, Tramill, Skrtic, & Oas, 1996). The next level of the pyramid represents several types of special education environments, such as special classes or a portion of the day spent in a "resource room," in which CWDs receive some specialized education, but they spend most of their day in the general classroom. The next level represents residential schools or boarding schools in which children live at school, and the very top represents hospital schools in which tutors and teachers come to hospitals to teach children who are patients.

As the pyramid narrows, there are fewer children in the group, the disabilities become more severe, and the settings become more restrictive, leading to separation of CWDs from CWODs and their isolation from society, including their own families (Bryom, 2004; Leinhart & Pallay, 1982). As the pyramid narrows, teachers also require more training and must have more skills, such as knowledge of American Sign Language (ASL) or Braille.

Robert Neumann was diagnosed with rheumatoid arthritis as a teenager in the 1950s. In the excerpt below, he described his education during his high school years:

> During my high school days, my social life was virtually nonexistent. Because I received physical therapy at home in the afternoon and because my stamina was poor in any event, I attended school until about 1 p.m. This eliminated any possibility of interacting with peers in extracurricular activities. To complicate the situation further, because my life revolved around classes and studying, I routinely received unusually good grades and routinely broke the class curve— much to the animosity of those peers I did interact with. But perhaps most significantly, the school I attended was a Catholic, all-boy high school. This removed me from any contact whatsoever with the female part of the population at a time when my interest was anything but dormant. I literally had only one date, with the daughter of family friends, during my entire 4 years of high school....These less than satisfying experiences have led me to be a strong advocate of mainstreaming.... Unfortunately, neither the school authorities nor my parents understood how important it was to ensure that deficits in social skills would not develop through lack of informal, out-of-classroom socialization with male peers and the total lack of contact with any female ones. (Dell Orto & Power, 2007, pp. 726–727)

RESIDENTIAL SCHOOLS

Residential schools in the United States began in late 1800s for children who were deaf, or blind, or both. Until the 1960s these schools were the only educational option for children with these types of disabilities, and 80% of all children in the United

FIGURE 12.2

Different school environments.

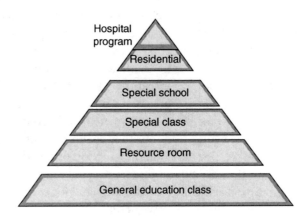

States who were deaf attended residential schools (Lane, Hoffmeister, & Bahan, 1996). These schools offered education from preschool to high school and often provided night classes for adults. Mainstreaming (or inclusion in community schools) began in the late 1960s, using sign language interpreters or "itinerant" teachers (teachers who teach at several different schools during the course of a day) or providing a separate classroom for deaf children. Nonetheless, most children with severe hearing losses continue to attend at least a few years of residential schools.

In such schools very young children are separated from their families and visit their families during the summer and holidays. Many of these children are "school-sick" when they visit home, wanting to go back to school where they have a language with which to communicate. Because most deaf children are born to hearing parents, these children are often the only members of their families who are deaf. Some deaf children reported that their siblings did not know their "sign-name." It is becoming more common for families with a deaf child to learn ASL; however, until recently deaf children typically felt lonely and isolated at home. Residential schools provide socialization and communication skills for children, allowing them to participate in all school opportunities, such as sports, student body offices, and debates. In residential schools the teachers and administrators are available as role models to children and adolescents, modeling a productive and fulfilling life with a disability. These role models encourage children to fulfill their potential. Both Braille and ASL are difficult to learn, and many experts suggest that for several years in early childhood the focus should be on learning Braille and ASL.

The use of English in tests and measurements of individuals who first language is ASL will yield questionable, if not worthless results. Anyone who is tested in his or her second language is at a great disadvantage. Pollard, DeMatteo, Lentz, and Rediess (2007) described ASL:

> ASL is the primary sign language used by deaf individuals in the United States and Canada. Its structural properties, increasingly well documented by researchers, differ markedly from those of English... Psychologists unfamiliar with the unique properties of ASL, its differences from English, and the compromised

English reading abilities of many deaf people may inappropriately use English-based measures in cognitive, personality, and neuropsychological assessment of deaf individuals, which may yield invalid results. (p. 11)

The use of Braille is declining because of the difficulty of learning Braille, the increased reliance upon sound technology, and the declining enrollments in residential schools for the blind. According to the National Federation of the Blind, fewer than 10% of blind children are now learning Braille; in the 1950s on the other hand, more than half of the nation's blind children learned Braille. Nonetheless, an individual who is blind and does not know Braille is considered to be illiterate (without the ability to read or write). The employment rate of blind adults who know Braille is far higher than those who do not have skills in Braille, much as adults who cannot read or write typically find it difficult to find work. One study found that 44% of blind participants who used Braille were unemployed, but those blind individuals who did not know Braille had a 77% unemployment rate.

Residential schools focus on teaching Braille during the early elementary school years rather than on a great deal of content, much as sighted students learn reading without a great deal of emphasis upon content. Dr. Geerat Vermeji, a professor of evolutionary biological/paleontologist at the University of California, Davis, has been blind since infancy. As a young child he attended a residential school for blind children. Dr. Vermeji advocated that blind children be educated in separate classrooms for blind students during the first years of elementary school. Following their acquisition of basic skills, these children can be mainstreamed into classes with sighted children:

> The ideal situation, it seems to me, is for a blind child to attend a local school. At first, full attention should be devoted to learning the essential skills—Braille, independent travel, getting to know one's physical and social surroundings—in a class wholly dedicated to that purpose. Gradually, blind children should be eased into class with their sighted peers, with time set aside to hone and expand the fundamental skills of blindness. Whatever the right solution is for any particular child, the goal of providing the necessary techniques as well as the self-confidence and social adaptations to live and compete successfully in sighted society must remain clearly fixed at center stage. (Vermeji, 1997, p. 36)

Mainstreaming in the public community schools may not provide a better education. For example, until recently sign language interpreters were not very well trained nor was any type of professional certification or licensure required. Because deaf children's learning is dependent upon the skill and experience of the interpreter, interpreters must also be trained in the subject that they interpret, be it chemistry, Shakespeare, or calculus. Unfortunately these children simply "attended" school and learned very little.

Although a residential school may have positives aspects, it is important to discuss their negative aspects. Indeed, many in the Deaf Culture consider that the single most important factor in the creation of their culture was the reaction against residential schools. For decades deaf schools emphasized "oralism," in which deaf children were forced to speak vocally and punished for using ASL. Thus deaf children were subjected to years of frustration and failure. Oralist teachers also forced deaf children to learn to read lips, which provides very inaccurate information at best. Kisor (1990) wrote a memoir about growing up deaf and having to learn lip reading. The title of his book, *What's That Pig Outdoors? A Memoir of Deafness*, illustrates the inaccuracy of lip reading. In extreme cases deaf children in oralist schools had their hands tied behind their backs to prevent them from signing.

The most famous advocate of oralism is Alexander Graham Bell, considered to be the inventor of the telephone. Bell's wife was deaf and his inventions, including the telephone, were intended to be assistive devices for individuals who were deaf.

The Deaf culture holds that teachers and administrators at these residential schools, who were most often hearing individuals, contributed to the prejudice and discrimination toward PWDs and reduced and limited their range of choices after they left school (Bragg, 1989). These "graduates" could not speak orally, they had been allowed to learn ASL, and had lip reading skills that were not very helpful. Teaching oralism was an attempt to make deaf children "appear" to be hearing or "normal" children.

Residential schools for deaf children, in general, provided little academic education for their students but focused on teaching vocational skills and trades, thinking that these children would grow up to work in the trades. Of course these administrators and teachers were right; the children did grow up to work in the trades. However, they were entrapped in these occupational roles not because of their disability but from their lack of an academic education. Deaf boys were taught printing, and deaf girls were taught typing. Deafness was thought to be an asset for work around loud printing presses. This occupational role entrapment was in place for decades, perhaps centuries, and was determined by the disability (deafness) and the individual's gender. No one bothered to ask these children about their interests. At a very early age they were assigned their life's work (Gulati, 2003). Of course, printing and typing are both valid occupations, but only if the individual chooses these jobs.

David Wright, a poet/professor in the U.K., was born and educated in South Africa. He lost his hearing at age seven from an infection. He wrote eloquently of the occupational role entrapment perpetuated in schools for children who are deaf. Note that he questions if his school really was a school.

> Since then, I have had an aversion to doing anything with my hands. To this day, I cannot draw, or tie up a parcel properly, if it comes to that.... But, for a long time, dating from attendance at this school, if it was a school, I refused on principle to learn, or was deliberately bad at manipulatory skills like carpentry, painting, and so on. Schools of this type, where the teacher was usually untrained—they probably do not exist nowadays—took the line of least resistance and while teaching their deaf pupils a little speech and lip-reading, concentrated on instruction in handicrafts. This seemed to me, even then, to be equating deafness with stupidity; and I resented it. So much so that I took cleverness with the hands to be a badge of deafness, and I would not wear that badge. Instead of being taught to use my head, because I was deaf, I was being fobbed off with handicrafts. (Wright, 1994, p. 40)

Even as young boy David Wright was able to resist the occupational role entrapment that adults tried to enforce. He either refused to learn these manual skills or was deliberately bad. In the end David Wright won and did not "wear a badge" that the school wanted to pin on him. Perhaps David was able to resist because he understood that deafness did not mean lack of intellectual abilities.

Residential schools have a long history of physical and sexual abuse. Because of the isolation of the children and the power differential between adults and small children, abuse was easily hidden, and it was often tolerated when discovered (Zavirsk, 2002).

Parents assumed that they were placing their children in a safe, secure environment, but in reality their children were sometimes being mistreated (Smart, 2001, 2009). One houseparent stated, "You have to break these children when they're young." This houseparent whipped the children with a large leather belt when they "misbehaved" (Evans & Falk, 1986, p. 100). These beatings were given for many minor infractions. Sexual molestation was also prevalent, with some children experiencing abuse throughout the years from many different perpetrators (Sobsey, 1994; Sobsey & Doe, 1991). "A top administrator estimates that one-third of all students were 'abused and molested' children" (Evans & Falk, 1986, p. 99).

These schools were coercive, did not prepare students for life after graduation, and (perhaps most important), were not the family home. Children who attended residential schools were not socialized into their family's culture. All these factors over decades of time combined to create the Deaf culture. Some believe that deaf people have been subjected to more professional misjudgment, paternalism, and control than any other disability group (Bauman & Drake, 1997; Higgins, 1992).

The Deaf culture does not believe that deafness is a disability; instead deaf people use another language, which is as complex and sophisticated as any spoken language. To them deafness is a natural condition. The Deaf Culture, therefore, feels greater identity to Spanish speakers than to other disability groups, including those with blindness (Ree, 1999). By assuming this cultural identity, they are able to resist the inferior, pathological, deviant role that society has tried to impose upon them. Of all the groups of PWDs, the Deaf Culture has achieved the greatest group solidarity and common history. In the past they were felt to be an invisible part of American society, so the identity and social role that the Deaf Cultures provides is very important (Lane, Hoffmeister, & Bahan, 1996).

Much of the history and solidarity of the Deaf Culture can be traced to a common language (ASL) and the common experience of residential education (Lane, 1993). Any language is a repository of rich cultural traditions, and ASL has a body of literature, including plays and poetry. As might be expected, jokes in ASL often deride hearing people (Lane, Hoffmeister, & Bahan, 1996).

Membership in the Deaf Culture can be quite restricted, excluding those who were not born deaf, did not attend residential schools, or are not fluent in ASL (Lane, 1993). As with any language, a native speaker finds it relatively easy to spot another native speaker/signer. Like other cultures, the Deaf Culture strives to preserve its identity and existence. Obviously prenatal screening and cochlear implants will probably greatly reduce the number of individuals who are deaf. Prenatal screening for deafness has a different meaning for deaf parents because as prospective parents they worry that their baby will be hearing, and many deaf parents oppose cochlear implants for their deaf children. Tucker (1998) explained the dilemma facing the Deaf Culture:

> The primary argument against deliberately seeking to produce deaf children is that it violates the child's own autonomy and narrows the scope of her choices when she grows up; in other words, it violates her right to an "open future." Insisting that children who are deaf be raised in a Deaf cultural community denies those children the right to choose for themselves to accept or reject the larger hearing world.

When most deafness becomes correctable, which for many people has already occurred and for others may well happen in the near future, an individual who chooses not to correct his or her deafness (or the deafness of his or her child) will lack the moral right to demand the others pay for costly accommodations to compensate for the lack of hearing of that individual. In this age of budget crises and cries for tax reform, when there is talk of, and some action with respect to, the need to cut funding for welfare, Medicaid, Social Security, federally supported food banks, and other social welfare programs, it is unrealistic, at best, to expect society to fund expenditures that could be eliminated. (Tucker, 1998, p. 8)

An example will show how membership in the Deaf Culture is narrowly defined. The first Miss America who was deaf was Heather Whitestone, who won the title in 1995. Ironically, in 1992 Ms. Whitestone competed in the Ms. Alabama D/deaf Alabama completion "where she was trounced because...[she was] unable to fully understand the ASL of the interviewer (or the judges)—and their inability to understand her ironically 'handicapped' Whitestone." Whitestone's parents had insisted that she learn to speak when she was a preschooler, so she was not fluent in ASL. "Just because I spoke...they [Miss D/d Alabama pageant officials] decided that I could not fit into the D/deaf culture, that I was not a an 'ideal D/deaf person'" (Burch 2007, p. 255). Therefore, Ms. Whitestone was not considered D/deaf enough and lost the Miss D/deaf Alabama competition; however, the Miss America pageant considered her to be deaf.

COCHLEAR IMPLANTS

Cochlear implants (CIs) are electronic devices with three basic components: a microphone worn behind the ear to pick up sound, a speech processor also worn behind the ear, and a small device surgically implanted in the ear, specifically in the cochlea. Simply speaking, the cochlea contains the auditory nerves that make hearing possible. When these nerves are damaged or absent, an implant performs the functions of these nerves. The signals produced by sounds are then sent to the brain, and the individual hears. Cochlear implants were first developed in France in the 1950s and gained popularity in the United States in the 1970s.

Around the world the Deaf Culture has consistently and vehemently been opposed to CIs for these three reasons: (1) CIs pathologize deafness, (2) CIs will weakness the Deaf Culture, and (3) the Deaf Culture resists being controlled by others outside their culture. The hearing world views deafness as a medical and biological concern, but the Deaf Culture thinks of deafness in cultural terms (Tucker, 1998). One French Deaf Leader asked "Why not bleach the blacks?" (Albinhac, D., 1978 cf Edwards, 2010, p. 407)

Terms to Learn

Academic self-concept
Atypical childhood
   experiences
Behavioral intentionality
Cochlear implants

Continuum of school
   placement
Deaf Culture
Decentration
Homophilous

Hyperactivity and atten-
   tion deficit disorder
Learning disabilities
Residential schools
Social comparison

Videos to View

- View the film *Sound and Fury.* This film was a 2001 Academy Award nominee for Best Documentary Feature. Then view the *Sound and Fury: Six Years Later.* The producer described these videos: "These films show the struggle of one extended family deciding whether to provide cochlear implants to their deaf children. Two cousins of Long Island, New York, are deaf. Heather age 6½, has deaf parents and Peter, age 1½ has hearing parents. Their grandparents are deaf. Heather's parents are resistant to the idea of implants because they want their daughter to be raised in the Deaf Culture." Both of these videos are available from Aquarius Health Care Media.
- View the 15-minute video *Understanding Learning Disabilities,* available from Insight Media. The producers describe this video: "Explaining that a child may have a learning disability in one academic area, yet excel in other subjects, this program examines the nature of learning disability and social disorders and presents techniques that help compensate for specific deficiencies."
- View the 30-minute video *Dyslexia,* available from Insight Media. The producers describe this video: "Featuring teenagers with dyslexia and offering commentary from medical and mental health professionals, this program examines the experience of growing up with dyslexia and considers the challenges facing students with the condition in schools. It explores the biological bases for dyslexia."

Learning Activities

(Note: These may also be used as class presentations.)
- Debate the advantages and disadvantages of simulation exercises. Divide the class into two groups. Have one group present the advantages and the other the disadvantages.
- Debate the advantages and disadvantages of lowered expectations, "pity grades," and "mercy graduations." Divide the class into two groups. Have one group present the advantages and the other the disadvantages.
- Read the following books, which are compilations of first-person experiences of polio survivors:
  A Nearly Normal Life: A Memoir (1999) by journalist and author Charles L. Mee, published by Brown and Little, Boston.
  Polio and Its Aftermath (2005) by polio survivor Marc Shell, published by Harvard University Press.
  Living With Polio: The Epidemic and Its Survivors (1990) by polio survivor Daniel J. Wilson, published by the University of Chicago.
- Discuss the childhood experiences of polio survivors, focusing your attention on the lack of services at the time of the epidemics.

Writing Exercises

- Write a short paper on the degree of neuroplasticity lost when a deaf infant is not taught signing immediately after birth.
- Read the article "A World of Their Own" by Liza Mundy, which first appeared in the *Washington Post Magazine*. This article can be found in the book *The Best American Science Writing 2003*, edited by Oliver Sacks and published by Harper-Collins. In this article deaf parents "worry" that they will have a hearing child. Write a paper explaining why deaf parents would want deaf children.
- Write a 10-page paper on the Deaf Culture, including the way in which its members define deafness. Do you think that the Deaf Culture is overly exclusive? Do you think the Deaf Culture will eventually cease to exist?
- Think back upon your own childhood. Write a 10-page autobiographical paper in which you compare your own experiences to the developmental tasks outlined in this chapter.

Web Sites

http://sports.yahoo.com/nfl/news?slug=lc-packers_draft_pick_overcomes_learning_disabilities_050311

This is a story about a football player who was diagnosed with several learning disabilities but earned a 3.5 GPA in college and was drafted by a professional football team.

http://learningdisabilities.about.com/od/infancyandearlychildhood/p/24to36monthsdev.htm

http://nichcy.org/

http://www.kidsource.com/kidsource/pages/toddlers.disabilities.html

Adolescence, Ages 13 to 18 and Emerging Adulthood, Ages 19 to 25

13

The term adolescent was not coined until the early 1900s. Before this there was no concept of a transition period between childhood and adulthood; the individual was expected to go from being a child to assuming adult roles and responsibilities, typically at the end of puberty. Adolescence is considered a transition period during which the individual is allowed time to develop an adult identity, explore ("try on") new identities and roles, and initiate the tasks of obtaining full-time work and getting married. Adolescence is considered to include the ages of 13 to 18.

Emerging adulthood is a new developmental stage, having been identified in the 1990s through the work of Jeffrey Arnett (Arnett, 1997, 2000). Emerging adulthood is considered a transition period between adolescence and adulthood that typically begins at age 19 and concludes at age 25, although Arnett stated that some individuals do not self-identify as adults until they reach the age of 30. Arnett's research included sending questionnaires to individuals between the ages of 19 and 30 to elicit information about their self-identities.

In addition to alterations in self-identities, biological changes have also contributed to redefining both adolescence and emerging adulthood. For example, boys and girls now tend to enter puberty earlier than in previous historical periods, a trend that has been observed over several generations of Americans and Western Europeans. In the early 1900s the average age of menarche (the beginning of menstruation) was 15 or 16, but it is 12½ in the early 2000s. Boys in developed nations are becoming taller and heavier and show earlier signs of genital maturation. Health demographers speculate that these earlier signs of the onset of puberty are the result of better nutrition and improved public health. Papalia and Olds (1992) concluded:

> This...trend appears to have ended, at least in the United States, probably as a reflection of higher living standards in most segments of our population.... The leveling of the trend suggests that the age of sexual maturity has now reached some genetically determined limit and that better nutrition is unlikely to lower the age any further. (p. 311)

Therefore today's adolescents are more likely to resemble their parents in physical growth than at any time during the previous 130 years (Berk, 2001).

Little more than 100 years ago, there was no transition period between childhood and adulthood, in contrast to the present in which there can be a total of 18 years (12–30) of an intermediate period (Modell, 1989). Therefore adolescence and emerging adulthood are a response to a complex interplay of biological changes, the social and cultural interpretations of these transition years, and societal expectations (such as the need for more postsecondary education for today's labor market).

ADOLESCENCE

One developmental theorist stated, "The way in which one grows up is closely related to what one becomes" (Modell, 1989, p. 26). The word adolescence is derived from a Latin root that means "to grow up." In addition an expanding body of empirical evidence indicates that a person's coping style and adaptive strategies in early adolescence are important in determining his or her life course. Because the beginning of adolescence means the end of childhood, obviously the earlier adolescence begins, the earlier childhood ends. This is termed the "compression of childhood" (Newman & Newman, 2009). Society places many demands upon adolescents while simultaneously providing adolescents with the resources of money, education, and a "social moratorium," a time when they can explore and "try on" new identities and roles (Clausen, 1991a, 1991b). All of these ideas underline the importance of the teenage years.

One developmental psychologist (Havighurst, 1972) outlined eight major psychological tasks to be accomplished during adolescence.

Developmental Tasks of Adolescence

- Accept one body and use it effectively
- Achieve emotional independence from parents and family
- Achieve a feminine or masculine social-sex role
- Achieve both new and more mature relationships with age mates of both sexes
- Achieve socially responsible behavior
- Acquire a set of values and an ethical system
- Prepare for a career
- Prepare for marriage and family life

These eight tasks require the individual to make important, far-reaching decisions in a relatively short period of time and to experience many different types of changes in self-identity. There are ways to remediate some adolescent and young adult decisions, such as changing careers or divorcing a spouse. Nonetheless, the societal expectations listed above may not always coincide with individual needs. These eight developmental tasks may be considered epigenetic because people tend to become more skilled and more effective as they mature and age at each developmental task. For example, Kohlberg stated that as an individual becomes older, he or she becomes more moral and socially responsible.

Adolescents experience "partial adult status" (Berk, 1998, p. 355), shown by actions such as receiving a driver's license, graduating from high school, or obtaining a job. Adolescents in nations (like Germany) that have structured apprenticeships beginning at age 14 are also given partial adult status. Therefore, the adolescent is considered to be an adult in some settings, such as on the highway or at the job. Adolescents in the military are also considered adults. Finally, in the developed nations there are no rites of passage for entrance into puberty.

PHYSICAL MATURATION

The physical maturation of childhood tends to occur gradually. In contrast, early adolescence is marked by rapid physical changes, among them an increase in height, increased muscle strength, redistribution of body weight, maturation of the reproductive system, and the appearance of secondary sex characteristics. In adolescence the cephalocaudal growth pattern of infancy and childhood reverses, and the hands, feet, and torsos grow. In fact the accelerated growth of the torso accounts for most of the adolescent growth spurt. Gormly (1997) explained the different types of growth experienced by adolescents:

> Different parts of the teenager's body grow at differing rates, so that at times adolescents look a bit awkward. Growth during adolescence violates the proximodistal (from the center of the body outward) trend characteristics of other development growth periods. Big feet and long legs are the early signs of a changing body. First the hands and feet grow, then the arms and legs, and only later do the shoulders and chest grow to fit the rest of the developing body. The stereotype of the gangling and clumsy teenager may be fueled by an awkward-appearing body. (p. 334)

At the beginning of adolescence, girls tend to be both taller and heavier than boys their same age. Girls tend to outweigh boys until about the age of 14 when boys begin to surpass girls (Santrock, 2009). Beginning at approximately age 14 for boys, their growth spurt adds about 4 inches of height per year until they attain their adult height at age 18. Girls tend to add about 3½ inches per year and attain their adult height at age 14 or 15.

The brain also continues to develop, and these changes increase emotionality and gradually improve connections between various parts of the brain, improving impulse control and expression of emotion. However, there is great variability in the rate of maturation among those in early adolescence (Newman & Newman, 2009). The structures of the brain change during adolescence, and some changes are not completed until age 25. Before the development of neuroimaging techniques, most of these brain changes were thought to be a result of experiences the adolescent had with school, peers, parents, and other adults. Now, it is known that the brain structure changes anatomically, but whether experiences or changes in brain anatomy come first is still not known, nor which changes the other.

The seat of an individual's emotions, the amygdala, matures more quickly than other parts of the brain. During adolescence the fibers of the corpus callosum, which connects the brain's right and left hemisphere, thicken and strengthen this connection. A stronger connection between the right and left hemispheres of the brain allows the adolescent to process information faster and more accurately. The area that controls the highest level of reasoning, self-control, and decision making, the prefrontal cortex, also matures during adolescence. This cortical development enables the development of "executive functioning," or the ability to reason, weigh alternatives, ignore irrelevant information, plan ahead, complete complex tasks, perform multistep processes, self-evaluate, organize data and information, and inhibit impulses. With the maturation of the prefrontal cortex, individuals are eventually capable of coordinating their emotions with their behavior. However, because the prefrontal cortex matures at a slower rate than other parts of the brain, adolescents are capable of feeling very strong emotions, such as love, anger, or frustration, but they may need years before they acquire the cognitive skills to moderate their emotions.

Puberty is a biological life course transition with many social definitions. Puberty is defined (biologically) for girls as the beginning of menstruation and the development of secondary sex characteristics, such as the emergence of breasts and the widening of the hips. Puberty may also be defined as the period or age at which a person reaches sexual maturity and becomes capable of having children (Rice, 1998). For boys puberty is defined as the maturation of the genitalia and the onset of secondary sex characteristics, such as facial hair and voice change. During childhood the bodies of girls and boys have both testosterone and estrogen. However, the concentration of these hormones increases during puberty, with testosterone dominating in boys and estrogen dominating in girls. Great age variability is seen in the onset and completion of puberty. For girls the average age range of puberty is as early as age 9 to a late onset at age 15. For boys the average range is 10 to 17. Moreover, individuals who complete puberty relatively early are not necessarily mature socially, intellectually, or emotionally, regardless of their physical maturity.

When girls and boys complete puberty at a relatively young age, they reap advantages of improved self-esteem and may have a head start on intellectual development. Both physically and emotionally girls tend to mature earlier than boys, creating a developmental gap. Thus boys who mature early are at the same developmental level as girls and have a dating advantage. Early maturing boys also have an advantage in athletics due to their increased muscular and strength development. The disadvantages for both early maturing boys and girls come from increased expectations of adults. Early maturing girls are developmentally ahead of other girls and very much ahead of most boys. Simply because these adolescents *appear* older than they actually are, adults may expect more mature behaviors and attitudes from them.

Late maturity has the advantage of a longer childhood that allows these individuals increased time to respond to the societal demands of adolescence. Nonetheless, most developmental psychologists feel that late maturation in adolescence leads to reduced self-esteem, introversion, and poor body image. Both early and late maturation are off-time transitions that usually make adolescents feel different from their peers, and off-time transitions tend to be stressful and difficult.

At puberty the individual's identity becomes sexualized. Children are thought to be asexual, but this belief may be changing now that preschool and elementary school children compete in beauty pageants.

STORM AND STRESS

Developmental psychologists once widely believed that most adolescents experienced a type of stress and anxiety that was termed "storm and stress" (or *Sturm und Drang* in

German). This tension was thought to be caused by the number of biological, emotional, intellectual, and social changes found in adolescence. Anna Freud agreed with the storm and stress hypothesis because she reasoned that adolescents experience intensified sexual urges and aggressive drives. Evidence mounted when it was thought that many adolescents have negative, troubling, and adversarial relationships with their parents and other family members and were always challenging parental authority. The "storm and stress" hypothesis was first advanced in 1904 in a classic work on adolescence by a prominent Harvard developmental psychologist, G. Stanley Hall.

Although the storm and stress hypothesis has been discarded, this does not mean that adolescence is completely stress-free. Dealing with academic pressures, coordinating many different activities, making choices that have lifelong consequences, and living up to parental expectations are experiences that often create turmoil, stress, and anxiety. Nonetheless few adolescents experience years of continuous storm and stress.

Developing an Identity

- Social
- Sex roles
- Ethnic
- Vocational

A self-identity is a synthesis of many different components, such as spiritual, sexual, ethnic, vocational, social, and physical self-images. Self-identity includes development of the individual's personal standards of behavior, such as becoming a vegetarian or converting to a religion and joining a church or similar organization. The acquisition of self-identity is a process in which many steps are repeated or remediated. Although identity formation does not begin in adolescence, during the adolescent years self-identity becomes most important. Parents, other family members, religious organizations, peers, and school all contribute to the many dimensions of an adolescent's self-identity. An adolescent may have a firm, well-developed, well-tested identity in one area without achieving an identity in other areas of his or her life.

Families provide both a sense of individuality and connectedness to others. Individuality means having an identity separate from the family and the ability to assert one's viewpoints, attitudes, and wishes, while connectedness involves sensitivity to and respect for the viewpoints of others and openness to differing opinions (Farrell & Hutter, 1984). Both individuality and connectedness are necessary, because connectedness provides a secure base of support from trustworthy people who encourage exploration and mastery of new skills and environments by remaining available to provide help and comfort when they are needed. Families also model behaviors that are trustworthy and consistent. When families combine encouraging individuality and providing connectedness, they provide a bridge to full adulthood for adolescents. For many adolescents, it is easier to separate from parents physically than emotionally. Studies have shown that 89% of adolescents with problems sought help from their friends, while 81% consulted parents and other family members. Interestingly, those who asked their parents for help had a better self-image than those who did not (Schonert-Reichl, Offer, & Howard, 1995).

In the past adolescents detached themselves completely from their parents and moved both physically and emotionally into a world that did not include their parents or family. This view may have built upon the idea of constant parent–adolescent stress and discord that ended only when the adolescent left home. The newer conceptualization of family–parent–adolescent relationships recognizes that conflict and negotiation can serve a positive developmental function. Parental monitoring and guidance have been found to be related to lower rates of self-destructive behaviors such as smoking, drinking, and the illegal use of marijuana (Council of Economic Advisors, 2000). However, one family in five experiences intense, repeated, and unhealthy discord, resulting in highly stressful parent–adolescent relationships (Santrock, 2009).

Determining one's sex-role identities (often termed "gender roles") includes examining the masculine and feminine roles of one's culture or subculture and deciding if these are appropriate. Sorting out the available sex roles is more difficult today, simply because a much wider range of choices is available than 50 years ago. Girls and women tend to test their identities and eventually choose identities that are self-defined but also integrate needs for connectedness and supportive relationships (Gilligan, 1977, 1982, 1987). This is not to suggest that women's self-defined identities do not also include professional and financial achievement (Holcomb, 1990).

Wheelchair athletics provide an important source of recreation and a way in which to express gender role identity. However, wheelchair sports did not exist before the 1980s because sports wheelchairs were not invented until then. Today sports wheelchairs are so specialized that each sport has its own chair that meets its particular demands. Some sports wheelchairs have three, four, or six wheels. It was World War II veterans who pushed for better wheelchairs (and other adaptive technology, such as hand controls for cars). Indeed, World War II provided the impetus for developing a wide range of assistive technology, just as the wars in Iraq and Afghanistan have led to the development of more functional prostheses. In the wars of the 1990s and 2000s soldiers wear body armor that prevents or reduces deaths and injuries to the trunk of the body, but the arms and legs are injured. In World War II antibiotics saved the lives of many soldiers who survived with paraplegia and quadriplegia. Because the wars in Iraq and Afghanistan have resulted in many limb amputations, they have spurred the development of better prostheses.

The popular movie *Murderball* shows the intense rivalry between the Canadian and American wheelchair rugby teams. Most of the team members are between the ages of 20 and 30. The film includes the stories of various athletes, some of whom acquired their disabilities in thrills and chills activities. One athlete spoke succinctly: "I'm not here for a hug. I'm here for a medal." Wheelchair sports allow athletes of both sexes and of all ages to continue their predisability activities or to develop new interests (Sherrill, 1997).

As adolescents begin to form a sexual self-identity, they confront the need to regulate their sexual emotions at the same time they initiate romantic relationships. Children are considered to be asexual, while adults are considered sexual. The media provide sexual content that is readily and universally available. Sexual identity is one dimension of a person's self-identity whose formation becomes important at puberty.

The exploration of vocational identity becomes more realistic during the adolescent years. Seventy-five percent of all high school students hold some type of part-time employment (Rice, 1998). Part-time paid employment during high school assists adolescents in learning the "soft skills" of employability, such as being punctual; responding to supervision and authority; maintaining the pace of the workplace; and relating properly to coworkers, customers, and clients. These soft skills are not tied to any one particular occupational or job skill set but are transferable to a wide range of jobs. Because part-time jobs during high school typically do not require a great deal of skill and there is a large turnover in employees, adolescents can learn these work personality skills in a relatively low-stakes environment. Being terminated from this type of job has fewer long-range consequences than losing a postcollege professional job. Part-time employment during high school can provide the type of "hands-on" skills that Piagetian formal operational thinking does not. One criticism of Piaget's theory is that it does not provide real-life skills, only academic skills of developing deductive hypotheses and other scientific processes.

There has been criticism of adolescent part-time jobs during the high school years, based on the premise that jobs decrease the time and effort spent on schoolwork or participating in extracurricular activities. The criticism of part-time work during high school years is related to the *number* of hours worked. These critics cited the number of days of missed school and lowered grade-point averages of adolescents who held part-time jobs. Closer inspection showed that problems did not necessarily arise *if* the adolescent held a part-time job but rather the *number of hours* the job required determined whether there would be difficulties. According to Gormly (1997), working more than 20 hours per week resulted in these negative outcomes, and adolescents who worked fewer than 20 hours tended to reap social and vocational benefits. In one longitudinal study (Steinberg, Fegley, & Dornbusch, 1993), many adolescents who worked more than 20 hours per week were attempting to "distance" themselves from difficult family situations.

Religious and spiritual identity answers the existential questions about the meaning of life, adversity, and one's place in the world (Arnett & Jensen, 2002; Edgell, 2006; Milevsky & Levitt, 2004). Arnett and Jensen titled their article on the religiosity of emerging adults "A Congregation of One," describing the individualistic nature of the religious experiences of emerging adults. Newly gained abstract thinking skills allow adolescents to imagine a world that is both ideal and perfect. Therefore adolescents begin to explore new ideologies, spiritualities, political systems, and organized religions (Milevsky & Levitt, 2004). In contrast, their parents tend to have a more realistic view of the world because of their age, understanding that most situations have both positives and negatives. Relating to a higher power through activities such as praying or meditating affects one's self-identity, often positively because the individual believes that he or she is worthy of love and attention (Milevsky & Leh, 2008; Rooehlkepartian, 2005). Communion with the universe helps individuals to feel they are a part of something larger than themselves. In addition, church congregations can be cultural capital, providing social support and a sense of belonging. Religious affiliation has been found to be a positive influence in the lives of adolescents, with evidence that adolescent church or synagogue attenders tend to engage in more community service, feel a sense of affiliation with others, and are less likely to engage in illegal acts.

Relationships with peers are an important source of one's self-identity because they fill needs for intimacy, reassurance of worth, and a safe context in which adolescents can confide to friends. Negotiating the positive and negative aspects of friendship can assist adolescents in gaining more highly developed social skills.

The developmental researcher James Marcia (1980, 1994) divided Erikson's theory of identity formation into four distinct stages, recognizing that formation of an identity is a process in which the steps build upon each other. These steps or stages are based on adolescents' questioning, exploration and investment, and willingness to develop an identity. The first stage is *identity diffusion*, in which adolescents have not experienced any turning point nor do they have an interest or commitment in achieving an identity. The second stage is termed *identity formation*, which is found in adolescents who have made a commitment to an identity but have not explored this identity. This stage typically occurs when adolescents from authoritarian homes with very strong belief systems unquestioningly accept their family's ideologies. The third stage is called *identity moratorium* and describes the individual who is engaged in active exploration but has not yet committed. Identity moratorium corresponds to Erikson's psychosocial moratorium, in which the adolescent is given time to experiment with various roles and identities. The last stage is called *identity achievement*, which describes the experiences of those who have successfully explored, investigated, and "tried on" identities and have as a result made a commitment. Marcia emphasized that these stages do not always occur in this sequence; at times individuals may cycle through these stages several times. Furthermore, individuals can reach identity achievement in a single aspect at a fairly young age. For example, many individuals marry their high school sweethearts and stay married throughout their lives.

Research on adolescent identity formation is beginning to show that key changes in identity are more likely to take place in emerging adulthood rather than in adolescence. In adolescence high school tends to be the central organizer of life, and responding to its demands may not leave time or energy for identity exploration.

James Marcia asserted that one's first identity is not necessarily the last and that healthy, adaptable, flexible individuals are open to changes in society, relationships, and careers. There may be many different reorganizations of identity throughout the life span. We hear expressions of such adaptability when someone states, "I'm reinventing myself."

Self-esteem differs from self-identity; self-identity answers the question, "Who am I" and self-esteem answers the question, "How good am I?" Both academic performance and physical appearance contribute to an individual's evaluation of himself or herself. Self-esteem tends to improve as people move from the earlier years of adolescence to the later years; in the process teenagers become more comfortable with who they are, their appearance, and their relationships with others.

THE GRAND THEORISTS' VIEWS ON ADOLESCENCE

Sigmund Freud focused most of his study and writing upon the stage of early childhood because he considered development to be determined during the first 5 or 6 years of life. However, he did devote some attention to the period after latency, which he termed "genital" and which coincides with the adolescent years. According to Freud, adolescents can begin the genital stage only after all of the psychosexual stages that precede the genital stage are resolved. In this way Freud's theory of development is sequential and hierarchical. Freud also thought that self-identity is forged during adolescence, and identifying with a role model, either fictional or real life, can help mold the adolescent's superego in a way that is acceptable to the standards of society. According to Freud, one task of the teenage years was to shift from same-sex friends to friends of the opposite sex.

Freud was clear in stating that he considered puberty to be easier and more understandable for boys. It is understood that Freud was more concerned with the biological process of puberty, rather than the socially defined developmental stage of adolescence. Moreover, Freud lived in a historical period which preceded the creation of the transitional stage of adolescence.

One developmental psychologist summarized her interpretation of Freud's views on differences in adolescent development between boys and girls:

> In *Three Essays on the Theory of Sexuality*, written in 1905, Freud once again showed little knowledge of women. He felt that in adolescence the sexual development of boys and girls differs greatly and that what happens for boys is more straightforward and understandable. He saw puberty as the period when there is a sharp distinction between boys' and girls' characters, and this contrast has a decisive influence on the rest of their lives. Puberty, he felt, brings up a strong resurgence of libido in boys and of repression. Freud believed that girls have a greater inclination to view sexuality in terms of shame and disgust, leading to repression and a tendency to passivity in sexual relations. (Austrian, 2002, p. 127)

Erikson considered that "identity versus role confusion" was the developmental task of adolescence and that the completion of this stage strengthens identity, especially for males. Erikson seemed to have accepted some of Freud's bias in favor of males or perhaps his thinking was distorted because he studied only male children to construct his theory. In any event, Erikson was clear in stating that adolescent boys develop a strong identity while adolescent girls defer identity development, waiting until marriage when they will take their husbands' surname and achieve their status through their husbands' positions. Therefore, Erikson held that girls attain their self-identity through attachment and boys attain theirs through separation.

Other vestiges of Freud are found in Erikson's theory, especially in Erikson's view that the developmental demands of adolescence can cause the return of earlier crises that were once resolved. Erikson thought that the physical changes of puberty made the earlier "crises" reemerge.

Erikson conceptualization of the developmental process of adolescence has two strengths: the idea that continuity and discontinuity may be present simultaneously and the idea of a "social moratorium." When the opposites of continuity and discontinuity are seen as part of adolescent development, one understands that the adolescent remains who he or she was (as an infant and child) but also changes in significant ways. Successful completion of adolescence is considered to results from the combination of acquiring new roles and responsibilities while integrating them with the former identities of childhood. The second idea (the existence of a social moratorium) appears to be a concept that was ahead of its time and foreshadows Arnett's emerging adulthood stage.

A social moratorium can be seen as societal-endowed resources of time, money, and experiences that allow adolescents to test out identities and try new experiences without a sense of high stakes. In the past adolescents, especially those in the lower socioeconomic groups, were encouraged (or pressured) to marry upon reaching sexual maturity, have children immediately following marriage, and initiate their life work. Furthermore, the structures of the labor market and the stigma and difficulty of divorce provided few escape routes or further choice points to individuals who had incurred these life responsibilities while still in adolescence. Many adolescents married the girl/boy next door; the girl became a lifelong mother and homemaker, and the boy worked at the same job that his uncle got him when he was 18 years old.

At the end of the 20th century and the beginning of the 21st century, adolescents in developed nations are given time to investigate and explore options before making commitments. During World War II one half of all American young men enlisted in the military, in contrast to 17% in the previous generation (Goldscheider & Goldscheider, 1999). In the second chapter we learned of two longitudinal studies of male military veterans of World War II. The war acted as a social moratorium but only for young veterans. Two Harvard professors, Eleanor and Sheldon Glueck (1950, 1968), studied young men who had been incarcerated in juvenile facilities and entered the military during World War II. For these relatively young soldiers and sailors, military duty did not cause a great deal of life disruption even when the risk of disability, injuries, and death from combat was considered. The war years acted as a social moratorium, giving them time to redirect their lives and to delay marriage and parenthood. World War II provided a social distancing from a world of juvenile crime, a steady income, and opportunities for leadership and other skill building; when they returned home, the white veterans were able to use a very generous G. I. Bill to get training and university educations, start-up money for businesses, and home mortgages. The war probably helped these young men form a self-identity as a valued, contributing members of very cohesive, supportive groups striving for important outcomes.

For those men who entered the military after age 26, service in World War II acted as a negative disruption. The demographers were surprised at the very clear difference between the early-enterers and late-enterers. They surmised that men older than 25 were usually married and had well-established jobs, and many of them had children. Military service was a disruption from which many did not recover, or at least it took years to regain their social and occupational positions. Shanahan (2000) cited a study that found "entry into the military at a late age often coincided with the disruption of nascent family life and careers, leading to, for example, a greater likelihood of divorce" (Pavalka & Elder, 1990, p. 673). Even in peacetime, without the need for mass mobilization, the same difference was found between men who enter the military early and those who enter after age 26.

The developmental stage of emerging adulthood does not quite correspond to Erikson's stage of young adulthood, so Erikson's developmental tasks do appear to be appropriate. Erikson divided the adolescent years into early adolescence (12–18) and late adolescence (18–24). Early adulthood was considered to be 24 to 34 years. The developmental task was that of intimacy versus isolation, and the specific goals were exploring intimate relationships such as marriage or long-term romantic relationships, initiating a lifelong career track, and becoming a parent. Although the years of Erikson's theory do not match the time period of Arnett's emerging adulthood, it is more significant that the developmental tasks of each theory are very divergent. Culturally prescribed pressures to shift one's identity have become more blurred. Erikson thought that adulthood (and all its attendant tasks) started at an earlier age, but Arnett believes that the important choices of adulthood can be deferred to a later age, often as late as age 30.

Piaget thought that "decentering" continues to evolve throughout adolescence. Decentering begins in infancy and allows individuals to approach situations from a more analytic point of view. In adolescence decentering includes the discovery that an individual's ideals are not shared by everyone. Adolescents still retain some vestiges of egocentrism, including a strong commitment to their personal thoughts, feelings, and goals. However, having a wide range of peers requires adolescents to understand that each individual has his or her own thoughts, feelings, and goals. Formal operational thinking allows the adolescent to become less egocentric.

Piaget's concept that a stage of formal operational thought was the final stage in the development of logical thought has met with criticism, especially the idea that this is the final stage. Formal operational thought involves the manipulation of information with flexibility and complexity; therefore several researchers question if all adults (without disabilities) attain this level of cognitive development. Research studies of first year college students showed that only between 40% and 60% reason at the level of formal operational thought (Commons, Miller, & Kuhn, 1982; Gormly, 1997). Another criticism of Piaget's theory of cognitive development states that Piaget defined cognitive development only in academic terms, thus ignoring "common sense" skills, "street smarts," and other interpersonal social skills.

We have learned that the physical structure of the brain undergoes changes that result in a higher level of executive function, including the ability to pay attention, encode information, plan, organize, and remember. When combined with this increased brain capacity, the high school curriculum teaches adolescents formal operational thought processes through developing scientific hypotheses in science and math courses; perspective taking in psychology, sociology, and anthropology classes; and providing new ideas about how the world can be represented and understood in art and humanities classes. Adolescents are able to think more abstractly and consider several possibilities simultaneously. Indeed, many adults acknowledge that a single teacher in one course changed their lives and started them down the developmental path that led to their vocational identity.

Adolescents assume a larger number of roles than children. For example, adolescents often have part-time work, engage in volunteer service activities, and may have a boyfriend/girlfriend even as they maintain the relationships of childhood, such as daughter, sister, niece, granddaughter, and neighbor. Adolescents also enter into relationships with adults who are neither their parents nor teachers, such as club or church leaders or sport coaches. The increased number of relationships and roles leads to numerous expectations placed upon adolescents, and often these expectations can compete for time and attention. For example, a teenage boy may be required to choose between an after-school part-time job or participation in school sports.

The peer groups of adolescents become less homogenous, allowing them greater psychosocial opportunities for development. Because high schools tend to draw students from a larger geographic area than elementary schools, adolescents are given the propinquity and the opportunity to socialize with individuals who are different, perhaps racially or ethnically or in other ways. (Propinquity means proximity or nearness.) Peer interaction is important in every developmental stage of life, but it is thought to be most important during adolescence because during this period adolescents are forging their self-identities. A person's peers provide the feedback and evaluation that are essential to acquiring a self-identity. It is a real friend who will tell you that you look fat in those jeans.

Although there is a tendency for adolescents to initiate friendships with those who are different from themselves, there is also the tendency for the formation of small friendship groups, sometimes referred to as cliques, on the basis on some shared characteristic. Frequently these cliques include all computer geeks, all athletes, or all individuals of a certain ethnic or racial groups. Cliques are large, visible groups with distinct patterns of interaction. Nonetheless, most cliques are school-based and often disband upon graduation.

As part of the process of individuation from the family and as part of the need for peer relationships, adolescents begin to spend more time away from home (Houser & Seligman, 1991). For the first time in life since early childhood dyadic friendships also become more important (both same-sex dyads and different-sex dyads). Conformity is an important quality of adolescent friendships, which is perhaps used as a defense against rejection and disapproval. It is thought that American adolescent dating was an invention of the 1920s (Modell, 1989), providing more proof that as times change each generation experiences different types of developmental stages.

Emerging Adulthood

- Identity exploration
- Instability
- Self-focus
- Feeling in-between
- Time and resources to make choices

AGES 19 TO 25

One developmental psychologist made an interesting observation: In American culture, the birthdays that end in 0 (zero) are often the most meaningful, such as 30, 40, 50, and 60. However, the 20th birthday is not as important as the 21st birthday (Capps, 2008). For a long time, the age of 21 was considered the legal age of adulthood. One birthday card reads, "Here's a joke for your 21st birthday. A guy goes into a bar....Finally!"

Emerging adulthood is considered a distinct, unique developmental stage because individuals in their late teens and early 20s do not consider themselves either adolescents or adults. Erikson first promulgated the idea that self-identity was a primary criterion for defining development stages. Emerging adults know that they have left adolescence but feel that they have not taken adult roles. A combination of biological processes, societal expectations, labor market constraints, and economic conditions has created the need for a transition or intermediate period between adolescence and adulthood. The need for more postsecondary education to enter many parts of the 21st century labor market shows one way that economic and labor market trends help define developmental stages.

Arnett (2006) identified these key features of the stage of emerging adulthood: (1) identity exploration, (2) instability, (3) self-focus, (4) feeling in-between, and (5) emerging adults who have had difficult childhoods are given the time and resources to direct their lives in more positive directions. The combination of added time, and few social commitments, allows the emerging adult to develop a positive self-identity. Indeed, one feature of the developmental stage of emerging adulthood is the use of self-identified criteria to determine when adulthood has been achieved. Throughout history individuals in their late teens and early 20s became heavily involved in political movements and ideologies of their times, perhaps because of their autonomy and freedom combined with their idealistic nature. When asked to recall one period of their lives, most individuals remember their adolescence and early adulthood, claiming that this period had the greatest influence on the person they became.

Another way in which the developmental stage of emerging adulthood differs from the stage of early adulthood is the use of self-identified, subjective markers by today's emerging adults. In the past adulthood was achieved when the individual completed the societal-defined, objective tasks of (1) leaving the parental home, (2) obtaining a full-time job or embarking upon a lifelong career, and (3) becoming married or entering into a lifelong romantic relationship. Arnett (1997) stated that young people, especially those from the individualistic culture of the United States, identify taking responsibility for one's actions, independent decision-making, and financial independence from parents as the criteria for reaching adulthood. Perhaps emerging adults place a great deal of importance upon adulthood and desire to "do it right the first time." In addition, if adulthood starts at age 18 or 20 and ends at 65, it is by far the longest stage of life. Why hurry?

Emerging adults are taking increased periods of time in order to investigate, explore, and try out educational and vocational choices. In the past 18- to 25-year-olds in the higher socioeconomic classes, perhaps had the time and money to defer adulthood. They had time to change majors in college, spend time traveling, and undertake foreign volunteer work. Using a Maslowian "hierarchy of needs" perspective, Ingehart (1977, 1986, 1990) argued that as entire generations become more educated and affluent, these societal conditions allow most 18 to 25 years to undertake these exploratory experiences, while earlier, poorer generations of 18 to 25 years were forced to meet lower-level needs earlier in their lives. Indeed, previous generations would have viewed today's emerging adults as self-involved and frivolous for spending years in these pursuits.

Exploration and experimentation in romantic attachments are more common among emerging adults, who are entering into long-term cohabiting relationships at a greater rate than any other generation. Emerging adults can point to the high divorce rates of their parents' generation as one motivator. Arnett (2000) suggested that the transitional and unpredictable nature of emerging adulthood leads to greater religious and belief diversity among this age group. For the first time in history, young adults are very religiously diverse, using elements from popular cultures and Eastern religions to form a unique combination of belief systems. This generational shift from mainstream

Christianity or Judaism may derive from the emerging adults' need to explore self-identity and challenge societal-imposed identities in the process. Two researchers (Milevsky & Leh, 2008) examined the religious beliefs of emerging adults by dividing the participants into two groups: the extrinsically religious and the intrinsically religious. Extrinsically religious individuals were affiliated with mainstream Christian churches or Jewish synagogues, while intrinsically religious individuals considered themselves to have a well-developed religious orientation but did not affiliate with a mainstream religion. They found that in this sample the intrinsically religious reported higher self-esteem.

One objective measure of achievement of adulthood is leaving the childhood home. For centuries this has been a straightforward and easily understood event. However, defining what leaving home means is complicated today; for example, in the past almost all people left the parental home to begin their own homes with their marriage partner and never returned to their parental homes for an extended time. Now adolescents leave the parental home for many different types of living arrangements; moreover, they often return to live for extended periods of time. The new joke is, "Your adult children have not left home until their storage boxes are out of your basement." Developmental psychologists use the terms "nest leaving" or "residential independence" to describe leaving home. Until the 1960s most women left the parental home in order to marry. Today most adolescents and young adults leave home in order to attend university or other educational institutions. In the 1970s 30% of this age group left home simply for greater independence or to form "nontraditional families" (Goldscheider & Goldscheider, 1999, p. 205), and 40% in the 1980s followed the same path for the same reason. "Non-traditional families are defined as single-parenthood or cohabitation" and "these new pathways began a spectacular increase in the 1960s" (p. 205).

The nest the children leave becomes the empty nest, but perhaps not for long, because increasing numbers of young adults are returning to live at home after substantial periods of time of living away from home. These young adults are no longer the same children who lived at home, and their parents often have become accustomed to their newfound freedom from responsibility. This is such a widespread occurrence that the present generation of young adults has been nicknamed the "Boomerang Generation." Moreover, these young adults often return home two or three times in order to "refuel" and "regroup." Interestingly, researchers have identified a gender-differentiated pathway to returning to the parental homes. Daughters are far less likely than sons to return home, and the rate of men returning home continues to climb. Rates for returning home are lower in homes with a stepparent or stepsiblings. Remember, it was Hansel and Gretel's wicked stepmother who took them into the woods and abandoned them.

BODY IMAGE

An individual's body image is the mental picture of himself or herself, including the physical self, physical appearance, sexuality, health, and physical skills. Body image is thus how one appears to himself or herself (Smart, 2001, 2009). The body is a reflection of oneself, and in a society obsessed with beauty, athletic prowess, and sexual allure, probably no one is entirely satisfied with her or her body image (Marantz, 1990).

Developmental stages influence the ways in which individuals view their bodies (Lerner & Jovanovic, 1990). Infants have no sense of a body image; although small children begin to develop a body image, it becomes very important in adolescence and emerging adulthood. Two authors explained: "adolescence is a time of exquisite body image sensitivity" (Bramble & Cukr, 1998, p. 285).

Perhaps most individuals are not aware that the comparison between their bodies and the idea of the ideal body has a great impact on their body image. However, the ideal body or bodily perfection does not exist (Etcoff, 1999). Therefore, many individuals, especially girls and women, judge themselves against an unattainable standard and find themselves lacking and falling short. Of course, it is possible to believe that one's body or one's appearance is of little importance. However, it is much more common to overvalue one's body image, most often in a negative way. All adolescents "know" that their entire self-identification should not be related to their body image. However, an individual's perceptions and evaluations about his or her body can affect social adjustment, interpersonal relationships, and general well-being (Biordi, Warner, & Knapik, 2006). Moreover, studies have shown that the personal appearance of individuals affects their lifetime earning potential. For men, these studies have shown that inches of height add up to greater earning power, while for women, weight can decrease earning power. Therefore, regardless of what our mothers have told us, there is more than just being beautiful on the inside (Macgregor, 1951; Macgregor et al., 1953; Love et al., 1987; Pruzinsky, 1990; Pruzinsky & Cash, 1990). Adults who considered themselves attractive during adolescence tend to have higher self-esteem and report higher levels of happiness (Paplia & Olds, 1992).

Two leading developmental scholars stated: "Bodily alterations, transitions, and turning points have the potential to open up new opportunities, alter life goals, and create stress" (McLeod & Almazan, 2004, p. 395). Acquiring a visible, disfiguring disability during adolescence would be a "bodily transition," especially for a girl, but probably would not be considered an event that created new opportunities.

Body image includes the individual's perception of his or her attractiveness, and body attractiveness is at times confused with the more inclusive concept of body image (Bramble & Cukr, 1998; Marantz, 1990). Part of a positive body image is the degree to which individuals are able to control their bodies, as seen in athletes and others who invest time and energy in exercise and other healthy practices in order to improve and control their bodies. Later in this chapter, a woman whose arms shake uncontrollably states that she wishes she could amputate her arm because of her desire to control her arm (Clare, 2010). Disabilities that have tremors or spasticity as common symptoms can lead to feeling a lack of control of one's body. In addition disabilities that are episodic, such as seizure disorders, and multiple sclerosis can also create a lack of control, although individuals with some of these types of episodic disabilities become expert in recognizing prodromal (warning) signs and can either abort the episode or find a safe place before the symptoms emerge.

Beauty is often considered a symbol or sign of virtue and goodness, a belief derived in part from our media (Hahn, 1988a, 1993a). For example, in Disney animated films the heroine is beautiful, young, and nondisabled, while the villains are unattractive and often have a disability. For example, children are often afraid of Captain Hook in *Peter Pan*. However, many people with disabilities (PWDs) use a hook at home because it is much more functional than a prosthetic hand; however, upon leaving home they often put on their plastic hand. Everyone knows that the individual is wearing a prosthetic hand, but others find it less distressing than the hook. This is not to assert that *Peter Pan* has singlehandedly created a fear of people who wear hooks. However, in a culture saturated with media, it is an easy step to assume that PWDs are twisted, tortured people who are continuously angry and bitter and that attractive people are automatically good and happy. Before the electronic media, the print media used the same analogies. For example, of the 16 books Charles Dickens wrote, 14 of them had characters with disabilities.

Though perhaps not on a conscious level, many believe that beautiful, attractive people are fulfilled people and that those who are not beautiful experience miserable lives. The study of physiognomy, the art of discovering personal character and personality by looking at an individual's outward appearance, contributed to the modern focus on beauty. Two authors (Mitchell & Synder, 2010) described physiognomy and its effect:

> Physiognomy became a paradigm of access to the ephemeral and intangible workings of the internal body. Speculative qualities such as moral integrity, honesty, truthworthiness, criminality, fortitude, cynicism, sanity, and so forth, suddenly became available for scrutiny by virtue of the "irregularities" of the body that enveloped them. For the physiognomist, the body allowed meaning to be inferred from the outside in; such speculative practice resulted in the ability to anticipate intangible qualities of one's personhood without having to await the "proof" of actions or the intimacy of a relationship developed over time. By "reasoning from the exterior to the interior," the trained physiognomist extracted the meaning of the soul without the permission or participation of the interpreted. (p. 282)

A feminist disability scholar (Thompson, 1997a) asserted that the cultural valuing and devaluing of physical appearance often make PWDs, especially women, feel that they have no place in the world.

In Beatrice Wright's theory of adjustment to physical disability, we learn that subordination of the physique and re-directing one's self-identity to aspects such as character, past experiences, relationships, or intelligence assists in adjusting to a physical disability. Elderly individuals are faced with the task of subordinating their physique as they age and their appearance and body changes.

For adolescents with disabilities, two disability scholars have suggested that negative feedback about their appearance will impede their adaptation to the disability:

> It is therefore conceivable that the social appraisals of a person's differences, vis-à-vis stigma and causal attributions, could impact the adjustment process of an individual with a visible disability....Yet what seems pivotal is the extent to which the inducement of OSA [objective self-awareness] may lead the individual to interpret the negative appraisals as being *realistically* based. In other words, can one's personal beliefs about oneself stand up against the perception that others believe differently—and for how long? (Phemister, & Crewe, 2007, p.150)

Adolescent men with disabilities also believe in the false stereotypes that beauty means virtue, intelligence, and happiness. Robert Neumann was diagnosed with arthritis as a teenager and recalled that these false stereotypes were worse than the arthritis.

> But as I look back on it now, I believe that seeing myself as I really was, was the first step in becoming comfortable with the person I am. Of course, what I did not realize then was that I was a victim, not just of a disease, but of that even more insidious social phenomenon...identified as the idolization of the normal physique....We believe that what is beautiful in conventional terms is good and we equate physical attractiveness with greater intelligence, financial success, and romantic opportunities. Lose that attractiveness, lose that physical perfection, the images imply, and gone as well are the chances for success in love and life. This is definitely not the type of foundation on which an adolescent's fragile self-concept is likely to develop a solid, confident base. (Neumann, 2007, p. 725)

DATING

Adolescent dating is an American innovation of the 1920s that is considered the gateway to romantic and sexual relationships and thus to long-term, committed relationships such as marriage. Erikson (1968) also viewed dating as an important part of identity formation in adolescence, especially the development of emotional intimacy. Individuals who were adept at forming close friendships in middle childhood tend to date more in adolescence (Newman & Newman, 2009). Thus dating can be considered a transition from same-sex friendships to more romantic relationships.

Early adolescence dating is different from late adolescence dating. Early dating relationships are typically of limited contact and short duration, and they may include "group dates." Late adolescence dating tends to have more of a couples orientation, is of longer duration, often involves sexual activity, and seems much like adult romantic relationships.

The biological stage of pubertal development involves the emergence of sexual attraction, while the greater autonomy of adolescents and their need to individuate from the family combine to make dating a very important activity. Erikson considered that establishing an identity is the task of adolescence, and dating provide one way to accomplish this. Self-disclosure may lead to sexual intimacy.

GENDER IDENTITY AND SEXUAL ORIENTATION

During adolescence one's gender identity, agreement with gender role expectations, and sexual orientation crystallize. Adolescent dating is an important part of each of these identities. Gender identity is the individual's combination of beliefs, attitudes, and values about being a man or a woman. In order to form a gender identity, the three components of gender must be integrated. These are biological, psychological, and social meanings.

Gender role expectations are created by cultures, governments, societies, religions, and relationships within the family and the peer group (Houser & Seligman, 1991).

These role expectations determine the appropriate behavior for each sex. Gender role standards change on a societal basis, and they change for an individual throughout the individual's lifetime. In the United States gender role standards are becoming more flexible, providing more choices and goals as well as fewer obstacles to achieving these goals.

Nonetheless, some gender role standards persist. For example, men and boys are thought to be more active, competitive, assertive, and achievement oriented than women and girls. In most cultures (including the United States), women are thought to be more nurturing and relationship oriented. Gender role preference is the degree to which an individual believes that he or she can meet role expectations and also the value the individual places on the role expectation of his or her sex. In some ways acceptance of one's gender role identity is an individual choice; however, in other important ways society makes these decisions. First, societal resources are allocated in terms of gender role expectations. For example, in the past athletic opportunities and access to higher education were not available to girls. Boys and men used to take pride in not knowing how to cook, and cooking classes in high school were not offered to boys. Second, society can enforce these gender role expectations by shaming or avoiding individuals who chose not to accept these roles.

Up until the 1950s, for example, the goals of adolescent girls often included finding a good husband (especially a husband who had status, position, and money) and becoming a good mother and housekeeper after the marriage (Dush, Taylor, & Kroeger, 2008). Occasionally, when the children were a bit older, the woman could engage in community and civic activities. Therefore, the behavior expectations of adolescent girls included being perceived as a nurturing and caring friend, as being attractive as possible, and dating. Gender role expectations of men required adolescent boys to determine a career path, prepare to enter university, become assertive and competitive (especially through athletics) and date many girls. As we read about these expectations, they seem to reflect a quaint, sweet, and innocent time. On the other hand, these expectations can also appear restrictive, simplistic, and confining for both sexes. Some vestiges of these gender role expectations can be seen in the workplace, where women typically earn less than men, a situation that has been stable for decades in spite of higher educational levels for women and the women's movement.

Sexual orientation refers to the erotic, romantic sexual attraction to members of the opposite sex, one's own sex, or both sexes. Sexual orientation can be understood as a continuum with one end being completely heterosexual (attracted to the opposite sex) or completely homosexual or gay (attracted to the same sex). The disability community has used the methods of the Gay Rights movement; PWDs understand that there is nothing wrong, pathological, or deviant about gay, and likewise know that there is nothing wrong with people with disabilities or the disability itself (Cohler & Hammack, 2007; Corbett & Bregante, 1993). Just like the gay pride movement, the disability rights movement knows that deviance is in the eye of the beholder. Gays in the United States have moved away from attempting to pass as straight to managing the unwarranted stigma of being gay then finally to becoming an identity group in the United States (Rosenfield, 2003). PWDs have followed the same evolutionary path. First, they tried to pass as nondisabled if they had an invisible disability; second, they were taught stigma management techniques; presently PWDs are beginning to see themselves as a political force, part of which entails taking pride in their disabilities.

Dating can enhance self-esteem, stimulate emotional growth, and create stronger self-identity. On the other hand, dating can be a source of frustration and disappointment and may lead to decreased self-esteem (Bregman & Castles, 1988). Not all romantic feelings are reciprocated. Dating can be an exciting, novel experience and a source of status among one's peers. Furman and Wehner (1997) asserted that dating fills four important needs: affiliation, attachment, caregiving, and sexual gratification.

MARRIAGE

Until recently marriage was considered one of the defining criteria of adulthood. It may appear that marriage is still important when we hear of 30-year-olds being pressured to marry and "grow up." For centuries marriage was considered a necessary and positive part of adulthood and a relationship that religion sanctioned. Indeed, in the past God (or some other deity) was considered part of the marital relationships. Marriage was a contract in which two individuals shared a vision of the future, had children, and worked together—at least that was the ideal of marriage. In preindustrial societies the family worked together at home, doing hard physical labor. Family life was like *Little House on the Prairie,* with Pa working in the fields and Ma working in the kitchen. Without a network of government-sponsored social and health agencies, the family took care of most of the social and medical needs of their members. High infant mortality rates, the lack of reliable birth control methods, and the need for child labor all contributed to the large number of children in families. Both women and men married early in life.

Since the end of the Baby Boom families have had fewer children. Significantly, the age of first marriage for both men and women has risen, and types of cohabitation other than marriage became common in the 1980s. Until recently children were thought necessary for adults to have fulfilled and happy lives. The first decade of the 21st century saw a proliferation and acceleration of all these trends. About 29% of children under the age of 18 now live with a parent or parents who are not married, a 500% increase from 1960. Fifteen percent of children have parents who are divorced or separated, and 14% have parents who were never married. Almost half of all American adults (44%) report that they have lived with a partner without being married, and for those within the 30 to 49 year age range, the percentage rose to 57%.

Both the perception and reality of family life and marriage have changed drastically, and the changes are driven by emerging adults in the age range of 18 to 29. Most Americans agree with the statement, "There are several ways to have a successful family life" (Pew Research Center, 2010). Same-sex couples with children, single parents, parents who have never married, interracial parents, and blended families with stepparents and stepsiblings are now perceived in a positive light. According to the Pew Research Center, the U.S. Census data show that marriage in the United States has hit an all-time low of 52% for all adults 18 and older. In 1972 72% were married. Obviously, in 1972 those children not in a conventional mother–father married relationship were a distinct minority. In 1960 68% of all individuals in the 20- to 30-year-old range were married, compared with 26% in 2008. Demographers are now questioning if this decrease in marriage will continue.

There is also a new "marriage gap" related to income. College-educated adults with good incomes are more likely to marry, while those without a college education and in lower socioeconomic levels marry less frequently, citing economic security as a condition of marriage. The Pew Research Center (2010) stated

> In 2008, a 16 percentage point gap separated marriage rates of college graduates (64%) and those with a high school diploma or less (48%). In 1950, this gap had been just four percentage points (76% vs. 72%). The survey finds that those with a high school diploma or less are just as likely as those with a college degree to say that they want to marry. But they place a higher premium than college graduates (38% vs. 21%) on financial stability as a very important reason to marry. (p. 1)

Whatever the configuration of the family, the Pew Research Center found that most American adults consider their family to be the most important and satisfying aspect of their lives.

CAREER DEVELOPMENT

Like theories of human growth and development, career development theories emerged in the United States after World War II, and most of these theories envisioned career development as a process rather than a one-time event. Also, like theories of human development, career theories considered white, middle-class males without disabilities, thinking that these individuals would have careers with an upward trajectory while the remainder of Americans would simply have jobs. These career development theories were based on the concept of individual choice with many different options. During the 1960s, 1970s, and 1980s, these theories expanded to include women and racial and ethnic minorities. Americans with disabilities were not included in any of the career development theories.

There were career theories that held that boys began a developmental process of choosing a career, and, therefore, an individual could be considered "on-time" or "delayed" in his career choice (Crites, 1973; Super, 1977; Ginzberg, 1984). Other theories held that individuals' personality types played a significant role in the choice of work environment (Holland, 1985), and one theorist, Anne Roe (1956), considered the family of origin and the home environment to influence the choice of career.

Only one of these theories (Krumboltz, Mitchell, & Gelatt, 1975) considered the labor market and the economic climate and the idea that only affluent, well-educated males in developed nations have the possibility of choosing from among a wide array of opportunities. Individuals who have families who can provide resources during appropriate choice points in life have more possibilities.

Career development is thought to be based on the individual's expression of his interests, use of skills learned at college, and the provision of advancement opportunities for the individual's growth, learning, increased responsibility, contribution, and pay. Upward progress through the various levels of careers is clearly demarcated, and individuals are aware of being "on-time," "ahead of the curve," or "delayed." Careers, therefore, define the individual, and the individual defines his career. Those in the lower socioeconomic groups (without college educations) find their job choices to be circumscribed to a few options. Obviously developing one's career track is more satisfying than working a job.

Feminist scholars hold that the women's movement and affirmative action policies have rewarded white women with college educations. For racial and ethnic minorities, recent immigrants, and PWDs, it is difficult to initiate a meaningful lifelong career.

For PWDs, a combination of governmental work disincentives and the unwarranted prejudice and discrimination of society prevents them from working. If PWDs have a double minority status (women, gays, or racial and ethnic minorities), their reported rates of employment are even lower than for men with disabilities. An archaic complex system of governmental work disincentives consists of providing subsistence-level support with medical care to PWDs. To take responsibility for their disability-related and living expenses and to forfeit their government aid, PWDs would need a very large income. For most PWDs it is economic stupidity to work, simply because they cannot earn enough to risk losing their benefits. The British scientist and author Steven Hawking can afford to pay for a personal care attendant and expensive medications from his own pocket. Most PWDs (or people without disabilities for that matter) cannot earn enough to pay for these costs. Harris polls have consistently shown that most PWDs state that they would like to work. The federal government is experimenting with laws and policies that would allow PWDs to work while maintaining some of their benefits.

World War II was considered the "Golden Age of Employment" for PWDs. Both women (Rosie the Riveter) and PWDs were needed to fuel the war economy when large numbers of men left for military service. PWDs in large numbers found work (Hahn, 1997). Indeed, PWDs have been termed the "industrial reserve army," allowed to work when the nation needs workers (Hahn, 1997, p. 173). Obviously neither PWDs nor their disabilities changed; to the contrary, it was fluctuations in the labor market that suddenly made PWDs employable. Like women, PWDs left their jobs at the end of the war when the men returned to reclaim their jobs. Hahn (1997) described this trend as follows:

> In World War II, physical exams and other conditions of employment were waived by many corporations to open jobs for disabled persons, and other members of the industrial reserve army, who compiled favorable records of productivity and work performance. During the war, the unemployed rate among disabled adults temporarily declined, only to rise again when these job requirements were reinstated to permit the hiring of returning veterans. (p. 173)

Since 1990 the Americans with Disabilities Act (ADA) provides PWDs protection under the law to ensure that PWDs do not experience discrimination in the job market. The ADA is clear in mandating that PWDs must meet all the job qualifications and be able to perform the essential functions of the job. Clear, specific, written job qualifications and functions must be in place. The ADA does not mandate blind bus drivers or hiring any PWD whose disability prevents him or her from performing essential job functions.

Assistive technology, such as computerized equipment, voice recognition software, and other job-related devices, has allowed many PWDs to work. We have learned that the first theories of career development were based on the idea of almost unlimited choice. In the past most PWDs had a very limited choice of jobs. Indeed, entrapment in occupational roles or occupational stereotyping was so common that it gained a derisive nickname, the "Bulova Syndrome." Such occupational role entrapment was obviously enforced by PWODs, and the interests, skills, and talents of PWDs were not considered when they were placed in jobs. The name Bulova Syndrome refers to the practice of enrolling men in wheelchairs in watch repair schools. This is not a criticism of the Bulova watch company, which indeed was one of the few companies to provide work for PWDs. It is a criticism of assigning PWDs to only a limited range of jobs because of their disability and their gender. For example, deaf men were placed in printing press work because their deafness would be an asset in a noisy workplace, deaf women were typists and data encoders, and blind men were often trained to be piano tuners or to work in photographic dark rooms (Holcomb, 1990; Sinick, 1969).

This occupational role entrapment was supported by the irrational idea that those with physical disabilities also had intellectual disabilities, while having PWDs work in the "solitary trades," such as watch repair, would let PWODs avoid the sight of a PWD. Individuals of racial and ethnic minority groups understand occupational role entrapment. For many PWDs it was simply easier to accept the assigned jobs than to fight a system that had been in place for centuries.

For a young PWD, it necessary to have role models who are professionally successful, have disabilities, and have a personal relationship with the young PWD (rather than a poster of a "celebrity" disability superhero, whom the young person will never meet). Consider the differences in these two types of role models.

> When I was about twenty-two, I had an unexpected, important experience. I worked for one summer for a prominent woman economist who happened to have cerebral palsy. I can't tell you my surprise when I met her at the job interview. It was a bit like looking at myself in the mirror. Betty had a powerful effect on me. I was impressed that a woman with cerebral palsy, not a very socially acceptable disability in our culture, could become so successful in her career, particularly in a "man's field," anti-trust economics. I was even more impressed that she was married.... It never occurred that I had any alternative, that I could have *both* a career and a romantic life. Betty's lifestyle, her successful marriage to an interesting, dynamic man made me question for the first time the negative assumptions that I had made about my social potential. (Rousso, 1993, p. 2)

In the National Public Radio's *Disability History Project,* a man with a disability recalled seeing an adult with a disability at work and it "scared this young man to death."

> One of the first people I saw working with a disability was the crippled newsie on the corner—the guy who couldn't use his legs who had a little knuckle board who dragged himself around to sell newspapers. I knew that except for the money my family had, that could very easily be me and it scared me to death. (Tomorrow's Children, 1998c).

SPINAL CORD INJURIES

Traumatic spinal cord injuries (SCIs) occur most frequently to young men between the ages of 16 and 30, the years of adolescence and emerging adulthood. Richards, Kewman, and Pierce (2000) explained:

> A great deal of what is known about the demographics and etiology of SCI comes from the collaborative database...funded by the National Institute on Disability and Rehabilitation Research. From that source, we know that more than half of all injuries occur in the 16–30 year old age group and that men make up 82% of the cases.... This percentage has changed little in the more than 20 years that the database has been in operation. (p. 11)

The survival rate of individuals who sustain a SCI has increased dramatically, as has their life expectancy. Overall their life expectancy is approximately 85% of the general populations. Therefore, those with SCIs do not live as many years on average as those without SCIs, but they may live decades after their accidents. In spite of these improvements in life expectancy, societal attitudes and architectural accessibility have tended to lag behind these medical successes.

Car accidents cause 46% of all traumatic SCIs, 16% are the result of falls, stab and gunshot wounds cause 12%, and diving accidents account for 10%. Traumatic SCIs are differentiated from other types of SCIs caused by cancer or neuromuscular diseases. There are well-coordinated government programs for the prevention of traumatic SCIs such as promoting using seat belts, wearing helmets, and avoiding alcohol and drugs while driving or participating in sports (see Table 13.1).

SCIs are defined as producing paraplegia, quadriplegia, or tetraplegia, according to the level of the injury to the spinal column. The classifications of these types of paralysis is based upon the lowest level at which useful motor function is spared. Although these are somewhat arbitrary demarcations, paraplegia is produced by an injury at the 12th thoracic vertebrae, and the individual typically has motor function above the waist. Quadriplegia results from injury at the eighth cervical vertebrae or higher, and the individual is usually paralyzed from the neck down. Therefore, the higher the spinal lesion, the more of the body is paralyzed. SCIs are also defined as either complete or incomplete. Complete injuries typically result in total sensory and motor loss below

TABLE 13.1

Grouped Etiology by Age at Injury

Etiology n (%)	<15	16–30	31–45	46–60	61–75	76–98	Total
Vehicular Accidents	343 (37.4)	6,347 (46.5)	2,809 (44.5)	1,405 (38.5)	535 (30.1)	132 (24.4)	11,571
Violence	214 (23.3)	3,196 (23.4)	1,050 (16.6)	270 (7.4)	47 (2.6)	7 (1.3)	4,784
Sports	219 (23.9)	1,967 (14.4)	435 (6.9)	137 (3.8)	40 (2.2)	3 (0.6)	2,801
Falls	73 (8.0)	1,439 (10.5)	1,438 (22.8)	1,359 (37.3)	880 (49.5)	349 (64.5)	5,538
Other	68 (7.4)	699 (5.1)	568 (9.0)	468 (12.8)	275 (15.5)	47 (8.7)	2,125
Unknown	0 (0.0)	11 (0.1)	10 (0.2)	6 (0.2)	2 (0.1)	3 (0.6)	32
Total	917	13,659	6,310	3,645	1,779	541	26,851

Source: National Spinal Cord Injury Statistical Center, University of Alabama at Birmingham, 2009 Annual Statistical Report, February 2010.

the level of the lesion. Finally, there can be multilevel crush injuries of the spinal cord. In a single sentence, a young man tells of the acute onset of an SCI, his accompanying feelings of shock, and his need to deal with a diagnosis: "I was 22, a recent college graduate, and all of a sudden, I'm a T8 bilateral paraplegic, whatever the hell that is!" (Crewe, 1997, p. 32)

The educational level of people with SCIs tends to be lower than that of the general population, even when considering the median age of this population (Richards, Kewman, & Pierce, 2000). In the age range of 18 to 21, 66% of patients are at least high school graduates compared to 86% in the general population (Krause & Anson, 1997).

Substance abuse is often found among individuals with SCIs, and in acute care and physical rehabilitation centers detoxification becomes part of the program of care. Most surveys of SCI individuals reveal a substantially higher lifetime and immediate preinjury frequency of substance abuse. Therefore, substance abuse often has contributed to the accident or injury. There is also growing evidence that a "disproportionate number of persons with SCI" have preinjury histories of alcohol abuse, difficulty in coping with life, and depression (Elliott & Frank, 1996; Judd, et al., 1989; Tate, 1993). Individuals with SCIs are routinely monitored for suicide, especially during the first few years after the injury. Suicide rates among SCI individuals are thought to range between 5% and 10%, compared to a 1% rate in the general population. Suicide is carried out through overt means (such as a gunshot), self-neglect (such as allowing pressure sores to become infected), or a refusal of necessary care. Those SCI individuals most prone to suicide have histories of drug and substance abuse, psychiatric care, criminal activities, family problems, and prior suicide attempts.

There are many secondary conditions of SCIs including spasticity, autonomic hyper-reflexia (HR), and pain. HR is considered a life-threatening emergency, characterized by a sudden onset of headache and high blood pressure, fast heartbeat, sweating, and blurred vision (Krause et al., 1999). Because blood pressure can reach dangerous levels very quickly, HR must be closely monitored. Occasionally fluid collects within the spinal at the site of the injury and can cause further nerve damage. Urinary tract infections are common, and pressure sores must be cared for to prevent infection. Pain is caused by abnormal sensations below the level of injury and can become chronic. One estimate of the incidence of pain is 48% to 98% (Ragnarsson, 1997), although any estimate of pain is based on subjective self-reporting. Interestingly, "people who are injured from gunshot are more likely to develop post-SCI pain" (Richards, Kewman, & Pierce, 2000, p. 16).

Treatment of SCIs is expensive, and the functional limitations are extensive. Pain and depression often follow SCIs and may last for years. One of the most effective treatments for SCI is peer counseling, in which people with similar injuries provide emotional support and model successful coping. Independent Living, a federally funded service, provides activities, socialization, and assistive technology. Perhaps more important, peer counselors and Independent Living Centers can decrease the isolation of those with SCIs. Many individuals with SCIs are able to return to work or enroll in further schooling.

TRAUMATIC BRAIN INJURIES

Like SCIs, traumatic brain injuries (TBIs) are most likely to occur during the years of adolescence and emerging adulthood (Perlesz, Kinsella, & Crowe, 1999). The decade of the 1970s marked the beginning of brain injury rehabilitation because the development of emergency medicine allowed individuals with TBIs to survive their injuries. Before the 1970s there were very few TBI survivors. According to the National Head Injury Foundation, a TBI is

> an insult to the brain caused by an external force, that may produce a diminished or altered state of consciousness of varying length and which results in impairment of cognitive abilities or physical functional. It can also result in a disturbance of behavior or emotional functioning. These impairments may be either temporary or permanent, and may cause partial or total functional disability or psychological maladjustment. (Dikmen & Jaffe, 1994, p. 130)

There are many unreported cases of TBIs; when someone complains of a headache, one of the first questions asked is "Have you been in a car accident?" There are two basic types of TBIs: open-head TBIs, in which missiles penetrate the brain, and closed-head injuries caused when a moving object strikes the head and accelerates the brain inside the skull. Most open-head, noncombat injuries are the result of gunshots. For closed-head noncombat injuries, car accidents are the single largest cause of TBIs, followed by falls.

Many TBIs are also accompanied by other injuries causing physical disabilities, such as SCIs. The symptoms and results of TBIs often make returning to work or school difficult, simply because of the broad range of cognitive deficits (Kozloff, 1987). These cognitive deficits may include an inability to focus and maintain attention, a diminished ability to remember or to learn new information, basic language difficulties, difficulty in analyzing new and complex situations, impulsivity and lack of behavioral regulation, and reduced information processing skills. Physicians and rehabilitation specialists consider each TBI to be unique because of this wide range of cognitive deficits. Perhaps the most difficult result of a TBI can be impaired self-awareness. Malec and Ponsford (2000) explained:

> Impaired self-awareness [makes individuals with TBIs] oblivious to adjustment issues and behavioral problems apparent to staff and to their close others. Sexuality and intimacy were often problematic, not because of physical sexual dysfunction, but because of reduced libido, relationship problems resulting from personality changes, or disinhibited and inappropriate sexual and interpersonal behaviors resulting from frontal cerebral damage.
>
> A...major set of obstacles to a circumscribed cognitive rehabilitation approach to brain injury rehabilitation was the impaired self-awareness that commonly resulted from brain injury and the catastrophic emotional reactions that occurred as more accurate self-awareness of deficits began to emerge. Some people are difficult to engage in any type of rehabilitation after brain injury because they do not recognize the deficits that are the focus of rehabilitation efforts.... However, increased self-awareness of deficits is commonly associated with the onset of depression or other negative emotional reactions. (pp. 418–419)

We have learned that disabilities are categorized not according to cause, but by symptoms. Although TBIs are caused by physical damage to the brain, they are considered cognitive disabilities because the symptoms impair cognitive functioning. Any type of vocational rehabilitation would be difficult if the individual is not capable of learning new information and cannot remember previously used knowledge and skills (Weinberg & Sterritt, 1991).

One sister described her adult brother with a TBI:

> My brother is in a wheelchair. He can no longer walk. He has problems eating and talking. My brother had a high IQ before the accident. As a result of this he remembers all that he could do before the car accident. He can no longer dress himself or go to the bathroom by himself. So what kind of quality of life is left for him? No one can answer that for us. (Degeneffe, & Lee, 2010, p. 32)

Individuals between the ages of 15 and 24 years have the highest incidence of TBIs, and males outnumber females by more than a ratio of two to one. Dikmen and Jaffe (1994) stated, "Alcohol intoxication is a contributory factor in approximately 50 percent of the cases" (pp. 130–131).

"THRILLS AND CHILLS" PERSONALITY

Especially for males, the years of adolescence and emerging adulthood are a time when sensation seeking, impulsivity, and seeking out unduly dangerous recreational activities are common. After people reach adulthood, many of these behaviors cease, or individuals enter professions that have the possibility of danger, such as the military or police work. The "thrills and chills" personality describes someone who is easily bored, is competitive, seeks out new and difficult adventures, likes physical activity, and often engages in "extreme" sports "that provide unusual sensations of speed or defiance of gravity, such as parachuting, scuba diving or skiing... They continue seeking sensation through social activities like, parties, social drinking, and sex" (Goma-i-Freixanet, 2004, p. 187).

These types of experiences and activities can result in disabilities, especially SCIs and TBIs. Impulsivity is defined as "actions that are poorly conceived, prematurely expressed, unduly risky, or inappropriate to the situation and result in undesirable outcomes" (Tansey, 2010, p. 4). Because impulsive individuals are less likely to learn from experience, either their own or that of others, they often repeat the same mistakes (Stelmark, 2004). One author explained that rather than taking precautions, the sensation-seeking individual will tend to abandon them when the perceived risk is greater.

The popular belief is that people tend to think that they are invulnerable, that is, they expect misfortunes to happen to others and not ourselves. This optimistic bias holds for a wide range of health conditions and other outcomes. Weinstein (1980) used the term unrealistic optimism to define it. This theory draws attention to risk perception and the ways in which it might be mediated by experience. A recent work on a nation sample of motorcyclists (Rutter et al., 1998) showed that the perceptions of risk predicted subsequent behavior, though generally not in the direction of precaution adoption but of precaution abandonment: the greater the perceived risk at time one, the more frequent the risky behavior at time two (one year later) (Goma-i-Freixanet, 2004, p. 186).

Another developmental scholar (Berk, 2001) cited "the adolescent personal fable, which leads teenagers to be so wrapped up in their uniqueness" that they conclude that they cannot be injured or acquire a disability or die (p. 632). Berk concluded that individuals gain the capability to think relativistically only in adulthood and can therefore weigh the risks and dangers of activities only then.

Zuckerman (1994) is considered the leading authority on sensation-seeking (SS). He determined that SS is highly correlated with drug abuse and other types of risky behaviors. Zuckerman proposed that SS is a result of neurological and biological factors, finding that levels of certain neurotransmitters, hormones, and immature development of the dorsolateral prefrontal cortex of the brain contributed to SS. Further, as the person ages, changes and maturation in these brain structures and changing levels of hormones and neurotransmitters often decrease levels of SS.

Arnett recognized the importance of the individually defined goals and activities of the emerging adulthood years. However, he also recognized the opportunity for risky, impulsive behaviors that these added years of independence and autonomy allow. These neurological and biological factors of SS also correspond to the high rates of SCI and TBI of young males between the ages of 18 and 25.

Avoiding disability can be viewed as a form of efficiency, relieving society of the responsibility and expense of rehabilitation. Cockerham (1998) explained the relationship between differing political systems and their views of accountability for both the causes of disability and its treatment.

> Marxist scholars like Howard Waitzkin and Vicente Navarro claim that an emphasis on individual responsibility for leading a healthy life excuses the larger society from direct accountability in health matters. Waitzkin (1999) maintains that capitalism puts the burden of being healthy squarely on the individual, rather than seeking collective solutions to health problems. The emphasis in capitalist societies on healthy lifestyles is seen as an effort to displace the responsibility for health from the social system and its health sector down individuals. (p. 99)

Substituting "safety-oriented lifestyle" for "healthy lifestyle," we can read this excerpt as an opinion that if individuals willingly choose to engage in risky, dangerous activities, then it is not reasonable to expect the public purse to pay for their rehabilitation. The public purse consists of insurance and tax dollars. Are individuals expected to change their entire personality and lifestyle simply to avoid illness, injury, or disability?

ALCOHOL AND SUBSTANCE ABUSE AMONG ADOLESCENTS AND EMERGING ADULTS

We have learned that both SCIs and TBIs are more common among adolescents and emerging adults than individuals in any other developmental stage (Yoshida, 1993). Often alcohol and substance abuse are also contributing factors in the cause of these injuries. According to the U.S. Department of Health and Human Services 2006 National Survey of Drug Use and Health (NSDUH), an estimated 22.6 million individuals aged 12 or older (9.2% of the American population) were classified with substance dependence. The illegal drugs with the highest levels of use were marijuana, followed by cocaine and pain relievers. In 2006 the age group with the highest percentage of substance dependence was adults aged 18 to 25, with 21.3% of this age group involved. Youths aged 12 to 17 was the age group that had the next highest level of use, with 8%

reporting substance dependence. After age 25 substance use drops substantially; only 7.2% of adults aged 26 or older were substance dependent.

When only the population of individuals with substance abuse or dependence is considered, in 2006 57.4% were youths aged 12 to 17, 36.9% were young adults between the ages of 18 to 25, and 24.1% were adults aged 26 or older. If we consider ages 12 to 25 to encompass adolescence and emerging adulthood, by far the majority of Americans who abuse substances are adolescents and emerging adults. There are also gender differences in the use of illegal substances. Among males aged 12 or older, the rate of substance dependence or use is twice as high as the rate for females (12.3% vs. 6.3%). However, among youths aged 12 to 17 rates for both males and females were about equal.

After reviewing "six long-term prospective national and regional prospective national and regional studies from Britain, Finland, and the United States that together encompass birth through to the late 40s," researchers were able to predict adult alcohol use and abuse (Schulenberg & Maggs, 2008, p. 1). Schulenberg and Maggs summarize:

> Developmental timing is an important consideration when understanding the causes and course of alcohol use and abuse. It matters *when* experiences occur and characteristics become manifest in regard to their meaning, and sequelae across the lifespan.... Many problem behaviors become normative during adolescence and early adulthood. (p. 2)

DISABILITY AND ALCOHOL AND SUBSTANCE ABUSE

Alcohol and substance abuse often play a role in causing disabilities such as TBIs and SCIs (see Table 13.2). Indeed, drug and alcohol rehabilitation is often a routine part of TBI and SCI rehabilitation. Acute hospitalization immediately following the trauma is often considered a "detox" period. Substance abuse counselors determine whether the

TABLE 13.2

Estimated Percentage of Illicit Drug Usage in the United States Population According to Gender, Age, and Race

	Ever used (%)	Used past year (%)	Used past month (%)
Total Population	46.1	14.4	8.1
Gender			
Male	50.8	16.8	10.2
Female	41.6	12.1	6.1
Age (Years)			
12–17	27.7	11.7	6.1
18–25	59.2	34.2	20.1
26–34	46.3	10.2	5.8
Race			
Caucasians	48.9	14.5	8.1
Hispanics	37.3	13.9	7.6
African Americans	44.7	16	9.7

Source: National Household Survey on Drug Abuse: Population Estimates 2005.

alcohol or substance abuse was preinjury or postinjury. Typically preinjury substance and alcohol abuse is more difficult to overcome because the individual has a longer history of abuse. One author who wrote about TBIs and SCIs explained:

> A preinjury pattern of chronic alcohol abuse or dependence is predictive of numerous negative outcomes after TBI and SCI. Preinjury alcohol abuse is associated with increased risk of mortality and more severe brain lesions. Patients with a history of alcohol abuse demonstrate poorer neuropsychological test performance 1-month and 1-year postinjury..., are less likely to successfully integrate back into the community and are at higher risk for recurrent TBI.
>
> People with SCI who had premorbid alcohol problems were found to spend less time in productive activities such as rehabilitation activities...and to have higher rates of suicide...than SCI patients who did not have a history of alcohol problems. (Bombardier, 2000, p. 401)

For all age groups PWDs have a much higher rate of alcohol and substance abuse than the general population. The causes for these higher rates of use are thought to be self-medication for pain and/or depression, the PWDs' sense of entitlement (they "deserve something for having a disability"), the "turning a blind eye" or enabling by others who also think that PWDs "deserve something," and the legitimate use of narcotic painkillers during medical rehabilitation that often leads to illegal substance abuse. For PWDs who spend long periods of time in rehabilitation centers, boredom and a sense of isolation from friends and families may be causative factors. Often PWDs are receiving prescriptions from two or more physicians, who may be unaware that patients are getting prescriptions from other doctors.

According to the *American Journal of Psychiatry*, opiates have a powerful "muting" effect on the disorganizing and threatening effects of rage and aggression. An individual with schizophrenia might be using narcotics to become organized and to decrease depression. Alcohol is often used as a sleeping aid.

The use of drugs and alcohol can delay recovery and healing for individuals with traumatic injuries and may produce serious secondary conditions. In those with SCIs alcohol and drug use interfere with health maintenance behaviors (such as caring for pressure sores), impede coordination, and impair memory and judgment so that compliance with medication regimens is often difficult. For individuals with TBIs, alcohol and other drugs can cause further cognitive damage and impairments. For those with seizure disorders, alcohol, cocaine, and amphetamines lower the seizure threshold. Many individuals with intellectual disabilities take anticonvulsant medications that interact with alcohol and drugs. The use of alcohol can mask the symptoms of psychiatric disabilities, thus lengthening the prediagnostic period. In diabetes and blindness caused by glaucoma, the vascular damage caused by alcohol exacerbates these conditions. In individuals with degenerating disabilities, such as some types of blindness, alcohol and other drugs may be used at each level of loss. Those with intellectual disabilities (mental retardation) and learning disabilities often use drugs and alcohol to deal with the social isolation and constant rejection. Everyone, or almost everyone, likes to be liked.

> ### Developmental Tasks of Adolescents and Emerging Adults With Disabilities
> - Continued management of the disability
> - Acceptance by peers
> - Integration of body image and self-concept
> - Establishment of sexual identity
> - Establishment of interdependence

A mother of a child with a disability described adolescence:

> Puberty, hormones, growth spurt, sexual maturation, decision making, risk taking, moodiness, peers, identity—the descriptors of adolescence are the essence of the challenge. Moreover, the broadening world of the adolescent is often a source of parental anxiety. It has been said that all adolescents think they are immortal, invincible, and infertile. This may be a bit too broad, but there is truth in it, nonetheless. All of this is compounded when disabilities, particularly those involving cognition, behavior, communication, and impulsivity, are present. (Berry, 2009, p. 145)

ACCEPTANCE BY PEERS

A survey of individuals with psychiatric disabilities asked, "What are some examples of the worst discrimination you have experienced?" Many replied "I'm sick of losing friends," and another wrote "friends who have abandoned me." Another question asked respondents if their psychiatric disabilities limited them in any way. One individual wrote, "no job, no friends" (Stefan, 2001, p. 14).

A sister of a man with a TBI related the following:

> The hardest thing for me to see is the way his friends and girlfriends treat him. Once the center of attention, now nobody wants to be around him. Inside he's the most friendly, kind-hearted, and loving person I know. I guess it pisses me off when people that used to love him have completely deserted when being with him takes more effort than it did before. I'm afraid he's lonely, and that he always will be somewhat lonely because of something he can't control. (Degeneffe & Lee, 2010, p. 32)

A survey of individuals with physical disabilities revealed the same type of responses, but there were such responses as "there are certain people that I love dearly that I have to restrict association with, because they're not positive" (Putnam et al., 2003, p. 41). A trainer of mental health workers who also has a mental illness teaches the importance of hope. Although she is speaking to professionals, this advice could be given to friends and family members. Note the way in which she writes "just one person" twice.

> I think hope is really a major issue. Professionals must instill a sense of hope in people and their families. Always give the individual logical, concrete examples

of why they should be hopeful. When I speak to consumers (clients), I ask them, "In your suicidal days, were you able to hang on because you had one, just one person who believed in you?" I also ask, "How many of you have come farther in your recovery than you thought possible because someone, just one person had hope for you?" When I ask just those questions, almost all the hands in the audience go up. They tell me that they got through suicidal times because someone had hope for them. The best advice I can give to professionals is to encourage people. Provide a sense of hope. You may be saving someone's life. You may be making a lifelong difference to an individual. (Mackelprang & Salsgiver, 1999, 186)

In the following story a teenager with a spinal cord injury described his friends as "drifting away." This phrase captures the gradual loss of friends.

Of course, there are some things that I wish I could have changed. Initially, everyone rallies around you, you know—they're supportive. All of the friends I had at the time of the accident were right there—right at the beginning. Then, as time went on, one by one they kind of drifted away, slowly. I think it was because they obviously didn't know how to react to me—and I certainly didn't know how to make things easier on them. I was having a hard enough time trying to figure out what was happening to me. I don't know if I pushed them away or if they felt that I wasn't the same person. It was a very gradual thing, but most of them just kind of drifted off. And I drifted off into myself. (Souders, 1993, pp. 153–154)

When friends and peers "drift away," the family must assume more responsibility.

There are also stories in which friends provided support and acceptance and, in some cases, helped the PWD with the disability (Anson, Stanwyck, & Krause, 1993). In the first story, the teen-aged boy acquired a spinal cord injury and friends gave him a personally defined reason (a Grateful Dead concert) to engage fully in his physical rehabilitation.

My friends came up to visit as usual and said that [my favorite group] the Grateful Dead were playing here in November. My mind was back, but I had to get my strength. The doctors said I would have to sit 4 to 5 hours straight if I were to go to the concert. Every time I got into the wheelchair, I blacked right out. Each day for only a short time, I would sit in a semi-reclined position determined to reach my goal. After a couple of days, I was up to three hours. The day of the show I reached my goals and I was psyched. The concert was the first time I had been out of the hospital. I had reached my destination. (Scherer, 1993, p. 22)

A teenager who sustained extensive burns came to the rehabilitation center and played ping pong with him.

When I got burned at age 18, I found out who my real friends were: They were the ones who came to see me and they still are my friends. . . . They made me use my burned hand to play games like ping-pong, so it wouldn't get stiff. (Holaday & McPhearson, 1997, p. 349)

INTEGRATION OF THE BODY IMAGE AND THE SELF-CONCEPT

One PWD wrote about the difficulty of integrating her body image with her disability:

> I think about my disabled body. For too long, I hated my trembling hands, my precarious balance, my spastic muscles so repeatedly overtaken with tension and tremors, [and I] tried to hide them at all costs. More than once I wished to amputate my right arm so it wouldn't shake. Self-mutilation is shame of the baldest kind. All the lies contained in the words, *retard, monkey, defect;* in the gawking, the pats on my head, and the tears cried on my shoulder; in the moments where I became someone's supercrip or tragedy: all those lies became my second skin. (Clare, 2010, p. 567)

In Ms. Clare's excerpt, it is apparent that (as for everyone else), part of her self-identity, self-esteem, and body image is derived from the perceptions of others. The years of harassment and teasing have resulted in feeling that "those lies became my second skin." On one level she realized that the perceptions of others were lies; however, she could not keep these lies from becoming part of her self-image. Based upon the degree of visibility of the disability and the coping strategies of the PWD, the individual can be subjected to staring, whispering, or shunning, which can negatively affect body image and self-esteem (Thomson, 1996). Many PWDs state that they *are* the disfiguring disability.

Nancy Mairs was diagnosed with multiple sclerosis. In this excerpt she related the time of diagnosis in an unusual way:

> I was never a beautiful woman, and for that reason I've spent most of my life (together with probably at least 95 percent of the female population of the United States) suffering from the shame of falling short of an unattainable standard.... When I first noticed the symptoms of that would be diagnosed as MS, I was probably looking my best.... The beginning of MS wasn't too bad. The first symptom, besides the pernicious fatigue that had begun to devour me, was "foot drop," the inability to raise my left foot at the ankle. As a consequence, I'd started to limp, but I could still wear high heels.... My self-esteem diminishes further as age and illness strip from me the features that made me, for a brief while anyway, a good-looking, even sexy, young woman.... No more lithe, girlish figure. (Mairs, 1997, pp. 55–56)

One 14-year-old girl, Lucy Grealy, worked at the Diamond D Horse Stables. Lucy had cancer and had undergone extensive therapeutic surgery on her face. She gave the following self-description: "half my jaw was missing, which gave my face a strange triangular shape, accentuated by the fact that that I was unable to keep my mouth completely shut" (Grealy, 1997, p. 14) and "I *was* my face, I *was* ugliness" (p. 17). Part of her job at the horse stables was transporting ponies to children's birthday parties and helping the children to ride the ponies. In the following excerpt she described her way of dealing with her disfigurement:

> While the eyes of these perfectly formed children swiftly and deftly bored into the deepest part of me, the glances from their parents provided me with an exotic sense of power as I watched them inexpertly pretend not to notice

me. After I passed the swing sets and looped around to pick up the next child waiting near the picnic table littered with cake plates, juice bottles, and party favors, I'd pause confrontationally, like some Dickensian ghost, imaging that my presence served as an uneasy reminder of what might be. What happened to me was any parent's nightmare, and I allowed myself to believe that I was dangerous to them.... They were uncomfortable because of my face. I ignored the deep hurt by allowing the side of me that was desperate for any kind of definition to staunchly act out, if not exactly relish, this macabre status. (Grealy, 1997, p. 19)

Eventually Lucy Grealy committed suicide.

Another young man, Leroy, had enjoyed photography as a hobby before he contracted polio. In the same way that Grealy had used her facial disfigurement as a weapon, Leroy used his camera as a weapon against curious people who made him feel like an object of curiosity instead of a person to be acknowledged and respected, the people who "without a word, they would stand and stare."

Leroy [was a person] who must spend the rest of his life flat on his back. Sometimes, the curious ones would make so bold as to stand directly above him. Without a word, they would stand and stare.

Photography has long been Leroy's hobby and he decided that a splendid opportunity has come to get unusual shots. Slightly concealed in his clothing so that no one would suspect, he planted his candid camera. Now let the curious ones come!

Slowly as before, they approached his cot. Now, they stood beside him. Now, they were bending over to *really* get a look. Eyes were opened wide. The jaw had dropped a bit. Then *click* went the camera. And bewildered, nonplussed onlookers fled speedily away.

What a collection Leroy must have now. (Lee, 1948)

If PWDs have visible disabilities, they often compartmentalize their body image, thinking of their bodies as separate parts rather than a whole. Compartmentalizing the part of the body with the disability allows the PWDs to isolate the body part with the disability, while at the same time maintaining a positive self-image (Biordi, Warner, & Knapik, 2006). Certainly the American ideal of feminine beauty or masculine attractiveness has not included a visible physical disability (Patterson et al., 1993). One woman considered her facial disfigurement a "mask, like the ones in the fairy tales."

Over and over I forgot what I had seen in the mirror. It could not penetrate into the interior of my mind and become an integral part of me. I felt as if it had nothing to do with me; it was only a disguise which is put on voluntarily by the person who wears it, and which is intended to confuse other people as to one's identity. My disguise had been put on me without my consent or knowledge like the ones in fairy tales, and it was on me for life. It was there, it was there, it was real. Every one of those encounters was like a blow on the head. They left me dazed and dumb and senseless every time, until slowly and stubbornly my robust persistent illusion of well-being and of personal beauty spread all through me again. (Wright, 1960, p. 157)

Robert Neumann was diagnosed with rheumatoid arthritis as a teenager. Note his use of the third person when describes seeing himself in the mirror ("the person looking back at me in the mirror").

> One day, almost by chance, I could avoid it no longer. I caught a good look at myself in a full-length mirror and was appalled at what I saw. The person I saw looking back at me had a face swollen from high doses of cortisone, hands with unnaturally bent fingers, and legs that could barely support his weight. (Power, Dell Orto, & Gibbons, 1988, p. 157)

Aspects of attractiveness include appearing healthy, sexually desirable, and physically fit—characteristics many PWDs are not often perceived as possessing (Bernstein, 1989, 1990; Bernstein, Breslau, & Graham, 1988). Another aspect of human attractiveness is symmetry, and many disabilities take asymmetrical forms (Bradway, Malone, Racy, Leal, & Poole, 1984). For example, an upper limb amputation is considered more handicapping than a lower limb amputation. Although losing an arm is functionally less impairing than losing a leg, societal reaction to the asymmetrical appearance of a person with one arm greatly limits the individual's acceptance in society (Rybarczynk et al., 1995). Many disabilities (such as strokes or polio) paralyze the muscles in asymmetrical ways. Many polio survivors had the muscles on one side of their face paralyzed, so they appeared to have a permanent grimace.

There are medically, anatomically derived norms of body image that are not cosmetic. Nonetheless, most individuals base their body image on these cosmetic perceptions or ideas of attractiveness. During adolescence body image assumes the greatest importance. When reaching adulthood, most individuals have a strong sense of their body image and base a great deal of their self-image on this. In childhood, perhaps because their bodies are changing rapidly and they are unable to understand societal perceptions, the body image of children is vague. The importance of body image is also gender differentiated, with greater demands and expectations placed upon girls and women to appear attractive; indeed, women's value is often based on the sole attribute of attractiveness. This is not to say that there are not societal expectations for male to appear masculine, strong, and tall (Shakespeare, 1999; Shakespeare, Gillespie-Sells, Davies, 1996). These gender-differentiated expectations at one time had a rational basis. Men did physical labor and women had to reproduce.

At times the disability itself is not is disfiguring (or visible) but the assistive technology, such as hearing aids and prostheses, or the treatment, such as medication that may cause swelling or weight gain. In fact many individuals sacrifice functioning in order to appear "normal" (Blood, 1997; Mann & Stuenkel, 2006). For example, teenagers often do not wear their hearing aids on dates because they want to appear hearing, but their hearing is very poor until they return home and re-insert their hearing aids.

Therefore, individuals born with disfiguring congenital disabilities often feel unattractive and socially unaccepted when they begin adolescence. Moreover, acquiring a disfiguring disability during adolescence can be devastating (Knight, 1989). Many individuals with disfiguring disabilities work at nights or alone, often termed the "solitary trades."

Indeed, in the past most prostheses (artificial limbs) were made to be as invisible (or "discreet") as possible. One designer explained: "The priority for design for disability has traditionally been to enable, while attracting as little attention as possible" (Pullin, 2009, p. 15). Prostheses are made of pink plastic and have wrinkles, veins, and sometimes fingernails. In spite of the addition of these realistic features, prosthetic arms have been highly visible and dysfunctional. The top priority for hearing aids is concealment. Designers of prostheses, in addition to engineering prostheses, consider themselves to be redesigning the body of the PWD.

Eyeglasses were once considered medical appliances and there was a certain degree of shame in wearing them. Now eyeglasses are considered fashion accessories. Indeed it is estimated that 20% of all eyeglasses sold have clear glass rather than prescription lens. There is a growing group of designers who want to make prostheses beautiful, visible, and functional, using the same evolutionary pathway of eyeglasses from medical appliance to fashion accessory (Pullin, 2009).

DATING

In all types of dating and romantic relationships, it is possible that the relationship may become unbalanced, with one individual dominant and the other submissive. With or without a disability, one individual may be perceived as a "saint" or a "loser" for choosing to date his or her partner. The saint image derives from the idea that one partner is being altruistic, and the loser image probably derives from the idea that this individual would not be able to get a "real" date. (A PWD is rarely considered a "real" date.) Intimate relationships between PWDs and PWODs, especially romantic ones, are often viewed as asymmetrical or unbalanced. Often, when a PWOD dates a PWD, the PWOD is thought to be either a loser or a saint, showing that PWDs are automatically assumed to have a lower social status than PWODs (Asch & Fine, 1999; Wade, 1994). An individual with a visible disability is rarely considered a "trophy date" or "arm candy." PWDs are often perceived as burdens without anything to contribute. Who would want to marry someone who is a burden without anything to contribute? A professor who was diagnosed with multiple sclerosis after she had been married for a long time continued with her university teaching duties. She was told repeatedly, "How *lucky* you are to have your husband" (Toombs, 1995, p. 16). The professor reports that most of these comments came from people who did not know her husband. However, statements like these communicate that others automatically viewed her as a burden.

Although most PWDs have difficulty in establishing all types of equal social status relationships, many say that dating is the most difficult. A woman psychologist reported:

> For people with disabilities, dating is Mount Everest. Disability discrimination is most felt in the romantic realm. Studies of attitudes toward disability repeatedly show that people's attitudes become more and more negative as the relationship with the person with the disability gets closer. Those who indicate that they would be fine with the idea of a neighbor with a disability draw the line at their children dating a person with a disability, and most people indicate that they would not marry a person with a disability. (Olkin, 1999, p. 223)

Olkin described the difficulty of dating by using the analogy of climbing Mount Everest. Dating and other types of relationships are a quality of life issue, and most people, with or without disabilities, seek out dating opportunities (Schover & Jensen, 1988). In the past institutionalization, segregation, and isolation contributed to the social distance between PWDs and PWODs. Often PWDs are told, sometimes subtly, sometimes not so subtly, that they should associate with their own kind (Shakespeare, 1999). In the video *My Body Is Not Who I Am,* a young man in a wheelchair is asked if he has a girlfriend. He replies, "Of course." The next question ("Does she have a disability?") fully indicates that the questioner thinks that PWDs should date other PWDs. The answer is, "No, my girlfriend does not have a disability."

A man in a wheelchair spoke of the difficulty of initiating and establishing romantic relationships:

> On the romantic side, women have a tendency to move away from me....It's like "see ya later." I mean, it's easy to find someone to say, "Okay, let's go out," but when it comes to the romantic side of it, they're not quite sure of what to do, what to expect. Too, it's hard to approach someone when you're in a wheelchair, as opposed to the way it was before. I mean, what do you say? "Can I buy you a drink, and, by the way, would you help me with mine?" (Scheer, 1993, p. 9)

One woman with a disability summarized: "I have a lot of people who respect me, but I have no friends." Abby Kovalsky told of her experience, "I joined a dating service a year and a half ago. All I hear from the agency is that anyone who reads my profile and then sees my photo is basically not willing to meet anyone with my disability" (Mackelprang & Salsgiver, 1999, p. 17).

A man who is legally blind and therefore was unable to obtain a driver's license as a teenager reported on one of the drawbacks of not having a driver's license:

> In my teen years, I was frustrated because I couldn't drive a car and pick up attractive young women and take them out to the park to do all the things in the back seat that everybody else was getting to do. But that was overcome when I got to the University of Texas; you didn't need a car for a date. I discovered nirvana. (Covington, 1993, p. 33)

Nonetheless PWDs often date, enter long-term romantic relationship, or marry, but they tend to do so at a later stage in life.

VIOLENCE, ABUSE, AND CRIME AGAINST PWDs

PWDs of both sexes and all ages experience more abuse, violence, and crime than PWODs. Surveys have found that noninstitutionalized women with disabilities were twice as likely to experience physical abuse as women without disabilities. The National Research Council (1996) found that rates of physical and sexual abuse of PWDs, for both men and women, were double the national rates for PWODs. These estimates do not reveal the full extent of the violence and abuse due to two factors: (1) the reluctance and failure of victims to report these crimes and (2) the fact that when surveys ask PWODs, "Have you been a victim of violence, abuse, or crime?" it elicits only a yes/no answer. PWDs typically experience abuse at a younger age, are abused for longer periods of time, and report a larger number of perpetrators; in addition the abuse goes unreported for a longer period of time (McFarlane et al., 2001).

Women with intellectual disabilities, communication difficulties, and deafness are more likely to experience abuse, violence, and crime than women with other types of disabilities. PWDs experience the same types of crime, abuse, and violence as do PWODs, including physical and sexual assaults, robbery, money theft, abuse of children and pets, and threats of physical harm. In addition many types of abuse and violence are unique to PWDs, such as medication manipulation, withholding or destroying equipment (such as wheelchairs), failure to provide needed services (such as toileting and feeding), and personal care attendants who come to work drunk or who handle the PWD roughly (Chang, et al., 2003). PWDs are often stalked and/or followed home from work. For example, bus drivers may become perpetrators because they know the schedules, routines, and homes of PWDs (Hughes et al., 2010). In addition these bus drivers also know if these PWDs live alone. At universities deaf students are very visible because of the use of sign language interpreters, and there have been reports of campus rapes of deaf students.

Why is abuse so prevalent among PWDs? There are many answers, including the large power differential between the PWD and the PWOD (Sobsey, 1994). For example, a large differential exists between PWDs who require the services of a personal care attendant or small children with intellectual disabilities who are cared for by many adults. Some PWDs have tolerated abuse for long periods because they fear abandonment or reprisals.

The lack of privacy and the visibility of the disability put PWDs at greater risk (Powers et al., 2002; Smart, 2001, 2009). The stalking of deaf university students is an example of this visibility. (The deafness is not visible; rather, it is the accommodation, the use of sign language interpreters which is visible.) This lack of privacy also tends to lead to identity theft and theft of money or checks. Until recently there were no locks on the bedroom doors at some schools and institutions. PWDs are often assisted by many caregivers during the day, and these caregivers are frequently alone with a PWD.

This power differential can be appealing to perpetrators because they understand that PWDs are often unable to get help and are often not believed when they report crimes. Abusers enjoy the power over someone who is physically weak and often deliberately target PWDs. Also it is easy to isolate a PWD (Powers et al., 2002). PWDs with intellectual disabilities might not be aware that they are being abused because they have been examined numerous times by physicians, nurses, and other caregivers (McFarlane et al., 2001). Indeed, of all disability types, girls with intellectual disabilities (especially severe intellectual disabilities) were raped far more often than girls with any other type of disability (M. McCarthy, 1999).

Before the Americans with Disabilities Act, the Deaf Culture lobbied for "communication violence" to end. Communication violence has resulted in the deaths or injuries of many deaf people. Communication violence is the lack of emergency telephone service for deaf people, the absence of visual "alarms" in public buildings, and the lack of ASL interpreters for reporting crimes to the police. Often deaf individuals were told by the police to write everything down because ASL interpreters were not available. The ADA now mandates the availability of these emergency communication services.

The centuries-old prejudice and discrimination against PWDs also play a part in the violence and crime against PWDs. Myths, such as the ones that PWDs are insensitive to pain or are less than human, often make it difficult for abusers to feel empathy for their victims. Personal care attendants have justified their abuse with the distorted logic that because of their low wages and highly stressful work, they were somehow "entitled to something."

Abuse and crimes against PWDs are gender differentiated in three respects: (1) the rate of abuse, (2) the willingness to report, and (3) the readiness of authorities to believe the victim. Michelle McCarthy (1999) summarized that there are "different thresholds of belief and intervention.... Among disabled people there are more girls who are abused, and the girls are less often believed than boys" (p. 146). Finally, boys and men are less likely to report abuse, crime, and violence.

PWDs who are the victims of crime and abuse have been asked why they failed to report these incidences to the police. Some replied that "the cops won't do anything" (Saxton et al., 2006, p. 7). At other times PWDs were blamed for the abuse or not believed (Cole, 1991, 1993). When trying to report a crime, some victims are been told that they need more medication, provoked the violence, or are lying. PWDs are often not accorded due respect, prestige, or status, especially those with severe intellectual abilities. Furthermore, their low social status is often reflected in the justice system when perpetrators receive lighter and shorter sentences (Zavirsek, 2002).

Men with disabilities are less likely to report abuse, violence, or crime committed against them, perhaps thinking that to be a victim is somehow not masculine (Saxton et al., 2006). In an article titled "We're All Little John Waynes" (Saxton et al., 2006), men with disabilities related stories of being abused by their personal care attendants. One man told this story:

> He and I got into the verbal altercation...so he thought he would put me in my place by throwing me upon the back of the chair, then letting me hang there. I'm on a ventilator.... I had already been off for an hour and a half, and I was getting winded... [H]e just kept screaming at me, (forced me) to apologize to him...hardly able to breathe, and I'm supposed to apologize to some guy. He really scared the hell out of me. (p. 4)

Attention is now focused on crime, violence, and abuse against PWDs. There are screening instruments (McFarlane et al., 2001) that seek to determine the extent of the problem and to help individuals report abuse. Most caregivers, including bus drivers, are now required to undergo criminal background checks, and preventive measures are used in institutions. Some of these preventive measures include teaching those with intellectual disabilities the meaning of boundaries and what boundary violation entails.

ACHIEVING AN IDENTITY

A polio survivor who became paralyzed as a teenager believed that PWDs are not allowed to define themselves. Rather PWODs determine the identity of PWDs.

> The world of the crippled and disabled is strange and dark, and it is held up to judgment by those who live in fear of it. The cripple is the creature who has been deprived of his ability to create a self.... He is the other, if for no other reason than that only by being the other will he be allowed to presume upon the "normals." He must accept definition from outside the boundaries of his own existence. (Kriegel, 1987, p. 66)

Basically, everyone gains a self-identity through the opinions of others, or to state it more accurately, everyone gains a self-identity through his or his *perception* of others' opinions. The accumulation of feedback gathered throughout the years is typically coalesced into an image of oneself. When attitudes of others are consistently negative, including well-intentioned sympathy and pity, the adolescent understands that he or she is considered to be a burden on others or an inferior, deviant person.

Often the disability of an individual is considered to be his or her most important, defining characteristic, and little else is noticed about the individual. Often PWDs state, "People meet my disability before they meet me." Nothing else about the individual is acknowledged or noticed, including, race, gender, or sexual orientation (Smart, 2001, 2009). In the National Public Radio Disability History Project (1998a) a PWD said, "People want you to be your disability when you want to be yourself." Uhlberg, a child of deaf parents in Brooklyn, New York, described the way in which his parents' disabilities defined both his parents and the entire family:

> It was one thing to be singled out on my street as the son of the "deafies" in 3A, which is all my parents were ever known as on our block. Not as Louis and Sarah; not as Mr. and Mrs. Uhlberg; but rather as the "deaf and dumb mutes in 3A." The unthinking consignment as objects of curiosity, and even pity, was something I had adapted to. (Uhlberg, 2008, p. 58)

By making a single characteristic so salient or relevant, a disability in this way exaggerates and heightens the difference between those with and those without disabilities (Fries, 1997). The individual's other characteristics and achievements, such as profession, level of education, or personality, are not noticed. Most PWDs state that most PWODs ascribe far more importance to their disability than they themselves do; furthermore, most PWODs ascribe more limitations to the disability than actually exist. In the following excerpt, it is clear that medical providers can also make the disability the defining characteristic. Note that the woman sacrifices "competence" in exchange for being treated as an individual.

> Right now I have a very nice doctor who's like really good in terms of trying to work with me. She's just not as competent as I would like...there are some doctors who might be better, but what they do to me emotionally it's not worth it.... [I]t always feels like I'm walking a tightrope.... I'd love to find somebody that's both a really good doctor and who's not prejudiced against me...who can really see me for, for [me]. (Putnam et al., 2003, p. 41)

The media can act as an important source of feedback. Whether consciously or not, everyone likes to identify with characters on television or in films or tries to find a character who seems to be like himself/herself. For adolescents and emerging adults with disabilities, the portrayal of PWDs in the print media and the electronic media can be damaging. Rod Michalko, who is blind, wrote about watching television as a teenager and seeing misfortune, sadness, incompetence, and poverty.

> In my teens, I saw blind people on television and in the movies and sometimes came across a blind character in a book. They were all portrayed as victims of a misfortune.... When I saw blind people in the movies or on television and even when I saw the "real" blind ones, I saw incompetence, sadness, and poverty.

And I saw misfortune. Whether my perception was accurate or not is irrelevant; that's just what I saw. What I did not see when I saw these blind people is just as significant as what I did see: I did not see me. Still, when I saw them, I experienced a nebulous fear that I later understood was the fear of seeing myself. (Michalko, 2002, p. 24)

Charles Mee, the historian and author who contracted polio as a teenager in the 1950s, described marginality perfectly when narrating his first awareness of it: "The world seemed too foreign to me, and at the same time so familiar" (p. 131). As a teenager, the only way in which he can describe this realization is to compare his situation with that of a racial minority.

I spent many hours in the living room, watching Ed Sullivan's *Toast of the Town,* and Sid Caesar's *Your Show of Shows* and *Ozzie and Harriet,* and *I Love Lucy.*

These shows, and their commercials, made me dizzy with their vision of a world so wholesome, intact, healthy vigorous, upbeat, smooth-skinned, smiling, sleek, plumb; with all the unattainable girls in swimming suits, each one of them incredibly sexy even as they were evidently not thinking about sex or anything other than purity, purity of soap and purity of complexion and purity of thought, the purity of a perfect Ipana toothpaste smile; clean people, good people, winning people, with their milk shakes and hamburgers and French fries, bobby sox and swirling skirts and snug sweater, their pep and vigor. This world seemed too foreign to me, and at the same time so familiar: actually, in many confusing ways, this vision of the close-knit, happy family, secure in the possession of basic consumer durables, described my life. But at the same time, in some way I couldn't put my finger on, I knew this was not my world at all. I thought: Oh, I think I know how *Negroes* feel. I thought: These people on the television could be from the moon. (Mee, 1999, p. 131)

A women diagnosed with a mental illness stated that the little information she had about mental illness came from the book *One Flew Over the Cuckoo's Nest.* After her diagnosis, the book became her self-identity.

At that time, I was not involved at all in the community mental health (CMH) system; I didn't even know there was such a thing as CMH. I hardly knew anyone with mental illness. My education about mental illness consisted of the book, *One Flew Over the Cuckoo's Nest,* which was really bad news. I felt all alone, and I believed that there were a lot of really bad things wrong with me. (Mackelprang & Salsgiver, 1999, p. 181)

The negative and inaccurate portrayal of PWDs in the media is slowly changing to show PWDs as ordinary, meaning people with ordinary roles, emotions, goals, and lives. In the past PWDs were viewed as the "other" or as symbols as dichotomous characteristics: either extremely good or extremely bad, either extremely brave or extremely pitiful, either extremely wise or extremely stupid, or either extremely weak or extremely strong (Hyler, 1988; Hyler, Gabbard, & Schneider, 1991). The actor Robert David Hall is a double amputee who plays a coroner on the popular television series *CSI*. He is quoted in a *New York Times* article as stating, "It used to be that if you were disabled and on television, they'd play soft piano behind you. The thing I love about *CSI* is that I'm just Dr. Robbins" (Navarro, 2007). The author of the article concluded by pointing out that the portrayal of PWDs is changing:

> The heart-wrenching movie of the week and fund-raising telethons striving for cures have given way to amputees rock climbing on reality shows like *The Amazing Race* and doing jive on *Dancing with the Stars*. Sitcoms and crime shows have jumped on the bandwagon, too: An actor who is a paraplegic, for instance, depicts a member of the casino surveillance team on *Las Vegas*. (Navarro, 2007)

The developmental tasks of adolescence and emerging adulthood are often assumed to be unsuitable or impossible for PWDs. This is true for some with severe and multiple disabilities. However, most PWDs want to undertake and complete these developmental tasks. At times their disability may require them to change the method or the timing of completion of these tasks, and occasionally they must redefine some of these tasks, such as complete independence (Thomson, 1997).

Terms to Learn

Body image	Identity diffusion	Soft skills of employability
Compression of childhood	Identity formation	Storm and stress
Emerging adulthood	Identity moratorium	hypothesis
Gender identity	Puberty	"Thrills and chills"
Identity achievement	Social moratorium	personality

Videos to View

- View the 25-minute video *Animated Neuroscience and the Action of Nicotine, Cocaine, and Marijuana in the Brain*, available from Insight Media. The producers describe this video: "Featuring three-dimensional animations, this program examines the human brain and considers the effects of psychoactive drugs on brain activity. The program demonstrates the effects of nicotine, cocaine, and marijuana and considers the cellular targets of each drug, drug-cell interactions, and the bodily effects of drug use."
- View the 30-minute video *Adolescent Cognition: Thinking in a New Key*, available from Insight Media. The producers describe this video: "This program addresses the cognitive changes that occur in adolescence. Citing the work of Piaget, Erikson, and Goffman, David Elkind explores the intellectual, emotional, and social consequences of changes in thinking."
- View the 30-minute video *The Becoming Years: Adolescence to Older Adults*, available from Insight Media. The producers describe this video: "Featuring gerontologist James Birren and his Guided Autobiography participants, this program explain that social and cognitive develop continue throughout

the life span. It describes the key developmental tasks of adolescence and adulthood."

- View the two videos *Traumatic Brain Injury Part 1* and *Traumatic Brain Injury Part 2*, available from Insight Media. Each of the videos is 30 minutes in length. The producers describe these videos: "This set emphasizes that traumatic brain injury (TBI) has profound physical, mental, emotional, and social effects on patients. Part 1 explores rehabilitating individuals during the early and middles phases of TBI. Part 2 looks at rehabilitation during the late phases of TBI and offers suggestions for maximizing patient outcomes."

- View the 30-minute video *Occupational Theory and Spinal Cord Injuries*, available from Insight Media. The producers describe this video: "Emphasizing the importance of functional assessments of patients with spinal cord injuries, this program discusses interventions for patients who require extensive rehabilitation."

- View the popular film *Murderball*. The producers describe this film: "Better known as Wheelchair Rugby, Murderball is a game created by quadriplegic athletes that is every bit as aggressive as the name would lead one to expect; played with bone-breaking intensity, a typical game of Wheelchair Rugby involves plenty of trash-talking, a few head-on collisions, and the occasional player being thrown from his modified wheelchair. The game has become an official event at the Paralympics, a worldwide competition for handicapped athletes, and the United States and Canada have become fierce rivals." After viewing *Murderball*, go to the website www.abledata.gov and type in "sports wheelchairs."

Learning Activities

(Note: These may also be used for class presentations.)

- Ben Mattlin was born with spinal muscular atrophy, and as a child he never looked forward to Halloween. As an adult he wrote:

  I never thought about a connection between disabilities and Halloween until I learned of the once-common fear of deformities—the limping, hunchbacked, hook-handed or one-eyed monsters of ancient fairy tales and old horror movies. Even the word "creepy" comes from the same word as the oldest term for folks like me, the politically incorrect "cripple." . . . For people Halloween is an *escape* from conformity, but for those of us who don't quite fit the norm, that's nothing special. In fact, demonstrating that you're not exactly what people expect is pretty much what disabled folks do every day. (October 28, 2010)

  Visit http://www.npr./org and access Mattlin's story. As a class, discuss some possible meanings of Halloween for those with visible disabilities.

- Read these two books:
  Helen Keller: A Life by D. Hermann (1998), published by Alfred A. Knopf.
  Blind Rage: Letters to Helen Keller by G. Kleege (2006), published by Gallaudet University.

In her book Kleege wrote about her anger at being constantly compared throughout her childhood and adolescence to Helen Keller. This comparison made Kleege angry, and to work through her anger, she wrote letters to Helen Keller, telling her how difficult Keller had made her childhood. She never mailed the letters. Discuss the way in which "disabled heroes" may be counterproductive.

- Read these three books:

Helen Keller: A Life by Dr. Hermann (1998), published by Alfred A. Knopf.

The Education of Laura Bridgman: First Deaf and Blind Person to Learn Language (2001) by Ernest Freeberg, published by Harvard University.

The Imprisoned Guest: Samuel Howe and Laura Bridgman, the Original Deaf-Blind Girl by Elisabeth Gitter, published by Farrar, Straus, & Giroux. Laura Bridgman was the most famous woman in America during her lifetime. Today very few know about her; however, without Laura Bridgman there would have been no Helen Keller. Helen Keller is the most famous deaf/blind individual and is typically the only deaf/blind individual most Americans can name. However, it was with Laura that Samuel Gridley Howe developed the communication technique of finger spelling at the Perkins Institute for the Blind in Boston. Howe taught this technique to a young Irish immigrant girl who was both sighted and hearing. This girl's name was Annie Sullivan.

From the age of 7, Laura Bridgman lived all her life at the Perkins Institute for the Blind until she died at an early age. In contrast, Helen Keller lived a rich and varied life, traveling the world and becoming friends with many of the celebrities of her day. What was the difference between Laura and Helen? Both women had the same disability, lived in somewhat the same time period, and learned the same communication technique. However, Helen Keller had a life-long hearing/sighted companion for 47 years, Annie Sullivan. Few, if any, deaf/blind individuals have such a long-term companion.

Writing Exercises

- Write a 10-page paper in which the new developmental stage Emerging Adulthood is described. Be sure to include the reasons why such a stage is necessary. In addition, write about the usefulness of this stage 50 years in the future.
- Write a five-page paper in which you define the concept of beauty and the way in which it affects the lives of adolescent and young adult women.
- Think back upon your adolescence and young adulthood. Write an autobiographical 10-page paper in which you compare your experiences to some of the developmental tasks outlined in this chapter.

Web Sites

http://jpepsy.oxfordjournals.org/content/28/4/233.abstract
http://www.disabilitypolicycenter.org/links/specialed.htm
http://www.aifo.it/english/resources/online/apdrj/apdrj204/adolescent.pdf

Adulthood, Ages 25 to 40 and Midlife, Ages 40 to 60

14

Astrong self-identity and autonomy are considered the twin goals of growth and development, according to the grand theorists of human development. Most individuals reach the peak of their self-identity, autonomy, professional success, and family integration during adulthood and midlife. Also the years of adulthood and midlife are the times of life with the greatest responsibilities, such as caring for children and aging parents, strengthening marriages or other long-term living arrangements, and achieving positions of authority and responsibility in their professions (Carr, 2009). The leading authority on midlife (Moen, 2004) termed this stage "the rush-hour of life." A disability, especially a disability acquired during adulthood or midlife years, often appears to be a stunning blow to one's identity, with losses in status, position, and job; the results of years' of sacrifice, work, and careful planning vanish. Further the acquisition of a disability in adulthood is rarely considered when constructing life plans (Mishel, 1993; J. Morris, 1991).

ETERNAL CHILDREN

For centuries PWDs have not been accorded adult status. Adults with disabilities are subjected to many behaviors that infantilize them, including intrusive touching by strangers, pats on the head, having their wheelchairs or other assistive devices moved, being called insulting endearments such as "honey," or being asked personal, sensitive questions by strangers. Many adults have told of being in public with a companion and having salespersons or wait staff ask the companion what "their little disabled friend would like." Of course most of these behaviors are well-intentioned and motivated by kindness; however, they are also perpetuated by lack of awareness.

Ruth Tollifson (1997) tells of "healing conversations" in a group of women with disabilities. Tollifson learned that all of the adults in the support group had been treated as children, and she began to understand that she was not to blame for being treated as less than an adult. (Many people with disabilities [PWDs] falsely think that they are responsible for the prejudice and discrimination directed at them.)

> They shared so many of what I had always thought were my own isolated, personal experiences that I began to realize that my supposedly private hell was a social phenomenon. We had eye-opening, healing conversations. We discovered, for example, that we had all had the experience of being patronized and treated like children even though we were adults. It wasn't simply some horrible flaw in my

own character that provoked such a reaction, as I had always believed, but rather, this was part of a collective pattern that was much larger than any one of us. It was a stereotype that existed in the culture at large. (Tollifson, 1997, p. 107)

Tollifson wrote on her experiences of being treated as an eternal child, while Wolfensberger (1981) wrote about institutionalized policies that do the same thing:

> Adults [with disabilities] may be cast into roles of eternal children by being encouraged to play children's games and to follow children's school schedules rather than adult work schedules; by children's decoration and children's clothing; by funding of services for adults coming from departments charged with serving children; and by such names as "day-care center" for day programs for adults. (p. 205)

A medical social worker who had a congenital bone disease that resulted in her small stature stated, "It's difficult to cross that border from childhood to adulthood." In the video *My Body Is Not Who I Am,* a woman described her experiences: "It's as if I am child and I have no boundaries. Complete strangers can ask me any question they want." Fifty years ago a college-educated woman (with a disability) described her experiences when she attempted to enter a career.

> With one extremely painful exception, as long as I was in the protective custody of family life or college, scheduled and lived without exercising my rights as an adult citizen, the forces of society were kindly and unruffling. It was after college, business schools and innumerable stretches as a volunteer worker on community projects that I was often bogged down by the medieval prejudices and superstitions of the business world. Looking for a job was like standing before a firing squad. Employers were shocked that I had the gall to apply for a job. (Goffman, 1963, p. 34)

A single mother who is an elementary school teacher is paralyzed and uses a wheelchair. She describes the reactions of others when they see that she has children.

> It's not easy. The stares that I get, just rolling down the mall taking my kids trick-or-treating. People in wheelchairs don't have kids, "What do you mean those are *your* kids?" The things they can say are amazing. They look you in the face and say, "You have kids? What are you doing with kids?" I say, "Well, I'm doing very well with kids, thank you. Look at them—they look pretty good! I love my kids, like anyone else." (Boggess, 1993, p. 8)

The last three words of this excerpt, "like anyone else," express this mother's two wishes: (1) not to be defined *entirely* by her disability, and (2) to be viewed as a "normal" person with ordinary emotions and functions, and as part of a family. Her first words ("It's not easy") describe her difficulty—not with the disability but with the societal reaction to the disability.

DISABILITY IN ADULTHOOD AND MIDLIFE

In this book we have learned about congenital disabilities for which there is no predisability (or premorbid) identity, and we have learned that traumatic onset disabilities are common in adolescence and emerging adulthood. With disabilities acquired as a result of trauma or injury, there is a clearly delineated time of onset, often as a result of engaging in dangerous activities. This sudden onset is also called an "acute onset." Therefore both the *time* and *type* of onset affect the way in which the individual responds. Broadly speaking disabilities acquired in adulthood or midlife tend to be chronic illnesses with insidious onsets. However, there are also acute-onset and traumatic-onset disabilities acquired in adulthood and midlife. Chronic illnesses are considered to be a type of disability.

An insidious onset is defined as a slow, gradual, subtle beginning of which the individual is not aware. This is often called asymptomatic (meaning without symptoms) or "silent" onset. In insidious-onset disabilities the time of diagnosis is referenced, rather than the time of acquisition or onset. There is less support, acknowledgment, or even awareness for insidious onset disabilities. In contrast, with many acute-onset disabilities there tends to be a great deal of support simply because it is a medical emergency.

Younger individuals (especially males) tend to acquire disabilities through injuries, accidents, and other types of trauma; but adults, especially those in midlife, tend to be diagnosed with chronic illnesses, such as multiple sclerosis, autoimmune diseases, and neuromuscular diseases. Such chronic illnesses with insidious onsets are often considered "silent transitions," transitions that are not socially acknowledged or supported. The typical age of onset of many of these disabilities occurs at the years of peak career development and the beginning of parenthood (Gordon, Lewis, & Wong, 1994). A young man who was diagnosed with multiple sclerosis explained, "Anyone's early years out of school and in the world are all about empowerment. Confidence in the future suddenly was neutralized" (Cohen, 2004, pp. 26–27). A disability diagnosed or acquired in early adulthood interferes with career development and also presents obstacles in establishing intimate and sexual relationships.

By midlife most individuals have established strong self-identities as capable, successful, and achieving individuals with both status and prestige. They expect to reap the rewards of careful planning, hard work, sacrifice, and progressive success. A disability in midlife may appear to be a cruel disappointment. Especially in midlife, many individuals are anticipating their time of retirement, when they will have more time and resources to spend on long-deferred goals and activities. Those in the midlife years have a well-defined place and identity in the larger community, an identity and status for which they worked years. The artist Chuck Close described his acute onset disability that resulted in paralysis:

> I was at Gracie Mansion in New York [the residence of the mayor of New York City] giving an award to someone. I suddenly had a tremendous pain in my chest that went through my back and my arms. I thought it was a heart attack. I went across the street to Doctors Hospital, where, within a very short time, I was totally paralyzed from the neck down. It was several days before they figured out what had happened, which was that an occluded or collapsed spinal artery had cut off the flow of blood to my spine and knocked out nerves over all my body. Virtually everything from the shoulders down was affected. (Close, 1993, p. 17)

Additionally, adult people without disabilities (PWODs) often have internalized the mistaken negative and pathological prejudices about PWDs. Therefore, for individuals in midlife their prejudices become self-identifiers. For example, those who view PWDs as "pathetic losers" may think of themselves in the same way following the onset or diagnosis of a disability. Those who have falsely thought of life with a disability as an unbearable tragedy often experience difficulties in responding to a disability, simply from their own prejudices. Lifelong attitudes and beliefs, even false ones, can be difficult to change. One man with a psychiatric disability described the way in which he accepted society's prejudice and the effect this had on his life. Also, note that even though he did not have a physical disability, he thought of himself as "deformed."

> Because of my history and because of the society in which I lived, I easily turned the notion of illness into thinking there was something wrong with me. I was the problem. I felt deformed, everything I did was wrong. I had no place in the world. I was a freak. I was deeply ashamed of who I was and I tried my best to cover up my abnormality. I learned from those around me that psychiatric disability and its aftereffects were something to hide. As a result, I lived marginally. I worked in a constant state of terror and tried to look normal. For the most part I succeeded—but at a tremendous cost to myself in terms of my energy, my self-image, my fear, and my inferiority. There were times when the stresses got to be too much and I ended up hospitalized, defeated, and feeling a failure. (Dell Orto & Power, 2007, p. 111)

Irving Zola, a polio survivor, describes the prejudices of "normal families" and the result:

> Born for the most part into normal families, we are socialized into that world. The world of sickness is one we enter only later, poorly prepared and with all the prejudices of the normal. The very vocabulary we use to describe ourselves is borrowed from that society. We are de-formed, dis-eased, dis-ordered, abnormal, and most telling of all, called an invalid. (Zola, 1982, p. 206)

One advantage of disabilities and chronic illnesses acquired in adulthood is that most individuals have completed their educations and entered their professional lives. Therefore, those with adult-onset disabilities tend to have higher rates of employment than those with adolescent-onset disabilities or congenital disabilities. For example, Stephen Hawking, the British theoretical physicist and author of such books as *A Brief History of Time*, has a progressive neuromuscular disease (ALS) that requires him to use a communication board and a power wheelchair. Because Hawking's symptoms appeared after he had been accepted for a PhD program, he was able to continue with his profession. If the onset of his neuromuscular disease had occurred in childhood or adolescence, Hawking probably would not have been able to attend Oxford University in England and obtain a doctoral degree. His first symptoms appeared while he was a student at Cambridge, when he began to lose his balance and fell down a flight of stairs. Hawking's inability to speak is not due to his ALS but is a secondary condition. While presenting a paper in Geneva, Switzerland he contracted pneumonia, an illness that is very serious for him because individuals with ALS have limited respiratory capacity. A doctor at a hospital emergency room performed a life-saving tracheotomy that resulted in the loss of speech.

PWDs who were entering their adult years in 2011, have little or no memory of life without the Americans with Disabilities Act (ADA). The ADA was enacted in 1990, giving PWDs their civil rights as Americans in employment, education, public transportation, voting, and participation in recreational and social activities. Before the ADA it was legal to exclude PWDs from airline travel, jobs, institutions of higher learning, restaurants, hotels, movie theaters, and stores. Such exclusion was not ethical, moral, or humane; however, it was legal, and there was no redress under the law. Perhaps, in the same way that African Americans view the 1964 Civil Rights Act, PWDs see the ADA as a defining event. The executive director of the National Council on Disability, Paul Hearne, considered the ADA to have two broad effects, regulatory and empowering:

> This law is very regulatory. It regulates states, municipalities, agencies, behavior, and they all have to comply with the Access Board. But the law also empowers people with disabilities to recognize that they have a role in society. (*National Council on Disability Bulletin*, 1997, March)

In the opinion of some experts, one of the most significant results of the ADA has been to build a group identity for Americans with disabilities. Later sections of this chapter will present the typical developmental tasks of adults and those in midlife. The inclusion of PWDs in the discussion of these developmental tasks may be traced to the ADA, because of governmental enforcement of its provisions and the influence on individual empowerment that the ADA has given to PWDs.

As life spans increase, the developmental stages of adulthood and midlife now offer greater diversity in roles, relationships, and resources. The combination of decreased fertility and longer life spans has "led to an unprecedented explosion of lifestyle possibilities" (Perrig-Chiello & Perren, 2005, p. 169). The growing tolerance of and appreciation for different lifestyles are also important factors in the wider range of choices possible.

THE CHANGING CONCEPTUALIZATIONS OF ADULTHOOD

Most developmental theorists consider adulthood the least structured of all the developmental stages, with the possible exception of the "old elderly." The idea of a somewhat "standardized" developmental stage of adulthood, in which the *majority* of individuals engage in such normative, predictable activities as marriage, parenthood, professional success, and grandparenthood, may be changing to the idea of adulthood as an *individualized* developmental stage without normative transitions. We have learned that a newly identified developmental stage, "emerging adulthood," has delayed the transition to adulthood. When an individual assumes adult roles and responsibilities early, his or her adult years will obviously be longer. For example, someone who marries at age 20 and has children in his or her early twenties will have 45 years of adulthood. However, we have learned that it is becoming less common for individuals to marry at 20. Another way to gauge the wide variation in defining adulthood is a comment such as "fifty is the new thirty." Phrases such as these are difficult to interpret because if we do not know what the age of 50 is as a developmental stage, how do we know what 30 is? Would the age of 30 be the new 10?

Nonetheless, biology does play a role, albeit reduced, in defining adulthood and midlife. Parenthood continues to be determined by biological age, but not to the extent that it once was. Women now have children at later ages; career and professional development require longer periods of education and training. At the beginning of adulthood individuals are in their prime years of physical and intellectual functioning. In midlife signs of physical and cognitive decline begin to appear. In spite of these changes, there are nevertheless some basic commonalities in the experience and role tasks of adulthood.

Early Adulthood

- Marriage
- Parenthood
- Vocational Identity

MARRIAGE

Early adulthood is considered to be a time of building (Erikson, 1982), constructing marriages or other long-term relationships, entering a career path, and becoming parents, all of which contribute to a strong sense of self-identity. Goals often become more clearly defined and refined in the decade of the 30s (Austrian, 2002). Today the marriages of same-sex couples and their parenthood are widely accepted (Pew Research Center, 2010). However, we have seen that not all adults consider either marriage or parenthood as essential for a satisfying and fulfilling life. For example, in 2004 28% of all women ages 30 to 34 were childless (Newman & Newman, 2009). Up until the mid-1900s most adults married, stayed married, and had children, and there were well-established roles for men and women. However, these norms changed as the older Baby Boomers became adults in the 1960s. Alternatives to marriage were widely accepted, including long-term cohabitation, with some of these relationships short in duration and others a long-term alternative to marriage.

In some ways the factors affecting the choice of marriage partner have changed, while in other ways these factors have remained the same. The greatest changes in American marriages are the later age of first marriage and the increasing rates of interracial and intercultural marriages. However, marriage partners continue to select each other based on perceived similarity and propinquity (being geographically close). The greatest indicators of perceived similarity are similar age (within 5 years), similar educational level, and similar values, such as religious orientation. Marriage includes more than two individuals, because both families become part of the marriage.

Marriage and co-parenthood require a sustained, collective sense of efficacy, and these two major life tasks are reflected in Erikson's development task of intimacy versus isolation. Marriage includes a shared vision of the future, sexual intimacy, and companionship, with love and commitment as major elements. In spite of high divorce rates, most people spend the majority of their lives with one partner (Berk, 2001). A developmental psychologist (Rice, 1998) determined that marital happiness was the greatest determinant of overall life satisfaction, stating that "data from six national studies conducted in the United States revealed that marital happiness contributed more to personal global (overall) happiness than did any other kinds of satisfaction, including satisfaction from work" (p. 568). At the same time, unhappiness in marriage often has a negative effect on all other areas of life.

The more balanced (or equal) the partners' contribution to the marriage, the happier the couple tends to be. Strain and tension enter the relationship when one partner feels that the other is not contributing equally or (in other words) when one partner feels that the marriage is asymmetrical. The partner who thinks that he or she is contributing more feels taken advantage of, and the partner who thinks that he or she is not contributing enough fears abandonment. Equal resources do not mean the *same* resources, nor are all of the resources tangible, such as money or help with the housework. Love, emotional support, and companionship are examples of intangible resources. The concept of a balanced, symmetrical marriage seems straightforward; however, shifting gender roles for both men and women make the determination of equal contribution more ambiguous.

Marriage meets a number of needs, including the economic benefits of division of labor and/or two incomes, an environment in which to raise children, and a source of intimacy, love, sexual fulfillment, and companionship. However, it is often difficult to have all three of these benefits simultaneously. Work, children, and a fulfilling marriage may at times conflict. Marriage is also physically healthy; fewer married people have disabilities and they report fewer sicknesses and illness. Married people also tend to live longer. The relationship between physical health and marriage is difficult to interpret, because marriage may cause better health, better health may cause marriage, or both. Certainly most adults are more likely to consider healthy individuals as potential marriage partners, and most married couples monitor the others' health and care. Indeed, many "thrills and chills" behaviors of young men end when they become married.

Does marriage limit one's autonomy and independence, or do the companionship, sexual fulfillment, and economic benefits provide a greater sense of control? One author (Rice, 1998, p. 570) provided a list of twelve marriage adjustment tasks, each with several subtypes. Some of these tasks are emotional fulfillment and support, sexual adjustment, personal habits, sex roles, power and decision making, family and relatives, and moral values and ideology, along with work, employment, and achievement. The list is daunting; furthermore, it assumes that neither partner has a disability. Obviously the list would become longer if it took into account the tasks of managing a disability and the changes resulting from disability.

PARENTHOOD

Having children is no longer considered the primary reason for marriage, nor is parenthood necessary in order for a person to be considered an adult. Nonetheless, most adults have children, but they tend to have fewer children and have them at a later age. The educational level of the woman is the most important predictor of when she will have her first child. Generally, more educated women tend to have children at later ages. According to the Pew Research Center (2010), the number of babies born to women 35 and older rose 64%. A record 41% of 2008 births also occurred outside of marriage. There are greeting cards with messages like "A dog is my grandchild," perhaps indicating that older adults place a higher value on parenthood. Furthermore, not all young children live in the traditional, conventional type of families with married parents. Indeed, U.S. Census Bureau statistics show that only a minority of children live in homes with two continuously married parents.

Marriage can be a difficult, stressful transition in which individuals feel that they are relinquishing the freedoms of single life. Parenthood is also a difficult transition, simply because of the abrupt nature of the transition, its irreversibility, and the continuous demands for care and love. In these ways parenthood may be considered a more demanding role transition than marriage. New parents change their identity from being the children of their parents to being parents themselves and are required to resolve the conflicts between career or educational goals and the needs of a child. Parental responsibilities take priority over almost all other activities and plans of life. Simply contemplating the financial costs in raising a child can be daunting. However, some adults consider parenthood a natural evolution in their lives, albeit a difficult and demanding one, and derive great pleasure and satisfaction in caring for a baby and planning his or her early years. For many, both marriage and parenthood are thought to be fulfilling and meaningful. Furthermore, parenthood is considered a significant developmental task, one which they willingly and happily assume.

VOCATIONAL IDENTITY

Success and satisfaction in work tend to generalize to other areas of life. Furthermore, work identity constitutes a great deal of overall self-identity, as shown by the phrase "you are what you do." When there were fewer vocational choices, it was easier to choose a career, but the narrow range of choices was also confining and constricting. For example, in the past most professional women were in "pink collar" jobs, such as teacher, librarian, nurse, social worker, or secretary. Most of these professions required a college degree, but their pay was low and men rarely entered these jobs. They were considered "women's work," hence the title of "pink collar." Of course this does not suggest that a teacher, librarian, nurse, social worker, or secretary does not do meaningful work, but simply that women were limited to these choices and men were not encouraged to enter these fields.

Men's work, on the hand, has remained strongly gender based (Gottfredson, 1996), and the idea that the low salaries of "pink collar" jobs are unattractive to men may have some validity. Also, "as late as 1950, only 11.9 percent of women with children under age 6 were in the labor force" (Glenn, 2010, p. 21). Just as theories of human development were developed with white, middle-class males in mind, most theories of career development also have a white male bias.

It was the capitalist industrialied economies that brought women (mostly single women without children) into the workforce. Factories required clerical workers to keep track of the production and distribution of goods, manage payrolls, maintain records, and record sales. Clerical positions increasingly became "pink collar" jobs. Today increasing gender equity has correspondingly increased the number of women who work, including those women with small children. The increased number of women attending and graduating from college explains some of the increase in working women. (Another significant factor is the number of single mothers who have the responsibility to support children.)

Some individuals defer making a career choice, at times preferring to keep their options open even beyond the university years. Although vocational development and career choice are no longer as irreversible as they once were, it is still true that individuals who make the transition to full-time work tend to become good family members and responsible citizens. Access to career information and role models is critical. Many adolescents and emerging adults have made career choices but lack a clear understanding of the steps involved in reaching their goals. Those with a great deal of knowledge about specific careers tend to make more meaningful choices.

The single most important predictor of career choice is the number of years of education completed. Another important factor in young adults' vocational identity and career choice is the jobs held by their parents. Although not specifically job training, children grow up observing their parents work and listening to them talk about work, including attitudes toward work in general, and they also tend to have more information on the steps involved in obtaining such employment. Teachers also play an important role in career choice. In one study, college freshmen were asked which individual had the most influence on their choice of a field of study. The single largest group (39%) identified a high school teacher (Rice, 1998). Young adults who attend college tend to be more influenced by teachers and professors, while young adults who do not attend college are more influenced by their parents.

Another important aspect of vocational choice is self-knowledge, specifically understanding one's needs and skills. Work not only provides adult status and financial independence but also offers a sense of affiliation (I work for a great organization), a feeling of belonging, a sense of contribution, social and friendship opportunities, and opportunities for learning and personal development. There are also idiosyncratic motivators for work (that is, motivators specific to an individual). These work motivators may shift over the lifetime of an individual. For example, a primary work motivator for a young man may be financial rewards (because he and his wife have children to support); however, when the children become financially independent, he may wish to find work that allows him to contribute to environmental causes and would be willing to take a substantial cut in pay.

Opportunity structures are the last factor to consider. Much of the previous discussion of vocational choice was based on the concept that people have unlimited choice, but of course no one has unlimited choice. Almost everyone has been faced with the need to compromise in career choices. However, some people have more choice than others. Opportunity structures developed by society and government provide opportunities for some types of people, but not for others. Historically, the only group considered to have careers were white, middle-class men without disabilities. Other groups of people had work and jobs, but these were low-paying, high turnover jobs without much status and prestige. For the most part careers that expressed the interests and skills of the worker were available only to white males without disabilities.

Paul Longmore (2003) described work disincentives in his essay "Why I Burned My Book." Because he contracted polio as a child, Longmore is paraplegic and has been receiving Social Security Disability Insurance (SSDI) for years. Although the amount of SSDI money was not very large, SSDI made Longmore eligible for Medicaid. Without Medicaid benefits, he could have been forced to live in a nursing home. Longmore was thus careful to ensure that he did not earn an amount of money that would have made him ineligible for SSDI. He earned a PhD in American history and wrote a book titled *The Invention of George Washington*, which was published by the University of California Press. Subsequently he was offered a research fellowship at the world-famous Huntington

Library. In a letter, the Social Security Administration informed Longmore that if he accepted any book royalties or salary from the Huntington Library, he would no longer be eligible for SSDI (or Medicaid). An academic's salary would be insufficient for many disability-related expenses. In order to register his protest, he carefully staged a book-burning demonstration with disability rights activists present and received both television and newspaper coverage. He carefully rehearsed the book-burning because "I didn't want to set *myself* on fire." He explained his feelings:

> I somberly watched the fire consume my book. I had planned the protest. I had rehearsed how to burn the book. I had even thought about what sort of expression I should have on my face. But I could never have prepared for the emotional effect on me of the act itself. I was burning my own book, a book I had spent ten years of my life laboring over, a book that had earned me my Ph.D. in history, a book I felt proud of and, in fact, loved. It was a moment of agony. (p. 253)

Longmore concluded the essay:

> We [PWDs], like all Americans, have talents to use, work to do, our contributions to make to our communities and country. We want the chance to work and marry without jeopardizing our lives. We want access to opportunity. We want access to work. We want access to the American Dream. (p. 258)

The provisions of government policies like SSDI made it impossible for PWDs to work, including those with a great deal of education. Obviously Longmore, even in his wheelchair, is capable of working in his field of history. The Social Security Act was passed in 1935 when assistive technology (AT) and psychotropic medications were rare, and many PWDs were residents of institutions. In 1935 there was no Americans with Disabilities Act. Without these resources and accommodations (and with the prejudices and discrimination of the time), the Social Security Administration made a wise choice to provide financial benefits for PWDs. However, there is presently a federal civil rights act for PWDs, all of the accommodations and resources are available, and PWDs can and want to work. Of course, the current large bureaucratic system of financial disincentives is slowly being dismantled, which will allow PWDs to work while maintaining disability benefits. A disability advocate described SSDI:

> Did you know that only one-half of one percent of those Americans with disabilities presently receiving Social Security Supplemental Insurance (SSDI) or Supplemental Security Income (SSI) are employed? How many more of us do you think would like to work but cannot, because we would lose cash benefits if we earn over $500 a month and Medicare and Medicaid health coverage if we work more than three years? (Pendergast, 2010, p. 293)

Robert P. Winske describes himself: "I am 41 and the middle son of three boys born with a rare form of muscular dystrophy known as Nemaline Rod Myopathy." He described the importance of work:

> Feeling sorry for ourselves was not an option. While in high school it was instilled in us that we were expected to go to college, and that to get ahead in

life and get a good job, continued education was a necessity. Though I received social security benefits as an individual with a disability, my parents made it clear that it was only while in school would I collect benefits and not do so for life. Having a job was an important value for my parents, and they insisted that my brothers and I were to have jobs every summer, with a majority of the money to be set aside to pay for college. This value is one that stuck with me. Since earning a bachelor's degree, I have always had a job, even when because of a dramatic change in my impairment I had to take time off from work. Each time I knew I would return to work. Not working was never an option in my mind, though the doctors would have preferred that I only collect disability benefits. I believe that having a job is important because it allows people to understand that individuals with disabilities are capable of working and can be productive members of society who shouldn't feel sorry for themselves because of their limitations. (Winske, 2007, p. 407)

Winske's positive outlook, hard work, parental support, and strong intellectual skills have combined to make it possible for him to work. Nonetheless, unless his employer or employers were willing to allow time off for his relapses ("dramatic changes in my impairment") and subsequently return him to his job, his employment would not have been possible.

Another factor that keeps PWDs from working is the prejudice and discrimination of employers (Bordieri & Drehmer, 1988; McCarthy, 2003; Rossides, 1990). Such prejudice and discrimination are now illegal due to the legal protection offered by the 1990 Americans with Disabilities Act. Reread Eric Weihenmayer's account of trying to find a job as a dishwasher in the Boston/Cambridge area. Most PWDs, like Longmore, want to work for the same reasons that most others express.

The following sections present short explanations of a few typical adult-onset disabilities.

AMYOTROPHIC LATERAL SCLEROSIS

Amyotrophic lateral sclerosis (ALS) is a progressive, degenerating motor neuron disorder that is the most common motor neuron disorder in adults. The peak age of onset is midlife (most often between the ages of 55 and 75), and the disease is more common in men. Most people with ALS die within 2 to 4 years after the onset of symptoms. Nonetheless, individuals diagnosed early in life tend to have longer survival rates. Stephen Hawking was diagnosed at age 21; his decades of survival have amazed his physicians. When he proposed to his wife, he told her that he only had about three years to live.

Weakness is the most common presenting symptom (Bronfin, 2005). Other symptoms include muscle cramps, weight loss, respiratory distress, difficulty swallowing, and fasciculations (rapid, irregular, painless twitching of the skin). ALS is caused by destruction of the motor neurons in the spinal cord and brain stem. One type of ALS is bulbar palsy, in which the brain stem (or bulb) experiences damage to the lower motor neurons, including those of the muscles in the face and tongue. In a rapidly progressing case, a person may not be able to eat or swallow 12 months after onset. In this type of

ALS there is muscle atrophy, muscle paralysis, fasciculations of the tongue, and loss of other important motor functions. Patients at first are able to walk with a cane, progress to using a walker, and finally a wheelchair.

As the word "lateral" in the name implies, the onset of symptoms is typically on one side of the body and involves one arm and one leg. A famous baseball player, Lou Gehrig of the New York Yankees, brought attention to this disease and it is often called "Lou Gehrig's Disease."

MULTIPLE SCLEROSIS

Multiple sclerosis (MS) is a chronic, invisible, episodic, and degenerating disability and chronic illness. The cause of multiple sclerosis (MS) is unknown; however, it is considered an autoimmune disease and is thought to be caused by a virus. In autoimmune diseases the body attacks its own cells as if they were foreign substances. In MS the body mistakenly destroys the protective covering (the myelin) of the message-carrying nerve fibers in the brain and spinal cord. Scar tissues form over the destroyed myelin, interfering with the transmission of electrical impulses and causing neurological defects. The severity of MS is related to the extent of the scar tissues. (The word "sclerosis" means "scarring.") Symptoms vary in intensity over time and include dizziness (vertigo or a false sense of spinning), weakness, spasticity, lack of balance, numbness (paresthesia) visual problems (diplopia or double vision), and poor bladder control. Although intellectual functioning remains intact, changes to cognitive functioning may occur, such as memory impairment and slowing of psychomotor responses. At times these symptoms may become visible, but at other times they are invisible. Generally these symptoms increase over time as more scar tissue develops. No known treatment will prevent or reverse the course of MS.

The typical age of diagnosis is 20 to 40 years, and the disease is twice as common in women as in men. The average age of onset of symptoms is about 30 years of age for women, although men tend to have a somewhat later onset. The presentation of symptoms and patterns of progression vary greatly, so each case is different. Individuals experience different combinations of symptoms. Furthermore, there is no predictable pattern of symptom development or progression. For some individuals there is a rapid onset of symptoms, but for others symptoms present very slowly. MS is considered an episodic disability in which there are periods of remission during which the symptoms get better, along with periods of relapse or exacerbation when the symptoms become worse. Nancy Mairs (1997) described the episodic course and autoimmune nature of her disability as "alien invaders." She also feels a lack of control.

> I have known that I have multiple sclerosis for about seventeen years now, though the disease probably started long before. The hypothesis is that the disease process, in which the protective covering of the nerves in the brain and in the spinal cord is eaten away and replaced by scar tissue, "hard patches," is caused by an autoimmune reaction to a slow-acting virus. Research suggests that I was infected by this virus, which no one has ever seen and therefore, technically doesn't even "exist," between the ages of four and fifteen. In effect, living with this mysterious mechanism feels like having your present self, and the past selves it embodies, haunted by a capricious and mean-spirited ghost, unseen

except for its footprints, which trips you even when you're watching where you're going, knocks glassware out of your hand, squeezes urine out of your bladder before you reach the bathroom, and weights your whole body with a weariness that no amount of rest can relieve. An alien invader must be at work. But, of course, it's not. It's your own body. That is, it's you. (pp. 52–53)

One woman with MS describes the loss of bowel and bladder control:

The loss of bowel and bladder control is much more than simply a mechanical or neurological dysfunction. Incontinence reduces an adult to the status of a helpless victim. One is no longer the master of even the most basic of bodily functions. So great is the threat of public humiliation that many afflicted patients simply choose to withdraw from society, rather than risk embarrassment. (Toombs, 1995, p. 18)

RHEUMATOID ARTHRITIS

Rheumatoid arthritis (RA) affects approximately 1% of the total adult population (ages 18 and older) and 2% of the male population and 5% of the female population by age 65. Its cause is unknown, and it presents with a slow, insidious onset and a slow progression. It is a disorder of the connective tissues, especially the joints, that presents with inflammation, swelling, pain, and loss of joint motion. One physician described the progression of RA: "The process is locally invasive, and the rheumatoid tissue can erode cartilage, bone, and support tissues. Additionally, the body produces enzymes harmful to tissue that can degrade the articular (joint) cartilage" (Beardmore, 1995, p. 355).

RA is a chronic, degenerating illness (or disability) that is not invisible but rather disfiguring. RA is degenerating because it eventually affects all the joints in the body and produces deformities in the joints of the hand. There may be flexion deformities, or the fingers may appear misaligned. The only treatments available are often slow acting and act only to relieve symptoms. In advanced stages individuals may require walking assistance, such as canes, walkers, or wheelchairs.

Women are three times more likely to develop RA than men, and the peak onset years are in the 20s and 30s. One woman described her experience of RA (although she has juvenile-onset RA rather than the more common adult-onset RA).

I've been in the hospital every year—for a week or so. It's progressive. I know where it's heading. But I don't really think about it too often. I have termites and they're just eating, having a good time. That's how I describe juvenile rheumatoid arthritis—having termites eating away at my bones and joints. It's not something that can be fixed. You can't slow it down. Gold shots retard it a little bit, but they're still in there having a picnic. They're eating away at the shoulders, so I've lost the rotator cuffs. This hip has to be redone because the termites that eat the bone eat the glue. It just stinks. (Penn, 1993, p. 111)

SYSTEMIC LUPUS ERYTHEMATOSUS

Systemic lupus erythematosus (SLE) is a disorder of the immune system that affects multiple organs of the body, most commonly the skin, joints, kidneys, and blood. Ninety percent of those with SLE are women, with the peak onset years in the 20s and 30s. The cause of SLE is unknown. SLE can be either mild or very severe, with the degree of severity based upon the organs involved. Some individuals may have only joint pain for several years; however, for others there is kidney failure and eventual death. SLE is an episodic disability, in which periods of remission alternate with periods of symptom exacerbation.

Fatigue is the most common presenting symptom, and there are laboratory tests to diagnose SLE. Because of the variable nature of SLE, treatment is based upon the organ(s) involved. For some individuals treatment consists of nonsteroidal antiflammatory drugs, corticosteroids, and immune system modulating medications. For others dialysis and kidney transplants are necessary. SLE is an invisible, episodic, degenerating disability that can be terminal.

POST-POLIO SYNDROME

Poliomyelitis was once a common disease in the developed nations from the 1890s until the introduction of the polio vaccine in the 1950s. Individual cases of polio are caused by poor sanitation. The virus is found in human feces and enters the body through the mouth. For this reason swimming pools were often the source of contagion. Before the 1890s and the development of clean water supplies and sewage systems, all infants were infected with the polio virus. Newborn infants infected with the polio virus either had a mild case of polio, did not become sick at all, or died. Before widespread public health measures, everyone had a naturally acquired immunity to polio.

This may appear to be contradictory, but the polio epidemics in the United States (and other developed nations) can be considered to have been caused by cleanliness. For the first time in history, large populations had no natural immunity because they had never contracted the polio virus. Therefore when the virus was introduced into a community, an epidemic occurred and did not end until everyone had been exposed. In 1955 the polio vaccine became widely available with accompanying motto, "Swim and dive in '55." All research on polio ended in 1955. Americans, scientists, medical practitioners, and the government thought that the problem of polio had been solved. To this day it is not known why the virus remained in the digestive tracts of some polio-infected individuals and was excreted, leaving them without any residual paralysis. For others the virus went into the spinal cord and central nervous and caused permanent paralysis. Currently physicians and other medical personnel are typically not trained or educated about polio, nor are younger physicians likely to see (or treat) an individual with an acute case of polio. The absence of polio education/training in medicine has resulted in a lack of expertise in diagnosing and treating post-polio syndrome (PPS) (Marks, 1990; Shell, 2005).

In the early 1980s a new term was coined, "post-polio syndrome," to describe the muscle weakness and pain experienced by those who had contracted polio during the epidemics. The virus had reappeared. The results of post-polio syndrome have been summarized:

> Since poliomyelitis is not a progressive disease, many individuals have adapted and adjusted to the functional limitations and residual effects associated with the condition, going on to lead full and productive lives. For symptoms to again

occur can be frightening, as well as frustrating for the individual who must again adjust and adapt to continuing limitations in function, potential use of new assistive devices, and alterations of lifestyle.... Since post-polio syndrome occurs many years after the original occurrence of the disease, individuals experiencing post-polio syndrome are often in middle age and experiencing other changes associated with aging as well. The combination of symptoms, readjustment, and life circumstances can result in personal stress as well as strain on family, work, and social relationships. (Falvo, 1999, pp. 67–68)

Chronic Illness and Disabilities

- Difficult to diagnose
- Invisible
- Episodic
- Female prevalent

According to the Commission on Chronic Diseases (1957) chronic illness (or disability) is caused by a nonreversible pathological alteration that produces permanency, long-term residual loss, and the need for rehabilitation and management. Larsen (2006) compiled a list of definitions that included "an ongoing medical condition with spectrum of social, economic, and behavioral complications which require meaningful and professional involvement" (p. 5). Simply stated, an individual with a chronic illness or disability is never "cured." A health care system designed for acute, curative medicine was never intended to serve PWDs. In acute, curative care there were two patient outcomes: the patient died or the patient lived, entirely cured without any residual effects. Because the date of the first Commission on Chronic Diseases is 1957, we can see that the identification of long-term illness or disability is a relatively recent occurrence.

Traditionally the goal of health care has been to cure the client. Even today health care providers tend to measure success in this way. Because chronic disease is more prevalent than infectious disease or acute illness, this criterion of success may be inappropriate. Cure is neither essential nor necessary for the client to receive a benefit. Instead the criterion should be caring, demonstrated by valuing and assisting. As the number of people with chronic diseases increases, providers must learn to accept the characteristics of chronic disease, relapses, and multiple treatment modalities (Mann & Stuenkel, 2006, pp. 59–60).

We have learned that medical advances, improved public health measures, and widespread insurance coverage have produced three societal changes: Americans tend to have longer life spans, there are more PWDs than ever before, and PWDs have longer life spans. All three of these successes result in more disabilities. An increase in life span results in more disability because the rate of disability is positively correlated with age; in other words, as society ages the rate of disability goes up. Because antibiotics and better care produce longer life spans for PWDs, aging services for the first time will become necessary for persons with many different types of disabilities. Indeed, a wide variety of specialized services will be necessary to respond to chronic illnesses and disabilities (Corbin & Strauss, 1988). The idea that an individual would manage and treat his or her disability for the rest of his or her life is a relatively new approach.

The course of a disability or illness is considered its trajectory and includes three factors: (1) the direction of the course, such as stable, degenerating, or improving; (2) the pace of movement; and (3) the degree of predictability (White & Lubkin, 1998). This idea of a course or trajectory is a relatively novel concept in medicine because of the centuries-old history of a two-outcome paradigm—life or death. The flu epidemics of 1918 in the United States and the polio epidemics of 1893 to 1955 show the difference between the two-outcome paradigm and the chronic disability paradigm. In the flu epidemics, individuals who contracted the disease either recovered fully or died. No one experienced residual effects from the flu. In the polio epidemics there were three results: individuals who contracted the virus were fully cured, died, or recovered but with life-long disabilities. Indeed, physicians are now seeing patients with post-polio syndrome, in which the polio virus has returned. Many of these post-polio patients thought they had been completely cured of polio.

Chronicity is an inherent part of the definition of disability and chronic illness (Curtin & Lubkin, 1998; Dell Orto, 1988). Thus a broken arm or a bad case of the flu is not a disability, because the individual eventually recovers. A professor of English described the difficulty of accepting chronicity.

> I was not going to get well—ever. Though I might have periods of remission, I would not (and could not) be cured. My expectation has been that the (profession of) medicine would restore me to health. Now, that expectation was dashed, along with my cherished illusion that I was in control of my life. The future disappeared. (Toombs, 1995, p. 4)

From this short excerpt it can be seen that both medical providers and the individuals with long-term disabilities and chronic illnesses find lifelong care and management less satisfying than a total cure.

Most chronic illnesses occurring in adulthood are difficult to diagnose, presenting with symptoms of fatigue, vision disturbances, numbness, weakness, and pain (Agich, 1995). All of these symptoms are not very easily recognized, but they are easily dismissed. Standardized, objective laboratory diagnostic testing often is not available, so physicians are frustrated and impatient because they cannot provide a clear-cut diagnosis and patients often wonder if they will die before anyone figures out what is wrong. Patients have often been told to take a vacation, learn to deal with stress better, take more vitamins, or see a psychiatrist. Family members feel frustration, helplessness, confusion, and eventually perhaps resentment. As a result of this long diagnostic odyssey, the individual can become angry or depressed; some individuals begin to wonder if they are "crazy."

One study showed that for men with MS, arriving at a diagnosis was a 40-month process, during which these men lived in an ambiguous world, simultaneously being sick and not being seen as having a disease. Many disabilities and conditions that are more common in one sex are more difficult to diagnose in the other sex. Physicians who do not have any expectation of a specific type of disease or condition often overlook or ignore the symptoms. For example, many elementary school–age girls were not diagnosed with learning disabilities because psychologists focused on diagnosing boys. Many chronic illnesses are female prevalent, so it often takes longer to arrive at a diagnosis for men.

A Harris national survey of Americans (of all ages) with chronic illness identified these challenges: (1) 45% reported that the cost of care is a financial burden, (2) 89% reported difficulty in obtaining adequate health insurance, (3) 14% reported that physicians diagnosed the same symptoms as caused by different chronic illnesses, (4) 17% reported that they received contradictory information from health care providers, and (5) 78% reported difficulty in obtaining assistance from family and friends (Rossi, 2003).

Individuals with invisible disabilities, whether physical, cognitive, or psychiatric, are the target of more prejudice and discrimination than those with visible disabilities. "Some disabilities are readily apparent to others; other disabilities are not apparent to others unless the PWD chooses to disclose; and other types of disabilities are invisible even to the individual himself or herself" (Smart, 2009, p. 529). There is no correlation between degree of visibility and degree of impairment. Nonetheless many believe that degree of visibility is related to degree of impairment, thinking that disabilities that cannot be seen are not very limiting while disabilities that can be seen must be severely impairing. Many individuals with invisible disabilities state, "You get tired of defending yourself all of the time." For example, many people with invisible disabilities have been followed into stores by strangers and then publicly berated for parking in a handicapped spot.

All disabilities appear to be ambiguous to PWODs (and to PWDs with other types of disabilities), and this ambiguity causes tension in PWODs. Often they do not know what to do or say. However, invisible disabilities create more ambiguity than disabilities that are readily apparent. There is also more prejudice and discrimination toward episodic disabilities. A stable course disability presents less ambiguity to both PWODs and the PWD. The questions "Do you or don't you have a disability?" or "Do I or do I not have a disability?" are often asked. A national survey of individuals with psychiatric disabilities (chronic, invisible, episodic disabilities) revealed:

> One of the most striking aspects of the survey responses was the percentage of people who described themselves as disabled but said that other people did not regard them as so, saying things such as, "even the people who know of my psychiatric history do not know what a struggle it is for me to maintain my balance." Another wrote, "Friends and family—they don't understand my illness/disability—they think I'm getting away with something—that there is nothing wrong with me." (Stefan, 2001, p. 57)

Disabilities with an episodic course are only visible during times of symptoms exacerbation or "flare-ups." Furthermore, it is often not possible to predict accurately when these relapses will occur, which makes planning and setting long-term goals difficult. Individuals may not know from day to day what to expect. What is life without plans?

When asked how they are doing, individuals with chronic, invisible disabilities understand that most people do not really want to know the answer, so they generally reply "I'm doing okay," even when they are so fatigued they can hardly stand or are experiencing horrible pain. Those with chronic, invisible illnesses understand that it is important to meet the needs of others by keeping them comfortable instead of explaining honestly how they are feeling. Because all people have experienced *acute* illness, they mistakenly think that they understand *chronic* illness. Acute illnesses are not pleasant, yet everyone understands that they will eventually recover. Even unconsciously, comparing acute illness with chronic illness is impossible. Richard Cohen, a journalist with MS, described the ambiguity of an invisible, episodic illness as "shadow-boxing."

> Finally, I had been drafted, only this time into the army of 350,000 Americans who shadowbox with this neurological enemy they cannot see. (2004, p. 23)

A man with a psychiatric disability described chronicity as more than symptom relief and stated that even though a cure is not possible, recovery is. Note also that he considers that the stigma toward him and his disability is something from which he must "recover."

> Recovery is not a return to a former level of functioning. I have heard so many people—professionals and survivors alike—say that mental illness is not curable. I agree that we can never go back to our "premorbid" selves. The experience of the disability, and the stigma attached to it, changes us forever. Instead, recovery is a deeply personal and unique process of changing one's attitudes, values, self-concept, and goals. It is finding ways to live a hopeful, satisfying, active, and contributing. Everyone is changed by major happenings in their lives. We cannot return to the past. Recovery involves the development of a new meaning and purpose in one's life. It is looking realistically at both the limitations and the possibilities. It is much more than symptom relief. (Walsh, 2007, p. 113)

Others have described the emotional response of those with episodic disabilities:

> Clients have compared times of adjustment to riding a roller coaster; constantly challenged or angered by uphill struggles, never knowing when another curve will come, and unable to stop the motion. During this period of mixed and conflicting emotions, they have a sense of instability, of bewilderment, and of helplessness. (Kohler, Schweikert-Stary, & Lubkin, 1998, p. 129)

During relapses and flare-ups, individuals may wonder if they will be able to return to their work or to their education. They ask, such questions as: "Will this relapse be severe or mild?" "How long will this relapse last?" Response demands are not great when relapses are infrequent and mild; however, when relapses are frequent and severe, perhaps requiring hospitalization, the individual and his or her family view the relapse as an acute emergency. Therefore the frequency, level of severity, and the predictability of the relapses are important considerations. Family members, spouses, and friends become skilled at recognizing prodromal (warning) symptoms. Family members are required to live with permanent uncertainty that oftens produces compassion, fatigue, or burnout (Peterson, Maier, & Seligman, 1993). One wife explained:

> I guess I'm okay with it, but...I have tons of anger, not really to him—sometimes to him—but more to, you know, "Why me? Why did this happen to me?

Why did my husband happen to be the one who got ill?" Because when we got married, we were the perfect little couple...So, yes, I've had to revise a lot.... I can't think far in advance any more. That is probably the biggest thing that has changed my life because I used to be a planner, all the time planned—ten years ahead.... With an illness like this that runs in cycles...I just think it's too much to put on yourself to expect things when you don't know what's going to happen. (Karp, 2001, p. 143)

A woman with a psychiatric disability described a relapse. She awoke "a madwoman."

First, I had a mini-anxiety attack ... and then I had trouble sleeping, and one morning, two weeks into my Kentucky trip, I woke up a madwoman again. The Prozac simply stopped working. That's impossible. No, it's not. I started to tap and touch things and to have to count until my mind clenched closed. Where are you, Prozac? Come home, come home. Back to my body again.... My mental illness came rushing back in. As fast as Prozac had once, like a sexy firefighter, doused the flames of pain, the flames now flared up, angrier than ever and my potent pill could do nothing to quell the conflagration. (Karp, 2001, pp. 171–172)

Public places in our society, including workplaces and schools, are not structured to accommodate episodic disabilities. For example, the winner of the Ms. Wheelchair Wisconsin, Janeal Lee, had her title rescinded after a newspaper photo showed her standing up. Ms. Lee has muscular dystrophy and is able to stand for short periods of time, although she uses a wheelchair the majority of the time. In response the World Association of Persons With Disabilities created a new title, Miss disAbility International, and presented it to Ms. Lee. In a book on legal issues of disabilities, the author echoed the same idea:

Society is most comfortable with disabilities that are permanent and chronic; either one is disabled or not. Even with people who sometimes have to use a wheelchair find themselves regarded with skepticism and suspicion bordering on hostility. (Stefan, 2001, p. 10)

Stefan (2001) continued to explain the prejudice and discrimination against those with episodic disabilities as part of the larger legal and economic systems of the United States.

The economic, mental health, and legal structures, however, cannot accommodate the central truth of alternating or concurrent crisis and functioning at all. The U.S. legal system, mental health system, and labor market are marked by a static and dichotomous vision: One is either disabled or not, and once identified as disabled, residence in the category is presumed permanent. There is no place for the complexities and contradictions of people's real lives....Defeats...are also not seen as temporary, but as permanent. One bad episode can mean the termination of parental rights, or involuntary commitment or involuntary medication. It is all or nothing in American society. (p. 59)

Developmental Tasks of Adults With Chronic Illness and Disabilities

- Managing pain
- Acting as caregivers
- Avoiding secondary conditions
- Responding to the interaction of the aging process with the effects of the disability

Many individuals in the age range of 25 to 60 have congenital disabilities or disabilities acquired earlier in life. These individuals either have had time in which to develop a self-identity that includes the disability or have no pre-disability identity. Nonetheless these individuals are required (and want) to negotiate the developmental tasks of adulthood and midlife.

For individuals who acquire a disability or are diagnosed with a disability during adulthood or midlife, a change of identity is necessary (Krapfl, 1983). The distinction between acquiring a disability and receiving a diagnosis is important. Acquiring a disability typically includes an acute onset, often traumatic. With this type of onset, the individual can state the exact time when his or her life changed—the time of an accident or the loss of some function. Often this is termed a "flashbulb memory," because the individual remembers in exquisite detail the time of onset, which he or she retains for life. Some PWDs describe the experience of receiving a diagnosis as "the scene is frozen in my mind" (Labroit, 2006, p. 417).

When time of diagnosis is referenced, the onset is considered insidious, meaning hidden or stealthy. Diabetes, MS, and many of the autoimmune diseases have insidious onsets so that neither the individual nor the physicians can pinpoint an exact date when the illness began. Receiving the diagnosis of a chronic illness often is also a "flashbulb memory." Read again that portion of Chapter 1 in which Cohen describes receiving the diagnosis of MS over the telephone. Because Cohen can remember the exact wording of the diagnosis and recall his thoughts and feelings, it is a flashbulb memory. Occasionally individuals report that they have not felt "quite right" or "something was not quite right" for a long time. The individual who receives a definitive diagnosis of a chronic illness often feels ambivalence. On the one hand, he or she is relieved that the symptoms have a name and diagnosis, and the person may feel validated and relieved. Even receiving a very serious diagnosis may end imagining an array of frightening possibilities. On the other hand, the individual may be horrified to learn that he or she has a condition that is serious and sometimes fatal. More support is given for acute onset disabilities because they occur during a clearly delineated emergency (Gulick, 1994). On the other hand, those with insidious onset diseases must at some point seek emergency care, undergo hospitalizations, and disengage from their lives; however, they may return from their hospitalizations without a diagnosis. Nonetheless, insidious onset disabilities are rarely acknowledged or understood as well as acute onset disabilities (Lubkin & Larsen, 1998, 2006; Power & Rogers, 1979). Carolyn Strite lost some of the most important things in life when she was diagnosed with MS:

When my symptoms were at their worst and I was diagnosed, my life literally collapsed around me. My husband left; my son was placed with another family; I lost my home (could not make the payments); my job retention was in question; my body did not seem to be my own anymore. My previous outlets for anxiety, frustration, and anger had been tennis, running, and bicycling. Those were out of the question at that time. Yet, when I attempted to write one last note to my exceptionally caring boss to explain why I had chosen this way out of my pain [suicide], I could not do it. (Vash, 1981, p. 254)

Until age 30 (especially for males) disability is primarily caused by injury (sometimes referred to as "trauma"), but after age 40 disability is primarily caused by chronic illness, most of which have insidious onset. Some individuals with chronic illness report the day of their diagnosis as the "happiest day of my life," a response that appears unusual at first glance. A woman with a husband with mental illness described her reaction to receiving her husband's diagnosis:

I'll tell you one of the best days of my life was when I got a phone call from the hospital telling me what they decided was wrong with my husband, and they couldn't understand why I was so excited or happy. (Karp, 2001, p. 50)

It can be a relief to end a long prediagnostic period of uncertainty, stress, and ambiguity and a prolonged "diagnostic odyssey" by simply learning that the symptoms have a name or a diagnosis. The book *Sick and Tired of Feeling Sick and Tired: Living with Chronic Invisible Illness* (Donoghue & Siegel, 1992) referred to a study that examined the psychological impact of multiple sclerosis. The outcome of the study surprised the researchers. Even though they had fewer functional limitations, men in the study tended to be more depressed than the women. The researchers found that these men had endured longer prediagnostic periods (an average of 40 months) than women and reported low feelings of self-worth and the need to defend and explain themselves constantly to skeptical physicians and family members. Thus the stress, ambiguity, and skepticism of others were more depressing than the actual physical impairments.

Lack of a diagnosis does not mean absence of impairment. As one woman explained,

It's so hard to justify my fatigue to friends and relatives; my husband often asks, "Why are you so tired?" It took an article in the *National Arthritis News* to finally help me to convince myself and him that my fatigue was real, physiologically, as well as emotionally. (Kohler, Schweikert-Stary, & Lubkin, 1998, p. 129)

Clare was an Englishwoman diagnosed with MS, and after the diagnosis friends told Clare that they had thought she was lazy.

One interesting piece of information that came to light after I told people that I had MS was the opinions that they and others had had of me. I guess I was both hurt and mildly angry to discover that I had been seen as a lazy and workshy person. . . . I was just left feeling betrayed by friends of many years. (Morris, 1991, p. 181)

Responding to Disability in Midlife

- The changing definition of autonomy and independence
- Little social role guidance
- Physicians are often untrained to deal with disability in midlife
- As the disability worsens, the physical environment becomes less accessible

One woman described the sudden onset of her disability and her gradual change in identity.

> In 1985, I fell ill overnight with what turned out to be a disabling chronic disease. [In t]he long struggle to come to terms with it, I had to learn to live with a body that felt entirely different to me—weak, tired, painful, nauseated, dizzy, unpredictable. I learned at first by listening to other people with chronic illness or disabilities; suddenly able-bodied people seem to me profoundly ignorant of everything I most needed to know.... I realized after a year of waiting to get well, hoping to recover my healthy body was a dangerous strategy. I began to slowly identify with my new, disabled body and to learn to work with it. (Wendell, 2010, p. 336)

Paul Longmore, a polio survivor who uses a wheelchair, summarized the importance of independence and autonomy in American culture and how PWDs can thought of as not "real Americans":

> Autonomy and dependency and quality of life are highly value-laden concepts. They are rooted in American values that uphold complete physical self-sufficiency and absolutely personal autonomy as cultural ideals. They express a myth, a myth that real Americans are rugged individualists who quite literally stand on their own two feet. The ideal, the authentic American is not in any way dependent on others. To become sick or disabled in American is to lose one's social validity. It is to acquire a relentlessly and radically negative identity. It is to become the inversion of what a real American is supposed to be. (2003, p. 190)

Randy Souders became paralyzed in a diving accident as a teenager. He described his experiences shortly after his accident and the ways in which obsolete laws and government policies (rather than his disability) fostered dependence. Souders, who became a successful artist, used the term "underchallenge" to describe "lowered expectations."

> It was the art that provided the motivation for me to get up every morning and do something instead of sitting in front of the TV. It's very easy to get sucked into a dependency routine—you know, this "give me, give me, give me" kind of attitude. Society has such limited expectations of the disabled person. It doesn't expect you to be able to do much of anything. It [society] underchallenges us to perform.... And that's what I take the most pride in—the fact that what

I'm doing today is well received all over, even with people who haven't a clue to my physical condition. Then, when they learn about the paralysis and the story behind it, their mouths just drop and hang open. The gallery owners, for example, are flabbergasted that I can do anything. So that's what I take some measure of pride in: They don't say, "Gee, this is good considering your condition…blah, blah," they say, "Boy, this is good *period*. And they dig into their pockets and pull out their wallets. That, for me, is a kick." (Souders, 1993, p. 151)

Linton (1998) observed that PWODs often think that PWDs should not ask for "luxuries" or "pleasures" such as sex education, sexual health care, and access to social and cultural events. She gives three reasons for these ideas: (1) because PWDs are an economic drain on America they really should not ask for "non-necessities," (2) PWDs should be grateful and satisfied with basic medical care, and (3) pleasure is not important for PWDs.

Society's choice, and I see it as a choice, to exclude disabled people from social and cultural events that afford pleasure, or deny them sex education, sexual health care, and, at times, marriage, privacy, and friendship are indications that pleasure is less consequential to disabled people than to nondisabled people. Yet that belief is likely a rationalization for more virulent impulses. Are disabled people denied access to pleasure by the unspoken notion that they are not entitled to it, because they cause displeasure to others?…How dare we crippled, blind, and crazy folks ask for parity? Shouldn't we be satisfied with the provision of medical care and sustenance, and leave the luxuries for those who are thought to drain fewer resources from society? (Linton, 1998, p. 111)

Another woman expressed the lack of dignity she experienced while using some of the accommodations provided:

I'd love to be able to get into the spa. And they have a wonderful spa where I swim, but there is not a decent lift to get into it. They have a sling-type, which just doesn't work for us anymore. It's so fatiguing to use. It's so dehumanizing that it's just not worth it. (Putnam et al., 2003, p. 42)

Robert Murphy (1987) was a professor of anthropology at Columbia University who became paralyzed as a result of a tumor of the spinal cord, from which he eventually died. He describes his new identity (as a PWD) as going on a long trip (sojourn) to a foreign country and leaving his native culture.

Just as an anthropologist gets a better perspective on his culture through long and deep study of a radically different one, my extended sojourn in disability has given me, like it or not, a measure of my estrangement far beyond the yield of any trip. I now stand somewhat apart from American culture, making me in many ways a stranger. And with this estrangement has come a greater urge to penetrate the veneer of cultural differences and reach an understanding of the underlying unity of all human experience. (pp. 102–103)

A woman who awoke with polio described how she was a stranger to herself, even in her dreams:

Something happened and I became a stranger. I was a greater stranger to myself than anyone. Even my dreams did not know me. They did not know what they ought to let me do—and when I went to dances or parties (in my dreams), there was always an odd provision or limitation—not spoken of or mentioned, but there just the same. I suddenly had the very confusion and mental and emotional conflict of a lady leading a double life. It was unreal and it puzzled me, and I would not help dwelling on it. (Goffman, 1963, p. 35)

The woman continued by stating that there is little social role guidance for adults who acquire disabilities. Note the way in which this lack of social role guidance made her feel like a child.

But suddenly, I woke up one morning and found that I could not stand. I had had polio and polio was simple as that. I was like a very young child who had been dropped into a big, black hole.... The education, the lectures, and the parental training which I had received for twenty-four years didn't seem to make the person who could do anything for me now. (Goffman, 1963, p. 35)

Reynolds Price, an author, playwright, and poet, wrote about his paralysis acquired at the age of 51. He wrote about the onset of his disability as a war, and because Price is a writer, he compared himself to the great war novelists.

Then, I got to go to a war that in many ways was even more challenging than Hemingway, William Styron, and James Jones got to go to. I was a whole army that the war was declared against. The cancer was out to get me and nobody else. (Price, 1993, p. 127)

Initially, I didn't want to go out at all. I got very agoraphobic. If you're in this condition, there are all kinds of problems. I mean going to the bath-room, you've got to learn a whole new way of doing that—just everything, your clothing, your dress, the way you eat a meal; it's like having to learn Chinese at the age of fifty-one. But damn it, you either learn it, or you die. Or you become someone who is so wretched and miserable and mean that no one can stand to be around you. I call it my after-life, this new life I have. (Price, 1993, p. 126)

George Covington was Special Assistant for Disability Policy in the office of the vice-president and was born legally blind, "a combination of what we've come to know as astigmatism, nystagmus, eccentric fixation, and myopia—all of which were acute—and probably even further back, a degenerating retina." Covington graduated from law school at the University of Texas and subsequently wrote the regulations for Section 504 of the 1973 Rehabilitation Act. Section 504 is considered the forerun-ner of the Americans with Disabilities Act that mandates civil rights for PWDs.

As a white southern male, I never thought I would have to worry about my civil rights. But as I wrote the 504 regs for the Department of Interior—the Handicapped Civil Rights rights—I realized that there is a lot of discrimina-tion against those with disabilities. (Covington, 1993, p. 41)

Adults with disabilities have expressed disappointment in physicians and other medical care givers who did not address sexual issues. In one study, adults with disabilities were asked to describe wellness factors in their disability and factors that did not contribute to wellness. The authors summarized:

> Participants also expressed aggravation at physicians who do not provide specific health and wellness issues relevant to their conditions. One woman said, "I'm tired of people dancing around the information we need to know. For instance, very specifically about sexual dysfunction...why not tell us? Are we not all adults? Do most of us not have husbands and wives? Do we not have sex? Why can't you talk to us in plain English about things that are affecting us?" (Putnam et al., 2003, p. 42)

One woman described the devastating loss of her career:

> I felt dreadful when I had to give up work. It was the most shattering experience I had had because going out to work you felt a part of society, you were contributing, you were earning your own money. You also had your friends that you went to work with, and then suddenly, you were cut off. You were in the house alone. Also, of course, financially you were worse off. You were lonely, you felt useless, on the scrap heap, finished, and it really was a bad time. (Campling, 1981, p. 115)

Managing a disability in midlife becomes more expensive. For an individual with a stable course disability, the effects of aging begin to interact with those of the disability, and people with degenerating disabilities must not only respond emotionally to each level of loss but also deal with increasing financial demands. Medical crises and equipment breakdown make budgeting difficult. A team of researchers interviewed individuals with spinal cord injuries, cerebral palsy, polio, and amputations in Portland, Oregon; Houston, Texas; and San Francisco and asked them what factors contributed to or decreased their sense of well-being. The researchers described this often-expressed concern.

> Many spoke about fears related to financing new equipment when their current devices needed replacing. Others relayed concerns about ongoing maintenance expenses. One participant said, "Once my scooter gives up, what am I going to do? Once my van goes toes up, what am I going to do? So, it's not so much . . . about obtaining the assistive device the first time, but replacing them. Because once my scooter gives up, how do I walk?" (Putnam et al., 2003, p. 42)

A young man with a type of progressive blindness described the emotional results of the degeneration of his vision.

> As my disability becomes worse, I am becoming less and less at home in the world. This is the world of the normal. The world of the normal is the background against which disability stands the figure of blindness....Still, I belong here, but not naturally anymore. Now that I am blind, belonging is a struggle. (Michalko, 2002, p. 38)

CHRONIC PAIN

Chronic Pain

- Not time limited
- No physical purpose
- Not socially acceptable
- Risk of self-medication
- Expensive, both personally and to the economy

Pain is a highly subjective experience defined as an unpleasant sensory and emotional experience with actual or potential tissue damage. There are two basic types of pain, acute and chronic. Acute pain is a "protective physiological mechanism that informs us when something is wrong with our bodies" (Jeffrey, 2006, p. 68). With acute pain, there is a cause-and-effect relationship because an identifiable pathology causes the pain and the pain remits when the pathology is cured. Therefore, acute pain is time limited and does not limit the individual's functioning for long periods of time. Acute pain can usually be controlled by medications. Understanding that the pain is only temporary and being able to control the pain make the experience of acute pain very different from that of chronic pain.

Chronic pain "no longer serves the purpose of acute pain" and "can be so pervasive that it becomes a condition unto itself that requires daily management" (Jeffrey, 2006, p. 68). With chronic pain, there is no evidence of underlying pathology, so the focus of treatment is on the relief of symptoms. Chronic pain is unremitting and intractable, and it can affect every area of the individual's life. Further clouding the picture are the negative stereotypes held by many medical professionals of individuals who have chronic pain. Indeed, many physicians believe that chronic pain is not as intense as acute pain (Taskahashi et al., 2000).

Acute pain is typically caused by pathology, while chronic pain typically results from musculoskeletal disabilities, such as lower back pain. (In the United States back problems are the most frequent cause of chronic pain.) There is no end to chronic pain. Individuals with severe chronic pain may change from being energetic, productive individuals with many roles (family member, worker, friend, community worker) to people who are only identified with pain, becoming dependent and depressed. Chronic pain can lead to sleep disturbances, fatigue, poor concentration, and depression. Family members are required to take on more responsibilities while they also try to understand the pain and feel powerless to help their loved one. Depression and chronic pain may have a circular relationship. As Gallaghter (2000) explained, "depression may lower the pain threshold and tolerance" (p. 28).

Thus chronic pain entails a great deal of ambiguity. It cannot be measured in any objective manner, it is invisible, the individual may be in severe pain and still appear to be pain-free, there is no end in sight, there is no identifiable pathology, and often there is no medical relief. Physicians are frustrated by these same aspects of chronic pain, and "many professionals have become desensitized to the client's pain experience and rate pain as less important than clients do" (Lubkin & Jeffrey, 1998,

p. 151). "Chronic pain often defies medical explanation, the pain and suffering experienced by the client is often conceptualized as something which must be stopped and never experienced again" (Burns, 2010, p. 483).

Although chronic pain is far more common in midlife, children also experience chronic pain. In children chronic pain is diagnosed as pain lasting a minimum of three months. Often chronic pain in children is not treated or fully treated due to three widely held myths:

a) very young children, especially neonates and infants are erroneously believed to feel little, if any pain, experience pain to a lesser degree, tolerate pain better than adults, and recover more quickly that adults;

b) the potential side effects of narcotics, including addiction, are believed to make the use of such medication too dangerous with small children;

c) pain is not thought to be life-threatening in young children, and young children do not remember pain. (Jeffrey, 2006, p. 75)

Like adults, children with chronic pain often experience depression and helplessness as well.

Reynolds Price, a novelist and professor of English at Duke University, wrote eloquently about constant pain. His pain may not fit all the criteria for chronic pain because the cause (spinal cancer) was known. Price underwent three surgeries and weeks of radiation, and eventually he lost the use of his legs. The following is an excerpt from his book *A Whole New Life*:

The pain was high and all-pervading from the neck to the feet; it generally peaked in blinding storms late in the day if I was tired. It intensified in conditions of low barometric pressure; and for dozens of other mysterious reasons, by now it had seized frank control of my mind, my moods, and my treatment of friends. Patience had ebbed to its lowest reach. (1994, p. 151)

Chronic pain is also socially unacceptable. No one wants to hear about someone's pain or see someone who is suffering. There simply is no socially acceptable way to express pain. Americans often praise those who overcome pain, ascribing heroic status to those who seem able to surmount their pain. Here is one such example:

Athletes are repeatedly praised by the media for overcoming extreme pain, like the astonishing Olympic gymnast from Japan who completed his dismount with a broken leg. Yet such praise and its implicit meaning (to overcome pain is heroic) leave a difficult legacy for chronic pain patients, who cannot surmount their affliction in a supreme moment of glory but must live with it, unpraised and often unobserved day after day. (Morris, 1998, p. 129)

Occasionally those with chronic pain seek to self-medicate through the use of alcohol and other types of drugs. Ironically, it is thought that alcohol may lower the pain threshold. Prescription drug abuse is another type of another way of attempting to alleviate pain.

We have learned that pain with no identifiable cause is one of the symptoms of some chronic illnesses, such as lupus, MS, or post-polio syndrome. Therefore it is necessary to rule out the presence of true organic causes for the pain, but we have seen that this is a long and difficult process and as the words "rule out" imply, a process of elimination.

Susan Wendell (1997) described the way in which we blame others for their pain in order to distance ourselves from the possibility that we might experience chronic pain.

> If someone tells me she is in pain, she reminds me of the existence of pain, the imperfection and fragility of the body, the possibility of my own, the *inevitability* of it. The less willing I am to accept all these, the less I want to know about her pain. If I cannot avoid it in her presence, I will avoid her. I may even blame her for it. I may tell myself that she *could have* avoided it, in order to go on believing that I *can* avoid it. I want to believe that I am not like her: I cling to the differences. (p. 268)

In a later work Susan Wendell (2010) states that most of us are afraid of pain, wish to deny its possibility and, therefore, actively avoid those who experience chronic pain. According to Wendell, this approach only *increases* our fear of pain:

> People with painful disabilities can teach us about pain, because they can't avoid it and have had to learn how to face it and live with it. The pernicious myth that it is possible to avoid almost all pain by controlling the body gives the fear of pain greater power than it should have and blames the victims of unavoidable pain. The fear of pain is also expressed or displaced as fear of people in pain, which often isolates those with painful disabilities. All of this is unnecessary. People in pain and knowledge of pain could be fully integrated into our culture, to everyone's benefit. (Wendell, 2010, p. 245)

Chronic pain imposes economic costs upon society and is a contributing factor to many negative life events, such as divorce, alcoholism, drug abuse, family violence, job loss, depression, and suicide (Burns, 2010). Chronic pain is expensive; it is estimated that in the United States, $70 to $100 billion are lost each year due to health care costs, job absenteeism, and job loss (Holmes et al., 2006; Libby, 2006; Turk & Burwinkle, 2005). No calculation of these costs and results takes into account the individual experience of pain.

FATIGUE AND SLEEP DISTURBANCES

Beginning in the 40s, fatigue tends to increase with the normal aging process from reduction in the number of muscle fibers, decreased muscle strength and endurance, and loss of cartilage and bone density. Malfunctions of the central nervous system and impaired neuromuscular transmissions are other types of organic causes for fatigue. There are two basic types of fatigue, acute fatigue and chronic fatigue. Acute fatigue is short term and can be traced to a known cause. In contrast, the cause of chronic, long-term fatigue cannot be determined. American society has long-enshrined values of energy, ambition, vim, and vigor, reflected in advertisements that admonish, "Just do it!" In active, achievement-oriented cultures, fatigue can appear to be laziness or lack of motivation. Conditions that include fatigue, such as Chronic Fatigue Syndrome (CFS), are given derisive nicknames like "yuppie flu" and the "shirker syndrome" (*New York Times*, 2007).

Chronic fatigue can affect every aspect of an individual's life and is not relieved by rest and sleep, nor is it related to activity or exertion. Endless tiredness, weakness, and lack of energy pervade the individual's life. Physicians try to determine the time of onset, including the time of day, and ask the patients if anything has helped relieve the fatigue. Fatigue typically does not occur in isolation from other symptoms of disability and chronic illness. Symptoms that frequently appear with fatigue include pain, depression, irritability, and frustration. Of course, with some of these other symptoms, it is difficult to separate the cause from the effect. For example, many fatigued individuals will avoid social contact, withdraw from an active lifestyle that includes exercise, and may retreat from their sexual partner. In these circumstances, when the symptoms of fatigue and depression are considered, it may be unclear which caused which. Chronic fatigue is stigmatized and ill-understood, and those individuals who experience fatigue are blamed and held responsible. Further, most PWODs confuse acute fatigue with chronic fatigue, even physicians. Therefore individuals who experience chronic fatigue are told to take a vacation, take vitamins, or buy a new hat. A feminist disability scholar explained:

> Some disabled people spend tremendous energy being independent in ways that might be considered trivial in a culture less insistent on self-reliance; if our culture valued *interdependence* more highly, they could use that energy for more satisfying activities. (Wendell, 1997, p. 273)

Canadian World War II veterans who returned home with spinal cord injuries told of physicians who wanted these men to walk on crutches so they would appear more "normal." In an oral history entitled "Going Back to Civvy Street," veterans said that they refused the crutches as a wasteful expenditure of energy. There was no doubt that the men were capable of walking on crutches. However, they knew that they had limited energy.

> It didn't make much sense spending all that energy covering a short distance (on crutches)...when you could do it quickly and easily with a wheelchair. . . It didn't take long for people to get over the idea that walking was that essential. (Tremblay, 1996, p. 153)

Sleep disturbances may be difficult to separate from the effects of middle age and late adulthood. Sleep habits change over an individual's life span; on average most adults over the age of 50 sleep 1 hour less, and "among the elderly, deep sleep generally disappears. Consequently, older adults sleep more fitfully and are more easily disturbed....Generally, the hours spent in bed are not as restful as they once were" (Rice, 1998, p. 466). Changes in the structure of the brain controlling sleep and higher levels of stress hormones in the blood stream are also thought to cause sleep disturbance in midlife (Berk, 2001).

Lack of accommodations and an inaccessible environment can deny the basic rights of citizenship for PWDs:

This particular discrimination, of course, has had a profound effect on the lives of disabled people. It has a psychological effect, among other things, but it also prevents [PWDs] from participating in society actively, getting jobs, paying taxes....This lack of mobility in many cases even affects the participation in the fundamental democratic process, the right to vote. Without transportation, in many cases, it is impossible even to cast your ballot, something which means that, at least in part, disabled people are excluded far more or just as much from the process as black people were by closed polls and poll taxes. (Fleischer & Zames, 2001, p. 69)

IN SICKNESS (DISABILITY) AND HEALTH

All marriages require that both partners agree on finances, their vision of the future, the decision to have or not have children, and the way in which to spend time. Thus the partners make compromises, and these decisions, needs, and desires also change over time. A marriage or partnership in which one individual (or both) has a disability includes all of these choices and additional disability-related decisions. For example, as the individual ages, the AT tends to become more expensive simply because the disability degenerates. For low-incidence disabilities, AT is very expensive, because it must be custom designed instead of purchased "off-the-rack."

A disability diagnosed in the early years of marriage requires the couple to confront loss, especially the loss of a normal life span and perhaps children and career. A psychiatrist explained:

When a disabling or life-threatening disorder occurs earlier, it is out of phase in both chronological and social time. When such events are untimely, spouse and family lack the psychosocial preparation and rehearsal that occur later, when peers are experiencing similar losses. The ill member and the family are likely to feel robbed of their expectation of a normal life span.... As one young woman explained whose husband had metastatic cancer confided, "As long as Jim has cancer, we have no future." Suffering is compounded for couples when peers distance themselves from them because they want to avoid facing the possibility of a similar loss of spouse or child. (Rolland, 1994, p. 186)

The pace of life is an area of compromise in all marriages. Multiple role demands and how much an individual decides to cram into a single day, especially an individual with a demanding job and small children at home, can be termed the "busyness of life" or "activity level" (Newman & Newman, 2009, p. 436). The need and desire for achievement is another aspect of pace of life. How active should an "active" life be? One partner may be an excellent time manager, a good organizer, achievement oriented, and energetic, while the other may be a "smell the roses" type of person who prefers a slower pace. Pace-of-life issues change throughout the course of the marriage, with more role demands and functions being typical in the younger adult years. In midlife, pace-of-life issues may resurface because extra time becomes available when children achieve independence and leave the family home and/or when one of the partners (or both) retires.

When descriptions are read of chronic illnesses and other disabilities that are episodic and may involve pain and fatigue, it becomes clear that these pace-of-life decisions are very difficult (O'Brien, 1993). Neither spontaneity nor well-planned calendars work with episodic disabilities in which relapses are not predictable. Fatigue and pain, separately or in combination, can cause individuals to become homebound with few activities. If the other partner does not have a disability (which is usually the case), the chronic illness of his or her partner has an effect. Many partners of individuals with chronic illness resent the chronic illness, and sometimes they find it difficult to separate this resentment from the partner who has the chronic illness. They may not feel that life is as fun as it used to be or that the loss of income necessitated by the illness has greatly reduced their standard of living. Sexual intimacy may be affected, either by illness itself or the medications required. A man who acquired a traumatic brain injury and a spinal cord injury related the story of his accident.

> After drinking beer … I got into my car to drive home. Halfway home, I fell asleep and struck a utility pole while sitting atop my seatbelt. My life was instantaneously altered. As my pregnant wife entered the hospital emergency room at 4:00 a.m., the neurosurgeon blasted her about my high alcohol reading and prognosis. If I survived I would need constant attention.
>
> After 6 months in the hospital, I was allowed to go home for weekends.… My foremost thought was to resume sexual activity with Valerie and provide for both our needs. At 27, I had serious doubts about being a person or a man and felt the only way to prove my virility was in the bedroom. Valerie was very patient and empathic to my needs. My hygiene was terrible, a tracheostomy was done on my throat, my bladder and bowel needed to be emptied prior to commencing intimacy, and there was always the chance of having an accident. To this day, I will always be indebted to her for allowing me to believe "I was the man." I told her she gave Oscar winning performances when I needed them. (Collins, 2007, p. 721)

When one partner requires a great deal of assistance and care, a relationship between two equals may become a relationship of a child with a caregiver. David Collins related that one sign of his recovery progress was "I was becoming less competitive with the girls." Collins had two small daughters, and he and his daughters competed for their mother's and wife's attention. The partner without the chronic illness may feel anger, resentment, and disappointment; furthermore, he or she may feel guilty for feeling angry. The other partner may question if divorce or separation will occur.

One woman described her husband's acquisition of a disability:

> One day I have a family member who is the strength of the family, who makes everyone proud, and the next, I have this person who scares everyone with his temper and who thinks everything is fine when it's a sorry mess. But life is getting better. The two of us get along. Sometimes I even like the fact that my husband is around all the time. He can be good company … I guess we'll be a good old twosome until the day we die.… Life is hard. I'm a survivor. (Dell Orto & Power, 2007)

PARENTHOOD WITH A DISABILITY

According to the Centers for Disease Control and Prevention (2001), approximately 13% to 14% of children have a parent with a disability. Typically, the older the child is when the parent acquires a disability, the more difficult the transition will be, simply because of the stress of change in the family and the threat of loss. Children who are born to parents who are disabled seem to adjust more easily, simply because for these families "abnormal is normal."

Many children who have a parent (or parents) with a disability think of their parent as simply "just my mom" or "just my dad." Naturally, the extent to which young children think of their parent as typical is based on the type and severity of the disability. "Living with losses can bring opportunities for everyone to have a fuller, deeper, and richer life," is a statement of a parent with disability (Aquarius Health Care Videos, 1999). Children are required to be more responsible, learn more patience, and tolerate differences. Often comparison with other families is the only setting in which the child sees himself or herself or the family as abnormal. One little boy stated, "Just because my dad can't walk like other daddies doesn't mean he is any different, really" (Aquarius Health Care Videos, 1999). A graduate student whose father had bipolar disorder (or manic depression) wrote:

> My father did not have a physical disability so it was difficult to understand that he did have a disability, especially when I was a young child. I wanted my dad to be dependable—there were times we couldn't even get him out of bed. As I look back on my childhood and the experiences I have had with my father, I am thankful, and would not change it for anything in this world.

Children can develop a stronger self-identity with pride in helping master a disability. These children also have a very close-up and personal view of a role model who manages a difficult situation.

Another graduate student is blind, and his 2-year-old son wears hearing aids. The little boy came to his dad and took his dad's hand and placed his dad's hand on his hearing aid to show him that the hearing aid was falling out of his ear. This father said that when his little boy goes to his mother about hearing aids that are falling out of his ear, he simply points at them. The 2-year-old son understands that his father cannot see and that his mother can. Another father who is blind told of an experience in which his 4-year-old daughter asked, "Daddy, when will you be able to see?" The father replied, "Probably never in this lifetime; but I was born this way and this is all I have ever known." Interestingly, both of these men's wives were told by others (before their marriage) that "life married to a blind man would be horrible." A mother with MS said that when she loses her balance and falls, it is a family affair. Her husband and some of the children help her up, and another child runs to the freezer to get packages of frozen peas to ice her knees.

Those outside of the family may not understand the family's responses and adaptation to a parental disability. One woman with MS told of being scolded by relatives for allowing her 6-year-old daughter to carry her newborn sister up and down the stairs in the home; the relatives felt it was putting too much responsibility upon the 6 year old. The mother explained that she was afraid of dropping the baby because of her MS.

On the other hand, a parent with a disability can create new stress and new responsibilities and demand sacrifices from everyone in the family, including the youngest children. Some children may think they have lost their childhood or were required to assume adult responsibilities at too early an age. Children who have a parent with a disability also experience "stigma by association."

Lee Martin's father lost both his arms in a farming accident when Lee was a year old, so he had no memory of his father with hands. However, Lee recalled the stigma by association. People stared at his father's hooks, asked inappropriate and intrusive questions, and sometimes simply avoided the entire family. As the son, Lee thought his father's angry, abusive behavior was caused in part by the stigma of being a man with a visible, disfiguring disability. Lee recalled looking at photographs of his father and thinking how different the lives of everyone in the family would have been if his father's hands had not been traumatically amputated:

> When I look at photographs of my father before his accident, my eyes go immediately to his hands. I try to figure out whether they resemble my own, but I can never really decide. His appear to be small, his fingers shorter, but that may only be the perspective of the camera. All I can be certain of is the sadness that comes over me whenever I look at those photographs. I want to tell my father about that moment in the cornfield when the shucking box will clog. "Shut off the tractor," I want to tell him, but of course, I can't. He's there in the photographs, and I'm here over forty years later, recalling the cold steel of his hooks. (Martin, 2000, pp. 7–8)

Children of Deaf Adults (CODAs)

- Bilingual in both signed and spoken languages
- Designated interpreter
- The power and responsibility placed on a child

When children undertake a great deal of responsibility in caring for a parent (or other older family member), it is termed "the parentification of the child," a negative term that implies the child has sacrificed childhood to assume adult responsibilities. Perhaps the most clear-cut example of the possibility of becoming parentified is children of deaf adults or CODAs. Smart (2009) described CODAs in this way:

> There is another situation in which a disability is present from the individual's birth; however, the disability is not the individual's disability, but rather the disability of his or her parents. Children of deaf adults (or CODAs) grow up bilingual, learning both sign language and spoken language. CODAs, unlike parents of deaf children, assume that deafness is "normal," have a way in which to communicate with their parents, and do not feel that their parents should try to enter the hearing world. (p. 449)

One child in the family is the "designated interpreter," typically the oldest daughter. Thus both age and gender are important determinants in choosing the designated interpreter. Even when there is an older son, the oldest daughter becomes the interpreter. If there are no daughters, the oldest son becomes the interpreter.

The role of designated interpreter places great responsibility on the child, but at the same time accords power that most children do not typically experience. These children must interpret for their parents in the adult hearing world, often as very young children (Filer & Filer, 2000). They must speak to the neighbors, the auto mechanic, doctors, and school teachers. There have been some autobiographical books about being CODAs, some of these which tell almost identical stories of attempting to fool their parents at school parent–teacher conferences. These stories are told by male CODAs and involve misinterpreting the teacher's negative feedback to their parents as glowing praise. In all these stories the father, either at home or in the car, signs to the son that he wants the "real truth." The deaf parents understood the teacher's body language and facial language and understood that that teacher was telling them that their son was a terrible student (Preston, 1994; Uhlberg, 2008). Most CODAs relate that they "protected" their parents from rude comments or intrusive curiosity by "editing" and omitting these comments from their signed interpretation to their parents (Filer & Filer, 2000; Sidranksy, 1990; Walker, 1986).

Some CODAs are proud of their service, feeling that their childhood gave them entry into two worlds—the hearing world and the deaf world—and many become professional teachers or counselors to deaf people (Couser, 1997). These CODAs remember that their childhoods gave them power and visibility that other children did not have and they saw their childhood as advantaged in a unique way. Other CODAs feel that their childhood was filled with responsibility and that they were often forced to "abandon our dreams and take care of our deaf mothers and fathers. They were our children, and we were their parents. We, the children, were invisible" (Sidransky, 1990, p. 96). Uhlberg (2008) perceptively described his life as a CODA:

> Many years later, when we were both living in Los Angeles, I was riding in a car with my uncle when he asked me if I remembered my eleventh birthday and the silver dollar he had pulled from my ear.
>
> He then explained what he had meant to say to me that day when he had set the coin spinning. As a child, David [my uncle] said, I always seemed to him to be two sides of the same coin, both one thing and it's opposite. I was cleaved into two parts, half hearing, half deaf, forever joined together. And, he had observed, very astutely, that I vacillated and vibrated between the child that I was in years and the adult I was forced to be in thought and action. When he looked at me, he saw that I stood at the crossroads of sound and silence, of childhood and adulthood, and that I would have to struggle to find my own way. (p. 219)

ASSISTIVE TECHNOLOGY

Throughout this book, we have seen the way in which PWDs view their AT. More than providing mobility, allowing access to job opportunities, or even sustaining life,

AT serves "as a replacement for parts of themselves to get the job done" (Reid, 2004, p. 572). Many PWDs speak of having a relationship with their AT, and some give their AT names. Remember how Weiskopf referred to his prosthetic hand as "Pretty Boy" how Mark O'Brien, the playwright and polio survivor, referred to his iron lung as "my second skin," or that Leonard Kriegel said he "loved his first wheelchair with a passion that embarrasses me now." Many PWDs remember the day they received their AT as the beginning of their lives. Self-esteem, integration into the wider society, and the provision of more privacy constitute some of the accommodations afforded by AT. AT also increases privacy because the PWD can use AT to preform functions that once required an aide, attendant, or family member. To cite a simple example, the use of a mouth-stick allows individuals with quadriplegia to complete their banking via the computer instead of having someone else write checks and keep track of the balance.

PWDs often view AT as an extension of themselves (which explains why they typically do not like others touching their wheelchairs) and as means of independence and autonomy. Quality of life for everyone is partially based on AT. Very few of us would like to live without electricity, computers, or cars. Up until the 1960s, most AT for PWDs was mechanical and homemade. Typically the husband or the father built whatever was needed in the garage. Now most AT is computerized and customized. For example, computer programs allow an individual to control the environment with his or her tongue, locking doors, turning lights and appliances on and off, and regulating heat and air conditioning. We have seen how wheelchair athletics have contributed to the quality of life of PWDs; however, athletic wheelchairs were not developed until the 1980s. We have also learned that deaf people died because of lack of access to emergency phone lines. Before the ADA many PWDs reported that they attended public schools and universities by having others carry them up and down stairs, a practice that is both humiliating and dangerous. Not many PWODs would submit to this treatment, so obviously the PWDs were forced into this position. Even worse, when accommodations (such as elevators or emergency telephone services for deaf people) or AT (such as wheelchairs and computerized voice recognition software) are missing, most PWODs do not notice. However, PWDs notice when AT and accommodations are not available.

It would seem to be without question that an accessible environment for everyone (curb cuts for wheelchairs and so on) is an excellent investment for everyone. For example, we have learned that the American population is aging and that accommodations and AT would increase their quality of life. Simply in terms of tax dollars, the provision of accommodations and AT would allow more individuals to work and thus pay for themselves. AT can be expensive, but not always. Remember the story of Brenda Premo, who is legally blind and wanted a $1.50 magnifying glass as AT. Although this is a simplistic statement, it is also true. It may not be possible to cure SCIs, but an easily obtained elevator (and other AT and accommodations) would ameliorate the effects of a SCI.

ROLE MODELS AND DISABLED HEROES

In his social learning theory, Albert Bandura identified the availability of role models and the principle of vicarious learning as central to learning new behaviors and increasing self-esteem. Bandura would probably state that if someone wanted to learn to golf, he or she should hire a highly skilled golfer as a teacher. In this book we have learned that there have not been many role models for PWDs, yet at the same time, the use of "disabled heroes" has been questioned.

The Disability Rights movement refers to disabled heroes as "Super Crips," a derisive term. Some examples of disabled heroes are Albert Einstein, Helen Keller, Beethoven, Christopher Reeve, Stephen Hawking, and Eric Weihenmayer. All of these individuals had (or have) disabilities yet achieved accomplishments that were remarkable for anyone, with or without a disability. Perhaps in an attempt to "normalize" disability to PWODs, these disabled heroes often appear on posters. The message implies something like this: "See, PWDs can accomplish great things." This message is true, but it also carries meaning for those who do have disabilities.

However, the message's effect on PWDs is often not recognized. For those who understand the experience of disability, it is readily apparent that many of these disabled heroes had exceptionally uncommon resources and did not have congenital disabilities, but rather achieved much of their success and fame *before* the onset of the disability. For some, such as Einstein, it is questionable if they were indeed disabled. The disabled hero posters state that Einstein, the British prime minister Winston Churchill, and the Danish fairy tale writer Hans Christian Andersen, all had a learning disability (dyslexia), but experts in learning disabilities often discount these post hoc diagnoses. These diagnoses of dyslexia are generally based on samples of poor handwriting with spelling errors and reports of difficulties in school. One expert explained:

> Frequently, in books and article on dyslexia, writers report a number of notable adults reputed to have had dyslexia. Repetition of these names has become almost a litany. These names are usually just listed in a series in books with rarely any explanation or evidence given why the person is considered to have been dyslexic. The few times any evidence is given it is scanty—often irrelevant or questionable.... Often there are more simple explanations for the difficulties these persons are said to have had. (Huston, 1987, pp. 151–152)

Covington (1997, as cited in Pelka) summarized the way in which PWDs view disabled heroes:

> Super crip is usually a character struck down in the prime of life who fights to overcome insurmountable odds to succeed as a meaningful member of society. Through strength of will, perseverance, and hard work, the disabled achieves a *normal* life....Too often, the news media treats an individual with disabilities who has attained success in his field or profession as though they were one-of-a-kind. While this one-of-a-kind aspect might make for a better story angle, it perpetuates in the mind of the general public how rare it is for the citizen with disabilities to succeed. (p. 292)

By focusing on *individuals*, society can reassure itself that the difficulties encountered by PWDs can be solved through individual effort. These posters also subtly communicate to PWODs that perhaps all individuals with the same type of disability could also accomplish at the same level (Brueggemann & Burch, 2007). In this way, the disabled hero becomes the standard by which all PWDs are judged.

Helen Keller acquired her deaf/blindness not in midlife but as a toddler. However, her remarkable resource, one most deaf/blind individuals do not have, was Annie Sullivan, her companion of more than 40 years (Angier, 2001). Most experts state that without Sullivan, Americans would never know who Helen Keller was. One blind woman wrote a book titled *Blind Rage: Letters to Helen Keller* (Kleege, 2006). In this book Ms. Kleege wrote letters to Helen Keller expressing her anger that she had to endure a childhood and adolescence in which she was always compared to Helen Keller. Ms. Kleege felt that she never measured up to Helen Keller.

Unlike poster Super Crips, role models can provide practical information on ways in which to manage the disability and share their experiences of having a disability. One SCI patient wrote about the importance of having a role model with whom he could identify.

> And then [the hospital staff] are showing people [with a spinal cord injury] in a $2 million yacht or on farms with 40 horses, you know; I mean that was for real?...[My mentor] is a real guy, you know, who lives a real life that's not easy and that's different than it was before ... Most of the things [in the video] are way out of reach for the average spinal-cord injured person.... [There are] not many Chris Reeves. (Veith et al., 2006, p. 294)

Developmental Tasks of Midlife or Late Adulthood

- Raise teen-aged children
- Develop adult relationships with maturing children
- Assume social and civil responsibility
- Achieve and maintain satisfactory performance in one's career or begin a second career
- Develop a strong, understanding relationship with one's life partner
- Care for aging parents
- Cope with the death of one's parents

AGES 40 TO 60

When this list is read, it becomes clear that there are differing tasks for early adulthood and old age, making midlife or late adulthood a separate and unique stage of life. Developmental tasks are considered to be normative when these tasks are undertaken by large groups of people of approximately the same age and when they are completed at the "right time." For example, regardless of an individual's age when he or she first becomes a parent, most people in midlife are reaching the end of day-to-day parenting of small children and begin to view their children as equals and friends. In spite of these differences, most individuals will not spend the majority of their active adult years raising children as parents did in the early 1900s. Because of smaller families with fewer children, the advent of universal birth control, and the longer life spans, the majority of the adult years will be "empty nest" years.

The "empty nest" or the tendency of emerging adults to leave the parental home does not mean that communication between parents and children ceases. In the chapter on emerging adults, we have seen that male children tend to return home for substantial periods of time more often than female children and that the presence of a stepparent or stepsiblings is related to fewer returns of adult children. The biological aspects of fewer children and the longer lives of parents coincide with the societal held views that women have other identities than caring for children, especially when they approach midlife. Fathers are no longer considered to be the sole authority of the home; for most young adults home-leaving is not forced or acrimonious.

Throughout adulthood, parents tend to give more support to their children than they receive; however, in midlife this pattern reverses, and adult children give more support to their midlife parents. Children begin to give their midlife parents advice, household aid, companionship and support, and financial resources. Adult children begin to reassess their relationships with their parents, viewing parents as equals and as individuals. Often adult children become more aware of and appreciative of their parents' strengths and the sacrifices they have made for their children. Interestingly, in spite of the geographic mobility of Americans, "proximity increases with age. Elders who move usually do so in the direction of kin, and younger people tend to move in the direction of their aging parents" (Berk, 2001, p. 538). These patterns of proximity communicate that family bonds remain strong throughout life.

In midlife individuals often review and evaluate their careers and measure their accomplishments with their expectations. Some may feel satisfied; indeed, some feel that they have exceeded their expectations. Some may redouble their efforts, in a type of "swan song," while others may seek an entirely different type of work. With the increased self-identity of midlife, new skills and talents are often discovered. Others are simply bored out of their gourds and are desperate to make a meaningful change. Despite the women's movement, empirical research has shown that men tend to measure their life in terms of occupational achievements, while women tend to define their age status in terms of family events.

The individual's self-identity changes in midlife, in part because the individual becomes aware that he or she no longer has as many possible self-identities or "possible selves." Berk (2001) described these changes:

> Adults in their early twenties mention many possible selves, and they are lofty and idealistic—being "perfectly happy," "rich and famous," "healthy throughout life," and not being "down and out," or "a person who does nothing important." With age, possible selves become fewer in number and more modest and concrete. Most middle-aged people no longer desire to be the best and the most successful. Instead, they are largely concerned with performance of roles and responsibilities already begun—being "competent at work," "a good husband and father," "able to put my children through the colleges of their choice," and not being "in poor health" or "without money to meet my daily needs." (Berk, 2001, p. 529)

One definition of autonomy is a lack of concern for the opinions and evaluations of others and deciding to follow self-chosen standards instead. When the individual is in midlife, the ambition and competition of early adulthood may be viewed as a lack of autonomy. Adding to this sense of freedom from the need to impress others is the transfer of personal fulfillment from oneself to one's children.

In every previous developmental stage, it was emphasized that the individuals' self-identities and self-esteem were derived from their perceptions of what others thought of them. According to Freud and most other developmental theorists, self-identity is derived first from the mother or other principal caregiver and progresses to parents, then teachers, and peers. At midlife a major shift in the *source* of self-identity occurs, and individuals begin to find self-chosen identities rather than looking to others.

Midlife was often viewed very negatively, as illustrated by the greeting card that stated "You're young only once. How was it?" The vitality, attractiveness, sense of mastery, and growth of youth was gone, and decline, sickness, and death waited (Levinson, 1986). Levinson, a psychologist at Yale, posited that these negative views are obsolete. One developmental psychologist (Neugarten, 1968) viewed midlife as the time of life when the "executive processes of personality" are at a lifetime peak. Neugarten defined these executive processes as self-awareness, the ability to change and control one's environment, increased selectivity, and a broad range of cognitive functioning. Acting on impulses is greatly reduced and more self-controlled and self-reflective strategies are used instead. Individuals in midlife are also able to interpret experiences (past, present, and future) in many different ways. Individuals in midlife tend to be decisive. Neugarten's theory parallels the empirical research that indicates older adults and elderly individuals adjust to disabilities better than younger people. These researchers suggest that three factors may cause this greater adaptation.

The midlife years are often years of stronger interpersonal skills, better coping abilities, and increased personal growth (Boerner, 2004). Such tangible resources as financial stability, a close circle of friends and family, and more free time contribute to a sense of well-being. However, the midlife years can be a time of economic hardships, loss of jobs, divorce, problems with adult children, and the death of parents.

Caring for aging parents may require more years than caring for children because of the combination of fewer children (decreased childbearing) and increased longevity of parents. Thus a woman who has two children born fairly close together may experience 20 to 22 years of child care; however, the woman's parents may require care for more than 30 years. Women in midlife may be providing care to parents, adult children who have returned home, and grandchildren. Furthermore, if the American government decreases Social Security or if other pension programs fail, many elderly individuals will see their standard of living decrease and may be forced to rely on their middle-aged children for financial aid. Indeed, middle-aged adults may provide resources, such as care and money, across several generational lines. In a book titled *Forced to Care: Coercion and Caregiving in America*, Glenn (2010) discusses the competing demands for income and caregiving. The following list of facts illustrates these competing demands:

- The average American couple now has more parents living (more than two) than children (fewer than two).
- Women now spend more years providing care for elderly parents (18 years) than for dependent children (17 years)
- The burden of elder care... falls most heavily on women who constitute around 70 percent of informal caregivers. Women are not only more likely to be primary

family caregivers for elderly kin, but they are more likely to care for those with more severe disabilities and to put in more hours of caregiving.

- Employed women are only slightly less likely to be primary caregivers compared to their age peers who are not in the labor force. Overall, about half of all employed women also care for a relative.
- Women of color, especially African American women, are more likely to have to combine elder and disabled care with employment outside the home. (Glenn, 2010, p. 2)

The midlife years entail a great deal of caregiving, and there will be greater responsibilities for individuals who have children with disabilities, a spouse or life partner with a disability, a disability themselves, or some combination (Asch & Fine, 1997; Conway-Giustra, Crowley, & Gorin, 2002). Individuals who acquire disabilities in midlife tend to experience more chronic illnesses, which are often invisible, episodic, and degenerating, making their experience much more difficult than living with a visible, stable-course disability.

We have learned that Dr. Beatrice Wright developed a theory of adjustment to physical disability with four components, one of which was "subordination of the physique." Subordination of the physique means that individuals shift their identity from their body, appearance, and physical abilities to other aspects, such as personality, character, and past history. Wright recognized that subordination of the physique is a common and important coping device when individuals enter midlife. There are many outward signs of growing older, including grey hair, balding, wrinkly skin, and body builds that become rounder and shorter. Women tend to become shorter as their spinal columns shrink. Men and women lose their secondary sex characteristics. Women develop facial hair, and their vocal cords thicken, making their voices lower, while men lose their facial hair and their vocal cords thin, making their voices higher.

Men in midlife become more tolerant of their seemingly feminine traits of nurturing and affiliative impulses, becoming more loving, compassionate, and emotionally sensitive, and women become more tolerant of their aggressive, autonomous, and ego-centric impulses. Gender identity becomes more androgynous in midlife as men and women become more like each other. Men no longer have the stamina and the strength of their youth, and women are released from the constant demands of caring for young children. Although gender-differentiated roles are becoming less salient, there are still many gender-specific roles held by society and by individuals. Nonetheless, when men become more nurturing and women more autonomous, the changes are widely experienced in midlife.

Midlife is also a time when physical losses first become apparent. Decline in body systems is very gradual and may not be noticeable because these changes are so small. On the other hand, some of the most noticeable losses are in vision and hearing. There is a gradual loss of vision as the lens of the eye becomes progressively less elastic and loses its ability to focus and the pupil of the eye becomes smaller; this loss of vision in middle age is termed presbyopia. There is a gradual loss of hearing, mostly of high-pitched sounds, called presbycusis. The prefix "presby" means old. Reaction time slows and coordination declines, each of which can make driving more difficult. Therefore, midlife adults are faced with the tasks of staying healthy while adjusting to limitations. Women's fertility comes to an end.

Midlife adults are not considered elderly; however, they are entering a stage of life when many disabilities are considered high incidence. High-incidence disabilities are ones that are very common, such as presbycusis and presbyopia. Although presbyopia is not considered a disability because an easily available piece of adaptive technology (eyeglasses) is available, presbycusis or late-onset hearing loss can impair functioning, and there remains stigma toward those who wear hearing aids. The effects of presbycusis and presbyopia are overgeneralized because others often assume automatically that individuals with these conditions lack cognitive functioning when, in reality, they cannot hear or see well. High-incidence disabilities have the advantages of greater acceptance (especially among age mates because everyone is looking for his or her eyeglasses) and are easier to manage due to the greater ease of diagnosis and the wider availability of services.

Relationships between the sexes (and for gays, with the same sex) change in midlife, becoming less sexualized. Rather than viewing others as possible sexual partners, individuals view each other more as complete people, and relationships become deeper and more companionable. As they shift from the perspective of sexualization, individuals are free to engage in relationships with individuals from a far wider range of ages, roles, and professions, resulting in feeling connected to the world.

Marriages are often strengthened in midlife when the demands and stresses of raising children, climbing career ladders, and managing tight budgets are eliminated. Partners now have time and money for each other and the marriage. Unlike divorce in the first ten years of marriage, divorce in midlife is often viewed as personal failure. Further, there is less social support for divorced people who are middle-aged.

However, some individuals in midlife often undergo dramatic restructurings of their lives, obtaining divorces, getting remarried, making major career changes, or moving to a new location. Generally most individuals in midlife tend to make smaller changes, typically reinforcing or strengthening components of their lives, such as marriage, career, or friendships. Typically those in the higher socioeconomic groups tend to make major changes in midlife, perhaps because they have more resources, such as money, job security, and education. Levinson considered midlife to be a time of great creativity for some people, for example Picasso or Grandma Moses.

Grandparents are becoming more important in the lives of children; as life spans increase, most individuals will spend one-third of their lives as grandparents. In addition grandparents are not elderly; the average age of grandparenthood in the United States is 46 for women and 49 for men.

Obviously, the identification of a new life stage (in this case midlife) delays the transition to later changes. Therefore the need to restructure one's life to meet the demands of retirement is delayed until 60 or even 70. On the other hand, the ambitions, struggles, and pressures of adulthood continue longer. The addition of a new developmental stage of life (in this case, midlife) requires new societal and institutional support structures, such as phased exits from one's primary career, the provision of second or third careers, continuing health insurance coverage for those who retire earlier, and various bridges to full retirement (Moen, 2003).

THE GRAND THEORISTS' VIEWS ON ADULTHOOD AND MIDLIFE

Freud did not apply his psychosexual stage theory of development to adults because he asserted that development had been achieved at the end of adolescence and that personality was established in the very early ages of life. Erikson was the first developmental theorist who extended his theories to include adulthood and the elderly years, for he viewed development as a series of tasks to be undertaken that established resulting strengths. The difficulties of Erikson's theories (and those of all the theorists who worked in the post–World War II years) are the biological changes in people (such as increased longevity), different demographic conditions, and shifting educational and labor environments. For example, no Eriksonian ego-crisis corresponds to the stage of "emerging adulthood," and there is only one stage for the years from 60 to death, even though many developmental theorists today divide these years into the "young old" and the "old old." Someone who is 60 years old certainly faces different tasks than someone who is 90. Indeed, if the longevity revolution continues, there might be a third stage. perhaps termed, "the very old old."

For adulthood the Eriksonian task is acquiring a sense of intimacy versus a sense of isolation, which is at first glance a radical departure from the task of adolescence, which is gaining a sense of identity rather than identity diffusion. Self-identity means that people know who they are, while intimacy is affiliation without the fear of losing one's ego identity. Thus the sequence or epigenetic nature of Erikson's theory becomes clear. In order to affiliate with others, one must have a strong self-identity. The ability to see one's self clearly requires a continuous perspective. Such affiliation, which often requires sacrifice and compromises, includes friendships, sexual relationships, work colleagues, and a partner with whom one can share mutual trust. Independence is still required in this stage for the individual to remain productive.

Isolation is remaining separate and unrecognized (Austrian, 2002). When the conflict between intimacy and isolation is resolved, the ego strength developed is love. In midlife, death enters the lives of most individuals because their parents pass away or some friends and acquaintances die. The sense of time changes from a perspective of "time since birth" to one of "time before death." In adulthood (especially midlife) individuals begin to change to being "an elder" with responsibility and leadership requirements in support of younger people, whether family members or children in the community. In this way adults in midlife begin to assume responsibility for the next generation. For centuries a recognized goal of each generation was to leave the world a better place for the upcoming generation. On a family level, this translates into providing children the resources for education and job training, lending them money for down payments on houses, and helping when babies are born. On a community level, middle-aged adults engage in community work with children and adolescents, most often through their churches or synagogues. Studies have found that those in the elderly years tend to do volunteer work with other elderly people. In midlife, individuals tend to become less egocentric; one study reflected this in finding that 70% of the respondents reported providing some kind of assistance to relatives, friends, and neighbors (Harootyan & Vorek, 1994).

Kohlberg theorized that individuals became more skilled at moral reasoning as they grew older, and there is some evidence for this. For example, we have seen that individuals in midlife (1) tend to be more skilled in problem solving with a greater degree of self-reflection and self-control; (2) tend to be autonomous, meaning less concerned about the expectations and opinions of others instead choosing self-evaluations; and (3) become more androgynous, which is related to higher moral reasoning.

Terms to Learn

Amyotrophic lateral sclerosis

Insidious onset

Multiple sclerosis

Parentification of the child CODAs

Pink-collar jobs

Post-polio syndrome

Rheumatoid arthritis

"Rush hour" of life

Systemic lupus erythematosus

Videos to View

- View the 49-minute video *The Anatomy of Pain*, available from Insight Media. The producers describe this video: "This program discusses the evolutionary purpose of pain and outlines the neurological aspects of pain. It presents methods for alleviating pain, distinguishes between acute and chronic pain, outlines the process by which pain signals travel though the human nerve network, and considers research regarding pain-generated depression and complex regional pain syndrome."

- View the 28-minute video *Chronic Pain,* available from Films for the Humanities and Sciences. The producers describe this video: "Medicine is gaining ground against chronic pain. This program explores what causes pain and looks at treatments, involving medication, physical therapy, and alternative methods. Presenting interviews with physicians who have dedicated their careers to fighting chronic pain—including University of California San Diego doctors Mark Wallace and Armelia Sani—this program also features commentary from patients who cope with it every day."

- View the 30-minute video *Chronic Care*, available from Films for the Humanities and Sciences. The producers describe this video: "A chronic condition is a long-term or permanent illness with no known cure. This program provides a framework for dealing with chronic illnesses—such as stroke, emphysema, or rheumatoid arthritis—whether viewers are seeking general knowledge, attending to their own health concerns, or caring for a loved one. This program explores way for family members and other caregivers to develop a realistic chronic care plan."

- View the 28-minute video *Making Connections: The Challenges, Fears and Hopes*, available from Aquarius Health Care Media. The producers describe this video: "Living with a parent with MS can be very hard or challenging. The coping skills that teens and young adults have influence in their lives. The more informed they are, the more comfortable they are and better able to deal with both the good and difficult times. This film looks at the feelings, interactions, and relationships that teens and young adults have and how they share with siblings, parents, and friends."

- View the 25-minute video *Family Challenges*, available from Aquarius Health Care Media. The producers describe this video: "When a parent has a disability, everyone in the family is affected. For children, these experiences may profoundly influence their lives and views of the world. In this sensitive film, you will hear about different roles that all the family members take on at varying times."

Learning Activities

(Note: These may also be used as class presentations.)
- As a class discuss the adjustment demands of an episodic disability. Also consider the added prejudice and discrimination directed toward those with episodic disabilities.
- Discuss the differences between chronic pain and acute pain. What conditions must be ruled out before the diagnosis of chronic pain can be made? Why is chronic pain socially unacceptable? What can people with chronic pain teach us? Do we avoid people with chronic pain for the same reason that we avoid PWDs?
- Read the following books about CODAs (children of deaf adults) and discuss the possibility of the "parentification" of these children:
  Hands of My Father: A Hearing Boy, His Deaf Parents, and the Language of Love (2008) by Myron Uhlberg, published by Bantam Books.
  A Loss for Words: The Story of Deafness in a Family (1986) by Lou Ann Walker, published by Harper.
  In Silence: Growing up Hearing in a Deaf World (1990) by Ruth Sidransky, published by St. Martin's.
  Mother Father Deaf: Living between Sound and Silence (1994) by Paul Preston, published by Harvard University.
- Would Vygotsky consider CODAs to have more learning opportunities? Remember that Vygotsky theorized that children who were bilingual were more skilled at problem solving and planning, and possessed greater abilities to think, understand, and construct the world. Vygotsky was probably thinking of children who were bilingual in two *spoken* languages. Would Vygotsky consider CODAs to be bilingual? CODAs are bilingual in a *spoken* language and in a *signed* language
- Discuss the ways in which old age and disability are often thought to be synonymous.

Writing Exercises

- Write a five-page paper supporting this statement, "Parenthood is no longer considered necessary in order to have a fulfilling life."

- Write a 10-page paper contrasting chronic illnesses with traumatic injuries that result in disabilities.
- Write a 10-page paper in which you describe the ways PWDs redefine such concepts as autonomy, freedom, and independence.
- Write a 10-page paper in which you outline the effects upon marriage of a disability acquired in midlife. Do you think the losses caused by a disability are the greatest when the individual is in midlife? Be sure to include the effects of pace-of-life issues.

Web Sites

http://nichcy.org/families-community/help/foradults
http://www.ldanatl.org/aboutld/adults/index.asp
http://www.php.com/support/adult-children-developmental-disabilities
http://esciencenews.com/articles/2010/04/06/middle.aged.americans.report.more.mobility.related.disabilities
http://www.medicinenet.com/script/main/art.asp?articlekey=115235
http://psychsocgerontology.oxfordjournals.org/content/59/1/P35.full

The Young Elderly, Ages 60 to 75 and the Old Elderly, Ages 75 to Death

15

For all of the developmental stages, demographic changes in the population have changed their definition, the appropriate tasks, and the disability issues seen in each of these stages. However, these demographic changes have changed the "elderly" stage to the greatest extent. The "silver tsunami," the growing number of elderly people, is a relatively new phenomenon. (Also the color "silver" is a euphemism for "gray," as in "the graying of the population.") The most obvious change is the addition of an entirely new stage, "the old old," to describe how the experiences of individuals who are 60 or 65 differ from those who are 90 or older. Without longer life spans, there would be no stage of "old old." Indeed, in the past adulthood was considered the longest stage of life, because it covered approximately three and a half decades. Today the late-life years or the elderly years can extend for four decades. In 1935 the federal government defined the retirement age as 65 years when it enacted the Social Security Act. Obviously, in 1935 American life spans were more than 20 years shorter than they are today.

These increased life spans have been termed an "age-quake." Another demographic shift has been the decreasing birth rate that has led to a larger proportion of older people in the population and given elderly Americans a greater voice and power in the national agenda. As someone said, "The geezer is king." The U.S. Bureau of the Census estimates that by the year 2050 more than 20.4% of the American population will be age 65 or older, in contrast to 12.5% today. It will be difficult to predict what the elderly age roles will be 40 years from now because of rapid changes in demographic, economic, and social conditions.

The generation currently entering the ranks of the young elderly is the Baby Boomers, the most racially and culturally diverse and best educated generation in history. On the one hand, the Baby Boom generation has experienced more financial success than their parents; on the other hand, Boomers have saved less than their parents' generation. Baby Boomers have been accustomed to being the focus of the national agenda throughout their life span. When they were infants and children in the post–World War II years and the 1950s, "the child was king." Throughout their youth, adulthood, and midlife, Boomers have redefined each stage of life. As the Boomers enter retirement and the elderly years, they will continue this trend and redefine both retirement and old age.

Considering only racial/ethnic identity, Hispanics, African Americans, Asian Americans, and Native Americans are also experiencing increases in the proportion of those over the age of 65, thus creating intragroup shifts. Between 1990 and 2050, it is estimated that the proportion of the population age 65 or older who are Native Americans, Eskimo, and Aleut will increase from 5.6% to 12.6%. Asians and Pacific

Islanders will see an increase from 6% today to 12.6%. African Americans will see an increase from 8.2% to 13.6%. The proportion of Hispanics who are age 65 or older will rise from 5.1% to 14.1%. For whites there will be increase from 13.4% to 22.8%. These statistics do not reveal the full extent of these increases. For example, immigration and high birth rates tend to cause ethnic and racial groups to be younger populations on average. Individuals over the age of 65 rarely immigrate; instead young adults immigrate. The younger age (as a group) of immigrants offsets the effect of the older age (as a group) of other American groups, thus lowering the "average" age of all Americans.

As a point of comparison, the proportions of European populations that are aged 65 and older are considerably higher than those of the United States. The average proportion of individuals over the age of 65 in the European Union (EU) is 16.6% (compared to 12.5% in the United States). Italy has 19.2% and Germany has 18.6%, and the projections for the year 2030 are 24.7% for the EU and 27.5% for Italy and Germany. These high proportions of elderly people in European nations are caused by "baby busts" rather than the post–World War II baby booms. First, after World War II much of Europe experienced baby busts because a large portion of a generation of men had died in the war. Second, the average fertility rate for the EU is 1.5 children for each woman, which is below the necessary replacement rate of 2.3 children per woman. Of course these are mathematical averages; it is not possible to have a half or a third of a baby. Freund, Nitiken, and Ritter (2009) maintain that there are other causes for the declining birthrates in Europe.

> Birth rates are decreasing in all industrialized countries, although there are differences among countries in the steepness of the decline and its causes. For example, in Germany, the decrease is not based on a trend towards one-child families as was assumed previously, but on an increase in childless families. A large proportion (32.1%) of German women born in 1965 have no children, and among those who are university graduates, this number is even larger. (p. 16)

Effects of the Longevity Revolution

- Structural lags
- Lack of role models
- Absence of role expectations

Role expectations, social norms, and societal institutions tend to lag behind all large demographic shifts. This lack of norms and institutions is termed "structural lag." Freund, Nitkitin, and Ritter (2009) explained, "Given that, historically old age is a fairly young phenomenon affecting a large number of people, it might take more time for norms and expectations...to develop" (p. 7). Bronfenbrenner (2005) believed that the number of available resources and supports has a great influence on individual growth and development. Therefore, the combination of structural lags and the ambiguity about role expectations contributes to difficulty in negotiating this life stage. Moreover, there may be few role models when demographic shifts occur quickly.

Chronological or biological age is not the most salient factor in the way in which individuals attach meaning to their stage of life. Although it is thus important to gain a sense of these large numbers and proportions in the population, it is more significant to recognize that everyone ages differently and to, take into consideration their past experiences, the time of history when they lived, their personal and familial situations, and the opportunity structures available to them (Neugarten, 1986). Some researchers assert that it makes more sense to study groups of individuals who self-identify as belonging to a certain developmental stage rather than to select samples of participants based on their chronological age. Two researchers concluded:

> In essence, a rigid metric of physical time (or chronological age here) may not be of direct relevance to the internal dynamic of many real-life physical and biological systems,... an issue which has been confronting researchers of dynamic processes in general. (Schu-Chen & Schmiedek, 2002, p. 8)

Atchley (2003) described using other indicators of aging in addition to chronological age when three other types of aging were considered: psychological aging, social psychological aging, and social aging. Psychological aging includes the individual's personality assets and coping skills; social psychological aging concerns the individual's interaction with the environment, including values, beliefs, and social roles. Finally, social aging is an interaction between the individual and his or her society. On one level this environment includes availability of health care, the economy, and the safety of the community. On another level social aging is related to the way society views old age. We have learned that when individuals are repeatedly given information, even if false, they tend to internalize these beliefs and prejudices into their self-identities. Furthermore, the most obvious outward signs of aging (gray hair, wrinkles, sagging skin, and baldness) are not related to either longevity or cognitive, sensory, or other functional losses.

Every period of the life span has role transitions and role loss. For example, infants must grow up, attend preschool, and relinquish their "babyhood," while teenagers must surrender the freedom of adolescence for full-time employment. However, the elderly years have more role transitions and role losses than any other stage, and although the other stages have a succeeding stage to anticipate, for elderly individuals there is a clear-cut, irreversible end point, death. The elderly years include the experience of physical and cognitive loss, the death of lifetime partners and friends, and the loss of visibility, status, and prestige. Certainly the resources and capacities that have been accumulated during earlier stages, both tangible and intangible, act as buffers against the inevitable losses of late-life. In addition to coping with losses, the developmental tasks of the elderly years include making decisions and choices concerning the use of free time and adjusting to reduced responsibilities and demands. In a chapter entitled "The Process of Successful Aging: Selection, Optimization, and Compensation," M. Baltes and Carstensen (2003) defined "successful aging":

> [A] useful model of successful aging must account for the dynamics between gains and losses—that is, on the one hand, for a reduction in reserves and an increasing number of specific losses and challenges in the biological, social, and psychological spheres, and, on the other hand, for potential growth and plasticity in old age. Such a metamodel should be able to harbor a great diversity of outcomes and goals, accommodate different success criteria, and emphasize

how elderly people obtain personal goals, accommodate different success criteria, and emphasize how elderly people obtain personal goals—that is, age successfully—in the face of simultaneous losses. (p. 87)

Selective optimization means that to maintain functioning, elderly individuals must narrow their goals and choose only those goals that are personally meaningful. Maintenance goals are those involving retaining life skills and knowledge, often by continuing to engage in activities that are well established. To compensate for losses, the individual must first become aware of these losses and then find other ways to accomplish the same results.

Developmental theories of late life are beginning to focus on its positive and growth-producing aspects, viewing these years as healthy, normal, and enjoyable. Some theorists have reframed such key developmental concepts as autonomy, independence, and contribution, conceptualizing the late-life years as the cumulation of a lifelong process of developing strengths and acquiring resources.

A unique challenge of this adaptive process may be seen in the way the Baby Boom generation differs from the previous generations. Health demographers predict high disability rates for elderly Baby Boomers. A study at the University of California at Los Angeles (Seeman et al., 2009) summarized their findings: "Ours is the first data to suggest disability rates may be going up. If it's true, it certainly suggests the Baby Boomers, whatever health benefits they've enjoyed up until now, may not enjoy such a rosy old age" (p. 1). Although the cause is not entirely clear (some have posited higher rates of obesity as a factor), Baby Boomers will experience higher rates of disability than their parents did at the same age.

DEMOGRAPHICS OF THE SILVER TSUNAMI

The statistics of aging and longevity are stunning, especially when life spans of the generation currently entering late life are compared to the shorter ones of earlier generations. Furthermore, many causes and factors that cause longer life spans, such as societal conditions of better nutrition, widespread insurance coverage, and more education for greater numbers of people, are also factors in the rising numbers of people with disabilities (PWDs) of all ages. Education is the single exception among the similar factors associated with longer longevity and higher rates of disability. Although higher levels of education are associated with longer longevity, they are associated with lower rates of disability. Another cause of the increasing numbers of both elderly individuals and PWDs is medical, scientific, and technological advances that both save and prolong lives.

Deaths from infectious diseases have decreased dramatically because of public health measures (clean water and sewage systems) and immunizations. Genetically based diseases, such as breast cancer, colon cancer or adult-onset diabetes, generally occur only in the second half of life. However, with improved screening procedures and the mapping of the human genome, the number of individuals affected by genetically based diseases will decline (see Table 15.1).

The rising numbers of elderly individuals and their corresponding greater proportion in the population are related to a combination of the following factors: (1) reduced childbearing (below the replacement rates), (2) medical advances, (3) the introduction of birth control, and (4) female empowerment. In 2011 approximately 12.5% of the American population is over the age of 65, compared to only 7% in 1950. In the year 2030 the percentage of elderly Americans is expected to increase to 20%, or one in every five Americans. Demographers think of the Baby Boom generation as "a blip on the radar screen," meaning that after the death of the last Boomers, the proportion of elderly people in the population will drop drastically.

When we consider Maslow's hierarchy of needs, some believe that the concept of self-actualization has changed. The altruistic motivations of child-rearing found in previous generations have changed to more materialistic and self-involved desires for upward mobility and material goods (Santrock, 2009). Although researchers find it difficult (if not impossible) to determine motivations and incentives, the statistics and correlations are clear. To give one example, it is known that on average, the more education women attain, the fewer children they have. Therefore, as larger proportions of women graduate from university and/or obtain graduate and professional education, the national birthrate declines.

One author described these longer life spans: "Twentieth century gains in life expectancy were so extraordinary that they equaled those of the previous of 5,000 years!" (Berk, 2001, p. 421). Rice (1998) stated that "the aging of the population is the most important demographic event occurring in the United States today" (p. 429). In the year 2000 persons aged 65 or older composed about 12.4% of the American population (Vasunilashorn & Crimmins, 2009). As noted before, in 1900 the life expectancy of Americans was 47 years; less than 100 years later, the life expectancy is about 77 years. As of 2011 there were 68,000 Americans aged 100 or older. In spite of these positive statistics, it should be noted that life expectancy is differentiated by gender, social class, and race. Those who live in poverty die younger, and on average racial and ethnic minority individuals tend to have lower life expectancies. Simply stated, whites live longer than nonwhites as a result of societal conditions that could be changed. For example, on average African Americans live seven fewer years than white Americans. Two authors pointed out a *drop* in life expectance for black Americans in the 1980s.

> In the United States, life expectancy is about 10 percent higher for white men than for black men, and about 7 percent higher for white women than for black women. A troubling aspect of this disparity is that life expectancy has not increased every year for black people as it has for white people. In fact, life expectancy for black people has declined from a peak of 69.7 years in 1984 to 69.4 years in 1987.... The decrease—although small—is a major public health concern; this is the only time in the twentieth century that life expectancy has decreased for black people while it increased for white people. Increases in death rates from several causes have affected the African American community disproportionally. (Papalia & Olds, 1992, p. 478)

These authors provide an explanation for the shorter life spans of African Americans.

> The largest single factor is poverty, which results in poor nutrition, substandard housing, inadequate prenatal care and poor access to health care throughout life.... Even when black people do have access to health care, they are less likely

TABLE 15.1

Noninstitutionalized Adults 18 Years and Older

- Number of adults with hearing trouble: 34.5 million
- Percent of adults with hearing trouble: 15%
- Number of adults with vision trouble: 19.4 million
- Percent of adults with vision trouble: 8.6%
- Number of adults unable (or very difficult) to walk a quarter mile: 15.9 million
- Percent of adults unable (or very difficult) to walk a quarter mile: 7.0%
- Number of adults with any physical functioning difficulty: 35.6 million
- Percent of adults with any physical functioning difficulty: 16%

Source: Summary Health Statistics for U.S. Adults: National Health Interview Survey, 2009, Tables 11, 12, 18, 19.

than white people to receive coronary bypass surgery, kidney transplants, and certain other treatments. (Paplia & Olds, 1992, p. 435)

The shorter life spans of racial/ethnic minority groups parallel the higher rates of disability for minorities. Furthermore, the same societal conditions are considered to be the cause for these higher rates of disability (Smart & Smart, 1997d). Dangerous jobs, which result in an increase in both disability and death rates, are often jobs that do not require a university education, and these types of jobs also have large numbers of minorities. Commercial fishing, mining, and construction are all physically demanding and dangerous jobs that often do not provide insurance coverage.

Women tend to live longer than men. Their longer life expectancies are thought to be caused by both biological and social factors. Women are much less likely to die (at any age) as a result of dangerous activities (or to acquire disabilities in this way), while men engage in these types of activities far more often than women. Women are also thought to be protected by their reproductive physiology, hormones, and genetic advantages. Santrock (2009) suggested that the extra X chromosome of women may be associated with the production of more antibodies to prevent infections (p. 529). Another social cause is the greater propensity of women to engage in preventative care and receive routine physical check-ups.

Obviously there are more older women than older men, and the gap widens with each age group. In 1991 55% of those in the 65–69 age group were women, 57% of those in the 70–75 age group were women, and 72% of those 85 and older were women. Austrian (2002) termed this greater proportion of elderly women to the "feminization of older populations," and cited a higher, worldwide statistic: "among persons 80 and over, there were 190 females for every 100 males in 1998, most of whom were widows" (United Nations, 1999, pp. 3–4).

THE OLD OLD

A recent trend has required demographers to coin a new term—supercententarians. Supercentenarians are those who are 110 years and older. The age group of 85 or older is the fastest-growing one in the United States and is expected to triple in size by 2020. Demographers, sociologists, psychologists, and gerontologists will be required to identify age norms and develop programs and agencies to serve a new group of Americans.

Another new term is "life endurance," which is defined as the age to which 1 person in 100,000 can be expected to survive. According to Santrock (2009), between 1900 and 1980 life endurance increased from 105 to 111 for men and from 105 to 114 for women. As we have learned, increasing life spans redefine not only late-life but also adulthood and midlife. For example, if someone retires at 55, he or she has the possibility of more than 40 years of nonworking life. If the individual in this example attended medical school, law school, or graduate school, he or she might have entered a career track as late as age 30. The math looks like this: 25 years of education, then 30 years of productive work, and finally 40 years of retirement.

Obviously each generation of elderly individuals benefits from the educational benefits and medical advances accrued during their lifetimes. For example, those adults who were over 75 years of age in the year 2000 were most likely to be high school graduates, thus benefitting from expanded educational opportunities and medical advances. Baby Boomers (and subsequent generations) will be more likely to have university educations when they retire. Therefore, as educational requirements and opportunities proliferate, adult working life will be delayed, as Arnett's new developmental stage of emerging adulthood predicted. Medical advances will allow longer life spans. It therefore seems that the proportion of full-time working years will decrease for coming generations. Perhaps the age norms of retirement will change, with delayed adulthoods and longer life spans pushing retirement age to older ages. It appears that opportunity structures are being instituted to accommodate these demographic changes. For example, forced retirements are now illegal, and the Social Security Reform Act of 1983 increased the retirement age (or the age when retirement benefits were paid) from 65 to 67. However, this revised higher retirement age was not put into effect until 2003 (Hudson, 2009).

Simply speaking, there are two theories on human aging. One is commonly referred to as "programmed aging," and the other as "wear-and-tear aging." All aging involves a complex interaction of heredity, health, and environmental factors. The programmed aging theory maintains that all organisms in each species have a built-in developmental pattern, subject only to minor modification. Therefore, each species (including humans) has its own pattern of maturation and aging, along with its own life expectancy. In contrast the wear and tear theory describes aging as the accumulated damage (or insults) to the body. In this theory the human body is considered a machine that eventually deteriorates and dies. Such theories are intuitively straightforward because many types of body cells, such as heart or brain cells, cannot repair themselves or reproduce. The wear and tear theory of aging is intuitively appealing because it allows individuals to take actions to increase their life spans by engaging in healthy activities (eating and exercising) and avoiding body insults (such as drugs, alcohol, and tobacco). The programmed aging theory, in contrast, does not allow for personal choice because the organism (the body) has been programmed at birth to live a certain number of years.

As would be expected, many gerontologists maintain that a combination of both theories is more likely to be true, carefully distinguishing between physical and mental declines that are *related to* aging and those declines that are *caused by* aging. In order to make this distinction clear, gerontologists and health demographers refer to those genetically influenced declines that affect all humans as "primary aging" and consider "secondary aging" to be declines caused by hereditary defects and negative environmental influences such as infectious diseases, lack of exercise, poor diet, and stress. Nonetheless, it remains difficult to separate these two theories. For example, is arteriosclerosis a degenerative process or a disease?

Physical Aspects of Aging

- Hearing
- Vision
- Balance
- Cognitive declines

The functioning of all five senses declines in old age. At age 65 most adults begin to experience visual problems that affect their daily functioning and often cause accidents, especially when they are driving a car. Age-related vision loss is termed presbyopia, and these losses can range from minimal loss to complete blindness. Approximately 1/6 of elderly individuals develop cataracts, a clouding of the lens of the eyes that causes blurred vision because light cannot pass through the lens. Half of all individuals in the United States who are legally blind are over the age of 65. Glaucoma occurs when fluid builds up in the eyes, causing pressure. Diabetic retinopathy, in which the retina detaches, affects one-half of all individuals with diabetes. Some of these conditions can be treated with surgery, laser treatments, or medicines. Individuals (of all ages) whose vision loss can be corrected to normal levels with the use of glasses or contact lens are not considered to have a vision loss. Approximately 21% of older Americans experience dual sensory impairments, loss of both hearing and vision (to some degree).

Between the ages of 65 to 74, approximately 30% of the American population experiences some degree of hearing loss, termed presbycusis. The U.S. Census (2000) estimates that about 46% of men and 32% of women over the age of 75 have some level of hearing loss. Age-related hearing losses tend to involve sounds at higher frequencies, which includes most speech, and to make people unable to filter out background noise. Men are more likely to experience hearing loss, perhaps as a result of "greater levels of exposure to occupational and recreational noise compared to older women" (Cimarolli, 2009, 360). Although hearing aids are available, many elderly individuals find these difficult to use, and for some hearing loss leads to social isolation because they find social activities too difficult. The effects of hearing loss in the later years are described:

> Loss of hearing interferes with a basic mode of human connectedness—the ability to participate in conversation. Hearing impairment may be linked to feelings of isolation or suspiciousness. A person may hear things imperfectly, miss parts of conversations, or perceive conversations as occurring in whispers rather than in ordinary tones. (Newman & Newman, 2009, p. 537)

Elderly individuals with hearing loss can feel excluded and rejected. With the advent of captioned television (as mandated by the Americans with Disabilities Act), many elderly individuals with hearing impairments are able to watch television.

Old age can also produce losses of two other senses related: taste and smell. After age 60 most individuals experience a decline in their sense of smell, more than 80% of individuals over the age of 80 have major impairments in smell, and more than half of these have no sense of smell at all. Impairments in the sense of taste include the inability to taste sour, salty, and bitter flavors; as a result individuals lose their appetites and subsequently fail to eat properly, leading to malnutrition and a host of other health problems. Medications (to treat other conditions) often have the side effect of loss of appetite, which compounds the effect of loss of taste.

Loss of strength, delayed reaction time, and loss of coordination are all related to the aging process. Loss of muscle coordination can result in incontinence, which can cause elderly people to withdraw from social activities. Most elderly people are aware of all these losses, impairments, and declines and develop compensating strategies that are individualized to their needs and situations. Driving a car becomes more difficult, and many elderly people choose to drive only during the daylight hours, avoid the freeways, and make shorter trips. The ability to drive is more than a convenience; as a part of an individual's lifestyle it allows autonomy, gives a sense of control over one's life, increases the individual's quality of life, and provides opportunities for socialization. Not being able to drive means dependence upon others , and the elderly often find it difficult to request rides from others. Nonetheless, it has been noted that:

> Older drivers are driving more miles than ever before; the current cohort of older drivers is driving more than past cohorts (i.e., so the number of miles driven on average by a 75 year old in the early 21st century is greater than the number of miles driven by the same in prior years). (Ball, 2009)

Affective disorders, such as depression, have been found to be associated with age-related sensory loss, including loss of motivation, reduced feelings of self-worth, and social isolation. Of course, depression in old age is related to many factors, such as marital status, the death of a partner or friends, and the loss of professional status upon retirement (Swett & Bishop, 2003; Wrosch, Schultz, & Heckhausen, 2004).

COGNITIVE DECLINES IN OLD AGE

Older adults process information more slowly and have a reduced capacity to retrieve information from their long-term memory. Their working memory declines in both speed and function, so they forget names, locations of important objects, appointments, and medication schedules. There are two types of memories: retrospective memories recall past events and prospective memories recall events planned for the future. Older individuals recall their adolescent and early adulthood experiences more readily than experiences and events that occurred during midlife. Rubin, Rahal, and Poon (1998) posited that:

> Perhaps youthful events are remembered best because they occurred during a period of rapid life change. In times of rapid change, people are likely to have many more novel experiences—ones that stand out from the humdrum of daily life. Adolescence and early adulthood are also times of identity development, when many personally significant experiences occur. . . . Such events are likely to become part of the individual's life story and to be long-lasting. Even

public events linked to this period—World Series winners, Academy Award winners, and current events—are especially salient to elders. (Rubin, Rahhal, & Poon, 1998, p. 3)

Also, the older the individual, the more memories he or she has, and memories in the later years tend to resemble one another. Prospective memory is an important aspect of any stage of life. Older individuals are more likely to use memory aids, such as writing (often compiling long to-do lists), buzzers, talking watches, and other types of timers. Interestingly many of these "memory aids" were first developed as assistive technology for individuals with brain injuries or blindness.

Word retrieval becomes more difficult as individuals age, so their speech is often slowed and somewhat disorganized because they are trying to remember a certain word or date. However, older individuals also have a lifetime of experience and education upon which to draw. Nonetheless, as they age these individuals are less capable of simultaneously retrieving multiple sources of information from their working memories. Problem-solving skills also deteriorate, but older individuals learn compensating strategies as they do in other areas of cognitive functioning. Real-life, practical problems are easier to resolve than recalling information simply for the purpose of recalling it, such as playing a memory board game like Trivial Pursuit. After someone answers the Trivial Pursuit question correctly, the elderly individual "remembers" the right answer. However, without the prompt of the correct answer, individuals in old age cannot retrieve these types of impractical information.

Measurements such as the Wechsler Adult Intelligence Scale (WAIS) have shown that intelligence declines with age. The WAIS has eleven different subtests (or scales), six of which measure verbal abilities, and five performance abilities. Longitudinal studies of older individuals have shown that verbal scales, such as information, comprehension, vocabulary, and arithmetic, tend to remain constant throughout the life span, but performance subtests, such as picture arrangement and block design, tend to decline with age. Other research has shown that there are small gains in intelligence from young adulthood to early middle age, but beginning at approximately age 60, gradual declines in intelligence are found. At age 80 the declines increase.

The use of such testing instruments as the WAIS is questionable, because these tests were originally designed for academic purposes, so the test questions are more familiar to children and young adults. The tasks of late-life are different from tasks of other life stages. Children are typically presented with problems and tasks by their school teachers who also evaluate the quality of the children's problem-solving. There is often an "answer key," such as the correct response to #10 is "true" and the right answer to #12 is "d," that places an overall emphasis on narrow aspects of memory. Intelligence tests mirror academic achievement tests and are unable to measure practical problem-solving.

Researchers (Horn & Cattell, 1966) introduced the ideas of crystallized and fluid intelligence. Fluid intelligence includes abstract thinking, reasoning, relational thinking, and short-term memory, and crystallized intelligence is the accumulation of knowledge. Fluid intelligence is the ability to deal with novel situations and involves the individual's working memory, such as giving an individual a list of five numbers and asking him or her to recite them in reverse order. We can see that tests of fluid intelligence measure how well new information (which is not committed to long-term memory) is learned and manipulated, such as reciting the numbers backwards. Another test of fluid knowledge includes inductive reasoning, such as presenting the individual with a large pattern of numbers, with a single blank. Those with a great deal of fluid knowledge are capable of discerning the correct number to complete the pattern. Fluid knowledge tends to peak in young adulthood. Older individuals lose some of their capacity to process new information and ignore irrelevant information. The movie character Indiana Jones demonstrates a great deal of fluid intelligence because he is always confronting novel situations and life-threatening problems. If we ever find ourselves in a snake-ridden jungle with native people chasing us, we would want a leader with a great deal of fluid intelligence. Crystallized intelligence, such as being able to recite all the presidents of the United States in order or name the planets, would not help us.

At any age the individual's amount of crystallized intelligence is based on the opportunities available to him or her, including level of education and the number and variety of stimulating experiences. It thus seems reasonable that longitudinal studies would show any age-related declines. However, Horn and Cattell used cross-sectional studies or studies completed at only point in time. Horn and Cattell found that memory, crystallized intelligence, and fluid knowledge all decreased after the age of 70.

Hence, we can see that it is difficult to measure declines in cognitive functioning of older individuals. Using standardized intelligence tests that were designed for school use artificially lowers (or deflates) the scores of older adults, and the research design used in previous studies has produced questionable results. Measuring age-related cognitive declines requires a longitudinal research design. Finally, intelligence tests cannot measure creativity or wisdom.

Measuring creativity is often a simple evaluation of the quality of work produced by artists, scientists, and inventors. There is the well known creativity of famous older individuals ("poster geezers") who have done important work when older, some as a continuation of a life of achievement, and others who began their creative work in late-life. Some poster geezers include Sigmund Freud (who wrote his last book at age 83) Sophocles (who wrote *Oedipus Rex* at age 75), and Claude Monet (who painted his *Water Lily* series at 73). Creative, groundbreaking work produced in late-life is often considered the individual's masterpiece. Lehman (1962, 1966) found that many people are most creative and produce their superior work during their 30s, and about 80% of their creative work was completed by age 50. Defining and measuring creativity only as the quantity of work produced has allowed researchers to conduct biographical reviews of the great composers, writers, and painters. Such a retrospective measurement is questionable simply because creativity is evaluated only by the amount of work produced.

Wisdom is also difficult to measure. However, wisdom is thought to be practical knowledge based on a lifetime's accumulation of expertise in dealing with tasks and problems. Wisdom is the capacity to apply this knowledge, expertise, and understanding to problems.

All the effects of the aging process are termed "high-incidence" conditions. Such conditions are accepted more readily simply because many individuals are experiencing the same losses and impairments, so they are, in some way, considered "normal," "common," or "expected." We have learned that 30% of individuals in the age range of 65 to 74 experience some degree of hearing loss. To show the contrast, 30% of young adults do not have spinal cord injuries, so spinal cord injuries are considered low-incidence disabilities. Services, programs, agencies, and assistive technology are readily available for high-incidence conditions, and more peer support groups are available. Finally, there is less blame or responsibility placed on the individual for his or her condition. Because these age-related impairments or conditions are age related, society does not hold elderly people responsible for these conditions.

PERSONALITY CHANGES

It seems self-evident that older individuals have had more time in which to accumulate knowledge and experiences, and one of the most important types of knowledge is self-knowledge. Lifelong personality affects intellectual functioning. Generally those who are sociable, outgoing, open to new ideas and experiences, and motivated to learn and seek out learning opportunities across a wide range of fields are happier, higher functioning people. Positive self-evaluations lead to greater life satisfaction.

Individuals tend to become more cautious with age, but rigidity is not always associated with aging (Rice, 1998). The ageist stereotype of the elderly person who tends to cling to a self-identity that is no longer possible or who constrict his or her social interactions has been found to be untrue. This is not to say that there are no such individuals, but as an entire group, late-life individuals tend to re-organize, substituting new roles and identities to replace the identities that are no longer possible. Personality tends to be stable throughout the life span; however, personality does change when the individual is required to deal with life changes. Therefore, lifelong personality traits and a willingness to accept the changes and losses of late-life both contribute to late-life satisfaction.

Psychologists have found that five factors are associated with life satisfaction in later life (Costa, Metter, & McCrae, 1994). These are extroversion, lack of neuroticism, a sense of usefulness and competence, optimism, and a sense of control. Extroverted individuals tend to seek out social activities and relationship. Anxiety, hostility, and impulsivity are characteristics of neuroticism, and older individuals with neurotic tendencies tend to be discouraged, dissatisfied, and unhappy, viewing everything in a negative light. Because optimism includes feeling that one's life is full of positive experiences, it makes sense that optimistic individuals tend to experience less depression and a greater sense of well-being (Wrosch, Schultz, & Heckhausen, 2004). A sense of control leads to the ability to select one's goals and to engage in healthy activities (Huppert, 2009). Those who were generous, good-natured, and agreeable tend to have greater capacities for accepting life circumstances.

Developmental Tasks of Late-Life

- Responding to physical declines
- Marriage in late-life
- Planning for retirement
- Maintaining productivity in the workforce
- Responding to changing roles, such as widowhood
- Caregiving of parents
- Making meaning of one's life

These researchers developed the list of these five factors after interviewing a large sample of elderly individuals, and it seems intuitive that extroversion, lack of neuroticism, a sense of competence/usefulness, optimism, and a sense of control are associated with life satisfaction.

RESPONDING TO PHYSICAL DECLINES

In the first chapter, we learned of Beatrice Wright's theory of adaptation to physical disability that included four basic principles. One of these is "subordination of the physique," in which PWDs redefine themselves as more than their physical body, their athletic abilities, or their appearance, which allows them to maintain their self-esteem and self-acceptance. Almost everyone expects to become older and experience the associated physical declines, so they are able to consider ways in which to redefine themselves. Aikin (1978) explained the concept of shifting one's identity away from his or her physical attributes:

> [The self-concept] includes not only the person's evaluation of his own body and behavior, but the overall value that he places on himself as a personality. Biological factors such as physical appearance, health, innate abilities, and certain aspects of temperament are important in determining the frequency and kinds of social experience that a person has and the degree of social acceptance that he attains. But these biological factors interact in complex ways, and they always operate in a social context. (p. 77)

It is easier to accept physical declines and to redirect self-identity when the individual associates with age mates who are also experiencing the loss of physical abilities. Turner and Helms (1979) expanded on this concept of body transcendence. Note how they refer to the physical declines of old age as "the gravest of insults."

> The retirement years bring most people a marked decline in resistance to illness, a decline in recuperative powers, and an increase in bodily aches and pains. For those who equate comfort and pleasure with physical well-being, this decline in health may represent the gravest of insults. There are many retired people whose lives seem to move in a decreasing spiral because of their growing concern with the state of their bodies. (p. 432)

Middle age is typically the stage of life when individuals begin to shift their identities from their bodies and start to value identities such as wisdom and greater ego identification.

MARRIAGE IN LATE-LIFE

In late-life, romantic love, sexuality, and intimacy remain important parts of life. We have learned that the concept of gender roles tends to converge during midlife, with men becoming more nurturing and loving and women becoming more independent, achievement oriented, and assertive. This gender role convergence may partially account for relaxed, companionate, and sexually satisfying marriages, as men and women become more similar in their emotional and sexual needs. There is evidence that many couples in late-life report that their marriages have improved over the years, and this appears reasonable because there are now fewer pressures to stay in an unhappy marriage in late-life (Gilford, 1986; Weishaus & Field, 1988). Earlier in life, couples may have remained married for the sake of their children or from a lack of financial resources.

The role transitions of one partner affect the other, or to state it more accurately, the interpretation and meaning that one partner gives to these role transitions affect the other. Retirement (which may be viewed as positive or negative), the death of one's parents (which may be devastating even though expected and common in this stage of life), or diverging views on the use of (previously unavailable) leisure time are developmental tasks of marriage in late-life. For some long-married partners, money has never been an issue; however money problems may arise for the first time because of the reduced financial resources of retirement, often coupled with adult children who need financial help. One partner may feel anxious about living on a fixed income in an inflationary economy and may be concerned about failing health and the rising costs of health care, while simultaneously acknowledging that his work skills and education are becoming obsolete. For such a husband, as carefully and skillfully as he has planned his retirement income, he now understands that the preparation phase is complete. On the other hand, his wife may not have these financial worries and could view the same income as more than sufficient for their retirement needs and actually feel proud of and satisfied with their retirement planning.

RETIREMENT

As an age-normed event with a predictable normative course requiring preparation, redefinition of self, and continuing psychological adjustment, retirement is a relatively new development. Until the 1940s or 1950s, retirees did not have parents who were also retired. Many older Americans did not retire because shorter life spans meant that most Americans did not live long enough to retire; without government- and employment-sponsored retirement plans, even many Americans who did live long enough could not afford to retire. With its national pension plan for workers, the Social Security Act of 1935 radically institutionalized retirement. The history of retirement in the United States has progressed from (1) no one retiring to (2) the first generation to retire feeling guilty about doing nothing and receiving retirement benefits to (3) the second generation of retirees feeling that financial benefits were an entitlement for which they had worked to (4) many in Baby Boom generation finding ways to prolong their work life and defer retirement.

Another change in retirement is the increasing number of options available. Rather than withdrawing completely from the workplace at a certain point in time, Americans may choose to work a reduced number of hours with the same employer (partial retirement or phased retirement), embark upon a second career (nonretirement), or seek part-time employment (bridge retirement.) From 1960 to 2002, the proportion of older men who worked part-time rose from 30% to 43.6%, and the proportion of older women who worked part time rose from 44% to 58.2%. About 40% of men and 35% of women who received a pension in 2005 were still employed (Rix, 2004).

In the 21st century, both the longer life spans and the numerically large Baby Boomer generation will combine to redefine the concept of retirement. The mass retirement of the Baby Boom generation presents two challenges: (1) the loss of a large number of skilled and eexperienced workers that will cause the American workforce to decrease 1.1% each year and (2) the fiscal burden placed on society. One author (Jacoby 2010) described the aging Baby Boomers as "greedy geezers." Mellor and Rohr (2005) seem to agree with Jacoby by pointing out that Baby Boomers have had more financial success than their parents but have saved less than their parents. These authors also point out that the older Baby Boomers will encounter a different economic environment upon retirement than the younger Baby Boomers.

> We can expect to see a growing divide between the haves and have-nots, between the "pension elite" and low wage, non-pensioned workers. In addition, younger Booms may be more adversely affected by the pension decline than older Boomers; younger Boomers entered a tighter labor market and are likely to receive weaker benefit packages than their counterparts. (p. 87)

We have learned that the American workplace has been more accommodating to white males without disabilities, but other groups such as women, racial and ethnic minorities, and PWDs have not experienced the career trajectories of white males. Career development theory and research has also focused on white males. Retirement is a different experience and has different meanings for those who have experienced stable, high-paying, orderly, upwardly mobile careers. Occupational pathways are an important factor in retirement as described by Moen (2003):

> Minority men and women from all race and ethnic backgrounds also tend to experience employment discontinuities, often being the last hired, the first fired. Consequently, most women and minority men come to the midcourse years without the same duration of employment or accumulation of work experience as White men.... Gendered and racial/ethnic occupational segregation, along with less stable employment histories, means that midcourse women and minority men are less likely to be covered by a pension than are White men and those who do have pensions have incomes far lower than those of White men. (p. 282)

Although Moen does not include PWDs, elderly individuals with congenital disabilities or disabilities that were acquired early in life tend to have employment histories much like those of racial and ethnic minority individuals and women of all ethnic groups. Furthermore, an individual may belong to two or more of these groups, such as an African American woman with a disability. Retirement is both a psychological adjustment and a socially defined event related to available opportunity structures. Pension plans, legislation that eliminates mandatory retirement ages, and indeed the entire American economic system are all types of opportunities; furthermore, these opportunities and resources are not equally available to all types of Americans.

The type of job held also contributes to retirement decisions. Those who have high-paying, high-prestige jobs are less likely to retire early, so they provide more options in retirement. According to Gormly (1997):

> Retirement age in the United States is often regarded as an "artifact" of Social Security and other pension systems. As many psychologists, physicians, and

social planners note, chronological age is a poor indicator of a person's ability or desire to work. (p. 640)

Just as the Social Security Act of 1935 defined who had a disability and who did not have a disability, it also defined who was of retirement age and who was not. Furthermore, the definitions of retirement age or disability are often not self-definitions. For example, PWDs are often told, "You get a Social Security check just because you have a label or a diagnosis." However, it is rare that someone is told, "You get a Social Security check just because you are old." The Social Security Act was a product of the Great Depression of the 1930s that had a benevolent intent, and for decades it had far-reaching positive effects. However, much has changed since the year 1935, both demographically and in the definition and management of disabilities. For example, a "forced retirement age" is now prohibited by law.

Retirement is not an event but rather a process that takes place gradually and is unique to each individual. However, it may be less of a process for those who are offered "early retirement incentives" (the financial packages that encourage workers to retire) or for those who must leave the workforce to provide care to an ill or disabled spouse. However, most individuals tend to move from the stage of planning, to actual retirement, to reorientation of goals and values, and finally to stability in retirement. This process is termed "mutual disengagement," in which both the employer and employee gradually adjust.

Retirement may be viewed as the gift of time, the opportunity of engaging in activities that have been postponed due to the demands of work, finding satisfaction in family life, especially grandchildren, and enjoying community and volunteer work. Retirement may also be viewed as a loss of financial security, prestige, social contact, and self-identity. In a work and productivity-oriented culture, those who do not work may feel that their identity is not complete. American culture has not placed a great deal of importance upon nonobligatory activities, especially those that appear to be self-centered. Many of these individuals seek part-time employment or initiate a second career.

On a societal basis, the retirement of the Baby Boomer generation has been couched in terms of "generational equity" (Williamson & Watts-Roy, 2009, p. 161). Generational equity maintains that each generation should provide for itself and not rely on the younger generations to care for them in old age. The conflict between the Baby Boomer generation and the younger generations is based on the assumption that benefits for elderly Americans result in sacrificing benefits for younger Americans, especially children. For example, if the federal government funds the (long) retirements of the (large) Baby Boom generation, will it become necessary to reduce federal loans for college students or curtail services for young children? A second point concerns the "dependency ratio," which compares the large number of nonworking, nonproductive elderly Americans to the shrinking number of younger, working Americans. Williamson and Watts-Roy concluded:

In general, advocates of the generational equity perspective make claims based loosely on fact, but overlook other important factors. However, the frame has appeal to many Americans because it resonates with individualism, a dominant value in the American culture. Individualism is linked to values of autonomy, person ownership, and personal freedom.... Social Security programs and

Medicare, by this argument, infringe on individual freedoms and make people less likely to rely on themselves to plan their retirement. Those who favor generational equity suggest that (those who oppose generational equity) lack an ethic of work and individual responsibility. (p. 159)

Intergenerational equity has often been called the "right to retire." One way to respond to these challenges is the postponement of retirement. Estimates suggest that in the future, 21% of men and 12% of women over the age of 65 will remain in the work force. Many Baby Boom women who delayed their entry into the workplace due to child-rearing responsibilities often wish to work into their 60s and 70s.

RESPONDING TO ROLE TRANSITIONS

Role transitions occur in every stage of loss; however, in old age role transitions tend to encompass greater change that necessitates revisions and redirection in all areas of life. Widowhood is an intense disruption that involves grief, loss of emotional and financial support, and loss of companionship. Widowhood is considered an "on-time" transition for late-life (but an "off-time" transition when it occurs earlier in life), most commonly experienced in the decade of the 70s. For those who have been married without divorce since early adulthood, their spouses are often an important part of their lives, because they have lived together for longer periods of time than they did in their childhood homes or when raising their own children. Especially during the elderly years, those who have experienced the death of a spouse find support and help from their adult children, extended family, and friends. As would be expected, emotional support is the type most needed and includes allowing them to speak about their spouse, rehearsing family memories, and providing time and space in which to grieve and find a new identity.

Fourteen percent of men and 43% of women aged 65 or older are widowed. Not only are men less likely to be widowed (because they have a greater tendency to die before their wives), men are more likely to remarry when their wives die. Men experience greater depression upon the loss of their spouse than women do, which perhaps partially explains men's greater tendency to remarry. Newman and Newman (2009) explained:

This [depression] may result in an immediate search for a new marriage partner. In a 2-year follow-up study of dating and remarriage after widowhood, 61% of men and 19% of women had remarried or were in a new romantic relationship by 25 months after the death of their spouses. For men, a higher monthly income and level of education were the best predictors of being remarried. (p. 512)

When people become single during late-life (either as a result of death or divorce), dating requires a change of orientation. For most of their lives, most men and women have interacted with the opposite sex in nonsexual ways, such as at the workplace or in friendships of married couples. In addition, remarriage in later life is often associated with a return to a younger stage of life. Nonetheless, reviewing the statistics of the preceding paragraph, we can see that the majority of elderly widows do not remarry, especially when other sources of social support are available.

Another way to forge a new identity as an older single individual is leisure, social, and community activities. Widows and widowers may meet many of their psychosocial needs through companionship, social integration, the growth and learning that result from new activities, and a sense of contribution. Social support often includes such practical needs as transportation, assistance with activities of daily life, and health care. It is thought that meaningful, consistent social support is associated with greater longevity. Although social relationships include both positive and negative aspects, many gerontologists maintain that social relationships in later life tend to be more positive because elderly individuals tend to make wiser choices in selecting friends and have more accepting and tolerant attitudes. The negative aspects of late-age social relationships include the possibility the person will be taken advantage of by elderly abuse, stealing, or an invasion of one's privacy.

Age is a major predictor of the size of the individual's social support group, although a large social support group is not necessarily better than a small one. It is true that younger people tend to have larger social networks because of their mobility, greater number of activities, and employment opportunities. Older individuals tend to have smaller social networks, but they consider their social networks closer and engage in more frequent contact.

Grandparenthood and great-grandparenthood are often reciprocal sources of satisfaction that change the family configuration. The average age of grandparenthood is in the 50s, which may allow grandparents to have relationships with their grandchildren from their birth to their adulthood. The adult children who are the parents of the grandchildren determine, in large part, the type of interaction grandparents will enjoy. Grandchildren help grandparents to see a sense of continuity in their lives and to believe that something of themselves will persist after their death. Emotionally close relationships and frequent contact with grandchildren are often viewed by grandparents as one of the gifts of old age.

Grandparents often provide benefits for grandchildren. Grandparents can provide an important stabilizing influence, especially with the demographic changes in American families, such as the entry of mothers into the workforce, parental divorce, and single parent homes. The more involved grandparents are in the lives of their grandchildren, the more important grandparents become to the child's sense of security and feeling loved. This sense of security is reciprocal because it allows grandparents to feel needed and to be significant, contributing members of their extended families.

In 2001 the Longitudinal Study of the Generations (LSOG) was completed after 35 years of interviewing families (Bengtson, 2001). The LSOG identified five aspects of intergenerational solidarity: (1) affectional solidarity, which is mutual love and emotional closeness; (2) associational solidarity, which is based on the type and frequency of contact; (3) consensual solidary, which is agreement in opinions and expectations; (4) functional solidarity, which involves giving and receiving emotional and instrumental support; and (5) geographic proximity, which allows interaction.

CAREGIVING OF PARENTS

Although caregiving of aging parents and grandchildren was formerly a typical task of midlife rather than late-life, longer life spans have increased both the number of individuals requiring care and the number of years such care is necessary. Perhaps care-giving for an ill or disabled is more commonly expected in late-life. Of course, parents of children with disabilities provide care throughout the life span.

Surveys have shown that most Americans feel a high degree of filial obligation or a moral obligation to care for their aging parents, thus reciprocating the love and care their parents gave to them when they were children. Adult children are more likely to care for their aging parents in their parents' home, which is a change from earlier times, when grandparents often lived with their adult children and their grand-children. Caring for an elderly parent, especially a parent in the old-old age category, can be both demanding and depressing. Even though they might be in the elderly category themselves, children tend to view their parents in the way they remember them, as high-functioning, active, achieving individuals. Regardless of the age of the adult children, they often view their parents as some sort of "buffer" against the world. Although it is a typical and expected experience, the death of parents results in grief and also changes a person's self-identity. After the death of their parents, many report that they feel like an adult for the first time in their lives. Judy Teplow (2007) described caring for her mother:

> It took 5 months for the doctors to make an accurate diagnosis. An electromyo-gram (EMG) was performed…and it was this test that ultimately determined that my mother had amyotrophic lateral sclerosis (ALS), Lou Gehrig's disease, a progressive, degenerative disease that is terminal. It is probably the most dreaded neurological disease, and is one with no known cause or cure.
>
> My initial reaction to the diagnosis was one of disbelief, devastation, and helplessness. How could such an active and health-conscious person be stricken with such a catastrophic illness? I felt a sadness for my parents, and I had real concerns about my dad's health also. It was conceivable to me that this tragedy could destroy him as well, and I prepared myself for the worst. (pp. 709–710)

Approximately one-third of all caregivers are spouses, predominantly female (Feinberg, Wolkwitz, & Goldstein, 2006). The American Association of Retired Persons (AARP) estimates that 66% of aged, ill, and disabled people receive extended care at home, primarily from family members. Demographically, it makes sense that women provide more caregiving because women live longer than men and women tend to marry older men. Socially, it is thought that women are more nurturing and loving, so caregiving roles are considered "women's work." Although caring for an ill or disabled spouse is becoming more common, caregivers have frequently done their work without support or acknowledgment and in obscurity. We have seen that when a child is born with a disability or acquires a disability, generally the mother provides most of the care, even when she has greater earning power than her husband.

A psychiatrist (Rolland, 1994) explained the gender differentiation of receiving care:

> Men, socialized to be tough and invulnerable, often feel that being nurtured and dependent is acceptable, if at all, only when they are ill or injured. For many men their early memories of being nurtured are associated with mother-ing in times of illness.…powerful voices desire dependency and disability as

evidence of infantilism, and failure to fulfill the dominant male role of self-reliant provider for one's family. (p. 254)

Rolland continues to discuss the ways in which giving care is also gender differentiated:

> Men tend to tackle the practical or instrumental aspects of coping, avoiding the emotional side of their partner and themselves. Women are typically expected to tend to the emotional needs of their husbands, children, and others and to stifle their own needs. At the time of the initial illness crisis, couples tend to divide up coping tasks according to habitual patterns or stereotyped expectations....This division of psychosocial labor can become skewed and rigidified depending on who is the patient and who the caregiver and on role assignments according to gender..... A chronic disorder gives couples an opportunity to reexamine habitual role constraints; this should be done with an understanding of the psychosocial demands of the disorder over time. (p. 254)

Long-term care for a husband or wife involves many responsibilities and stresses. In late-life, both the caregiver and the care-receiver are elderly. Functional losses, reduced ability to handle stress, lowered immunity, and sleep disturbances make caregiving difficult. When the management of medical treatment, legal and financial concerns, and responsibilities are added, caregiving may become burdensome. Certainly it is more economic and humane to provide care at home, in the individual's familiar surroundings. The increased costs of institutionalized care and the longer life spans have made care at home necessary. As new and recurring losses in the health and functioning of one's spouse occur, they require the caregiver to adjust and grieve almost continuously. Rossheim and McAdams (2010) described this grief:

> It is the nature of progressive illness to diminish life with unpredictable but inevitable losses. Those confronted with the progressive decline of a long-time companion and familiar lifestyle naturally react to each milestone of decrement with shock and dismay, triggering a host of emotions including anxiety, grief, and depression. There is, however, a particular form of suffering characteristic to long-term spousal caregivers which should be considered. It is known as *chronic sorrow.* (p. 478)

The solution to chronic sorrow of the caregivers includes social support and acknowledgment of their contributions. Both of these require others to accept (and be comfortable with) the uncertainty and losses of caregiving. Often spouses who are receiving long-term care find it demeaning and unpleasant and consider themselves weak and helpless. It is often necessary for a person to conserve strength by using it for highly valued activities, which requires the individual to accept help for other, less important tasks.

Practical help on a consistently planned basis, assistance for the caregiver in developing a routine of daily activities, and surveillance of the elderly caregiver's physical and mental health are necessary. The quality of care provided at home by family members is directly related to the patient's survival, and quality of life and has been termed "caregiver burden" (Caplan & Moelter, 2000, p. 97). Physical care is demanding, especially when the caregiver is elderly, but the personality changes of the family members are the most difficult thing to cope with. Respite time from the home and the spouse is an example of a simple but effective type of practical help. For example, such care occurred when a spousal caregiver received dinner delivered to her doorstop anonymously every Wednesday evening for a year. The caregiver never learned who was providing the meals until the last one came with a note. Shortly thereafter the husband was hospitalized and died. The Wednesday night dinners were a practical help but perhaps more important, they were an acknowledgment and awareness of the caregiver's responsibilities.

DISABILITY IN LATE-LIFE

Research has shown that individuals in late-life adjust to disability more positively and productively than individuals in any other stage of life. Factors that are thought to influence this greater acceptance are that (1) disability is common among elderly people, (2) elderly people have had a lifetime of successful problem-solving and decision-making, and (3) elderly individuals have fewer role demands, such as working or child care. Often medical caregivers will construct a "biography" of the ways the individual and his or her family have dealt with illness, injury, and hospitalizations to allow these caregivers to understand their idiosyncratic methods of coping. Older individuals experience age-related challenges and problems, but they also have some of the problems experienced during the younger stages. As one researcher notes, "[in] some ways old age is familiar territory, that experiences of earlier years reappear in slightly altered forms" (Austrian, p. 301). Although individuals in late-life are typically good problem-solvers (a skill that helps them respond to disability), they typically do not accept assistive technology and prostheses as well as younger individuals do. For example, elderly individuals who undergo a therapeutic amputation often prefer to use wheelchairs rather than submit to the rigorous process of learning to use a prosthesis.

Disabilities with onsets in late-life tend to be chronic illnesses rather than traumatic injuries or acute illnesses. With chronic illness, the focus is on shaping the experience rather than curing the individual. When a severe disability is acquired in the 50s or the 60s, the individual often changes his or her self-identity from middle aged to elderly. This is termed an early transition to old age; not only is the acquisition of a disability a factor in early transition, but the death of a spouse, forced retirement, or the need to provide care for a family member can also create a need for a a person to make an early transition into late-life. Although there may be fewer functional demands, the onset or acquisition of a disability in later life may require retirement from an enjoyable career and forfeiting retirement plans (such as travel), and the individual painfully understands that his or her spouse will probably be required to provide most of the necessary care. Caring for a spouse with a disability or chronic illness over a period of years results in role ambiguity. Is the caregiver married or single? In many ways the ill spouse is no longer a marriage partner in the conventional ways, but it is a dependent patient.

Biordi (2006) described how chronic illness often leads to self-isolation for the individual and his or her family.

> People with chronic illness struggle to understand their body failure and its effect on their activities and lives.... In doing so, they also struggle to maintain

their sense of personal and social identity, often in the face enormous financial, psychological, and social obstacles. If individuals with chronic illness lose hope or become otherwise incapacitated, they may withdraw from their social networks, isolating themselves from others important to them. (p. 131)

The elderly often experience social isolation or at least reduced social contact because of retirement from work, the deaths of friends and family members, and their lack of transportation. The addition of a chronic illness or disability increases the probability of social isolation for both the individual and his or her spousal caregiver.

Congenital disabilities or disabilities that have been acquired early in life present other types of challenges in the elderly years. First, the effects of the disability interact with the effects of aging, so it is often not possible to separate these effects. Nonetheless, each (the disability and the effects of aging) accelerates and exacerbates the other. Monitoring for secondary conditions requires vigilance and consistency, because a secondary condition (for example, an infection of pressure sores or the urinary tract) could result in the individual's death. There are positive aspects of living to old age with a congenital disability, such as the individual's skill and mastery of the disability and providing role models of adaptive functioning. It often becomes difficult to maintain the highest quality of life during the later years of life because medical expenses tend to escalate, assistive technology expenses rise, and there is often pressure to live in a nursing home or assisted living facility.

THE GRAND THEORISTS' VIEWS OF LATE-LIFE

Erikson was the first grand theorist to consider late-life as a developmental stage, and when later theorists included late-life as part of the developmental life span, they did not think of this period as one of continued growth and development but as one of decline and loss. Freud believed that in the elderly years, an internal process overcomes the instinct for life, and unlike some other aspects of his theory, he never wavered from the idea that all humans have a silent death wish. One psychologist noted that Freud's development of the idea of a universal death wish coincided with his struggles with cancer.

> His certainty [about the death wish] may have been due to his own physical struggles. He began experiencing a painful swelling on his palate in 1917 due to a longstanding addiction to cigar smoking, and by early 1923, a cancerous growth had developed on his palate and jaw.... The growth was surgically removed, but it returned at various times in subsequent years, and by 1939 several cancerous lesions in his jaw were causing what he called "paralyzing pain," and his ulcerated cancer would give off such a disagreeable smell that his dog would cringe from him and could not be lured into his presence.... Why would Freud's struggle with cancer convince him that the idea we have a silent death drive within ourselves was really true? (Capps, 2008, p. 197)

It must be remembered that Freud was suffering from a self-inflicted, terminal, and painful disease, an experience that many elderly individuals do not have. Although Freud eventually asked for (and received) physician-assisted suicide, he clearly wrote that the universal death wish was not meant to be understood as advocating suicide.

Instead Freud thought that the death wish was simply a universal desire not to continue living. Some have also speculated that because he witnessed the death and destruction of the First World War, he began to feel that human beings are somehow drawn to the inevitability of death and that death must be a motive force in his theories.

Like Freud, Erikson felt that his theories were associated with his own life stages. Erikson (1977) wrote "Have my students not long suspected that all these neat listings are my own ceremonial reassurances?" (p. 116). He proposed that the developmental tasks of the first part of late-life (ages 60 to 75) were to resolve the conflict between integrity versus despair, and in very old age (ages 75 until death) the conflict to be resolved was achieving immortality versus extinction. By the age of 60 and certainly by the age of 75, most people have completed their parenting responsibilities and have retired from their professional life. For most individuals, parenting and professional duties have consumed the majority of their lives and are the major components in their self-identity. Erikson viewed the concept of integrity as the culmination of all the preceding stages and defined integrity as completeness or wholeness. Erikson (1959) described integrity:

> Only he who in some way has taken care of things and people and has adapted himself to the triumphs and disappointments to being, by necessity, the originator of others and the generators of things and ideas—only he may gradually grow the fruit of these seven stages. I know of no better word for it than ego identity. (p. 98)

The mere fact that Erikson identified these developmental crises of old age demonstrates his adherence to the principle of active choice, even in old age. He stated that rather than becoming dependent and demanding, elderly people seek out opportunities to contribute in ways that strengthen both themselves and those whom they assist. Indeed, later in life Erikson embarked upon a study of Jesus. Erikson believed that as the individual matures and ages, he or she becomes more individuated, or more himself or herself. Individuals in late-life may contribute by an increased concern for the world and all of its inhabitants. According to Erikson, older individuals define themselves as more tolerant, open, compassionate, and less critical, rather than becoming rigid, inflexible, judgmental, selfish, and cynical. Instead of thinking that nothing can be done about global concerns, older individuals tend to be more hopeful. Erikson cited the tendency of older individuals to return to the spiritual and religious organizations of their childhood as a manifestation of this compassionate and loving acceptance. One author (Peck, 1968) termed this revision of self-identity "the night of the ego."

> To live so generously and unselfishly that the prospect of personal death—the night of the ego, it might be called—looks and feels less important than the secure knowledge that one has built for a broader, longer future than any one ego could every encompass. Through children, through contributions to the culture, through friendships—these are the ways in which human beings can achieve enduring significance for their actions which goes beyond the limit of their own skins and their own lives. It may, indeed, be the only *knowable* kind of self-perpetuation after death. (p. 91)

In his 80s Erikson and his wife Joan developed a more detailed description of the ways in which the strengths, skills, and knowledge of all of the previous developmental stages contributed to the elderly years (Austrian, 2002). Erikson thought that older individuals engage in retrospective reviews of their lives; however, rather than engaging in self-blame and regret, they can avoid being overwhelmed by these feelings. Late-life individuals who regret missed opportunities or think that they have not met many of their goals see time as short, without any opportunity to pursue these meaningful goals (Schuster et al., 2003). Finally, at approximately age 90 individuals begin the process of releasing, sensing a freedom from tension, worries, and responsibilities.

One expert on life span development (Moen, 2003) considered how Albert Bandura's social behaviorism theory would influence retirement:

> Psychologist Bandura (1977, 1986) points to the importance of personal control in shaping behavior. How competent individuals feel affects what activities they take on and their persistence in them. One can expect, therefore, that a sense of mastery or personal control is an important resource facilitating active retirement planning, as well as a productive old age. (p. 276)

Individuals who have had an upward, stable career trajectory have the advantage of determining their time of retirement. Moen refers to these types of jobs as "advantaged occupational positions" (2003, p. 279). Because these types of career trajectories are most likely to have pension plans, good health insurance options, and perhaps opportunities for phased retirements and part-time employment, individuals in these advantaged occupational positions can choose early retirement and use these available resources. On the other hand, these individuals are most likely to feel in control of their work life (and thus enjoy it more than people who feel that they have little power or influence at work) and therefore may choose to retire at a later time. Also, "advantaged occupational positions" typically provide a sense of accomplishment and achievement, which many workers do not relinquish easily.

Bandura recognized the importance of individual effort and also the strong influence of structural, institutionalized opportunities. For example, regardless of talent and initiative, some individuals have not enjoyed advantaged occupational positions. Therefore, their work has not been considered significant by society, has not paid much nor provided benefits, and (most important) has not engaged the full potential of these individuals. If they are financially able, many of these nonadvantaged career people thus retire as soon as possible.

The behavioral theorist B. F. Skinner felt that as individuals enter late-life, their environments become more constricted, offering fewer social relationships and stimulating professional opportunities, along with a restricted, smaller world due to transportation problems. Skinner felt that the quality of an individual's thinking is directly related to the learning opportunities of the environment. Therefore, systematic reinforcement for learning is lacking. For most elderly individuals, there are reduced opportunities for learning and, therefore, elderly individuals tend to repeat themselves.

AGEISM

Society often views elderly people negatively, stereotyping this group as noncontributing drains on the national pocketbook. It is true that the health care costs of individuals over the age of 65 account for a large portion of total health care costs. When a society values youth, productivity, independence, and achievement, elderly people may be considered obsolete (Smart, 2009). The stereotype of an elderly person includes feebleness, incompetence, and narrow-mindedness (Papalia & Olds, 1992). Two authors (Rowe & Kahn, 1998) called the idea, "To be old is to be sick," a myth, and Austrian (2002) referred to this myth as the "pathologization of old age" (p. 269). "Ageism is defined as stereotyping, prejudice, and discrimination against people on the basis of age. Stereotyping is the formation of beliefs and expectations about an age group" (Leifheit-Limson & Levy, 2009, p. 20). Very elderly individuals may invoke "death anxiety" in others (Leifheit-Limson & Levy, 2009, p. 21). Society often wishes to deny the inevitability of death, and seeing elderly individuals acts as a painful reminder. Society may therefore avoid elderly people or ridicule them, both defenses against death anxiety.

Negative stereotypes of aging people are widespread in Western cultures, and surveys have shown that people of all ages think of elderly individuals very negatively. Men especially viewed elderly women negatively. Often older individuals incorporate societal ageism into their self-concepts, which may result in less adaptive coping to old age.

Another type of ageism is the idea that older adults are physically and sexually unattractive, even considering that it is "morally wrong and perverted for older adults to be sexually active" (Newman & Newman, 2009, p. 332). Ageist prejudices dictate that older people are sexless and should be sexless. The larger generation of Baby Boomers will dispel many of these negative social attitudes toward elderly people.

Ageism is related to other types of illogical prejudices and discriminations, such as sexism, racism, and handicappism. These different types of prejudices have many similarities, and of course an individual may be a target of all of these, if she is an older woman of a racial/ethnic group who has a disability. Old age itself is often viewed as a disability, an idea that makes little sense. It is true that age is positively correlated with disability, or to state it differently, the older the individual, the more likely that he or she will acquire a disability. Nonetheless, many elderly individuals do not have disabilities. There is another parallel between the disability experience and the aging experience. PWDs and elderly individuals have been falsely viewed as expensive drains on society who have no possibility of contributing to society. Both groups are thought to be "dependent" upon the working population. The last parallel concerns "death anxiety" and the fear of acquiring a disability. Disability is a normal and natural part of life, and everyone has the potential to acquire a disability. Therefore, PWDs are often avoided or segregated because society does not want to be reminded of this possibility, just as society often avoids elderly people to avoid being reminded of the inevitability of death.

Another parallel between elderly people and PWDs is society's response. For both groups, accommodations in society are needed, including both the physical environment (ramps, elevators, or sign language interpreters) and attitudinal changes in society to view these groups more accurately. Unfortunately, society often thinks that elderly people and PWDs must adapt and "take the world as it is." When speaking about elderly people, Datan and Ginzberg (1974) termed this dichotomy "neglect" and "accommodation."

Industrialization and globalism may render some older people's skill sets obsolete, and even if these individuals do not "impose" upon society for services and resources, they may have little effect on the national political and economic agenda. According to some theories of "sociological aging" (Dowd, 1975; Rosow, 1976), those who do not occupy valued roles are invisible or socially inconsequential. Indeed, some theories of sociological aging consider the older person a member of a devalued group, regardless of an individual's independence, health, and financial resources. Their social position is defined by loss. This parallels handicappism because society (rather than the individual and/or his disability) judges PWDs only on their losses, and regardless of the achievements and resources of a PWD, he or she understands that he or she is a member of a devalued group.

Elderly individuals occasionally ridicule ageism by adopting derisive words such as "geezer" to describe themselves. For the same reasons, PWDs often use insulting words to describe themselves, such as "gimp" or "crip." For both groups, these are "in-group" words that are used only by those in that particular group.

Sociological aging seems more logical when we consider that a person's old age experience is related to his or her peer group. Carried to one possible extreme and stated bluntly, life can be viewed as a contest between age peers for limited resources. Of course, there are limited resources for each developmental stage. For example, some toddlers are not admitted to exclusive preschools, and not all women who wish to marry are able to do so. In old age, the 30 widows at the senior center may compete to dance with the five available widowers. Nonetheless, if old age is considered the stage in which there are the fewest resources available, old age might be thought of as a desperate competition. Gilligan, who stated that girls and women tend to view development at all ages in more relational terms, would probably reject this competitive viewpoint and instead view old age as a time when age mates engage in dynamic noncompetitive relationships.

Disengagement theory holds that withdrawal from the work force, invisibility in the community, and loss of family roles are inevitable and contribute to negative outcomes for individuals in late-life. Erikson thought that middle age, old age, and old-old age all include possibilities for generativity and integration. Generativity, a word invented by Erikson, involves leaving some type of legacy or inheritance to one's children and to the world. These legacies and inheritances are more than financial resources or the family silverware, but include a sense of continuity for the generations and valuable wisdom and insights. For example, elderly people often write family histories and their life stories. Related to the idea of generativity is ego integrity in which the individual puts his or her life into context and concludes that it has been generally good.

Disabilities in Late-Life

- Dementias
- Alzheimer's
- Diabetes
- Cerebrovascular accidents (strokes)

DEMENTIAS

Cognitive skills and abilities, which include reasoning, memory, and problem-solving, are closely associated with independence. Individuals with high cognitive functioning typically experience more autonomy and self-direction. In addition, higher cognitive functioning is related to health outcomes, because those with high cognitive functioning engage in healthful behaviors such as undergoing routine physical exams, taking medications in the correct way, exercising, and eating nutritionally. There are age-related cognitive declines that are not considered pathological or given a diagnosis, and the key component for a diagnosis of dementia is impairment of functioning. Therefore, misplacing an object occasionally or forgetting an appointment is not a symptom of dementia. Finally, prevention, enhancement, and intervention techniques are possible for many types of dementia.

Dementias are syndromes involving a cognitive decline that is sufficiently severe to interfere with daily functioning, all of which are symptoms of an underlying disease process in the brain (Mast & Healy, 2009). There are several types of dementias, although the most well-known is Alzheimer's disease. Many dementias are treatable and often reversible. When symptoms appear in the first stages of dementias, it is then possible to identify each type of dementia. Diagnosis becomes more complex when individuals experience two or more types of dementia simultaneously. Also, physicians must rule out a hearing impairment before progressing to the consideration of a type of dementia.

Individuals experiencing clinical depression tend to (unconsciously) exaggerate their cognitive declines, while individuals with dementias tend to minimize their cognitive declines and are not fully aware of these impairments. The side effects of many medications often mimic dementia. A combination of treating depression and changing medications often reverses these dementias. For this reason, physicians must eliminate (or exclude) other types of dementias before considering the diagnosis of Alzheimer's. Alcohol and other drugs can cause dementias, as can infections of the brain and brain injuries. These types of dementia are typically reversible. Another common type of dementia is vascular dementia, typically a result of a stroke.

Dementias are extremely frightening to experience, especially in the early stages when the individual understands that he or she is losing cognitive abilities and also knows that this deterioration of functioning will continue. Considering only financial costs, it is thought that $315 billion each year is spent worldwide on treating dementias (Durand & Barlow, 2010). These costs do not factor in the costs to businesses for health care insurance or the financial losses that result when family members must leave their jobs to care for someone with a dementia. In the United States, the cost is estimated to be $100 billion a year.

ALZHEIMER'S DISEASE

The German psychiatrist Alois Alzheimer first described what he called "a strange disease of the cerebral cortex," in which the individual manifested a progressive memory loss. The syndrome that now bears his name, Alzheimer's disease (AD), is the most prevalent and most feared of all dementias (Papalia & Olds, 1992). However, differentiating

Alzheimer's from other types of dementia is difficult. Currently AD is irreversible and incurable; it is not considered a part of "normal" of aging, because it affects only 5%–10% of individuals over the age of 65 and up to 40% of individuals older than 85. However, Alzheimer's does account for approximately one-half of all nursing home admissions. Although Alzheimer's is not an inevitable result of the aging process, it is a severe disability that affects many areas of functioning, so individuals with Alzheimer's often require the type of care and monitoring that nursing homes can provide. Margrett and Deshpande-Kamat (2009) explained: "cognitive changes such as dementia are considered 'nonnormative' or atypical and do not constitute the majority of cases" (p. 77). AD causes severe and widespread damage to multiple regions of the brain. After the diagnosis has been established, the average time of survival is 8 to 10 years.

In the earlier years of old age (age 65), Alzheimer's is a low-incidence disability, but it becomes a high-incidence disability after the age of 85. We can see that the higher rate of Alzheimer's is directly linked to the longevity revolution. Indeed, prevalence rates of AD differ markedly between the developed nations and undeveloped nations, with developed nations showing much higher prevalence rates. However, demographers consider that these higher rates are caused by longer life spans. Health demographers have found higher rates of AD among women, again because women live longer than men.

Thinking only in terms of the various dementias, AD by far is the most common type and accounts for 50%–60% of all cases of dementia. The first symptoms of AD are memory loss, such as repeatedly forgetting to turn off the stove or to lock the house, or losing one's keys. Disorientation and faulty judgment then become apparent. The individual forgets familiar routes to the grocery store, the post office, or his or her children's homes. Unable to make sensible decisions, the individual with AD may insist on persisting in activities that have become dangerous, such as driving. Family members tire of repeating directions, acting as walking dictionaries, and hear the same story endlessly.

Symptoms include early onset (in the course of Alzheimer's) of cognitive impairments, behavioral changes such as agitation, lack of impulse control, and irritability. Memory loss and the inability to express oneself become very frustrating for both the individual and those around him or her. Aphasia, agnosia, and apraxis often result. Aphasia is the lack of ability to use or understand spoken or written language, and agnosia is the lack of ability to perceive objects through the senses, including facial agnosia, which makes the individual unable to recognize others. Finally, apraxis is the lack of ability to perform purposeful movements; the individual falls, develops a lurching gait while walking, and may have convulsive seizures. In the later stages, the individual often becomes rigid, unable to walk or stand, and incontinent. We have learned about the stresses of spousal caregiving, especially in old age when the caregiving spouse is most often elderly and may have functional impairments. The effects of Alzheimer's have been described:

> Other research shows that even in the earlier to middle stages, Alzheimer's disease has a significant impact on marital companionship and total marital quality. Part of the tragedy is that afflicted spouses either seem unable to perceive problems and to view interactions between themselves and their caregivers as positive, or they distort interactions—either because of the cognitive impairment or perhaps as a way of coping with fears of abandonment. (Rice, 1998, p. 548)

The individual with AD can be reduced to a socially dependent patient through a combination of the effects of AD, such as loss of employment, incontinence, and the inability to drive, manage financial affairs, and perform such simple activities of daily living as dressing oneself or brushing teeth. Due to personality changes, such as lack of impulse control and irritability, the individual with AD often becomes difficult to be around. If there is a spousal caregiver, he or she also becomes homebound. We have learned how marriages in which one partner has a disability, especially a severe disability such as AD, may become asymmetrical or unbalanced. This same pattern occurs when one partner has AD. The caregiver feels resentment, and the spouse with AD often feels like a burden and fears abandonment.

This disability is characterized by rapid deterioration and atrophy of the cerebral cortex that is combined with chemical changes, including lowers levels of neurotransmitters that are necessary for communication between neurons (Berk, 2001). Nerve cells shrink and decrease in number. Two major structural changes in the brain occur: amyloid plaques (clusters of degenerating nerve cell endings) and neurofibrillary tangles (masses of twisted threads in the nerve cells) develop. Amyloid plaques destroy the surrounding neurons and their communication networks and reduce the flow of blood to the brain. Although AD was once considered a diagnosis of exclusion, the advent of functional brain imaging has made AD diagnosis more accurate.

There are two main types of AD: familial (which runs in families) and sporadic (which has no family history). Familial AD typically has an early onset (before the age of 65) and progresses more rapidly than sporadic AD. Although more than half of the individuals diagnosed with AD show no genetic markers, it is known that genes on chromosomes 1, 14, and 21 are linked to familial AD. For this reason, individuals with Down syndrome who live past age 40 almost always develop AD. Chromosome 21 is a factor in both Down syndrome and AD.

DIABETES

Diabetes is actually a group of diseases characterized by the body's inability to metabolize glucose (sugar). There are two basic types of diabetes: Type 1, which affects 5% to 10% of individuals diagnosed with diabetes and has an onset in early life, and Type 2, which is far more common and affects as much as 90%–95% of all Americans diagnosed with diabetes. In Type 1 diabetes, the body cannot produce insulin, so "exogenous" (external) insulin must be administered, typically by injection. In Type 2 diabetes, the body cannot utilize insulin. A third type, gestational diabetes, affects pregnant women. In addition, some physicians diagnose a condition known as "prediabetes" in which the individual is considered to have a high risk for developing diabetes. Type 1 diabetes is considered the most severe type of diabetes and requires a great deal of management of exercise, food intake, and the use of insulin injections. "All diabetic diets are designed to balance the number of proteins, carbohydrates, and fats ingested and to exclude foods that contain large amounts of sugar" (Falvo, 1999, p. 210).

About 1.7 individuals in 1,000 have Type 1 diabetes, making it one of the most prevalent chronic disabilities of childhood. (Remember that childhood disabilities tend to be low-incidence disabilities.) Early symptoms of Type 1 are polyuria (frequent urination), polydipsia (frequent drinking), polyphagia (frequent eating), and weight loss. Even though there is more than sufficient glucose in the blood stream, because the pancreas no longer produces insulin that glucose cannot be transferred to the organs and muscles. The individuals continue to eat more and more and drastically increase their caloric intake, but they still feel fatigued and weak and lose weight. In some cases, the individual is in a state of starvation. In extreme cases, the individual may develop diabetic ketoacidosis (DKA), a dangerous high level of acid in the bloodstream that may result in coma and eventually death.

Although the onset of Type 1 diabetes is acute, with presentation of clear symptoms, the onset of Type 2 diabetes is insidious and symptoms may not be evident for several years after the onset. With Type 2 diabetes, the onset is not referenced, but rather the date of diagnosis. With the typical onset of Type 2 diabetes late in life, individuals often consider the symptoms of this slow, insidious onset normal signs of aging, such as loss of energy, frequent urination, and vision problems. All types of diabetes are considered generalized, multisystem disorders, so they have many complications and secondary conditions. The secondary conditions include retinopathy (12% of all cases of new blindness in the United States each year result from diabetes). Nephropathy and renal disease affect approximately 10%–21% of individuals with diabetes and can result in end-stage renal failure. Diabetic individuals often require dialysis because their kidneys are not receiving a sufficient supply of blood.

Diabetes results in a generalized pathological process that affects the entire body and produces lowered resistance to infection. Because there is often vascular disease through-out the body, including the heart, brain, legs, feet, and kidneys, diabetics are at greater risk for heart attacks, congestive heart failure, and stroke. Major arteries, medium-sized veins, and capillaries are damaged, often resulting in tissue necrosis (death of the tissue) or gangrene. Individuals whose diabetes was diagnosed early in life are more susceptible to these complications, or in other words, the duration of the disease is related to the number and severity of complications.

Those with Type 2 diabetes are at increased risk for developing large blood vessel disease, which is the leading cause of death for this group. Damage to the blood vessels is diffuse, resulting in peripheral vascular disease that greatly constricts the blood and oxygen flow to the legs and feet. Half of all therapeutic leg and foot amputations in the United States are the result of diabetes-related neuropathy. As the population ages, the rate of diabetes rises, and the number of amputations thus increases. As one author explained, "the disproportionate number of lower limb amputation (versus upper limb amputation) relates to the etiology of limb loss.... Approximately 70 percent of all lower extremity amputees have vascular disease, and of these, approximately 80 percent have diabetes" (Czerniecki, 1994, p. 197). Moreover, the survival rate of diabetes-related amputation is about 61%, and the amputee has a far higher likelihood that the other leg will also be amputated. There is a 12% incidence of secondary amputation within one year of the ini-tial amputation, 18% after two years, 27% after three years, and 44.3% after four years.

Decreased blood flow commonly leads to sexual dysfunctions in both men and women. For young people considering marriage or a long-term romantic relationship, diabetic-related sexual dysfunction will affect these plans. Unless the individual wears a visible insulin pump, diabetes is an invisible disability. We have learned that there is no correlation between degree of impairment and visibility of the disability, and diabetes illustrates this relationship. Although diabetes is invisible, at the same time it is a very impairing, life-threatening disability. We have also learned that many invisible disabilities are invisible to the individuals themselves, who first fail to notice symptoms and then may "forget" that they have a disability. Many different areas of the individual's lifestyle are affected by diabetes, including monitoring every bite of food. Therefore, any form of denial of diabetes can be life-threatening.

Like people with any type of invisible disability, the individual with diabetes must carefully weigh the advantages of disclosure against the disadvantages. At parties where food and alcohol are a major focus, individuals with diabetes must plan ahead and monitor their intake. At times it may be simpler to disclose, but at other times and in other situations with other people, it may be wiser not to disclose. The activities necessary to manage diabetes, such as eating on regular schedules, performing blood tests several times a day, and injecting insulin, may also influence the disclosure decision (see Table 15.2).

Clearly, the management of diabetes requires a high degree of self-discipline and support from family members. Services from nutritionists are important, as are frequent eye examinations by ophthalmologists.

CEREBROVASCULAR ACCIDENTS (STROKES)

The incidence of stroke is common, and the resulting implications of strokes are widespread. One author stated that "in the elderly, stroke is the most common neurological disorder that results in permanent disability" (Gitter, 1994, p. 117), while other authors summarized, "stroke constitutes the major cause of paralysis in the United States, and its survivors comprise the largest diagnostic category of referrals to rehabilitation hospitals" (Caplan & Moelter, 2000, p. 75). Finally, "stroke is the third leading cause of death in the USA and the leading cause of disability. Approximately 550,000 people suffer strokes each year" (Diller & Moroz, 2005, p. 650).

A stroke has an acute onset that affects a wide range of functioning and typically occurs in late-life. Health demographers find it difficult to determine prevalence rates for stroke, because only those who have moderate impairments tend to receive services. Those with severe strokes typically die or are judged to be too disabled to benefit from post-stroke services and rehabilitation, and those with mild strokes are often discharged from emergency rooms and sent home. When a stroke occurs while the person is in the 50s or 60s, the individual often moves from an identity as a middle-aged person to that of an elderly person. Not only is the onset of stroke acute, but the warnings signs are also invisible or are attributed to the effects of aging. Some early warning signs are ignored, but the risk factors, such as the use of alcohol and smoking, are well known. Because of the greater number of elderly individuals, the prevalence of stroke will continue to increase. Indeed, with each decade of life after the age of 55, a person's risk of having a stroke doubles (see Figure 15.1).

Some risk factors can be changed, but others cannot. Factors such as high blood pressure, diabetes, alcohol use, and smoking can be modified, while such factors as

TABLE 15.2

Average, Annual Crude, and Age-Adjusted Incidence Rates of Diagnosed Diabetes* Among Adults Aged >18 Years, by State and U.S. Census Region—Behavioral Risk Factor Surveillance System, 33 States, 1995–1997 and 2005–2007

Regional/State	1995–1997					2005–2007					% Increase in age-adjusted rate
	Crude rate	(95% CI†)	Age-adjusted rate	(95% CI)	No. of cases (1,000s)§	Crude rate	(95% CI)	Age-adjusted rate	(95% CI)	No. of cases (1,000s)	
Northeast	4.6	(3.8–5.4)	4.6	(3.8–5.4)	78	8.3	(7.5–9.1)	8.2	(7.4–9.0)	145	78¶
Maine	4.1	(2.3–5.7)	4.1	(2.4–5.9)	4	8.5	(6.9–10.2)	8.3	(6.6–10.0)	8	102¶
New Hampshire	3.2	(1.8–4.6)	3.4	(1.9–4.9)	3	8.0	(6.4–9.6)	8.0	(6.4–9.6)	8	135¶
New Jersey	4.6	(2.9–6.1)	4.7	(3.0–6.3)	27	7.7	(6.5–8.8)	7.7	(6.6–8.9)	4.7	64¶
Pennsylvania	4.8	(3.6–6.0)	4.7	(3.6–5.9)	42	8.9	(7.4–10.4)	8.6	(7.1–10.0)	79	83¶
Vermont	4.4	(2.8–6.0)	4.6	(2.9–6.2)	2	6.8	(5.6–8.0)	6.6	(5.4–7.8)	3	43¶
Midwest	4.2	(3.4–5.0)	4.2	(3.4–5.0)	92	7.5	(6.7–8.3)	7.4	(6.6–8.2)	174	76¶
Indiana	5.6	(3.4–7.6)	5.8	(3.6–8.0)	23	10.0	(8.5–11.5)	10.2	(8.6–11.7)	43	76¶
Iowa	4.9	(3.3–6.5)	4.9	(3.3–6.5)	10	8.2	(6.8–9.6)	8.0	(6.6–9.3)	18	63¶
Minnesota	2.9	(2.1–3.7)	3.0	(2.1–3.9)	9	5.0	(3.6–6.3)	5.0	(3.6–6.3)	18	67¶
Missouri	5.4	(3.1–7.7)	5.2	(3.1–7.4)	21	8.8	(7.2–10.5)	8.8	(7.1–10.4)	36	69¶
Ohio	3.2	(2.0–4.4)	3.3	(2.0–4.5)	26	6.4	(4.6–8.2)	6.3	(4.6–8.1)	52	91
North Dakota	5.0	(3.1–6.9)	5.2	(3.2–7.1)	2	7.2	(5.8–8.5)	7.0	(5.7–8.3)	3	35
South Dakota	2.7	(1.3–4.1)	2.6	(1.3–4.0)	1	7.5	(6.2–8.8)	7.3	(6.1–8.6)	4	181¶
South	4.3	(3.7–4.9)	4.5	(3.9–5.1)	234	10.3	(9.7–10.9)	10.5	(9.9–11.1)	642	133¶
Alabama	5.2	(3.2–7.2)	5.4	(3.3–7.5)	16	11.3	(9.4–13.2)	11.3	(9.4–13.1)	36	109¶
Arkansas	4.5	(2.5–6.3)	4.6	(2.6–6.6)	8	10.4	(8.9–11.9)	10.2	(8.7–11.7)	20	122¶
Florida	3.4	(2.2–4.6)	3.4	(2.2–4.6)	36	10.9	(9.5–12.3)	10.3	(9.0–11.7)	139	203¶
Georgia	5.5	(3.2–7.8)	6.2	(3.5–8.8)	28	10.3	(8.5–12.1)	11.2	(9.3–13.0)	64	81¶
Kentucky	3.9	(2.6–5.2)	4.0	(2.7–5.3)	11	10.6	(8.9–12.2)	10.5	(8.8–12.1)	31	163¶
North Carolina	5.4	(3.9–6.9)	5.7	(4.1–7.3)	29	9.8	(8.8–10.8)	10.1	(9.1–11.1)	59	77¶
South Carolina	5.2	(3.3–7.1)	5.4	(3.4–7.5)	13	11.4	(10.0–12.6)	11.5	(10.1–12.9)	34	113¶
Tennessee	5.1	(3.5–6.5)	5.2	(3.6–6.8)	19	11.0	(8.9–13.1)	11.0	(8.9–13.2)	46	112¶
Texas	3.2	(2.0–4.4)	3.6	(2.2–4.9)	42	10.2	(8.2–12.2)	11.1	(9.0–13.3)	156	208¶

Virginia	5.1	(3.3–6.9)	5.5	(3.6–7.5)	24	7.5	(6.1–8.9)	7.6	(6.2–9.0)	40	38
West Virginia	5.8	(3.4–8.2)	5.8	(3.5–8.2)	8	13.3	(11.2–15.4)	12.7	(10.7–14.7)	17	119¶
West	5.3	(4.5–6.1)	5.7	(4.7–6.7)	189	8.1	(7.1–9.1)	8.6	(7.6–9.6)	332	51¶
Arizona	4.9	(2.3–7.5)	5.2	(2.3–8.0)	15	10.2	(7.6–12.8)	10.4	(7.7–13.1)	41	100¶
California	6.0	(4.5–7.5)	6.6	(5.0–8.1)	134	8.3	(4.8–9.7)	9.0	(7.4–10.6)	208	36¶
Colorado	3.2	(1.8–4.6)	3.6	(2.0–5.2)	9	5.8	(4.8–6.8)	6.2	(5.2–7.2)	20	72¶
Hawaii	4.0	(2.1–6.0)	4.2	(2.2–6.3)	3	6.1	(4.6–7.6)	5.9	(4.5–7.4)	6	40
Idaho	3.1	(3.1–4.1)	3.1	(2.1–4.2)	2	9.5	(7.9–11.2)	9.8	(8.1–11.5)	9	216¶
Montana	3.6	(2.0–5.2)	3.6	(2.0–5.2)	2	7.5	(6.3–8.7)	7.1	(6.0–8.3)	5	97¶
New Mexico	5.0	(2.2–7.8)	5.3	(2.2–8.5)	6	8.8	(7.0–10.6)	8.7	(6.8–10.6)	12	64¶
Oregon	4.6	(3.3–6.0)	4.7	(3.4–6.1)	11	6.9	(5.4–8.4)	6.7	(5.2–8.2)	18	43
Utah	3.7	(2.0–5.4)	4.5	(2.4–6.5)	5	6.4	(5.2–7.7)	7.8	(6.3–9.2)	11	73¶
Wyoming	5.0	(3.4–6.6)	5.3	(3.9–7.0)	2	6.3	(5.2–7.4)	6.1	(5.0–7.2)	2	15
All states combined	4.6	(4.2–5.0)	4.8	(4.4–5.2)	590	9.0	(8.6–9.4)	9.1	(8.7–9.5)	1,293	90¶

*Per 1,000 population.

†Confidence Interval

§Annual weighted number of incident cases.

¶Significant differences between age-adjusted rate for 1995–1997 and 2005–2007 ($p < 0.05$, by t-test).

Source: CDC.

prior stroke, age, sex, ethnicity, and family history cannot be changed. Men tend to have more strokes than women, and African Americans have higher rates of stroke than white Americans. One source (Gorelick, 1994) estimated that lifestyle modifications could prevent 378,500 strokes each year, and with the longevity revolution, it is safe to state that education and prevention campaigns will increase. These personal choices that put people at greater risk for stroke parallel the debate about the dangerous activities younger people engage in ("thrills and chills").

There are basically two types of strokes, although each type has many subtypes. The first type is the most common and is termed ischemic. In ischemic strokes, the flow of blood is reduced and cell death results. Veins and arteries are occluded (clogged) by the build-up of plaque, or small bits of blood clots break loose and become lodged in a vessel. The second type of stroke is termed hemorrhagic stroke; it occurs when the rupture of a blood vessel in the brain produces bleeding. A subtype of hemorrhagic type is caused by an aneurysm, a small ballooning of the walls of an artery that ruptures and causes bleeding in the brain. There is swelling and pressure in the brain, and death often occurs.

The amount and type of brain damage from a stroke depends upon the size of the lesion and the specific regions of the brain that are damaged. Generally, damage on one side of the brain affects the opposite of the body. For example, left brain damage generally affects the right side of the body. Left cerebral hemisphere damage causes impairments in language and communication skills, often termed aphasia, which may make the individual unable to speak or understand language. Right cerebral damage often results in unilateral neglect, causing the individual to fail to dress or groom the left side

FIGURE 15.1

Percentage of people who were ever told that they had a stroke, 2008.

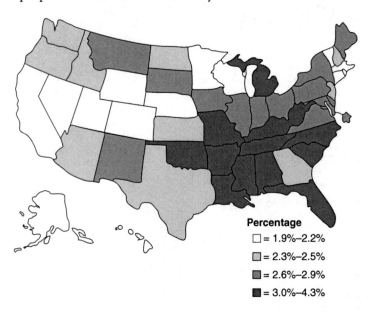

Percentage
□ = 1.9%–2.2%
▨ = 2.3%–2.5%
▩ = 2.6%–2.9%
■ = 3.0%–4.3%

Source: CDC.

of his or her body, eat food off one side of the plate, and bump into walls that are on the left.

Right brain damage results in severe and persistent perceptual problems, such as difficulty in judging distance, determining shapes (such as recognizing squares, triangles, and circles), and being unable to discern important visual information from a complex background (such as reading maps). Depression often results from frontal lobe damage or from strokes that damage both sides (bilateral) of the brain. Hemiplegia on the opposite side of the brain damage often results, so that the individual is paralyzed on one side of his or her body.

Jill Bolte Taylor experienced a stroke at the age of 37 from a congenital malformation of a blood vessel. Ironically, she was a scientist trained in neuroanatomy. She described the experience:

> I didn't know exactly what type of stroke I was experiencing, but the congenital arteriovenous malformation (AVM) that burst in my head was spewing a large volume of blood over the left hemisphere of my brain. As the blood swept over the higher thinking centers of my left cerebral cortex, I began losing my skills of higher cognition—one precious ability at a time (Taylor, 2006, p. 47).

> When I lost my left hemisphere and its language centers, I also lost the clock that would break my moments into consecutive brief instances. Instead of having my moments prematurely stunted, they became open-ended, and I felt no rush to do anything. Like walking along the beach, or just hanging out in the beauty of nature, I shifted from the doing-consciousness of my left to the being-consciousness of my right brain. I morphed from feeling small and isolated to feeling enormous and expansive. I stopped thinking in language and shifted to taking new pictures of what was going on in the present moment. I was not capable of deliberating about past or future-related ideas because those cells were incapacitated. (p. 68)

Losing one's communication skills from left cerebral damage can effectively isolate the individual. Speech retraining and other cognitive skill training will be necessary. The effects of hemiplegia includes paralysis, the tendency to become easily fatigued, impairment of fine motor coordination, and weakness on one side of the body. Mobility skills training is initiated while the individual is in the hospital, and it begins with sitting balance, standing balance, and finally walking. Apraxia results in approximately 25% of patients with left hemisphere strokes, which makes the individual unable to carry out motor tasks despite having adequate strength, sensation, coordination, and comprehension (Gitter, 1994). Apraxia impairs the individual's abilities to learn new motor skills, such as standing and walking.

Margaret Robison described her apraxia following a stroke:

> To lose my ability to walk was to lose all sense of safety. Who would come when I needed to be propped up in bed so I wouldn't choke on a sip of water, or when I needed a bedpan or a blanket? To lose my ability to walk was to be thrown back to memories of being an infant left in a closed room for hours, screaming. To lose the use of my left arm and hand felt like a cruel amputation...I *needed* my left. I *needed* my arm. I *needed* my hand.

A booklet explaining apraxia lay under a pile of books where I'd hidden it. As long as I didn't read it, as long as I didn't put words to what had happened…my own acknowledgment of it didn't have to cut so deeply. I could postpone the pain of acceptance. (Robison, 1997, pp. 88–89)

Thus, the after effects of stroke can be widespread and may affect motor abilities, speech, and cognitive skills. Recovery and rehabilitation are dependent upon the degree and type of damage, the availability of a caregiver in a home, and the premorbid (before the stroke) functioning. Widespread damage usually translates to a need for extensive case management, requiring the services of speech language pathologists, physical therapists, physicians, and rehabilitation counselors to deal with the emotional aspects.

MAKING MEANING

The motivation for achievement and the competitive drives of young adulthood and midlife dissipate in late-life, and a need and desire to understand one's life and relationships takes precedence. These introspective tasks of making meaning of the life that the individual has lived are considered growth and development, so the elderly years, including the old-old, are a time of continued progress. Freund, Nikitin, and Ritter (2009) explained succinctly: "Time perception extends into the past and into the future. With respect to longevity, the longer we live, the longer the past we have to look back on" (p. 5). The authors also maintain that the longer lives of elderly individuals result in a greater capacity for self-regulation and also provide more "diachronic weakening." Self-regulation and diachronic weakening mean that older individuals have fewer functional demands and more free time. In all the earlier stages of life, individuals live by the clock and the calendar, because they must attend school at certain hours of the day, go to work in the morning, take the children to soccer practice at 4:00, and remember to tip the paper girl at Christmas. Late-life, in contrast, is diachronic, lacking a great deal of temporal structure and allowing great freedom in the choice of lifestyle.

When people look back on the major activities of life, such as marriage, child-rearing, and job, it usually reveals both successes and failures; for most individuals, successes outnumber failures and disappointments. For some failures, self-corrective actions are still possible, but not for all. Also, in spite of longer life spans and increased opportunities, no one completes everything he or she wanted to do. Retrospective contemplation of one's life is much like viewing a "time budget" and asking, "Where did all the time go?" Personal decisions account for some time expenditures, and societal opportunity structures and role expectations influence other time allocations. Indeed, until old age societal expectations dictate many of an individual's decisions and choices, but in old age personal decisions take precedence in the use of time.

In Terman's longitudinal study of gifted children, the men who had been studied since early childhood were interviewed about their satisfaction with life. The men, who were aged 58 to 72, were also asked about their life goals. Health and socioeconomic status were found to be related to general life satisfaction, and goals related to family life and religious life provided a greater sense of meaning and emotional support than occupational goals. Those men who had focused on career goals were found to be more poorly adjusted (Crosnoe & Elder, 2002). Terman's study was one of the first large-scale longitudinal studies, so it was possible for it to compare life satisfaction at various stages of life; consequently, self-reports of satisfaction in late-life combined with reflection on important life choices and the consequences of these choices provide an insight into possible causes of life satisfaction. It must be remembered, however, that Terman's study participants were highly intelligent white males without disabilities, so it is safe to assume that, as a group, they had more opportunities for and fewer barriers to success.

Erikson's theory of development maintained that during late-life, individuals tend to identify themselves in broader terms, seeing themselves as a part of the world rather than identifying with their professional work or their immediate family. Late-life individuals are typically satisfied with their work and family accomplishments, but they continue to grow and develop a deeper sense of self, often redefining their self-worth. Perhaps the combination of a long life to review and the freedom from role obligations that retirement provides allows the opportunity for self-evaluation. Erikson expressed this shift in self-identity as moving from procreation to creativity.

DEATH

Young adults tend to die from accidents, while elderly people die from chronic illnesses and the effects of lifelong disabilities. Women tend to live longer than men. The experience of death has changed drastically in the last 100 years; formerly death was a part of everyday experience, with loved ones providing care for dying family members in the home. Medical advances have contributed to the shift in how death occurs and how it is viewed. For example, 77% of all deaths in the United States now occur in the hospital.

Death in the United States has been described in this way:

> Changing profiles both in population demographics and in acute treatment service delivery influence family decision making. Advances in medical technologies and gains in standards of living have combined to create a large group of people whose end-of-life course unfolds slowly from long-term chronic illnesses at an advanced age. (Tilden, Tolle, Nelson, Thompson, & Eggman, 2007)

In the past, individuals often died quickly, typically contracting an infectious disease and dying within days. Without antibiotics, everyone feared infectious diseases. Infectious diseases are not stratified by social glass or gender; everyone is equally at risk. Up until 1950, people often died from acute pneumonia, tuberculosis, diarrhea, and enteritis. The length of a serious illness or disability was measured in days or weeks, certainly not years. Childbirth often resulted in the mother's death. Two hundred years ago, almost one of every two children died before the age of 10, and on average one parent died before the children grew up (Santrock, 2009). Therefore, in the past the death of a child or a young adult did not appear to be an off-time transition. Such a death was tragic but still very common. In contrast, today the death of children and young adults are considered off-time transitions. Kübler-Ross (1969) focused national attention on the structural lag between the changing ways in which Americans die and the lack of agencies and services for dying individuals and their families. For example, Kübler-Ross initiated the hospice movement, which allowed people to die relatively pain-free in a "home-like" setting. When people died quickly at home and did not experience today's lingering deaths in hospitals, hospices were not necessary.

According to the U.S. Census (Edmondson, 1997), white Americans live longer than minority Americans. This discrepancy in life expectancies becomes lower throughout the life course because death at younger ages, often from childhood infectious diseases, decreases the average life span of African Americans, Asian Americans, and Native Americans. At age 85 whites live on average only one month longer than minority Americans, but at birth whites have a life expectancy that is 7 years longer than these other groups. In contrast, the gender gap in death increases with age. For example, more than two-thirds of Americans who die at age 85 or older are women.

Edmondson (1997) described the relationship between death rates and life expectancies:

> Death has a contract with everyone, but 20th century Americans have renegotiated the deal. . . . A baby girl born in the U.S. in 2000, will expect to live almost 80 years. Thanks to advances in medicine, sanitation, and basic nutrition, the annual age-adjusted death rate per 100,000 Americans will decline from 2,296 in 1900 to a projected 731 in 2000. If this decline had never occurred, half of Americans alive in 2000 would never have been born. (p. 1)

Today, as a society we make death invisible. One developmental psychologist explained:

> We try to solve the problems of death by hiding it or denying it. We lie to dying people about their condition because death is unmentionable. They, in turn, try to convince us that they are getting better. . . . When people die, they are made to look healthy and alive, as though they were sleeping. . . . The denial of death has become the orthodoxy of our culture. (Rice, 1998, p. 602)

SUICIDE IN LATE-LIFE

Elderly individuals have much higher rates of suicide than younger people, with elderly men completing suicide five to eight times more often than elderly women. The difference in the rates is related to coroner's reports. Coroners will often record the cause of death as accidental or unintentional poisoning when it is in fact a suicide. Elderly white males have a higher suicide rate than elderly black men, and white women have suicide rates at least triple that of black women. One reason for the lower rate of elderly suicide among women may be their tendency to seek counseling and medical treatment more readily than do men. Because of monitoring provided, living in a nursing home results in a 59% reduction in rate of elderly suicide.

There are multiple factors related to the high suicide rate among elderly individuals, including depression, social isolation, lack of purpose, severe chronic pain, and visual impairments. One of the factors is "cultural support" of suicide for elderly people who are in a great deal of pain. Interestingly, approximately 40% of the elderly individuals who committed suicide saw a physician during the last month of their lives.

As the Baby Boom generation moves into the elderly years, larger numbers of elderly suicides will occur. Suicide rates are lower in states in which elderly incomes are higher and in states with larger numbers of individuals that have strong religious identification. Divorce is a trigger for suicide in the elderly, for both men and women. Divorced men and women who are elderly have suicide rates nearly twice that of their married age mates. States in which guns are more easily available tend to have high elderly suicide rates. The two states with the lowest elderly suicide rates are Rhode Island (7.25 per 100,000) and Massachusetts (6.48 per 100,000). Both these states have high rates of church attendance and high proportions of Catholics. The three states with the highest elderly suicide rates are Nevada (26.15 per 100,000), Idaho (26.15 per 100,000), and Montana (25.87 per 100,000).

In 2004 42.9% of elderly women and 78.7% of elderly men used guns in their suicides, making guns the principal method of suicide. Elderly people who had a gun in their home were 4.6 times more likely to die from suicide than people who did not own a firearm.

ASSISTED SUICIDE AND PWDs

PWDs have a motto: "Pity is lethal." Society incorrectly views the experience of disability as an unbearable tragedy and may feel that death would be preferable to life with some disabilities. Most who hold these views are peoplr without disabilities (PWODs). Disability rights advocates point out the discrepancy between the heroic lifesaving measures taken on behalf of a PWOD and the supposed "humanity" of allowing a PWD to die. Smart (2009) summarized:

> [The assisted suicide of PWDs is justified by] the strong pressure to accord everyone autonomy and personal liberty. However, when a PWOD threatens suicide, an array of services is mobilized to *prevent* the suicide. In contrast, when a PWD asks for assistance in committing suicide, an array of services is mobilized to *facilitate* the suicide. (p. 158)

The following excerpt was written by playwright, filmmaker, and writer Mark O'Brien, who won an Academy Award in 1997 for his documentary film *Breathing Lessons*. O'Brien lived in an iron lung since 1955 and died in 1999. When he refers to the "death train," he may be alluding to Nazi methods used in the Holocaust.

> It is tempting to pity a man in an iron lung. But pity has become a lethal weapon. On January 8, 1997, the Supreme Court heard arguments in favor of killing people like me—out of pity—to end our suffering. An iron lung has been my second skin since the 1955 polio epidemic. For forty years, people have said, "That poor thing—how he must suffer. He's terminally ill, you know." I'm not "suffering," "terminal," or even "ill." Don't waste your pity on me. I want to live. Every year, practitioners of mercy death kill thousands of people against our will—out of pity. If the Supreme Court declares mercy death legal, that's like declaring open season on people with disabilities. We're not contagious or dangerous. And we aren't affiliated with any political party. We are people who hear the death train. We will not board that train willingly. (Fleischer & Zames, 2001, p. 132)

Life with a disability is often thought to be "life unworthy of life." In the few widely publicized assisted suicides for PWDs, no examination of the person's quality of life was discussed (Shapiro, 1997). One such ill-informed perspective is seen in the Clint Eastwood/Hilary Swank film *Million Dollar Baby*, in which Eastwood, a boxing coach, assists a young woman, Swank, to commit suicide because she has a severe disability. Those in the disability community were appalled when Eastwood's character was considered a hero and applauded for his actions. Although this film is simply an invented story, it literally shows society's view of "pity" and its definition of "humanity." Thousands of PWDs who have the same type of disability experienced by Swank's character live happy, productive lives for a long period after the acute hospitalization stage, learning to manage their disability, to mobilize social support, and to use assistive technology. The disability community considers it outrageous to show favorably the assisted death of someone in the acute hospitalization stage only a few days post-injury, before that person attempts to learn how to deal with the disability.

The story of Larry McAfee illustrates this point. This is a true story of a 34-year-old man from the state of Georgia who in 1989 was injured in a motorcycle accident that left him a quadriplegic and on a respirator. At the time of the accident, he was nearing graduation from Georgia Tech as an engineer. McAfee contacted a lawyer, asking for the legal right to end his life. The case went to the Georgia Supreme Court and McAfee was granted his wish. However, by the time his case was decided in 1990, McAfee no longer wished to die and was indeed a disability rights activist who testified before the Georgia State Senate. In the intervening three years, nothing had changed in McAfee's disability. So what had changed?

First, McAfee was a young man who had to live in a nursing home because Medicaid and Medicare policies would only pay for his care in an institution. McAfee reported that he "escaped" from the nursing home, stating that "Medicaid and Medicare policies that do not work in the best interest of the disabled have caused me and those like me to become prisoners of the bureaucracy" (Shapiro, 1997, p. 177). In the nursing home, McAfee felt that he was stripped of the ability to make decisions for himself. Second, a man named Russ Fine (which is his real name) stepped forward and admitted that he supported McAfee's right to die, but Russ insisted that McAfee first consider all his options. The first option was assistive technology, the second was finding ways around Medicaid's funding requirements so that McAfee could leave the nursing home—Fine simply took McAfee out for rides in the van, to restaurants, movies, and other types of entertainment. A computer engineer from California, Bob Stockwell, heard of McAfee's case on television and flew out to Georgia to set up a voice-activated computer. Stockwell knew nothing about disability, but he did know computers. Stockwell also set up a computer system that allowed McAfee to make architectural drawings by directing a sonar beam from a strap on his head. McAfee has a power wheelchair and a modified van that allow him to go anywhere he wants. All of this process was lengthy (3 years) and difficult, but at the end of it McAfee no longer wanted to die. Nothing about his disability changed; rather, his environment changed, including the freedom to live in his home, the assistive technology, and the availability of transportation.

Assisted suicide for PWDs is a sensitive issue and is related to abortion of fetuses with disabilities, infanticide of newborns with disabilities, and euthanasia of PWDs. Most adults with disabilities are capable of speaking for themselves, while babies are not. Those nations, such as the Netherlands, that have legalized euthanasia tend to have a fairly racially and ethnically homogenous citizenry and almost universal health care coverage. In contrast, the United States has many marginalized groups in addition to PWDs and no universal health care coverage. If such laws were passed, would "society" unwittingly encourage PWDs to die? In the case of Larry McAfee, society was the Supreme Court of the state of Georgia, which was willing to assist him to die.

Assisted suicide for anyone, with or without a disability, is a difficult decision, and without doubt the principles of autonomy and individualism are important American values. There are strong arguments both for and against assisted suicide, all with merits. However, when a nation allows assisted suicide for one group of people, the question of humanity must be raised. People in vulnerable categories realize that they will be more likely to be considered for euthanasia. A 1996 *Washington Post* poll showed that 70% of African Americans and 58% of those termed "elderly" opposed legalized assisted suicide. African Americans were submitted to the most horrific medical exploitation in American history, followed by people who had mental retardation or who were mentally ill. It is understandable why African Americans and PWDs view the legalization of assisted suicide with outright hostility.

Those with power make decisions, and they are often physicians in cases of PWDs. The legal scholar Stefan (2001) related an account in which the triple combination of disability, parental race, and perceived poverty resulted in the deliberate deaths of infants.

> Researchers at the University of Oklahoma decided to investigate the effects of treatment on the survival rates of infants born with spina bifida. To further their research, they divided the infants born at the hospital with spina bifida into two categories, those who would receive treatment, and those who would not— obviously without the knowledge or consent of the parents of the children who did not receive treatment. The way the children were divided was based on the researchers' perceptions of the parents' ability to take care of their children, so the children of poor, minority parents did not receive treatment, and the children of more economically stable parents did receive treatment. Virtually every one of the children who did not receive treatment died. Virtually every one of the children who did receive treatment lived. (p. 155)

In 1992 the parents of the dead children sued (*Johnson v. Thompson, 1992*), and the court ruled that the parents did not have a case based on race, because a few white babies were not treated, even though the majority of the dead babies were African American. Additionally, the court ruled that there was no discrimination based on disability because all the babies had spina bifida. Therefore the parents lost the case. Every baby born to an African American single mother was allowed to die. The perceptions and "clinical" judgments of the physicians determined who lived and who died.

Widespread euthanasia of a specific group of people, such as PWDs, is often presented as a "release" or "mercy" (Marks, 1999). In Nazi Germany, 200,000 Germans with disabilities were murdered (Friedlander, 1995; Gallagher, 1990; Fleischer & Zames, 2001; Wolfensberger, 1981). These PWDs were killed before the start of World War II, and there is documented evidence that other nations knew of these killings. Hitler and the Nazi waited to see if an international crisis would develop, and when none of the nations protested, the killings continued. The gas chambers and crematoria used in the Holocaust were first used for PWDs. Hugh Gallagher's book *By Trust Betrayed: Patients, Physicians, and the License to Kill in the Third Reich* (1990) pointed out that doctors worked with the Nazis in order to facilitate efficient, cost-effective murders. In the following excerpt, Gallaher quotes the statement of a psychologist, Dr. Ludwig Lehner, at the Nuremburg trials. A physician, Dr. Pfannmuller, killed children with disabilities by starving them. Part of the Lehner's deposition stated: "I remember the gist of the following remarks of Pfannmuller":

> "These creatures (he meant the children) naturally present for me as National Socialist only the burden for the healthy body of our *Volk* [people]. We do not kill (he could have used a euphemistic expression for this word kill) with poison, injections, etc.: then the foreign press and certain gentlemen in Switzerland (the International Red Cross) would only have new inflammatory material. No, our method is much simpler and more natural, as you see." With these words, he pulled, with the help of a…nurse, a child from its little bed. While exhibiting the child like a dead rabbit, he asserted with a knowing expression and cynical grin, "For this one it will take two or three more days." (Gallagher, 1990, p. 127)

Another author (Friedlander, 1995) described the way in which the expense of caring for Germans with disabilities played a part in their deaths. The following excerpt was written by the publisher:

> The move to rid Germany of institutionalized handicapped adults might have been expected. As we have seen, the funds spent for the upkeep of institutionalized patients had already been reduced drastically, and it had become customary to refer to them as "life unworthy of life." Hitler, who had told Gerhard Wagner in 1935 that he would institute compulsory euthanasia once war came, had not been alone in the desire. At a 1938 meeting of government officials responsible for the administration of mental institutions, for example, one speaker concluded that "a solution for the field of mental health would simply require that one eliminates these people." Fritz Bernotat, the Nazi radical who administrated state hospitals in Hessen-Nassau, was later more explicit when he told a meeting of institutional directors who were complaining about overcrowding: "If you have too many patients in your institution, just beat them to death, and then you will have space."
>
> In the summer of 1939 Hitler initiated the policy of killing handicapped adults. This killing operation would involve far larger numbers of victims than the relatively limited operation against children [who were disabled]. Hitler first turned to the government agency normally responsible for public health. The Fuhrer sent for Leonardo Conti, who would soon succeed the deceased Wagner as Reich physician leader. Unlike Wagner, who had held only a Nazi party office, Conti also occupied the newly created position of state secretary for health in the RMI [Reich Ministry of Interior].

Disability scholars recognize the significance of the Nazis' first choice of victims, PWDs. Not a single physician or administrator who participated in these killings was convicted at the Nuremberg trials after World War II. Indeed Dr. Hans Sewering, whose part in the mass killings of Germans with disabilities has been documented, was elected president of the World Medical Association in 1992. However, he was forced to resign when protesters objected to his history of killing (Sobsey, 1994).

Obviously the families of these PWDs did not know about the killings. Recently declassified East Germany documents provided evidence that many Germans were aware of the government-sponsored murders of PWDs and attempted to solicit international support to stop the killings. The following excerpt comes from a newspaper article of 1999 titled "The Holocaust Foreshadowed."

> The death notices appeared in German newspapers in suspicious numbers in the fall of 1940, twenty-two in two weeks, and the families placing them using strikingly similar phrases about the fates of their loved ones, patients in mental asylums.
>
> "After days of uncertainty we received the unbelievable news of the sudden death of my beloved wife, the mother of our little Christa," said one.
>
> "After anxious uncertainty, I received from Grafeneck in Wurtemberg the unbelievable news that my beloved husband, our dear son-in-law and brother-in-law, the glass handycraftsman...closed his dear eyes forever," said another.
>
> On they went, "unbelievable" deaths after periods of "uncertainty."
>
> In their bewildered sorrow, these families were uncovering a Nazi horror. They were signaling to fellow citizens that terrible acts were going on in the sanitariums of southern Germany. The U.S. vice consul in Leipzig, Paul Dutko, understood what was happening and cabled superiors.
>
> But recently declassified documents do not show anything was done about that warning and others in the months before Germany's "euthanasia" program became undeniably known and the full weight of the Holocaust descended.
>
> "Details, so far gather[ed] concerning these notices give them a 'Frankenstein' setting; their attendant circumstances, described in this dispatch, are fantastic and gruesome," Dutko wrote in his October 1940 cable.
>
> "Opinion has been expressed that incurable mental patients of Germany are being eliminated in this manner to reduce mouths to feed and that this is but a beginning."
>
> Documents founds in the National Archives by the Simon Wiesenthal Center, a Los Angeles research organized named after the famed Nazi hunter, point to a series of early communications by U.S. officials about Nazi Germany's systematic killing of its own mentally or [physically] deformed citizens.
>
> In one German letter, an anonymous correspondent wrote to NBC in New York saying thousands of mental patients were being killed monthly in southern Germany.
>
> "Hurry," the correspondent wrote, "and with your expressions of horror prevent further murders! Humanity will thank you." ("Holocaust Foreshadowed," 1999)

In 1996 PWDs formed a protest group named "Not Dead Yet" in response to the Supreme Court decisions involving the constitutionality of physician-assisted suicide. Vulnerable populations, such the elderly and PWDs, fear that the "*right* to die," might become the "*duty* to die," and they will feel that they are burdens to their loved ones.

In abortion, infanticide, euthanasia, and assisted suicide of PWDs, the principles of "mercy," and "release" are invoked. However, the idea of cost-savings underlies many of these arguments, and disabilities are undoubtedly expensive. Many PWDs are aware that some people think they are an expensive drain or burden on "society." Remember when the mother of two boys with MD heard her doctor say about her youngest son,

"This could have been prevented." Carolyn Vash, the disability scholar and polio survivor, stated that she did not have the graciousness to die early, and Harriet McBryde Johnson, a disability rights lawyer, was told by Dr. Peter Singer that she should have been killed at death. In Germany this account was published:

> Another German, Gunther Schirmer, had lost his leg in a car accident in 1979. He had learned to ride a tricycle. One afternoon...his wife saw boys harassing her husband, spitting on him and saying repeatedly, "You live off our taxes. You'd have been gassed under Hitler."...Shortly after this incident, Gunther Schirmer committed suicide. He wrote to his wife that people with disabilities do not have a chance in this world and that he would now personally "destroy the cripple." (Holzbauer & Berven, 1996, p. 480)

The Netherlands allows euthanasia for newborn infants with disabilities. A Dutch professor concluded that "the killing of handicapped children...denotes the end, or the beginning of the end, of care for the mentally retarded" (Fenigsen, 1997, p. 163). Dutch parents of a child with a disability have reported hearing these statements: "What? Is that child still alive?" "How can one love such a child?" "Nowadays such a being need not be born at all," and "Such a thing should have been given an injection."

A psychologist undertook a search of professional scholarly journals that are research oriented and looked for articles about PWDs with the word "burden" in their titles. She excluded articles published before 1990. She found a large body of what she termed the "burden literature" (Olkin, 1999, p. 94). This psychologist understands that PWDs are perceived as burdens and drains, even in scholarly professional writing.

Society often requires PWDs to defend and justify their existence and their right to live. Assisted suicide may or may not be ethical; the issue is yet to be decided, and there are many sensible arguments in favor of it. However, vulnerable groups such as PWDs are justifiably opposed to assisted suicide.

Terms to Learn

Advantaged occupational positions	Dependency ratio	"Silver tsunami"
Baby busts	Diabetes	Structural lags
Cerebrovascular accidents	Generational equity	Supercentenarians
Chronic sorrow	Programmed aging	"Wear-and-tear" aging
	Selective optimization	

Videos to View

- View the 29-minute video *Late Adulthood: Death, Dying, Bereavement, and Widowhood,* available from Insight Media. The producers describe this video: "This program offers sociocultural and multicultural perspectives on dying and bereavement. This DVD also explores the work of Elisabeth Kübler-Ross, who introduced the five stages of grief."

- View the video *Alzheimer's Today: A Caregiver's Guide*, available from Films for the Humanities and Sciences. The producers describe this video: "This program, offers an insightful look at Alzheimer's disease and related disorders. Section one deals with understanding Alzheimer's disease and discusses how to communicate with people affected by Alzheimer's. Section two focuses on behavior management that beings with symptom recognition and concludes with specific strategies and techniques for dealing with challenging behaviors. A thorough and accessible primer."
- View the 57-minute video *Forever Young: Nanotechnology and Medicine—A Fred Friendly Seminar*, available from Films from the Humanities and Sciences. The producers describe this video: "With nano-enabled drugs that destroy diseased cells and enable tissue repair, doctors may one day extend life expectancy far beyond our current capabilities—at least in countries wealthy enough to afford the technology. But the medicine that so radically redefines our standards of health and mortality will also profoundly challenge our social support systems and cultural values. Moderator and Peabody award-winning journalist John Hockenberry leads a panel of experts through provocative scenarios that shed light on the issue. What kinds of cures and therapies will nanomedicine make possible? Should access to them be universal, even if they are prohibitively expensive? Does everyone have the right to live forever? Or does immortality present a danger, ironically to human survival?"
- View the 31-minute video *Understanding Stroke*, available from Insight Media. The producers describe this video: "Featuring physicians who specialize in the diagnosis and treatment of stroke, this program provides an in-depth introduction to strokes. It covers such topics as cerebral vascular accidents and transient attacks."

Learning Activities

(Note: These may also be used as class presentations.)
- Create a new developmental stage "emerging retirement" or "pre-retirement." Review Arnett's addition of "emerging adulthood" as a new developmental stage to Erikson's eight stages, which is dicussed in the chapter on adolescence. Consider the rationale for identifying this new stage (emerging adulthood) and the tasks that are not found in either the preceding stage (adolescence and early adulthood) or the succeeding stage (adulthood). Conceptualize pre-retirement as a stage with tasks that are not appropriate for midlife or for old age. Justify this new developmental stage in terms of changes in the labor market, the longevity revolution, and the risk and importance in planning for one's retirement. Would the Social Security Retirement Fund benefit from a widely accepted developmental stage of pre-retirement?
- Schafer (2009) stated: "Remaining subjectively youthful is associated with increased life satisfaction, morale, and self-esteem (Logan, Ward, & Spizte, 1992; Mutran & Reitzes 1981; and Westerhof & Barrett, 2005) and recent longitudinal evidence even suggests that a young age identity enhances multiple aspects

of health and reduces disease among middle-age and older adults (Demakakos, Ghonca, & Nazroo, 2007)" (p. 76). Schafer also asserted that a sense of age is related to workforce participation, with those who "feel" younger than their actual age remaining in the workforce longer. Do you think that "you're only as old as you feel?"

Writing Exercises

- Write a 10-page paper that defends the practice of assisted suicide.
- Write a 10-page paper that argues against the practice of assisted suicide.
- Write a five-page paper that explains this statement, "Retirement in the United States is often regarded as an 'artifact' of Social Security and other pension systems."
- Write a five-page paper outlining your plans for retirement. Do you plan to have enough money? Do you plan to have a disability?
- Interview an elderly person with a congenital disability. Interview another elderly person who has a disability that was acquired or diagnosed after age 50. Ask them about their adjustment, the effect of their disability on their marriage, and any prejudice and discrimination they have experienced.

Web Sites

http://www.prb.org/Articles/2010/oldagedisability.aspx
http://mars.hhj.hj.se/hhj_sql/ifg/files/FinalReport.pdf
http://cirrie.buffalo.edu/encyclopedia/en/article/189

Conclusion

16

DEVELOPMENTAL THEORIES AND PEOPLE WITH DISABILITIES

It may seem somewhat contradictory to consider demographic shifts, the changing labor market, and medical advances while simultaneously discussing theorists who mostly developed their theories of human development more than 50 years ago. Nonetheless, many principles of these so-called "grand theorists" have stood the test of time and remain relevant today. However, without exception none of the human development theorists addressed the experience of PWDs.

Human development theories include the concept of humanity. Perhaps the psychological and psychoanalytic theorists considered individuals with disabilities so different that the typical or "normal" stages of development did not apply to them. Those theorists who regarded biology as destiny might have thought that individuals with disabilities could not be considered normal in any biological sense, or the theorists who looked at social forces thought that people with disabilities did not (or could not) participate in the wider society. The experience of disability and the individuals who experience disabilities were thought to be the responsibility of practitioners in the medical field (Smart, 2001, 2009). No field of psychology or general counseling has included people with disabilities.

Disability may seem to be an unbearable tragedy to those who do not have disabilities, yet all people know that they may acquire a disability. Therefore, to avoid the anxiety and fear of acquiring a disability they find it easier simply to avoid people with disabilities (PWDs). Ironically, if people without disabilities (PWODs) were to have more experience with PWDs, they would gain a better understanding of the disability and thus reduce some of their fears. Scholars, psychologists, and sociologists may have some of these feelings coupled with the false idea that there are no general, broad theories that can be applied to PWDs.

When we discussed demographics, we learned that the demographers projected longer life spans, but the demographers did not foresee the full extent of the effects of lengthening life spans. In much the same way, demographers did not recognize the full impact of the growing number of PWDs, an increase caused mostly by medical and scientific advances and the higher standard of living. Now a large segment of population needs services, funding, and most important, a social place and group identity. Thus structural lags are caused by the demographic shifts of larger numbers of PWDs, paralleling the structural lags of the longevity revolution, and elderly people require services, funding, health care, and a social identity in place in the larger society.

We have learned that the major goals of these theories of human development are autonomy, competence, and strength. PWDs consider themselves autonomous, competent, and strong; they simply redefine these terms. Armed with civil rights and protection under the law, assistive technology, and perhaps personal care attendants, PWDs view themselves as directing their own lives. America is a nation that glorifies independence, freedom, and physical strength and ability. During the polio epidemics, many polio survivors stated that "it felt un-American to have a disability." These are positive values. However, we can conceptualize that these values require redefinition or reframing and that others, such as physical strength and ability, are unnecessary for some individuals. Indeed, PWDs have historically been judged by standards that very few PWODs achieved.

In addition to conceptualizing the typical developmental stages of life as part of the disability experience, we have also increased our understanding of (1) the value of theories, (2) the importance of stage theories in general, and (3) the ways in which demographic and historical shifts have influenced the developmental stages of life. When discussing the value of theories, we must remember that all theories of human development have received criticism, some valid, some not. Further, each grand theorist had disciples who expanded upon or changed some aspects of their mentor's theory; however, with only one or two exceptions, few of these disciples or their ideas are remembered. Finally, theories affect lives by influencing government policy and providing the base to develop testing and assessment instruments, the results of which determine important aspects of people's lives. These theories also stimulate the identification of plans for treatment, therapy, and intervention. None of these uses include the important areas of research, writing, or teaching professionals-to-be. Professionals who have not had access to training and education in the developmental aspects of disability will be unprepared to provide services to PWDs or (even worse) may unintentionally do harm. "Theoretical" and "practical" often appear to be opposing concepts; furthermore, the practical is thought to be superior to the theoretical. However, there can be no practical applications without theory, and the difference between theory and practice may also not be large.

Viewing theory and practice as inextricably linked does not suggest that every theory is valid. Theories always reflect the values and the social and historical environments of their creators. This explains why we understand the theories better when we know something about the theorist's life. In the case of disability, we have seen how the Nazis in Germany developed a theory in which PWDs were defined as "life unworthy of life." Numbers (quantification) were applied to these observations. The Nazis carefully calculated the costs to feed and house PWDs and found the costs to be expensive. (Undoubtedly the care of PWDs is expensive.) The practical results of this Nazi theory led to the mass murder of 200,000 Germans with disabilities. On the other hand, in the chapter on pregnancy and infancy, we learned about the Apgar score that is given to neonates. This scale revolutionized childbirth all over the world, has saved the lives of countless babies, and provided the impetus for a new medical specialty, neonatology. Virginia Apgar had a theory that was derived from her observations, then she applied numbers to her observations. A physician described the way in which Dr. Apgar developed her theory:

> [By the 1950s], one in thirty newborns still died at birth—odds that were scarcely better than they were a century before—and it wasn't clear how that

could be changed. Then a doctor named Virginia Apgar, who was working in New York (as an anesthesiologist) had an idea, but it transformed childbirth and the care of the newly born. Apgar was an unlikely revolutionary for obstetrics. For starters, she had never delivered a baby—not as a doctor and not even as a mother.

Throughout her career, the work she loved most was providing anesthesia for child deliveries. She loved the renewal of a new child's coming into the world. But she was appalled by the care that many newborns received. Babies who were born malformed to too small or just blue and not breathing well were listed as stillborn, placed out of sight, and left to die. They were believed to be too sick to live.... (Apgar) devised a score. (Gawande, 2007, pp. 185–186)

The Apgar Score is simple, perhaps even simplistic. Every baby is scored on skin color and whether or not the baby cries, is breathing, and is moving all four limbs. A perfect score is 10. Newborns are tested 1 minute postbirth and again at 5 minutes postbirth. Physicians found that infants with poor Apgar Scores at 1 minute postbirth could, without any intervention, improve drastically. Furthermore, when interventions were given to an infant with a low score, many more infants survived. Even simple interventions, such as warming the infant and giving oxygen, saved their lives. In the United States today, only one infant dies in 500 full-term births.

When we contrast the Nazis' views of "life unworthy of life" with Dr. Apgar's theory of neonatal survival, it is easy to understand that a theory is not valid simply because a theory is sophisticated, technical, and accurately quantified. The Nazis' theory killed many PWDs, while Apgar's theory saved untold numbers of lives; nonetheless both started with observations and quantifications. Apgar's example teaches us that by making simple observations and quantifications (a scale of 1–10), one individual can make remarkable contributions.

Second, we have learned the value of stage theories. In addition to their application to human development, stage theories have been applied to many life experiences, such as racial identification, religious development, and adaptation to disability. Critics of stage theories point to the undisputed fact that some individuals skip stages, others recycle through stages, and still others often do not complete the stages in the prescribed sequence. These critics may be missing the point. The major contribution of all stage theories is their emphasis upon a *process* rather than an *event*. Conceptualizing the responses to life's demands as a long-term process, rather than a one-time event, is both powerful and useful. One illustration of this is Kübler-Ross's theory of the stages of death and dying (1969) that is currently receiving criticism because of her lack of empirical research methodology. Nonetheless, Kübler-Ross was the first to write about death and dying as a process, rather than as an event. Higher standards of living, better public health measures, and medical advances had affected the experience of death *demographically*. Instead of dying within hours or days of infectious diseases or injuries, individuals died of chronic illnesses over months or years. Kübler-Ross observed, identified, and documented this process. Her work brought a taboo subject, death, into an arena in which it could be discussed; her book was a national best seller. It brought about the hospice movement, the development of grief counseling as a new specialty, and on a personal level, Kübler-Ross's work supported many individuals and their families through the difficult process of dying.

Because the stage theory of acceptance of disability is based upon Kübler-Ross' theory of dying and loss, as would be expected, it has met with the same criticisms. It is indisputable that not everyone progresses through every stage or that some individuals do not repeat stages when responding to a disability. However, the stage theory of acceptance of disability recognizes the long-term process and also views acceptance of disability as more than medical and physical stabilization. Many PWDs recount that they were given excellent medical care, but no one provided emotional and psychological counseling.

Finally, we have increased our understanding of the way in which demographic and historical changes have transformed the experience of developmental stages of life. For PWDs two historical events have altered the experience of disability, but another can be considered a missed opportunity. World War II and the Americans with Disabilities Act of 1990 are considered positive events for PWDs, but the American polio epidemics of 1893 to 1955 are thought to be a missed opportunity to provide civil rights and accommodations for Americans with all types of disabilities.

We have learned that World War II is considered to be the golden age of employment for PWDs. Just as women and men of racial minorities were encouraged to enter the labor market when white males entered the military, large numbers of PWDs were also allowed to work. Women, racial minorities, and PWDs—individuals who had been disenfranchised in the American job market up to that time—made tremendous contributions to the American war effort; however, when the white veterans returned home, many of these workers quit or were forced out of their jobs, allowing the veterans to return to their jobs. Nonetheless, the contributions of these marginalized groups demonstrated their competence and abilities.

The polio epidemics could have provided the impetus for an Americans with Disabilities Act in the first half of the 20th century, rather than in the year 1990. Polio was justifiably feared, because no one was immune and the United States had more epidemics that affected greater numbers of people than any other nation. Scientists could not determine the method of infection, and physicians could do nothing to prevent or cure polio. Physicians simply waited while the disease ran its course and then discharged their patients to a society with no accommodations or civil rights for polio survivors. Polio survivors were told that "No one is going to make accommodations for you," "You must take the world as it is," "Don't expect any special considerations," and "Don't talk about your polio. We don't want to hear about it." Nonetheless, for 60 years the fear of polio epidemics dominated American public life. When the polio vaccines were developed, the "problem" of polio was considered solved and polio was forgotten. Survivors of polio, especially those who were paralyzed, felt that they were painful reminders of the failure of American medicine. Even though there are living polio survivors (who are aging) today, no one is interested in their experiences.

The Americans with Disabilities Act of 1990 (ADA) provided civil rights to Americans with disabilities. The prejudice, discrimination, institutionalization, forced sterilization, and lack of education and professional services that affected PWDs are becoming history. In the same way that the 1964 Civil Rights Act was a watershed event for African Americans, the ADA is a defining point for Americans with disabilities. Moreover, just as the Civil Rights Act unleashed the potential of a large group of Americans and allowed the nation to benefit economically and socially, the ADA will also allow a large group of Americans to participate in the social, political, and economic life of the United States and thus benefit everyone.

Medical and technological advances and demographic shifts have changed the world. Freud's theories are practiced in psychiatrists' offices today, and the single alteration in Erikson's theory of psychosocial stages has been the suggestion of adding a stage for emerging adulthood. Piaget's, Vygotsky's and Bronfenbrenner's theories are used in schools; Maslow's theory of self-actualization continues to be used, especially in counseling interventions; and Kohlberg's stages of moral reasoning are taught in schools. Therefore, the developmental theories remain essentially unchanged, thus confirming the explanatory power of these grand theories.

References

Abroms, K. I., & Hodera, T. L. (1979). Acceptance hierarchy of handicaps: Validation of Kirk's statement "Special education often begins where medicine stops." *Journal of Learning Disabilities, 12,* 15–20.

Achenbaum, W. A. (2009). A history of productive aging and the Boomers. In R. B. Hudson (Ed.), *Boomer or bust? Economic and political issues of the graying society* (pp. 47–109). Westport, CT: Praeger.

Adams, M. (2006). Toward an existential phenomenological model of life span human development. *Existential Analysis, 17,* 261–280.

Addison, J. T. (1992). Urie Bronfenbrenner. *Human Ecology, 20*(2), 16–20.

Adolph, K. E., & Berger, S. E. (2006). Motor development. In D. Kuhn, R. S. Siegler, W. Damon, & R. M. Lerner (Eds.), *Handbook of child psychology: Vol. 2, Cognition, perception, and language* (6th ed.). Hoboken, NJ: Wiley.

Affleck, G., Tennen, H., Pfeifer, C., & Fifield, J. (1987). Appraisals of control and predictability in adapting to a chronic disease. *Journal of Personality and Social Psychology, 53,* 273–279.

Agich, G. J. (1995). Chronic illness and freedom. In S. K. Toombs, D. Barnard, & R. A. Carson (Eds.), *Chronic illness: From experience to policy* (pp. 129–153). Bloomington: University of Indiana.

Agosta, J., & Melda, K. (1995). Supporting families who provide care at home for children with disabilities. *Exceptional Children, 62,* 271–282.

Aikin, L. R. (1978). *The psychology of later life.* Philadelphia, PA: W. B. Saunders.

Albon, J. (1984). *Little people of America: The social dimensions of dwarfism.* New York: Praeger.

Albon, J. (1989). Families with dwarf children. In S. C. Hey, G. Kiger, & D. Evans (Eds.), *The changing world of impaired and disabled people in society* (pp. 350–358). Salem, OR: The Society for Disability Studies and Willamette University.

Albrecht, G. L. (Ed.). (1976). *The sociology of physical disability and rehabilitation.* Pittsburgh, PA: University of Pittsburgh Press.

Albrecht, G. L., Seelman, K. D., & Bury, M. (Eds.). (2001). *Handbook of disability studies.* Thousand Oaks, CA: Sage.

Alder, A. B., Wright, B. A., & Ulicny, G. R. (1991). Fundraising portrayals of people with disabilities: Donations and attitudes. *Rehabilitation Psychology, 36,* 231–240.

Alfano, D. P., Nielsen, P. M., & Fink, M. P. (1993). Long-term psychosocial adjustment following head or spinal cord injury. *Neuropsychiatry, Neuropsychology, and Behavioral Neurology, 6,* 117–125.

Allen, B. P. (2000). *Personality theories: Development, growth, and diversity* (3rd ed.). Needham Heights, MA: Allyn & Bacon.

Allen, M. C. (2008). Neurodevelopmental outcomes of preterm infants. *Current Opinion in Neurology, 21,* 123–128.

Allen, K. E., & Cowdery, G. E. (2009). *The exceptional child* (6th ed.). Belmont, CA: Wadsworth.

Alwin, D. F., & McCammon, R. J. (2004). Generations, cohorts, and social change. In J. T. Mortimer & M. J. Shanahan (Eds.), *Handbook of the life course* (pp. 23–49). New York: Springer.

Ambron, S. R., & Brodzinsky, D. (1979). *Lifespan human development.* New York: Holt, Rinehart & Winston.

American Association on Intellectual and Developmental Disabilities. (1992). *Mental retardation: Definition, classification, and systems of support* (Special 9th ed.). Washington, DC: Author.

American Psychiatric Association. (1994). *Diagnostic and statistical manual of mental disorders* (4th ed.). Washington, DC: Author.

American Psychiatric Association. (2000). *Diagnostic and statistical manual of mental disorder* (4th ed., text rev.). Washington, DC: Author.

Americans with Disabilities Act of 1990, 42 U.S.C. 12101 *et seq.* Retrieved from www.usdoj. gov/crt/ada/adahomal.htm.

Anderson, V., Jacobs, R., & Harvey, A. H. (2005). Prefrontal lesions and attentional skills in childhood. *Journal of International Neuropsychological Society, 11,* 817–831.

Andrews, N. R., Chaney, J. M., Mullins, L. L., Wagner, J. L., Hommel, K. A., & Jarvis, J. N. (2009). The differential effect of child age on the illness intrusiveness. Parent distress relationship in Juvenile Rheumatic Disease. *Rehabilitation Psychology, 54,* 45–50.

Angier, N. (2001, May 27). Before the miracle. *New York Times Book Review,* pp. 12–13.

Angold, A., & Costello, E. J. (1991). Developing a developmental epidemiology. In D. Cochetti & S. L. Toth (Eds.), *Rochester symposium on developmental psychopathology: Models and integrations* (pp. 75–96). Rochester, NY: University of Rochester.

Anson, C. A., Stanwyck, D. J., & Krause, J. S. (1993). Social support and health status in spinal cord injury. *International Journal of Paraplegia, 31,* 632–638.

Antonak, R. F. (1980). A hierarchy of attitudes toward exceptionality. *The Journal of Special Education, 14,* 231–241.

Antonak, R. F. (1985). Societal factors in disablement. *Rehabilitation Counseling Bulletin, 28,* 188–201.

Antonak, R. F. (1988). Methods to measure attitudes toward people who are disabled. In H. E. Yuker (Ed.), *Attitudes toward persons with disabilities* (pp. 109–126). New York: Springer.

Antonak, R. F., & Livneh, H. (1991). A hierarchy of reactions to disability. *International Journal of Rehabilitation Research, 14,* 13–24.

Appel, T. (1988). Personal statement: Living in spite of multiple sclerosis. In P. W. Power (Ed.), *Family interventions throughout chronic illness and disability* (pp. 253–257). New York: Springer.

Aquarius Health Care Videos. (1999). *Family challenges: Parenting with a disability: Exploring family relationships when a parent has a disability.* Retrieved from www.aquariusproductions. com

Arnett, J. J. (1992). Reckless behavior in adolescence: A developmental perspective. *Developmental Review, 12,* 339–373.

Arnett, J. J. (1997). Young people's conceptions of the transition to adulthood. *Youth & Society, 29,* 1–23.

Arnett, J. J. (1998). Learning to stand alone: The contemporary transition to adulthood in cultural and historical context. *Human Development, 41,* 295–314.

Arnett, J. J. (2000). Emerging adulthood: A theory of development from the late teens through the twenties. *American Psychologist, 55,* 469–480.

Arnett, J. J. (2004). *Emerging adulthood.* New York: Oxford University.

Arnett, J. J., & Jensen, L. A. (2002). A congregation of one: Individualized religious beliefs among emerging adults. *Journal of Adolescent Research, 17,* 451–468.

Asch, A., & Fine, M. (1997). Nurturance, sexuality, and women with disabilities: The example of women and literature. In L. J. Davis (Ed.), *The disability studies reader* (pp. 241–259). New York: Routledge.

Asch, A., & Scotch, R. (2001). Disability politics. In J. Krieger, M. E. Crahan, L. R. Jacobs, W. A. Joseph, G. Nzongola-Ntalaja, & J. A. Paul (Eds.), *The Oxford companion to politics of the world* (2nd ed., pp. 223–225). Oxford, UK: Oxford University.

Ashford, J.B., LeCroy, C. W., & Lortie, K. L. (2001). *Human behavior in the social environment* (2nd ed.). Belmont, CA: Wadsworth.

Associated Press. (2009). *Revised formula determines 1 in 6 Americans living in poverty.* Washington, DC: Author.

Associated Press. (2010). *Poverty to touch half of kids in the U.S.* Washington, DC: Author.

Austin, J. K. (1990). Assessment of coping mechanisms used by parents and children with chronic illness. *Maternal and Child Nursing, 15,* 98–102.

Austrian, S. G. (Ed.). (2001). *Developmental theories through the life cycle.* New York: Columbia University.

Azar, B. (1997, October). Was Freud right: Maybe, maybe not. *Monitor of the American Psychological Association.* Washington, DC: American Psychological Association.

Bailey, D. B., Skinner, D., & Warren, S. F. (2005). Newborn screening for developmental disabilities: Reframing presumptive benefit. *American Journal of Public Health, 95,* 1889–1893.

Bailey, D. B., & Winton, P. J. (1987). Stability and change in parents' expectations about mainstreaming. *Topics in Early Childhood Special Education, 7,* 73–88.

Baird, G. L., Scott, W. D., Dearing, E., & Hamill, S. K. (2009). Cognitive self-regulation in youth with and without learning disabilities: Intelligence, learning vs. performance goal preferences and effort attribution. *Journal of Social and Clinical Psychology, 28*(7), 881–908.

Ball, K. (2009). Older drivers. In D. Carr (Ed.), *Encyclopedia of the life course and human development, Vol. 3: Later life* (pp. 275–278). Detroit, MI: Gale Cengage Learning.

Ball, S. A. (2004). Personality traits, disorders, and substance abuse. In R. M. Stelmack (Ed.), *On the psychobiology of personality* (pp. 203–221). Amsterdam, The Netherlands: Elsevier.

Baltes, M. M., & Carstensen, L. L. (1996). The process of successful aging. *Aging and Society, 16,* 397–422.

Baltes, M. M., & Carstensen, L. L. (2003). The process of successful aging: Selection, optimization, and compensation. In U. M. Staudinger & U. Lindenberger (Eds.), *Understanding human development: Dialogues with lifespan psychology* (pp. 83–104). Dordrecht, The Netherlands: Kluwer Academic Publishers.

Baltes, P. B., Featherman, D., & Lerner, R. M. (Eds.). (1988). *Life span development and behavior.* Hillsdale, NJ: Lawrence Erlbaum.

Baltes, P. B., & Reese, H. W. (1984). The life-span perspective in developmental psychology. In M. H. Bornstein & M. E. Lamb (Eds.), *Developmental psychology: An advanced textbook* (pp. 493–531). Hillsdale, NJ: Lawrence Erlbaum.

Baltes, P. B., Reese, H. W., & Lipsitt, L. P. (1980). Life span developmental psychology. *Annual Review of Psychology, 31,* 65–110.

Baltes, P. B., & Schaie, K. W. (Eds.). (1973). *Life-span development psychology: Personality and socialization.* New York: Academic Press.

Baltes, P. B., Staudiner, U. M., & Lindenberger, U. (1999). Lifespan psychology: Theory and application to intellectual functioning. *Annual Review of Psychology, 50,* 471–507.

Bandura, A. (1977). *Social learning theory.* Englewood Cliffs, NJ: Prentice-Hall.

Bandura, A. (1982). The self and mechanisms of aging. In J. Suls (Ed.), *Psychological perspectives on the self* (pp. 3–40). Hillsdale, NJ: Lawrence Erlbaum.

Bandura, A. (1986). *Social foundations of thought and action: A social cognitive theory.* Englewood Cliffs, NJ: Prentice-Hall.

Bandura, A. (1997a). *Self-efficacy: The exercise of control.* New York: W. H. Freeman.

Bandura, A. (1997b). Self-efficacy: Toward a unifying theory of behavioral change. *Psychological Review, 84,* 191–215.

Bandura, A., Ross, D., & Ross, S. A. (1963). Imitation of film-mediated aggressive males. *Journal of Abnormal and Social Psychology, 67,* 601–607.

Barnes, C., Mercer, G., & Shakespeare, T. (1999). *Exploring disability: A sociological introduction.* Cambridge, England: Polity.

Basheda, L. (2006, July). No arms, no legs—no worries. *Orange County Register, 1,* 7.

Bashford, J. B., LeCroy, C. W., & Lortie, K. L. (2001). *Human behavior in the social environment: A multidimensional perspective.* Belmont, CA: Brooks/Cole.

Batavia, A. I., & Schriner, K. (2001). The Americans with Disabilities Act as an engine of social change: Models of disability and the potential of a civil rights approach. *Disability Policy Studies Journal, 29,* 690–702.

Bateson, P. (1998). Problems and possibilities in fusing developmental and evolutionary thought. In L. E. Berk (Ed.), *Development through the lifespan* (pp. 3–21). Needham Heights, MA: Allyn and Bacon.

Batshaw, M. L. (Ed.). (1998). *Children with disabilities* (4th ed.). Baltimore, MD: Paul H. Brookes.

Batshaw, M. L. (Ed.). (2001). *When your child has a disability.* Baltimore, MD: Paul H. Brookes.

Batshaw, M. L. (2001). Why my child? Causes of developmental disabilities. In M. L. Batshaw (Ed.), *When your child has a disability* (pp. 11–12). Baltimore, MD: Paul H. Brookes.

Batshaw, M. L., Pellegrino, L., & Roizen, N. J. (Eds.). (2007). *Children with disabilities* (6th ed.). Baltimore, MD: Paul H. Brookes.

Bauman, H. D. L., & Drake, J. (1997). Silence is not without voice: Including D/deaf culture within the multicultural curricula. In L. J. Davis (Ed.), *Disability studies reader* (pp. 307–314). New York: Routledge.

Bayles, M. D. (1987). The value of life. In D. Van De Veer & T. Regan (Eds.), *Health care ethics: An introduction* (pp. 265–289). Philadelphia: Temple University.

Bayton, D. (1995). Chronic illness and the dynamics of hoping. In S. K. Toombs, D. Barnard, & R. A. Carson (Eds.), *Chronic illness and the dynamics of hoping.* (pp. 38–57). Bloomington: University of Indiana.

Beardmore, T. D. (1995). Rheumatic diseases. In M. G. Brodwin, F. Tellez, & S. K. Brodwin (Eds.), *Medical, psychosocial, and vocational aspects of disability* (pp. 353–367). Athens, GA: Elliott & Fitzpatrick.

Beck, U. (1992). *Risk society.* Newbury Park, CA: Sage.

Becker, G., & Kaufman, S. (1988). Old age, rehabilitation, and research: A review of the issues. *The Gerontologist, 28,* 459–468.

Beisser, A. (1989). *Flying without wings: Personal reflections on being disabled.* New York: Doubleday.

Bendell, R. D. (1984). Psychological problems of infancy. In M. G. Eisenberg, L. C. Sutkin, & M. A. Jansen (Eds.), *Chronic illness and disability through the life span: Effects on self and the family* (pp. 23–38). New York: Springer.

Bengston, V. L. (2001). Beyond the nuclear family: The importance of multigenerational bonds. *Journal of Marriage and the Family, 63,* 1–16.

Berk, L. E. (1986). Relationship of elementary school children's private speech to behavioral accompaniment to task, attention, and task performance. *Developmental Psychology, 22*(5), 671.

Berk, L. E. (1998). *Development through the lifespan.* Needham Heights, MA: Allyn & Bacon.

Berk, L. E. (2001). *Development through the lifespan* (2nd ed.). Needham Heights, MA: Allyn & Bacon.

Berkowitz, E. D. (1987). *Disabled policy: America's programs for the handicapped.* London, England: Cambridge University.

Bernbaum, J. C., & Batshaw, M. L. (1998). Born too soon, born too small. In M. L. Batshaw (Ed.), *Children with disabilities* (4th ed., pp. 115–139). Baltimore, MD: Paul H. Brookes.

Bernstein, N. R. (1976). *Emotional care of the facially burned and disfigured.* Boston: Little Brown.

Bernstein, N. R. (1989). Psychological problems associated with facial disfigurement. In B. W. Heller, L. M. Flohr, & L. S. Zegans (Eds.), *Psychosocial interventions with physically disabled persons* (pp. 147–161). New Brunswick, NJ: Rutgers University.

Bernstein, N. R. (1990). Objective bodily damage: Disfigurement and dignity. In T. F. Cash & T. Pruzinsky (Eds.), *Body images: Development, deviance, and change* (pp. 131–148). New York: Guilford.

Bernstein, N. R., Breslau, J. J., & Graham, J. A. (Eds.). (1988). *Coping strategies for burn survivors and their families.* Westport, CT: Praeger.

Berry, J. O. (1995). Families and deinstitutionalization: An application of Bronfenbrenner. *Journal of Counseling and Development, 73,* 379.

Berry, J. O. (2009). *Lifespan perspectives on the family and disability* (2nd ed.). Austin, TX: PRO-ED.

Berube, M. (1996). *Life as we know it: A father, a family, and an exceptional child.* New York: Pantheon Books.

Berube, M. (1998). Foreword. In S. Linton (Ed.), *Claiming disability: Knowledge and identity* (pp. vii–xv.). New York: New York University.

Bettelheim, B. (1967). *The empty fortress: Infantile autism and the birth of the self.* New York: Free Press.

Bettelheim, B. (1969). *Children of the dream.* New York: Macmillan.

Bickenbach, J. E. (1993). *Physical disability and social policy.* Toronto, Ontario: University of Toronto.

Biordi, D. L., Warner, A. M., & Knapik, G. P. (2006). Body image. In I. M. Lubkin & P. D. Larsen (Eds.), *Chronic illness: Impact and interventions* (6th ed., pp. 181–197). Sudbury, MA: Jones and Bartlett.

Birren, J. E. (1990). Spirituality maturity in psychological development. In J. J. Seeber (Ed.), *Spiritual maturity in later years* (pp. 41–53). New York: Haworth.

Bishop, C. (2009). The looming economic of Boomer health care. In R. B. Hudson (Ed.), *Boomer bust? Economic and political issues of the graying society* (pp. 95–109). Westport, CT: Praeger.

Blackburn, J. (1988). Chronic health problems of the elderly. In C. S. Chilman, E. W. Nunnally, & F. M. Cox (Eds.), *Chronic illness and disability: Families in trouble* (pp. 108–122). Newbury Park, CA: Sage.

Blanchflower, D. G., & Oswald, A. J. (2008). Is well-being U-shaped over the lifecycle? *Social Science and Medicine, 66,* 1733–1749.

Blumberg, B. D., Lewis, M. J., & Susman, E. J. (1984). Adolescence: A time of transition. In M. G. Eisenberg, L. C. Sutkin, & M. A. Jansen (Eds.), *Chronic illness and disability through the life span: Effects on self and the family* (pp. 133–163). New York: Springer.

Blood, I. M. (1997). The hearing aid effect. *Journal of Rehabilitation, 63*(4), 59–63.

Boerner, K. (2004). Adaptation to disability among middle aged and older adults: The role of assimilative and accommodative coping. *Journal of Genontology: Psychological Sciences, 59,* 35–42.

Boerner, K., & Jopp, D. (2007). Improvement/maintenance and reorientation as central features of coping with major life change and loss: Contributions of three life-span theories. *Human Development, 50,* 171–195.

Bogdan, R. (1988). *Freak show: Presenting human oddities for amusement and profit.* Chicago: University of Chicago.

Bogdan, R., & Taylor, S. (1987). Toward a sociology of acceptance: The other side of the study of deviance. *Social Policy, Fall, 17,* 34–39.

Bogdan, R., & Taylor, S. J. (1992). The social construction of humanness: Relationships with severely disabled people. In P. M. Ferguson, D. L. Ferguson, & S. J. Taylor (Eds.), *Interpreting disability: A qualitative reader* (pp. 275–294). New York: Teachers College, Columbia University.

Boggess, P. S. (1993). Pamela Spurlock Boggess. In J. K. Smith & G. Plimpton (Eds.), *Chronicles of courage: Very special artists.* New York: Random House.

Bombardier, C. H. (2000). Alcohol and traumatic disability. In R. G. Frank & T. R. Elliot (Eds.), *Handbook of rehabilitation psychology* (pp. 399–416). Washington, DC: American Psychological Association.

Bordieri, J. E. (1993). Self-blame attributions for disability and perceived client involvement in the vocational rehabilitation process. *Journal of Applied Rehabilitation Counseling, 24*(2), 3–6.

Bordieri, J. E., & Drehmer, D. E. (1988). Causal attribution and hiring recommendations for disabled job applicants. *Rehabilitation Psychology, 33,* 239–247.

Bornstein, M. H., & Lamb, M. E. (Eds.). (1984). *Developmental psychology: An advanced textbook.* Hillsdale, NJ: Lawrence Erlbaum.

Bowbly, J. (1958). The nature of the child's tie to his mother. *International Journal of Psycho-Analysis, 39,* 350–373.

Bowlby, J. (1969). *Attachment.* New York: Basic Books.

Bowbly, J. (1973). *Attachment and loss: Vol. 2. Separation: Anxiety and anger.* New York: Basic Books.

Bowbly, (1980). *Attachment and loss: Vol. 3. Loss: Sadness and depression.* New York: Basic Books.

Bradsher, J. E. (1997). Disability among racial and ethnic groups, #10 [online]. *Disability statistic's abstract.* San Francisco: University of California, San Francisco. Retrieved from www.dsc.ucsf.edu

Bradway, J. K., Malone, J. M., Racy, J., Leal, J. M., & Poole, J. (1984). Psychological adaptation to amputation: An overview. *Orthotics and Prosthetics, 38,* 46–50.

Bragg, B. (1989). *Lessons in laughter: The autobiography of a deaf actor. As signed to Eugene Bergman.* Washington, DC: Gallaudet University.

Brain Awareness Week. (2001, March 12–18). *What is neuroscience?* http://www.sfn.org./BAW/resources/what.is.neuro.html

Bramble, K., & Cukr, P. (1998). Body image. In I. M. Lubkin & P. D. Larsen (Eds.), *Chronic illness: Impact and interventions* (pp. 283–298). Sudbury, MA: Jones & Bartlett.

Brandist, C. (2006). The rise of Soviet sociolinguistics from the ashes of Völkerpsychologie. *Journal of the History of the Behavioral Sciences, 42,* 261–277.

Brandtstadlter, J., & Rothermund, K. (2003). Intentionality and time in human development and aging: Compensation and goal adjustment in changing developmental contexts. In U. M. Staudiner & U. Lindenberger (Eds.), *Understanding human development: Dialogues with lifespan psychology* (pp. 105–124). Boston: Kluwer Academic.

Breaslau, N., & Marshall, I. A. (1985). Psychological disturbances in children with physical disabilities: Continuity and change in a 5-year follow-up study. *Journal of Abnormal Child Psychology, 13,* 199–216.

Breaslau, N., Paneth, N. S., & Lucia, V. C. (2004). The lingering academic deficits of low birth weight children. *Pediatrics, 114*, 1035–1040.

Breggin, P. R. (2001). *Talking back to Ritalin.* Braintree, MA: Perseus.

Bregman, S., & Castles, E. E. (1988). Insights and intervention into the sexual needs of the disabled adolescent. In P. W. Power, A. E. Dell Orto, & M. B. Gibbons (Eds.), *Family interventions throughout chronic illness and disability* (pp. 184–200). New York: Springer.

Brew-Parrish, V. (2004). HEY, HEY, HEY, it's Disability Awareness Day! Still. Even in the 21st century! *The Ragged Edge.* http://www.raggededgemagazine.com/focus/wrong message04. html

Britell, C. W., & Hammond, M. C. (1994). Spinal cord injury. In R. M. Hayes, G. H. Kraft, & W. C. Stolov (Eds.), *Chronic disease and disability: A contemporary approach to medical practice* (pp. 142–160). New York: Demos.

Bronfenbrenner, U. (1974). Developmental research, public policy, and the ecology of childhood. *Child Development, 45,* 1–5.

Bronfenbrenner, U. (1977). *The experimental ecology of human development.* Cambridge, MA: Harvard University.

Bronfenbrenner, U. (1986). Ecology of the family as a context for human development: Research perspectives. *Developmental Psychology, 22,* 723–742.

Bronfenbrenner, U. (Ed.). (2005). *Making human beings human: Bioecological perspectives on human development.* Thousand Oaks, CA: Sage.

Bronfin, L. (2005). Neuromuscular disorders. In H. H. Zarestsky, E. F. Richter, & M. G. Eisenberg (Eds.), *Medical aspects of disability: A handbook for the rehabilitation professional* (3rd ed., pp. 383–426). New York: Springer.

Brookes, T. (1995). *Catching my breath: An asthmatic explores his illness.* New York: Vintage.

Brooks, D. (2011, January 17). Annals of psychology: Social animal. *The New Yorker,* 26–32.

Brown, S. C. (1991). Conceptualizing and defining disability. In S. Thompson-Hoffman & I. F. Storck (Eds.), *Disability in the United States: A portrait from national data* (pp. 1–14). New York: Springer.

Bruce, S. & Muhammad, Z. (2009). The development of object permanence in children with intellectual disability, physical disability, autism, and blindness. *International Journal of Disability, 56*(3). doi: 10.1080/10349120903102213

Brueggemann, B. J., & Burch, S. (Eds.). (2007). *Women and deafness: Double visions.* Washington, DC: Gallaudet University.

Bryan, W. V. (1996). *In search of freedom: How people with disabilities have been disenfranchised from the mainstream of American society.* Springfield, IL: Charles C Thomas.

Bryant, C. D. (Ed.). (2003). *Handbook of death and dying.* New York: John Wiley.

Buckbinder, M., & Clark, C. D. (2009). Illness and disease, childhood and adolescence. In D. Carr (Ed.), *Encyclopedia of the life course and human development* (Vol. 1, pp. 253–256). New York: Macmillan.

Buki, L. P., Kogan, L., Keen, B., & Uman, P. (2007). In the midst of a hurricane: A case study of a couple living with AIDS. In A. Dell Orto & P. Power (Eds.), *The psychological and social impact of illness and disability* (6th ed., pp. 329–350). New York: Springer.

Burch, S. (2007). Beautiful, though D/deaf: The D/deaf American beauty pageant. In B. J. Brueggemann & S. Burch (Eds.), *Women and D/deafness: Double visions* (pp. 242–261). Washington, DC: Gallaudet University.

Burgdorf, R. (2002). *Supreme Court decisions thwart intent of ADA.* San Diego, CA: Center for an Accessible Society.

Butcher, J. N., Mineka, S., & Hooley, J. M. (2010). *Abnormal psychology* (14th ed.). Boston: Allyn & Bacon.

Butterworth, G., Rutkowka, J., & Scaife, M. (Eds.). (1985). *Evolution and developmental psychology.* New York: St. Martin's.

Byrd, E. K. (1979). Magazine articles and disability. *American Rehabilitation, 4,* 18–20.

Byrd, E. K., Byrd, P. D., & Allen, C. (1977). Television programming and disability: A descriptive study. *Journal of Applied Rehabilitation Counseling, 8,* 28–32.

Byrd, E. K., & Elliott, T. R. (1985). Feature films and disability: A descriptive study. *Rehabilitation Psychology, 30,* 47–51.

Byrd, E. K., & Elliott, T. R. (1988). Media and disability: A discussion of the research. In H. E. Yuker (Ed.), *Attitudes toward persons with disabilities* (pp. 82–95). New York: Springer.

Byrd, E. K., Williamson, W., & Byrd, P. D. (1986). Literary characters who are disabled. *Rehabilitation Counseling Bulletin, 30,* 57–61.

Byrom, B. (2004). A pupil and a patient. Hospitals-schools in progressive America. In S. Danforth & S. D. Taff (Eds.), *Crucial readings in special education* (pp. 25–37). Upper Saddle River, NJ: Pearson.

Callahan, E. J., & McCluskey, K. A. (Eds.). (1983). *Life-span developmental psychology: Nonnormative life events.* New York: Academic Press.

Campling, J. (1981). *Images of ourselves: Women with disabilities talking.* London: Routledge Kegan Paul.

Caplan, B., & Moelter, S. (2000). Stroke. In R. G. Frank & T. R. Elliot (Eds.), *Handbook of rehabilitation psychology* (pp. 75–108). Washington, DC: American Psychological Association.

Capps, D. (2008). *The decades of life: A guide to human development.* Louisville, KY: Westminster John Knox Press.

Carnegie Corporation of New York. (1994). *Starting points.* New York: Carnegie Corporation of New York.

Carr, D. (Ed.). (2009). *Encyclopedia of the life course and human development, Vol. 1: Childhood and adolescence.* Detroit, MI: Gale Cengage Learning.

Carr, D. (Ed.). (2009). *Encyclopedia of the life course and human development, Vol. 2: Adulthood.* Detroit, MI: Gale Cengage Learning.

Carr, D. (Ed.). (2009). *Encyclopedia of the life course and human development, Vol. 3: Later life.* Detroit, MI: Gale Cengage Learning.

Carroll, T. J. (1961). *Blindness: What it is, what it does, and how to live with it.* Boston: Little-Brown.

Case-Smith, J. (2004). Parenting a child with a chronic medical condition. *American Journal of Occupational Theory, 58,* 551–560.

Case-Smith, J. (2007). Parenting a child with a chronic medical condition. In A. E. Dell Orto & P. W. Power (Eds.), *The psychological and social impact of illness and disability* (5th ed., pp. 210–328). New York: Springer.

Casey, P. H. (2008). Growth of low birth weight preterm children. *Seminars in Perinatology, 12,* 20–27.

Cataldo, M. F., Kahng, S. W., DeLeon, I. G., Martens, B. K., Friman, P. C., & Cataldo, M. (2005). Behavioral principles, assessment, and therapy. In M. L. Batshaw, L. Pellegrino, & N. J. Roizen (Eds.), *Children with disabilities* (6th ed., pp. 539–555). Baltimore, MD: Paul H. Brookes.

Cate, I. M. P., & Loots, G. M. P. (2000). Experiences of siblings of children with physical disabilities: An empirical investigation. *Disability and Rehabilitation, 22,* 399–408.

Centers for Disease Control and Prevention. (2007a). *Fetal alcohol spectrum disorders.* Retrieved from http://www.cdc.gov/ncbddd/fas

Centers for Disease Control and Prevention. (2007b). Prevalence of ASDs—Autism and Developmental Disabilities Monitoring Network, United States, 2002. *Morbidity and Mortality Weekly Report, 56,* 12–18.

Centers for Disease Control and Prevention. (2008). Cytomegalovirus Disease: The congenital disease mothers don't know about. http://www.cdc.gov/features/dscytomegalovirus

Chang, J. C., Martin, S. L., Moracco, K. E., Dulli, L., Scandlin, D., Loucks-Sorrel, M. B., et al. (2003). Helping women with disabilities and domestic violence: Strategies, limitations, and challenges of domestic violence programs and services. *Journal of Women's Health, 12,* 699–708.

Chang, R. & Page, R. C. (1991). Characteristics of the self-actualized persons: Visions from the East and West. *Counseling and Values, 36,* 2–11.

Chapman, S. B., Sparks, G., & Levin, H.S. (2004). Discourse macrolevel processing after severe pediatric traumatic brain. *Developmental Neuropsychology, 25,* 37–60.

Charlton, J. I. (1998). *Nothing about us without us: Disability oppression and empowerment.* Berkeley, CA: University of California.

Chesler, M. A., & Chesney, B. K. (1988). Self-help groups: Empowerment attitudes and behaviors of disabled and chronically ill persons. In H. E. Yuker (Ed.), *Attitudes toward individuals with disabilities* (pp. 230–244). New York: Springer.

Chilman, C. S., Nunnally, E.W., & Cox, F. M. (Eds.). (1988). *Chronic illness and disability: Families in trouble.* Newbury Park, CA: Sage.

Chisholm, K. (1998). A three-year follow-up of attachment and indiscriminate friendliness in children adopted from Romanian orphanages. *Child Development, 69,* 1092–1106.

Chudacoff, H. P. (2011). *Children at play: An American history.* New York: New York University.

Cicchetti, D., & Toth, S. L. (1991). *Rochester symposium on developmental psychopathology: Models and integrations* (Vol. 3). Rochester, NY: University of Rochester.

Cimarolli, V. R. (2009). Sensory impairments. In D. Carr (Ed.), *Encyclopedia of the life course and human development, Vol. 3: Later life* (pp. 358–362). Detroit, MI: Gale Cengage Learning.

Cincotta, N. F. (2002). The journey of middle childhood: Who are "latency"-age children? In S. G. Austrian (Ed.), *Developmental theories through the life cycle* (pp. 69–122). New York: Columbia University.

Cirillo, L., & Wapner, S. (Eds.). (1986). *Value presuppositions in theories of human development.* Hillsdale, NJ: Lawrence Erlbaum.

Clair, E. B., Church, R. P., & Batshaw, M. L. (2007). Special education services. In M. J. Batshaw, L. Pellegrino, & N. J. Roizen (Eds.), *Children with disabilities* (6th ed., pp. 523–538). Baltimore, MD: Paul H. Brookes.

Claire, E. (2010). Stones in my pockets, stones in my heart. In L. J. Davis (Ed.), *The disability studies reader* (3rd ed., pp. 563–572). New York: Routledge.

Clark, R. L., Glick, J. E., & Bures, R. M. (2009). Immigrant families over the life course: Research directions and needs. *Journal of Family Issues, 30,* 852–872.

Clark-Stewart, A. (1977). *Child care in the family: A review of research and some propositions for policy.* New York: Academic.

Clausen, J. (1991a). Adolescent competence and shaping of the life course. *American Journal of Sociology, 96,* 805–842.

Clausen, J. (1991b). Adolescent competence and the life course, or why one social psychologist needed a concept of personality. *Social Psychology Quarterly, 54,* 4–14.

Clausen, J. (1998). *American lives: Looking back at the children of the great depression.* Berkeley: University of California.

Cloninger, C. R. (2003). Completing the psychobiological architecture of human personality development: Temperament, character, and coherence. In U. M. Staudiner & U. Lindenberger (Eds.), *Understanding human development: Dialogues with lifespan psychology* (pp. 160–181). Boston: Kluwer Academic.

Close, C. (1993). In J. K. Smith & G. Plimpton (Ed.), *Chronicles of courage. Very special artists.* New York: Random House.

Clydesdale, T. (2009). Religion and spirituality, childhood and adolescence. In D. Carr (Ed.), *Encyclopedia of the life course and human development, Vol. 3: Later life* (pp. 388–392). Detroit, MI: Gale Cengage Learning.

Cockerham, W. C. (1998). *Medical sociology* (7th ed.). Upper Saddle River, NJ: Prentice Hall.

Cockerham, W. C. (2005). Health lifestyle theory and the convergence of agency and structure. *Journal of Health and Social Behavior, 46,* 51–67.

Cohen, R. M. (2004). *Blindsided: Living a life above illness: A reluctant memoir.* New York: HarperCollins.

Cohler, B. J., & Hammack, P. L. (2007). The psychological world of the gay teenager: Social change, narrative, and "normality." *Journal of Youth and Adolescence, 36,* 47–59.

Colapinto, J. (2010, December 20, 27). Medical dispatch: Mother courage. The Duchenne campaigner. *The New Yorker,* New York.

Colby, A., Kolberg, L., Gibbs, J. C., Kandee, D., Hewer, R., Kaufman, K., et al. (1983). *Assessing moral stages: A manual.* New York: Cambridge University.

Cole, M. & Gajdamaschko, N. (2007), Vygotsky and culture. In J. W. Daniels & M. Cole (Eds.), *The Cambridge companion to Vygotsky.* New York: Cambridge University.

Cole, S. S. (Ed.). (1991). Sexual exploitation of people with disabilities [Special issue]. *Sexuality and Disability, 9,* 3–6.

Cole, S. S. (1993). Facing the challenges of sexual abuse in persons with disabilities. In M. Nagler (Ed.), *Perspectives on disability* (2nd ed., pp. 273–282). Palo Alto, CA: Health Markets Research.

Coleman, L. M. (1997). Stigma: An enigma demystified. In L. J. Davis (Ed.), *The disability studies reader* (pp. 216–231). New York: Routledge.

Coles, R. (1970). *Erik H. Erikson: The growth of his work.* Boston: Little, Brown.

Collins, C. (2007). For better or for worse. In A. Dell Orto & P. Power (Eds.), *The psychological and social impact of illness and disability* (6th ed., pp. 719–723). New York: Springer.

Collins, W. A. (2002). Historical perspectives on contemporary research in social development. In P. K. Smith & C. H. Hart (Eds.), *Blackwell handbook of childhood social development* (pp. 3–23). Oxford, UK: Blackwell.

Collins-Moore, M. S. (1984). Birth and diagnosis: A family crisis. In M. G. Eisenberg, L. C. Sutkin, & M. A. Jansen (Eds.), *Chronic illness and disability through the life span: Effects on self and the family* (pp. 39–66). New York: Springer.

Commission on Chronic Illness. (1957). *Chronic illness in the United States: Prevention of chronic illness.* Cambridge, MA: Harvard University.

Commons, M. L., Miller, P. M., & Kuhn, D. (1982). The relation between formal operational reasoning and academic course selection among college course selection and performance among college freshmen and sophomores. *Journal of Applied Developmental Psychology, 3,* 1–10.

Conrad, P. (2004). The discovery of hyperkinesis: Notes on the medicalization of deviant behavior. In S. Danforth and S. D. Taff (Eds.), *Crucial readings in special education* (pp. 18–24). Upper Saddle River, NJ: Pearson.

Conway, C. M., Pisoni, D. B., Anaya, E. M., Karpicke, J., & Henning, S. C. (2011). Implicit sequence learning in deaf children with cochlear implants. *Developmental Science, 14,* 69–82.

Conway-Giustra, F., Crowley, A., & Gorin, S. H. (2002). Crisis in caregiving: A call to action. *Health and Social Work, 27,* 307–311.

Cook, D., & Ferritor, D. (1985). The family: A potential resource in the provision of rehabilitation services. *Journal of Applied Rehabilitation Counseling, 16*(2), 52–53.

Cook, D. T. (2009). *The commodification of childhood.* Durham, NC: Duke University.

Cook, L. D. (1979). The adolescent with a learning disability: A developmental perspective. *Adolescence, 14,* 697–707.

Coplan, J., & Trachtenberg, S. W. (2001). Finding out your child has a disability. In M. L. Batshaw (Ed.), *When your child has a disability* (pp. 3–10). Baltimore, MD: Paul H. Brookes.

Corbett, J. O., & Bregante, J. L. (1993). Disabled lesbians: Multicultural realities. In M. Nagler (Ed.), *Perspectives on disability* (pp. 261–271). Palo Alto, CA: Health Markets Research.

Corbin, J., & Strauss, A. (1988). *Unending work, and care: Managing chronic illness at home.* San Francisco: Jossey-Bass.

Cornell University (2010). Prevalence of disability among non-institutionalized people of all ages in the United States in 2008. Ithaca:NY: Cornell.

Corrigan, J. D. (1995). Substance abuse as a mediating factor in outcome from traumatic brain injury. *Archives of Physical Medicine and Rehabilitation, 76,* 302–309.

Costa, P. T., Metter, E. J., & McCrae, R. R. (1994). Personality stability and its contribution to successful aging. *Journal of Geriatric Psychiatry, 27,* 41–59.

Cott, C., & Wilkins, S. (1993). Aging, chronic illness, and disability. In M. Nagler (Ed.), *Perspectives on disability* (2nd ed., pp. 363–377). Palo Alto, CA: Health Markets Research.

Council of Economic Advisors. (2000). *Teens and their parents in the 21st century: An examination of trends in teen behaviors and the role of parent involvement.* Washington, DC: Author.

Couser, G. T. (1997). *Recovering bodies: Illness, disability, and life writing.* Madison, WI: University of Wisconsin.

Cox, A., Rutter, M., Newman, S., & Bartak, L. (1975). A comparative study of infantile autism and specific developmental receptive language disorder: II. Parents characteristics. *British Journal of Psychiatry, 126,* 146–159.

Crain, W. C. (1985). *Theories of development.* New York: Prentice-Hall.

Crewe, N. M. (1993). Aging and severe physical disability. Patterns of change and implications for change. In M. Nagler (Ed.), *Perspective on disability* (2nd ed., pp. 355–361). Palo Alto, CA: Health Markets Research.

Crewe, N. M. (1997). Life stories of people with long-term spinal cord injury. *Rehabilitation Counseling Bulletin, 41,* 26–42.

Crites, J. O. (1973). *Theory and research handbook: Career maturity inventory.* Monterey, CA: CTB-MacMillan-McGraw-Hill.

Crosnoe, R. (2000). Friendships in childhood and adolescence: The life course and new directions. *Social Psychology Quarterly, 63,* 377–391.

Cruickshank, W. M. (1990). Definition: A major issue in the field of learning disabilities. In M. Nagler (Ed.), *Perspectives on disability* (2nd ed., pp. 389–406). Palo Alto, CA: Health Markets Research.

Curry, R. L. (1995). The exceptional family: Walking the edge of tragedy and transformation. In S. K. Toombs, D. Barnard, & R. A. Carlson (Eds.), *Chronic illness: From experience to policy* (pp. 24–37). Bloomington, IN: University of Indiana.

Curtin, M., & Lubkin, I. (1998). What is chronicity? In I. M. Lubkin & P. D. Larsen (Eds.), *Chronic illness: Impact and interventions* (4th ed., p. 325). Sudbury, MA: Jones & Bartlett.

Damrosch, S. P., & Perry, L. A. (1989). Self-reported adjustment, chronic sorrow, and coping of parents of children with Down syndrome. *Nursing Research, 38,* 30.

Daniels, H. (2007). Pedagogy. In J. W. Daniels & M. Cole (Eds.), *The Cambridge companion to Vygotsky.* New York: Cambridge University Press.

Darling, R. B. (1979). *Families against society: A study of reactions to children with birth defects.* Beverly Hills, CA: Sage.

Darling, R. B. (1983). The birth defective child and the crisis of parenthood: Redefining the situation. In E. J. Callahan & K. A. McCluskey (Eds.), *Life-span developmental psychology: Nonnormative life events* (pp. 115–143). New York: Academic Press.

Darling, R. B., & Baxter, C. (1996). *Families in focus: Sociological methods in early intervention.* Austin, TX: Pro-Ed.

Datan, N., & Ginsberg, L. H. (Eds.). (1975). *Lifetime developmental psychology: Normative life crises.* New York: Academic Press.

Datan, N., Greene, A. L. & Reese, H. W. (Eds.). (1986). *Life-span developmental psychology: Intergenerational relations.* Hillsdale, NJ: Lawrence Erlbaum.

Davis, L. J. (Ed.). (1997). *The disability studies reader.* New York: Routledge.

Davis, L. J. (Ed.). (2010). *The disability studies reader* (3rd ed.). New York: Routledge.

Davis, L. J. (1997). Constructing normalcy: The bell curve, the novel, and the invention of the disabled body in the nineteenth century. In L. J. Davis (Ed.), *Disability studies reader* (pp. 307–314). New York: Routledge.

Dean, V. J., Burns, M. K., Grialou, T., & Varro, P. J. (2006). Comparison of ecological validity of learning disabilities diagnostic models. *Psychology in the Schools, 43*(2), 157–168.

Deegan, P. E. (1991). Recovery: The lived experience of rehabilitation. In R. P. Marinelli & A. E. Dell Orto (Eds.), *The psychological and social impact of disability* (3rd ed., pp. 47–54). New York: Springer.

Deegan, P. E. (1997). Recovery: The lived experience of rehabilitation. In L. Spaniol, C. Gagne, & M. Koehler (Eds.), *Psychological and social aspects of psychiatric disability* (pp. 92–98). Boston: Center for Psychiatric Rehabilitation, Boston University.

Degeneffe, C. E., & Lee, G. K. (2010). Quality of life after traumatic brain injury: Perspectives of adult siblings. *Journal of Rehabilitation, 76,* 27–36.

DeJong, G., & Batavia, A. I. (1990). The Americans with Disabilities Act and the current state of U.S. disability policy. *Journal of Disability Policy Studies, 1,* 65–75.

Dell Orto, A. E. (1988). Respite care: A vehicle for hope, the buffer against desperation. In P. W. Power, A. E. Dell Orto, & M. B. Gibbons (Eds.), *Family interventions throughout chronic illness and disability* (pp. 265–284). New York: Springer.

Dell Orto, A. E., & Power, P. W. (Eds.). (2007). *The psychological and social impact of illness and disability.* (5th ed.). New York: Springer.

DeLoach, C., & Greer, B. G. (1981). *Adjustment to severe disability: A metamorphosis.* New York: McGraw-Hill.

Demo, D. H. (1992). The self-concept over time: Research issues and directions. *Annual Review of Sociology, 18,* 303–336.

Deshen, S. A. (1992). *Blind people: The private and public life of sightless Israelis.* Albany, NY: State University of New York.

De Vos, S., & Ruggles, S. (1988). The demography of kinship and the life course. In P. B. Baltes, D. Featherman, & R. M. Lerner (Eds.), *Life span development and behavior* (pp. 259–281). Hillsdale, NJ: Lawrence Erlbaum.

Dien, D. S. (2000). The evolving nature of self-identity across four levels of history. *Human Development, 43,* 1–18.

Diessner, R., & Tiegs, J. (2001). *Notable selections in human development* (2nd ed.). Guilford, CT: McGraw-Hill.

Dikmen, S. S., & Jaffe, K. M. (1994). Head injury. In R. M. Hayes, G. H. Kraft, & W. C. Stolov (Eds.), *Chronic disease and disability: A contemporary rehabilitation approach to medical practice* (pp. 130–140). New York: Demos.

Diller, L., & Moroz, A. (2005). Stroke. In H. H. Zarestsky, E. F. Richter, & M. G. Eisenberg (Eds.), *Medical aspects of disability: A handbook for the rehabilitation professional* (3rd ed., pp. 649–673). New York: Springer.

Dinsmoor, J. A. (1992). Setting the record straight: The social views of B. F. Skinner. *American Psychologist, 47,* 1454–1463.

Dixon, R. A., & Lerner, R. M. (1984). A history of systems in developmental psychology. In M. H. Bornstein & M. E. Lamb (Eds.), *Developmental psychology: An advanced textbook* (pp. 1–35). Hillsdale, NJ: Lawrence Erlbaum.

Dixon, T. M., Layton, B. S., & Shaw, R. M. (2005). Traumatic brain injury. In H. H. Zarestsky, E. F. Richter, & M. G. Eisenberg (Eds.), *Medical aspects of disability: A handbook for the rehabilitation professional* (3rd ed., pp. 119–149). New York: Springer.

Donoghue, P. J., & Siegel, M. E. (1992). *Sick and tired of feeling sick and tired: Living with invisible chronic illness.* New York: Norton.

Donohew, L., Bardo, M. T., & Zimmerman, R. S. (2004). Personality and risky behavior: Communication and prevention. In R. M. Stelmack (Ed.), *On the psychobiology of personality* (pp. 223–245). Elsevier: Amsterdam, The Netherlands.

Dotson, J. (2010, December). The individuality of Asperger Syndrome. *The Utah Special Educator, 33*(2), pp. 22–23.

Douard, J. W. (1995). Disability and the persistence of the "Normal." In S. K. Toombs, D. Barnard, & R. A. Carson (Eds.), *Chronic illness: From experience to policy* (pp. 154–175). Bloomington: University of Indiana.

Dowker, A. (2006). What can functional brain imaging studies tell us about typical and atypical cognitive development of children. *Journal of Physiology, Paris, 99,* 333–341.

Drew, C. J., Logan, D. R., & Hardman, M. L. (1992). *Mental retardation: Life cycle approach* (5th ed.), Columbus, OH: Merrill.

Drotar, D., Crawford, P., & Bush, M. (1984). The family context of childhood chronic illness: Implications for psychosocial intervention. In M. G. Eisenberg, L. C. Sutkin, & M. A. Jansen (Eds.), *Chronic illness and disability through the life span: Effects on self and the family* (pp. 103–235). New York: Springer.

Dunn, D. S. (1996). Well-being following amputation: Salutary effects of positive meaning, optimism, and control. *Rehabilitation Psychology, 41,* 285–301.

Durand, V. M., & Crimmins, D. B. (1988). Identifying the variables maintaining self-injurious behavior. *Journal of Autism and Developmental Disorders, 18,* 99–117.

Durston, S., & Casey, B. J. (2006). What have we learned about cognitive development from neuroimaging. *Neuropsychologia, 44,* 2149–2157.

Dush, C. M. K., Taylor, M. G., & Kroeger, R. A. (2008). Marital happiness and psychological well-being across the life course. *Family Relations, 57,* 211–226.

Dyson, K. (1980). *The state tradition in Western Europe.* Oxford: Robertson.

Ebner, N. C., Freund, A. M., & Baltes, P. B. (2006). Developmental changes in personal goal orientation from young to late adulthood: From striving for gains to maintenance and prevention of losses. *Psychology and Aging, 21,* 664–678.

Edgell, P. (2006). *Religion and family in a changing society.* Princeton, NJ: Princeton University.

Edmonson, B. (1997, April). The facts of death—statistics, demographics. Washington, DC: *American demographics.* Retrieved from http://findarticles.com/p/articles/mi_m4021/is/_n4_v19/ai_19310644

Edwards, R. A. R. (2010). "Hearing aids are not deaf": A historical perspective on technology in the deaf world. In L. J. Davis (Ed.), *The disability studies reader* (3rd ed., pp. 403–416). New York: Routledge.

Eisenberg, M. G., Sutkin, L. C., & Jansen, M. A. (Eds.). (1984). *Chronic illness and disability through the life span: Effects on self and the family.* New York: Springer.

Elder, G. H., Jr. (1980). Adolescence in historical perspective. In J. Adelson (Ed.), *Handbook of adolescent psychology.* New York: Wiley.

Elder, G. H., Jr. (1997). The life course and human development. In R. M. Lerner (Ed.), *Handbook of child psychology: Volume 1: Theoretical models of human development* (pp. 939–991). New York: Wiley.

Elder, G. H., Jr. (1998). The life course as development theory. *Child Development Theory, 69,* 1–12.

Elder, G. H., Jr. (1999). *Children of the Great Depression.* Boulder, CO: Westview.

Elder, G. H., Jr., Johnson, M. K., & Crosnoe, R. (2004). The emergence and development of life course theory. In J. T. Mortimer & M. J. Shanahan (Eds.), *Handbook of the life course* (pp. 3–19). New York: Springer.

Elliot, T. R., & Frank, R. G. (1996). Depression following spinal cord injury. *Archives of Physical Medicine and Rehabilitation, 77,* 815–823.

Elliott, T. R., Frank, R. G., Corcoran, J., Beardon, L., & Byrd, E. K. (1990). Previous personal experience and reactions to depression and physical disability. *Rehabilitation Psychology, 35,* 111–119.

Elliott, T. R., Shewchuk, R. M., & Richards, J. S. (1999). Caregiver social problem-solving abilities and family member adjustment to recent onset physical disability. *Rehabilitation Psychology, 44,* 104–123.

Elms, A. C. (1981). Skinner's dark year and Walden Two. *American Psychologist, 36,* 627–632.

Entwisle, D. R., Alexander, K. L., & Olson, L. S. (2004). The first-grade transition in the life course perspective. In J. T. Mortimer & M. J. Shanahan (Eds.), *Handbook of the life course.* (pp. 229–250). New York: Springer.

Entwisle, D. R., Alexander, K. L., & Pallas, A. M., & Cadigan, D. (1987). The emergent academic self-image of first-graders: Its response to social structure. *Child Development, 58,* 1190–1206.

Equal Access to Software and Information. (1999). Retrieved from http://www.rit.edu/-easi

Erikson, E. (1977). *Toys and reason: Stages in the ritualization of experience.* New York: W. W. Norton.

Erikson, E. H. (1950). *Childhood and society.* New York: Norton.

Erikson, E. H. (1959). The problem of ego identity. *Psychological Issues, 1,* 101–164.

Erikson, E. H. (1964). *Insight and responsibility.* New York: Norton.

Erikson, E. H. (1968). *Identity: Youth and crisis.* New York: Norton.

Erikson, E. H. (1970, December 21). The quest for identity. *Newsweek,* pp. 84–89.

Erikson, E. H. (1975). *Life history and the historical moment.* New York: Norton.

Etcoff, N. (1999). *Survival of the prettiest: The science of beauty.* Cambridge, MA: Harvard University Press.

Evans, A. D., & Falk, W. W. (1986). *Learning to be deaf.* Berlin: Mouton de Gruyter.

Falvo, D. R. (1991). *Medical and psychosocial aspects of chronic illness and disability.* Gaithersburg, MD: Aspen.

Falvo, D. R. (1999). *Medical and psychosocial aspects of chronic illness and disability* (2nd ed.). Gaithersburg, MD: Aspen.

Farrell, F. Z., & Hutter, J. J., Jr. (1984). The family of the adolescent: A time of challenge. In M. G. Eisenberg, L. C. Sutkin, & M. A. Jansen (Eds.), *Chronic illness and disability through the life span: Effects on self and the family* (pp. 150–163). New York: Springer.

Farrow, M. (1997). *What falls away: A memoir.* New York: Doubleday.

Featherstone, H. (1980). *A difference in the family: Living with a disabled child.* New York: Basic Books.

Federal Interagency Forum on Child and Family Statistics. (2007). *America's children: Key indicators of well-being 2007.* Washington, DC: Federal Government Printing Office.

Feist, J. (1990). *Theories of personality* (2nd ed.). Fort Worth, TX: Holt, Rinehart & Winston.

Fenigsen, R. (1997). Euthanasia of disabled infants is not morally acceptable. In B. Stalcup (Ed.), *The disabled* (pp. 160–164). San Diego, CA: Greenhaven.

Fennel, M. (1999). The boy who could not speak. *Exceptional Parent, 29*(9), 132.

Ferguson, P. M., Ferguson, D. L., & Taylor, S. J. (Eds.). (1991). *Interpreting disability: A qualitative reader.* New York: Columbia University.

Ferster, C. B. (1961). Positive reinforcement and behavioral deficits of autistic children. *Child Development, 32,* 437–456.

Filer, R. D., & Filer, P. A. (2000). Practice considerations for counselors working with hearing children of deaf parents. *Journal of Counseling and Development, 78,* 38–43.

Films for the Humanities and Sciences. (1999). *Autism: The child who couldn't play* [Film]. Retrieved from www.films.com

Fine, M., & Asch, A. (1988a). Disability beyond stigma: Social interaction, discrimination, and activism. *Journal of Social Issues, 44,* 3–21.

Fine, M., & Asch, A. (Eds.). (1988b). *Women with disabilities.* Philadelphia: Temple University.

Fine, M., & Asch, A. (1988c). Introduction: Beyond pedestals. In M. Fine & A. Asch (Eds.), *Women with disabilities: Essays in psychology, culture, and politics* (pp. 1–37). Philadelphia: Temple University.

Finger, A. (1991). *Past due: A story of disability, pregnancy, and birth.* Seattle, WA: Seal Press.

Fishler, K., & Koch, R. (1991). Mental development in Down syndrome mosaicism. *American Journal of Mental Deficiency, 96,* 345–351.

Fishman, T. C. (2010). *The shock of gray: The aging of the world's population and how it pits young against old, child against parent, worker against boss, company against rival, and nation against nation.* New York: Scribner.

Fleischer, D. Z., & Zames, F. (2001). *The disability rights movement: From charity to confrontation.* Philadelphia, PA: Temple University.

Fletcher, J. F. (1979). *Humanhood: Essays in biomedical ethics.* Buffalo, NY: Prometheus.

Fowler, C. A., & Wadsworth, J. S. (1991). Individualism and equality: Critical values in North American culture and the impact on disability. *Journal of Applied Rehabilitation Counseling, 22,* 19–23.

Frank, A. W. (1995). *The wounded storyteller: Body, illness, and ethics.* Chicago: University of Chicago.

Frank, R. G., & Elliot, T. R. (Eds.). (2000). *Handbook of rehabilitation psychology.* Washington, DC: American Psychological Association.

Frankel, M. (1971). Personality as a response: Behaviorism. In S. R. Maddi (Ed.), *Perspectives on personality.* Boston: Little, Brown.

Frese, F. (1997). Twelve aspects of coping for persons with serious and persistent mental illness. In L. Spaniol, C. Gagne, & M. Hoehler (Eds.), *Psychological and social aspects of psychiatric disability.* Boston: Center for Psychiatric Rehabilitation, Boston University.

Freud, S. (1925/1961). Some psychical consequences of the anatomical distinction between the sexes. In J. Strachey (Ed.), *The standard edition of the complete psychological works of Sigmund Freud* (Vol. 19, pp. 248–258). London: Hogarth.

Freud, S. (1952). *An autobiographical study* (J. Strachey, Trans.). New York: Norton.

Freud, S. (1969). *General introduction to psychoanalysis.* New York: Crown.

Freund, A. M., Nikitin, J., & Ritter, J. O. (2009). Psychological consequences of longevity: The increasing importance of self-regulation in old age. *Human Development, 52,* 1–37.

Freund, A. M., & Riediger, M. (2001). What I have and what I do—The role of resource loss and gain throughout life. *Applied Psychology,* 371–380.

Frieden, L. (2010, July 26). Impact of the ADA: Results from 20th Anniversary Survey. http://www.southwestada.org/html/whatsnew/whats_new.html

Friedlander, H. (1996). *The origins of the Nazi genocide: From euthanasia to the final solution.* Chapel Hill, NC: University of North Carolina.

Friedman, D., Holmbeck, G. N., DeLucia, C., Jandasek, B., & Zebracki, K. (2009). Trajectories of autonomy development across the adolescent transition in children with spina bifida. *Rehabilitation Psychology, 54,* 16–27.

Friedman, L. J. (1999). *Identity's architect: A biography of Erik H. Erikson.* New York: Schribner.

Fries, K. (Ed.). (1997). *Staring back: The disability experience from the inside out.* New York: Plume.

Friesen, B. J. (1996). Family support in child and adult mental health. In G. H. S. Singer, L. E. Powers, & A. L. Olson (Eds.), *Redefining family support: Innovations in public private partnerships* (pp. 259–274). Baltimore, MD: Paul H. Brookes.

Furman, W., & Wehner, E. A. (1997). Adolescent romantic relationships: A developmental perspective. In S. Shulman & W. A. Collins (Eds.), *Romantic relationships in adolescence: Developmental perspectives* (pp. 21–36). San Francisco: Jossey-Bass.

Furstenberg, F. (2004). Reflections on the future of the life course. In J. T. Mortimer & M. J. Shanahan (Eds.), *Handbook of the life course* (pp. 661–680). New York: Springer.

Furstenberg, F. F., Brooks-Gunn, J., & Morgan, S. P. (1987). *Adolescent mothers in later life.* New York: Cambridge University.

Gaier, E. L., Linkowski, D. C., & Jaques, M. E. (1968). Contact as a variable in the perception of disability. *The Journal of Social Psychology, 74,* 117–126.

Galambos, C. M., & Rosen, A. (2000). The aging are coming and they are us. In S. M. Kergher, A. E. Fortune, & S. L. Witkin (Eds.), *Aging and social work: The changing landscape* (pp. 1–19). Washington, DC: NASW Press.

Gallagher, H. G. (1985). *FDR's splendid deception.* New York: Dodd and Mead.

Gallagher, H. G. (1990). *By trust betrayed: Patients, physicians, and the license to kill in the Third Reich.* New York: Henry Holt.

Gallotti, K. M., Kozberg, S. F., & Farmer, M. C. (1991). Gender and developmental differences in adolescents' conceptions of moral reasoning. *Journal of Youth and Adolescence, 20,* 13–20.

Garmon, L. C., Basinger, K. S., Gregg, V. R., & Gibbs, J. C. (1996). Gender differences in stage and expression of moral judgment. *Merrill-Palmer Quarterly, 42,* 418–437.

Gartner, A., & Lipsky, D. K. (1987). Beyond special education: Toward a quality system for all students. *Harvard Educational Review, 57,* 367–395.

Gay, P. (1988). *Freud: A life for our time.* New York: Norton.

Gecas, V. (2004). Self agency and the life course. In J. T. Mortimer & M. J. Shanahan (Eds.), *Handbook of the life course* (pp. 369–388). New York: Springer.

Gehlen, A. (1956). *Urmensch und spätkultur.* Bonn: Germany Athenäum.

Gerber, P. J., & Brown, D. S. (Eds.). (1997). *Learning disabilities and employment.* Austin, TX: PRO-ED.

Gilford, R. (1988). Marriages in later life. *Generations, 10*(4), 16–20.

Gill, C. J. (2001). Divided understandings: The social experience of disability. In G. L. Albrecht, K. D. Seelman, & M. Bury (Eds.), *The handbook of disability studies* (pp. 351–373). Thousand Oaks, CA: Sage.

Gilligan, C. F. (1977). In a different voice: Women's conception of self and morality. *Harvard Educational Review, 47,* 481–517.

Gilligan, C. F. (1982/1993). *In a different voice.* Cambridge, MA: Harvard University.

Gilligan, C. F. (1987). Adolescent development reconsidered. In C. E. Irwin (Ed.), *Adolescent social behavior and health.* San Francisco, CA: Jossey-Bass.

Gindis, B. (1995). The social/cultural implication of disability: Vygotsky's paradigm for special education. *Educational Psychologist, 30*(2), 77–81.

Ginsberg, S. D., Hof, P. R., McKinney, W. T., & Morrison, J. H. (1993). Quantitative analysis of tuberoinfundibular tyrosince hydrooxylast- and corticotrophin-releasing-factor-immunoreactive neurons in monkeys raised with differential rearing conditions. *Experimental Neurology, 120,* 95–105.

Ginsburg, F., & Rapp, R. (2010). Enabling disability: Rewriting kinship, reimagining citizenship. In L. J. Davis (Ed.), *The disability studies reader* (3rd ed.). New York: Routledge.

Ginzberg, E. (1984). Career development. In D. Brown, L. Brooks, & Associates (Eds.), *Career choice and development* (3rd ed., pp. 179–228). San Francisco: Jossey-Bass.

Gitter, A. (1994). Stroke syndromes. In R. M. Hayes, G. H. Kraft, & W. C. Stolov (Eds.), *Chronic disease and disability. A contemporary rehabilitation approach to medical practice* (p. 117–129). New York: Demos.

Glanzman, M. M. & Blum, N. J. (2007). Attention deficits and hyperactivity. In M. L. Batshaw, L. Pellegrino, & N. J. Roizen (Eds.), *Children with disabilities* (6th ed., pp. 345–365). Baltimore, MD: Paul H. Brookes.

Glass, P. (2001). Your baby was born prematurely. In M. L. Batshaw (Ed.), *When your child has a disability.* (pp. 59–71). Baltimore, MD: Paul H. Brookes.

Glenn, E. N. (2010). *Forced to care: Coercion and caregiving in America.* Cambridge, MA: Harvard University.

Gliedman, J., & Roth, W. (1980). *The unexpected minority: Handicapped children in America.* New York: Harcourt, Brace, Jovanovich.

Glueck, S., & Glueck, E. (1950). *Unraveling juvenile delinquency.* Cambridge, MA: Harvard University.

Glueck, S., & Glueck, E. (1968). *Delinquents and non-delinquents in perspective.* Cambridge, MA: Harvard University.

Glueckauf, R. L., & Quittner, A. L. (1984). Facing physical disability as a young adult: Psychological issues and approaches. In M. G. Eisenberg, L. C. Sutkin, & M. A. Jansen (Eds.), *Chronic illness and disability through the life span: Effects on self and the family* (pp. 167–183). New York: Springer.

Goeke, J. (2003). Parents speak out: Facial plastic surgery for children with Down syndrome. *Education and Training in Developmental Disabilities, 38,* 323–333.

Goffman, E. (1963). *Stigma: Notes on the management of spoiled identity.* Englewood Cliffs, NJ: Prentice Hall.

Gold, J. T. (1996). Growth hormone treatment of children with neural tube defects. *Journal of Pediatrics, 129,* 771.

Goldscheider, F., & Goldscheider, C. (1999). *The changing transition to adulthood: Leaving and returning home.* Thousand Oaks, CA: Sage.

Goma-i-Freixanet, M. (2004). Sensation seeking and participation in physical risk sports. In R. M. Stelmack (Ed.), *On the psychobiology of personality* (pp. 185–201). Elsevier: Amsterdam, The Netherlands.

Gordon, P. A., Lewis, M. D., & Wong, D. (1994). Multiple sclerosis: Strategies for rehabilitation counselors. *Journal of Rehabilitation, 62,* 34–38.

Gorelick, P. B. (1994). Stroke prevention: An opportunity for efficient utilization of health care resources during the coming decade. *Stroke, 25,* 220–224.

Gormly, A. V. (1997). *Lifespan human development* (6th ed.). Philadelphia: Harcourt Brace College Publishers.

Gottfredson, L. S. (1996). Gottfredson's theory of circumscription and compromise. In D. Brown, L. Brooks, & Associates (Eds.), *Career choice and development* (3rd ed., pp. 179–228). San Francisco: Jossey-Bass.

Graliker, B. V., Fishler, K., & Koch, R. (1962). Teenage reaction to a mentally retarded sibling. *Journal of Mental Deficiency, 66,* 838–843.

Grandin, T. (1996). *Thinking in pictures and other reports from my life with autism.* New York: Vintage Books.

Grealy, L. (1997). Pony party. In K. Fries (Ed.), *Staring back: The disability experience from the inside out.* (pp. 13–21). New York: Plume.

Grealy, L. (1999). Pony party. In K. Fries (Ed.) *Staring Back: The disability experience from the inside out.* (pp. 14–21) New York: Plume.

Green, S. E. (2003). "What do you mean 'what's wrong with her?'": Stigma and the lives of families of children with disabilities. *Social Science and Medicine, 57,* 1361–1374.

Green, S. E. (2007). "We're tired, not sad": Benefits and burdens of mothering a child with a disability. *Social Science and Medicine, 64,* 150–163.

Greenough, A. (2007). Late respiratory outcomes after preterm birth. *Early Human Development, 83,* 785–788.

Greve, W., & Wentura, D. (2007). Personal and subpersonal regulation of human development. Beyond complementary categories. *Human Development, 50,* 201–207.

Grossman, H. J. (Ed.). (1983). *Classification in mental retardation.* Washington, DC: American Association on Mental Deficiency.

Grotevant, H. D., & Cooper, C. R. (1988). The role of family experience in career exploration: A life span perspective. In P. B. Baltes, D. Featherman, & R. M. Lerner (Eds.), *Life span development and behavior* (pp. 231–258). Hillsdale, NJ: Lawrence Erlbaum.

Gulati, S. (2003). Psychiatric care of culturally deaf people (pp. 33–107). In N. S. Glickman & S. Gulati (Eds.), *Mental health care of deaf people: A culturally affirmative approach.* Mahwah, NJ: Lawrence Erlbaum.

Gulick, E. E. (1994). Social support among persons with multiple sclerosis. *Research in Nursing and Health, 17*(3), 195–206.

Gunnar, M. (2001). Effects of early deprivation: Findings from orphanage-reared infants and children. In C. A. Nelson & M. Luciana (Eds.), *Handbook of developmental cognitive neuroscience* (pp. 617–630). Cambridge, MA: MIT Press.

Guralnick, M. J. (Ed.) (2001). *Early childhood inclusion: Focus on change.* Baltimore, MD: Paul H. Brookes.

Hahn, H. (1988a). Can disability be beautiful? *Social Policy, 18,* 26–32.

Hahn, H. (1988b). The politics of physical differences: Disability and discrimination. *Journal of Social Issues, 44,* 39–47.

Hahn, H. (1993a). Can disability be beautiful? In M. Nagler (Ed.), *Perspectives on disability* (2nd ed., pp. 213–216). Palo Alto, CA: Health Markets Research.

Hahn, H. (1993b). The political implications of disability definitions and data. *Journal of Disability Policy Studies, 4,* 41–52.

Hahn, H. (1997). Advertising the acceptably employable image: Disability and capitalism. In L. J. Davis (Ed.), *The disability studies reader* (pp. 172–186). New York: Routledge.

Hahn, H. (2005). Academic debates and political advocacy: The U.S. disability movement. In G. E. May and M. B. Raske (Eds.), *Ending disability discrimination: Strategies for social workers* (pp. 1–24). Boston: Pearson.

Hall, C. S., Lindzey, G., & Campbell, J. B. (1998). *Theories of personality* (4th ed.). New York: Wiley.

Hall, E. (June, 1983). A conversation with Erik Erikson. *Psychology Today, 17*(6), 22, 24–30.

Hannah, M. E., & Midlarsky, E. (1987). Differential impact of labels and behavioral descriptions on attitudes toward people with disabilities. *Rehabilitation Psychology, 32,* 227–238.

Hardman, M. L., Drew, C. J., Egan, M. W., & Wolf, B. (1993). *Human exceptionality: Society, school, and family* (4th ed.). Boston: Allyn & Bacon.

Hardy, M. A. (2006). Older workers. In R. H. Binstock & L. K. George (Eds.), *Handbook of aging and the social sciences* (6th ed., pp. 201–216). Boston: Academic Press.

Harley, D. A., Greer, B. G., & Hackerman, A. E. (1997). Substance abuse and rehabilitation. *Rehabilitation Education, 11,* 353–372.

Harootyan, R. A., & Vorek, R. E. (1994). Volunteering, helping and gift giving in families and communities. In V. L. Bengtson & R. A. Harootyan (Eds.), *Intergenerational linkages: Hidden connections in American society* (pp. 77–111). New York: Springer.

Harper, D. C., & Peterson, D. B. (2000). Neuromuscular and musculosketetal disorders in children. In R. G. Frank and T. R. Elliot (Eds.), *Handbook of rehabilitation psychology* (pp. 123–144). Washington, DC: American Psychological Association.

Harris, R. W. (1992). Musings from 20 years of hard-earned experience. *Rehabilitation Education, 6,* 207–211.

Harter, S. (1982). The perceived competence scale for children. *Child Development, 53,* 87–97.

Harter, S. (1990). Issues in the assessment of the self-concept of children and adolescents. In A. LaGreca (Ed.), *Through the eyes of a child* (pp. 292–235). Boston: Allyn & Bacon.

Harter, S. (1998). The development of self-representations. In N. Eisenberg (Ed.), *Handbook of child psychology Vol. 3. Social, emotional, and personality development* (5th ed., pp. 533–618). New York: Wiley.

Hartup, W. W. (1983). Peer relations. In P. H. Mussen (Ed.), *Handbook of child psychology, Vol. 4: Socialization, social development, and personality* (pp. 96–103). New York: Wiley.

Havighurst, R. J. (1951). *Developmental tasks and education.* New York: Longman Green.

Havighurst, R. J. (1972). *Developmental tasks and education* (3rd ed.). New York: David McKay.

Hawking, S. D. (2011). Disability advice. Retrieved from http://www.hawking.org.uk/index.php/disability.

Hayes R. M., Kraft, G. H., & Stolov, W. C. (Eds.). (1994). *Chronic disease and disability: A contemporary rehabilitation approach to medical practice.* New York: Demos.

Head, D. W., Head, B., & Head, J. (1985). Life or death of severely disabled infants: A counseling issue. *Journal of Counseling and Development, 63,* 621–624.

Heckhausen, J. (2003). The future of lifespan developmental psychology: Perspectives from control theory. In U. M. Staudiner & U. Lindenberger (Eds.), *Understanding human development: Dialogues with lifespan psychology* (pp. 383–400). Boston: Kluwer Academic.

Heinemann, A. W., & Rawal, P. H. (2005). Spinal cord injury. In H. H. Zarestsky, E. F. Richter, & M. G. Eisenberg (Eds.), *Medical aspects of disability: A handbook for the rehabilitation professional* (3rd ed., pp. 696–721). New York: Springer.

Heinz, W. R. (2004). From work trajectories to negotiated career: The contingent work life course. In J. T. Mortimer & M. J. Shanahan (Eds.), *Handbook of the life course.* New York: Springer.

Heller, A., Rafman, S., Zvagulis, I., & Pless, I. B. (1985). Birth defects and psychosocial adjustment. *American Journal of Diseases of Children, 139,* 257–263.

Hendry, C. N. (2000). Childhood disintegrative disorder: Should it be considered a distinct diagnosis? *Clinical Psychology Review, 2,* 77–90.

Herbert, M. (2010, December). From the editor—Neurodiversity pride. *The Utah Special Educator, 33*(2), 4–5.

Herman, D. (1998). *Helen Keller: A life.* New York: Knopf.

Hersen, M., & Van Hasselt, V. B. (Eds.). (1990). *Psychological aspects of developmental and physical disabilities.* Newbury Park, CA: Sage.

Heumann, J. (1999). Personal narrative. In R. Mackelprang & R. Salsgiver (Eds.), *Disability: A diversity model in human service practice* (pp. 51–54). Pacific Grove, CA: Brooks/Cole.

Heumann, J. E. (1979). *Disability: Our Challenge.* New York: Columbia University.

Higgins, P. C. (1992a). *Making disability: Exploring the social transformation of human variation.* Springfield, IL: Charles C. Thomas.

Higgins, P. C. (1992b). *Outsiders in a hearing world: A sociology of D/deafness.* Newbury Park, CA: Sage.

Higo, M., & Williamson, J.B. (2009). Retirement. In D. Carr (Ed.), *Encyclopedia of the life course and human development, Vol. 3: Later life* (pp. 328–336). Detroit, MI: Gale Cengage Learning.

Himmelstein, D. U., Woolhander, S., & Wolfe, S. M. (1992). The vanishing health care safety net: New data on uninsured Americans. *International Journal of Health Services, 22,* 381–396.

Hirandini, V. (2005). Rethinking disability in social work: Interdisciplinary perspectives. In G. E. May & M. B. Raske (Eds.), *Ending discrimination in social work: Strategies for social workers* (pp. 71–81). Boston: Allyn & Bacon.

Hitlin, S., & Elder, G. H. (2007). Time, self, and the curiously abstract concept of agency. *Sociological Theory, 25,* 170–191.

Hockenberry, J. (1995). *Moving violations: War zones, wheelchairs, and declaration of independence.* New York: Hyperion.

Hofsiss, J., & Laffey, M. (1993). In J. K. Smith, & G. Plimpton. *Chronicles of courage. Very special artists* (pp. 78–87). New York: Random House.

Holcomb, L. P. (1990). Disabled women: A new issue in education. In M. Nagler (Ed.), *Perspectives on disability* (pp. 381–388). Palo Alto, CA: Health Markets Research.

Holden, K. C. (2009). The Boomers and their economic prospects. In R. B. Hudson (Ed.), *Boomer bust? Economic and political issues of the graying society* (pp. 63–75). Westport, CT: Praeger.

Holland, J. L. (1985). *Making vocational choices: A theory of vocational personality and environments.* Englewood Cliffs, NJ: Prentice Hall.

Holmes, C. P., Gatchel, R. J., Adams, L. L., Stowell, A. W., Hatten, A., Noe, C., et al. (2006). An opioid screening instrument: Long-term evaluation of the utility of the Pain Medication Questionnaire. *Pain Practice, 6,* 74–88.

Holocaust foreshadowed in newspaper obituaries. (199, July 30). *The Herald Journal,* 5.

Holzbauer, J. J., & Berven, N. L. (1996). Disability harassment: A new term for a long-standing problem. *Journal of Counseling and Development, 74,* 478–483.

Hoover, K. (Ed.). (2004). *The future of identity: Centennial reflections on the legacy of Erik Erikson.* New York: Lexington Books.

Horn, J. L., & Cattell, R. B. (1966). Age differences in primary mental ability factors. *Journal of Gerontology, 21,* 210–220.

Horne, M. D., & Ricciardo, J. L. (1988). Hierarchy of response to handicaps. *Psychological Reports, 62,* 83–86.

Horowitz, F. D. (1987). *Exploring developmental theories: Toward a structural/behavioral model of development.* Hillsdale, NJ: Lawrence Erlbaum.

Houser, R., & Seligman, R. (1991). Differences in coping strategies used by fathers of adolescents with disabilities and fathers of adolescents without disabilities. *Journal of Applied Rehabilitation Counseling, 22,* 7–10.

Howard, V. F., Williams, B., & Lepper, C. E. (2010). *Very young children with special needs: A foundation for educators, families, and service providers* (4th ed.). Upper Saddle River, NJ: Pearson.

Hubbard, R. (2006). Abortion and disability: Who should and who should not inhabit the world. In L. J. Davis (Ed.), *The disability studies reader* (2nd ed., pp. 93–103). New York: Routledge.

Huberty, D. J. (1980). Adapting to illness through family groups. In P. W. Power & A. E. Dell Orto (Eds.), *Role of the family in the rehabilitation of the physically disabled* (pp. 433–443). Austin, TX: Pro-Ed.

Hudson, R. B. (Ed.).(2009). *Boomer bust? Economic and political issues of the graying society.* Westport, CT: Praeger.

Hughes, M. E. (2009). Baby boom cohort. In D. Carr (Ed.), *Encyclopedia of the life course and human development, Vol. 3: Later life.* Detroit, MI: Gale Cengage Learning.

Hughes, R. B., Robinson-Whelen, R., Pepper, A. C., Gabriella, J., Lund, E. M., et al. (2010). Development of a Safety Awareness group intervention for women with diverse disabilities: A pilot study. *Rehabilitation Psychology, 55,* 263–271.

Humphrey, J. C. (1999). Disabled people and the politics of differences. *Disability & Society, 14,* 17–188.

Hunt, S. (2005). *The life course: A sociological introduction.* New York: Palgrave Macmillian.

Huppert, F. A. (2009). Psychological well being: Evidence regarding its causes and consequences. *Applied Psychology: Health and Well-Being, 1,* 137–164.

Hurst, R. (1998). Forget pity or charity: Disability is a rights issue. *Disability International, 5*(3), 14–16.

Huston, A. M. (1987). *Common sense about dyslexia.* New York: Madison.

Hyler, S. E. (1988). *DSM-III* at the cinema: Madness in the movies. *Comprehensive Psychiatry, 29,* 195–206.

Hyler, S. E., Gabbard, G. O., & Schneider, I. (1991). Homicidal maniacs and narcissistic parasites: Stigmatization of mentally ill persons in the movies. *Hospital and Community Psychiatry, 42,* 1044–1048.

Hyman, S. L., & Towbin, K. E. (2007). Autism spectrum disorders. In M. L. Batshaw, L. Pellegrino, & N. J. Roizen (Eds.), *Children with disabilities* (6th ed., pp. 325–343). Baltimore, MD: Paul H. Brookes.

Idler, E. L., & Kasl, S. V. (1997). Religion among disabled and nondisabled persons 1: Cross sectional patterns in health practices, social activities, and well-being. *Journal of Gerontology, 52B,* S294–S305.

Imrie, R. (1996). *Disability and the city: International perspectives.* New York: St. Martin's Press.

Individuals with Disabilities Education Act of 1990, 20 U.S.C. § 1400 *et seq.*

Individuals with Disabilities Education Improvement Act of 2004, Pub. L. No. 108–466, 20 U.S. C. 1400 *et seq.*

Inglehart, R. (1977). *The silent revolution: Changing values and political styles among western publics.* Princeton, NJ: Princeton University.

Inglehart, R. (1986). Intergenerational changes in politics and culture: The shift from materialist to postmaterialist value priority. In R. G. Braungart & M. M. Braungart (Eds.), *Research in political sociology* (pp. 81–105). Greenwich, CT: JAI Press.

Inglehart, R. (1990). *Culture shift in advanced industrial society.* Princeton, NJ: Princeton University.

Ireys, H. T. & Burr, C. K. (1984). Apart and a part: Family issues for young adults with chronic illness and disability. In M. G. Eisenberg, L. C. Sutkin, & M. A. Jansen (Eds.), *Chronic illness and disability through the life span: Effects on self and the family* (pp. 184–206). New York: Springer.

Ivey, A. E., & Ivey, M. B. (1998). Reframing the *DSM-IV*: Positive strategies from developmental counseling and therapy. *Journal of Counseling and Development, 76,* 334–350.

Jack, M. (1984). Verbal behavior. *Journal of the Experimental Analysis of Behavior, 42,* 363–376.

Jacoby, S. (2002). Living, better, longer. *American Association of Retired Persons Bulletin, 11,* 14.

Jacoby, S. (2011). *Never say die: The myth and marketing of the new old age.* New York: Pantheon.

Jahoda, A., Dagnan, D., Kroese, B. S., Pert, C., & Trower, P. (2009). Cognitive behavioral therapy: From face to face interaction to a broader contextual understanding of change. *Journal of Intellectual Disability Research, 53*(9), 759–771.

Jason, L. A., Jordan, K. M., Richman, J. A., Rademaker, A. W., Huang, C., McCready, W., et al. (1999). A community-based study of prolonged and chronic fatigue. *Journal of Health Psychology, 4,* 9–26.

Jason, L. A., Porter, N., Hunnell, J., & Brown, A., Rademaker, A., & Richman, J. A. (2011). A natural history study of Chronic Fatigue Syndrome. *Rehabilitation Psychology, 56,* 32–42.

Jeffrey, J. E. (2006). Chronic pain. In I. M. Lubkin & P. D. Larsen (Eds.), *Chronic illness: Impact and interventions* (6th ed., pp. 67–104). Sudbury, MA: Jones and Bartlett.

Johnson, D. L. (1993). Grieving is the pits. In G. H. S. Singer & L. E. Powers (Eds.), *Families, disability, and empowerment: Active coping skills and strategies for family interventions* (pp. 151–154). Baltimore, MD: Paul H. Brookes.

Johnson, H. B. (March/April 2005). Too late to die young. *American Association of Retired Persons Bulletin, 44,* 46 & 99.

Johnson, H. M. (2003, February 16). Should I have been killed at birth? The case for my life. *The New York Times Magazine, 50,* 52–56, 74.

Johnson, S. K. (2008). *Medically unexplained illness: Gender and biopsychosocial implications.* Washington, DC: American Psychological Association.

Jones, E. (1957). *The life and work of Sigmund Freud* (Vol. 3). New York: Basic Books.

Jones, M., Stanford, J., & Bell, R. B. (1997). Disability demographics. How are they changing? *Team Rehab Report, 38,* 36–44.

Jorde, D. (2010). *Eight fingers and eight toes.* Salt Lake City, UT: Author.

Joseph P. Kennedy, Jr. Foundation. (1991). *Facts about mental retardation.* Washington, DC: Author.

Joshi, S., & Kotecha, S. (2007). Lung growth and development. *Early Human Development, 83,* 789–794.

Judd, F. K., Stone, J., Webber, J. E., Brown, D. J., & Burrows, G. D. (1989). Depression following spinal cord injury: A prospective in-patient study. *British Journal of Psychiatry, 154,* 668–671.

Judson, L. (2004). Global childhood chronic illness. *Nursing Administration Quarterly, 28,* 60–61.

Juengst, E. T. (2005). Can aging be interpreted as a healthy, positive process? In M. Wykle, P. J. Whitehouse, & D. L. Morris (Eds.), *Successful aging throughout the lifespan* (pp. 3–18). New York: Springer.

Jungers, C. M. (2010). Leaving home: An examination of late-life relocation among older adults. *Journal of Counseling and Development, 88,* 416–423.

Kagan, J. (1986). Presuppositions in developmental inquiry. In L. Cirillo & S. Wapner (Eds.), *Value presuppositions in theories of human development* (pp. 63–88). Hillsdale, NJ: Lawrence Erlbaum.

Kanner, L. (1943). Autistic disturbances of affective contact. *Nervous Child, 2,* 217–250.

Kanner, L. (1949). Problems of nosology and psychodynamics of early infantile autism. *American Journal of Orthopsychiatry, 19,* 416–426.

Karp, D. A. (2001). *The burden of sympathy: How families cope with mental illness.* Oxford, UK: Oxford University.

Katznelson, I. (2005). *When affirmative action was white.* New York: W. W. Norton.

Kaye, J., & Raghavan, S. K. (2002). Spirituality in disability and illness. *Journal of Religion and Health, 41,* 231–242.

Keeter, S., & Taylor, P. (2009, December 11). The millennials. Washington, DC: Pew Research Center.

Keller, H. (1990). *The story of my life.* New York: Bantam.

Keller, M. (2006). The development of obligations and responsibilities in cultural context. In L. Smith & J. Voneche (Eds.), *Norms in human development* (pp. 168–188). Cambridge, UK: Cambridge University.

Keller, M., Edelstein, W., Krettenauer, T., Fang, F., & Fang, S. (2005). Reasoning about moral obligations and interpersonal responsibilities in different cultural contexts. In W. Edelstein & G. Nunner-Winkler (Eds.), *Morality in context* (pp. 317–340). Advances in Psychology, 137. Amsterdam: Elsevier.

Kelly, T. E. (1996). The role of genetic mechanisms in childhood disabilities. In R. Haslam, A. Haslam, & P. J. Valletutti (Eds.), *Medical problems in the classroom. The teacher's role in diagnosis and management* (3rd ed., pp. 125–159). Austin, TX: PRO-ED.

Kerckhoff, A. C. (1993). *Diverging pathways: Social structure and career deflections.* New York/ London: Cambridge University.

Kerckhoff, A. C. (1995). Building conceptual and empirical bridges between studies of education and labor force careers. In A. C. Kerckhoff (Ed.), *Generating social stratification: Toward a new research agenda* (pp. 37–56). Boulder, CO: Westview.

Kiesler, D. J. (1999). *Beyond the disease model of mental disorders.* Westport, CT: Praeger.

Kiger, G. (1992). Disability simulations: Logical, methodological, and ethical issues. *Disability, Handicap, & Society, 7,* 71–78.

King, L. A., Scollon, C. K., Ramsey, C., & Williams, T. (2000). Stories of life transition: Subjective well being and ego development in parents of children with Down syndrome. *Journal of Research in Personality, 34,* 509–536.

Kisor, H. (1990). *What's that pig outdoors? A memoir of deafness.* New York: Hill and Wang.

Kleege, G. (2006). *Blind rage: Letters to Helen Keller.* Washington, DC: Gallaudet University.

Klein, N. K., & Safford, P. L. (2001). Application of Piaget's theory to the study of thinking of the mentally retarded: A review of research. *The Journal of Special Education, 11*(2), 201–216.

Klemm, D., & Schimanski, C. (1999). Parent to parent: The crucial connection. *Exceptional Parent, 29*(9), 109–112.

Klobas, L. (1988). *Disability drama in television and film.* Jefferson, NC: McFarlan.

Kneezel, T. T., & Emmons, R. A. (2006). Personality and spiritual development. In E. C. Rooehlkepartian, P. E. King, L. Wagener, & P. L. Benson (Eds.), *The handbook of spiritual development in childhood and adolescence* (pp. 266–278). Thousand Oaks, CA: Sage.

Knight, S. E. (1989). Sexual concerns of the physically disabled. In B. W. Heller, L. M. Flohr, & L. S. Zegans (Eds.), *Psychosocial interventions with physically disabled persons* (pp. 183–199). New Brunswick, NJ: Rutgers University.

Kohlberg, L. (1973). Continuities in childhood and adult moral development revisited. In P. Baltes & K. W. Schaie (Eds.), *Lifespan developmental psychology: Personality and socialization* (pp. 180–204). New York: Academic.

Kohlberg, L. (1976). Moral stages and moralization: The cognitive-development approach. In T. Likona (Ed.), *Moral development and behavior: Theory, research, and social issues* (pp. 31–53). New York: Holt, Rinehart, & Winston.

Kohlberg, L. (1981). *Essays on moral development.* San Francisco: Harper & Row.

Kohlberg, L. (1984). *The psychology of moral development: The nature and validity of moral stages.* San Francisco: Harper & Row.

Kohlberg, L. (1987). *Child psychology and childhood education: A cognitive developmental view.* New York: Longman.

Kohlberg, L., & Gilligan, C. (1971, Fall). The adolescent as a philosopher: The discovery of self in a postconventional world. *Daedalus,* 1051–1086.

Kohler, K., Schweikert-Stary, T., & Lubkin, I. (1998). Altered mobility. In I. M. Lubkin & P. D. Larsen (Eds.), *Chronic illness: Impact and interventions* (4th ed., pp. 122–148). Sudbury, MA: Jones & Bartlett.

Konigsberg, R. D. (2011). *The truth about grief.* New York: Simon & Schuster.

Kopriva, P., & Taylor, J. R. (1993). Cerebral palsy. In M. G. Brodwin, F. Tellez, & S. K. Brodwin (Eds.), *Medical, psychosocial, and vocational aspects of disability* (pp. 519–536). Athens, GA: Elliott & Fitzpatrick.

Kosciulek, J. F., & Lustig, D. C. (1998). Predicting family adaptation from brain injury-related family stress. *Journal of Applied Rehabilitation, 29*(1), 8–12.

Kozloff, R. (1987). Networks of social supports and the outcome from severe head injury. *Journal of Head Trauma Rehabilitation, 2,* 14–23.

Krapfl, J. E. (1983). Traumatic injury in midlife. In E. J. Callahan & K. A. McCluskey (Eds.), *Life-span developmental psychology: Nonnormative life events* (pp. 265–280). New York: Academic Press.

Krause, J. S. (1992). Adjustments to life after spinal cord injury: A comparison among three participant groups based on employment status. *Rehabilitation Counseling Bulletin, 35,* 218–229.

Krause, J. S. (1997). Adjustment after spinal cord injury: A nine-year longitudinal study (1985–1994). *Archives of Physical Medicine and Rehabilitation, 78,* 651–657.

Krause, J. S. (1998a). Changes in adjustment after spinal cord injury: A 20-year longitudinal study. *Rehabilitation Psychology, 43,* 41–55.

Krause, J. S. (1998b). Dimensions of subjective well-being after spinal cord injury: An empirical analysis by gender and race/ethnicity. *Archives of Physical Medicine and Rehabilitation, 79,* 900–909.

Krause, J. S., & Anson, C. A. (1997). Adjustment after spinal cord injury: Relationship to participation in employment or educational activities. *Rehabilitation Psychology, 42,* 31–46.

Krause, J. S., & Crewe, N. M. (1991). Chronologic age, time since injury, and time of measurement: Effect on adjustment after spinal cord injury. *Archives of Physical Medicine and Rehabilitation, 72,* 91–100.

Krause, J. S., Coker, J., Charlifue, S., & Whiteneck, G. G. (1999). Depression and subjective well being among 97 American Indians with spinal cord injury: A descriptive study. *Rehabilitation Psychology, 44,* 354–372.

Kriegel, L. (1953). *The long walk home.* New York: Appleton-Century.

Kriegel, L. (1982). Claiming the self: The cripple as American male. In M. G. Eisenberg, C. Griggins, & R. J. Duval (Eds.), *Disabled people as second-class citizens* (pp. 52–63). New York: Springer.

Kriegel, L. (1987). The cripple in literature. In A. Gartner & T. Joe (Eds.), *Images of the disabled, disabling images* (pp. 31–46). New York: Praeger.

Kriegel, L. (1997). Falling into life. In K. Fries (Ed.), *Staring back: The disability experience from the inside out* (pp. 37–50). New York: Plume.

Krumboltz, J. D., Mitchell, A., & Gelatt, H. G. (1975). Applications of social learning theory of career selection. *Focus on Guidance, 8,* 1–6.

Kübler-Ross, E. (1969). *On death and dying.* New York: Macmillan.

Kusmer, K. (2010, October 27). Indiana parents told to drop disabled kids at shelters. Indianapolis: Associated Press.

L'Abate, L. (Ed.). (1994). *Handbook of developmental family psychology and psychopathology.* New York: Wiley.

Laborit, E. (1998). *The Cry of the Gull.* Washington, DC: Gallaudet University.

Laborit, E. (2010). Selections from the *Cry of the Gull.* In L. J. Lennard (Ed.), *The Disability Studies Reader* (3rd ed., pp. 599–618). New York: Routledge.

Lambie, G. W., & Milsom, A. (2010). A narrative approach to supporting students diagnosed with learning disabilities. *Journal of Counseling and Development, 88,* 196–203.

Lamphear, B. (2005). Origins and evolutions of children's environmental health. *Environmental Health Perspectives, 113,* 24–40.

Lane, H. (1993). Cochlear implants: Their cultural and historical meaning. In J. V. Van Cleve (Ed.), *Deaf history unveiled: Interpretations from the new scholarship* (pp. 272–291). Washington, DC: Gallaudet University Press.

Landers, A. (1989, January 27). Alert the boneheads. Houston, TX: *Houston Chronicle.*

Landers, A. (2010, October 31). Looks can be deceiving. Salt Lake City, UT: *Salt Lake Tribune.*

Lane, H., Hoffmeister, R., & Bahan, B. (1996). *A journey into the deaf-world.* San Diego, CA: Dawn Sign Press.

Languis, M. & Wilcox, J. (2001). A life-span human development model of learning for early education. *Theory into Practice, 40,* 79–85.

LaPlante, M. P. (1991). *The demographics of disability.* In J. West (Ed.), *The Americans with Disabilities Act: From policy to practice* (pp. 55–80). New York: Milbank Memorial Fund.

LaPlante, M. P. (1993). State estimates of disability in America. *Disability Abstracts No. 3.* Washington, DC: National Institute on Disability and Rehabilitation Research.

LaPlante, M. P. (1996). Health conditions and impairments causing disability. *Disability Abstracts, No. 16.* Washington, DC: National Institute on Disability and Rehabilitation Research.

LaPlante, M. P. (1997). How many Americans have a disability: #5 [On-line]. *Disability Statistics Abstract.* San Francisco: University of California at San Francisco. Retrieved from http://www.dsc.ucsf.edu.

Larsen, P. D. (2006). Chronicity. In I. M. Lubkin & P. D. Larsen (Eds.), *Chronic illness: Impact and Interventions* (6th ed.). Sudbury, MA: Jones and Bartlett.

Laub, J. H., & Sampson, R. J. (2006). *Shared beginnings, divergent lives: Delinquent boys to age 70.* Cambridge, MA: Harvard University.

Lavaas, O. I. (1987). Behavioral treatment and normal education and intellectual functioning in young autistic children. *Journal of consulting and Clinical Psychology, 55*(1), 3–9.

Lawton, M. P. (1996). The aging family in a multigenerational perspective. In G. H. S. Singer, L. E. Powers, & A. L. Olson (Eds.), *Redefining family support: Innovations in public private partnerships.* (pp. 135–149). Baltimore, MD: Paul H. Brookes.

Lee, A. (1948). *My soul more bent.* Minneapolis, MN: Augsburg College.

Leete, E. (1991). The stigmatized patient. In P. J. Fink & A. Tasman (Eds.), *Stigma and mental illness* (pp. 17–25). Washington, DC: American Psychiatric Association Press.

Lefley, H. P. (1991). The stigmatized family. In P. J. Fink & A. Tasman (Eds.), *Stigma and mental illness* (pp. 127–138). Washington, DC: American Psychiatric Association Press.

Lehman, H. C. (1962). The creative production rates of present versus past generations of scientists. *Journal of Gerontology, 17,* 409–417.

Lehman, H. C. (1966). The psychologist's most creative years. *American Psychologist, 21,* 363–369.

Lehr, D. H. & Brown, F. (1996). *People with disabilities who challenge the system.* Baltimore, MD: Paul H. Brookes.

Leifheit-Limson, E., & Levy, B. (2009). Ageism/age discrimination. In D. Carr (Ed.), *Encyclopedia of the life course and human development, Vol. 3: Later life* (pp. 20–23). Detroit, MI: Gale Cengage Learning.

Leinhardt, G., & Pallay, A. (1982). Restrictive educational settings: Exile or haven. *Review of Educational Research, 52,* 557–558.

Leininger, M., Dyches, T. T., Prater, M. A., & Health, M. A. (2010). Newbery Award winning books 1975–2009: How do they portray disabilities? *Education and Training in Autism and Developmental Disorders, 45,* 583–596.

Leisering, L. (2004). Government in the life course. In J. T. Mortimer & M. J. Shanahan (Eds.), *Handbook of the life course* (pp. 205–225). New York: Springer.

Lerner, R. M., & Jovanovic, J. (1990). The role of body image in psychosocial adjustment across the lifespan: A developmental contextual perspective. In T. F. Cash & T. Pruzinsky (Eds.), *Body images, development, deviance, and change* (pp. 110–127). New York: Guilford.

Lerner, R. M., Schwartz, S. J., & Phelps, E. (2009). Problematics of time and timing in the longitudinal study of human development: Theoretical and methodological issues. *Human Development, 52,* 44–68.

Levinson, D. (1986). A conception of adult development. *American Psychologist, 41,* 3–13.

Lewis, B. (2010). A mad fight: Psychiatry and disability activism. In L. J. Davis (Ed.), *The Disability Studies Reader* (3rd ed.). New York: Routledge.

Leytens, J. P., Paladino, P. M., Rodriguez-Torres, R., Vaes, J., Demoulin, S., Rodriguez-Torres, A., et al. (2000). The emotional side of prejudice: The attribution of secondary emotions to ingroups and outgroups. *Personality and Social Psychology Review, 4,* 186–197.

Li, S.C., Lindenberger, U., Hommel, B., Aschersleben, Prinz, W., & Baltes, P. B. (2004). Transformations in the couplings among intellectual abilities and constituent cognitive processes across the life span. *Psychological Science, 15,* 155–163.

Liachowitz, C. H. (1988). *Disability as a social construct: Legislative roots.* Philadelphia, PA: University of Pennsylvania.

Libby, R. T. (2006). Treating doctors as drug dealers: The Drug Enforcement Administration's war on prescription painkillers. *Independent Review, 10,* 511–545.

Lindenberg, R. E. (1980). Work with families in rehabilitation. In P. W. Power & A. E. Dell Orto (Eds.), *Role of the family in the rehabilitation of the physically disabled* (pp. 516–525). Austin, TX: Pro-Ed.

Lingerman, J. (2007). In A. Dell Orto & P. Power (Eds.), *The psychological and social impact of illness and disability* (6th ed., pp. 408–417). New York: Springer.

Linton, S. (1998). *Claiming disability: Knowledge and identity.* New York: New York University.

Liptak, G. S. (2007). Neural tube defects. In M. L. Batshaw, L. Pellegrino, & N. J. Roizen (Eds.), *Children with Disabilities* (6th ed., pp. 419–438). Baltimore, MD: Paul H. Brookes.

Living with Tourette Syndrome: (2011, March.) A Family Portrait. Retrieved from http://www.tsa-usa.org/LivingWith TS/Images

Livneh, H. (1991). On the origins of negative attitudes toward people with disabilities. In R. P. Marinelli & A. E. Dell Orto (Eds.), *The psychological and social impact of disability* (3rd ed., pp. 181–196). New York: Springer Publishing.

Livneh, H., & Antonak, R. F. (1997). *Psychosocial adaptation to chronic illness and disability.* Gaithersburg, MD: Aspen.

Livneh, H., & Cook, D. (2005). Psychosocial impact of disability. In R. M. Parker, E. M. Szymanski, & J. B. Patterson (Eds.), *Rehabilitation counseling: Basics and beyond.* (4th ed., pp. 187–224). Austin, TX: PRO-ED.

Longmore, P. K. (1985). Screening stereotypes. *Social Policy, 16,* 31–37.

Longmore, P. K. (2003). *Why I burned my book and other essays on disability.* Philadelphia: Temple University.

Love, B., Bryne, C., Roberts, J., Browne, G., & Brown, B. (1987). Adult psychosocial adjustment following childhood injury: The effect of disfigurement. *Journal of Burn Care and Rehabilitation, 8,* 280–285.

Lubkin, I. M., & Larsen, P. D. (Eds.). (1998). *Chronic illness: Impact and interventions* (4th ed.). Sudbury, MA: Jones and Bartlett.

Lubkin, I. M., & Larsen, P. D. (Eds.). (2006). *Chronic illness: Impact and interventions.* (6th ed.). Sudbury, MA: Jones and Bartlett.

Luria, A. R. (1976). *Cognitive development: Its cultural and social foundations.* Cambridge, MA: Harvard University.

Luria, A. R. (1981). *Language and cognition.* New York: Wiley.

Lynch, R. T., & Thomas, K. R. (1994). People with disabilities as victims: changing an ill-advised paradigm. *Journal of Rehabilitation, 69*(1), 8–11.

Macgregor, F. C. (1951). Some psycho-social problems associated with facial deformities. *American Social Review, 16,* 629–638.

Macgregor, F. C., Abel, J. M., Bryt, A., Laver, E., & Weissmann, S. (1953). *Facial deformities and plastic surgery: A psychosocial study.* Springfield, IL: Charles C. Thomas.

Mackelprang, R., & Salsgiver, R. (1999). *Disability: A diversity model approach in human service practice.* Pacific Grove, CA: Brooks/Cole.

Macmillan, M. (1997). *Freud evaluated.* London: MIT Press.

Maddi, S. R. (1996). *Personality theories* (6th ed.). Pacific Grove, CA: Brooks/Cole.

Magee, B., & Milligan, M. (1995). *On blindness.* Oxford, UK: Oxford University.

Magnusson, D., & Torestad, B. (1992). The individual as an interactive agent in the environment. In W. B. Walsh, R. H. Price, & K. H. Craik (Eds.), *Person-environmental psychology: Models and perspectives* (pp. 95–124). Norwood, NJ: Ablex.

Mairs, N. (1997). Carnal acts. In K. Fries (Ed.), *Staring back: The disability experience from the inside out.* New York: Plume.

Malec, J. F., & Ponsford, J. L. (2000). Postacute brain injury. In R. G. Frank & T. R. Elliot (Eds.), *Handbook of rehabilitation psychology* (pp. 417–439). Washington, DC: American Psychological Association.

Mangeot, S., Armstrong, K., Colvin, A., Yeates, K., & Taylor, H. (2002). Long-term executive function deficits in children with traumatic brain injuries: Assessment using the behavior rating inventory of executive function (BRIEF). *Child neuropsychology, 8*(4), 271. Retrieved from Academic Search Premier database.

Mann, R. J., & Stuenkel, D. (2006). Stigma. In I. M. Lubkin & P. D. Larsen (Eds.), *Chronic illness: Impact and interventions* (6th ed., pp. 45–66). Sudbury, MA: Jones and Bartlett.

Mannion, E. (1996). Resilience and burden in spouses with mental illness. *Psychiatric Rehabilitation Journal, 20,* 13–24.

Maples, M. F., & Abney, P. C. (2006). Baby boomers mature and gerontological counseling comes of age. *Journal of Counseling and Development, 84,* 3–9.

Marantz, P. R. (1990). Blaming the victim: The negative consequences of preventive medicine. *American Journal of Public Health, 80,* 1185–1187.

Marcia, J. (2004). Why Erikson? In K. Hoover (Ed.), *The future of identity: Centennial reflections on the legacy of Erik Erikson* (pp. 43–59). New York: Lexington Books.

Marcia, J. E. (2002). Identity and psychosocial development in adulthood. *Identity, 2,* 7–8.

Margrett, J. A., & Deshpande-Kamat, N. (2009). Cognitive functioning and decline. In D. Carr (Ed.), *Encyclopedia of the life course and human development, Vol. 3: Later life* (pp. 77–82). Detroit, MI: Gale Cengage Learning.

Marks, D. (1999). *Disability: Controversial debates and psychosocial perspectives.* London: Routledge.

Marlow, N., Hennessy, E. M., Bracewell, M. A., Wolke, D., & The EPICure Study Group. (2007). Motor and executive function at 6 years of age and older after extremely preterm birth. *Pediatrics, 120,* 793–804.

Marrero, D. G., & Guare, J. C. (2005). Diabetes mellitus. In H. H. Zarestksy, E. F. Richter, & M. G. Eisenberg (Eds.), *Medical aspects of disability: A handbook for the rehabilitation professional* (3rd ed., pp. 241–265). New York: Springer.

Marsh, D. T. (1992). *Families and mental illness: New directions in professional practice.* Westport, CT: Praeger.

Marsh, D. T., & Lefly, H. P. (1996). The family experience of mental illness: Evidence for resilience. *Psychiatric Rehabilitation, 20*(2), 3–13.

Martin, L. (2000). *From our house.* New York: Dutton.

Martinelli, R. P., & Dell Orto, A. E. (1991). *The psychological and social impact of disability* (3rd ed.). New York: Springer.

Maslow, A. H. (1968). *Toward a psychology of being* (2nd ed.). Princeton, NJ: Van Nostrand.

Maslow, A. H. (1970). *Motivation and personality* (2nd ed.). New York: Harper.

Maslow, A. H. (1971). *The further reaches of human nature.* New York: Viking.

Mason, M. (1992). Internalized oppression. In R. Reiser and M. Mason (Eds.), *Disability Equality in the Classroom: A Human Rights Issues.* London: Disability Equality in Education.

Mast, B. T., & Healy, P. J. (2009). Dementias. In D. Carr (Ed.), *Encyclopedia of the life course and human development, Vol. 3: Later life* (pp. 107–111). Detroit, MI: Gale Cengage Learning.

Mavoa, H. (1999). Tongan children with asthma in New Zealand. *Pacific Health Dialog, 6,* 236–239.

May, G. E. (2005). Changing the future of disability: The disability discrimination model. In G. E. May & M. B. Raske (Eds.), *Ending discrimination in social work: Strategies for social workers* (pp. 82–98). Boston: Allyn & Bacon.

Mayer, K. U. (1988). German survivors of World War II: The impact on the life course of the collective experience of birth cohorts. In M. W. Riley (Ed.), *Social structures and human lives* (pp. 211–228.) Newbury Park, CA: Sage.

Mayer, K. U., & Schoepflin, U. (1989). The state and the life course. *Annual Review of Sociology, 15,* 187–209.

McAdams, D. P., de St. Aubin, E., & Logan, R. L. (1993). Generativity among young, midlife, and older adults. *Psychology and Aging, 8,* 221–230.

McCarthy, H. (1993). Learning with Beatrice A. Wright: A breath of fresh air that uncovers the unique virtues and human flaws in us all. *Rehabilitation Education, 10,* 149–166.

McCarthy, H. (2003). The disability rights movement: Experiences and perspectives of selected leaders in the disability community. *Rehabilitation Counseling Bulletin, 46,* 209–223.

McCarthy, M. (1999). Consent, abuse, and choices: Women with intellectual disabilities and sexuality. In R. Traustadottir & K. Johnson (Eds.), *Women with intellectual disabilities: Finding a place in the world.* London/Philadelphia: Jessica Kingsley Publishers.

McEachin, J., Smith, T., & Lovaas, O. I. (1993). Long-term outcome for children with autism who received early intensive behavioral treatment. *American Journal on Mental Retardation, 97*(4), 359–372.

McFarlane, J., Hughes, R. B., Nosek, M. A., Groff, J. Y., Swedlend, N., & Mullen, P. D. (2001). Abuse Assessment Screen-Disability (AAS-D): Measuring frequency, type, and perpetrator of abuse toward women with physical disabilities. *Journal of Women's Health & Gender-Based Medicine, 10,* 861–866.

McLeod, J. D., & Almazan, E. P. (2004). Connections between childhood and adulthood. In J. T. Mortimer& M. J. Shanahan (Ed.), *Handbook of the life course* (pp. 391–411). New York: Springer.

McMahon, B. T., Shaw, L. R., & Jaet, D. N. (1995). An empirical analysis: Employment and disability from an ADA litigation perspective. *NARPPS Journal and News, 10*(1), 3–14.

McNulty, M. A. (2003). Dyslexia and the life course. *Journal of Learning Disabilities, 36,* 363–381.

McPhee, N. (1982, June). A very special magic: A grandparent's delight. *Exceptional Parent, 20,* 13–16.

Mee, C. L. (1999). *A nearly normal life.* Boston: Little-Brown.

Mellor, M. J., & Rehr, H. (Eds.). (2005). *Baby boomers: Can my eighties be like my fifties?* New York: Springer.

Mettler, S. (2005). *Soldiers to citizen: The G.I. Bill and the making of the greatest generation.* New York: Oxford University.

Meyer, D. (2005). *The sibling slam book.* Bethesda, MD: Woodbine.

Meyer, G. A. (2001). Genetic syndromes. In M. L. Batshaw (Ed.), *When your child has a disability.* Baltimore, MD: Paul H. Brookes.

Michalegko, P. M. (1993). A sibling born without disabilities: A special kind of challenge. In S. D. Klein and M. J. Schleifer (Eds.), *It isn't free!* (pp. 51–54). Westport, CT: Bergin & Garvey.

Michalko, R. (2002). *The difference disability makes.* Philadelphia: Temple University.

Milevsky, A., & Leh, M. (2008). Religiosity in emerging adulthood: Familial variables and adjustment. *Journal of Adult Development, 15,* 47–53.

Milevsky, A., & Levitt, M. J. (2004). Intrinsic and extrinsic religiously in preadolescence and adolescence: Effect on psychological well-being. *Mental Health, Religion, and Culture, 7,* 307–321.

Miller, J. (1988). Personal statement: Mechanisms for coping with the disability of a child—A mother's perspective. In P. W. Power, A. E. Dell Orto, & M. B. Gibbons (Eds.), *Family interventions throughout chronic illness and disability* (pp. 136–147). New York: Springer.

Miller, M. M., & Menacker, S. J. (2007). Vision: Our window to the world. In M. L. Batshaw, L. Pellegrino, & N. J. Roizen (Eds.), *Children with disabilities* (pp. 137–156). Baltimore, MD: Paul H. Brookes.

Miller, S., & Morgan, M. (1980). Marriage matters: For people with disabilities, too. *Sexuality and Disability, 3,* 203–211.

Mirzoeff, N. (1997). Blindness and art. In L. J. Davis (Ed.), *The disability studies reader* (pp. 382–398). New York: Routledge.

Mishel, M. (1993). Reconceptualization of the uncertainty in illness theory. *Image: The Journal of Nursing Scholarship, 22*(45), 256–262.

Mitchell, D., & Snyder, S. (2010). Narrative prosthesis. In L. J. Davis (Ed.), *The disability studies reader* (3rd ed., pp. 274–287). New York: Routledge.

Mitsos, S. B. (1972). The grieving process of parents with atypical children. *Journal of Rehabilitation, 38*(2), 5–7.

Modell, J. (1989). *Into one's own. From youth to adulthood in the United States 1920–1975.* Berkeley: University of California.

Moen, P. (1996). Gender, age, and the lifecourse. In R. H. Binstock & L. K. George (Eds.), *Handbook of aging and the social sciences* (pp. 171–187). San Diego: Academic Press.

Moen, P. (1998). Recasting careers: Changing reference groups, risks, and realities. *Generations, 22*(1), 40–45.

Moen, P. (2004). Midcourse: Navigating retirement as a new life stage. In J. T. Mortimer, & M. J. Shanahan (Eds.), *Handbook of the life course* (pp. 269–291). New York: Springer.

Moore, D. F. (1987). *Educating the D/deaf: Psychology, principles, and practices* (3rd ed.). Boston: Houghton Mifflin.

Moreno, S., Neiner, M. A., & O'Neal, C. (2010, December). Considerations in teaching more advanced students with Autism, Asperger Syndrome and other Pervasive Developmental Disorders. *The Utah Special Educator, 33* (2), 12–15.

Morris, D. B. (1998). *Illness and culture in the postmodern age.* Berkeley: University of California.

Morris, J. (1991). *Pride against prejudice: Transforming attitudes towards disability.* Philadelphia: New Society

Morris, R. J., Morris, V. P., & White, P. A. B. (2005). Developmental disabilities. In H. H. Zarestsky, E. F. Richter, and M. G. Eisenberg (Eds.), *Medical aspects of disability: A handbook for the rehabilitation professional* (3rd ed., pp. 343–382). New York: Springer.

Morrison, F. J., Lord, C., & Keating, D. P. (Eds.). (1984). *Applied developmental psychology.* New York: Academic.

Mortimer, J. T., & Shanahan, M. J. (Eds.). (2004). *Handbook of the life course.* New York: Springer.

Mottern, R. (2008). Choice theory as a model of adult development. *International Journal of Reality Therapy, 27*(2), 35–39.

Mueller, A. S. (2009). Body image, childhood, and adolescence. In D. Carr (Ed.), *Encyclopedia of the life course and human development* (Vol. 1, pp. 58–62). New York: Macmillan.

Mukulincer, M., & Florian, V. (1998). The relationship between adult attachment styles and emotional and cognitive reactions to stressful situations. In J. A. Simpson & W. S. Rholes (Eds.), *Attachment theory and close relationships* (pp. 143–165). New York: Guilford.

Munkata, Y. (2006). Information processing: Approaches to development. In W. Damon & R. Lerner (Eds.), *Handbook of educational psychology.* New York: Wiley.

Murphy, C., & Barnes-Holmes, D. (2009). Establishing derived manding for specific amounts with three children: An attempt at synthesizing Skinner's verbal behavior with relational frame theory. *The Psychological Record, 59,* 75–92.

Murphy, R. F. (1987). *The body silent: An anthropologist embarks on the most challenging journey of his life: Into the world of the disabled.* New York: W. W. Norton.

Mutchler, J. E., & Burr, J. (2009). Boomer diversity and well-being: Race, ethnicity, and gender. In R. B. Hudson (Ed.), *Boomer bust? Economic and political issues of the graying society* (pp. 23–45). Westport, CT: Praeger.

Nagi, S. Z. (1991). Disability concepts revisited: Implications for prevention. In Institute of Medicine (Ed.), *Disability in America: Toward a national agenda for prevention* (pp. 309–327). Washington, DC: National Academy Press.

National Organization on Disability (2004, June 24). Press Release. "Landmark survey finds pervasive disadvantages." Washington, DC: Author.

National Public Radio. (1998a, May). *Disability history project. Inventing the poster child.* Retrieved from http://iris.npr.org/programs/disability/ba_shows.dir/work.dir/

National Public Radio (1998b, May). *Disability history project. The Overdue Revolution.*

National Public Radio. (1998c, May). *Disability history project. Tomorrow's children.* Retrieved from http://iris.npr.org/programs/disability/ba_shows.dir/work.dir/

National Public Radio. (1998d, May). *Disability history project. What's work got to do with it?* Retrieved from http://iris.npr.org/programs/disability/ba_shows.dir/work.dir/

National Research Council. (1996). *Understanding violence against women.* Washington, DC: National Academy Press.

Naugle, R. I. (1991). Denial in rehabilitation: Its genesis, consequences, and clinical management. In R. P. Marinelli & A. E. Dell Otto (Eds.), *The psychological and social impact of disability* (3rd ed., pp. 139–151). New York: Springer.

Navarro, M. (2007, May 17). Clearly, frankly, unabashedly disabled. *New York Times.*

Neergaard, L. (2009, October 5). Report: One in 10 babies worldwide born premature. *The Salt Lake Tribune,* pp. A6, A10.

Neill, C. M., & Kahn, A. S. (1999). The role of spirituality and religious social activity on the life satisfaction of older widowed women. *Sex Roles, 40,* 319–329.

Neugarten, B. L. (1968). Adult personality: Toward a psychology of the life science. In B. J. Neugarten (Ed.) *Middle age and aging. A reader in social psychology* (pp. 137–147). Chicago: University of Chicago Press.

Neugarten, B. L. (1986). The aging society. In A. Pifer & L. Bronte (Eds.), *Our aging society: Paradox and promise.* New York: W. W. Norton.

Neugarten, B. L., & Hagestad, G. O. (1976). Age and the life course. In R. Binstock, & E. Shanas, (Eds.), *Handbook of aging and the social sciences.* New York: Van Nostrand Reinhold.

Neumann, R. J. (1988). Personal statement: Experiencing sexuality as an adolescent with rheumatoid arthritis. In P. W. Power, A. E. Dell Orto, & M. B. Gibbons (Eds.), *Family interventions throughout chronic illness and disability* (pp. 156–163). New York: Springer.

Newman, B. M., & Newman, P. R. (2009). *Development through life: A psychosocial approach.* (10th ed.). Belmont, CA: Wadsworth.

New York Times (2007, July 17). Chronic Fatigue gaining respect as serious syndrome. Retrieved from http:www.nytimes.com/2007/02/17/science/17fatigue.html.

Ng, T. W. H., Sorensen, K. L., & Eby, L. T. (2006). Locus of control at work: A meta-analysis. *Journal of Organizational Behavior, 27,* 1057–1087.

Nielsen, K. E. (2006). Was Helen Keller deaf? Blindness, deafness, and multiple identities. In B. J. Brueggemann, & S. Burch (Eds.), *Women and deafness: Double visions* (pp. 21–39). Washington, DC: Gallaudet University.

Nixon, C. D. (1993). Reducing self-blame and guilt in parents of children with severe disabilities. In G. H. S. Singer & L. E. Powers (Eds.), *Families, disability, and empowerment: Active coping skills and strategies for family interventions* (pp. 175–201). Baltimore, MD: Paul H. Brookes.

Norden, M. F. (1994). *The cinema of isolation: A history of disabilities in the movies.* New Brunswick, NJ: Rutgers University.

Nordqvist, I. (1980). Sexual counseling for disabled persons. *Sexuality and Disability, 3,* 193–198.

O'Brien, M. T. (1993). Multiple sclerosis: Stressors and coping strategies in spousal caregivers. *Journal of Community Health Nursing, 10,* 123–135.

Ochse, R., & Plug, C. (1986). Cross cultural investigation of the validity of Erikson's theory of personality development. *Journal of Personality and Social Psychology, 50,* 1240–1252.

Oeppen, J., & Vaupel, J. W. (2002). Demography: Broken limits to life expectancy. *Science, 296,* 1029–1031.

O'Keeffe, J. (1994). Disability, discrimination, and the Americans with Disabilities Act. In S. M. Bruyere & J. O'Keeffe (Eds.), *Implications of the Americans with Disabilities Act for psychology* (pp. 1–14). Washington, DC: American Psychological Association [co-published with Springer Publishing, New York].

Oliver, M. (1996). *Understanding disability: From theory to practice.* London: Macmillan.

Olkin, R. (1999). *What psychotherapists should know about disability.* New York: Guilford.

O'Neill, G. (2009). The Baby Boom age wave: Population success or tsunami? In R. B. Hudson (Ed.), *Boomer bust? Economic and political issues of the graying society* (pp. 3–22). Westport, CT: Praeger.

O'Rahilly, R., & Tanner, J.M. (Eds.). (1987). Human growth during the embryonic period proper. In F. Falkner, & J. M. Tanner (Eds.). Human growth: A comprehensive treatise (2nd ed.). (pp. 245–252). New York: Plenum.

Orrin, D. (1997). Past the struggles of mental illness, toward the development of quality lives. In L. Spanoil, C. Gagne, & M. Hoehler (Eds.), *Psychological and social aspects of psychiatric disability* (pp. 138–144). Boston: Center for Psychiatric Rehabilitation, Boston University.

Oser, F., & Reichenbach, R. (2005). Moral resilience—the unhappy moralist. In W. Edelstein & G. Nunner-Winkler (Eds.), *Morality in context* (pp. 203–224). *Advances in Psychology,* 137. Amsterdam: Elsevier.

Oshinsky, D. M. (2005). *Polio: An American story.* Oxford, UK: Oxford University.

Paris, J. (2000). *Myths of childhood.* Philadelphia, PA: Taylor & Francis.

Parisi, T. (1987). Why Freud failed: Some implications for neurophysiology and sociobiology. *American Psychologist, 42,* 235–242.

Papalia, D. E. & Olds, S. W. (1992). *Human development* (5th ed.). New York: McGraw-Hill.

Paquette, D., & Ryan, J. (2001). *Bronfenbrenner's Ecological Systems Theory.* Retrieved from http://pt3.nl.edu/paquetteryanwebquest.pdf

Passel, J. S., Wang, W., & Taylor, P. (2010, June 4). *Marrying out: One in seven new U.S. marriages is interracial or interethnic.* Washington, DC: Pew Research Center Publications.

Patterson, D. R., Everett, J. J., Bombardier, C. H., Questad, K. A., Lee, V. K., & Marvin, J. A. (1993). Psychological effects of severe burn injuries. *Psychological Bulletin, 113,* 362–368.

Patterson, J. M. (1988). Chronic illness in children and the impact upon families. In C. S. Chilman, E. W. Nunnally, & F. M. Cox (Eds.), *Chronic illness and disability* (pp. 69–107). Beverly Hills, CA: Sage.

Pavalko, E. K., & Elder, G. H. Jr. (1990). World War II and divorce: A life course perspective. *American Journal of Sociology, 95,* 1213–1234.

Pearson, J. E., & Sternberg, A. (1986). A mutual project for families of handicapped children. *Journal of Counseling and Development, 65,* 213–216.

Peck, R. C. (1969). Psychological developments in the second half of life. In B. K. Neugarten (Ed.), *Middle age and aging.* Chicago: University of Chicago.

Pelka, F. (1997). *The ABC-CLIO companion to the disability rights movement.* Santa Barbara, CA: ABC-CLIO.

Pellegrino, L. (2007). Patterns in development and disability. In M. L. Batshaw, L. Pellegrino, & N. J. Roizen (Eds.), *Children with disabilities* (6th ed., pp. 217–228). Baltimore, MD: Paul H. Brookes.

Pelletier, L. (1988). Personal statement: The challenge of cerebral palsy: Familial adaptation and change. In P. W. Power, A. E. Dell Otto, & M. B. Gibbons (Eds.), *Family interventions throughout chronic illness and disability* (pp. 54–59). New York: Springer.

Pendergast, C. (2010). The unexceptional schizophrenic: A post-postmodern introduction. In L. J. Davis (Ed.), *The disability studies reader* (3rd ed., pp. 288–297). New York: Routledge.

Penn, A. (1993). Audrey Penn. In J. K. Smith & G. Plimpton (Ed.), *Chronicles of courage: Very special artists* (pp. 109–117). New York: Random House.

Perkins, R. (1996). *Talking to angels: A life spent in high latitudes.* Boston: Beacon.

Perlesz, A., Kinsella, G., & Crowe, S. (1999). Impact of traumatic brain injury on the family: A critical review. *Rehabilitation Psychology, 44,* 6–35.

Perrig-Chiello, P., & Perren, S. (2005). Biographical transitions from a midlife perspective. *Journal of Adult Development, 12,* 169–181.

Perrin, J. (2004). Chronic illness in childhood. In R. Behrman, R. Kleigman, & H. Jensen (Eds.), *Nelson textbook of pediatrics* (17th ed.). Philadelphia: Saunders.

Perrone, K. M., Gordon, P. A., & Tschopp, M. K. (2006). Caregiver marital satisfaction when a spouse has multiple sclerosis. *Journal of Applied Rehabilitation Counseling, 37,* 26–32.

Pervin, L. A., & John, O. P. (2001). *Personality: Theory and research* (8th ed.). New York: John Wiley.

Peterson, C., Maier, S. F., & Seligman, M. E. P. (1993). *Learned helplessness: A theory for the age of personal control.* New York: Oxford University.

Pew Research Center (2010, November 18). *The decline of marriage and rise of new families.* Washington, DC: Author.

Pfeiffer, D. (2005a). Changing the future of disability: The disability discrimination model. In G. E. May & M. S. Raske (Eds.), *Ending disability discrimination* (pp. 82–98). Boston: Allyn & Bacon.

Pfeiffer, D. (2005b). The conceptualization of disability. In G. E. May & M.B. Raske (Eds.), *Ending disability discrimination: Strategies for social workers.* (pp. 25–44). Boston: Pearson.

Phillips, M. J. (1990). Damaged goods: Oral narratives of the experience of disability in American culture. *Social Science Medicine, 30,* 849–857.

Phillips, M. J. (1992). "Try harder": The experience of disability and the dilemma of normalization. In P. M. Ferguson, D. L. Ferguson, & S. J. Taylor (Eds.), *Interpreting disability: A qualitative reader* (pp. 213–227). New York: Columbia University.

Piaget, J. (1952). *The language and thought of the child.* London: Routledge.

Piaget, J. (1954). *The construction of reality in the child.* New York: Basic Books.

Piaget, J. (1962). *Play, dreams, and imitation in childhood.* New York: Norton.

Piaget, J. (1965). *The moral judgment of the child.* New York: Free Press.

Pickar, D., & Tori, C. (1986). The learning disabled adolescent: Eriksonian psychosocial development, self-concept, and delinquent behavior. *Journal of Youth and Adolescence, 15,* 429–440.

Pimpare, S. (2009). The failures of American poverty measures. *Journal of Sociology and Social Welfare, 36,* 103–122.

Plutchik, R. (1980). A general psycho evolutionary theory of emotion. In R. Plutchik & H. Kellerman (Eds.), *Theory, research, and experience* (pp. 3–33). New York: Academic.

Pollard, I. (2000). Substance abuse and parenthood: biological mechanisms—bioethical challenges. *Women and Health, 30,* 1–24.

Power, P. W., & Dell Orto, A. E. (1980). Approaches to family interventions. In P. W. Power & A. E. Dell Orto (Eds.), *Role of the family in the rehabilitation of the physically disabled* (pp. 321–330). Austin, TX: Pro-Ed.

Power, P. W., & Rogers, S. (1979). Group counseling for multiple sclerosis patients: A preferred mode of treatment for unique adaptive problems. In R. G. Lasky & A. E. Dell Orto (Eds.), *Group counseling and physical disabilities* (pp. 115–127). North Scituate, MA: Duxbury.

Powers, L. E. (1993). Disability and grief: From tragedy to challenge. In G. H. S. Singer & L. E. Powers (Eds.), *Families, disability, and empowerment: Active coping skills and strategies for family interventions* (pp. 119–149). Baltimore, MD: Paul H. Brookes.

Powers, L. E., Curry, M. A., Oschwalk, M., Maley, S., Saxton, M., & Eckels, K. (2002). Barriers and strategies in addressing abuse: Survey of disabled women's experiences. *Journal of Rehabilitation, 68,* 4–13.

Preston, P. (1994). *Mother father deaf: Living between sound and silence.* Cambridge, MA: Harvard University.

Price, R. (1994). *A whole new life: An illness and a healing.* New York: Atheneum.

Princeton Religion Research Center. (1994). *Religion in America.* Princeton, NJ: Gallup Poll.

Pruzinsky, T. (1990). Psychopathology of body experience: Expanded perspectives. In T. F. Cash & T. Pruzinsky (Eds.), *Body images: Development, deviance, and change* (pp. 170–189). New York: Guilford.

Pruzinsky, T., & Cash, T. F. (1990). Integrative themes in body-image development, deviance, and change. In T. F. Cash & T. Pruzinsky (Eds.), *Body images: Development, deviance, and change* (pp. 337–347). New York: Guilford.

Public Broadcasting Service (1999). *Paralyzing fear: The story of polio in America.* Retrieved August 2, 2007, from www.shoppbs.org

Pullin, G. (2009). *Disability meets design.* Cambridge, MA: Massachusetts Institute of Technology.

Putnam, M., Greenen, S., Powers, L., Saxton, M., Finney, S., & Dautel, P. (2003). Health and wellness: People with disabilities discuss barriers and facilitators to well being. *Journal of Rehabilitation, 69,* 37–45.

Putney, N. M. & Bengtson, V. L. (2004). Intergenerational relations in changing times. In J. T. Mortimer & M. J. Shanahan (Eds.), *Handbook of the life course.* New York: Springer.

Ragnarsson, K. T. (1995). Management of pain in persons with spinal cord injury. *The Journal of Spinal Cord Medicine, 20,* 186–199.

Rampal, A. (2003). Counting on everyday mathematics. In *Cross-cultural perspectives in human development: Theory, research, applications* (pp. 326–353). Thousand Oaks, CA: Sage.

Ree, J. (1999). *I see a voice: A philosophical history of language, deafness, and the senses.* New York: HarperCollins.

Reed, P. G. (1991). Toward a nursing theory of self-transcendence: Deductive reformulation using developmental theories. *Advances in Nursing Science, 13*(4), 64–77.

Reeve, C. (1998). *Still me.* New York: Random House.

Rehabilitation Act of 1973, 87 Stat. 355, 29 U.S.C. § *701 et seq.*

Reichart, D. C., Lynch, E. C., Anderson, B. C., Svobodny, L. A., DiCola, J. M., & Mercury, M. G. (1989). Parental perspectives on integrated preschool opportunities for children with handicaps and children without handicaps. *Journal of Early Intervention, 13,* 6–13.

Reid, D. (1988, August, September). Reflections on the pragmatics of a paradigm shift. *Journal of Learning Disabilities, 21,* 417–420.

Reid, D. (2004, December). Impact of the environment on role performance in older stroke survivors living at home. *International Journal of Therapy and Rehabilitation, 11,* 567–573.

Remley, T. R., & Herlihy, B. (2005). *Ethical, legal, and professional issues in counseling* (2nd ed.). Upper Saddle River, NJ: Prentice Hall.

Renninger, K. A., & Amsel, E. (Eds.). (1997). *Change and development: Issues of theory, method, and application.* Mahwah, NJ: Lawrence Erlbaum.

Resch, J. A., Mireles, G., Benz, M. R., Grenwelge, C., Peterson, R., & Zhang, D. (2010). Giving parents a voice: A qualitative study of the challenges experienced by children with disabilities, *Rehabilitation Psychology, 55,* 139–150.

Rice, F. P. (1998). *Human development: A life-span approach* (3rd ed.). Upper Saddle River, NJ: Prentice Hall.

Richards, J. S., Kewman, D. G., & Pierce, C. A. (2000). Spinal cord injury. In R. G. Frank & T. R. Elliot (Eds.), *Handbook of Rehabilitation Psychology* (pp. 11–27). Washington, DC: American Psychological Association.

Richardson, S. A., & Roland, L. (1977). The effect of a physically handicapped interviewer on children's expression of values toward handicap. *Rehabilitation Psychology, 24,* 111–128.

Riediger, M., & Ebner, N. C. (2007). A broader perspective on three lifespan theories: Comment on Boerner and Jopp. *Human Development, 50,* 196–200.

Riegel, K. F. (1975). Adult life crises: A dialectic interpretation of development. In N. Datun & L. H. Ginsberg (Eds.), *Lifetime developmental psychology: Normative life crises* (pp. 99–128). New York: Academic Press.

Rifkin, J. (1995). *The end of work.* New York: Putnam.

Rix, S. E. (2004, February). *Aging and work: A view from the United States* (AARP Public Policy Institute Paper No, 2004–02). Retrieved from http://assets.aarp.org/rgcenter

Rix, S. E. (2009). Will the Boomers revolutionize work and retirement? In R. B. Hudson (Ed.), *Boomer bust? Economic and political issues of the graying society* (pp. 77–93). Westport, CT: Praeger.

Robb, C., Chen, H., & Haley, W. E. (2002). Ageism in mental health and health care: A critical review. *Journal of Clinical Geropsychology, 8,* 1–12.

Roberts, B. W., & Caspi, A. (2003). The cumulative continuity model of personality development: Striking a balance between continuity and change in personality traits across the life course. In U. M. Staudiner & U. Lindenberger (Eds.), *Understanding human development: Dialogues with lifespan psychology* (pp. 183–214). Boston: Kluwer Academic.

Robinson, I. (1988). Managing symptoms in chronic disease: Some dimensions of patients' experience. *International Disability Studies, 10*(3), 112–119.

Robinson, M. (1997). Renascence. In K. Fries (Ed.), *Staring back: The disability experience from the inside out* (pp. 87–92). New York: Plume.

Rodger, S., & Tooth, L. (2004). Adult siblings' perceptions of family life and loss: A pilot case study. *Journal of Developmental and Physical Disabilities, 16,* 53–71.

Roe, A. (1956). *The psychology of occupations.* New York: Wiley.

Rogers, C. R. (1951). *Client-centered therapy: Its current practice, implications, and theory.* Boston: Houghton Mifflin.

Rogers, C. R. (1961). *On becoming a person.* Boston: Houghton Mifflin.

Rogers, C. R. (1980). *A way of being.* Boston: Houghton Mifflin.

Rolland, J. (1987). Chronic illness and the life cycle: A conceptual framework. *Family Process, 26,* 203–221.

Rolland, J. S. (1988). A conceptual model of chronic and life threatening illness and its impact on family. In C. S. Chilman, E. W. Nunnally, & F. M. Cox (Eds.), *Chronic illness and disability: Families in trouble* (pp. 17–68). Newbury Park, CA: Sage.

Rolland, J. S. (1994). *Families, illness, and disability: An integrative treatment model.* New York: Basic Books.

Rooehlkepartian, E. C., King, P. E., Wagener, L., & Benson, P. L. (Eds.). (2005). *The handbook of spiritual development in childhood and adolescence.* Thousand Oaks, CA: Sage.

Rosenfield, D. (2003). *The changing of the guard: Lesbian and gay elders, identity, and social change.* Philadelphia, PA: Temple University.

Rosenthal, B. P., & Cole, R. G. (2005). Visual impairments. In H. H. Zarestsky, E. F. Richter, & M. G. Eisenberg (Eds.), *Medical aspects of disability: A handbook for the rehabilitation professional* (3rd ed., pp. 611–647). New York: Springer.

Rosenthal, T., & Bandura, A. (1978). Psychological modeling: Theory and practice. In S. L. Garfield & A. E. Bergin (Eds.), *Handbook of psychotherapy and behavior change* (pp. 621–658). New York: Wiley.

Rossheim, B. N., & McAdams, C. R. III. (2010). Addressing the chronic sorrow of long-term spousal caregivers: A primer for counselors. *Journal of Counseling and Development, 88,* 477–482.

Rossi A, & Rossi, P. (1990). *Of human bonding: Parent-child relations across the life course.* New York: Aldine de Gruyter.

Rossi, P. (2003). Introduction to complex care. In P. Rossi (Ed.), *Case management in health care* (pp. 343–510). Philadelphia: Saunders.

Rossides, D. W. (1990). *Social stratification: The American class system in comparative perspective* (2nd ed.). Englewood Cliffs, NJ: Prentice-Hall.

Rousso, H. (1981). Disabled people are sexual, too. *The Exceptional Parent, 11,* 21–25.

Rousso, H. (1993). *Disabled, female and proud! Stories of ten women with disabilities.* Westport, CT: Bergin & Garvey.

Rowe, J., & Kahn, R. (1998). *Successful aging.* New York: Pantheon.

Rubin, D. C., Rahal, T. A., & Poon, L. W. (1998). Things learned in early adulthood are remembered best. *Memory and Cognition, 26,* 3–19.

Rustad, L. C. (1984). Family adjustment to chronic illness and disability in mid-life. In M. G. Eisenberg, L. C. Sutkin, & M. A. Jansen (Eds.), *Chronic illness and disability through the life span: Effects on self and the family* (pp. 222–242). New York: Springer.

Rutter, M., & English and Romanian Adoptees (ERA) Study Team. (1998). Developmental catch-up and deficit, following adoption after severe global early privation. *Journal of Child Psychology and Psychiatry, 39,* 465–476.

Rutter, M. L. (1989). Pathways from childhood to adult life. *Journal of Child Psychology and Psychiatry, 30,* 23–51.

Ryan, J. L., Ramsey, R. R., Fedele, D. A., Mullins, L. L., Chane, J. M., & Jarvis, J. N. (2010). A longitudinal examination of the parent-child distress relationship in children with Juvenile Rheumatic Disease. *Rehabilitation Psychology, 55,* 286–291.

Ryan, M. K., David, B., & Reynolds, K. J. (2004). Who cares? The effect of gender and context on the self and moral reasoning. *Psychology of Women Quarterly, 28,* 246–255.

Rybarczyk, B., Nyenhuis, D. L., Nicholas, J. J., Cash, S. M., & Kaiser, J. (1995). Body image, perceived social stigma, and the prediction of psychosocial adjustment to leg amputation. *Rehabilitation Psychology, 40,* 95–110.

Ryder, N. B. (1965). The cohort as a concept in the study of social change. *American Sociological Review, 30,* 843–861.

Safran, S. P. (1998). The first century of disability portrayal in film: An analysis of the literature. *Journal of Special Education, 31,* 467–479.

Sailor, W., Kleinhammer-Tramill, J., Skrtic, T., & Oas, B. K. (1996). Family participation in new community schools. In G. H. S. Singer, L. E. Powers, & A. L. Olson (Eds.), *Redefining family support: Innovations in public private partnerships* (pp. 313–332). Baltimore, MD: Paul H. Brookes.

Santelli, B., Turnbull, A. P., Lerner, E., & Marquis, J. (1993). Parent to parent programs: A unique form of mutual support for families of persons with disabilities. In G. H. S. Singer & L. E. Powers (Eds.), *Families, disabilities, and empowerment: Active coping skills and strategies for family interventions* (pp. 27–57). Baltimore, MD: Paul H. Brookes.

Santrock, J. W. (2009). *Life-span development* (12th ed.). Boston: McGraw-Hill.

Saraswathi, T. S. (Ed.). (2003). *Cross-cultural perspectives in human development: Theory, research, applications.* Thousand Oakes, CA: Sage.

Sautter, R. A., & LeBlanc, L. A. (2006). Empirical applications of Skinner's analysis of verbal behavior with humans. *Analysis of Verbal Behavior, 22,* 35–48.

Saxton, M. (2006). Disability rights and selective abortion. In L. J. L. Davis (Ed.), *The Disability Studies Reader* (2nd ed., pp.105–116). New York: Routledge.

Saxton, M., Curry, M. A., McNeff, E., Limont, M., Powers, L., & Benson, J. (2006). We're all little John Waynes: A study of disabled men's experience of abuse by personal assistants. *Journal of Rehabilitation, 72*(4), 3–13.

Scarr, S., & McCartney, K. (1983). How people make their own environments: A theory of genotype-environment effects. *Child Development, 54,* 424–435.

Scarr, S., Weinberg, R. A., & Levine, A. (1986). *Understanding Development.* Orlando, FL: Harcourt Brace Jovanovich.

Schafer, M. H. (2009). Parental death and subjective age: Indelible imprints from early in the life course. *Sociological Inquiry, 79,* 75–97.

Schaie, K. W. (2007). Generational differences: The age-cohort period model. In J. E. Birren (Ed.), *Encyclopedia of gerontology* (2nd ed.), Oxford, UK: Elsevier.

Scheer, J., & Groce, N. (1988). Impairment as human constraint: Cross cultural and historical perspectives on variation. *Journal of Social Issues, 44,* 23–37.

Scherer, M. J. (1993). *Living in the state of stuck: How technology impacts the lives of people with disabilities.* Cambridge, MA: Brookline.

Schlossberg, N. K. (1981). A model for analyzing human adaptation to transition. *The Counseling Psychologist, 9,* 2–18.

Schnorr, R. F. (1993). "Peter? He comes and goes...": First graders' perspective on a part-time mainstream student. In M. Nagler (Ed.). *Perspectives on disability* (2nd ed., pp. 423–435). Palo Alto, CA: Health Markets Research.

Scholar under fire for views on infanticide. (1999, October 2). *The Herald Journal, 2,* 4.

Schonert-Reichl, K. A., Offer, A. D., & Howard, K. I. (1995). Seeking help from informal and formal resources during adolescence: Sociodemographic and psychological correlates. *Adolescent Psychiatry, 20,* 165–178.

Schover, L. R., & Jensen, S. B. (1988). *Sexuality and chronic illness: A comprehensive approach.* New York: Guilford.

Schroots, J. F., & Birren, J. E. (1988). The nature of time: Implications for research on aging. *Contemporary Gerontology, 2,* 1–29.

Schu-Chen, L., & Schmiedek, F. (2002). Age is not necessarily aging: Another step towards understanding the "clocks" that time aging. *Gerontology, 48,* 5–12.

Schulenberrg, J. E., & Maggs, J. L. (2008). Destiny matters: Distal developmental influences on adult alcohol use and abuse. *Addiction, 103,* 1–6.

Schuster, E. O., Francis-Connolly, E., Alford-Trewn, P., & Brooks, J. (2003). Conceptualization and development of a course on aging to infancy: A life course retrospective. *Educational Gerontology, 29,* 841–850.

Scorgie, K., & Sobsey, D. (2000). Transformational outcomes associated with parenting children with disabilities. *Mental Retardation, 38,* 195–206.

Scotch, R. K. (1984). *From good will to civil rights: Transforming federal disability policy.* Philadelphia, PA: Temple University.

Scott, R. A. (1969). *The making of blind men: A study of adult socialization.* New York: Sage.

Seifert, K. (1999). *Constructing a psychology of teaching and learning.* Boston: Houghton Mifflin.

Settersten, R. A., Jr., & Mayer, K. U. (1997). The measurement of age, age structuring, and the life course. *Annual Review of Sociology, 23,* 233–261.

Shakespeare, T. (1999). The sexual politics of disabled masculinity. *Sexuality and Disability, 17,* 53–64.

Shakespeare, T., Gillespie-Sells, K., & Davies, D. (1996). *The sexual politics of disability: Untold stories.* London: Caswell.

Shanahan, M. J. (2000). Pathways to adulthood in changing societies: Variability and mechanisms in life course perspective. *Annual Review of Sociology, 26,* 667–692.

Shanahan, M. J., Hofer, S. M., & Miech, R. A. (2002). Planful competence, aging, and the life course. Retrospect and prospect. In S. Zarit, L. Pearlin, & K. Warner Schaie (Eds.), *Societal impacts on personal control in the elderly* (pp. 198–211). New York: Springer.

Shanahan, M. J., Hofer, S. M., & Shanahan, L. (2004). Biological models of behavior and the life course. In J. T. Mortimer & M. J. Shanahan (Eds.), *Handbook of the life course* (pp. 597–622). New York: Springer.

Shanahan, M. J., Miech, R. A., & Elder, G. H., Jr. (1998). Changing pathways to attainment in men's lives: Historical patterns of school, work, and social class. *Social Forces, 77*(1), 231–256.

Shapiro, B., Church, R. P., & Lewis, M. E. B. (2007). Specific learning disabilities. In M. L. Batshaw, L. Pellegrino, & N. J. Roizen (Eds.), *Children with disabilities, (6th ed.).* (pp. 367–385). Baltimore, MD: Paul H. Brookes.

Shapiro, J. P. (1993). *No pity. People with disabilities forging a new civil rights movement.* New York: Random House.

Shapiro, J. P. (1997). Assisted suicide devalues the lives of disabled people. In B. Stalcup (Ed.), *The disabled* (pp. 170–178). San Diego, CA: Greenhaven.

Sheehy, G. (1976). *Passages.* New York: Bantam.

Shell, M. (2005). *Polio and its aftermath: The paralysis of culture.* Cambridge, MA: Harvard University.

Sherrod, L. R. (2001). Using the selection, optimization and compensation model to take us one step further in developmental research. *Human Development, 44,* 51–64.

Sherrill, C. (1997). Disability, identity, and involvement in sport and exercise. In K. R. Fox (Ed.), *The physical self: From motivation to well-being* (pp. 257–286). Champaign, IL: Human Kinetics.

Shontz, F. C. (1991). Six principles relating to disability and psychological adjustment. In R. P. Marinelli & A. E. Dell Orto (Eds.), *The psychological and social impact of disability* (3rd ed., pp. 107–110). New York: Springer.

Sidransky, R. (1990). *In silence: Growing up hearing in a deaf world.* New York: St. Martin's.

Siegel, B., & Silverstein, S. (1994). *What about me?* New York: Plenum.

Silber, T. J. (2007). Ethical dilemmas. In M. L. Batshaw, L. Pellegrino, & N. J. Rolzen (Eds.), *Children with disabilities* (6th ed., pp. 591–600). Baltimore, MD: Paul H. Brookes.

Silber, T. J., & Batshaw, M. L. (2004). Ethical dilemmas in the treatment of children with disabilities. *Pediatric Annals, 33,* 752–761.

Singer, G. H. S. (1996). Introduction: Trends affecting home and community care for people with chronic conditions in the United States. In G. H. S. Singer, L. E. Powers, & A. L. Olsen (Eds.), *Redefining family support: Innovations in public private partnerships* (pp. 3–38). Baltimore, MD: Paul H. Brookes.

Singer, G. H. S., & Irvin, L. K. (1989). Family caregiving, stress, and support. In G. H. S. Singer & L. K. Irvin (Eds.), *Support for caregiving families* (pp. 3–25). Baltimore, MD: Paul H. Brookes.

Singer, G. H. S., & Powers, L. E. (1993). Contributing to resilience in families: An overview. In G. H. S. Singer & L. E. Powers (Eds.), *Families, disabilities, and empowerment: Active coping skills and strategies for family interventions* (pp. 1–25). Baltimore, MD: Paul H. Brookes.

Singer, G. H. S., Powers, L. E., & Olson, A. L. (Eds.). (1996). *Redefining family support: Innovations in public-private partnerships.* Baltimore, MD: Paul H. Brookes.

Singer, P. (1975). *Animal liberation.* New York: Random House.

Singer, P. (1981). *The expanding circle: Ethics and sociobiology.* New York: Farrar, Straus, & Biroux.

Singer, P. (1995). *Rethinking life and death: The collapse of our traditional values.* New York: St. Martin's Press.

Singer, P. (2000). *Writings on an ethical life.* New York: HarperCollins.

Sinick, D. (1969). Training, job placement, and follow-up. In D. Malikin & H. Rusalem (Eds.), *Vocational rehabilitation of the disabled: An overview* (pp. 129–153). New York: New York University.

Skeels, H. M. (1966). Adult status of children with contrasting early life experiences. *Monographs of the Society for Research in Child Development, 31,* 1–65.

Skinner, B. (1987). A humanist's alternative to A. A.'s Twelve Steps. *Humanist, 47*(4), 5. Retrieved from Academic Search Premier database.

Skinner, B. F. (1948). *Walden two.* New York: Macmillan.

Skinner, B. F. (1953). *Science and human behavior.* New York: Macmillan.

Skinner, B. F. (1971). *Beyond freedom and dignity.* New York: Knopf.

Skinner, B. F. (1979). *The shaping of a behaviorist.* New York: Knopf.

Smart, D. W., & Smart, J. F. (1997). *DSM-IV* and culturally sensitive diagnosis: Some observations for counselors. *Journal of Counseling and Development, 75,* 392–398.

Smart, J. F. (2001). *Disability, society, and the individual.* Austin, TX: PRO-ED.

Smart, J. F. (2004). Models of disability: The juxtaposition of biology and social construction. In T. F. Riggar and D. R. Maki (Eds.), *Handbook of Rehabilitation Counseling* (pp. 25–49). Springer Series on Rehabilitation. New York: Springer.

Smart, J. F. (2005a). Challenges to the biomedical model of disability: Changes to the practice of rehabilitation counseling. *Directions in Rehabilitation Counseling, 16*(4), 33–43.

Smart, J. F. (2005b). The promise of the International Classification of Functioning, Disability, and Health (ICF) [Special Issue]. *Rehabilitation Education, 19,* 191–199.

Smart, J. F. (2006). Challenging the biomedical model of disability. *Advances in Medical Psychotherapy and Psychodiagnosis, American Board of Medical Psychotherapists, 12,* 41–44.

Smart, J. F. (2007). *The promise of The International Classification of Functioning, Disability, and Health* (ICF) *the psychological and social impact of illness and disability* (5th ed., pp. 528–595). New York: Springer.

Smart, J. F. (2009a). The Americans with Disabilities Act. In D. Carr, R. Crosnoe, M. E. Hughes, & A. M. Pienta (Eds.), *Encyclopedia of the life course and human development* (Vol. 2). Farmington Hills, MI: MacMillan Reference.

Smart, J. F. (2009b). Counseling individuals with disabilities. In I. Marini & M. S. Stebnicki (Eds.), *Professional counselors desk reference* (pp. 639–646). New York: Springer.

Smart, J. F. (2009c). Disability in adulthood. In D. Carr, R. Crosnoe, M. E. Hughes, & A. M. Pienta (Eds.), *Encyclopedia of the life course and human development* (Vol. 2, pp. 95–100). Farmington Hills, MI: MacMillan Reference.

Smart, J. F. (2009d). *Disability, society, and the individual* (2nd ed.). Austin TX: PRO-ED.

Smart, J. F. (2009e). The power of models of disability. *Journal of Rehabilitation, 75,* 3–11.

Smart, J. F. (in press). Counseling individuals with physical, cognitive, and psychiatric disabilities. In C. C. Lee (Ed.), *Multicultural counseling: new approaches to diversity* (4th ed.). Washington, DC: American Counseling Association.

Smart, J. F., & Smart, D. W. (1997a). Culturally sensitive informed choice in rehabilitation counseling. *Journal of Applied Rehabilitation Counseling, 28,* 32–37.

Smart, J. F., & Smart, D. W. (1997b). Disability issues in translation/interpretation. In M. B. Labrum (Ed.), *American Translators Association scholarly monograph series,* IX. Amsterdam: John Benjamin.

Smart, J. F., & Smart, D. W. (1997c). Introduction. In *The Hatherleigh guide to vocational career counseling* (pp. xi–xvii). New York: Hatherleigh.

Smart, J. F., & Smart, D. W. (1997d). The racial/ethnic demography of disability. *Journal of Rehabilitation, 63,* 9–15.

Smart, J. F., & Smart, D. W. (2006). Models of disability: Implications for the counseling profession. *Journal of Counseling and Development, 84,* 29–40.

Smart, J. F. & Smart, D. W. (2007). Models of disability: Implications for the counseling profession. In A. E. Dell Orto & P. W. Power (Eds.), *The Psychological and Social Impact of Illness and Disability* (pp. 75–100). New York: Springer.

Smart, N. (1969). *The religious experience of mankind.* London: Macmillan.

Smart, N. (1978). Understanding the religious experience. In S. Katz (Ed.), *Mysticism and philosophical analysis* (pp. 10–21). New York: Oxford University.

Smith, D. D., & Tyler, N. C. (2010). *Introduction to special education: Making a difference* (7th ed.). Upper Saddle River, NJ: Merrill.

Smith, J. K. & Plimpton, G. (1993). *Chronicles of courage: Very special artists.* New York: Random House.

Smith, L. & Voneche, J. (Eds.). (2006). *Norms in human development.* Cambridge, UK: Cambridge University.

Smith, P. K., & Hart, C. H. (2002). *Blackwell handbook of childhood social development.* Oxford, UK: Blackwell.

Smith, R. P. (1957, 2011). *Where did you go? Out. What did you do? Nothing.* New York: Norton.

Smith, S. (2010, July) Distress and hope in families raising children with special needs. *Counseling Today, 52,* 54–56.

Smith, S. M., & Kampfe, C. M. (1997). Interpersonal relationship implications of hearing loss in persons who are older. *Journal of Rehabilitation, 63,* 15–20.

Snarey, J. R., & Keljo, K. (1991). In a gemeinschaft voice: The cross-cultural expansion of moral development model. In W. M. Kurtines & J. L. Gewirtz (Eds.), *Handbook of moral behavior and development* (Vol. 1, pp. 395–424). Hillsdale, NJ: Erlbaum.

Sobsey, D. (1994). *Violence and abuse in the lives of people with disabilities: The end of silent acceptance.* Baltimore, MD: Paul H. Brookes.

Sobsey, D., & Doe, T. (1991). Patterns of sexual abuse and assault. *Sexuality and Disability, 9,* 243–260.

Sobsey, D., & Mansell, S. (1993). The prevention of sexual abuse of people with developmental disabilities. In M. Nagler (Ed.), *Perspectives on disability* (2nd ed., pp. 283–292). Palo Alto, CA: Health Markets Research.

Sontag, J. C. (1996). Toward a comprehensive theoretical framework for disability research: Bronfenbrenner revisited. *The Journal of Special Education, 30*(3), 319–344.

Souders, R. (1993). Randy Souders. In J. K. Smith & G. Plimpton (Eds.). *Chronicles of courage: Very special artists* (pp. 147–155). New York: Random House.

Souter, S. (1993, August 16). Women with disabilities: How to become a boat rocker in life. Speech given at *Ethics in Rehabilitation Conference.* Dunedin, NZ: New Zealand Rehabilitation Association.

Stalcup, B. (Ed.). (1991). *The disabled, current controversies series.* San Diego, CA: Greenhaven.

Staudiner, U. M., & Lindenberger, U. (Eds.). (2003). *Understanding human development: Dialogues with lifespan psychology.* Boston: Kluwer Academic.

Steenbarger, B. N. (1991). All the work is not a stage: Emerging contextualist themes in counseling and development. *Journal of Counseling and Development, 70,* 288–296.

Steenbarger, B. N. (2001). Placing our counseling texts in context: A reply to Lyddon. *Journal of Counseling and Development, 73,* 570–571.

Stefan, S. (2001). *Unequal rights: Discrimination against people with mental disabilities and the Americans with Disabilities Act.* Washington, DC: American Psychological Association.

Steinberg, L., Fegley, S., & Dornbusch, S. M. (1993). Negative impact of part-time work on adolescent adjustment: Evidence from a longitudinal study. *Developmental Psychology, 29,* 171–180.

Steinem, G. (1994, March/April). Womb envy, testyria, and breast castration. *MS,* 49–56.

Stelmack, R. M. (Ed.). (2004). *On the psychobiology of personality: Essays in honor of Marvin Zuckerman.* Amsterdam: Elsevier.

Stewart, J. R. (1994). Denial of disabling conditions and specific interventions in the rehabilitation counseling setting. *Journal of Applied Rehabilitation Counseling, 25*(3), 7–15.

Stjernfeldt, M., Berglund, K., Lindsten, J., & Ludvigsson, J. (1989). Smoking during pregnancy and the maternal risk of childhood cancer. *Lancet,* pp. 1350–1352.

Stone, D. A. (1984). *The disabled state.* Philadelphia: Temple University.

Strachey, J. (Ed.) (1964). *The standard edition of the complete psychological works of Sigmund Freud.* London: Hogarth.

Strauss, A., & Glaser, B. (1975). *Chronic illness and the quality of life.* St. Louis, MO: Mosby.

Stubbins, J. (1988). The politics of disability. In H. E. Yuker (Ed.), *Attitudes toward persons with disabilities* (pp. 22–23). New York: Springer.

Summers, J. A., Behr, S. K., & Turnbull, A. P. (1989). Positive adaptation and coping strengths of families who have children with disabilities. In G. H. S. Singer & L. K. Irvin (Eds.), *Support for caregiving families: Enabling positive adaptation to disabilities* (pp. 27–40). Baltimore, MD: Paul H. Brookes.

Super, D. E. (1977). Vocational maturity in mid-career. *Vocational Guidance Quarterly, 25,* 297.

Suter, S. (1993, August 16). Women with disabilities: How to become a boat rocker in life. Paper presented at the *Ethics in Rehabilitation Conference.* Dunedin: New Zealand Rehabilitation Organization.

Sutkin, L. C. (1984). Introduction. In M. G. Eisenberg, L. C. Sutkin, & M. A. Jansen (Eds.), *Chronic illness and disability through the life span: Effects on self and the family* (pp. 1–19). New York: Springer.

Swartz, C. (2011, April). Leave those kids alone. *The Atlanta Monthly, 307*(3), 101–103.

Swett, E., & Bishop, M. (2003). Mental health and the aging population: Implications for rehabilitation counselors. *Journal of Rehabilitation, 69,* 13–18.

Takahashi, K. (2005). Toward a life span theory of close relationships: The affective relationships model. *Human Development, 48,* 48–66.

Takahashi, M., Yoshida, A., Yamanaka, H., Furuyama, Y. (2000). Lower s-endorphin content in peripheral blood mononuclear cells in patients with complex regional pain syndrome. *Journal of Back and Musculoskeletal Rehabilitation, 15,* 31–36.

Tansey, T. N. (2010). Impulsivity: An overview of a biopsychosocial model. *Journal of Rehabilitation, 76,* 3–9.

Tate, D. (1993). Alcohol use among spinal cord injured patients. *American Journal of Physical Medicine and Rehabilitation, 72,* 192–195.

Taylor, J. B. (2006). *My stroke of insight: A brain scientist's personal journey.* New York: Viking.

Taylor, J. J., & Achenbach, T. M. (1975). Moral and cognitive development in retarded and nonretarded children. *Journal of Mental Deficiency, 80,* 43–50.

Terman, L. (1925). *Genetic studies of genius: Volume 1. Mental and physical traits of a thousand gifted children.* Stanford, CA: Stanford University.

Terman, L. M., & Oden, M. H. (1959). *Genetic studies of genius: Vol. 5. The gifted at midlife: Thirty-five years of follow-up of the superior child.* Stanford, CA: Stanford University.

The Lighthouse. (1995). *The lighthouse national survey on vision loss: The experience, attitudes, and knowledge of middle-aged and older Americans.* New York: Author.

Thompson, V. C. (1997). Independent and interdependent views of self: Implications for culturally sensitive vocational rehabilitation services. *Journal of Rehabilitation, 63,* 18–20.

Thomson, R. G. (1996). *Freakery: Cultural spectacles of the extraordinary body.* New York: New York University.

Thomson, R. G. (1997). Feminist theory, the body, and the disabled figure. In L. J. Davis (Ed.), *The disability studies reader* (pp. 279–292). New York: Routledge.

Tichy, M., Johnson, D. W., Johnson, R. T., & Roseth, C. J. (2010). The impact of constructive controversy on moral development. *Journal of Applied Social Psychology, 40,* 765–787.

Tilden, V. P., Tolle, S. W., Nelson, C. A., Thompson, M., & Eggman, S. C. (2007). Family decision making in foregoing life-extending treatments. In A. E. Dell Orto & P. W. Power (Eds.), *The psychological and social impact of illness and disability* (pp. 77–291). New York: Springer.

Tollifson, R. (1997). Imperfection is a beautiful thing: On disability and meditation. In K. Fries (Ed.), *Staring back: The experience disability from the inside out* (pp. 105–112). New York: Plume.

Toombs, S. K. (1995). Sufficient unto the day: A life with multiple sclerosis. In S. K. Toombs, D. Barnard, & R. A. Carson (Eds.), *Chronic illness: From experience to policy* (pp. 2–23). Bloomington: University of Indiana.

Toombs, S. K., Barnard, D., & Carson, R. A. (Eds.). (1995). *Chronic illness: From experience to policy.* Bloomington, IN: University of Indiana.

Trachtenberg, S. W., Batshaw, K., & Batshaw, M. (2005). Caring and coping: Helping the family of a child with a disability. In M. L. Batshaw, L. Pellegrino, & N. J. Rolzen (Eds.), *Children with disabilities* (6th ed., pp. 601–612). Baltimore, MD: Paul H. Brookes.

Tremblay, M. (1996). Going back to civvy street: A historical account of the Everest and Jennings wheelchair for Canadian World War II veterans with spinal cord injuries. *Disability and Society, 11,* 149–169.

Trieschmann, R. B. (1987), *Aging with a disability.* New York: Demos.

Tringo, J. L. (1970). The hierarchy of preference toward disability groups. *The Journal of Special Education, 4,* 295–306.

Tucker, B. P. (1998, July/August). Deaf culture, cochlear implants, and elective disability. *Hastings Center Report, 28*(4), 6–15.

Tudge, J. & Rogoff, B. (1999). Peer influences on cognitive development: Piagetian and Vygotskian perspectives. P. Lloyd & C. Fernyhough (Eds.) *Lev Vygotsky critical assessments.* New York: Routledge.

Turk, D. C., & Burwinkle, T. M. (2005). Clinical outcomes, cost-effectiveness, and the role of psychology in treatment for chronic pain sufferers. *Professional Psychology: Research and Practice, 36,* 602–610.

Turkeltaub, P. E., Garaeau, L., Flowers, D. L. Zeffiro, T. A., & Eden, G. F. (2003). Developmental of neural mechanisms for reading. *Nature Neuroscience, 6,* 767–773.

Turnball, A., & Winton, P. (1983). A comparison of specialized and mainstreamed preschools from the perspectives of mothers of handicapped children. *Journal of Pediatric Psychology, 8,* 57–71.

Turnbull, A. P., & Turnbull, H. R. (1991). Understanding families from a systems perspective. In J. M. Williams & T. Kay (Eds.), *Head injury: A family matter* (pp. 37–64). Baltimore, MD: Paul H. Brookes.

Turnball, A., Turnball, R., & Wehmeyer, M. (2010). *Exceptional lives: Special education in today's school.* (6th ed.). Upper Saddle River, NJ: Merrill.

Turner, J. S., & Helms, D. B. (1979). *Life span development.* Philadelphia: W. B. Saunders.

Tuttle, D. W. (1984). *Self-esteem and adjusting with blindness: The process of responding to life's demands.* Springfield, IL: Charles C Thomas.

Uhlberg, M. (2008). *Hands of my father: A hearing boy, his deaf parents, and the language of love.* New York: Bantam Books.

United Nations Department of Public Information. (1999). *Towards a society for all ages, international year of older persons 1999: Demographics of older persons.* New York: United Nations.

U.S. Bureau of the Census. (1996). *65+ in the United States.* Current Population Reports, Special Studies, pp. 23–190. Washington, DC: Government Printing Office.

U.S. Department of Education. (1993). *Fifteenth annual report to Congress on the implementation of the Individuals with Disabilities Education Act.* Washington, DC: Author.

U.S. Department of Education. (2006, August 14). 34 *CFR* Parts 300 and 301, *Assistance to States for the Education of Children with Disabilities* and *Preschool Grants for Children with Disabilities. Final rule.* Federal Register.

U.S. Department of Education, National Center for Education Statistics. (2003). Table 52—Child 3 to 21 served in federally supported by programs for the disabled, by type of disability. Selected years 1976–1977 to 2001–2002. In *Digest of Education Statistics, 2003* (p. 72; NCES No. 2005–025). Washington, DC: U.S. Government Printing Office.

U.S. Depatment of Health and Human Services. (2000). *Healthy people 2010: Understanding and improving health* (2nd ed.). Washingtonm, DC: U.S. Government Printing Office.

U.S. Department of Health and Human Services. (2006). *2006 National Survey of drug use and health.* Washington, DC: Author.

Vaillant, G. E. (1977). *Adaptation to life.* Boston: Little, Brown.

Valliant, G. E. (1990). Avoiding negative life outcomes: Evidence from a forty-five year study. In P. B. Baltes & M. M. Baltes (Eds.), *Successful aging: Perspectives from the behavioral sciences* (pp. 323–358). New York: Cambridge University.

Van Royan, J. (1997, Autumn). "There's NO such thing as a building." *NewSquiggle: The Newsletter of the Squiggle Foundation, 1,* 5–6.

Vash, C. L. (1981). *The psychology of disability.* New York: Springer.

Vasta, R. (Ed.). (1998). *Annals of child development.* Philadelphia: Jessica Kingsley.

Vasunilashorn, S., Crimmins, E. M. (2009). Aging. In D. Carr (Ed.), *Encyclopedia of the life course and human development, Vol. 3, Later life approaches.* (pp. 23–32).

Veith, E. M., Sherman, J. E., Pellino, T. A., & Yasui, N. Y. (2006). Qualitative analysis of the peer-mentoring relationship among individuals with spinal cord injury. *Rehabilitation Psychology, 51,* 289–298.

Vermeij, G. (1997). *Privileged hands: A scientific life.* New York: Freeman.

Vernellia, R. R. (1994). Impact of managed care organizations on ethnic Americans and underserved populations. *Journal of Health Care for the Poor and the Underserved, 5,* 224–237.

Vilchinsky, N., Findler, L., & Werner, S. (2010). Attitudes toward people with disabilities: The perspective of attachment theory. *Rehabilitation Psychology, 55,* 298–306.

Vygotsky, L. A. (1962). *Thought and language.* Cambridge, MA: Massachusetts Institute of Technology.

Vygotsky, L. S. (1978). Interaction between learning and development. *Mind in Society.* Cambridge, MA: Harvard University.

Vygotsky, L. S. (1987). Genetic roots of thinking and speech. In R. W. Rieber & A. S. Carton (Eds.), *The collected works of L.S. Vygostky: Vol. 1: Problems of general psychology* (pp. 101–120). New York: Plenum.

Waaland, P. K. (1990). *Pediatric traumatic brain injury.* Richmond VA: Virginia Commonwealth University. Rehabilitation Research and Training Center on Severe Traumatic Brain Injury.

Wachs, H. (2001). Visual implications of Piaget's theory of cognitive development. *Journal of Learning Disabilities, 14*(10), 581–583.

Wade, C. (1994). It ain't exactly sexy. *The Ragged Edge,* 89–90.

Waitzkin, W. C. (1991). *The politics of medical encounters: How patients and doctors deal with social problems.* New Haven, CT: Yale University.

Walker, L. A. (1986). *A loss for words: The story of deafness in a family.* New York: Harper.

Walkup, J. (2000). Disability, health care, and public policy. *Rehabilitation Psychology, 45,* 409–422.

Wallis, C. (2007, January 22). What autism epidemic? *Time, 172,* 69.

Walsh, D. (2007). Coping with a journey toward recovery: From the inside out. In A. E. Dell Orto and P. Power (Eds.), *The psychological and social impact of illness and disability* (6th ed., pp. 110–117). New York: Springer.

Walsh, F., & Pryce, J. (2003). The spiritual dimension of family life. In F. Walsh, (Ed.), *Normal family process: Growing diversity and complexity* (3rd ed., pp. 337–372). New York: Guilford.

Warner, M.C. (1999). *The trouble with normal: Sex, politics and ethics of queer life.* New York: Free Press.

Warren, D. H. (1984). *Blindness and early childhood development.* New York: American Foundation for the Blind.

Warren, D. H. (1989). Implications of visual impairments for child development. In M. C. Wang, M. C. Reynolds, & H. J. Walberg (Eds.), *Handbook of special education: Research and practice. Vol. 3. Low-incidence conditions* (pp. 155–172). Oxford, England: Pergamon.

Wasak, F., Schneider, W. X., Li, S. C., & Hommel, B. (2009). Perceptual identification across the life span: A dissociation of early gains and late losses. *Psychological Research, 73,* 114–122.

Watson, J. (1924). *Behaviorism.* New York: Norton.

Watson, J. (1926/1960). *Behaviorism.* New York: Norton.

Waxman, B. F. (1991). Hatred: The unacknowledged dimension in violence against disabled people. *Sexuality and Disability, 9,* 185–199.

Wechsler, D. (1991). *Wechsler Intelligence Scale Children* (3rd ed.). San Antonio, TX: The Psychological Corporation.

Weihenmayer, E. (2001). *Touch the top of the world: A blind man's journey to climb farther than the eye can see.* New York: Dutton.

Weinberg, N. (1982). Growing up physically disabled: Factors in the evaluation of disability. *Rehabilitation Counseling Bulletin, 25,* 219–227.

Weinberg, N., & Sterritt, M. (1991). Disability and identity: A study of identity patterns in adolescents with hearing impairments. In M. G. Eisenberg & R. L. Glueckauf (Eds.), *Empirical approaches to psychosocial aspects of disability* (pp. 68–75). New York: Springer.

Weingarten, R. (1997). How I've managed my mental illness. In L. Spanoil, C. Gagne, & M. Hoehler (Eds.), *Psychological and social aspects of psychiatric disability* (123–129). Boston: Center for Psychiatric Rehabilitation, Boston University.

Weisgerber, R. A. (1991). *Quality of life for persons with disabilities: Skill development and transitions across life stages.* Gaithersburg, MD: Aspen.

Weishaus, S. & Field, D. (1988). A half century of marriage: Continuity or change? *Journal of Marriage and the Family, 50,* 763–774.

Weisskopf, M. (2006, October 2). How I lost my hand but found myself. *Time, 173,* 28–37.

Wendell, S. (1997). Toward a feminist theory of disability. In L. J. Davis (Ed.), *The disability studies reader* (pp. 260–278). New York: Routledge.

Wendell, S. (2010). Toward a feminist theory of disability. In L. J. Davis (Ed.), *The disability studies reader* (3rd ed., pp. 336–352). New York: Routledge.

West, T. G. (1994). Slow words, quick words—Dyslexia as an advantage in tomorrow's work place. In P. J. Gerber & D. S. Brown (Eds.), *Learning Disabilities and Employment* (pp. 349–370). Austin, TX: Pro-Ed.

White, N., & Lublin, I. M. (1998). Illness trajectory. In I. M. Lublin & P. D. Larsen (Eds.), *Chronic illness: Impact and interventions* (pp. 53–76). Sudbury, MA: Jones & Bartlett.

Whitney, C. R. (1993, January 19). Disabled Germans fear they'll be the next target. *The New York Times,* p. A3.

Whitt, J. K. (1984). Children's adaptation to chronic illness and handicapping conditions. In M. G. Eisenberg, L. C. Sutkin, & M. A. Jansen. *Chronic illness and disability through the life span: Effects on self and family* (pp. 69–102). New York: Springer.

Widmer, T. (2006, May 7). Magic man: How Franklin D. Roosevelt brought 85, America back from the brink. *New York Times Book Review.*

Wiener, J. (2004). Do peer relationships foster behavioral adjustment in children with learning disabilities? *Learning Disability Quarterly, 27,* 21–30.

Wilder, D. (1987). Personal responsibility for illness. In D. Van De Veer & T. Regan (Eds.). *Health care ethics: An introduction* (pp. 326–358). Philadelphia: Temple University.

Wilkins, S., & Cott, C. (1993). Aging, chronic illness and disability. In M. Nagler (Ed.), *Perspectives on disability* (2nd ed., pp. 363–377). Palo Alto, CA: Health Markets Research.

Williamson, J. B., & Watts, D. M. (2009). Aging Boomers: Generational equity, and the framing of the debate over Social Security. In Hudson (Ed.), *Boomer bust? Economic and political issues of the graying society* (pp. 153–169). Westport, CT: Praeger.

Wilson, D. J. (1990). *Living with polio: The epidemic and its survivors.* Chicago: University of Chicago.

Wilson, E. O. (1998). *Consilience: The unity of knowledge.* New York: Knopf.

Wilson, J. C. (2006). (Re)Writing the genetic body-text: Disability, textuality, and the Human Genome Project. In L. J. L. Davis (Ed.), *The Disability Studies Reader* (2nd ed., pp. 67–75). New York: Routledge.

Winske, R., & Lingerman, J. (2007). Dealing with spina bifida: A mother's perspective. In A. Dell Orto & P. Power (Eds.), *The psychological and social impact of illness and disability* (pp. 408–417). New York: Springer.

Winton, P. J. (1990). A systemic approach for planning in-service training related to Public Law 99–457. *Infants and Young Children, 3,* 51–50.

Wolbring, G. (2001). Where do we draw the line? Surviving eugenics in a technological world. In M. Priestley, (Ed.), *Disability and life course.* Cambridge, UK: Cambridge University.

Wolfensberger, W. (1972). *The principle of normalization in human services.* Toronto, Canada: National Institute on Mental Retardation.

Wolfensberger, W. (1981). The extermination of handicapped people in World War II Germany. *Mental Retardation, 85,* 1–7.

Wright, B. (1960). *Physical disability: A psychological approach.* New York: Harper & Row.

Wright, B. A. (1983). *Physical disability: A psychosocial approach* (2nd ed.). New York: Harper & Row.

Wright, B. A. (1991). Labeling: The need for person–environment individuation. In C. R. Snyder & D. R. Forsyth (Eds.), *Handbook of social and clinical psychology: The health perspective* (pp. 469–487). New York: Pergamon.

Wright, D. (1994). *Deafness: An autobiography.* New York: Harper Perennial.

Wrosch, C., Schultz, R., & Heckhausen, J. (2004). Health stresses and depressive symptomatology in the elderly: A control-process approach. *Current Directions in Psychological Science, 13,* 17–20.

Wuthnow, R. (2007). *After the baby boomer: How twenty-and thirty-somethings are shaping the future of American religion.* Princeton, NJ: Princeton University.

Yoshida, K. K. (1993). Reshaping of self: A pendular reconstruction of self and identity among adults with traumatic spinal cord injury. *Sociology of Health and Illness, 15,* 217–245.

Young, R., & Olsen, E. (1991). Introduction. In R. Young and E. Olson (Eds.), *Health, illness, and disability in later life: Practice issues and interventions* (pp. 1–7). Newbury Park, CA: Sage.

Young-Bruehl, E. (1996). *The anatomy of prejudice.* Cambridge, MA: Harvard University.

Zarestsky, H. H., Richter, E. F., & Eisenberg, M. G. (Eds.). (2005). *Medical aspects of disability: A handbook for the rehabilitation professional* (3rd ed.). New York: Springer.

Zarit, S. H., & Zarit, J. M. (1984). Psychological approaches to families of the elderly. In M. G. Eisenberg, L. C. Sutkin, & M. A. Jansen (Eds.), *Chronic illness and disability through the life span: Effects on self and the family* (pp. 269–288). New York: Springer.

Zavirsek, D. (2002). Pictures and silences: Memories of sexual abuse of disabled people. *Journal of Social Welfare, 11,* 270–285.

Zigler, E., & Finn, M. (1984). Applied developmental psychology. In M. H. Bornstein & M. E. Lamb (Eds.), *Developmental psychology: An advanced textbook* (pp. 451–492). Hillsdale, NJ: Lawrence Erlbaum.

Zigler, E., Piotrkowski, C. S., & Collins, R. (1994). Health services in head start. *Annual Review of Public Health, 15,* 511–534. Retrieved from http://www.annualreviews.org/doi/abs/10.1146/annurev.pu.15.050194.002455.

Zigler, E., & Valentine, J. (Eds.). (1979). *Project Head Start: A legacy of the war on poverty.* New York: Free Press.

Zimmerman, J. (2010, December). Epidemiology of Autism Spectrum Disorders: Utah prevalence rates likely to climb above 1 in 85. *The Utah Special Educator, 33*(2), 10–11.

Zola, I. K. (1982). *Missing pieces: A chronicle of living with a disability.* Philadelphia: Temple University.

Zola, I. K. (1983). *Socio-medical inquiries: Recollections, reflections, and reconsiderations.* Philadelphia: Temple University.

Zola, I. K. (1985). Depictions of disability-metaphor, message, and media: A research and political agenda. *The Social Science Journal, 22,* 5–17.

Zola, I. K. (1992). "Any distinguishing features?" The portrayal of disability in the crime-mystery genre. In P. M. Ferguson, D. L. Ferguson, & S. J. Taylor (Eds.), *Interpreting disability: A qualitative reader* (pp. 233–250). New York: Columbia University.

Zola, I. K. (1993). Disability statistics: What we count and what it tells us. *Journal of Disability Policy Studies, 4,* 9–39.

Zuckerman, M. (1994). *Behavioral expressions and biosocial bases of sensation seeking.* New York: Cambridge University.

Zunker, V. G. (1998). *Career counseling: Applied concepts of life planning* (4th ed.). Pacific Grove, CA: Brooks/Cole.

Zweig, S. (1962). Wider horizons on Freud. In L. Gerard (Ed.), *Sigmund Freud: The man and his theories.* New York: Fawcett.

Index